INTERNATIONAL
ENCYCLOPEDIA
OF
ELECTIONS

INTERNATIONAL

ENCYCLOPEDIA

OF

ELECTIONS

Richard Rose, Editor in Chief

CQ PRESS

A Division of Congressional Quarterly Inc.
Washington, D.C.

CQ Press
A Division of Congressional Quarterly Inc.
1414 22nd Street, N.W.
Washington, DC 20037

(202) 822-1475; (800) 638-1710

www.cqpress.com

Cover and interior design by Debra Naylor, Naylor Design Inc., Washington, D.C.
Book production by BMWW, Baltimore, Md.

Printed and bound in the United States of America

04 03 02 01 00   5 4 3 2 1

The paper used in this publication meets the minimum requirements of the American National
Standard for Information Sciences—Permanence of Paper for Printed Library Materials,
ANSI Z39.48-1984.

LIBRARY OF CONGRESS CATALOGING-IN-PUBLICATION DATA
International encyclopedia of elections / Richard Rose, editor.
    p. cm.
  Includes bibliographical references and index.
  ISBN 1-56802-415-0 (cloth : acid-free paper)
    1. Elections—Encyclopedias.   I. Rose, Richard, 1933–

JF1001.I57 2000
324′.03—dc21   99-056836

CONTENTS

ABOUT THE EDITORS

EDITOR IN CHIEF

Richard Rose has published millions of words about voting and elections on many continents and has commented frequently about elections on television and in the press. Since coauthoring *The British General Election of 1959*, he has edited the landmark comparative study of voting on three continents, *Electoral Behaviour* (1974), and coauthored the definitive text of election results in twenty-five democratic countries, *The International Almanac of Electoral History* (three editions), *How Russia Votes* (1997), and studies of party politics, such as *The Problem of Party Government* (1974) and *Do Parties Make a Difference?* (1984).

Rose is professor and director of the Centre for the Study of Public Policy at the University of Strathclyde, Glasgow, Scotland, and has been a visiting professor at the European University Institute, Florence; the Wissenschaftszentrum Berlin; Johns Hopkins University; and Stanford University. He has presented papers to seminars and conferences on six continents, and his writings have been translated into seventeen languages. Rose is a fellow of the British Academy and of the American Academy of Arts and Sciences and is a recipient of the Lasswell Award for lifetime achievement in public policy.

EDITORIAL BOARD

Joel D. Barkan is professor of political science at the University of Iowa. A specialist on issues of governance and electoral processes in developing countries, he has published extensively on these topics and on the relationship between democratization and macroeconomic reform. He is a coauthor of *Beyond Capitalism vs. Socialism in Kenya and Tanzania* (1994). In 1997–1998 he was a visiting senior fellow at the U.S. Institute of Peace.

André Blais is professor in the Department of Political Science at the University of Montreal. He has published extensively on voting behavior and electoral systems, most notably his forthcoming book, *To Vote or Not to Vote?* He is writing a book with Louis Massicotte with the working title *Establishing the Rules of the Game: Election Laws in Democracies*.

Walter Dean Burnham is professor of political science at the University of Texas at Austin and was formerly a professor at the Massachusetts Institute of Technology and the University of Chicago. His encyclopedic knowledge of election results in the United States at the state as well as national level is recorded in *Presidential Ballots, 1836–1892* (1955), in *Critical Elections and the Mainsprings of American Politics* (1970), and in articles interpreting American election results in a broad theoretical framework.

Gary W. Cox is professor of political science at the University of California, San Diego. His most recent book, *Making Votes Count: Strategic Coordination in the World's Electoral Systems* (1997), won the Woodrow Wilson prize of the American Political Science Association.

Larry Diamond is coeditor of the *Journal of Democracy* and a senior research fellow at the Hoover Institution on War, Revolution, and Peace, Stanford University, where he received his Ph.D. He is the author of *Developing Democracy: Toward Consolidation* (1999) and *Class, Ethnicity, and Democracy in Nigeria* (1988).

Richard S. Katz is professor of political science at Johns Hopkins University. He is the author of numerous books and articles on political parties and electoral systems, including *A Theory of Parties and Electoral Systems* (winner of the 1998 George H. Hallett Award) and *Democracy and Elections* (1997).

Arend Lijphart is research professor of political science at the University of California, San Diego. He is the author of *Electoral Systems and Party Systems: A Study of Twenty-Seven Democracies, 1945–1990* (1994) and many other books, as well as coeditor of *Choosing an Electoral System: Issues and Alterna-*

tives (1984) and *Electoral Laws and Their Political Consequences* (1986). He has served as an adviser on electoral system design to Bolivia, Colombia, Israel, and South Africa.

Tom Mackie is head of the Politics Division, Department of Government, University of Strathclyde, Glasgow, Scotland. He is a coauthor of *The International Almanac of Electoral History* (three editions) and of the *Europe Votes* series.

Dieter Nohlen is professor of political science at the University of Heidelberg, Germany. He is a well-known expert on elections and electoral systems in developing countries as well as Europe and has consulted extensively on electoral reforms. He has edited a number of handbooks and encyclopedias of political science in English, German, and Spanish, including *Elections in Africa* (1999). Nohlen is a recipient of the Max Planck award for outstanding research in comparative politics.

ALPHABETICAL
LIST OF ARTICLES

A

Absentee Voting
Michael Maley, *Australian Electoral Commission*

Acclamation, Election by (or Voice Vote)
Richard S. Katz, *Johns Hopkins University*

Accountability, Elections as One Form of
Robert E. Goodin, *Australian National University*

Additional Member System
Dieter Nohlen, *University of Heidelberg*

Administration of Elections
Michael Maley, *Australian Electoral Commission*

Age of Voting
Florian Grotz, *University of Heidelberg*

Alternative Vote
Colin A. Hughes, *University of Queensland, Brisbane*

Apparentement
Arend Lijphart, *University of California, San Diego*

Approval Voting
Steven J. Brams, *New York University*

At-Large Elections
Tom Mackie, *University of Strathclyde*

Australian Ballot
Tom Mackie, *University of Strathclyde*

B

Bandwagon Effects
William L. Miller, *Glasgow University*

Barometer Elections
Christopher J. Anderson, *Binghamton University (SUNY)*

Binomial Electoral System
Dieter Nohlen, *University of Heidelberg*

Bonus Seats
Richard Rose, *University of Strathclyde*

Boycott of Elections
Michael Bratton, *Michigan State University*

By-Elections
Richard Rose, *University of Strathclyde*

C

Campaigning
Dennis Kavanagh, *University of Liverpool*

Candidates: Legal Requirements and Disqualifications
Michael Maley, *Australian Electoral Commission*

Candidates: Selection
Michael Marsh, *Trinity College, University of Dublin*

Canvassing
David Denver, *Lancaster University*

Choice, Elections as a Method of
Richard Rose, *University of Strathclyde*

Citizen Juries (and Other Methods of Informed Citizen Consultation)
James S. Fishkin, *University of Texas at Austin*

Colonial Elections
Tom Mackie, *University of Strathclyde*

Compensatory Seats
Matthew Soberg Shugart, *University of California, San Diego*

Competitiveness of Elections
Michael Krennerich, *Institute for Ibero-American Studies, Hamburg*

Compulsory Voting
Wolfgang P. Hirczy de Miño, *University of Houston*

Condorcet Theorems
Iain McLean, *Nuffield College, Oxford University*

CONTRIBUTORS

A

ALEXANDER, HERBERT E.
Citizens' Research Foundation, University of Southern California
Election Finance

ANDERSON, CHRISTOPHER J.
Binghamton University (SUNY)
Barometer Elections

AUSTIN, RORY
George Washington University
Nonpartisan Elections

B

BARKAN, JOEL D.
University of Iowa
Elections in Developing Countries

BARTOLINI, STEFANO
European University Institute, Florence
Franchise Expansion

BLAIS, ANDRÉ
University of Montreal
Constitution and Elections
Day of Election
Majority Systems
Mixed Electoral Systems
Plurality Systems
Simultaneous Elections
Staggered Elections
Term of Office, Length of
Turnout, Minimum Requirement

BONEO, HORACIO
Observation of Elections

BRAMS, STEVEN J.
New York University
Approval Voting

BRATTON, MICHAEL
Michigan State University
Boycott of Elections
Founding Elections: Africa

BRIANS, CRAIG LEONARD
Virginia Polytechnic Institute
Registration of Voters in the United States

BUDGE, IAN
University of Essex
Manifesto, Election

BURNHAM, WALTER DEAN
University of Texas at Austin
Realigning Elections in the United States

C

CAIN, BRUCE E.
University of California, Berkeley
Positive Discrimination in Redistricting
in the United States

CAREY, JOHN M.
Washington University, St. Louis
Presidential Electoral Systems
Term Limits

COURTNEY, JOHN
University of Saskatchewan
Reapportionment and Redistricting

COX, GARY W.
University of California, San Diego
Coordination, Electoral
Cumulative Voting
Duverger's Law
Limited Vote
List
Pooling Votes
Proportional Representation
Tactical Voting

D

DALTON, RUSSELL J.
University of California, Irvine
Voting Behavior, Influences on

DENVER, DAVID
Lancaster University
Canvassing

DONSBACH, WOLFGANG
Technical University of Dresden
Public Opinion Polls: Legal Regulation

E

ELDER, JOSEPH W.
University of Wisconsin–Madison
Quaker Decision Making without Voting

ELKLIT, JØRGEN
University of Aarhus
Free and Fair Elections
Open Voting
Tendered Ballots

F

FISCHER, JEFFREY W.
International Foundation for Election Systems
Technical Assistance in Elections

FISHKIN, JAMES S.
University of Texas at Austin
Citizen Juries (and Other Methods of Informed Citizen Consultation)

G

GALLAGHER, MICHAEL
Trinity College, University of Dublin
Proportionality and Disproportionality
Referendums: Europe
Single Transferable Vote

GOODIN, ROBERT E.
Australian National University
Accountability, Elections as One Form of

GREELEY, ANDREW
University of Chicago
Papal Elections

GROFMAN, BERNARD
University of California, Irvine
Downsian Model of Elections

GROTZ, FLORIAN
University of Heidelberg
Age of Voting
Appendix: Electoral Systems in Independent Countries

GWYN, WILLIAM B.
Tulane University
Rotten Boroughs

H

HERMET, GUY
Institut d'Études Politiques, Paris
Unfree Elections

HIRCZY DE MIÑO, WOLFGANG P.
University of Houston
Compulsory Voting

HOLTZ-BACHA, CHRISTINA
University of Mainz
Regulation of Television at Elections

HUGHES, COLIN A.
University of Queensland, Brisbane
Alternative Vote
Donkey Votes

J

JEWELL, MALCOLM E.
University of Kentucky
Primary Elections

JONES, MARK P.
Michigan State University
Double Simultaneous Vote
Founding Elections: Latin America
Fused Votes
Gender Quotas
Second Ballot (or Runoff)

K

KARL, TERRY LYNN
Stanford University
Electoralism

KATZ, RICHARD S.
Johns Hopkins University
Acclamation, Election by (or Voice Vote)
Functions of Elections
Lot

Noncitizens and the Right to Vote
Preference Voting
Qualified Majority Voting
Suppléant

KAVANAGH, DENNIS
University of Liverpool
Campaigning

KENNEDY, J. RAY
International Foundation for Election Systems
Technical Assistance in Elections

KING, ANTHONY
University of Essex
Effect of Elections on Government

KOUSSER, J. MORGAN
California Institute of Technology
Poll Tax

KRENNERICH, MICHAEL
Institute for Ibero-American Studies, Hamburg
Appendix: Electoral Systems in Independent Countries
Competitiveness of Elections

KUMAR, KRISHNA
Carnegie Endowment for International Peace
Postconflict Elections

L

LAVER, MICHAEL
Trinity College, University of Dublin
Government Formation and Election Outcomes

LIJPHART, AREND
University of California, San Diego
Apparentement
Turnout

M

MACKIE, TOM
University of Strathclyde
At-Large Elections
Australian Ballot
Colonial Elections
Cross-Filing
Estate and Curia Constituencies
Gerrymandering
Plural Voters
Quotas and Divisors
Secret Ballot

MAGLEBY, DAVID B.
Brigham Young University
Initiative: United States
Recall Elections
Referendums: United States

MAIR, PETER
University of Leiden
Public Aid to Parties and Candidates
Volatility, Electoral

MALEY, MICHAEL
Australian Electoral Commission
Absentee Voting
Administration of Elections
Candidates: Legal Requirements and Disqualifications
Deposit
Disqualification of Voters, Grounds for
Nomination Procedures
Overseas Voting
Parties: Qualification for Ballot
Proxy Voting

MARSH, MICHAEL
Trinity College, University of Dublin
Candidates: Selection
Second-Order Elections

MASSICOTTE, LOUIS
University of Montreal
Constitution and Elections
Day of Election
Federal Countries, Elections in
Mixed Electoral Systems
Second-Chamber Elections
Simultaneous Elections
Staggered Elections
Term of Office, Length of
Turnout, Minimum Requirement

McLEAN, IAIN
Nuffield College, Oxford University
Condorcet Theorems
Paradox of Voting

MILLER, WILLIAM L.
Glasgow University
Bandwagon Effects
Election Forecasting

MITOFSKY, WARREN J.
Mitofsky International
Exit Polls

MONROE, BURT L.
Indiana University
Cube Law
Fractionalization Index

N

NOHLEN, DIETER
University of Heidelberg
Additional Member System
Appendix: Electoral Systems in Independent Countries
Binomial Electoral System
Threshold of Exclusion

NORRIS, PIPPA
Harvard University
Women: Representation and Electoral Systems

O

OTTAWAY, MARINA
Carnegie Endowment for International Peace
Postconflict Elections
Premature Closure of Democracy

R

REED, STEVEN R.
Chuo University
Single Nontransferable Vote in Multimember Districts

REYNOLDS, ANDREW
University of Notre Dame
Designing Electoral Systems

ROSE, RICHARD
University of Strathclyde
Bonus Seats
By-Elections
Choice, Elections as a Method of
Democracy and Elections
Election Studies, Types of
Founding Elections (Definition)
Founding Elections: Democratization without Interruption
Founding Elections: Refounding after Breakdown
Manufactured Majorities
Offices Filled by Direct Election
Safe Seat
Swing
Ticket Splitting
Unopposed Returns
Wasted Votes
Winning an Election

RULE, WILMA
University of Nevada, Reno
Women: Enfranchisement

S

SANDERS, DAVID
University of Essex
Political Business Cycle

SARTORI, GIOVANNI
Columbia University
Relevant Parties

SCARROW, HOWARD
State University of New York, Stony Brook
Weighted Voting

SHUGART, MATTHEW SOBERG
University of California, San Diego
Compensatory Seats
District Magnitude
Indirect Election

T

THIBAUT, BERNHARD
University of Heidelberg
Appendix: Electoral Systems in Independent Countries
Referendums: Latin America

TRECHSEL, ALEXANDER H.
University of Geneva
Initiative: Europe

U

ULERI, PIER VINCENZO
University of Florence
Plebiscites and Plebiscitary Politics

W

WATTENBERG, MARTIN P.
University of California, Irvine
Ticket Splitting in the United States

WHITE, STEPHEN
Glasgow University
Founding Elections: Postcommunist

WORCESTER, ROBERT M.
MORI International, London
Public Opinion Polls: How They Work

INTRODUCTION:
WHY ELECTIONS?

Today more than a billion people in countries all over the globe can vote in competitive elections. From the Republic of South Africa to Siberia and from Alaska to Australia, ordinary people are not only subjects of government but also voters choosing their governors. The audience of this book is broad in scope as well as space, including students, librarians, journalists, political activists, and scholars. Its 147 entries, ranging from "Absentee Voting" to "Women: Representation and Electoral Systems," are designed to explain how diverse features of elections work in different historical, geographical, and cultural settings.

DEMOCRACY AND ELECTIONS

Today, there are very few countries in the world that do not have national elections. Holding an election, however, does not make a country democratic. This is most obvious where more than 99 percent of the votes are cast for the governing party of a one-party state. Until the fall of the Berlin Wall in 1989, elections without choice were common throughout the communist bloc. Following the creation of new democracies in eastern Europe and in many other regions, the majority of countries in the world now have some form of competitive election, but fewer than half of the member states of the United Nations hold elections that are both free and fair.

For most of the history of the world, elections were unimportant because democracy was nonexistent or voting occurred under very different conditions than are normal today. Two and one-half millennia ago Athens held elections, but the right to vote was restricted and Greek philosophers were fearful of democracy, viewing it as rule by the mob. In the centuries following the decline of Athens, the authority of secular rulers around the globe was justified not by popular election but by tradition, inheritance, force, or success in intrigue and cabals. For example, the pope has been elected for more than a millennium by an electoral college that does not consist of everyday churchgoers but of leaders in the hierarchy of the Roman Catholic Church. The theory behind the papal electoral system is that the cardinals should elect the person who best represents the will of God.

Elections gained importance in nineteenth-century Europe when radical groups began questioning the authority of governments chosen by traditional leaders of society and demanded representative government responsible to the whole of the adult population (or, at least, all adult men) through competitive elections. The broadening of the franchise in some places took more than a century. In Britain the first steps were made in 1832; women gained the right to vote in 1918; and the goal of one person, one vote was not reached until 1949. Although the United States was early in granting the right to vote to white males, full adult suffrage was not federally guaranteed until the enactment of the 1965 Voting Rights Act. Until the outbreak of the First World War, in 1914, most countries of Europe greatly restricted the right to vote, and their governments were accountable to a king rather than an elected parliament. Between the two world wars many European countries expanded the right to vote, but many of the governments in these new democracies were overthrown and replaced by dictators. It was not until after the end of the Second World War, in 1945, that free competitive elections became the norm in western Europe, and only after the fall of the Berlin Wall did they become normal in eastern Europe.

THE CONDUCT OF ELECTIONS

In the predemocratic era, elections were easy to organize because the right to vote was restricted and traditional elites were often elected without any competition. Methods for casting ballots and counting votes were simple; for example, a group of voters might gather in the marketplace or a hall and choose a representative by acclamation. Even where paper ballots were used, voting was usually open rather than secret, a practice that made it easy for landowners and the nobility to influence how people voted.

The move to democracy brought about great changes in the conduct of elections. The number of individuals registered to vote increased by several thousand percent. Contested elections replaced the unopposed return of local notables. Secret ballots replaced voice votes. Political reformers wanting to make government more representative proposed new types of electoral systems. Old elites seeking to avoid being swept from office by a flood of new voters often accepted the changes; for example, the adoption of proportional representation offered old elites a chance of remaining in parliament once the franchise was expanded.

The organization of a national election is among the most difficult tasks that public officials must undertake. Voting takes place across the country within the space of a few hours, whereas tax collection is spread over months or throughout the year. A census, another public activity in which every adult citizen can participate, takes place less frequently than elections.

ELECTIONS IN THE DEMOCRATIZATION PROCESS

In a modern state, governors are subject to the rule of law; schools and universities, the press, interest groups, and other institutions of civil society are independent of the state; and the government is accountable to parliament, the courts, and civil institutions. In the oldest democracies, the creation of a modern state came long before free and competitive elections; introducing free elections in which every adult could vote was the final step in completing democratization. By contrast, the process leading to new democracies is often "democratization backwards." In the Russian Federation, for example, competitive elections are being held even though basic institutions of a modern state, such as the rule of law and civil society, are not yet secure. In Latin America many countries have oscillated between democratic and undemocratic forms of rule, while to some extent institutions of civil society and accountability have developed. In Africa institutional constraints on government tend to be weak; an elected president can turn into a dictator or the military can decide who governs.

The coexistence of elections and undemocratic practices in many countries leads some social scientists to conclude that, regardless of whether elections are held, countries that are underdeveloped economically or lack a cultural tradition favoring democratic norms cannot easily become democratic. India, however, contradicts such generalizations, for even though it is a sprawling, populous, and poor multiethnic society, free elections have been held there since 1952.

VARIETY OF ELECTORAL FORMS AND PROCEDURES

The spread of elections around the world has encouraged variety rather than uniformity in the conduct of elections. As the entries in this encyclopedia show, there are many ways to turn the ideal of free and fair elections into reality. The variety extends from the long-ballot tradition of the United States, in which many holders of executive office at the federal, state, and local levels are elected simultaneously, to the short-ballot tradition of European democracies. At national elections the number of parties competing ranges from two in U.S. congressional elections to more than a dozen in parliamentary elections in the Netherlands, Israel, and Spain. Most established democracies use one or another form of proportional representation, intended to award seats in parliament in proportion to each party's share of the popular vote. But some old democracies, such as the United States and Britain, use the plurality electoral system: the winner is the individual candidate who comes "first past the post," whether taking more or less than half the vote. Although the plurality system usually produces a less proportional distribution of seats among competing parties than does a proportional-representation system, it tends to reduce the number of parties in parliament and thus makes it easier for the parties to form a stable government with an absolute majority of seats in parliament.

To evaluate the merits and shortcomings of election procedures in a particular country, we will find it helpful to understand how elections are held in others; this observation is especially true when reforms are being contemplated. New Zealand, for example, has abandoned the plurality system of electing parliament in favor of proportional representation, whereas Italy has replaced proportional representation with the first-past-the-post plurality rule for the election of most members of its parliament. In the United Kingdom methods of election vary from one part of the country to the other. In Northern Ireland proportional representation is the norm, and in Scotland and in Wales it is used to elect devolved assemblies. The British Parliament continues to be elected by the first-past-the-post plurality system, while Britain's representatives in the parliament of the European Union are elected by proportional representation. In the United States the debate about drawing districts to give ethnic or racial groups representation echoes arguments heard in Britain at the end of the eighteenth century.

SCOPE OF THE ENCYCLOPEDIA

Because elections involve much more than the simple act of voting, this book aims to include everything that you ever thought of asking about elections. It is intended to stimulate fresh thoughts by calling attention to features of the electoral process often overlooked when the focus is on the "horse race" aspects of election campaigns. Although the entries emphasize contemporary events, references to the past show the origins of many things taken for granted today—for example, the right of women to vote. Historical references also make it possible to understand practices that once were common but today are rare, such as communal voting in colonial elections.

Elections of all kinds are included, from free and fair ballots to unfree elections. There are entries about elections to unique offices, such as the national presidency, and elections to national parliaments with hundreds of members. There are entries dealing with elections to the second-order, fifteen-country European Parliament; elections to multiple tiers of government in federal systems; and elections of nonpartisan local officials. There are entries about referendums, in which electors vote on policies rather than people. To complete our understanding of elections, there are also entries about ways of making choices without voting—for example, consumer behavior in the market place and the Quaker practice of decision making.

Because electoral conditions vary greatly among countries, contributors have been encouraged to draw examples from countries having different types of electoral and socio-economic systems. The members of the encyclopedia's editorial board live on two continents, and they write about elections on every continent. Joel Barkan is a professor in Iowa, but his primary field of interest is Africa; Dieter Nohlen's university in Germany is a continent away from Latin America, about which he has published extensively; and Larry Diamond of Stanford University has lived in and written about Asia and Africa.

To understand elections in a particular country, we need concepts identifying the basic elements of the electoral process. To understand how votes are converted into seats in Mexico or Japan, we do not need to know Spanish or Japanese; rather, we need to understand the workings of proportional representation and plurality electoral systems. Therefore, the primary entries in this book are generic terms referring to features of elections found almost everywhere, such as campaigning, counting votes, and the effects of elections. In this way, a reader can appreciate different ways of conducting a free and fair competitive election. For example, in some countries voting is conducted on the weekend; in others it is held on a weekday that is in some countries made a public holiday for the occasion.

A reader wanting information about a particular country should turn to the appendix, which contains descriptive information about the election of the national legislature in 144 countries and provides details of presidential elections in the many countries that fill this office by direct election. The format of the appendix makes it easy to find information about one particular country and to compare a particular feature of elections across many countries. It reports for the most recent election the turnout of voters, the share of the vote won by the most successful party, and the degree of proportionality in converting votes into seats. Thanks to the Internet, a reader wanting to keep abreast of the dozens of elections held every year can use the World Wide Web to update the figures reported here. A particularly useful site for global

information is the Parline section of the Inter-Parliamentary Union (www.ipu.org), an association of national parliaments from around the world.

Because it is important to understand both the broad purposes and the narrow mechanics of elections, the topics in this encyclopedia range from the grand to the microscopic. There are comprehensive entries about democracy and about accountability, and there are narrow, technical ones on topics such as proxy voting and recall elections. No claim is made to cover every feature of the political process of which elections are but one part. This focus avoids unnecessary duplication and keeps the work within a single volume. Differences in the importance and complexity of topics cause entries to vary in length. Some are brief, while others are as long as a chapter in a book. Because founding elections are of special importance in initiating the move toward democracy, the topic merits six lengthy entries that highlight the differences between the founding elections in the oldest democracies and those in the new democracies. Substantial parts of the encyclopedia can be read like the chapters of a book or assigned to students needing a clear and full exposition of a topic, whereas others may be read like entries in a dictionary or a pocket encyclopedia.

ACKNOWLEDGMENTS

The contributors to this encyclopedia are experts in the subjects on which they write and come from eleven different countries. Each was asked to define the key words in an entry; describe the topic's significance in the electoral process; provide illuminating examples from different countries, past and present; discuss problems and differences of opinion; cite books and articles that offer more details; and, as appropriate, propose cross-references to other entries in the encyclopedia.

The editor in chief thanks a cosmopolitan and scholarly editorial board: Joel Barkan, André Blais, Walter Dean Burnham, Gary Cox, Larry Diamond, Richard Katz, Arend Lijphart, Tom Mackie, and Dieter Nohlen. My task was to start the ball rolling by developing the encyclopedia's terms of reference and the initial list of entries. The editorial board members made comments and suggestions for topics, wrote entries, and reviewed other entries in their areas of expertise. The review process was essential to ensure that each entry is comprehensive and accurate. Each contributor played an important part, distilling knowledge acquired over many years into relatively short, clear, and authoritative entries on topics as esoteric as rotten boroughs or as commonplace and complex as proportional representation.

The editorial team at CQ Press deserves special praise, since it took only twenty-nine months from signing the contract to publishing this large and complex book. David Tarr, the executive editor, responded promptly and positively to the initial proposal and persistently kept track of an enormous volume of correspondence between authors and editors without losing anything, not even his temper. Grace Hill was indispensable in tracking authors and manuscripts, maintaining the database, and sending out reminders. Once the entries started coming in, Jerry Orvedahl, the senior editor, edited each entry carefully to make sure that information was clearly set out and that there were no inconsistencies or gaps in the exposition. He was assisted by staff member Tom Roche and freelance editors Nola Healy Lynch, Mary Y. Marik, and Tracy Villano. I hope the knowledge he gained about elections around the world was some compensation for the effort he put into editing.

For a bulky reference volume to be easily read and handled it must be well designed. If it is, the book will look and feel right in the reader's hands, and the designer's work may hardly be noticed. The editor in chief appreciates the quality of design, which was the handiwork of Debra Naylor. Deborah Patton compiled the compendious index. For a reference work to be useful to many people, it must also get into many hands—and the CQ marketing team led by Kathryn Suarez, director of Library Reference Publishing, and Kristen Beach has been efficient and active in pursuing this goal.

Richard Rose, editor in chief
University of Strathclyde
Glasgow, Scotland

INTERNATIONAL
ENCYCLOPEDIA
OF
ELECTIONS

ABSENTEE VOTING

Absentee voting is voting in accordance with prescribed procedures by persons who are away from the polling station or stations at which they would normally be expected to vote. Under most systems of election administration, voters are able to cast an "ordinary" vote at only a limited number of polling stations. Often, voters are required to cast such a vote at a designated polling station within a precinct or polling division, but depending on the arrangements in place they may be able to vote at more than one polling station. Constraints of this type may be implemented with the practical objective of limiting the size of the lists of voters used at polling stations. In many countries, however, it is also thought beneficial to require voters to vote, if possible, in or near their own communities, as a means of safeguarding against impersonation. But many systems with diverse and mobile populations recognize that it is impracticable to impose an absolute limitation on the places at which people can vote, since the effect might well be to disenfranchise significant numbers of voters.

Diverse mechanisms for absentee voting are available. Under some regimes, voters who wish to cast an absentee ballot are required to register their intention in advance, indicating where they will be voting. Associated with this requirement, there may be only a limited class of persons entitled to cast an absentee ballot. Under other systems, voters may be able to cast an absentee vote without making a prior application; at Australian federal elections, for example, a voter may cast an absentee vote, without prior notice, at any polling station located in the same state as the constituency for which he or she is registered to vote. Voters may also have the option of transmitting their completed ballots by mail; of casting a vote prior to election day; or of voting outside the country at specially created stations or at diplomatic missions.

Where voters have not been required to register in advance for an absentee ballot, they often are required to record some form of tendered ballot, since their eligibility to vote may need to be checked.

See also *Day of Election; Overseas Voting; Proxy Voting; Tendered Ballots.*

MICHAEL MALEY, AUSTRALIAN ELECTORAL COMMISSION

ACCLAMATION, ELECTION BY (OR VOICE VOTE)

Election by acclamation reflects a preference for spontaneity and unanimity over deliberation and disagreement. In its purest form, it harkens to the "elections" of the Homeric assembly, in which the warriors would shout their approval of choices made elsewhere by the aristocracy, or to the election of some early bishops, for example, St. Ambrose in Milan, of whom it is reported that when he arrived (in his capacity as governor) to calm a public disturbance, a child in the crowd shouted "Ambrose Bishop," with the cry taken up by the entire crowd.

A reasonably close approximation of this ideal type might take the form of an uncontested election by a mass meeting with voice voting or voting by show of hands. An example would be many elections of knights of the shire to the unreformed English parliament, in which personal standing or elite agreement often reduced the number of candidates to the number to be elected. These individuals would then be presented to the county court for approval rather than choice. Even when there was a contest, a second election might be held to confirm the choice unanimously.

This practice is formalized in a second sense of election by acclamation: a parliamentary procedure in which a formal motion to elect by acclamation is offered, usually to confirm the outcome of a previously contested election. This type of motion conventionally is introduced by a supporter of one of the losing candidates and often is accepted by a vote of one to nothing, with everyone except the introducer abstaining.

A third sense of election by acclamation would be "election" by plebiscite, in which the people are asked whether they accept a single candidate rather than which of several candidates they choose. The classic examples are the French plebiscite of 1851, in which Louis Napoleon was confirmed as president for ten years, and that of 1852, when his presidency was converted into a hereditary emperorship ("The French people wish the restoration of the Imperial dignity in the person of Louis Napoleon Bonaparte . . ."). Ballots that take the form of elections but limit the number of candidates to precisely the number to be elected are equivalent to this plebiscitary sense of election by acclamation. They were typical of many functionally nondemocratic governments that wanted to maintain the outward institutional trappings of democracy.

Finally, a substantially free election that simply is uncontested also may technically result in election by acclamation. When several individual elections of this sort are part of a larger and contested election, they can have a distorting effect on aggregate statistics, since they generally are included in the reported aggregate distribution of elected candidates but of necessity are excluded from the aggregate distribution of votes.

As the last two cases illustrate, election by acclamation need not be by voice vote. Conversely, voting by voices need not be limited to election by acclamation. At least into the sixteenth century, members of Parliament for the English counties might be chosen by voice vote in contested elections; although an individual polling of the voters might be demanded, it was not required, and was in any event directed at verifying their eligibility to vote rather than establishing a precise count of the number of votes received by each candidate. As the chief justice observed in 1555, "election might be by voices . . . or by such other way, wherein it is easy to tell who has the majority, and yet very difficult to know the certain number of them" (quoted in Edwards 1964, 189).

With a large crowd assembled in one place, voice voting has the obvious advantage of efficiency, and at least in the case of closely contested elections, the obvious danger of inaccuracy or intentional misrepresentation of the result. Voice voting additionally supports the idea of a single collective choice rather than the summation of a number of individual choices. It also affords more anonymity to voters than an individual open poll, while allowing illiterates to vote without requiring special assistance.

See also *Open Voting; Papal Elections; Plebiscites and Plebiscitary Politics; Quaker Decision Making; Secret Ballot; Unopposed Returns.*

RICHARD S. KATZ, JOHNS HOPKINS UNIVERSITY

BIBLIOGRAPHY

Dudden, F. Homes. *Life and Times of St. Ambrose.* Oxford: Clarendon Press, 1935.

Edwards, Goronwy. "The Emergence of Majority Rule in English Parliamentary Elections." *Transactions of the Royal Historical Society,* 5th series, 14 (1964).

Hirst, Derek. *Representative of the People.* Cambridge: Cambridge University Press, 1975.

ACCOUNTABILITY, ELECTIONS AS ONE FORM OF

Holding officials accountable for their actions at elections is one of the primary functions of elections and one of the primary mechanisms for ensuring that government is systematically responsive to citizens' desires.

THE CONCEPT

The concept of "accountability" has had a varied career from ancient Greece forward. The core of the concept, though, is well captured in its etymology. Accountability is a matter of giving an account; to give an account is to tell a story; and to hold persons to account is to require them to tell you a story, reserving to yourself the right to query and probe the story you have been told.

Accountability, thus understood, entails being answerable *to* someone *for* something. Some people or entities might be "unaccountable," not answerable to anyone for anything. (Critics claim multinational corporations are like that.) Other people might be accountable to some particular person for everything they do (as medieval vassals and Victorian wives were said to be). Typically, however, accountability is both agent-specific and subject-specific. Those who are accountable are accountable to particular others in respect of particular sorts of performances.

Such accountability might be strong or weak. The weak form, which may well be strong enough in most cases, amounts merely to asking embarrassing questions that the other must answer. The powers of the British House of Commons Public Accounts Committee arguably amount to little more than that. Strong accountability attaches real sanctions to unsatisfactory accounts. Administrative law tribunals declare an act unlawful if proper procedures cannot be shown to have been followed.

Within democratic theory, accountability mechanisms take on another, somewhat different, significance. Democracy is based on the rule of law, where laws themselves must be in accordance with (or at least not contrary to) the will of the people. Thus within democratic theory political accountability has the more specific aim of making political actors not only nonarbitrary but also systematically responsive to popular wishes, either (or both) in terms of the policies the electorate wants pursued or the results the electorate wants achieved.

Politically, the central purpose of accountability is to check the arbitrary exercise of power. The availability of mechanisms to do so is a necessary but insufficient condition for the rule of law. The simple fact that one's actions are subject to external scrutiny, in a system where reasons have to be given, offers overseers at least the opportunity to require that those reasons be based on principles and rules that are general in form, as the larger ideal of the rule of law would require.

ELECTORAL ACCOUNTABILITY

Systems of electoral accountability strive to achieve systematic responsiveness through the mechanism of periodic reelection, making the official's continuing tenure in office subject to the votes of the electorate.

Democratic accountability is a matter of politicians being called to account at the next poll for what they, and all those responsible to them, have done during their previous period in office. Strictly speaking, it is not election but reelection that constitutes the occasion for electoral accountability. Politicians have nothing to account for until they have had a chance to do something in public office. Aspirants may promise, but only incumbents can account.

In the course of elections, both challengers and incumbents make campaign promises. Such promises not only presuppose some subsequent accounting but also assist in it, providing a yardstick by which voters can judge whether elected officials have done what they said they were going to do. Connected though the two processes are, there is nonetheless a striking contrast between the retrospective accounting implied by models of democratic accountability and the prospective promising at the heart of models of democratic competition for people's votes.

A further consequence of electoral accountability being a post hoc check is that only those who expect to seek reelection have any (material) reason to take any notice of the threat that electoral accountability poses. If elected officials were eligible for only one term in office, then electoral accountability would be totally absent. (Politicians may, of course, care about other things, like their place in history or the fate of their party in the next election. But were we prepared to count on public officials being conscientious and public spirited, we could dispense altogether with the formalities of reelection and the political accountability that comes with it.)

Holding officials accountable through the mechanism of reelection implies, finally, an "omnibus" sort of accountability. In terms of the sanction attached, the mechanism of electoral accountability is a blunt instrument. A politician is either reelected or not. Furthermore, in making that summary judgment, voters are forced to pass judgment not just on the elected official but also on everyone accountable to and through that official for their performance.

The bluntness of their sanction combines with their essentially backward-looking nature to make systems of electoral accountability imperfect mechanisms for doing what

systems of democratic accountability are supposed to do, which is to make public officials systematically responsive to the wishes of the public at large.

RESPONSIVENESS BY OTHER MEANS

If our ultimate aim is democratic responsiveness, we ought not fixate on accountability mechanisms at all. All accountability mechanisms, electoral or otherwise, strive to ensure that X's actions will conform to Y's wishes by ensuring that Y can review X's actions and possibly reverse them. Such post hoc measures are not the only way of seeking to ensure X's responsiveness to Y's wishes, however.

Some familiar mechanisms for promoting democratic responsiveness work prospectively rather than retrospectively. Crucially, we try to ensure that X's actions will conform to Y's wishes through selection procedures that ensure that only people with Y-like preferences will be chosen to occupy the role of X. Or we devolve decision-making powers to subgroups of Xs, identified geographically (for example, federalism) or functionally (such as corporatism, subsidiarity), whose own preferences are more in accord with Y's. Sometimes we even try to ensure that decisions conform to Y's wishes by dispensing with X altogether, instead vesting decision-making power directly in Y (for example, through a referendum).

Or we try to ensure that X's actions conform to Y's wishes through procedures (as in administrative law) requiring simply that X consult Y, in a nonbinding way, before the decision is taken. We sometimes conjoin the requirement to consult with a further, but still largely toothless, requirement for officials to "take note" of the results of the consultation. Weak though such requirements may be, just being forced to "go through the motions" has been shown to make decision makers more sensitive and responsive to the considerations being canvassed, even in the absence of any binding requirements for them to respond.

Even within the realm of retrospective accountability, there are many alternatives to elections. One powerful mechanism for bringing X's actions into conformity with Y's wishes is by holding X up to public ridicule or private opprobrium. Question Time in the UK House of Commons (perhaps the most cherished mechanism for "accountability" in British political lore) might be an example of public ridicule; the prime minister's weekly audience with the monarch, who can ask penetrating questions but possesses no political power, might be an instance of private accountability. The threat of being "named in Parliament," even if no material consequences ensue, is conventionally regarded as a powerful deterrent to antisocial conduct. Administrators dread nothing more than a "please explain" memo from their superiors. And of course the "embarrassment factor" is the chief mechanism through which the Fourth Estate—the free press—holds politicians accountable and helps make them democratically responsive.

We can also try to ensure that X's actions conform to Y's wishes by subjecting X's actions to the discipline of markets in which Y's wishes are effectively expressed. Privatizing public functions might make the enterprise more responsive to the wishes of the public at large, or at least of those members of the public with money enough to buy shares in or products from the privatized enterprise. Introducing quasi-markets within public authorities, or vouchers that citizens can use to "purchase" services from them, might make those authorities more responsive to the public that they are meant to serve and might widen the range of that public.

The success of market strategies in promoting systematic responsiveness to the wishes of the public at large depends on Ys in general having sufficient resources to make their preferences felt in the markets. Markets respond only to "effective demand," and money is the element that classically makes demand economically effective. Where money is concentrated in the hands of a relatively few people, markets will be systematically responsive principally to their desires. That is the problem to which vouchers and quasi-markets are addressed, and that is the sense in which vouchers and quasi-markets must promote the democratic ideal of "systematic responsiveness to the public at large" better than privatizing public functions.

The success of market-oriented accountability mechanisms also depends on the perfect realization of the notoriously unrealistic conditions characterizing the economist's "ideal market." Privatizing public monopolies like water or railways in ways that leave them effective monopolies invites private profiteering at the expense of the public rather than enforces systematic responsiveness to it. In other cases, however, ideal market conditions might more nearly be approximated. In any case, before dismissing the ideal market out of hand, we must recall that the capacity of political systems to ensure that politicians' actions conform to citizens' wishes similarly depend on the satisfaction of certain ideal conditions (which are perhaps equally unrealistic) governing the political market for people's votes.

HOW WELL DOES ELECTORAL ACCOUNTABILITY PROMOTE DEMOCRATIC RESPONSIVENESS?

Systems of electoral accountability emphasize retrospective voting, rewarding or punishing elected officials for what they have done in the previous period in office, rather than evaluating competing candidates in terms of their promises and plans for the future. That is problematic in various ways. It presupposes that voters are adept at retrospective accounting, remembering what all the officials have done in the last pe-

riod. It further presupposes that the past will be like the future, and that a party that has done well in one set of circumstances will do likewise in future circumstances that might be very different.

Demanding though retrospective electoral accountability is in those respects, in other important respects it is minimally demanding. Comparative assessment of campaign promises entails complicated causal modeling, which is beyond the ken of most voters. Simply asking them whether they are better off than they were four years ago, or whether the country is better off than it was four years ago, does not. And tricky though it may be to prevent political money from contaminating the democratic ideal of political equality ("one person, one vote"), those difficulties are pale shadows of those that come in trying to equalize everyone's resources in markets or quasi-markets.

Systems of electoral accountability are not stand-alone institutions. Minimally, they must be supplemented by other mechanisms of judicial and administrative accountability, particularly in complex organizations where responsibility is otherwise so diffused as to be meaningless or is hierarchically lodged in the hands of someone with no effective control over the operations in question. Partial though it may be, holding politicians accountable at elections nonetheless constitutes the chief guarantor of democratic responsiveness in the contemporary world.

ROBERT E. GOODIN, AUSTRALIAN NATIONAL UNIVERSITY

BIBLIOGRAPHY

Bovens, Mark. *The Quest for Responsibility: Accountability and Citizenship in Complex Organizations.* Cambridge: Cambridge University Press, 1998.

Day, Patricia, and Rudolph Klein. *Accountabilities: Five Public Services.* London: Tavistock, 1987.

Fiorina, Morris. *Retrospective Voting in American National Elections.* New Haven, Conn.: Yale University Press, 1981.

Miller, Warren E., and Donald E. Stokes. "Constituency Influence in Congress." *American Political Science Review* 57 (March 1963): 45–56.

Taylor, Serge. *Making Bureaucracies Think: The Environmental Impact Statement Strategy of Administrative Reform.* Stanford, Calif.: Stanford University Press, 1984.

Wolf, Charles, Jr. *Markets or Governments: Choosing Between Imperfect Alternatives.* Cambridge, Mass.: MIT Press, 1988.

ADDITIONAL MEMBER SYSTEM

In English-speaking countries, the term *additional member system* refers to an electoral system in which some of the seats are allocated in single-member constituencies and the remaining seats are allocated according to a proportional-representation formula. By this definition, the German electoral system could be considered an additional member system. But in Germany and other countries with similar systems, the term is not used, probably because it implies—incorrectly—that some of the members of parliament are elected according to a plurality formula and others according to a proportional formula. To the contrary, *all* seats in the German Bundestag are allocated according to the proportional formula. Within this overall determination, however, the voter can choose among party candidates in single-member constituencies, and the candidate who wins a constituency is definitely elected.

The English definition implies that the single-member districts are complemented by a proportional-representation component, but this implication obscures the proportional-representation character of the German and similar systems, in which some deputies come from single-member constituencies, others from multimember constituencies. The Germans' term for their electoral system is *personalized proportional system*. It emphasizes the connection between proportionality as the basic principle of representation, on the one hand, and the ability of people to vote for individual candidates, on the other. In the German system, proportional representation is the most important element, while the allocation in single-member constituencies remains the complement. The term *personalized proportional system* expresses exactly this relationship.

The different terms express different conceptual perspectives. New Zealand tried to combine them in 1993, when it named its new electoral system, which was similar to the German one, a *mixed-member proportional system*. The different terminology would not be so important were it not reflective of differences in the type and functioning of the systems.

THE DECISION RULE AND PRINCIPLE OF PROPORTIONALITY

Before considering the German system in more detail, it is necessary to address some conceptual questions that are relevant for distinguishing between different types of electoral systems. First, it is important to distinguish between the principle of representation and the decision rule. In "classical" electoral systems, the two are identical. For example, in first-past-the-post, majority is both the decision rule and the principle of representation; in pure proportional representation, proportionality is both the rule and the principle. In the so-called additional member system, however, the principle of representation and the decision rule are segmented: the principle of proportionality is combined with the plurality decision rule. The term *mixed-member proportional system,* as used in New Zealand, means precisely that. The principles of representation are not mixed, which would in practice be impossible. Rather, in this new category of combined electoral systems, the decision on individual candidates at the constituency level is combined with proportionality as the principle of representation at the parliamentary level. Different combinations of decision rule and principle of representation distinguish the following combined electoral systems.

Personalized proportional systems or mixed-member proportional systems (the terminology used in Germany and New Zealand, respectively). All seats are allocated according to the proportional principle at the national level. The decisions that voters make on the individual candidates in the constituencies, who make up half of the parliament, do not affect the national proportional distribution of seats among parties, except in the case of extra seats (see below).

Compensatory systems. Under these electoral systems, a portion of the seats are allocated in single-member constituencies according to a plurality or majority formula, then, in a second step, a second portion of seats are allocated by proportional representation in order to compensate, at least roughly, for the disproportionality that resulted from the elections in single-member constituencies.

Parallel, segmented, or mixed systems. Under these electoral systems, one portion of the seats are allocated in single-member constituencies, and, *separately,* another portion of seats are allocated through party lists according to a proportional formula.

When classifying electoral systems, it is necessary to distinguish first between classical systems (meaning those in which the principle of representation and the decision rule correspond to each other) and combined systems (meaning those in which the principle of representation and the decision rule cross each other) and second between different combinations of the main elements within the combined systems.

The types of combined electoral systems mentioned above are in use in a large number of countries. For example, personalized proportional systems are in use in Germany and New Zealand, compensatory systems in Italy and Hungary, and parallel systems in Mexico, Japan, and Russia. Scholars often do not (yet) distinguish among the three types, although they affect the distribution of seats differently. Furthermore, scholars generally identify these very different electoral systems with the German system. This is why the German electoral system is treated as a model in discussions on electoral reform in many countries. Therefore, it should be described in detail.

THE GERMAN ELECTORAL SYSTEM

The German electoral system is a proportional system, not a mixed system. The proportional-representation system is personalized by virtue of a voter's ability to choose among party candidates in the single-member constituencies. Winners in the single-member constituencies comprise half of the seats in parliament. These candidates are elected according to the plurality formula. The voter has two votes: the first is cast for a party candidate in a single-member constituency, the second for a (closed and blocked) regional list of parties in one of the sixteen federal states (bundesländer). The allocation of all parliamentary seats is determined by the parties' proportional shares of the votes at the national level, applying the Hare-Niemeyer method (number of the party's votes multiplied by the total number of seats that are to be allocated divided by the total number of valid votes; the result is the same as Hare but it does not leave remaining seats). There is a 5 percent legal threshold at the national level, which is waived if a party attains three constituency seats.

After ascertaining how many seats a party is entitled to claim in parliament, these seats are allocated proportionally within each party according to the party's sixteen regional list shares, once again applying the Hare-Niemeyer method. Then, the number of seats the party attained in the single-member constituencies is subtracted from the number of seats to which it is entitled by proportional distribution. The remaining seats are filled by the regional lists' candidates. If a party attains more constituency seats than it is proportionally entitled to (so-called extra seats), then it keeps them. Thus, the voters determine with their first vote the composition of half of the Bundestag, but, with the exception of possible extra seats, they have no influence on the parliament's party composition. This structure and effect are typical for personalized proportional representation, although variations of some minor elements are possible. Variations arise in the electoral systems of some German federal states. Outside of Germany, variations arise where personalized procedures have been introduced, concerning, for example, the relationship between constituency seats and list seats, the proportional allocation of seats that may be distributed at the national level or in multi-member constituencies, or the treatment of extra seats, which in some cases are proportionally compensated.

Combined electoral systems have gained ground on classical electoral systems in the last decade. At least in eastern Europe, almost no classical electoral systems were introduced. The reasons are evident: Combined electoral systems are more amenable to political compromise and also to (ambitions of) political engineering. Above all, they are more suitable for fulfilling, simultaneously and in a well-balanced way, the different functions of electoral systems: providing fair representation, government stability, voter participation in making personal choices, and government accountability to voters.

See also *Compensatory Seats; Mixed Electoral Systems.*

DIETER NOHLEN, UNIVERSITY OF HEIDELBERG

BIBLIOGRAPHY

Irvine, William P. "Additional-Member Electoral Systems." In *Choosing an Electoral System,* edited by B. Grofman and A. Lijphart. New York: Praeger, 1984.

Kaase, Max. "Personalized Proportional Representation: The 'Model' of the West German Electoral System." In *Choosing an Electoral System,* edited by Bernard Grofman and Arend Lijphart, 155–164. New York: Praeger, 1984.

Nohlen, Dieter. *Elections and Electoral Systems.* New Delhi: Macmillan India, 1996.

ADMINISTRATION OF ELECTIONS

Election administration is the organization of the voting process and the counting of votes by authorities exercising power derived from the sovereignty of a state or from an appropriate international agreement, and it entails the creation and maintenance of a proper environment for election-related activities. Fair and effective administration of the electoral process is a necessary condition for free and fair elections.

DISTINCTIVE FEATURES OF ELECTION ADMINISTRATION

The way in which election administrators work is shaped by at least five challenges. The first is political neutrality. Since election administrators control the voting and counting processes, the extent to which election results are accepted as valid by all relevant actors often depends on the extent of public trust in the administrators. It is therefore most important that an election administration body should be, and should be seen to be, politically neutral.

The second challenging area is logistics. Since an election involves putting almost the whole adult population of a polity through a prescribed process in a short period, usually in the face of immutable deadlines, it is one of the most complex logistical exercises that a country ever faces in peacetime. Election logistics are made even more demanding by the fact that in many countries the date of an election is not fixed until a short time before polling takes place.

A third challenge is accountability. Election administrators are required not only to conduct elections properly but also to be in a position to demonstrate that they have done so, in order to respond to formal challenges to the result and to maintain public confidence in the election process. This requires the keeping of detailed records and the establishment of audit trails at all stages.

Fourth, there is the challenge of decentralization. Since a basic objective of polling is to enable universal and equal participation by those entitled to vote, facilities for voter registration and polling cannot be located in only a few places: they must be established throughout the country so as to ensure that all voters have ready access to them, and the staff managing them must have full authority to perform their tasks. Although a small commission or small central administration may have nominal overall responsibility for the conduct of an election, in practice it will always have to devolve that responsibility to a large number of subordinate bodies or officers, while maintaining accountability.

Finally, election administrators must meet the challenge of project planning. The simplest legislative election involves hundreds of interdependent tasks, and a complex one involves thousands. The only way to ensure that these will be done on time is to use comprehensive and structured project planning. Skills in project planning and management are taken for granted in fields such as civil engineering and the military but are much less common in professions from which senior electoral administrators are frequently appointed, such as law and the social sciences.

These five challenges tend not to be well understood by political decision makers, and as a consequence, election administrators are sometimes given unrealistic deadlines to work toward and inadequate resources. Such a failure of understanding at the political level led directly to major and well-documented problems at the 1994 South African elections and the 1996 elections in Bosnia-Herzegovina.

ETHICS OF ELECTION ADMINISTRATION

Electoral administrators should demonstrate respect for the law; be nonpartisan and neutral; operate transparently; be accurate; and serve the voters. Adherence to these principles will tend to enhance the validity and credibility of an election process, whereas a failure to adhere to them will have the opposite effect. They are spelled out and discussed in some detail in the *Code of Conduct for the Ethical and Professional Administration of Elections,* issued by the International Institute for Democracy and Electoral Assistance (Stockholm, 1997), which within a year of its publication had been endorsed by thirty election administration bodies around the world.

THE STRUCTURE OF ELECTION ADMINISTRATION BODIES

Around the world there is considerable variation in structures for administering elections, reflecting the administrative history of, and environment prevailing in, each country.

The simplest model is where election administration is undertaken by a branch of the executive government, in the same way as any other administrative task. In the United Kingdom, for example, electoral administration is a responsibility of local government officials, who function largely autonomously, though within a legislative framework administered by the home secretary. Similar arrangements prevail in France. In the United States, elections are locally administered, though the legislative framework, even for federal elections, is established largely at the state level, albeit with some constraints imposed by the Constitution, the federal Voting Rights Act, and the National Voter Registration Act, and with responsibility for federal campaign finance issues retained by the Federal Election Commission. In Sweden, elections are conducted by the National Tax Board, an arrangement that flows from the board's more general responsibility for the maintenance of the national civic register.

The conduct of elections by a branch of the executive government potentially raises questions about the neutrality of administration, since in a democratic environment the executive will itself be under the control of political actors who have an interest in the outcome of the election process. In some cases, especially where the concept of an apolitical civil service holds sway, this may not be a problem. Often, however, it has been thought desirable to reinforce public confidence in the neutrality of election administration by establishing a permanent electoral administration that is explicitly independent of the government of the day and not subject to political direction. Prominent examples of such bodies include Elections Canada (established in 1920), the Election Commission of India (established in 1950), and the Australian Electoral Commission (established in 1984).

Even among such administrations there are significant variations in aspects of their independence, reflecting nuances in the relationship between the administration and the broader executive government. Some, like Elections Canada, have a portion of their funding guaranteed by law, and a few even have extensive powers during an election period to commandeer resources from the government. Others, such as the Australian Electoral Commission, have to compete for funding in an annual budget process controlled by the government. Some have their own permanent staff, not only at the central level but also at the grassroots level; for example, the Australian Electoral Commission has a separate, permanent office corresponding to each constituency in the national parliament. In Canada, field officers operate full-time only at elections and are government appointees. Some, such as the Election Commission of India, have their independence guaranteed in the constitution, while others are established by a law that may be amended or repealed by the legislature. Appointments may be in the hands of the executive government or may require the approval of the legislature.

The degree of authority of an election administration is influenced by its relationship to the judiciary. Some election administrations not only administer elections but also pronounce on their ultimate validity. This can happen in transitional situations where the judiciary is seen as associated with the old order; for example, the Independent Electoral Commission, which conducted the 1994 South African elections, was given such a mandate. The work of an election commission can be subject to judicial review; in Australia and India, for example, the courts may be petitioned to overturn an election result. An alternative is to buttress the independence of an election administration by drawing some or all of its membership from the judiciary. In Costa Rica, the Supreme Electoral Tribunal is required, at election time, to consist of five magistrates. It not only manages the organization of elections but also has jurisdiction to rule on challenges to the election process. In Australia, the chairperson of the Electoral Commission must be a sitting or retired Federal Court judge. Members of the judiciary also chaired the electoral commissions established in 1994 in South Africa and Malawi.

Because of the diversity of election administration functions, sometimes more than one administrative body has a role in the process. In the United Kingdom, although voter registration and polling are administered locally, redistricting (an activity that by its very nature goes beyond the purely local) is undertaken by boundary commissions separately established for England, Scotland, Wales, and Northern Ireland. In New Zealand, four different bodies are involved in the election process: New Zealand Post, which maintains the electoral register; the Chief Electoral Office in the Ministry of Justice, which has responsibility for conducting general elections, by-elections, and referendums; the Electoral Commission, which registers political parties, conducts voter education, and administers certain legal provisions governing political party resources; and the Representation Commission, which is established intermittently to determine constituency boundaries. Arrangements of this type typically require close liaison between the responsible bodies, since areas such as registration of voters, registration of parties, and preparation for polling tend to overlap significantly.

The collapse of the Soviet Union gave rise in the 1990s to a need for election administrations in many countries that had previously had one-party systems, or in which there was significant public mistrust of the incumbent state authorities. As a consequence, many countries have had to establish ad hoc election administrations, often initially mandated to conduct a specific election. The Independent Electoral Commission, which conducted the first South African multiracial elections in 1994, is a prominent case in point, but other examples abound throughout eastern Europe and Africa.

Ad hoc administrations typically face a challenging environment. Especially where a transition to multiparty competition is involved, the legitimacy (and often the structures) of the old order will often have been brought close to collapse. In such cases, there tends to be great pressure on the election administration to conduct elections as quickly as possible, in order to establish a basis for legitimate government.

When the election administration is appointed, a premium is often placed on finding people who have a high degree of political credibility. This may lead to officials from the old order being overlooked in favor of academics and members of the judiciary, civil society, and the private sector. While this trend is understandable, such individuals are unlikely to have experience in election administration and often have little experience in the planning and execution of any other large-scale operations. As a consequence, they are often poorly placed to make an accurate assessment of the resources they will need.

An ad hoc election administration, faced with the need to establish a decentralized election machine, often has little choice but to make use at the grassroots level of functionaries drawn from the old regime. Such functionaries may have little personal commitment to the political transition that is underway and no experience in working neutrally in a multiparty environment. Their work therefore typically needs to be monitored closely. At the 1994 South African elections, a full-time Monitoring Directorate was established within the Independent Electoral Commission to deal with that issue.

In some cases a transition may involve a move not only to a multiparty system but also to a universal franchise. The latter change is harder to implement on the ground. For example, most of the practical problems that arose at the 1994 South African election stemmed from an inadequate assessment of the difficulties that would flow from multiplying the number of people for whom voting facilities had to be provided.

A problem with ad hoc election administrations is that because of their transitory nature, they may not provide a basis for the further development of democratic institutions. Even if moves have been made to establish the ad hoc commission as a permanent body, often those who organized the transitional election will not wish to make permanent careers in the field. This can create problems when the next election falls due: not only will institutional memory be gone, but an election administration will have to be established again, virtually from scratch. This was the case in South Africa after 1994.

Regardless of its status, an election administration must be able to establish a grassroots structure at election time, with staff at each polling place; as a rough rule of thumb, approximately ten thousand polling officials are required for every million voters. In practical terms it normally is necessary to have administrative structures between the central administration and the polling stations: these are often at the constituency level, but other levels of administration, frequently based on existing administrative units such as provinces or districts, tend also to be required.

The establishment of a decentralized field structure is not just a matter of having staff in the field: the tasks for which they are responsible, and the authority that they may exercise in performing those tasks, must be clearly defined in law.

PREPARING FOR THE ELECTION

The foundation of all election administration is an electoral law that expresses in a precise form the basic ground rules for the conduct of an election. The existence of such a law ensures that all political actors can have a common expectation of how the election process will proceed and prescribes and legitimizes the actions taken by election administrators. A failure to address critical aspects of the process in advance can seriously compromise an election; for example, at the 1998 elections in Cambodia, the formula for allocating seats in proportion to votes was not properly specified in the electoral law, which contributed to a bitter dispute between the contesting parties in the aftermath of the count.

The amount of detail in an electoral law varies greatly from country to country. Some laws, such as the Canada Elections Act, are highly detailed and prescriptive, whereas others deal only with broad principles and have to be supplemented by subordinate legislation or by rulings from the election administration. Highly prescriptive laws are by their nature inflexible, which can be a problem, particularly in transitional elections where unexpected difficulties are likely to arise; but when properly framed they provide definitive answers to the politically controversial questions that are likely to surface in the course of the election process. Less prescriptive laws provide flexibility but may leave controversial questions unanswered. Such questions then normally have to be resolved by the electoral administrators, in circumstances where there may be no obvious right or wrong answers; and in such situations, the credibility of the election administration may be diminished in the eyes of some of the political actors, regardless of the decisions made.

Once the electoral law is in place, the election administration can develop detailed, written operational procedures. The need for such documents arises, first, because even the most detailed electoral law will seldom spell out in sufficient detail the accountability mechanisms and audit trails that are necessary, and second because in cases where the election is centrally directed, much of the field staff will not be under direct day-to-day supervision from headquarters and will therefore need detailed instructions to ensure that the electoral law is implemented in a consistent way throughout the country. Since the movement of materials in an accountable way is a major part of day-to-day election operations, the process of designing forms, materials, and computer systems is not separate from the process of designing procedures, but is rather integral. The magnitude of these development and design tasks is largely independent of the number of voters.

Once the basic scheme for the conduct of an election has been determined, a project plan can list all the tasks required to bring the election to a successful conclusion; can identify how the tasks relate to one another and who will be doing them; and can be used to develop a budget for the process. From a practical point of view the quality of project planning is probably the single most important determinant of the mechanical quality of an election. Because of the number of tasks required to make an election succeed, it will rarely be possible for a policy maker to use instinct to assess the critical deadlines or the implications of slippages in important tasks (for example, delays in the printing of ballots). These assessments can be done in a reliable way only through the use of critical-path analysis. In the absence of a clear picture of precisely what has to be done, it is also impossible to produce an accurate budget.

VOTER REGISTRATION

The first aspect of the plan to be executed normally is voter registration, though this is not absolutely necessary. At the Rhodesian independence election of 1980 there was no separate registration, and voters were able to vote after presenting identification to a polling official. At the 1994 South African election, voters were able to support their claims to vote with a range of documents, but temporary voter cards were issued in the months preceding the polling for the benefit of persons who did not have any of the prescribed identification.

There are two major benefits to undertaking voter registration. The first is that it allows disputes about the right of a person to vote to be dealt with in a measured way well before the polling takes place, and thereby minimizes disputes on election day. This is of particular importance where there are major concerns that persons not entitled to vote might attempt to do so, a fear that often arises where an election is being held as part of a peace settlement, the UN-organized Cambodian election of 1993 being a good example. Second, registration provides finely structured data concerning the locations of voters, which can be used to considerable effect in planning the logistics of the polling. This is of particular benefit in developing countries, where adequate statistical information of this type is often difficult to obtain.

An essential output from any registration process is a mechanism for determining at the polling station whether a person should be allowed to vote there. Registrants may be given documents that identify them as registered voters and that can be produced at the polling station; or polling stations may be provided with lists of all registered voters entitled to vote there. Both schemes can be used concurrently. Voters may be given a photographic, nonphotographic, or machine-readable identity card, and such cards may be issued face-to-face or dispatched to voters after an election is called. The list of voters provided to a polling station may be in hard-copy or computerized form and may include all voters in a constituency or (if the scheme of polling constrains a voter to a predetermined polling station or to one of a predetermined set of polling stations) only a subset of those voters.

There are four main methods of producing a register. Under the first, there need be no separate register of voters; lists used at polling stations can be produced directly from a population database used for a range of administrative purposes. Under this system, no special steps are needed to update the register. Examples of countries using this system are Sweden and Denmark.

Under the second approach, there is a separate electoral register that is ongoing and is maintained between elections by adding the names of people who have newly qualified for registration, deleting the names of people who have died or become subject to disqualification, and amending records to reflect voters' changes of address. Since the register is not part of a broader national database, the election administration must obtain information from other government bodies for updating the register or the voters themselves must provide that information.

A register of this type can be designed so as to meet the needs of several levels of government, for example, national, state, and local. In the past, this tended to be done by registering voters for such subdivisions as a ward or parish and aggregating administrative units to create constituencies of a number of discrete subdivisions. Typically, subdivisional registers were printed periodically, and changes made to the registers between the time of the print and the time of the election at which they were to be used were reflected in a much smaller "supplementary register."

With the introduction of computerized registers, the need for subdivisions has largely disappeared, though in some cases they continue to be used. On a computerized register, every residence can be coded to a particular political jurisdiction, such as a national or state constituency or a local government area or ward. Where redistricting takes place, the changes can be reflected on the register by simply amending the territorial codes attached to addresses that have been moved from one jurisdiction to another. Voter identification cards or printed lists of voters can be produced for elections at any level of government at any time, providing considerable flexibility in cases where election dates are not fixed. Computerized maintenance of registers also facilitates the identification of duplicate entries and comparison of the register with other databases for the purpose of identifying invalid or outdated entries. Examples of countries with a continuously maintained register are Australia (which has had one for decades) and Canada (which developed one in the late 1990s).

A continuously maintained register also can be used to provide political parties, candidates, members of the legislature, authorities of the executive government, and other users such as geographers, demographers, medical researchers, and public opinion institutes with up-to-date information on population movements and the movement of individuals. In Australia, parliamentarians and political parties are entitled by law to obtain regularly updated information on changes to the register, and they use this information for direct-mail campaigns.

Under the third model, a register has a continuous existence but is created only periodically. The United Kingdom uses this system. Its electoral registration officers organize an annual canvass of all households in their areas of responsibility for the purpose of revising the register. Application forms for registration are given to each household to complete. A draft register is published each December, and members of the public have the opportunity to object to the presence or omission of particular names. A final register is then produced for use at all general elections and by-elections for a year. The emphasis is on public openness of the register, rather than rigorous checking of individual applications for registration, to provide confirmation that the names on the register are genuine and validly entered.

The fourth system is to develop a new register for each election. In Canadian national elections until the late 1990s an electoral register was enumerated only after an election had been called. Enumerators were sent to each address to identify individuals eligible to vote, and a preliminary register was published and revised on the basis of appeals against the omission of names and objections to the inclusion of names. In effect, this produced a potentially very accurate "snapshot" of the electorate at election time. The major disadvantages of the system were cost and delay: not only were similar data gathered repetitively at one national election after another, but since most Canadian provinces separately compiled provincial registers by enumeration, there was additional duplication. In some cases where this system is used, the onus to register is left with the voters, who may have to proceed to registration points rather than be visited at their homes. Such a system was used at the Namibian independence elections of 1989 and the UN-organized elections in Cambodia in 1993.

While most registration systems fall under one of the four systems described above, some features of one model may be reflected in another. For example, Australia's continuously maintained register is subject, between elections, to "electoral roll reviews" under which a door-to-door canvass (where feasible) is conducted to identify errors in the register to be corrected. These tend to be done when state or federal elections or federal redistricting is about to occur.

Regardless of the mechanics of the registration scheme, the process must involve a deliberative assessment of each individual's entitlement to registration. The most common requirements for registration include age (with a minimum voting age of somewhere between eighteen and twenty-one years being typical); citizenship or nationality; and residence. Residence requirements are often applied at two levels: residence for a certain period within a country is required for the person to be able to register at all; and residence for a prescribed time at a particular address is required for the person to be able to register for a particular constituency. Typically, there will also be a number of explicit disqualifications from the right to vote, including unsoundness of mind and being in prison or under a criminal conviction.

A major issue that arises in developing and administering a scheme of voter registration is that of achieving an acceptable balance between ensuring that only qualified persons are registered and ensuring that qualified persons are not deterred from registering by unduly inconvenient or oppressive registration requirements. The calculated use of such requirements in the American South to prevent the registration of African Americans gained worldwide notoriety following the protests of the civil rights movement in the 1950s and 1960s and led directly to the enactment of the federal Voting Rights Act in 1965.

ELECTION DAY

In terms of magnitude, the next most demanding tasks are the identification of premises that can be used as polling stations and the identification and training of persons able to work as polling officials. If these tasks are not substantially complete before an election is called, there usually will be insufficient time to do them before election day.

The election process moves into top gear with the promulgation of an election timetable specifying the deadlines for critical activities. The dates are often set by the executive government. Critical are the cutoff date for changes to the register of voters; the date for the close of registration of political parties and nomination of candidates; the polling day or days; and the day by which the election result must be announced.

Whether polling should take place over one or several days is a critical decision for administration as well as turnout. Polling on a single day is logistically simplest, as long as all voters have a reasonable opportunity to cast their ballots. Polling spread over several days gives rise to ballot security problems associated with the need to store sensitive materials, including ballots already in the ballot boxes, overnight. Particularly in developing countries, it is simply not possible to provide adequate polling facilities throughout the land on a single day. In India, where there are more than 600 million voters and some 800 thousand polling stations, the balloting process takes place on a staggered timetable across the country.

On the day or days of the election, even the simplest form of polling must provide four things: a mechanism for determining whether an individual claiming a right to vote is entitled to do so; a means for casting a secret ballot; controls to prevent multiple voting by an individual; and security against the count of fraudulent votes.

The first is intimately connected with the system of voter registration that has been chosen. Lists of voters may be provided to the polling officials, or voters may be given documents that establish their right to vote. In some cases, voters may be required to produce additional documentation: at the Namibian independence elections of 1989, voters were required to produce the nonphotographic voter registration card that had been issued to them plus one of a range of photographic identity documents. Arrangements are often made to cater to voters who have lost their documentation or whose names may have been wrongly omitted from the list of voters. Where a paper ballot is being used, these arrangements will often take the form of a "tendered ballot" (also known as a "declaration ballot" or a "provisional ballot"). The voter whose right to vote remains to be established will be given a ballot, but rather than placing it directly in a ballot box, the voter will place it in an unmarked "ballot paper envelope," which is then placed in an outer envelope on which the voter's particulars are recorded. Only when the voter's right to vote has been confirmed will the ballot paper envelope be withdrawn from the outer envelope and placed in a ballot box. Tendered voting runs the risk of being perceived as providing inadequate guarantees of the secrecy of the vote, but these perceptions can usually be overcome by adopting open and transparent procedures for opening the envelopes.

Tendered-voting mechanisms can also be used to enable a voter to vote at a polling station other than the one supplied with a list of voters containing his or her name and to enable the voting by mail of persons who cannot easily get to a polling station.

Numerous mechanisms have been developed over the years for secret balloting. The most widespread and simplest is the traditional paper ballot bearing the names of candidates, parties, or both; it is marked with a pen, a pencil, a stamp, or even a thumbprint and placed in a ballot box. Paper ballots can cope equally well with voting systems that require candidates or parties to be marked categorically and those that require an order of preference to be shown for candidates or parties. They also have sufficient flexibility to cope with systems that give voters relatively complex voting options. Examples include ballots on which voters may vote for either a party or a candidate of a party (as permitted in certain list systems of proportional representation used in Europe); those on which voters may vote for a constituency candidate and for a party list (as is the case in Germany); and those on which a voter may choose either to indicate an order of preference for the candidates or to adopt a preregistered ordering recommended by a political party (a system that has been used at elections for the Australian Senate since 1984, under the title of "group ticket voting," and that has also recently been adopted for elections in Fiji).

To ensure that the ballot is secret, ballot papers should ideally bear no markings that distinguish one from another. This is not the case, oddly enough, in the United Kingdom; UK ballot papers bear a unique serial number, and if a court finds after an election that one of the voters was not entitled to vote, his or her ballot paper may be extracted from the count. A number of Commonwealth countries have based their systems on the British approach, and while breaches of the secrecy of the ballot have been rare (though not unknown), the effect of using numbered ballot papers on the perceived secrecy of the ballot is probably a greater problem than actual breaches.

A significant issue with any paper ballot is that of making the voting process accessible to people who are blind, physically incapacitated, or illiterate. A typical approach is to allow the voter's ballot paper to be marked according to his or her instructions by a person he or she has nominated, perhaps a friend or relative. In the absence of such a person, the task may be performed by a polling official. This process has the potential to become controversial. Polling officials may be seen by the voters, particularly in transitional elections, to be associated with an unpopular old regime; this was the case at the 1989 Namibian independence elections. If, however, illiterate voters choose to be helped by a person who is perceived to be associated with a political party contesting the election, other parties tend to become suspicious. In some cases party agents at the polling station are entitled to observe the ballot paper being marked on behalf of the voter, but then the secrecy of the vote is clearly compromised. In some situations the problem can be overcome by printing photographs of candidates on the ballot papers or by printing symbols of parties as well as their names; the ballots used at the 1997 Liberian elections identified the parties and candidates in that way. Although some ballot papers are printed using Braille script, the use of Braille by the blind is declining with the passage of time.

Alternatives to the paper ballot are many. Voters may be supplied with tokens, each representing a candidate or party, one of which must be chosen and placed in a ballot box, with the others being returned to a discard bin; such arrangements have in the past been popular in Africa. They may have the option of placing an unmarked ballot paper in one of a number of ballot boxes, each of which represents a distinct candidate or party. Voters may be given a machine-readable ballot paper to mark with a pen or pencil, or a machine-readable punch card from which holes are to be punched with a stylus to indicate the party or candidate that is to receive the vote. Voters may vote by pulling one or more levers on a voting machine or by entering data into a computer system, sometimes using sophisticated "touch screen" technology. The more technically sophisticated methods of voting have been most widely used in the United States, where they are particularly efficient in handling the large number of elections for different positions that are held at the same time. Many of the voting machines were developed with the aim of minimizing the opportunities for fraud that are sometimes seen to arise with the use of a paper ballot; however, perceptions that voting machines may themselves be susceptible to fraud has held up their introduction in other places where they were being considered, for example, India. One factor influencing the use of machines for voting is that once an initial investment in the machines has been made, they eliminate the recurrent costs associated with printing new ballot papers for every election, though storage costs between elections are an issue. On the other hand, computer technology is evolving so quickly that voting machines based on the latest equipment may rapidly become obsolete.

Multiple voting can be minimized by a variety of methods. If a voter identity document has to be presented by the voter at a polling station, it can be punched, stamped, or otherwise marked to indicate that it has already been used to support a claim for a vote. If lists of voters are provided at polling stations, the voter's name can be marked on the list to indicate that he or she has voted. These mechanisms will not prevent multiple voting by a person who has obtained two or more voter identity documents or whose name appears on two or more lists (which can easily arise in countries, such as Australia, where electors are not constrained to vote at one particular polling station). Another approach, widely used in developing countries, is to mark the voter's fingers with indelible ink to indicate that he or she has voted. A visible ink is most easily used, but if there is a risk that voters may be subjected to intimidation after voting, an invisible ink, which can be seen only under ultraviolet light, may be used.

Security measures to prevent the inclusion of fraudulent votes in the count are many and varied. Typical measures associated with a paper-ballot system include strict accounting for ballot papers at all levels of operation; display of the empty ballot box prior to the start of polling; observation of the polling and counting by agents appointed by the parties and candidates; sealing of ballot boxes and containers of ballot papers with uniquely numbered seals; and guarding of sensitive materials at all times. The more sophisticated balloting methods give rise to commensurately more complex security and auditing mechanisms.

While most polling on election day takes place at polling stations, special arrangements often have to be made to enable voting by people who are in the country but unable to attend a polling station and by people who are outside the country. In the case of the former, mobile polling facilities may be provided in hospitals, nursing homes, military barracks, prisons, and remote areas; electoral workers may go to the homes of the infirm to take their votes; and pre–poll, postal, or proxy voting may be made available. In the case of the latter, pre–poll, postal, or proxy voting may be made available, or voting facilities may be provided by diplomatic missions or by the electoral authorities of another country. At the 1994 South African elections, eligible voters in Australia cast their ballots at premises provided by the Australian Electoral Commission.

DETERMINING THE RESULT AND AFTERWARD

At its simplest, counting can take place at the polling station immediately after the close of the poll. This has the advantage of providing prompt results and enables immediate confirmation that the results have been properly ascertained; party or candidate agents involved in monitoring polling can simply stay on for the count. In addition, it spreads the workload of counting as widely as possible, so that no individual count is unduly onerous. An early indication of the result of the election may be obtained through the conduct of a parallel vote count, which in many countries is the responsibility of election observers, local or international, who are separate from the election administration. Such observers may use statistical sampling techniques to enable projections of the overall results to be obtained on the basis of counting at a sample of polling stations.

Sometimes, however, it is deemed preferable to undertake the counting away from the polling stations. At some polling stations, so few votes may have been cast that there is a risk that all will be for the same party or candidate, and in that case to count them separately would compromise the secrecy of each voter's vote. There may be security concerns that make it desirable to count ballots at a limited number of places. Finally, it might be thought desirable to protect the secrecy of the votes of individuals and to disguise how a particular community has voted. This concern led counting at the 1993 Cambodian elections to be done only at the provincial level; there the contents of ballot boxes from different areas of the province were combined before any ballot papers were sorted to parties, so it was impossible to tell how individual villages had voted.

The polling method also influences the method of counting; paper ballots have to be physically sorted, and machine readable cards have to be processed. With some voting machines, the results can be read directly from the mechanism at the end of the poll.

Any counting process must commence with the identification and exclusion of invalid votes. Some methods of voting, particularly mechanized or computerized ones, do not permit an invalid vote to be cast in the first place. Invalid votes are, however, always possible when a paper ballot is used, and in some countries such as Australia, where compulsory voting forces to the polls people who without compulsion might well have abstained, deliberate as well as accidental invalid votes are cast. Electoral law typically charges officials with counting ballots to give effect to the voter's intention to the extent that it is clear. Ballot forms affect the extent to which clarity is readily ascertained. Where preferential voting systems are used, voters are sometimes required to rank a large number of candidates. At an election with one hundred candidates, all of whom have to be numbered, and 50,000 voters, close to 5 million numbers need to be checked by polling officials just to exclude the invalid votes.

Under preferential systems of voting, the counting process is normally more prolonged than under categorical systems, since the result of the election requires that regard be had not just to the first preference votes but also to the later preferences shown by the voters. This becomes particularly complicated when single-transferable-vote systems of proportional representation are used, since multiple vacancies have to be filled. The distribution of preferences can be done manually, by successively sorting ballot papers according to next available preferences and counting ballot papers so sorted, but the process often involves hundreds (and sometimes thousands) of separate counts and can takes days or weeks. An alternative approach is to keypunch into a computer the numbers marked by the voters on each ballot paper, and thereafter ascertain the result electronically.

After the counting at an election has been finished and the results announced, a period is normally allowed within which challenges to the result may be lodged. These may be dealt with by the election administration itself, by the courts, or by specially constituted tribunals.

The last phase of activity associated with a specific election is normally the publication of detailed statistics setting out the results of voting. These not only provide a basis for further research by political scientists and participants in the electoral process but also are part of the ritual of accountability on the part of the election administration.

See also *Absentee Voting; Candidates: Legal Requirements and Disqualifications; Deposit; Disqualification of Voters, Grounds for; Election Finance; Nomination Procedures; Overseas Voting; Parties: Qualification for Ballot; Registration of Voters in the United States; Regulation of Television; Tendered Ballots.*

MICHAEL MALEY, AUSTRALIAN ELECTORAL COMMISSION

BIBLIOGRAPHY

Administration and Cost of Elections Project Web site: *http://www.aceproject.org*

Dundas, Carl W. *Dimensions of Free and Fair Elections.* London: Commonwealth Secretariat, 1994.

———. *Organising Free and Fair Elections at Cost-Effective Levels.* London: Commonwealth Secretariat, 1993.

Goodwin-Gill, Guy S. *Free and Fair Elections: International Law and Practice.* Geneva: Inter-Parliamentary Union, 1994.

Gould, Ron, Christine Jackson, and Loren Wells. *Strengthening Democracy: A Parliamentary Perspective.* Aldershot: Dartmouth, 1995.

Leonard, Dick. *Elections in Britain Today.* 2d ed. London: Macmillan, 1991.

Mackenzie, W.J.M. *Free Elections: An Elementary Textbook.* London: George Allen and Unwin, 1958.

AGE OF VOTING

For all direct elections, legal provisions require the voters to have reached a certain minimum age. Like other basic conditions of voting, such as citizenship, residence, and full possession of mental faculties, an age limit is not considered an illegitimate reduction of the standard of general suffrage. Only great differences between the age of voting and the age of majority are seen as problematic, since the latter is usually regarded as the main formal criterion of political maturity. Therefore, some electoral laws simply concede the right to vote to "every adult citizen" instead of stating an age limit.

Sometimes the age of voting has been differentiated by sex or marital status. The age limit for Hungarian men in the 1920s, for example, was twenty-four years, whereas it was thirty for women. In Bolivia, from 1952 until adoption of a new constitution in 1994, the threshold for singles was twenty-one years, whereas for married people it was eighteen years.

In exceptional cases a differentiation of voting age is determined by the structure of the electoral system. Under the segmented electoral system of 1938 in Hungary, the minimum voting age was twenty-six for single-member constituencies and thirty for national proportional representation seats.

Whereas a minimum age of voting exists in every country, electoral provisions establishing an upper limit cannot be found. However, special regulations in Brazil and Peru release citizens older than seventy from compulsory voting without taking away their general right to vote.

Currently, the age of voting in most countries is eighteen years. The only European country with a higher limit (nineteen) is Austria. In Africa and Asia there are several states with a threshold of twenty-one (Azerbaijan, Côte d' Ivoire, Fiji, Kuwait, Lebanon, Malaysia, Pakistan, Singapore), twenty (Cameroon, Japan, Morocco, Nauru, South Korea, Taiwan, Tunisia), and nineteen years (Jordan). Lower limits have been established in Indonesia, North Korea, and the Palestinian Authority (seventeen years); in Cuba and Nicaragua (sixteen years); and in Iran (fifteen years). A special case is Brazil, where citizens have the right to vote at age sixteen but are exempt from compulsory voting until age eighteen.

In historical perspective, the voting age has developed toward a lower limit, but the variation in this general process has been immense, both across and within cultural areas. Nevertheless, three aspects of the process help identify specific patterns in the reduction of the age limit.

Date of lowering. Latin American states were the first in the world to reduce the age of voting from twenty-one to eighteen years, beginning in the nineteenth century (for example, Argentina, Costa Rica, Paraguay) and early twentieth century (among them Brazil, Uruguay, Venezuela). It was only in the 1970s that the United States and all west European countries did likewise. In most former colonies of Africa, Asia, and the Caribbean the process of lowering the threshold to eighteen years also began in the early 1970s (for example, Jamaica, Kenya) and lasted until the late 1990s (Gambia, Lesotho).

Process of lowering. In most countries the age of voting was reduced in a linear process. Whereas many west European and several African and Asian states lowered their age limit in a single step, it took four or five steps for the Scandinavian states and the Netherlands to reach their current level of eighteen years. In contrast to these linear developments, countries like Turkey, Sudan, and Costa Rica displayed cyclical processes of lowering and raising their voting age.

Main causes of lowering. In general, the reduction of the voting age was caused by either social change or political factors. On the one hand, the age of voting is usually adapted to a reduction in the age of majority caused by social change. This explains in large part the process that Western industrialized countries underwent in the 1970s. In the same manner, a lot of Asian and African states adapted their electoral rules during the "third wave" of democratization, which brought the reintroduction of direct elections (for example, Burkina Faso, Malawi, Nepal). On the other hand, the lowering of the age of voting can be a result of genuine political factors, especially after revolutionary regime changes. Historical examples are the establishment of communist rule in eastern Europe after World War II as well as the revolutions in Cuba, Nicaragua, and Iran in the 1960s and 1970s. The new regimes stressed the need to expand "democratic" participation, and thus lowered the voting age. Besides these ideological arguments, Machiavellian considerations of the new political elite played a significant role, as the younger generation was considered to be more open minded to revolutionary changes.

In summary, the regulation of the age of voting has not only a sociocultural but also a strong political dimension.

Therefore, even in nonrevolutionary countries, periodic debates about a further reduction of the voting age might reflect the self-interests of "progressive" parties hoping to increase their electoral chances by attracting most of the first-time voters.

See also *Franchise Expansion*.

FLORIAN GROTZ, UNIVERSITY OF HEIDELBERG

BIBLIOGRAPHY

Mackie, Thomas T., and Richard Rose, eds. *The International Almanac of Electoral History.* 3d ed. rev. London: Macmillan, 1991.

Nohlen, Dieter, ed. *Enciclopedia Electoral Latinoamerica y del Caribe.* San José, Costa Rica: IIDH/CAPEL, 1993.

Nohlen, Dieter, Florian Grotz, and Christof Hartmann, eds. *Elections in Asia. A Data Handbook.* Oxford: Oxford University Press, forthcoming.

Nohlen, Dieter, Michael Krennerich, and Bernhard Thibaut, eds. *Elections in Africa. A Data Handbook.* Oxford: Oxford University Press, 1999.

ALTERNATIVE VOTE

The alternative vote is a relatively rare equivalent of the second ballot, similarly intended to ensure the winning candidate is preferred by a majority of all voters. Under the alternative vote, voters record additional candidate preferences after their first, to be counted if no candidate receives an absolute majority of first preferences. Recording multiple preferences at the outset eliminates the cost and inconvenience of a second election and also avoids the sort of bargaining among parties that takes place between the first and second ballots in second-ballot systems. Under the alternative vote, political alliances and exchanges of support must be settled and made public before the first ballot takes place and the exact balance of political strengths is known. This system may also encourage moderation, because candidates and parties in the middle can draw second and subsequent preferences from both sides of the political spectrum. The alternative vote has been used in Papua-New Guinea (1964–1972) and western Canadian provinces, has been of recurring interest in Great Britain, and has recently been recommended by some scholars for use in countries like Fiji to encourage alliances across ethnic divisions.

AUSTRALIAN EXPERIENCE

Most experience with the alternative vote in parliamentary elections comes from Australia, where it is called "preferential voting." In Queensland it replaced the British first-past-the-post system in 1892, following a by-election won by the emerging Labor Party against several candidates from established parties. The alternative vote was preferred to the second ballot because of the widely dispersed electorate. Other Australian states subsequently adopted the alternative vote for one chamber or both; only one tried the second ballot, briefly. In 1919 it was introduced for both federal chambers, then abandoned for use in electing the upper house in 1949. The federal upper house and South Australia's upper house (1930–1973) used the alternative vote with multimember districts; all other alternative-vote elections have been in single-member districts.

In Australia alternative vote forms the last link in a majoritarian chain. Compulsory voter registration, compulsory voting, and (usually) compulsory expression of a full set of preferences are expected to ensure that the majority of members of parliament, and consequently the cabinet they support, were chosen by a majority of the whole population. However, the use of single-member electoral districts sometimes frustrates that objective; four of the twenty-one federal general elections from 1949 to 1998 produced a parliamentary majority lacking an electoral majority. Comparative studies of proportionality suggest the alternative vote to be no better than first-past-the-post and at times to be worse.

Counting subsequent preferences to achieve an absolute majority is required in only a minority of Australian electoral districts, since first preferences are usually adequate to give one candidate a majority. In federal general elections from 1919 to 1998, preferences had to be distributed in 30 percent of electoral districts; in 6 percent the outcome was changed from what would have resulted from first preferences. (The five states in which the lower house is elected by the alternative vote system record comparable figures: between 15 and 27 percent had to distribute preferences, and the results were affected in 3 to 7 percent of the cases.) In only 0.2 percent of federal districts (eight cases altogether) was the eventual winner other than one of the two candidates who led on first preferences. Of those eight cases, in two a coalition partner had nominated three candidates; multiple nominations had been expected to be common when alternative voting was introduced, but the danger of preferences "leaking" to other parties soon put a stop to the practice in all but exceptional circumstances. In the other six cases preferences from a strong independent or a minor-party candidate tipped the balance to move a third-place candidate up.

As had been intended, the principal beneficiary of the alternative vote has been the enduring coalition of the two right-of-center parties, which won 79 percent of the districts where the outcome was altered by preference distributions; Labor won only 18 percent, and independent candidates just 3 percent. Variations over time have appeared but have been slight. For example, between 1975 and 1998 the proportion of districts where second preferences had to be counted rose to 40 percent, but the proportion where outcomes were changed dropped slightly, to 5 percent; between 1955 and 1974, when the only alternative to the major parties was the schismatic Democratic Labor Party, 95 percent of changed outcomes favored the coalition.

IMPLEMENTING THE ALTERNATIVE VOTE

Two main choices have to be made when implementing the alternative vote. First, must all candidates be ranked, only some lesser number, or will a single first preference be valid? Two Australian states make additional preferences optional; approximately 25 percent of minor- and independent-candidate supporters now fail to record a full set of preferences. Second, should all candidates other than the leading two be eliminated simultaneously and their preferences allocated between those two, or should they be eliminated and their preferences distributed successively, starting with the one with the fewest votes?

Outcomes could be affected by such choices, but in Australian experience, with a strong party system this rarely happens. Because of the dominance of the major actors, the Labor Party and the coalition, negligible use has been made of tactical voting. One example of what might be done comes from Western Australia, where in two districts the Labor Party naturally ran third, and Labor supporters used their second preferences to defeat whichever coalition partner had won the seat previously, so as to strain relations within the coalition. Another example is New South Wales at the state and then federal level, where the Labor Party naturally ran second, but pro-Labor voters ensured a large share of their first preferences went to a popular independent so that Labor's candidate could be eliminated first and deliver preferences solidly to the independent, enabling the independent to overtake the coalition candidate.

See also *Apparentement; Designing Electoral Systems; Proportionality and Disproportionality; Second Ballot (or Runoff)*.

COLIN A. HUGHES, EMERITUS,
UNIVERSITY OF QUEENSLAND, BRISBANE

BIBLIOGRAPHY

Bean, Clive. "Australia's Experience with the Alternative Vote." *Representation* 34 (spring/summer 1997): 103–113.

Graham, B. D. "The Choice of Voting Methods in Federal Politics, 1902–1918." *Australian Journal of Politics and History* 8 (November 1962): 164–179.

Lal, Brij V., and Peter Larmour, eds. *Electoral Systems in Divided Societies: The Fiji Constitution Review.* Canberra: National Centre for Development Studies, The Australian National University, 1997.

Punnett, R. M. *The Alternative Vote with the Optional Use of Preferences: Some Irish Lessons for Britain and Australia.* Strathclyde Papers on Government and Politics No. 43. Glasgow: Department of Politics, University of Strathclyde, 1986.

APPARENTEMENT

Apparentement means the formal linking of party lists that is allowed in some list systems of proportional representation, and the term also denotes the set of parties that are thus linked. It is a French term, and English translations that have been proposed are the "blocking" of party lists and the "interparty electoral link"—but *apparentement* is the most commonly used term in English, too. The party lists that belong to an *apparentement* appear separately on the ballot, and each voter normally votes for one list only, but in the initial allocation of seats, all of the votes cast for the lists in the *apparentement* are counted as having been cast for the *apparentement*. The next step is the proportional distribution of the seats won by the *apparentement* to the individual party lists that belong to it.

Because, in practice, even the most proportional of proportional-representation systems favor the larger parties, the possibility of *apparentement* encourages the formation of alliances among medium-sized and small parties, since it gives them jointly the same advantage as a single large party with an equal number of votes. It may also enable very small parties to cross the electoral threshold that many list proportional representation systems impose. As a result, *apparentement* tends to increase the proportionality of election outcomes. Another consequence is that by removing the disadvantage of being a small party, *apparentement* removes an important incentive for small parties to merge.

Apparentement has been used in the list proportional representation systems of Israel, the Netherlands, Norway, Sweden, and Switzerland. Another well-known example of its use was in the partly majoritarian French system used in the 1951 and 1956 elections. Here an additional rule, designed to help the medium-sized parties in the political center, was that any *apparentement* that won an absolute majority of the votes in a multimember electoral district would receive all of the district's seats instead of a proportional share of the seats.

The formation of interparty electoral links not only is allowed as a special feature of some list proportional representation systems but is a logical consequence of the rules of several other electoral systems. The alternative vote, used in Australia, and the single transferable vote, used in Ireland, permit parties to form alliances in order to maximize their joint electoral gains by agreeing to ask their respective voters to cast first preferences for their own candidates but the next preferences for the candidates of the allied party. Australian and Irish parties frequently take advantage of this opportunity. Similarly, the French two-ballot system, used in most of the elections of the Fifth Republic, allows parties to link up for the purpose of reciprocal withdrawal from the second ballot in different districts; this possibility has encouraged the formation of electoral coalitions both on the right and the left of the political spectrum. Thus, *apparentement* can be seen as an integral part of several electoral systems, not including list proportional representation systems, but can be added to list proportional representation as a special rule.

See also *Alternative Vote; Binomial Electoral System; Coordination, Electoral; Cross-Filing; Fractionalization Index; List; Pooling Votes; Proportional Representation; Single Transferable Vote.*

AREND LIJPHART, UNIVERSITY OF CALIFORNIA, SAN DIEGO

BIBLIOGRAPHY

Carstairs, Andrew McLaren. *A Short History of Electoral Systems in Western Europe.* London: George Allen and Unwin, 1980.

Cox, Gary W. *Making Votes Count: Strategic Coordination in the World's Electoral Systems.* Cambridge: Cambridge University Press, 1997.

Lijphart, Arend. *Electoral Systems and Party Systems: A Study of Twenty-Seven Democracies, 1945–1990.* Oxford: Oxford University Press, 1994.

APPORTIONMENT

See *Gerrymandering; Reapportionment and Redistricting*

APPROVAL VOTING

Proposed independently by several analysts in the 1970s, approval voting is a procedure in which people can vote for, or approve of, as many candidates as they wish in multicandidate elections—that is, elections with three or more candidates. Each candidate approved of receives one vote, and the candidate with the most votes wins. In the United States the case for approval voting seems particularly strong in primary and nonpartisan elections, which often draw large fields of candidates.

BENEFITS AND ADVANTAGES

Supporters of approval voting argue that it has several compelling advantages over other voting procedures. First, it would give voters more options. They can do what they would under plurality voting—vote for a single favorite—but if they have no strong preference for one candidate, they can express this fact by voting for all candidates they find acceptable. In addition, a voter whose most preferred candidate has little chance of winning can vote for both a first choice *and* a more viable candidate without worrying about wasting his or her vote on the less popular candidate.

Second, approval voting would help elect the strongest candidate. Today, the candidate supported by the largest minority of voters often wins, or at least makes the runoff if there is one. Under approval voting, by contrast, the candidate with the greatest overall support will generally win. In particular, "Condorcet candidates"—those candidates who could defeat every other candidate in separate pairwise contests—almost invariably win under approval voting, whereas under plurality voting they often lose because they split the vote with one or more other centrist candidates.

Approval voting's third advantage is that it would reduce negative campaigning. It induces candidates to mirror the views of a majority of voters, rather than to cater to minorities whose voters could give them a slight edge in a crowded plurality contest. Approval voting is thus likely to cut down on negative campaigning, because candidates will have an incentive to broaden their appeals, to reach out to voters who might have a different first choice. Lambasting a prospective voter's first choice of candidate would risk losing his or her approval.

That approval voting would increase voter turnout is a fourth compelling advantage. By being better able to express their preferences, voters will be more likely to vote. Voters who think they might be wasting their votes, or who cannot decide which of several candidates best represents their views, will not have to despair about making a choice. By not being forced to make a single—perhaps arbitrary—choice, they will feel that the election system allows them to be more honest, which will make voting more meaningful and encourage greater participation in elections.

Approval voting would give minority candidates their proper due. Minority candidates will not suffer under this system: their supporters will not be torn away simply because there is another candidate who, although less appealing to them, is generally considered a stronger contender. Because approval voting allows supporters of minority candidates to vote for both the minority candidate and the strongest contender, they will not be tempted to desert the one who is weak in the polls, as under plurality voting. Hence, minority candidates will receive their true level of support under approval voting, even if they cannot win. This will make election returns a better reflection of the overall acceptability of candidates, which is important information often denied to voters today, and the returns will be relatively undistorted by strategic voting.

Finally, approval voting is eminently practicable. Unlike more complicated ranking systems, which suffer from a variety of theoretical as well as practical defects, approval voting is simple for voters to understand and use. Although more votes must be tallied under approval voting than under plurality voting, the former can readily be implemented on existing voting machines. Since approval voting does not violate any state constitutions in the United States (or, for that matter, the constitutions of most countries in the world), it requires only an ordinary statute to enact.

APPROVAL VOTING IN PRACTICE

Probably the best-known official elected by approval voting today is the secretary general of the United Nations. The political parties in some states, such as Pennsylvania, have used it in internal elections, and several state legislatures have introduced bills to implement it. In 1987 a bill to enact approval voting in certain statewide elections passed the North Dakota senate but not the house. In 1990 Oregon used approval voting in a statewide advisory referendum on school financing, which presented voters with five options and allowed them to vote for as many as they wished.

In 1987 and 1988 several scientific and engineering societies began using approval voting to aid in finding "consensus candidates"—those candidates with the greatest support among voters. With the exception of the Institute of Management Science (which no longer exists), the following societies continue to use it today:

- The Mathematical Association of America, with about 32,000 members

- The Institute of Management Science, with about 7,000 members

- The American Statistical Association, with about 15,000 members

- The Institute of Electrical and Electronics Engineers, with about 320,000 members

In addition, the Econometric Society has used approval voting (with certain emendations) to elect fellows since 1980; likewise, since 1981 the National Academy of Sciences, at the final stage of balloting, has utilized approval voting to select its members. In 1989 the American Mathematical Society, with about 29,000 members, adopted approval voting in several of its elections. In 1994 the Institute of Management Science and the Operations Research Society of America combined to form the Institute of Operations Research and Management Science, which has about 15,000 members and used approval voting from the start. Furthermore, many colleges and universities now use approval voting—at the departmental level and schoolwide. It is no exaggeration to say that several hundred thousand individuals have had direct experience with approval voting.

Beginning in 1987, approval voting was used in some competitive elections in eastern Europe and the Soviet Union, where it was effectively "disapproval voting" because voters were permitted to cross names off ballots but not to vote for candidates. But this procedure is logically equivalent to approval voting: candidates not crossed off are, in effect, approved, although psychologically there is almost surely a difference between approving and disapproving of candidates.

APPROVAL VOTING IN PRINCIPLE

As cherished a principle as "one person, one vote" is in single-winner elections, such as for president, supporters of approval voting consider it somewhat of an anachronism today. Democracies, they contend, could benefit from the alternative principle of "one candidate, one vote," whereby voters are able to judge whether each candidate on the ballot is acceptable or not.

The principle of one candidate, one vote ties the vote not to the voter but rather to the candidates, which is arguably more egalitarian than artificially restricting voters to casting only one vote in multicandidate races. This principle also affords voters an opportunity to express their intensities of preference, for example, by approving all candidates except the one they despise.

Although approval voting is a strikingly simple election reform for finding consensus choices in single-winner elections, in elections with more than one winner—such as for a council or a legislature—it would not be desirable if the goal is to mirror a diversity of views, especially of minority views. On the other hand, minorities may derive indirect benefit from approval voting in single-winner elections, because mainstream candidates, in order to win, will be forced to reach out to minority voters for the approval they (the mainstream candidates) need to win. While promoting majoritarian candidates, therefore, approval voting induces them to be responsive to minority views.

See also *Plurality Systems; Quaker Decision Making without Voting.*

STEVEN J. BRAMS, NEW YORK UNIVERSITY

BIBLIOGRAPHY

Brams, Steven J. "Approval Voting on Bills and Referenda." *The Good Society* 5, no. 2 (spring 1995): 37–39.

Brams, Steven J., and Peter C. Fishburn. *Approval Voting.* Cambridge, Mass.: Birkhäuser Boston, 1983.

———. "Approval Voting in Scientific and Engineering Societies." *Group Decision and Negotiation* 1 (April 1992): 41–55.

Brams, Steven J., and Samuel Merrill, III. "Would Ross Perot Have Won the 1992 Presidential Election under Approval Voting?" *PS: Political Science and Politics* 27, no. 1 (March 1994): 39–44.

Merrill, Samuel, III. *Making Multicandidate Elections More Democratic.* Princeton, N.J.: Princeton University Press, 1988.

Myerson, Roger B., and Robert J. Weber. "A Theory of Voting Equilibria." *American Political Science Review* 87, no. 1 (March 1993): 102–114.

AT-LARGE ELECTIONS

At-large elections are elections in nonproportional electoral systems in which all the seats in a multi-member district are filled by the votes of the district as a whole. Each voter normally has as many votes as there are seats to be filled. At-large elections have been a common feature in national, state, and local elections in the United States. Elections to the U.S. electoral college are also in effect elections at-large in almost every state, since the slate of candidates that wins a plurality of the vote wins all the seats in that state's delegation. In the United Kingdom most members of Parliament were elected at-large before the 1832 Reform Act, after which the number of single-member constituencies progressively increased, until the last two-member constituency was abolished in 1948. In Ireland, where representatives are chosen by single transferable vote in multimember constituencies, by-elections become elections at-large when a single legislator is elected.

In U.S. congressional elections, states with a single representative necessarily elect at-large, as is also the case with elections to the U.S. Senate. In the early nineteenth century, elections at-large were common in the United States. In 1842 six of twenty-eight states sent at-large delegations to Congress. In the same year, Congress mandated the use of single-member districts to prevent a party with an overall majority in a particular state from winning all of the state's seats. But this law subsequently lapsed and a few states continued to send at least some representatives at-large, sometimes to avoid or at least delay redistricting after federal reapportionment. In 1964, 22 of the 435 representatives were elected at-large. In 1967 Congress passed a law mandating single-member districts for elections to the House.

In the United States, political reformers from the late nineteenth century onward supported at-large elections in order to weaken a politics based on neighborhood or ethnic identity. In the mid-1970s nearly 80 percent of cities with a population over ten thousand elected their city councils either entirely (63 percent) or partly (15 percent) at-large. At-large elections were also a weapon in the civil rights battle. After passage of the 1965 Voting Rights Act, many local governments in the U.S. South moved from single-district to at-large systems in order to minimize the effectiveness of the ballots cast by newly enfranchised African Americans. So long as white majorities voted as a bloc, at-large voting severely restricted African Americans' chances of winning local office. Longitudinal studies, including that conducted by Chandler Davidson and George Korbel, demonstrate that this strategy of vote dilution was largely effective. Following the 1982 amendments to the 1965 Voting Rights Act and subsequent Supreme Court decisions and legal cases, many jurisdictions changed to single-member or mixed electoral systems, which resulted in dramatic increases in the number of African Americans elected.

See also *Gerrymandering*.

TOM MACKIE, UNIVERSITY OF STRATHCLYDE

BIBLIOGRAPHY

Davidson, Chandler, and Bernard Grofman, eds. *Quiet Revolution in the South: The Impact of the Voting Rights Act, 1965–1990*. Princeton, N.J.: Princeton University Press, 1994.

Davidson, Chandler, and George Korbel. "At-Large Elections and Minority Group Representation: A Re-examination of Historical and Contemporary Evidence." *Journal of Politics* 43 (November 1981): 982–1005.

Dixon, Robert. *Democratic Representation: Reapportionment in Law and Politics*. Oxford: Oxford University Press, 1968.

Engstrom, Richard, and Michael McDonald. "The Effect of At-Large Versus District Elections on Racial Representation in U.S. Municipalities." In *Electoral Laws and their Political Consequences*, edited by Bernard Grofman and Arend Lijphart. New York: Agathon, 1986.

Hacker, Andrew. *Congressional Districting: The Issue of Equal Representation*. Washington, D.C.: Brookings Institution, 1964.

AUSTRALIAN BALLOT

Australian ballot is an American term for a ballot prepared by public authorities and containing the names of all the candidates in an election, which each voter can mark in secret. This type of ballot was first introduced in the Australian colony of Victoria in 1856.

Until the 1880s U.S. political parties produced their own ballots, often in different colors, a process that inhibited the secrecy of the vote. The Australian ballot was first introduced in Massachusetts, in 1888, and within eight years at least 90 percent of the states had followed suit. The secret ballot was one of a series of measures introduced by Progressive reformers to weaken party control over the electorate and reduce corruption in elections; when the briber was no longer able to check that the recipient had delivered his side of the contract, the incentive to invest in bribery at election time was reduced.

The consequences of introducing the secret ballot varied from jurisdiction to jurisdiction. Jerrold Rusk demonstrated that its introduction led to an increase in split-ticket voting, although the extent of the increase depended, in part, on the kind of ballot adopted. Ballots that listed candidates by the office being contested made it difficult for the voter to vote a straight ticket with a single mark. Party-column ballots, on the other hand, grouped candidates by party and usually allowed voters to vote a straight ticket with a single mark at the head of each party column. Although the introduction of the secret ballot reflected antiparty sentiment, it was also used by political parties to protect their interests. For instance, the procedures by which parties could gain a place on the Australian ballot—such as surpassing a high threshold of votes at the previous election or amassing a large number of petition signatures—protected the major parties, as did burdensome regulations for the filing of nomination papers. Moreover, the use of an official ballot facilitated the introduction of "antifusion" laws, which prevented a candidate's name from being included more than once on the ballot. This device was intended to, and succeeded in, reducing the political weight of third parties that sought to collaborate with one of the two major parties.

See also *Administration of Elections; Open Voting; Secret Ballot; Tendered Ballots.*

TOM MACKIE, UNIVERSITY OF STRATHCLYDE

BIBLIOGRAPHY

Argersinger, Peter. *Structure, Process and Party: Essays in American Political History.* Armonk, N.Y.: M.E. Sharpe, 1992.

Fredman, Lawrence. *The Australian Ballot: The Story of an American Reform.* Lansing: Michigan State University Press, 1968.

Rusk, Jerrold. "The Effect of the Australian Ballot Reform on Split-Ticket Voting: 1876–1908." *American Political Science Review* 64 (December 1970): 1220–1238.

Rusk, J. "Comment: The American Electoral Universe: Speculation and Evidence." *American Political Science Review* 68 (September 1974): 1028–1049.

Wigmore, John. *The Australian Ballot System as Embodied in the Legislation of Various Countries.* Boston: Boston Book Company, 1889.

B

BALLOT FORMS

See *Administration of Elections; Australian Ballot*

BANDWAGON EFFECTS

The term *bandwagon* is used to describe a situation in which perceptions of strong or surprising support for a party or candidate generate even more support. That usage assumes the bandwagon is advancing. The term is seldom used to describe a bandwagon in retreat: a situation in which perceptions of a low level of support lead to even lower support. But whether the bandwagon is rolling forward or backward, the statistical model is the same: it is a "positive-feedback loop" between the level of and the trend in public support.

A positive-feedback loop makes the majority ever-larger and the minority ever-smaller. It would end in a total consensus if it continued to operate long enough. The rarity of total consensus is sometimes considered proof of the rarity, or the limited duration, of bandwagon effects. But a bandwagon can roll during an election campaign or even a little longer (producing a postelection surge of support for the victor, and a further postelection collapse of support for the loser) without operating so long as to produce total consensus.

THE SPIRAL OF SILENCE

The most frequently quoted and uncompromising statement of the bandwagon model is Elisabeth Noelle-Neumann's *The Spiral of Silence.* Fear of social or political exclusion encourages the minority first to fall silent, then to jump on the bandwagon of the expected winner, and finally, in her words, to "run with the pack." It is impossible to avoid the feeling that this model owes its inspiration, consciously or unconsciously, to the experience of interwar Germany. The "spiral of silence" is the dream of totalitarian dictators and the nightmare of democrats.

In reaction to that nightmare, democrats might place their hopes in the underdog model, in which voters swing against the expected winner and toward the perceived underdog. In decision-making terms, that behavior is just as irrational as the behavior of voters in the bandwagon model. But it may be rationally justifiable in terms of the need to limit the power, or at least the arrogance, of the victor.

THE UNDERDOG MODEL

In practice, the bandwagon model as outlined by Noelle-Neumann does not work well. As David Butler (in *Comparing Democracies,* pp. 241–242) points out: "Some temperaments may want to be on the successful side; others, suspicious of the arrogance of elected persons, may decide to reduce the scale of the predicted winner's victory. The evidence for either phenomenon is limited and inconsistent. There is certainly no systematic pattern." U.S. president Jimmy Carter's concession of defeat in the 1980 election, before voting had closed in the western states, does not seem to have caused a surge of support for the Republicans, though it may have depressed the turnout of Democrats in the West. And since the party that led in the opinion polls has usually not done as well as predicted at British general elections, Butler suggests the British have a weakness for underdogs.

HEGEMONIC, TACTICAL, AND MEDIA BANDWAGONS

The literature on bandwagon effects is unnecessarily confusing because it fails to distinguish sufficiently between hegemonic bandwagons, tactical bandwagons, and media bandwagons. They are quite different in character, in terms of rationality, and in their implications for democracy. Yet all three are indiscriminately termed bandwagons.

Noelle-Neumann's model describes a hegemonic bandwagon—a swing toward the expected winner caused not by superior policies or campaigning but by the desire to be associated with the winner. This is both irrational and undemocratic.

A tactical bandwagon requires more than an expected winner and an underdog. It requires at least three parties or candidates, and it requires some degree of political alliance as well as opposition among them. Moreover, in a tactical bandwagon model, voters shift their support between political friends or allies rather than between political enemies. It is a model of rational rather than irrational behavior. And it is consistent with the democratic ideal. It is not rational to swing from the losing side to the winning side for no reason, but it is rational to swing behind the best of several champions representing the same or similar causes. It is fundamentally undemocratic for supporters of the minority to switch to the majority side just to be on the winning side, but it is democratic as well as rational for supporters of a no-hope party in a multiparty contest to switch to a political ally in order to defeat an enemy.

The pattern of constituency voting at the 1997 British election suggests that Liberal and Labour supporters swung behind whichever of the two opposition parties appeared best placed to defeat the Conservatives in their locality. The Labour and Liberal Parties have not always been allies, and individual voters have different views about which parties they regard as similar and substitutable. But panel-survey studies of voting intentions conducted during British elections suggest that the final voting choice of voters who are almost equally attracted to a pair of parties is strongly—and progressively—influenced by their perceptions of the relative strength of their two preferred parties within their local constituency.

Butler and others who dismiss the importance of hegemonic bandwagon effects and incline toward the underdog model to explain the overall result in British general elections usually balance that conclusion about general elections by pointing to the obvious importance of tactical bandwagons in British by-elections. Tactical bandwagons roll within constituencies even in general elections (though in different directions in different constituencies). But they roll more strongly and more obviously in by-elections, which focus much more attention on the constituency as opposed to the national contest and provide much more polling information for voters about the relative standing of the parties within the constituency.

The significance of tactical bandwagons may be less in a proportional-representation system than in a plurality system since the "wasted vote" argument may not apply so strongly to third parties. Nonetheless, proportional-representation systems usually incorporate an explicit or implicit threshold below which votes for a party would indeed be wasted. A tactical bandwagon may then run in favor of parties whose support is well above the threshold, at the expense of those that are perceived to be in danger of falling below it. Interestingly, however, voter responses to the proportional-representation threshold in Germany provide a clear example of something

similar to a tactically driven underdog effect. When the Free Democratic Party has seemed in danger of falling below the threshold, supporters of its coalition ally have rallied to its aid by casting a tactical vote for the party in order to ensure that the coalition did not lose a valuable bloc of seats.

Finally, there are media bandwagons—publicity-driven bandwagons based on positive feedback between publicity and support. Candidates who receive little or no media coverage are not likely to be taken seriously by the electorate. Extensive media coverage does not by itself merit the title of a media bandwagon, of course. But insofar as media attention generates support, and that support then generates more media coverage, it is reasonable to regard the process as a media bandwagon. The behavior of individual voters in a media bandwagon model is rational. And the behavior of the media, allowing the voters to set its agenda, could be regarded as compatible with the democratic idea provided the media does not play too large a role in jump-starting the process. But a media bandwagon is less unambiguously rational and democratic than a tactical bandwagon.

A recurrent feature of British general-election campaigns is the gradual increase in support for the third-place Liberal Party, which is frequently attributed to increased media coverage. That should not be described as a media bandwagon, since the increased media coverage in this case largely reflects the attempts of public-service broadcasters to "level the playing field" during an election campaign, irrespective of whether Liberal support is low or high. But by contrast, the rapid increase in support for the Scottish National Party from 15 to 30 percent during 1974, or for the Social Democratic Party from zero to 50 percent during 1981, had all the characteristics of a media bandwagon. Initially modest but newsworthy levels of support initiated a cycle of increasing media attention and increasing levels of support.

MOMENTUM

The term *momentum* is often applied to bandwagon effects in primary elections in the United States. Candidates seeking a party's nomination for the presidential election compete against each other in primary elections among party supporters. These are held in different states on various dates throughout the first half of the election year, before the party's nominating convention in the summer and the presidential election in the autumn. The momentum model suggests that the candidate who establishes a lead (or performs unexpectedly well) in the early state primaries gathers ever-increasing support. Conversely, candidates who fail in the early primaries, by one criterion or another, find their support ebbing.

The anecdotal evidence for a momentum effect is stronger than the statistical, and its character is unclear. If the momentum process is driven by the desire of party supporters to achieve unity and consensus, it is a hegemonic bandwagon, albeit one that is confined within a party: party supporters swing behind the candidate who appears to have the most support within the party. Concurrently with the primary elections, however, numerous opinion polls are conducted purporting to show how each candidate would perform in a presidential election against candidates from the opposing party. If the momentum process is driven by these considerations, it has the character of a tactical bandwagon: party supporters swing behind the candidate most likely to win not their own party's nomination but the presidential election. Finally, the decentralized and unstructured nature of American politics puts a premium on media attention. If a surprisingly good performance in an early primary grabs the attention of a jaded and sensation-hungry media, and increased media coverage then leads to greater name-recognition, attention, and votes in later primaries, then the momentum effect has the character of a media bandwagon.

See also *Campaigning; Election Forecasting; Public Opinion Polls: How They Work; Public Opinion Polls: Legal Regulation; Regulation of Television; Tactical Voting; Voting Behavior.*

WILLIAM L. MILLER, GLASGOW UNIVERSITY

BIBLIOGRAPHY

Butler, David. "Polls and Elections." In *Comparing Democracies: Elections and Voting in Global Perspective,* edited by Lawrence LeDuc, Richard G. Niemi, and Pippa Norris, 236–253. Thousand Oaks, Calif.: Sage, 1996.

Goidel, Robert K., and Todd G. Shields. "The Vanishing Marginals, the Bandwagon, and the Mass Media." *Journal of Politics* 56, no. 3 (August 1994): 802–810.

Marsh, Catherine. "Back on the Bandwagon: The Effect of Opinion Polls on Public Opinion." *British Journal of Political Science* 15, no. 1 (January 1985): 51–74.

McAllister, Ian, and Donley T. Studlar. "Bandwagon, Underdog, or Projection? Opinion Polls and Electoral Choice in Britain, 1979–87." *Journal of Politics* 53, no. 3 (August 1991): 720–741.

Miller, William L., David Broughton, Niels Sonntag, and Duncan McLean. "Political Change in Britain During the 1987 Campaign." In *Political Communications: The General Election Campaign of 1987,* edited by Ivor Crewe and Martin Harrop, 108–125. Cambridge: Cambridge University Press, 1989.

Noelle-Neumann, Elisabeth. *The Spiral of Silence: Public Opinion—Our Social Skin.* 2d ed. Chicago: University of Chicago Press, 1993.

BAROMETER ELECTIONS

Elections are designed to serve many purposes. One function performed by a particular class of elections is that of a barometer. Similar to indicators of impending weather patterns, barometer elections measure the public mood about the government by reflecting changes in the political environment that have occurred since the last general election. Usually, these are contests in which representatives of governing and opposition parties compete for office between two national (or general) elections.

Although a number of elections may fit this general definition, an election performs the role of a barometer to a greater or lesser extent depending on whether officeholders and other political elites view them as performing such a role. Thus, the perception that elections are an indicator of public sentiment is critical to whether they truly are a barometer. The electorate may use these contests to send signals to political actors regarding the incumbent government's performance and changes that have occurred in the political environment since the last election. Barometer elections thus reveal changes in collective preferences in response to national political and economic conditions, absent the direct opportunity to reinstall or remove the party in power.

Barometer elections may exist in a variety of political systems. By-elections in Westminster systems (for example, Australia, Britain, Canada), German *land* (state) elections, and U.S. special (congressional) elections are particularly well-known examples. Other potential barometer elections include European Parliament elections and legislative (midterm) elections in the presidential systems of Latin America, since they take place within the context of national party systems yet have no immediate consequence for the distribution of executive power at the national level.

Given the importance attached to these contests by observers, the scholarly literature has focused on explaining why barometer elections come out the way they do. Anthony Mughan and Pippa Norris, working separately, found that incumbent parties almost invariably achieve lower levels of support in a barometer election than they received in the previous general election. Moreover, to explain the outcomes of barometer elections (that is, usually the magnitude of the loss), scholars have relied for the most part on national-level variables, such as the state of the economy, executive popularity, the national electoral cycle, and partisan support. The findings from this line of research indicate that the barometer contest is, by and large, a referendum on the ruling party's economic and political performance. Researchers thus have explained the outcomes of local contests with the help of national political and economic conditions because they are viewed as augurs of the national political situation.

Although they have been studied in different contexts, barometer elections have not been analyzed as extensively as general (national) elections. Sometimes characterized as unimportant or irrelevant, barometer elections provide scholars a chance to consider a class of electoral contests that matter in ways different from general elections. Specifically, Christopher Anderson found them to provide information about the public's preferences, to shape public and elite expectations, and to affect public support for government and opposition by providing momentum to the winners of such contests. They also can alter the internal dynamics of political parties by influencing the allegiance of party activists, the cohesion of party leadership, and the decisions of potential candidates to run or sit out. In addition, Pippa Norris and Frank Feigert found that barometer elections affect a country's party system by providing significant support for new parties that seek to enter the electoral arena.

See also *By-Elections; Second-Order Elections.*

CHRISTOPHER J. ANDERSON, BINGHAMTON UNIVERSITY (SUNY)

BIBLIOGRAPHY

Anderson, Christopher J. *Blaming the Government: Citizens and the Economy in Five European Democracies.* Armonk, N.Y.: M.E. Sharpe, 1995.

Anderson, Christopher J., and Daniel S. Ward. "Barometer Elections in Comparative Perspective." *Electoral Studies* 15, no. 4 (1996): 447–460.

Mughan, Anthony. "On the By-election Vote of Governments in Britain." *Legislative Studies Quarterly* 13, no. 1 (1988): 29–48.

Norris, Pippa. *British By-elections.* New York: Oxford University Press, 1990.

Norris, Pippa, and Frank Feigert. "Government and Third-Party Performance in Midterm By-Elections: The Canadian, British, and Australian Experience." *Electoral Studies* 8, no. 2 (1989): 117–130.

Shugart, Matthew. "The Electoral Cycle and Institutional Sources of Divided Presidential Government." *American Political Science Review* 89, no. 2 (1995): 327–343.

BINOMIAL ELECTORAL SYSTEM

A binomial system is a specific type of electoral system in which all members of the parliament are elected in two-member constituencies. The term is relatively new and refers to the type of electoral system that was established in Chile in 1988 in the context of the redemocratization of the country after sixteen years of authoritarian military rule. The Chilean system combines personal voting with a list element in order to structure the vote along party or party-alliance lines. The decision rule is plurality: the party with the most votes gets the first seat, the party with the second-highest plurality wins the second seat (mathematically, this is identical to d'Hondt). Technically, candidacy is organized in closed, nonblocked lists, that is, voters have the possibility of choosing between the two candidates within one list, and within the list the candidate who gets the most votes is elected. Only if the strongest list doubles the votes of the second-strongest does it get both seats of the constituency. Usually, the strongest and the second-strongest list each gain one of the two seats. Hence the binomial system protects (and in Chile was intentionally designed to protect) the second-strongest party or alliance.

On the aggregate level the empirical effect is similar to that of proportional representation in small constituencies with an even number of seats, which also favors the second-strongest party or alliance over the strongest one. Where the parties are permitted to form alliances, like in Chile, the binomial system tends to restructure party competition such that parties compete in two main alliances for strategic electoral reasons. Elitist nomination of candidates and preelectoral distribution of shares and seats among the parties forming an alliance are likely consequences, and these consequences may, in the long run, widen the gap between voters and their political representatives.

The strong tendency to protect the first minority and to inhibit the formation of an absolute majority in parliament distinguishes the binomial system—which often has been described misleadingly as a majority system—from other electoral systems under which all or a considerable number of the members of parliament are elected in two-member districts but with differing forms of candidacies, balloting, and seat allocation. For example, voters may dispose of one vote or two for individual candidates, and the two candidates with the most votes (regardless of their party affiliation) are elected. Alternatively, voters may cast one vote for a blocked list, and the list that gets a plurality or an absolute majority of votes wins the two seats. Such a system (with plurality as the decision rule) was applied in the Seychelles in the 1970s. These electoral systems adhere to the representation principle of majority and may even produce extreme majoritarian effects.

See also *Apparentement; Pooling Votes.*

DIETER NOHLEN, UNIVERSITY OF HEIDELBERG

BLOCK VOTE

See *Limited Vote*

BONUS SEATS

Bonus seats are awarded to a party in addition to seats won by the normal procedures in use for allocating seats in parliament. One justification for doing so is to correct anomalies between votes and representation. In Malta, if the party winning a majority of the popular vote does not win a majority of the seats, it can claim bonus seats in order to achieve a parliamentary majority. This happened in 1987, when the Nationalists won only thirty-one seats with 50.9 percent of the vote while the Labour Party won thirty-four seats with 48.9 percent of the vote. The Nationalist Party was able to claim four bonus seats in order to have a majority in parliament that matched its share of the popular vote. In 1996 the rule worked to the benefit of the Maltese Labour Party, which won 50.7 percent of the vote but only thirty-one seats; it could therefore claim four bonus seats to give it a parliamentary majority.

The bonus system may also be used to increase the representation of the party that already has the most seats. In Turkey, the party with the most members of parliament in districts returning five or more members is entitled to one bonus seat. This rule tends to help larger parties and to reduce the effects of fragmentation in a political system in which a half-dozen or more parties may be represented in parliament. At one time in South Korea a bonus system was used to give the party winning the most single-member plurality seats a majority of the seventy-five nationally allocated seats. In Italy a 1953 law authorized any party or alliance of parties winning more than half the popular vote to claim 64 percent of the seats in parliament, a procedure for creating a dominant party that smacked of the fascist era. The dominant Christian Democratic coalition narrowly failed to achieve this goal in 1953, and in 1956 the law was repealed.

In a sense, all first-past-the-post electoral systems normally give a substantial bonus of seats to the party or parties winning the most votes in single-member districts. But this bonus is an incidental consequence of that electoral system. Almost every proportional-representation system awards a small "bonus" to parties that clear the electoral threshold, as a consequence of parties that fall below the threshold not receiving any seats. In the extreme case of the election of the Russian Duma in 1995, almost half the proportional-representation vote was cast for parties that failed to clear the 5 percent threshold to qualify for Duma seats. In consequence, the four parties that did clear the threshold won 106 seats more than the 119 that they would have gained if seats had been awarded strictly in proportion to vote shares.

The award of bonus seats has few advocates, because it is inconsistent with the expression of popular preferences through a country's normal electoral procedures. The exception, the Malta law ensuring that the party with a majority of votes also has a majority of seats, has not been proposed for adoption in the United Kingdom, even though twice since 1945 the party with the largest share of the popular vote has come second in the distribution of seats in Parliament.

See also *Compensatory Seats; Manufactured Majorities; Proportional Representation; Winning an Election.*

RICHARD ROSE, UNIVERSITY OF STRATHCLYDE

BOYCOTT OF ELECTIONS

Election boycotts arise when political parties or candidates withdraw in protest from participation in an election and call upon voters to stay home on election day. The purpose of a boycott is to challenge the validity of a planned election and to call into question the political legitimacy of the resulting government. Usually mounted by opposition groups, such embargoes signal that contenders for political power have not yet agreed on rules for playing the democratic game.

Opposition boycotts also offer analysts a means to judge whether an election is free and fair. After all, the exit of an opposition party can be a potent emblem that all is not well with the electoral process. Insofar as walk-outs or stay-aways cast light on the quality of elections, they play a similar role to negative findings by election observers or the rejection of official election results by losing parties. Whereas these other devices offer ex post assessments of electoral quality, however, election boycotts are credible only to the extent that they are mounted ex ante, that is, prior to election day. Ex ante boycotts can potentially serve as an early warning system about malfunctions in the electoral system.

But, because not all boycotted elections are actually unfair, the claims of boycotters should be treated with caution. Rather than reflecting a flawed electoral process, a boycott can be a disruptive ruse by a party that has concluded that it has no chance of winning. Similarly, the disputation of announced election results may sometimes represent nothing more than the "sour grapes" of losers who find it hard to accept that they lack support among the electorate. For these reasons, analysts who seek to interpret the fairness of boycotted elections must carefully weigh the rival rhetorical appeals of incumbent and opposition groups.

THE CONDITIONS THAT GIVE RISE TO BOYCOTTS

The probability of election boycotts tends to vary with the nature of the regime that sponsors the election. Opposition boycotts are least likely where an elected government maintains a level electoral playing field that does not grant undue advantage to any participant. By adhering strictly to rules laid down in the constitution and electoral laws and running open and transparent electoral contests, sitting governments can undermine the rationale for opposition boycotts and defuse their effects. By contrast, boycotts are most likely where authoritarian governments permit competitive electoral contests but seek to stage-manage them in order to ensure their own political survival. Under these circumstances, boycotters can easily discredit the proceedings by drawing attention to the manipulation of election rules or the monopolization of electoral resources by the incumbents.

One would therefore expect election boycotts to be common in founding elections that terminate prolonged periods of authoritarian rule. Founding elections invariably pose a dilemma for opposition groups: should they participate in, or stand back from, contests organized by the old regime? On the one hand, a competitive election offers a welcome opportunity for regime opponents to take part in politics after many years of political exclusion. On the other hand, the motivations of the incumbent leader may be suspect, in which case the opposition would not wish to be lured into endorsing a fraudulent electoral process.

In practice, opposition forces usually resolve this quandary with careful reference to their own local circumstances. The principal consideration is the opposition's judgment of whether the incumbent, through choice or circumstance, has irrevocably embarked on a path of democratization. In countries where reform elements hold the political initiative and a regime transition is clearly under way—as with founding elections in Brazil in 1984, Poland in 1989, and Zambia in 1991—opposition leaders can safely and eagerly jump on the electoral bandwagon.

In countries where hard-line elements in the ruling elite hold power and threaten to control any election process, however, the case for a boycott is much more clear-cut. For example, in Greece in 1973 the Center Union Party and other opposition groups refused to participate in elections for a legislature that was regarded as a powerless tool of the military government headed by Col. Giorgios Papadopoulos. Three of four opposition parties urged resistance to 1974 presidential elections in the Dominican Republic when Joaquín Balaguer Ricardo gave every indication that he did not intend to surrender power. And, after 1983 in South Africa, opposition leaders resisted efforts by P.W. Botha to tempt them to run candidates for race-based legislatures and local government councils.

The boycott dilemma arises most sharply when elections are called by a liberalizing regime whose ultimate intentions with respect to democratization are uncertain. After intense debate, Philippine opposition leaders could not agree on whether to boycott the 1984 National Assembly elections and the 1986 presidential election sponsored by Ferdinand Marcos. In Pakistan opposition leaders encountered resistance from their own rank-and-file when they urged a boycott of the 1985 National Assembly elections organized by the liberalizing regime of Mohammad Zia ul-Haq. The incumbent's objective is to induce some (but not too much) opposition participation so that he can claim enhanced legitimacy from a competitive vote. For these reasons, some old-guard governments—as in Pakistan and South Africa—passed legislation making advocacy of an election boycott a punishable offense.

South Africa's founding elections illustrate how threats of withdrawal sometimes can amount to little more than a bluff by weak opposition elements. The campaign to resist apartheid, which included school and service protests in black townships and trade and financial sanctions from abroad, suffused South Africa's politics with a culture of boycott. Once an April 27, 1994, date was announced for a majority-rule election, the burning question became whether minority parties—especially the Zulu-based Inkatha Freedom Party—would join the process or seek to wreck it. Forming a rejectionist front with the white right, Inkatha's Mangosuthu Buthelezi opposed holding elections until he received guarantees of federal autonomy for his home region. Despite escalating violence, in which Inkatha militants interpreted the boycott as a call to prevent people from electioneering and voting, the authorities insisted on adhering to the announced election schedule. Faced with the prospect of being excluded entirely from power, Buthelezi reversed himself by adding his party to the ballot just days before the election.

Following democratic transitions, one would expect that elected governments would enjoy increased legitimacy and that the frequency of opposition boycotts therefore would decline. This scenario has come to pass in countries like Spain, the Czech Republic, and Argentina, where second and third elections have attracted a wide range of contenders and led to the rotation of governing parties. Evidence from sub-Saharan Africa, however, indicates that the incidence of opposition boycotts rises the second time around: whereas opposition parties mounted boycotts in just eleven founding elections between 1990 and 1994, they did so for 30 percent of second elections between 1995 and 1997. The opposition called these boycotts to protest manipulation of electoral rules (for example, to bar their leading presidential candidate in Côte d'Ivoire and Zambia) but also to avoid revealing their weaknesses at the polls. Unlike in other world regions, in Africa boycotted second elections have tended to entrench dominant parties, to reduce leadership turnover, and to demonstrate the continued absence of basic agreement on political rules.

THE EFFECTIVENESS OF BOYCOTTS

At a minimum, boycott campaigns have the effect of shifting the voters' attention from whom to vote for to whether to vote at all. Whether voters stay away from the polls, however, depends on the number and cohesion of the parties sponsoring the boycott; a divided opposition rarely sponsors an effective boycott. It also depends on the salience of the election; citizens are less likely to sacrifice a once-in-a-lifetime opportunity to vote in a historic founding election than to forgo a routine voting experience in a subsequent election.

For this reason, boycotts of founding elections—in which opposition forces share the objective of ousting a dictator and citizens are eager to exercise a political choice—have rarely worked well. In this regard, the abstention rate of 70 percent of voters in the general elections in the Dominican Republic in 1974 was an aberration. More typical was low abstention: 23 percent in the 1976 Spanish referendum, 20 percent in the 1984 Philippines election, and just 14 percent in the 1994 South African election. Indeed, in a public opinion poll conducted shortly before Inkatha re-entered the electoral race, fewer than 10 percent of South African blacks said they approved of a boycott; the overwhelming majority were determined to vote.

Boycotts have worked slightly better in second elections, at least in Africa. To be sure, the stay-away organized by Zambia's main opposition party in 1996 was a flop, with just 16 percent (concentrated mainly in one eastern province) saying the boycott affected their voting behavior. On the other hand, abstention rates in legislative elections of 65 percent in Niger in 1995 and 79 percent in Mali in 1997 bespeak electorates disengaged from politics, an outcome partly induced by opposition boycotts.

Election boycotts cannot be recommended as a strategy for democratic opposition. At best, their contribution to democratization is negative, calling into question the legitimacy of illiberal governments who win power through imperfect elections. At worst, election boycotts undermine democratization because they rarely put an end to autocratic regimes. More often, the withdrawal of opposition plays into the hands of the powers-that-be, allowing sitting governments to increase their majorities at the polls, at the same time reducing the plurality of voices in parliament and leading boycott proponents into the political wilderness. Even if elections are not conducted with full fairness, they still offer opportunities for upset, outsider victories. And even modest electoral gains by an opposition can be used to challenge repressive governments and strengthen the hands of reformers. Thus, democrats should probably prefer to keep election boycotts in reserve for use only as a very last resort.

See also *Elections in Developing Countries; Founding Elections; Turnout; Unfree Elections.*

MICHAEL BRATTON, MICHIGAN STATE UNIVERSITY

BIBLIOGRAPHY

Bratton, Michael. "Second Elections in Africa." *Journal of Democracy* 9 (July 3, 1998).

Huntington, Samuel. *The Third Wave: Democratization in the Late Twentieth Century.* Norman: University of Oklahoma Press, 1991.

Le Duc, Lawrence, Richard G. Niemi, and Pipa Norris, eds. *Comparing Democracies: Elections and Voting in Global Perspective.* London: Sage, 1996.

Linz, Juan J., and Alfred Stepan. *Problems of Democratic Transition and Consolidation: Southern Europe, South America, and Post-Communist Europe.* Baltimore, Md.: Johns Hopkins University Press, 1996.

Johnson, R.W., and Lawrence Schlemmer, eds. *Launching Democracy in South Africa: The First Open Election, April 1994.* New Haven, Conn.: Yale University Press, 1996.

Zakaria, Fareed. "The Rise of Illiberal Democracy." *Foreign Affairs* 76 (November–December 1997): 22–43.

BY-ELECTIONS

Vacancies occur between elections due to the death, resignation, or expulsion of an elected representative. A resignation may be voluntary or it may be required by law if an individual is appointed to a post incompatible with elected office, for example, a judgeship; a cabinet post in political systems that emphasize the separation of powers; or, in Britain, a seat in the House of Lords. Expulsion may be ordered for a nonpolitical offense, such as conviction on a criminal charge, or for actions arising from political activities, such as election fraud. The likelihood of a vacancy arising is partly a function of the term of office. In the U.S. House of Representatives, by-elections are infrequent because the term of office is only two years, whereas the six-year term of U.S. senators makes vacancies more likely to arise.

When a vacancy occurs in a parliament, the seat may be filled by holding a by-election, that is, a fresh vote with a fresh slate of candidates and an opportunity for voters to behave differently than at the previous ballot. They may vote differently because of shifts in the popularity of the contending parties, because of differences in candidates, or because a by-election rarely decides which party governs. Alternatively, the vacancy can be filled without an election according to provisions set out in legislation, or the seat can remain vacant.

VACANCIES IN A
FIRST-PAST-THE-POST SYSTEM

The by-election procedure in a first-past-the-post, single-member district such as in Great Britain, Canada, or India involves holding an election in the constituency with the same rules applying as at a general election. The number and types of candidates may differ, for it is easier to attract attention at a specially held by-election, which brings forward publicity-seeking individuals and advocates of causes with no hope of winning. In by-elections in Northern Ireland, the Irish Republican movement has nominated candidates pledged to refuse to take their seat in a British Parliament, including prisoners convicted on charges of using violence against the state. In Catholic districts, such candidates have sometimes won, only to be disqualified subsequently and another by-election held.

Voting at by-elections often differs somewhat from that at a general election. For example, in Britain turnout is almost always lower, since a by-election receives less publicity than a general election. By-elections usually show a swing against the government of the day. The extent of the governing party's loss of votes depends on the distance in time from the last general election and the anticipated date of the next election. Control of government is not at stake, since only one member of Parliament is elected at a by-election, and this encourages some people to support parties that do not have a chance of winning a parliamentary majority, for example, the Liberal Democrats or Nationalists. Normally, the closer the ballot is to the middle of the term of a parliament, the greater the government's loss of support. For this reason, the governing party can try to delay a by-election. In Canada in the late 1970s the governing Liberal Party left so many seats vacant for so long, for fear of by-election defeats, that the law was changed to compel a by-election to be held within a specified period of a vacancy arising.

Since members of the U.S. Senate were historically elected to represent states rather than voters within a state, the U.S. Constitution (Article I, sec. 3) initially gave state legislatures the right to fill vacancies, if in session, and state governors the right to make temporary, recess appointments. The Seventeenth Amendment (ratified in 1913), which made senators directly elected, mandated that states hold by-elections to fill Senate vacancies but left the state legislatures to determine how vacancies would be temporarily filled pending an election. Many state legislatures opted to empower their governor to make the temporary appointment, and governors normally appoint a member of their own party rather than of the party of the outgoing senator.

VACANCIES IN PROPORTIONAL-REPRESENTATION SYSTEMS

Because a by-election normally involves a single vacancy, it is inherently incompatible with proportional representation, which requires the election of a multiplicity of candidates to spread representation in proportion to the vote for different parties. In a proportional-representation electoral system, candidates are normally elected to represent a party; thus, when a vacancy arises, a seat can be filled by another candidate from the same party. The procedure is simplest in a list system; the highest-ranked candidate on the party's list not yet in parliament can succeed to the post. The American provision for the vice president to succeed to the presidency when a vacancy occurs is another example of "promoting" a candidate of the same party to avoid a by-election.

The logic of the party, rather than individual incumbents, holding a seat is extended in South Africa so that an individual who resigns or is expelled from the party with which he or she was affiliated at the time of a general election is thereby deemed to have resigned from parliament. In Sweden there are provisions for members of parliament to have a substitute temporarily replace them when they take leave so that their party is not unrepresented, and a substitute can fill a vacancy arising from death. In France parliamentary deputies may have a substitute fill their seat if, for example, they are appointed as a minister and compelled to resign from parliament.

The outcome of an Irish by-election is determined by majority voting, whereas the outcome in a general election is determined by a form of proportional representation. The Irish system of electing members of parliament from multi-member districts by the single transferable vote makes it inappropriate to fill vacancies by promoting the next candidate on a list. In Ireland a by-election is held for a single seat. The use of the transferable vote means that the winner obtains a majority of the valid votes, thus making the contest like the alternative vote in Australia, where candidates are also ranked by preference in single-member districts.

See also *Barometer Elections; Suppléant; Term of Office, Length of.*

RICHARD ROSE, UNIVERSITY OF STRATHCLYDE

BIBLIOGRAPHY

Cook, Chris, and John Ramsden. *By-Elections in British Politics.* London: University College London Press, 1998.

Feigert, Frank, and Pippa Norris. "Do By-elections Constitute Referenda? A Four-Country Comparison." *Legislative Studies Quarterly* 15, no. 2 (1990): 183–200.

Norris, Pippa. *British By-Elections: The Volatile Electorate.* Oxford: Clarendon Press, 1990.

CAMPAIGNING

The term *election campaigning* refers to the set of activities employed by political parties and candidates to seek electoral support in a bid to win political office. It includes such persuasive activities as speech making, passing out literature, broadcasting, advertising, distributing posters, and holding rallies.

In countries that have competitive party systems and free elections, the style of election campaigning is determined by a number of factors:

- Offices for election; for example, members of parliament, president, or federal officers

- Ballot form; for example, vote for party list or candidate

- Election rules; for example, raising and spending money by parties and candidates, access to broadcast media, entitlement to vote, definitions of illegal practices

- Culture; for example, what activities and appeals are deemed acceptable

- Technology; for example, extent of television penetration, number of computers and professional opinion research and opinion polling organizations

- Political system; for example, degree of party competition, organizational strength of political parties, extent to which a candidate campaigns as a representative of the party

THREE PHASES OF DEVELOPMENT

In the past one hundred years, election campaigns in the Western states have gone through three broad phases: traditional, modern, and postmodern.

In the traditional phase, campaigns relied heavily on public meetings, rallies, and canvassing. Much party activity was directed to maximizing turnout of voters who were predisposed toward them, and for many voters elections were an opportunity to reaffirm support for a party or a candidate.

For many voters, party identification was based on social class or religious or ethnic loyalties. One of the first voting studies in the United States, conducted by Paul Lazarsfeld et al. in 1944, compiled an "index of political predisposition," linking a voter's choice of party to his or her religion, social class, and residence in an urban or rural area. Voters were exposed largely to their own side of the political argument. Election turnout was high. In the United States this phase ended in the 1950s, and in western Europe, a decade or so later.

Ushering in the modern phase of campaigning, television and public relations techniques spread rapidly, particularly in the United States beginning around 1952, with western Europe following. There was some weakening of party identification; this was both cause and consequence of parties becoming more catch-all in their appeal. Parties appealed to an increasingly wider range of voters, even if it involved some dilution of ideology and ties with traditional, loyal voters. Social and economic change also weakened traditional party loyalties. Declining loyalty meant that election campaigns could have a greater impact on outcomes, as more voters were less tied to a party, and that created an incentive to sway more voters by campaigning. In presidential races, campaigning became more candidate- than party-oriented.

The postmodern phase, which started in the 1980s, sees the continuation of many of the features of modern campaigning. New media (videos, telephone canvassing, and computers) have continued to spread, and party identification and membership continue to decline. Even in parliamentary and party-list systems, campaigning focuses more on individual party leaders. Campaigning is less labor- and more capital-intensive, more media-oriented, and more computer-based. Parties increasingly use opinion polls and focus groups to learn about the voters' moods and preferences and to target key voters, usually potential "switchers." To make use of the new media, political parties and (in a presidential system) candidates employ experts, for example, opinion pollsters, public relations professionals, advertising agencies, and campaign consultants. This is sometimes called a "scientific approach" to campaigning.

TELEVISION

The spread of television has greatly expanded the opportunity for campaigners to address the mass electorate. Parties attach great importance to television coverage because they believe it can set the agenda for voters. Parties and candidates rely in part on *controlled media*—party broadcasts or advertisements on commercial outlets. In the United States, Russia, Germany, and Italy, for example, commercial channels allow candidates to purchase time, subject to regulation. In Britain, Russia, Spain, and Italy, broadcasters provide time as a public service, such as for debates between party leaders. Televised debates between the main-party candidates, as in the United States, Australia, Spain, and France, reflect personalization of the electoral choice. Political advertising on television has spread in Europe in recent years; with the development of cable and satellite television, it may spread even further. Where broadcasting systems exclude advertisements, they usually provide parties with opportunities via broadcasts of leaders' debates.

Parties also seek "free" coverage in television news and current affairs programming. They devise "photo opportunities" and other events to coax TV cameras to cover the party's leader and favored themes, and candidates prepare sound bites for news bulletins. Candidates who feel excluded or denied "fair" coverage by broadcasters may use the "new news"— talk-shows or phone-in programs. Television coverage usually exposes voters to more than one side of an issue or of the political spectrum. It is usually more interested in the "horse race" (who is winning), and also focuses more on personalities than other media.

These trends facilitate a greater central control of the campaign message and, if appropriate, a national message. Voters are exposed more to the centrally determined messages than to those of the constituency. But, paradoxically, party headquarters can also segment the electorate and target specialized appeals. Using opinion polls to select key audiences, parties can reach them through specialized media, for example, by advertising in magazines and newspapers with particular readerships and by using direct mail. Much of the campaign effort can be targeted in swing constituencies that will determine the overall result. In the United States television advertisements are concentrated in key swing states.

Modern campaigning is expensive, in part because of the prevalence of what are termed the three "T's" of electioneering: technology, technocrats, and techniques. The trend in Western countries is for the state to provide public funding for some of the election campaign costs and to provide subsidies in kind, such as free postage for leaflets. In Britain there are strict limits on the amount of spending in constituencies, although there has been no limit on the amount spent by na-

tional party headquarters. This will change following the Blair government's acceptance of an official committee's recommendations to ban foreign donations and to disclose sources of finance above a certain limit. In the United States candidates devote much time and effort to raising funds. The formal campaign in most parliamentary systems lasts about a month. In the United States and France a presidential campaign lasts longer. Expansion of the mass media and calculations by politicians are interacting to prolong the campaign, leading to what is now termed the "permanent campaign."

There is some scholarly debate in Britain about whether the present trends, including the growing importance of television and professional communicators, are best described as "Americanization." Many of the media- and public-relations centered techniques first emerged in the United States. But so far as these trends reflect technology and media developments, other countries may simply be catching up with the United States. Differences in national cultures and political institutions prevent a complete convergence in campaign style. Sweden and Britain, for example, do not allow parties to advertise on TV. But across many democracies there is a common tendency for modern campaigning to be regarded as political marketing, as more resources are devoted to media strategies and campaigns are adapted to the format requirements of television. Another force for convergence is the trend for campaign consultants and pollsters to ply their skills in many countries. Skills developed in the United States, and to a lesser extent in Britain, are being applied in many other countries, notably in eastern Europe. In eastern Europe and other newly emerged democracies, parties are not long-established and therefore have less scope to mobilize traditional loyalties. These states have moved quickly to media-centered campaigns.

There is no scholarly agreement on what constitutes a good or effective campaign; it is easier to recognize a bad one. In the disastrous Labour Party campaign of 1983 in Britain, the party lost, according to opinion polls, nearly a quarter of its support during the four weeks of the campaign. Election campaigns are only one of a number of influences on the voter. It is a short-term influence, to be compared with many long-term forces, such as economic conditions and social structure.

In the United States incumbents in the Senate and House of Representatives are better placed to raise funds than their challengers and run a perpetual campaign offering constituency services. In Britain studies of local campaigns show that a new member of Parliament benefits by 1 percent or so of the vote in his or her first defense of the seat, compared with other MPs, largely on account of the constituency services he or she has provided. Other studies have suggested that contacting voters, or surrogate indicators of campaign activities, such as the amount of money spent and the size and activity of local party membership, also help boost a candidate's vote.

It is sometimes claimed that the postmodern campaign reduces citizens to the role of spectators. An alternative view is that opportunities for participation have now increased via single-issue groups, referendums, focus groups, and broadcast phone-in programs. Many of the claims about broader campaign "effects" are not proven.

See also *Bandwagon Effects; Canvassing; Coordination, Electoral; Cross-Filing; Election Finance; Manifesto, Election; Public Aid to Parties and Candidates; Regulation of Television at Elections.*

DENNIS KAVANAGH, UNIVERSITY OF LIVERPOOL

BIBLIOGRAPHY

Butler, David, Austin Ranney, and Howard Penniman, eds. *Democracy at the Polls.* Washington, D.C.: American Enterprise Institute, 1981.

Butler, David, and Austin Ranney, eds. *Electioneering.* Oxford: Oxford University Press, 1992.

Farrell, David. "Campaigning Strategies." In *Comparing Democracies,* edited by Lawrence LeDuc, Richard Niemi, and Pippa Norris. London: Sage, 1996.

Rose, Richard. *Influencing Voters.* London: Faber, 1967.

Swanson, David, and Paolo Mancini, eds. *Politics, Media and Modern Democracy.* Westport, Conn.: Praeger, 1996.

CANDIDATES: LEGAL REQUIREMENTS AND DISQUALIFICATIONS

Electoral laws typically impose limitations on who may be a candidate for election. These limitations tend to fall into one of five broad categories.

First, there are certain minimal and basic requirements that do little more than define membership of the body politic in a country. An example is the typical requirement that candidates be citizens ("natural born citizens," in the case of candidates for the presidency of the United States). There is sometimes an associated requirement that a candidate not be a citizen of, or under some obligation of allegiance to, another country. In a similar vein, persons convicted of treason or treachery are normally disqualified from candidacy, since their crime represents a direct attack on the political system of which, as candidates, they would be seeking to form a part.

The second category of requirements covers those that reflect pragmatic judgments as to the qualities that a person will need in order to function effectively as a representative. The view is held almost universally that politics is a matter for adults; this is taken to imply a minimum age at which a person can be a candidate. Often the minimum age will be the same as the legal voting age in the country, typically eighteen or twenty-one years; but in some countries the representative is seen as performing a higher function than that of a voter, and the minimum age for candidacy is higher than for voting. In the United States, for example, a candidate for the presidency must be at least thirty-five years old. This category also covers the disqualification of persons of unsound mind; its purpose is simply to ensure that elected representatives will be capable of functioning effectively. A requirement that a candidate be capable of working in an official language of the country also falls into this category, since a person who did not speak that language would be unable to participate in debates in the legislature, and a person who did not read it would have difficulty in absorbing official documents. Another disqualification in this category arises in political systems that have as an underlying principle a doctrine of separation of powers: persons with direct links to the executive branch of government or the judiciary may be disqualified from seeking election to the legislature, on the basis of their ostensible conflict of interest. (A subordinate question that arises in the context of such a disqualification is whether a candidate who holds an office incompatible with membership in a legislature should be required to resign that office prior to being nominated or only after being elected.) In some cases, it is thought desirable to require candidates to have been resident for a specified period of time either in the country or in the territorial constituency that they aspire to represent.

Third, requirements may be imposed that reflect a desire to enhance the image or effectiveness of the body for which members are being chosen. Candidates may, for example, be required to have achieved a certain level of education.

Fourth, candidates who advocate political positions that are generally held to be inconsistent with the basic political norms of a society or of the international community may be disqualified (for example, candidates who advocate racial hatred or actions that would constitute a gross breach of international human rights agreements).

Finally, there may be disqualifications that reflect moralistic rather than pragmatic judgments. In many countries, undischarged bankrupts are prohibited from being candidates. Criminals and persons who have been convicted of certain categories of crime (often including crimes associated with the election process) are also frequently subject to disqualification.

Any precondition for candidacy has the effect of restricting, and to some extent prejudging, the choice to be made by the voters; and in severe cases, the application of qualifications or disqualifications that at first glance appear reasonable may be used as a means of manipulating an electoral process. An example of such manipulation arose in Zambia in 1996: the steps taken by the incumbent authorities to amend the qualifications for presidential candidates, apparently motivated by a desire to prevent the former president, Kenneth Kaunda, from recontesting the position, attracted widespread international criticism. Any qualifications based on supposed criteria of competence have the potential to be implemented in a discriminatory way, and, if the qualifications in question are not widely held, may have the effect of producing a legislature dominated by an unrepresentative elite. Disqualifications based on criminal convictions may affect, in particular, opposition politicians who have been subject to quasi-legal persecution. In the face of these difficulties, there is much to be said for maximizing the choice open to voters by applying only minimal qualifications for candidacy. Although maximizing choice may be controversial in societies where particularly obnoxious points of view may thereby be given expression in the legislature, it is a matter of judgment as to whether it is better for them to be given formal expression in the parliament or to be channeled into extraparliamentary activities.

See also *Administration of Elections; Constitution and Elections; Cross-Filing; Deposit; Nomination Procedures.*

MICHAEL MALEY, AUSTRALIAN ELECTORAL COMMISSION

BIBLIOGRAPHY

Administration and Cost of Elections Project website: *www.aceproject.org*

Blackburn, Robert. *The Electoral System in Britain.* London: Macmillan Press, 1995.

Mackenzie, W.J.M. *Free Elections: An Elementary Textbook.* London: George Allen and Unwin, 1958.

CANDIDATES: SELECTION

Candidate selection is the internal process by which parties choose the people who will contest elections on their behalf. Although candidate selection typically attracts only a small fraction of the attention given to the elections, it deserves more, for two reasons: first, because candidate selection can be at least as important as elections in determining the nature and the behavior of the people elected, and second, because candidate selection provides a valuable window into the parties themselves. Parties act as "gatekeepers" in their recruitment of politicians, organizing and necessarily restricting the choice made by the voters.

CENTRALIZATION OF SELECTION

The methods by which parties choose their candidates vary considerably. One important dimension is the degree to which the process is centralized. Some parties choose candidates at the national level, some at the regional level, and others, probably the largest number, at the local level, although in many cases local competence is subject to some oversight

and influence from the top. A second important dimension is the degree of participation in the selection process. The proportion of party supporters involved ranges from near zero, when the selection is made by a single person, to unity, when all supporters are consulted. These two dimensions are not entirely independent of one another. More centralized processes are typically more exclusive, and less centralized ones more inclusive, but there are exceptions. In particular, practices vary widely at the local level.

Normally, the individual party determines the method that it will use, but in some countries, such as Germany, the law lays down how candidates should be selected. In other countries the choice is influenced by many factors, including the centralization of the political system, the type of electoral system in place, and the values of the party. In recent years many parties have tried to increase the degree of central control over selection. Moves toward public financing of political parties and capital-intensive campaign techniques have strengthened party leaderships and weakened local branches. Yet at the same time, many parties have sought to provide a role for members, and making candidate selection more inclusive also confers a greater legitimacy on the candidates selected.

Outside one-party states, it is unusual for one person to control candidate selection. Indira Gandhi and later her son Sanjay did so as leaders of the Congress Party in India, as did Andreas Papandreou on behalf of the Greek socialist party PASOK. Where control is very centralized, it is usually exercised by a party's national executive committee. This has been the case in, for instance, Israel (until 1992), Venezuela, and France (in the major parties of the right), but decisions made at the central level can be informed and influenced by local requirements and concerns. The French party Rally for the Republic, for instance, has used a nomination commission, reporting to the national executive, but that commission has normally been influenced strongly by local notables, especially where a local organization secured internal consensus. In Japan the use of a similarly centralized system has contained and balanced factional rivalries.

In most parties, local organizations make the decision, even though the party leadership often supervises the process to some degree. ("Local" here means constituency-level organizations, not local party branches, although branches may well provide the units of the constituency organization.) The British Conservative Party's experience in 1997 illustrates the difficulty that can occur when a party's local associations are independent of central control. That party operates a central screening process for new candidates but not for incumbents. A member of Parliament cited by Parliament for grossly unethical conduct was nonetheless reselected by his local organization, causing considerable embarrassment to a party already burdened by a widespread public perception that it was ridden with "sleaze." He also failed to retain his seat. In contrast to the British case, the Irish Fine Gael Party, which could have faced a similar situation in the same year, was able to ensure that one of its disgraced deputies did not get an official nomination (although he was elected anyway as an independent!).

Leadership influence over local selections varies. Some leaderships exercise a veto over individual selections; others set rules to promote certain types of candidates (notably women). And even where central parties have no formal powers, they are not devoid of influence, and selection may in effect entail a collaboration between local and national levels. Collaboration between local and national elements of the party normally occurs away from the public gaze, and only when it breaks down does it become visible.

PARTICIPATION IN SELECTION

Local selection varies with the degree of participation by party supporters. At one extreme is the unique primary process in the United States, where the parties effectively abandon control over selection. Not only is there a lack of central control, there is little or no local party control over the process either. The voters decide who shall be a party's candidate, and they are free to choose anyone from among the individuals who present themselves. The procedure varies from state to state. A "closed" primary allows only those who register as a party member, for instance, a Democrat, to select the party's candidate, whereas an "open" primary allows all voters, regardless of their declared party affiliation, to participate. (Variations in the timing of party registration can blur this difference.) There are further variations. In "blanket" primaries, voters may choose among all candidates—Democratic as well as Republican—for president, Congress, and so on, with the limitation that voters can choose only one candidate for each office. Parties in places as diverse as Australia, Belgium, Canada, Finland, Israel, and Turkey have also experimented with primary elections, but without surrendering so much control. In those countries, voting is confined to party members, and their choice tends to be further restricted by factors such as eligibility criteria, reserved places, and rules making it difficult for them to amend a recommended slate.

Extensive participation may be encouraged by using a convention system, which is the most common method of selection. Some parties allow all members to attend selection conventions; others allow only delegates from the subunits of the party to attend. Conventions may be the real decision-making body, or they may be called simply to ratify a decision made by a constituency committee.

The central–local dimension is complicated in some countries by an intermediate layer of party organization. In Germany, for instance, the *land* (state) level of party organization is involved along with the local constituency organizations. The electoral system, which requires some candidates to be nominated in single-member districts and others on *land*-level lists, encourages some collaboration between local and regional organizations.

EXPLANATIONS FOR DIFFERENCES IN SELECTION METHOD

The German system illustrates the manner in which the electoral system can influence the locus of selection, and hence to some degree the extent of centralization. In Germany the parties need to choose a list of candidates for a large (multi-member regional) constituency and individual candidates for the smaller single-member constituencies within the same area. Other electoral systems set different requirements, but essentially each determines the mechanics of selection: how many candidates have to be selected for a constituency and how large the constituencies are. Even so, single-member districts are compatible with both centralized (India) and decentralized (UK) selection, as are list systems. The fact that Dutch elections use a single, national constituency does not deny local branches a significant role in the selection process in many parties. After an extensive review of the evidence, Michael Gallagher concluded that there was no simple relationship between electoral system and centralization. The fact that parties in the same political system often use different methods, with different degrees of centralization, only serves to underline that conclusion.

Other factors commonly described as playing a role in the choice of method include the ideology of the party, the national political culture, and the organization of government. However, none of these really explains very much. Centralized, exclusive methods are found in parties of the left as well as the right, as are decentralized, inclusive methods. Explanations rooted in political culture may raise as many questions as they purport to answer. Localistic political cultures could be expected to favor decentralized selection, but independent evidence of such a culture is hard to find. The populist, antiparty values that gave rise to the primary method in the United States may have been in part a consequence of the nature of late-nineteenth-century parties in that country. Certainly, parties often change their methods in response to criticism of existing methods, but some change them again at a later date. The growing emphasis on participatory democracy from the 1970s encouraged many parties to open selection to the party membership.

Governmental organization is another factor said to explain selection methods, with federal systems often alleged to be more inclined toward decentralized selection, but again there are exceptions: selection in Austria is quite centralized, although the country is a federation, and selection is decentralized in many unitary states.

Even the law has ambiguous effects on selection methods. Laws differ in that some instruct parties to behave in a particular manner, whereas others merely tie funding to the use of a particular method. German electoral law prescribes a number of party statutes as well as the use of the secret ballot in selection. Norwegian law allows subsidies for party nomination meetings on condition that they are organized in accord with the law, although these subsidies are relatively small and in themselves provide little incentive. Even where the law sets the methods, the law may simply reflect accepted practice.

CONSEQUENCES OF DIFFERENCES IN SELECTION METHODS

However it is achieved, selection provides a short list of candidates from whom representatives are chosen for local, regional, and national assemblies. Selectors thus play a central role in deciding who is elected: who gets the safe seats in single-member districts or the safe places in the lists. Even where preferential voting determines who is elected from a short list, the selectors decide the short list. Furthermore, inasmuch as they are important figures in the eyes of the representatives who want to retain their seats at the next election, selectors can be expected to influence the behavior of those elected.

Scholars have derived various hypotheses from these observations. For instance, some have suggested that more centralized candidate selection leads to stronger party discipline in assemblies, whereas local selection insulates deputies somewhat from the need to toe the party line and ensures that deputies respect local interests and concerns. Researchers have done little systematic comparative testing of such assertions, but they have observed that discipline may result as much from a common outlook among selectors as from a centralized selection mechanism. Deputies can be expected to respond to a number of incentives, only one of which is the demands of their potential selectorate at the next election.

The values of the selectors and the mechanisms of selection influence the composition of the elected assembly. Selectors' criteria for a good assembly member influence who is chosen. If selectors want someone to service the needs of the constituency, they are likely to reward individuals with proven records of local service; if they want to help the party maintain an effective legislative presence, they may be more inclined to reward specialist expertise. Some observers suggest that representatives in more centralized systems pay more attention to legislative requirements, while representatives in decentralized ones favor local effort. More inclusive methods might also be expected to reward those who have established

a broad public reputation. Evidence for the validity of such expectations is hard to find. Certainly, America illustrates the importance of having either a "name" or the money to establish one, but there is little echo of this in Belgium, where despite a decentralized selection process, selectors are not immune to the assembly's need for legislative competence. Methods of selection might also be expected to influence the composition of assemblies in ascriptive terms, but again there is no simple set of consequences.

Scholars, commentators, and political activists have given much attention to the gender imbalance in most parties. Many parties have addressed the imbalance through central control, using mechanisms like all-women shortlists in the British Labour Party or the "layering" of lists in many countries—giving alternate places to men and women. Yet these remedies have been compatible with local and even inclusive selection, largely because selectors and party leaders agreed that something had to be done. Central direction simply provides a means of coordinating the response. In itself, however, central direction does not guarantee a more representative slate of candidates. Where selection is more inclusive, parties may respond more easily to demands for the representation of new groups, since those voices can be heard in the selection process. However, the United States again demonstrates the limits to simple generalization. Women candidates are still rare, not so much because of the selection process as because of the limits of single-member districts and the absence of any mechanism through which the central parties can balance selection, as they have done in Britain. Furthermore, selection is only one element in the recruitment process. If certain sorts of candidates are in short supply, a disproportionately small number of them is likely to be selected, whatever method is used.

The variety of procedures for selecting presidential candidates is similar to that for selecting parliamentary candidates. In the United States the parties initially preferred the convention system, which allowed the appearance of widespread participation but enabled senior party people to manage the process quite effectively by making deals in "smoke filled rooms." After 1903 some states started to use primaries to constrain voting in the convention, and in recent years the primary system has become dominant, leaving the convention no option but to rubber-stamp the decision of the voters. By contrast, in France the convention system has prevailed, but normally there is only one candidate, and the convention simply gives the stamp of democratic legitimacy to the outcome of an elite power struggle. In 1995 the Socialist Party experimented with a system that allowed members to choose among rival candidates.

Candidate selection is important in what it shows us about parties. A decentralized and inclusive process of selection proves a significant exception to the general rule that parties are highly undemocratic organizations, dominated by an elected dictatorship. Just because members do not make policy does not mean they have no positive role to play. The analysis of interactions among various levels of the party in the selection process tends to show a more complex and subtle picture.

See also *Gender Quotas; Nomination Procedures; Primary Elections; Suppléant; Women: Enfranchisement; Women: Representation and Electoral Systems.*

MICHAEL MARSH, TRINITY COLLEGE, UNIVERSITY OF DUBLIN

BIBLIOGRAPHY

Epstein, Leon. *Political Parties in the American Mold.* Madison: University of Wisconsin Press, 1988.
Gallagher, Michael, and Michael Marsh, eds. *Candidate Selection in Comparative Perspective: The Secret Garden of Politics.* London: Sage, 1988.
Katz, Richard, and Peter Mair, eds. *How Parties Organise.* London: Sage, 1994.
Norris, Pippa, and Joni Lovenduski. *Political Recruitment.* Cambridge: Cambridge University Press, 1995.
Norris, Pippa, and Mark Franklin. "Social Representation." In *Political Representation in the European Parliament: European Journal of Political Research* 32, no. 2 (October 1997): 185–210.

CANVASSING

Canvassing originated in Britain during the nineteenth century as an electioneering technique in connection with voter registration. Registration was the responsibility of the individual voter. Canvassers working on behalf of a candidate or party attempted to identify people who were sympathetic to them and were qualified to vote, and then tried to ensure that such voters were properly registered. (They also challenged the qualifications of known opponents.) This process was the equivalent of contemporary "voter registration drives" in the United States.

As the qualifications for voting became less restrictive, however, and registration became almost automatic, canvassing evolved into the practice of candidates and their helpers soliciting support during election campaigns by means of face-to-face contact with individual voters. During the twentieth century, with the advent of mass democracy, mass media, and party domination of elections, campaigners came to realize that the party choice of most voters was relatively fixed and that voters were not easily persuaded to change their minds during campaigns. This view of voters' attachment to parties was confirmed by voting studies in the United States in the 1940s. Accordingly, although some element of persuasion remained, canvassing became predominantly a technique for identifying supporters so that they could be mobilized on election day.

In a traditional canvassing operation, typical of local campaigning in Britain from the 1950s to the 1980s, canvassers call at homes in the relevant electoral district during an election campaign to ascertain whether any voters in the household intend to support the canvasser's party. Responses are recorded on specially prepared lists of voters ("canvass cards"). The task of the canvasser is not to engage in debate or discussion with voters—this wastes valuable time—but simply to record their preferences. Toward the end of the campaign, lists are compiled of the names, addresses, and electoral registration numbers of probable supporters. On election day, party workers are posted outside polling stations to ask voters, as they enter or leave, for their registration number. At regular intervals the registration numbers of those who have voted are conveyed to a central location, where their names are crossed off the pre-prepared lists. From time to time, teams of volunteers go out to "knock up" (as it is known in the UK) or "fetch out" supporters who have not yet voted—to remind them to do so and, if necessary, to offer them transportation to the polls.

Canvassing is an essential element in an efficient "get out the vote" operation. Moreover, an efficient party organization can use canvass- and election-day records to build a picture of the electorate in its area—who is a loyal supporter, who is always for the other side, who always votes, and so on.

CHANGES IN CANVASSING TECHNIQUES

During the 1990s (although these developments began to appear in the United States in the 1960s) this traditional style of canvassing has been substantially modified. First, voters are now frequently contacted by telephone, both during the canvassing period and on election day, rather than face to face. This has clear advantages. It can be done in bad weather and by people who would be unable or unwilling to meet voters personally, and it enables the parties to contact voters who live in remote areas or are otherwise difficult to reach in person. Perhaps most important, telephone canvassing can be done from anywhere in the country, and parties frequently set up central telephone "banks" from which teams of volunteers can call voters. Second, canvass records are now normally kept on computers, which not only makes the storage and subsequent analysis of data more efficient but also minimizes the laborious copying out of names and addresses by hand. Third, parties no longer wait until the election campaign begins to gather information about voters' preferences. Rather, the operation begins months or years before an election is due. Fourth, more detailed information is now sought from voters. In addition to their current voting intention, they will typically be asked about their past voting record, opinions on issues, current concerns, and views of the party leaders or candidates. In addition, a range of demographic details—including age, sex, and occupation—will be collected. Subsequently, voters can be sent direct mail specifically tuned to their situation and, if necessary, arrangements can be made for party workers in the locality to pay a visit. This approach clearly represents something of a return to "canvassing as persuasion," and it also allows communication from voters to parties. To emphasize the change from traditional canvassing, the process is now sometimes called "voter identification."

ELECTORAL EFFECTS OF CANVASSING

In the past, some academic analysts have been skeptical about the efficacy of canvassing (and hence about local campaigning) in influencing election outcomes. Voters, it is suggested, may mislead canvassers about their true intentions, and hence the lists used on election day may be inaccurate. Local campaigning, in this view, is an elaborate ritual bringing some sense of gratification to the participants but making no difference to election results. All that matters is the national campaign, fought on and reported by television. In fact, party supporters have no incentive to deceive their own party, and even if some covert opponents find their way onto the lists, that is irrelevant. The party's aim is to maximize the turnout of its likely supporters, and as long as they are identified by the canvass, that is all that matters.

Although a lively debate continues about the effects of local campaigning on electoral outcomes (especially in the United States), recent research has been more positive about the impact of canvassing and campaigning at the local level. A number of studies have suggested that a well-organized and thorough canvassing operation followed up with efficient election-day activity can produce a significant electoral bonus for the candidate or party concerned. Canvassing, whether of the traditional or modern variety, remains a central element in the effort to mobilize voters on election day and is a campaign technique by which party organizations can attempt to maximize the number of votes polled for their candidate.

See also *Campaigning; Registration of Voters in the United States.*

DAVID DENVER, LANCASTER UNIVERSITY, UK

BIBLIOGRAPHY

Bochel, J. M., and David Denver. "Canvassing, Turnout and Party Support: An Experiment." *British Journal of Political Science* 2 (July 1971): 257–269.

Denver, David, and Gordon Hands. *Modern Constituency Electioneering.* London: Frank Cass, 1997.

Denver, David, Gordon Hands, and Simon Henig. "Triumph of Targeting?: Constituency Campaigning in the 1997 Election." In *British Elections and Parties Review,* vol. 8, edited by David Denver, Justin Fisher, Philip Cowley, and Charles Pattie. London: Frank Cass, 1998.

Hanham, H. J., *Elections and Party Management: Politics in the Time of Disraeli and Gladstone.* London: Longmans, 1959.

Huckfeldt, R. Robert, and John Sprague. *Citizens, Politics and Social Communication: Information and Influence in an Election Campaign.* Cambridge: Cambridge University Press, 1995.

CHOICE, ELECTIONS AS A METHOD OF

Elections are a form of decision making; collectively, votes decide which parties and individuals will hold specified public offices. However, elections are not the only form of decision making, and because they aggregate the decisions of the whole of the adult population, or at least that fraction that turns out to vote, they can aggregate millions of individual preferences, by contrast with an individual or household deciding what to eat for dinner, or choices made within face-to-face groups, such as a parent-teacher association or the board of directors of a large corporation.

ELECTION BY VOTE

Elections involve choice at two radically different levels. The choice that a voter makes with a ballot in his or her hand is that of an individual. By contrast, the winner in a national election is a collective choice produced by the aggregation of millions or tens of millions of votes. In the election of a French president, the winning individual is the choice of a majority of voters. But in the election of the U.S. Congress, the winning party is produced by the aggregation of votes for 435 winning candidates.

In every democratic system, the voter's choice is limited. First, only a restricted number of offices are filled by election. In parliamentary democracies such as Britain, the only national vote that a voter can cast is for one member of Parliament in his or her local constituency. In a proportional-representation system, an individual normally is restricted to a choice between parties that list candidates for a multiplicity of seats. In Europe most elected presidents are nonexecutive and primarily honorific officeholders, and no other executive officeholder is directly elected, with the exception of mayors. The long ballot characteristic of American state and local elections, in which a voter can endorse a large number of executive branch officials at every level from governor to county coroner is unknown in other established democracies. When representatives are elected at different levels—for example, the European Parliament and local government councils as well as the national parliament—the elections are usually held on different dates.

Second, only a restricted number of parties or candidates appear on the ballot. The United States is extreme in that a voter's effective choice for member of Congress or president is usually between candidates of two parties: the Republican and Democratic Parties. Candidates of other parties attract derisory numbers of votes or, even if they secure a significant number of votes, as has Ross Perot, have no chance of winning. Proportional-representation systems widen the choice of parties, but the number of parties with a chance of influencing the election outcome remains restricted. In economic terms, competition for national office tends to be oligopolistic, that is, a restricted number of parties compete, and many voters find that no party exactly matches their combination of preferences on major issues of the day.

A third and lesser restriction on choice is that voters cannot withdraw their endorsement when they lose confidence in an elected official, whereas shareholders in a public company can sell shares when they lose confidence in the firm or its leadership. Even though public opinion polls may indicate that a majority of the electorate has withdrawn its approval, elected politicians can remain in office until their term expires or, in a parliamentary system, elected representatives withdraw confidence from the prime minister while remaining in office themselves. Even in the United States, where some state and local governments formally permit the recall of an officeholder through a special vote, this is rarely used. At the national level, impeachment and conviction on an impeachment charge are rarer still.

The referendum offers a small extension of choice on specific issues of public policy. However, choice in referendums is restricted by their wording, which may be chosen by the government of the day. The initiative allows a group of citizens to place a question of their choice on the ballot. But since the great majority of voters do not sign an initiative petition, the initiative is often held on a question chosen by interested nongovernmental groups. Whatever the wording of a referendum question, voters can only vote yes or no or abstain; they cannot reformulate or amend the question.

All free and fair elections restrict choice. Depending on circumstances, voters may face a choice between a greater and lesser good, between a preferred alternative and alternatives that are disliked, or between a lesser and a greater evil. By increasing the number of parties or candidates on the ballot for a particular office or by increasing the number of offices filled by popular election, the range of choice can be expanded. But given the restricted starting point, choice is inevitably limited compared with the number of offices in government and the variety of opinions and interests that might seek representation.

The outcome of an election validates the choice of those who voted for the winner, but it may negate the choice of those who voted for losers. In a two-ballot presidential election, those who chose the winner will always be a majority, but a large number who support the winner on the second ballot will not have made that candidate their first-round choice. For example, Boris Yeltsin was elected Russian president even though 65 percent of Russians rejected him at the 1996 first-round vote, and Jacques Chirac became president of France even though he was not the first choice of 79 percent of French voters in the first round of the 1995 election. In five American presidential elections since 1948 the winner has received less than half the popular vote, and the same is true of every British parliamentary election since 1935.

ALTERNATIVES TO VOTING

Voting is not the only way in which the citizenry can make a choice. In classical Greece many major offices were filled by drawing lots; the person whose name was drawn from a list of eligible voters was chosen. Often, the "winners" regarded the offices as an onerous obligation, a doctrine that also applies to the modern selection of individuals for jury service. The selection of officeholders by lot was intended to curb the power of politicians by making their hold on office depend on chance. It also emphasized an egalitarian belief that all eligible persons (a minority of the Athenian population) were equally able to make the decisions required of an officeholder.

The neoclassical economic paradigm is based on the liberal political and economic ideal of individual choice. The consumer is sovereign, making choices in his or her self-interest in the marketplace. Instead of voting, a citizen as consumer makes a choice by spending money. Insofar as this theory of choice is accepted, it follows that the government should limit its activities to providing what cannot be bought and sold in the marketplace—collective or public goods, in the jargon of economists—and should let private individuals make choices (that is, select benefits for themselves and their families) in the marketplace. For economic liberals such as Nobel laureate economist Milton Friedman, the marketplace offers the ordinary individual far more freedom of choice than the ballot box, for an individual can purchase different goods and services from different sources, whereas electoral choice is usually reduced to endorsing one party or candidate to provide many goods and services.

The attempt to substitute market choice for political choice faces two fundamental difficulties. First, a significant minority of the population normally lacks the income to choose services of the sort that the welfare state routinely provides all citizens. While rich people can pay for superior education for their children, if public education were abolished, poor people could buy only inferior education. Second, some goods and services important for everyone in society are not sold in the marketplace, such as military defense or clean air. They are collective goods that must be provided to everyone or to no one. Taxation, and elections to choose a government that decides how to spend tax revenue, are therefore appropriate ways of deciding how to provide collective goods.

PUBLIC CHOICE THEORIES

Neoclassical economic theory has also spawned theories of public choice, in which voters are expected to maximize self-interest, as in the marketplace. However, this overlooks one obvious difference between the two types of choices. Individuals, in their role as consumers or as shopkeepers or other vendors of economic goods, are buying and selling particular products on a daily basis. By contrast, elections offer voters a restricted and blunt choice between one or another agent to provide them goods and services over the course of several years. Moreover, the choices that an individual makes as a voter are infrequent and cannot easily be switched. By contrast, the choices that an individual makes as a consumer can differ from one stall to another in the marketplace on a daily basis.

Traditional theories of representation, as stated by Edmund Burke, a late eighteenth century English member of Parliament, declared that representation was not a mechanical process of aggregating preferences but a matter of deliberation by elected members of Parliament. In Burke's terminology, voters chose a person to sit in Parliament as their representative, listening to debates there and forming an opinion in the light of what was said and the circumstances of the moment. Burke argued that a member should not be mandated or delegated to vote in a fixed way, since many circumstances could not be foreseen. Nor could a member be mandated on many issues about which the electorate was unconcerned or unaware. The Burkean theory of choice stressed the predemocratic value of elite deliberation yet is consistent with the modern evidence behind empirical theories of voting, which shows that most voters do not have any views, or at least stable views, about most issues on which their representatives vote.

Contemporary theories of deliberative or discursive democracy run parallel to Burkean theory. They meet the problem of collective choice by postulating that a democratic system ought to arrive at decisions after a period of collective discussion. Ideally, deliberation should involve all citizens, as in a town meeting, but it can also take place between elected representatives. The critical point about deliberation is that the representatives are not tied to what voters appear to have endorsed on election day or what the prospective representatives told their electorate prior to election. Instead, participants in a deliberative discourse are expected to exchange information and opinions in a discussion that is also a reciprocal exchange of influence. In theory, the outcome is a collective point of view that pools the wisdom of participants rather than simply represents positions that were endorsed by a majority of votes.

See also *Initiative: Europe; Initiative: United States; Lot; Offices Filled by Direct Election; Quaker Decision Making without Voting; Recall Elections; Referendums: Europe; Referendums: Latin America; Referendums: United States; Winning an Election.*

RICHARD ROSE, UNIVERSITY OF STRATHCLYDE

BIBLIOGRAPHY

Elster, Jon, ed. *Deliberative Democracy.* New York: Cambridge University Press, 1998.

Fishkin, James S. *The Voice of the People: Public Opinion and Democracy.* New Haven, Conn.: Yale University Press, 1997.

Heap, Shaun Hargreaves, Martin Hollis, Bruce Lyons, Robert Sugden, and Albert Weale. *The Theory of Choice: A Critical Guide.* Cambridge, Mass.: Blackwell, 1992.

Katz, Richard S. *Democracy and Elections.* New York: Oxford University Press, 1997.

Mueller, Dennis C. *Public Choice II.* Cambridge, England: Cambridge University Press, 1989.

Olson, Mancur. *The Logic of Collective Action.* Cambridge, Mass.: Harvard University Press, 1965.

CITIZEN JURIES (AND OTHER METHODS OF INFORMED CITIZEN CONSULTATION)

What methods are available to consult ordinary citizens about public policy? On many issues, ordinary citizens have little incentive to become informed. Having only one opinion or one vote in millions, an individual is unlikely to make much difference. In the classic phrase of the political economist Anthony Downs, ordinary citizens have incentives for "rational ignorance." If their opinions are consulted in polls, their views are likely to reflect top of the head impressions of sound bites or headlines. Or, as Philip Converse of the University of Michigan demonstrated, their views may even represent "nonattitudes," or phantom opinions offered in response to questions but concocted on the spot because a respondent does not wish to admit that he or she does not know.

In the face of this problem, a variety of academic institutions, foundations, and media organizations have undertaken efforts to foster informed and representative citizen consultation. These efforts harken back to the citizen juries and other deliberative microcosms chosen by lot in ancient Athens. But in a wave of experimentation, particularly in the last two decades in Britain, Denmark, Germany, and the United States, researchers have adapted versions of the idea to a modern context, often with modern random sampling and use of the electronic media to disseminate results. These efforts include citizen juries, deliberative opinion polls, consensus conferences, and planning cells. The basic idea is to gather citizens who are representative of the population in question and allow them to discuss an issue under conditions favorable for acquiring more information and getting their questions answered. The resulting conclusions represent what more-informed opinion might look like and provide a mechanism for citizen consultation that aspires to be both representative and deliberative.

Citizen juries, pioneered by the Jefferson Center in Minnesota and by the Institute for Public Policy Research in London, gather small groups of ordinary citizens, ranging usually from twelve to eighteen persons, who deliberate on a policy issue in dialogue with experts and decision makers, sometimes over a few days or even weeks. They call "witnesses" and often come to a consensual decision or write a report. The strength of the process is that it represents informed citizen deliberation. The weaknesses are that the numbers are too small to demonstrate the statistical representativeness of the group (so it becomes difficult to say that it is speaking for the community) and, by reaching a consensus in the manner of a jury, the process does not distinguish social pressures to conform to the group conclusion from individual considered opinions.

Deliberative opinion polls, pioneered by James Fishkin and his colleagues at the University of Texas at Austin, select individuals in a random sample of a population (a city, state, region, or nation) and, after completion of an initial questionnaire, transport them to a single place where they are separated into small groups with trained moderators for extended discussion on an issue with prepared briefing materials. After two-to-four days of discussion, with sessions alternating between small groups and larger plenary sessions with panels of competing experts or decision makers, the respondents take the same questionnaire. The samples of several hundred are large enough for their representativeness to be evaluated and for the changes of opinion to be statistically meaningful. By assessing the opinions in confidential questionnaires, the pressures toward group conformity are limited. Deliberative polls have usually been conducted in conjunction with a television broadcast, and the taped and edited discussions are usually presented with the statistical results in order to influence public dialogue.

Consensus conferences, pioneered in Denmark, have usually employed self-selected persons to reach consensus on some policy issue, usually a scientific or technical problem. They bring the voice of the public to issues that have normally been the province of experts.

Planning cells, pioneered in Germany, use small groups gathered in a variety of locations to deliberate on issues. Un-like consensus conferences, they employ random sampling, and unlike citizen juries, they employ large enough numbers to be statistically meaningful. However, random samples of localities that are not themselves randomly selected do not add up to random samples of the entire population under consideration. Hence planning cells lack the representativeness achieved by deliberative polls, which attempt to gather random samples of the entire population in question, even if that means bringing a national random sample to a single place. Planning cells may, however, achieve real deliberation in the small group discussions and avoid the expense and logistical difficulty of attempting to attract and transport a national random sample to a single place.

All of these efforts attempt to overcome rational ignorance by gathering representative groups of respondents to meet together to discuss issues and become more informed so as to form a considered judgment. These methods vary in their advantages and their costs. All have certain advantages when compared with public opinion polls, at least on issues for which the public has little information.

See also *Public Opinion Polls: How They Work; Quaker Decision Making without Voting; Voting Behavior.*

JAMES S. FISHKIN, UNIVERSITY OF TEXAS AT AUSTIN

BIBLIOGRAPHY

Coote, Anna, and Jo Lenagen. *Citizens Juries: Theory into Practice.* London: Institute for Public Policy Research, 1997.

Fishkin, James S. *The Voice of the People: Public Opinion and Democracy.* New Haven, Conn.: Yale University Press, 1997.

Renn, Ortwin, et al., eds. *Fairness and Competence in Citizen Participation.* Boston: Kluwer, 1995.

Sclove, Richard E. *Democracy and Technology.* New York and London: Guilford Press, 1995.

CITIZENSHIP AND THE RIGHT TO VOTE

See *Administration of Elections; Franchise Expansion; Noncitizens and the Right to Vote*

COLONIAL ELECTIONS

In the great majority of colonies, mass elections on the principle of one person, one vote, one value were introduced, at the earliest, only in the decades preceding independence, and this was especially true in the Belgian, French, Portuguese, and Spanish colonies and in British colonies in Africa. The chief exception was in the British colonies of European emigration—Australia, Canada, and New Zealand—where free elections evolved in accord with European practice.

BRITISH COLONIES

The British colonies in the West Indies, Africa, the Mediterranean, and the Pacific followed a common pattern of constitutional development, although the pace of change varied considerably from colony to colony. In the early days of each colony, the British authorities established a legislative council and an executive council of officials responsible to the governor. Initially, the legislative council also consisted mostly of government officials, but the governor also appointed a number of nongovernmental members to represent the colonial population and the European minority and commercial interests. At a later stage, a number of the nongovernmental members were elected on a narrow franchise, and the number of appointed nongovernmental members increased. As the franchise was broadened, the number of elected members grew until they became a majority. As these changes occurred in the legislative council, the number of nongovernmental members on the governor's executive council also increased, and with the granting of self-government the executive council was transformed into a council of ministers responsible to the legislative council. This was the penultimate stage before the achievement of full independence.

Although British authorities introduced legislative bodies very early in many colonies, the franchise was usually very limited. In the West Indies several islands had enjoyed effective self-government since the seventeenth century, but since the franchise was limited to the planters and wealthy merchants, elections were infrequent and nonpartisan. The franchise in the West Indies remained on a very restricted property basis until the British granted adult suffrage in Jamaica in 1944. The other West Indian colonies had achieved adult suffrage by the end of the 1950s. During the late 1940s and 1950s durable patterns of party competition and responsible government were established, leading to independence in the early 1960s.

The first elections to legislative councils took place in The Gold Coast (now Ghana), Nigeria, and Sierra Leone in the 1920s. In central and east Africa—Kenya, Uganda, Tanganyika, and Zanzibar (the last two now united as Tanzania), Northern Rhodesia (now Zambia), Southern Rhodesia (now Zimbabwe), and Nyasaland (now Malawi)—legislative elections did not take place until the 1950s, except in Kenya and Northern and Southern Rhodesia, where a large European settler minority successfully demanded a political voice for themselves and, for a time, successfully resisted the African population's demand for the vote. In the east and central African countries, complex franchises with communal electorates for Africans, Asians, and Europeans became the norm.

As in west Africa, universal suffrage came only on the eve of independence.

In west Africa the pre–Second World War franchise, although nonracial in character, was limited in two important respects. First, it was property-based; and second, only the small minority of the population living in a few towns was eligible. In consequence, only a few thousand Africans were able to vote. In the decade after the Second World War the electorate was extended geographically to include the interior of the west African colonies. However, elections at first were usually indirect, a provision that was designed to protect the political role of the traditional chieftaincy. Only in the late 1950s or early 1960s, shortly before independence, did west African colonies adopt universal suffrage.

In the Indian Empire British colonial authorities introduced elections at the local level in 1882. Under the 1909 Morley-Minto reforms, elected members gained a majority on both the provincial councils and the all-India Legislative Council, but most of them were elected indirectly by local authorities, trade associations, and universities. Britain introduced the principle of communal representation for the first time with the provision for separate electorates for Muslims, albeit on a very restrictive franchise. The principle of communal representation was extended in 1935 to create constituencies for Muslims, Sikhs, Europeans, Indian Christians, Anglo-Indians, backward areas, and tribes. Further limited liberalization of the franchise followed, but at the provincial elections of 1946 (the last all-India elections before independence), only about one-fifth of the adult population had the vote.

While the central government remained responsible to the viceroy alone, Britain granted a substantial measure of responsible self-government to the provinces in 1935. An electorate of some 40 million people and office-holding at the provincial level provided the base for the development of an effective party system from 1935 to independence in 1947. In Ceylon (now Sri Lanka) early colonial elections were held on a communal basis and with a very restrictive suffrage. In 1931 colonial authorities introduced universal adult suffrage and replaced the communal constituencies with territorial ones.

Communal representation has been a feature of elections in many, but not all, of the multiethnic colonies in the British Empire. In colonies where there were large numbers of incomers, whether of British or other origin, the British often introduced communal representation to give voice to these immigrant communities. In colonies that were largely self-governing, such as the Cape Colony or Southern Rhodesia, the local European minority typically legislated for a restrictive property- or education-based franchise, which was formally nonracial but in practice ensured an overwhelming European majority in the electorate. In other colonies with a sizable European minority, for example, Kenya, Northern Rhodesia, and Fiji, the European population pressed successfully for communal representation. In colonies such as Burma, Fiji, and Kenya, British authorities provided separate representation for the immigrant Indian population. Britain eschewed the principle of communal representation in other multiethnic colonies, for instance, Trinidad and Malaya.

FRENCH COLONIES

Some or all of the French colonies were represented in the French parliament from 1789 to 1799 and from 1847 to 1852 and have been continuously since 1871. Before the Second World War, Algeria, Senegal, the French colonies in the West Indies, Rèunion, the settlements in India, and part of Indo-China had representation in parliament. After 1945 representation was extended to include the remaining African colonies and territories in the Pacific. In 1936, 20 of 618 deputies, and in 1946, 75 of 619 deputies, represented France overseas. With the achievement of independence by Algeria and the African colonies in the early 1960s the number of overseas deputies was greatly reduced, to 22 of 577 today.

Within most French colonies elections played only a limited role before the Second World War. After 1945 French colonial authorities set up throughout sub-Saharan Africa territorial assemblies with modest financial powers. The franchise was initially quite limited. Citizens of metropolitan status (overwhelmingly European) voted in a communal constituency separate from citizens of local status. In the latter constituency a *vote capacitaire* limited the franchise to, for instance, local notables, ex-servicemen, and clergy. Over the next decade the franchise was gradually extended, and in 1956 France introduced a large measure of local self-government and universal suffrage. Soon after the establishment of the Fifth Republic in 1958, the sub-Saharan African colonies became independent. Constitutionally, Algeria remained an integral part of metropolitan France, although it also had its own elected assembly. This system was, however, largely a facade which concealed the political dominance of the European minority. The two communal constituencies elected the same number of deputies even though 90 percent of the population was Algerian, and widespread intimidation and fraud ensured that elections in Algeria were, for the Algerian population, without any real meaning.

PORTUGUESE, BELGIAN, AND SPANISH COLONIES

Elections in the Portuguese colonies reflected a colonial policy similar to the French policy. Portugal regarded its colonies as overseas provinces of Portugal, and thus they were represented in the National Assembly. However, the majority of these provinces' voters were from mainland Portugal, because only mainland Portuguese and "assimilated" Africans were entitled to vote. In 1955 Portugal established local legislative councils in Angola and Mozambique but not in the other colonies. The very limited extent of contestation in Portugal prior to the 1974 revolution further restricted the significance of colonial elections. As in Algeria, the path to independence was armed struggle.

In the Belgian and Spanish colonies no territorywide elections took place until the eve of independence. The first local elections in the Belgian Congo's major cities were held in 1957 and 1958, the first territorywide local elections in 1959, and the first election for a national parliament under manhood suffrage in May 1960, only one month before independence. In the Belgian UN trusteeship territory of Ruanda-Urundi (after independence the separate states of Rwanda and Burundi), local elections were introduced in 1953, but the first legislative elections under universal suffrage were not held until 1961, only a year before independence.

CONCLUSION

What impact did the experience of elections in colonial times have on subsequent developments? Where colonial authorities introduced elections late in the day, stable democracies did not emerge. This category includes all of the Belgian, French, Portuguese, and Spanish colonies and some, but not all, of the British colonies. In the non-African parts of the British Empire, where the British introduced elections early on, relatively free and democratic political systems developed, for example, in India and Sri Lanka. Even in some British colonies where elections were introduced late—in the West Indies and the South Pacific, for example—democratic regimes have nearly always been sustained, but this did not happen in formerly British Africa.

See also *Elections in Developing Countries; Founding Elections: Africa; Founding Elections: Latin America; Postconflict Elections.*

TOM MACKIE, UNIVERSITY OF STRATHCLYDE

BIBLIOGRAPHY

Campbell, Peter. *French Electoral Systems and Elections.* London: Faber and Faber, 1958.

Chiriyandkandath, J. "Democracy Under the Raj: Elections and Separate Representation in British India." *The Journal of Commonwealth and Comparative Politics* 30 (March 1992): 1–64.

Collier, Ruth C. *Regimes in Tropical Africa: Changing Forms of Supremacy.* Berkeley: University of California Press, 1982.

Mackenzie, W.J.M., and Kenneth Robinson, eds. *Five Elections in Africa.* Oxford: Oxford University Press, 1960.

Nohlen, Dieter, Michael Krennerich, and Bernard Thibaut. *Elections in Africa: A Data Handbook.* Oxford: Oxford University Press, 1999.

Smith, Trevor E. *Elections in Developing Countries: A Study of Electoral Procedures in Tropical Africa, South-East Asia and the British Caribbean.* London: Macmillan, 1960.

Tinker, Hugh. *Separate and Unequal: India and the Indians in the British Commonwealth, 1920–1950.* London: Hurst, 1906.

Weiner, Myron, and Ergun Özbudun, eds. *Competitive Elections in Developing Countries.* Washington, D.C.: American Enterprise Institute, Duke University Press, 1987.

COMMUNAL ROLL

See *Colonial Elections; Elections in Developing Countries; Estate and Curia Constituencies*

COMMUNITIES, REPRESENTATION OF

See *Elections in Developing Countries*

COMPENSATORY SEATS

Compensatory seats are allocated in an upper (or secondary) tier of a legislative body in order to compensate parties for deviations from proportionality that result from the employment of lower district magnitudes, less-proportional formulas, or both at a lower tier of allocation. Numerous variations on this basic theme are possible. For instance, there may be a single national compensation district, or compensatory action might take place in two or more regional districts (as in Belgium), or there might be multiple compensatory tiers (as in Greece and Venezuela). The important point is that compensatory seats are an upper tier of seats overlaid on a lower tier or tiers and allocated in such a way as to increase overall proportionality between votes and seats.

The precise means of allocating compensatory seats varies tremendously. In some cases, as in Austria and Nicaragua, votes that are unused in a lower tier and seats that are unfilled are transferred to the upper tier. For instance, if a quota formula is used in primary districts, instead of allocating remaining votes in the primary districts, the remainders, along with any seats not yet filled in the primary districts, are pooled in the upper tier and allocated there. In such a system there is no fixed number of seats in the upper tier. The number allocated at the upper tier depends on the number unallocated at the lower tier.

Elsewhere, fixed numbers of seats may be assigned to lower and upper tiers. In such systems, assuming that the upper tier is a nationwide compensation district, the total number of seats to which each party is entitled is determined as if there were a single nationwide district for the entire parliament. Then this result is compared with seats won by each party in the primary districts, and parties whose total primary-district seat allocation falls short of their national entitlement are compensated by receiving seats from the upper tier. In this respect, parties that were overrepresented in the allocation of seats at the primary tier will receive a smaller share of the upper-tier seats than will parties that were underrepresented at the primary tier. Systems that work on this basis include those of Denmark and Germany. Other systems employ a mix of compensatory mechanisms. For instance, in Hungary there is a fixed, minimum number of seats in an upper tier, into which are transferred the seats remaining unallocated at a lower tier.

Typically, voters vote only in the primary tier. Votes for the compensatory seats come solely from transfers of remainders at the lower tier or from an aggregation of votes cast in primary-tier districts. However, there are exceptions, particularly in the class of electoral systems often known as "mixed member" (or just "mixed"). In these systems voters typically cast one vote for a candidate in a primary (usually single-seat) district and another vote for a party list. The German and, since 1996, New Zealand systems are good examples. In these cases the votes cast for party lists determine the overall party makeup of parliament; votes cast in the primary level determine which candidate wins in each of the primary districts and also how many seats each party wins off the compensatory list as opposed to in the primary districts. These systems may be known as "compensatory-member" systems or as "mixed-member proportional" systems.

Mixed-member proportional systems are sometimes called "additional-member" systems; however, the latter term should be reserved for another type of mixed-member system in which the upper tier is noncompensatory. Additional-member systems are also known as "parallel systems" because seats in the two tiers are allocated independently, or in "parallel." Thus, the seats from the upper tier are not allocated so as to compensate parties for deviations from proportionality resulting from the primary tier, but are simply added to the total number of seats won there. Thus, even parties overrepresented at the primary tier will receive additional seats (provided they received votes cast for the upper tier, if separate votes are cast for the two tiers), although their overall degree of overrepresentation will be reduced owing to seats won by parties underrepresented in the primary tier. Variants of the additional-member system are currently used in Japan and Russia. There are also examples of parallel or additional seats in systems that use proportional representation at the primary tier as well, but these are fairly rare. One example is Ecuador.

Compensatory seats are a means of combining the perceived virtues of local representation (in small-magnitude, possibly single-seat, districts) with the goal of minimizing disproportionality. As long as the upper tiers are allocated in a compensatory rather than parallel manner, and as long as the share of total seats allocated in the upper tier is at least 25 percent, then a national tier of compensatory seats can produce a parliament that is as close to proportionality as would be produced by a single nationwide district for all seats, regardless of the magnitude employed in the primary tier. When the primary tier is already a form of proportional representation, nearly full nationwide proportionality can be obtained with a compensatory tier that is as little as 10 percent of the total.

See also *Additional Member System; Bonus Seats; District Magnitude; Mixed Electoral Systems; Proportionality and Disproportionality.*

MATTHEW SOBERG SHUGART,
UNIVERSITY OF CALIFORNIA, SAN DIEGO

COMPETITIVENESS OF ELECTIONS

Competitiveness is necessary for an election to be democratic. Competitive elections allow the voters to choose political officeholders in a free and fair multiparty environment. In noncompetitive and semicompetitive elections, freedom of choice and fair competition are not present or strongly restricted, and the voters do not decide who holds political power. In this sense, the term *competitive* is equivalent to "free and fair," "classical," or "democratic," whereas semi- or noncompetitive elections are nondemocratic.

PRINCIPLES OF COMPETITIVE ELECTIONS

In modern liberal democracies, competitive elections adhere to the following principles.

Freedom of candidacy. Are all social and political groups able to form political parties and to stand for election? Or is the electoral participation of parties and candidates restricted—either de jure (for example, formal and legal exclusion of particular parties or candidates) or de facto (achieved by means of political violence against particular parties or candidates or the imposition of unacceptable political conditions on candidature)?

Presence of electoral competition. Does more than one party participate (a quantitative criterion), and can the voter relate the multipartism to competition among individuals and programs for political power (a qualitative criterion)? Even multiparty elections may lack significant competition due to one-party dominance at the national, regional, or local level.

Equal opportunities for parties and candidates. Do the parties and candidates compete for votes on a level playing field? A level field entails, among other things, full and equal political rights, a fair electoral campaign, a free and pluralistic press, equal access of the parties to state-owned or state-controlled media, the impartial allocation of public funds to the parties, and no misuse of government facilities for campaign purposes, especially by the ruling party.

Freedom of voting. Is universal suffrage given and its application secured by appropriate mechanisms of voter registration and identification, among other safeguards? Can the voters decide freely how to vote? Voter freedom requires an effective secret ballot and the absence of coercion, not only on election day but also before. It is important to note that elections may be held in a political climate that is not favorable to a free vote (for example, martial law, civil war, persistent violations of human rights, absence of the rule of law).

A correct ballot verification process and vote count. Are appropriate measures taken to prevent electoral fraud? The technical correctness of the election is particularly influenced by the body that is responsible for organizing elections, be it the executive or an independent electoral commission. It is important that this body works impartially.

An electoral system that satisfies democratic criteria. Does the electoral system translate votes into seats in a democratically acceptable manner? Although the many types of multiparty electoral systems (proportional-representation systems, plurality systems, absolute-majority systems, segmented systems, and so on) have different effects on such criteria as the vote-seat proportionality and the likeliness of "manufactured majorities," they are all usually held to be compatible with democratic elections. However, some extreme plurality systems (Djibouti's, for example) and bonus systems (the Italian system of 1924) can be regarded as problematic. In general, a wide variety of technical elements can affect the electoral outcome.

An electoral decision that holds for a limited period of time. Are elections held periodically in order to allow the voters to reexamine their preferences for a political party or candidate? Although no leader currently is elected for life, incumbents may try to prolong their term of office, as happened in the 1990s in some francophone African countries (Burkina Faso, Côte d'Ivoire, Gabon) and in some post-Soviet republics in Central Asia (Turkmenistan, Uzbekistan). Party systems in which one party or candidate perennially dominates the political landscape are not regarded by observers as a problem as long as political leaders are legitimized by periodic, free, and fair elections and exercise power democratically.

The elections really determine who will exercise political power. That is to say, do the votes determine who rules?

ANALYZING COMPETITIVENESS

The above catalog may be used to classify elections by the degree to which they are or are not competitive. The concept of competitiveness goes far beyond the question of whether multiple parties are competing. Multiparty elections do not necessarily meet competitive standards. In various Latin American countries (for example, Brazil, El Salvador, Guatemala, Mexico, Nicaragua, Paraguay), former authoritarian leaders used to hold multiparty elections, but the voters' freedom and multiparty competition were strongly restricted, and political power was not at stake in open contests. Thus, the elections were only semicompetitive and did not fulfil democratic functions; rather, they were held to serve the stability of the authoritarian regimes.

Only in the wake of redemocratization of the political systems from the late 1970s onward did the political and technical conditions of voting in Latin America improve. Almost all Latin American elections in the 1990s could be regarded as competitive.

In other parts of the world, multiparty elections still do not meet competitive standards. In various African countries, for example, political leaders controlled or manipulated elections in the 1990s even after the introduction or reintroduction of a multiparty system (among them, Burkina Faso, Cameroon, Côte d'Ivoire, Djibouti, Equatorial Guinea, Kenya, Mauritania, and Togo). Even where the opposition won the founding elections, subsequent elections were not guaranteed to maintain the same competitive standards (for example, Zambia 1996). Thus, it seems sensible to undertake a context-related, in-depth analysis of elections that examines their technical and political conditions in light of the above catalog of criteria.

The degree of competitiveness allows observers and scholars to differentiate one competitive election from another in a sensible way. The analysis may, for example, lay out the technical differences between competitive elections in well-established democracies and those in newly established democracies. Analysis of the degree of competitiveness also would allow observers to chart developments in the electoral procedures of a given country during the country's democratization (for example, an extension of party competition, an improvement in campaign conditions, a professionalization of the electoral commission). Since nondemocratic systems differ in how far they allow inter- and intraparty opposition and in how well they are able to control elections, analysis of their semi- or noncompetitive elections would illuminate the use of power by the ruling elite.

The concept of competitiveness is limited, insofar as it refers only to the technical and political conditions of elections. The concept excludes the sociocultural and economic conditions under which elections are held, even though free electoral choice may be restricted by poverty, illiteracy, social pressure, or social and economic dependency, among other factors.

See also *Free and Fair Elections; Unfree Elections.*

MICHAEL KRENNERICH, INSTITUTE FOR
IBERO-AMERICAN STUDIES, HAMBURG (GERMANY)

BIBLIOGRAPHY

Butler, David, Howard R. Penniman, and Austin Ranney, eds. *Democracy at the Polls. A Comparative Study of Competitive National Elections.* Washington, D.C.: American Enterprise Institute, 1981.

Harrop, Martin, and William L. Miller. *Elections and Voters. A Comparative Introduction.* New York: Meredith Press, 1987.

Hayward, Fred M., ed. *Elections in Independent Africa.* Boulder, Colo.: Westview Press, 1987.

Hermet, Guy, Richard Rose, and Alain Rouquié, eds. *Elections without Choice.* London: Macmillan, 1978.

Krennerich, Michael. *Wahlen und Antiregimekriege in Zentralamerika.* Opladen: Leske and Budrich, 1996.

Nohlen, Dieter. *Wahlsysteme der Welt.* München: Pieper, 1978.

———. *Elections and Electoral Systems.* New Delhi: Macmillan India, 1996.

Weiner, Myron, and Ergun Özbudun, eds. *Competitive Elections in Developing Countries.* Washington, D.C.: American Enterprise Institute, 1987.

COMPULSORY VOTING

Compulsory voting, also known as mandatory or obligatory voting, refers to electoral participation under conditions that make the exercise of the franchise a legal duty rather than merely a norm of good citizenship. Its primary purpose is to assure high voter turnout, which in turn entails a more faithful expression of the popular will. Such laws are the most obvious available means of raising the level of electoral participation, but they are not a necessary condition for high turnout.

Compulsory voting can take a variety of forms, both in its legal foundation and the manner in which it is implemented. The most common legal basis is statutory law (election code or act), but the obligation to vote can also be anchored in a constitutional provision, be it one that declares voting to be a citizen's duty or authorizes the legislature to enact a mandatory voting law. Implementation ranges from no enforcement at one extreme to universal enforcement, with imposition of real penalties, at the other. Variation exists in the nature of acceptable excuses for failing to vote (such as illness or absence from usual place of residence), the nature and severity of sanctions (fines; denial of passports, professional licenses, or government benefits; imprisonment), and the frequency with which penalties are imposed. Since in most countries voter registration is the responsibility of the authorities and most eligible voters are in fact enrolled, the authorities can monitor compliance easily: voters are checked off when they present themselves at the polling station. Those who fail to appear are subsequently contacted by mail and asked to provide a justification for their absence or pay a fine. This is how the system is administered in Australia, where voting has been compulsory since 1924. In some Latin American countries compulsory voting is enforced more indirectly through voting documents that are stamped at the polling place. These cards must be presented to obtain certain types of benefits (for example, a passport).

Strictly speaking, compulsory voting is a misnomer. To protect the secrecy of the vote, only attendance at the poll can be verified, at least as long as elections are conducted with conventional paper ballots, which voters mark and drop in a ballot box. Voters have as many as three options to avoid endorsing a party or candidate: cast no ballot, cast a blank ballot, or mark the ballot in a way that renders it invalid. Voting machines and voting by computer may enable election authorities to verify that the voters actually make a valid selection while at the same time safeguarding the secrecy of the vote, but these instruments are not used widely.

Democracies of long standing that have mandatory voting in some form—or did so until recently—are Australia, Austria, Belgium, Italy, Luxembourg, and the Netherlands (until 1970). Voting is also mandatory in Cyprus, Greece, Singapore, Turkey, and in most Latin American countries.

Even in the United States mandatory voting is not without precedent. According to Henry J. Abraham it existed in the colonies of Plymouth, Virginia, Maryland, Delaware, North Carolina, and in revolutionary Georgia. Three states—North Dakota (1897), Massachusetts (1918), and Oregon (1919)—adopted constitutional amendments authorizing their state legislatures to make voting obligatory. Popular referenda approved the North Dakota and Massachusetts amendments in 1899 and 1918, respectively, but the voters of Oregon rejected their amendment in 1920. More than fifty bills calling for some type of compulsory voting were introduced in various states between 1888 and 1952, but none of them passed. Compulsory voting was in effect in Kansas City, Missouri, from 1889 to 1895, when the state supreme court struck it down as unconstitutional.

Compulsory voting finds less and less favor today. Austria and the Netherlands have already repealed it, and Australia and Belgium have been embroiled in heated debates on whether to do so. On the other hand, there has been some renewed interest among academics and election-reform ad-

vocates, who see mandatory voting as a vehicle to reverse the downward trend in voter participation; but it is generally conceded that the chances for adoption are slim.

EMPIRICAL ASSESSMENT: MANDATORY VOTING LAWS AND THEIR EFFECTS

Does compulsory voting work, and if so, how well and why? The answer to the first question is well settled: mandatory voting laws do produce higher levels of turnout. This much is clear from cross-national comparisons as well as from more sophisticated analyses. In surveys conducted in countries with compulsory voting, more than a few respondents admit that they would not vote if they were not required to.

But the answers to the second and third questions are more complex. How much of a difference mandatory voting makes depends on how high voter participation is (or would be) under voluntary voting. The more numerous the nonvoters, the more new voters can potentially be mobilized. The percentage point gain in turnout is thus contingent on the circumstances. The strength and pervasiveness of citizens' other sources of motivation to vote play a key role. How much enforcement it takes to maximize compliance also depends on the context. Merely passing a law does not mean everyone will follow it, as the example of mandatory seat-belt use in automobiles illustrates. In some countries the authority of the law itself appears to suffice. In others the normative force of the law is not so effective in shaping citizens' behavior. This may be because the social norm to engage in the desired behavior is weak or nonexistent or because the government and its policies lack legitimacy generally. Evasion of other legal duties, such as the obligation to pay taxes, may also be widespread and socially condoned in some societies.

How does compulsory voting work? The seemingly obvious answer is that people vote to avoid punishment. But this does not explain why compulsory voting laws can be effective without enforcement. The social-norms model provides the most satisfactory explanation. According to this approach, people vote to comply with the norm, which is stronger and better internalized where the law backs it up. But the norm can also exist without the law, and can even be enforced informally by family, neighbors, and friends through social approval and ostracism.

People may, of course, vote for reasons having little to do with social norms and civic spirit. In a competitive race in which much is at stake, the desire to affect the outcome may be a powerful force, particularly when coupled with high partisanship, which induces people to make small individual sacrifices for the benefit of the group or political party they identify with. With a turnout rate consistently above 94 percent in recent elections, the island nation of Malta is a case in point.

To the extent that compulsory voting does promote turnout, it also promotes the integration of segments of the citizenry that otherwise would not vote as assiduously. Survey-based studies in a variety of countries attest to the higher turnout of the more privileged in society, particularly when turnout is low. Compulsory voting counteracts this bias and promotes the inclusion and more effective representation of those with less access to power. The franchise is the great equalizer because everyone's vote counts the same. In this regard, voting is indeed unique. Other modes of political participation invariably give those with superior resources an edge. Proponents of compulsory voting thus maintain that it contributes to fairness in the political system.

No doubt there are partisan implications to the differential turnout rates as well. To the extent that one or some parties might disproportionately benefit from better mobilization of less-well-off segments of the citizenry, vested interests might get in the way of reform efforts and participation-promotion schemes. Indeed, much of the heat in electoral reform debates is ultimately fueled by concern about likely gains and losses by different political parties.

Another effect of compulsory voting is a higher incidence of spoilt or blank ballots. This fact is sometimes invoked as an argument against mandatory voting. After all, such ballots do not contribute to the election outcome. But ultimately this is a weak argument—for two reasons: first, the increase in invalid ballots is lower than the increase in participation; second, even spoilt ballots carry political meaning. Indeed, explicit rejection of the available choices sends a stronger and clearer message than mere abstention. Furthermore, it is preferable that such sentiment be expressed through the electoral mechanism, rather than manifesting itself in disruptive anti-system activities. A sudden surge in the incidence of invalid ballots may provide a useful signal to the prevailing political forces that the concerns of a segment of the electorate are not being properly addressed. Such venting of frustration is likely to lead to a political response. It may thus help avert greater harm that could result from the establishment's neglect of an unrecognized but nonetheless real political problem.

NORMATIVE ASSESSMENT: ARGUMENTS FOR AND AGAINST

Although it is clear that mandatory voting laws are effective, their merits are vigorously contested on normative grounds. The controversy involves alternative conceptions of democracy and citizen rights as well as divergent assumptions about nonvoters and their attitudes toward the existing political order. Although the debate is ostensibly fought over lofty principles, it usually contains a hefty dose of self-interested calculations as well.

Proponents of mandatory voting stress its salutary effect on turnout. According to them, the principle of universal suffrage should be routinely achieved in fact—rather than merely being promulgated in law. They point out that all governments resort to compulsion to avoid free-riding and that they impose many other obligations on citizens for the benefit of the community as a whole. Voting entails only a very small burden compared with other state-imposed duties, such as paying taxes, wearing seat belts, and performing jury duty and military service. Moreover, it is a responsibility that many citizens already assume and exercise eagerly.

Opponents question the ends as well as the means, that is, the desirability of high turnout as a goal of electoral practice and the appropriateness of resorting to coercion in pursuit of it. Some argue that the citizen has a right to abstain as much as he or she has a right to vote. Some assert categorically that a legal duty to vote is incompatible with the tenets of liberalism. Compulsory voting laws can also be opposed on the grounds that they render voluntary voting altogether impossible because a blanket legal obligation covers even the most dedicated voters. According to this view, a legal duty to vote not only deprives citizens of their own choice to participate or abstain, it also deprives them of the ability to act morally. Mandated voting casts doubt on the motives and civic orientations of all, even those who need no prodding.

Critics also point out that totalitarian regimes sought turnout rates approximating 100 percent and that this hardly constituted proof of their legitimacy. Indeed, a good case can be made that forced mobilization of their subjects was a substitute for the genuine popular support they sorely lacked. A democracy, by contrast, enjoys greater legitimacy to begin with and is thus less in need of visible demonstrations of regime support. Not only are democracies expected to grant their citizens greater freedom and choice; they can also more easily afford to do so because of the inherent legitimacy they command in a time when popular sovereignty and individual rights have come to enjoy universal appeal. According to the opponents of mandatory voting, the decision not to vote is one such choice. Nor does abstention put the political order at risk. Indeed, opponents argue that a certain amount of apathy is a sign of a political system's health and success.

The experience of countries with a long history of compulsory voting, such as Australia and Belgium, makes it clear that it is an option that can work. But compulsory voting laws are not a necessary condition for high turnout. Some democracies achieve high levels of participation because their citizens are intensely invested in the electoral process and derive their motivation from sources other than a sense of civic duty. Still, as a factor promoting high levels of participation, mandatory voting is unique. Because it is an institutional feature, it is under the direct control of the policy makers. Other turnout-enhancing circumstances, such as competitiveness of the party system and strength and pervasiveness of partisanship, are not as amenable to direct intervention. Compulsory voting laws are an instrument that institutional engineers can use to good effect—assuming that high turnout is seen as desirable and that this time-proven method of obtaining a high poll is politically acceptable. Whatever its merits and effectiveness, however, compulsory voting is a tool that has been used only sparingly.

See also *Administration of Elections; Designing Electoral Systems; Federal Countries, Elections in; Functions of Elections; Noncitizens and the Right to Vote; Registration of Voters in the United States; Secret Ballot; Turnout; Unfree Elections.*

WOLFGANG P. HIRCZY DE MIÑO, UNIVERSITY OF HOUSTON

BIBLIOGRAPHY

Abraham, Henry J. *Compulsory Voting.* Annals of American Government. Washington, D.C.: Public Affairs Press, 1955.

Hasen, Richard L. "Voting Without Law?" *University of Pennsylvania Law Review* 144 (May 1996): 2135–2179.

Lijphart, Arend. "Unequal Participation: Democracy's Unresolved Dilemma. Presidential Address, American Political Science Association, 1996." *American Political Science Review* 91, no. 1 (March 1997): 1–14.

Rose, Richard. "Evaluating Election Turnout." In *Voter Turnout from 1945 to 1997: A Global Report on Political Participation,* 35–47. Stockholm: Institute for Democracy and Electoral Assistance, 1997.

Wertheimer, Alan. "In Defense of Compulsory Voting." In *Participation in Politics,* edited by J. Roland Pennock and John W. Chapman. New York: Lieber-Atherton, 1975.

CONDORCET THEOREMS

Several theorems are associated with the Marquis de Condorcet (1743–1794), the founder of the mathematical study of elections. Most of his massive *Essay on the Application of Analysis to the Probability of Majority Decisions* (1785) is devoted to what scholars now call the "Condorcet jury theorem." However, in passing, Condorcet also discovered voting cycles, and it is for this discovery that he is better remembered among scholars of elections. Nevertheless, interest in the jury theorem has lately revived strongly.

THE JURY THEOREM

The jury theorem formalizes Aristotle's insight that majority rule may be better than the rule of one person, just as a banquet to which all contribute may be better than a feast provided by one person. Mathematicians (most of them in France, as Condorcet proudly pointed out) developed classical probability theory in the eighteenth century to a point where they could make mathematical statements of probability. Building on the earlier work of Jacob and Daniel Bernoulli, Pierre-Simon de Laplace, and Thomas Bayes, Condorcet produced a formula for the reliability of a majority decision.

To illustrate Condorcet's formula, suppose that a number of jurors have each independently pronounced on whether the accused is guilty as charged. Whether the accused did or did not commit the crime cannot be directly known, and the jurors' estimates of guilt or innocence are based on the evidence. Condorcet's jury theorem states that

$$P(E) = \frac{v^{h-k}}{v^{h-k} + e^{h-k}}$$

where *P(E)* stands for the probability that the verdict of the jury (given the evidence *E)* is correct; *v* stands for the probability that a juror is correct (from *vérité,* meaning truth); *e* (which is equal to $1 - v$) stands for the probability that a juror is wrong (from *erreur,* meaning error); *h* stands for the number of votes cast on the majority side; and *k* stands for the number of votes cast on the minority side.

The equation assumes that each juror's chance of being correct on any one occasion—the value *v*—can somehow be observed. If it can, then for any value of *v* greater than one-half, Aristotle's insight is confirmed. If the average person is right more often than not, then majority rule is better than one person's decision, and the larger the size of the majority, the more reliable the decision. Furthermore, *v* need not be much greater than one-half for *P(E)* to be close to 1. Individuals may be unreliable, but a majority jury verdict is quite reliable.

The jury theorem was dismissed, soon after Condorcet's death in the French revolutionary Terror, as an absurd piece of mathematics. Since the mid-1980s, however, scholars have accepted that there are real-life situations to which it applies. One of them is the reliability of computer-controlled systems. If a controlling computer gives an error warning, which is malfunctioning—the computer or the system it is monitoring? The jury theorem can solve such problems.

THEORY OF VOTING CYCLES

Condorcet discovered voting cycles when he found that the jury theorem did not necessarily work when jurors (or voters) had more than two options. If there are at least three voters (say *P, Q,* and *R)* and at least three options (say *a, b,* and *c),* then *a* may beat *b,* which beats *c,* which beats *a.* Condorcet called this a "contradictory case," and it poses deep problems for democracy: Whatever society chooses, a majority of its members would have voted for a different alternative. When Condorcet's essay is cited in works on elections and electoral procedures, it is invariably for his discovery of cycles, sometimes known as "Condorcet's paradox" or "the Condorcet effect."

Condorcet's discovery of cycles was forgotten after his death. Voting cycles were rediscovered in 1874 by Lewis Carroll (whose real name was C.L. Dodgson), who did not know of Condorcet's earlier discovery. Condorcet's work on cycles was rediscovered in the 1940s by Kenneth Arrow and Duncan Black, and it now forms the foundation of social choice theory, that is, the mathematical study of the properties of choice procedures.

See also *Choice, Elections as a Method of; Paradox of Voting.*

IAIN MCLEAN, NUFFIELD COLLEGE, OXFORD UNIVERSITY

BIBLIOGRAPHY

Arrow, Kenneth J. *Social Choice and Individual Values.* 2d ed. New Haven, Conn.: Yale University Press, 1963.

Black, Duncan. *The Theory of Committees and Elections,* 2d ed., edited by Iain McLean, Alistair McMillan, and Burt L. Monroe. Norwell, Mass.: Kluwer Academic, 1998.

McLean, Iain, and Arnold B. Urken, eds. *Classics of Social Choice.* Ann Arbor: University of Michigan Press, 1995.

McLean, Iain, and Fiona Hewitt, eds. *Condorcet: Foundations of Social Choice and Political Theory.* Brookfield, Vt.: Edward Elgar, 1994.

CONSTITUENCY

See *District Magnitude; Estate and Curia Constituencies; Gerrymandering; Positive Discrimination; Reapportionment and Redistricting*

CONSTITUTION AND ELECTIONS

Strictly speaking, a constitution is the supreme law of a country, a legal document that defines the basic rights of citizens, establishes the various branches of government, and sometimes sets out the goals of the political community it governs. The vast majority of countries in the world now have written constitutions, Britain remaining a conspicuous if isolated exception.

Although election laws remain paramount sources of electoral rules, students of electoral rules cannot ignore the contents of formal constitutions. At a minimum, constitutions always establish legislative chambers and rulers and provide for their election. Constitutions often list and protect rights and freedoms of citizens that are basic to the conduct of elections, like the right to vote and to be elected and freedom of expression and association. Sometimes, constitutions go further by specifying which electoral system will be used, the age qualification for voting and being elected, who will supervise the electoral process, and how electoral districts will be de-

limited. The power of supreme courts to interpret the often broad language of constitutions may empower them to establish, through their decisions, rules that are binding on political actors, even if they are not specifically set out in the formal constitution.

SHOULD ELECTORAL RULES BE ENTRENCHED?

Constitutions help protect the integrity of the electoral process by curbing the ability of the government of the day to manipulate rules to its own advantage. Since constitutions normally are entrenched, meaning a qualified majority (two-thirds of legislators, for example) is required to amend them, citizens are protected against crude practices like the arbitrary postponement of elections or the selective disfranchisement of voters. Constitutions also provide some stability to the most basic electoral rules by demanding a wide consensus for their amendment or removal.

A case can be made for not including too many electoral rules in formal constitutions. For example, there is no place in constitutions for rules that govern the establishment of polling stations or the conditions for a ballot to be rejected. In such matters, it is preferable to give some leeway to legislators so as to ensure flexibility and adaptation to changing circumstances.

WHICH RULES SHOULD BE ENTRENCHED?

There is no pattern among contemporary democracies regarding which rules should be given constitutional protection. However, constitutions rarely fail to entrench items like freedom of expression and association, the term of elected assemblies, and the conditions, if any, for their dissolution. In only three of sixty-two countries commonly acknowledged as democratic does the constitution fail to entrench the right to vote.

In countries where the president is elected, the formula to be used is normally provided for by the constitution. A survey of ninety-five countries where the president is elected by the people found seventy-eight where the electoral formula was constitutionally entrenched.

When it comes to the formula for legislative elections, constitutions are less specific. Among sixty-two democracies, we found thirty-five where the formula for electing legislators was set out, if only in general terms. In the other twenty-seven, however, the electoral formula could be changed by a simple majority of legislators, since the constitution was mute on this topic. Well-established democracies can be found on both sides of the fence.

Britain is an example of a country where the ability of legislators to modify electoral rules is unhampered by constitutional obstacles. Parliament is supreme and is empowered to alter even the most basic rules. That comparatively little abuse has occurred is generally interpreted as evidence of British fair play, although many Britons argue that basic political rights should be formally entrenched and protected.

France, Germany, and Italy have constitutions that provide for some basic rules but leave much to legislators. All three provide for universal suffrage, but none specifies by which electoral system legislators will be elected. The German and Italian constitutions, but not the French, include the term of parliament. The Italian constitution sets out the size of each house of parliament, a topic the other two ignore.

Norway exemplifies a tendency to be much more detailed. In addition to providing for the right to vote, grounds for disfranchisement, and residential requirements for members, its constitution provides for the term of the Storting (parliament), the total number of seats, the number of national seats as well as the number of seats for each district, the formula for distributing seats among parties (Saint Laguë), and the threshold required for getting seats (4 percent). The law even directs that each municipality constitute a separate polling district.

A MATTER FOR POLITICAL JUDGMENT

Whether a constitution will specify electoral rules in great detail or leave them to legislators to enact is a political judgment that the constitution makers must make, taking into consideration a wide range of local factors. Whether the constitution should be a long or short document, whether electoral rules reflect or not reflect a wide consensus within the polity, whether politicians wish to be or wish not to be in a position to alter the rules to their own advantage are some contributing factors for the constitution makers to consider.

Nineteenth-century constitutions tended to be relatively short documents that often made no mention of the electoral formula to be used. In those days, no one realized the potential of electoral formulas to structure the party system by providing incentives for a two- or a multiparty system. More recent constitutions, reflecting a keener appreciation of the importance of electoral formulas, tend at least to determine whether proportional representation, plurality, or majority will be used for electing legislators. However, recent constitutions, like those of Russia, Romania, Slovakia, and Bulgaria, fail to specify which electoral system will be used for elections.

Constitutional entrenchment of rights and freedoms opens avenues for citizens who are dissatisfied with electoral rules. This is illustrated by the experience of the United States and of Canada, two countries where judicial review is solidly established. In the former, after the Supreme Court's decision in *Baker v. Carr* (1962), the courts began to strike down reapportionment plans that discriminated against urban and suburban areas as infringements on the principle of equality under the law. Since then the courts have frequently affirmed the principle that, as far as possible, votes should carry the same weight in different districts. In 1976 *(Buckley v. Valeo)*, the Supreme Court declared spending limits for congressional elections to be a breach of freedom of expression. In Canada the disfranchisement by the Elections Act of prison inmates, mentally deficient persons, and judges was declared by the courts in the late 1980s and early 1990s to be an unreasonable limit to the constitutionally entrenched right to vote that could not be justified in a free and democratic society. Similarly, Canadian courts struck down (in 1984 and 1986) successive attempts by parliament to prohibit or limit election spending by interest groups as an infringement on freedom of expression.

See also *Administration of Elections; Candidates: Legal Requirements and Disqualifications; Compulsory Voting; Democracy and Elections; Disqualification of Voters, Grounds for; Federal Countries, Elections in; Franchise Expansion; Noncitizens and the Right to Vote; Parties: Qualification for Ballot.*

LOUIS MASSICOTTE AND ANDRÉ BLAIS, UNIVERSITY OF MONTREAL

BIBLIOGRAPHY

Abernathy, M. Glenn. "Should the United Kingdom Adopt a Bill of Rights?" *American Journal of Comparative Law* 31 (summer 1983): 431–479.

Lowenstein, Daniel Hays. *Election Law: Cases and Materials.* Durham, N.C.: Carolina Academic Press, 1995.

Massicotte, Louis. "Electoral Reform in the Charter Era." In *The Canadian General Election of 1997,* edited by Alan Frizzell and Jon H. Pammett, 167–191. Toronto: Dundurn Press, 1997.

Smiley, Donald V. "The Case against the Canadian Charter of Human Rights." *Canadian Journal of Political Science* 2 (1969): 277–291.

Wade, Lord. "A Bill of Rights for the United Kingdom." *The Parliamentarian* 61 (April 1980): 65–71.

CONTESTING RESULTS

See *Administration of Elections*

COORDINATION, ELECTORAL

Electoral coordination refers to a variety of processes by which groups of voters and politicians coordinate their electoral actions in order to win more legislative seats or executive portfolios. Since what it takes to win more seats or portfolios is partly determined by the electoral system, electoral coordination takes different forms in different systems. There are three broad categories of coordination problems that voters or parties face, which vary in severity depending on the nature of the electoral system.

First, individual parties face the problem of nominating the optimal number of candidates. In some cases, the optimal number is obvious, and the problem is routinely solved. In single-member districts, for example, every party understands that it should nominate only a single candidate, and most parties succeed in establishing a nomination process that produces just one nominee. Even in single-member districts, however, there is a mixture of common and opposed interests that can sometimes make coordinating on a single nominee difficult: all the Democrats may understand that in order to beat the Republicans they must agree on a single nominee; at the same time, however, different factions within the party may each strongly prefer that a person from their wing of the party get the nod. In other electoral systems, such as those using limited or cumulative votes, nomination problems are more difficult to solve, and one finds parties going to great lengths in solving them.

Second, similar parties face the problem of making sure that their nominees do not all go down to defeat because they have split a given bloc of votes too many ways. This is a much bigger risk in plurality than in proportional-representation systems. It is possible to negotiate a merger of the parties concerned (which transforms the problem into one of regulating nomination). In systems with more than one district, it is also possible to negotiate mutual withdrawals, with party A refraining from entering the race in one constituency in return for party B returning the favor elsewhere. In some systems, the electoral law allows parties to issue joint nominations (joint lists or fusion candidates). Thus, if they can agree on the candidates that both are to nominate, they can coordinate without having to merge. In yet other systems, *apparentement*—whereby different lists pool their votes for purposes of seat allocation—is allowed. In *apparentement* systems, the parties gain the benefits of alliance without even having to agree on a joint slate of candidates, much less merging.

Third, groups of similar voters face the problem of tactical voting. If, for example, the parties of the left fail to coordinate their nominations, leaving too many leftist candidates in the field and opening the possibility of losing seats to the center and right, leftist voters may choose to concentrate their votes on a smaller number of leftists, those with a chance at winning seats. In the process, some leftists forgo voting for their favorite candidates in order to secure the election of a second or third choice and avert the victory of more right-wing candidates. Depending on the electoral system in use, tactical voting can take a variety of forms and serve a variety of purposes.

The simplest form of tactical voting occurs in single-member districts, such as those used in the United States or United Kingdom, when a minor party nominates a candidate in a district that is closely contested by two major parties. In such a situation, supporters of the minor-party candidate may decide to support the lesser of the two major-party evils rather than "waste" their vote on their favored candidate. Other forms of tactical voting arise when parties and voters face incentives to help potential alliance partners at election time. Germany, for example, has a national 5 percent vote threshold that parties must pass before they are eligible for a share of the nationally distributed seats. The Free Democrats, perennial coalition partners to one of the two larger parties (the Christian Democrats and the Socialists), sometimes appeal for help to supporters of whichever of the two large parties is their ally. Thus, in this and similar systems (such as New Zealand), tactical considerations at the coalition level can sometimes help small parties.

See also *Apparentement; Cumulative Voting; Duverger's Law; Limited Vote; List; Nomination Procedures; Tactical Voting; Wasted Votes.*

GARY W. COX, UNIVERSITY OF CALIFORNIA, SAN DIEGO

BIBLIOGRAPHY

Cox, Gary W. *Making Votes Count: Strategic Coordination in the World's Electoral Systems.* Cambridge: Cambridge University Press, 1997.

Duverger, Maurice. *Political Parties.* Translated by Barbara and Robert North. New York: John Wiley and Sons, 1954.

COUNTING VOTES, METHODS OF

See *Administration of Elections; Manufactured Majorities; Quotas and Divisors*

CRITICAL ELECTIONS

See *Realigning Elections in the United States*

CROSS-FILING

Cross-filing is an American term for running for nomination in the primary of more than one political party. It is closely related to cross-endorsement (or fusion), when a candidate is supported by more than one political party.

Cross-endorsement is a form of electoral alliance. Electoral alliances in other countries share some of the characteristics of cross-endorsement in the United States. One example of electoral alliance was that between the Liberal Party and ex-Labour Party Social Democrats in the United Kingdom in the early 1980s, where the two parties ran a single candidate in nearly every constituency before merging to form the Liberal Democrats. Cross-endorsement was common in the United States in the nineteenth century in presidential, gubernatorial, and congressional elections. The joint Democratic Party–Populist Party presidential candidacy of William Jennings Bryan in 1896 is one example. After the introduction of the Australian ballot at the end of the nineteenth century, U.S. states increasingly adopted antifusion laws and laws requiring contestants in a primary to be members of that party. By 1920 at least twenty-five states had antifusion laws on their books. In the 1990s only ten states permitted cross-endorsement of candidates.

Cross-filing and cross-endorsement make it easier for minor parties to exercise influence in a party system dominated by two large parties. Cross-filing in California allowed that state's Progressive Republicans to establish a separate party in 1913 but to still compete in Republican primaries. Cross-endorsement in New York allowed the state's third parties—the American Labor Party and later the Liberal, Conservative, and Right to Life Parties—to offer or deny their support to Republican or Democratic Party candidates who shared their policy preferences or were prepared to share political patronage. The state's minor parties should not be regarded as simply factions of the Republicans and the Democrats. For example, although the Liberal Party has usually supported liberal Democrats, it has also backed Republican mayoral candidates such as John Lindsay (1966–1974) and Rudolph Giuliani (1994–) in New York City. While two-party competition is characteristic of the rest of the United States, cross-filing and cross-endorsement in New York State provide the framework for a five-party system.

See also *Apparentement; Cumulative Voting; Nomination Procedures; Tactical Voting; Wasted Votes.*

TOM MACKIE, UNIVERSITY OF STRATHCLYDE

BIBLIOGRAPHY

Argersinger, Peter. *Structure, Process and Party: Essays in American Political History.* Armonk, N.Y.: M.E. Sharpe, 1992.

Kirschner, W. "Fusion and the Associational Rights of Minor Parties." *Columbia Law Review* 95 (1995): 683–723.

Scarrow, Howard. "Cross-endorsement and Cross-filing in Plurality Partisan Elections." In *Electoral Laws and Their Political Consequences,* edited by Bernard Grofman and Arend Lijphart, 248–256. New York: Agathon Press, 1986.

———. *Parties, Elections and Representation in the State of New York.* New York: New York University Press, 1982.

CUBE LAW

The cube law is a mathematical relationship often purported to govern the relationship between seats and votes in a plurality electoral system. It is a common starting point for discussions of the "mechanical effect" in Du-

verger's Law, under which differences in votes are exaggerated into larger differences in legislative seats. The cube law states that each party's share of seats (σ_i) will be proportional to its share of the vote (v_i) cubed: $\sigma_i \propto v_i^3$. Consider an example in which two parties receive 60 percent and 40 percent of the vote, respectively. The cube law states that the first party will receive about $0.6^3/(0.6^3 + 0.4^3)$ or about 77 percent of the seats, and the other about 23 percent. The 20 percent vote differential is exaggerated into a 54 percent seat differential.

Scholars first observed and applied the cube law to the votes and seats of the Conservative and Labour Parties in Britain. Many scholars subsequently investigated whether the cube law applied in all cases of plurality election, such as national and state elections in the United States, other two-party systems like New Zealand, or even multiparty systems like Canada. Others took the cube law to be a norm against which deviations could be viewed as evidence of bias for or against particular parties. Still others investigated possible explanations for the cube law, such as the tendency of like-minded voters to take up residence within the same geographic district or the strategic allocation of resources by political parties.

It soon became clear that the cube law was not really a law. It is obvious, for example, that it does not apply to proportional-representation systems, where seats are nearly proportional to votes, not to votes cubed. It also became clear that the cube law did not closely match observations in all plurality systems or even in Britain.

A generalization of the cube law to a "power law," where seats are proportional to votes raised to some exponent, not necessarily three, has wider applicability: $\sigma_i \propto v_i^\rho$. The exponent, ρ, might take on any value greater than or equal to zero. If ρ equals one, then we have proportional representation. If ρ equals zero, then every party receives the same number of seats regardless of its vote share. As ρ grows infinitely large, we have a winner-take-all situation, such as a single plurality district or a presidential election. The cube law, then, is the special case where $\rho = 3$, in which the larger parties are advantaged relative to proportional representation but not to the extent of winner-take-all.

There are many ways to estimate ρ in any given electoral system, and scholars do not yet agree on the best method. In general, however, they estimate ρ to be a little larger than one for proportional-representation systems and to be between two and five for plurality systems. The value of ρ seems to be closer to two than to three in contemporary British elections. While the cube law is a reasonable rule of thumb for estimating seats from votes in a plurality system, it should not be taken literally.

Research into the cube law has suggested several powerful concepts for the study of electoral systems. In particular, the value of ρ can be interpreted as an indicator of an electoral system's "responsiveness," that is, the extent to which seats change when votes change. Another related concept is the "swing ratio," or how much swing there is in seats for any given swing in votes.

Responsive systems are neither more nor less *fair* than unresponsive ones. High responsiveness—the cube law is high—just indicates that a losing party may be under-represented at this election, but it will be over-represented at the next one if it wins. There is still debate, however, over whether more or less responsiveness is *desirable*. More responsive systems tend to have higher rates of disproportionality—which some people view as bad—but also tend to have greater competitiveness—which some people view as good.

Scholars have noticed, however, that there are often deviations from a general pattern of responsiveness to the advantage or disadvantage of specific parties. Such bias is obvious in elections where the ranking of parties by seats is not the same as their ranking by votes (for example, Britain in 1974 or St. Vincent and the Grenadines in 1998), but typically the bias is more subtle. It appears primarily through differences in the nature of party competition across districts and can be caused by gerrymandering, malapportionment, or differences in turnout among parties. More general forms of the power law also include parameters for these party-specific biases.

Power laws can be generalized even further to reflect the fact that responsiveness is not the same for all parties even in the same electoral system. Consider, for example, the British system and the Conservative, Labour, and Liberal Democratic Parties. The Liberal Democratic vote is spread fairly evenly across the country, and the party frequently finishes second in any given district. As a consequence, small swings in votes might result in the party winning almost all seats instead of almost none. The other parties, however, draw their support from more specific areas (the Conservatives from rural England, and Labour from urban areas, Scotland, and Wales) and tend to win or lose by large margins. Similar swings in votes would result in much smaller swings in seats. Historically, the cube law "worked" because the margins of victory for the Conservative and Labour Parties were distributed across districts in just the right way. Responsiveness may now be different for some parties at some times, and the cube law may apply to one party and not the others.

In sum, the cube law is no "law," but it may serve as a useful rule of thumb for understanding plurality elections as well as a starting point for the investigation of many interesting questions in election studies.

See also *Competitiveness of Elections; Duverger's Law; Gerrymandering; Plurality Systems; Proportional Representation; Proportionality and Disproportionality; Swing; Turnout.*

BURT L. MONROE, INDIANA UNIVERSITY

BIBLIOGRAPHY

Katz, Richard. *Democracy and Elections.* Princeton, N.J.: Princeton University Press, 1997.

Kendall, M.G., and A. Stuart. "The Law of Cubic Proportions in Election Results." *British Journal of Sociology* 1 (1950): 183–196.

King, Gary. "Electoral Responsiveness and Partisan Bias in Multiparty Democracies." *Legislative Studies Quarterly* 15, no. 2 (1990): 159–181.

Monroe, Burt L. "Bias and Responsiveness in Multiparty and Multigroup Representation." Paper presented to the Society for Political Methodology, 1998.

Niemi, Richard G., and Patrick Fett. "The Swing Ratio: An Explanation and an Assessment." *Legislative Studies Quarterly* 11, no. 1 (1986): 75–90.

Schrodt, Philip A. "A Statistical Study of the Cube Law in Five Electoral Systems." *Political Methodology* 7, no. 1 (1981): 31–53.

Taagepera, Rein. "Reformulating the Cube Law for Proportional Representation Elections." *American Political Science Review* 80, no. 2 (1986): 489–504.

Tufte, Edward R. "The Relationship between Seats and Votes in Two-Party Systems." *American Political Science Review* 67, no. 2 (1973): 542–554.

CUMULATIVE VOTING

Cumulative voting refers to an electoral system in which electors voting in multimember districts are allowed to cast more than one vote for a single candidate. Consider, for example, the cumulative-voting system used to elect the lower house of the Illinois state legislature from 1870 to 1980. In this system, each district returned three members to the state assembly, each elector had three votes to cast, and electors could distribute their votes in any of the following patterns: one vote to each of three distinct candidates; one and a half votes to each of two candidates (partial cumulation); or three votes to a single candidate (full cumulation). The three candidates garnering the most votes were elected (plurality rule).

The main political consequence of cumulative voting, when combined with plurality rule, is to introduce an element of proportionality into multimember elections. When multimember plurality elections use the block vote (that is, each voter has as many votes to cast as there are seats to fill but can give at most one vote to any given candidate), the largest party can sweep all the seats. With the cumulative vote, in contrast, any group in an M-seat district constituting at least $1/(M+1)$ of the voting population can guarantee itself a seat (if it can get all its members to fully cumulate on a single candidate). For this reason, cumulative voting is often proposed as a method of securing minority representation, especially in the United States.

A secondary consequence of cumulative voting (again, when combined with plurality rule) is that it poses a coordination problem for parties at nomination time. Whereas parties in a block-vote system can simply nominate as many candidates as there are seats to be had, in a cumulative-vote system this strategy can lead to poor results. In the Illinois case, for example, if party A has 51 supporters in a 100-voter district, it can guarantee itself two seats by nominating two candidates (and getting its supporters to give 1.5 votes to each). But if the party nominates three candidates, then it may win only one seat: if the other 49 voters concentrate their votes on just two candidates, then each of these candidates will get 73 votes (49 × 1.5), which is more than the 51 votes that each of party A's three candidates will get. Thus, party A will win only one seat due to "over-nominating."

Cumulative voting is also used, in combination with proportional representation, in Luxembourg and Switzerland. In these systems, each citizen has as many votes to cast as there are seats to be filled in his or her constituency. These votes may be cast for candidates of the same or different parties (panachage), and they may also be cumulated. Votes cast for any candidate pool to the list level, with seats allocated first to lists, and then to the candidates on each list.

Cumulative voting is also widely used in elections of corporate boards in the United States. The usual rationale for using this method of voting is to secure minority stockholding interests a voice on the board.

See also *Coordination, Electoral; Limited Vote.*

GARY W. COX, UNIVERSITY OF CALIFORNIA, SAN DIEGO

BIBLIOGRAPHY

Bhagat, Sanjai, and James Brickley. "Cumulative Voting: The Value of Minority Shareholder Voting Rights." *Journal of Law and Economics* 27 (1984): 339–365.

Brams, Steven. *Game Theory and Politics.* New York: Free Press, 1975.

Guinier, Lani. "The Triumph of Tokenism: The Voting Rights Act and the Theory of Black Electoral Success." *Michigan Law Review* 89 (1991): 1077–1154.

DAY OF ELECTION

Day of election refers to the day or days of the week on which polling stations are open. In the eighty-six countries that Freedom House deemed to be democratic in 1996 (those that it gave a score of *1* or *2* on political rights), seventy-seven held their most recent election (at the time of writing) on a single day. Among these seventy-seven, almost half—thirty-five countries—conducted their election on a Sunday. Among them are Argentina, Belgium, France, Germany, Greece, Japan, Mexico, Poland, Spain, Sweden, and Turkey.

The two most popular days after Sunday are the days preceding and following it: Saturday and Monday. Eight countries had their election on the other rest day, Saturday. Among them are Australia and New Zealand. All in all, a majority of democratic elections are held on the weekend.

Among days of the week, Monday is the most popular for elections. This is the case in Canada and the Philippines, in particular. The least frequent day for elections is Friday.

Tuesday is election day in the United States. Interestingly, only a few countries have followed suit. In the same vein, only six countries had their most recent election on Thursday, the day British voters go to the polls. The United Kingdom may have been quite successful in exporting its main institutions, but its influence seems to be more limited with respect to the day of voting, although former British colonies are quite distinct in their avoidance of Sunday. Among the thirty-two former British colonies, only one (Cyprus) had its most recent election on a Sunday.

In nine of the eighty-six countries, elections took place over more than one day. In six of them, polling stations were open two days. The first election under universal suffrage in South Africa ran from Tuesday to Friday. In Papua New Guinea the election took place over a period of two weeks. Voters in the 1998 election in India went to the polls on four different days (a Monday, a Sunday, and two Saturdays), depending on the region where they lived, over a period of twenty days.

In most countries, elections are always held on the same day or days because the law so prescribes. In other countries, on the contrary, the law does not impose any constraint, and the day of election is determined by the government of the day. Among these countries are Brazil, Ireland, Israel, and the Netherlands.

Most elections are held on a rest day. In a few countries, the law prescribes that the day of election automatically becomes a holiday. This is the case in Samoa, Vanuatu, and the Philippines. The main arguments for having an election on a rest day are that most voters have more time to cast their ballots and most families find it easier to make arrangements so that all adult members can go to the polling stations. Two different studies, one by Jerome Black and another by Mark Franklin, suggest that turnout is indeed higher in elections held on a rest day.

We should note, finally, that more voters have been voting before the official election day. Opportunities for absentee voting have increased in a number of countries.

See also *Absentee Voting; Turnout.*

ANDRÉ BLAIS AND LOUIS MASSICOTTE, UNIVERSITY OF MONTREAL

BIBLIOGRAPHY

Black, Jerome. "Reforming the Context of the Voting Process in Canada: Lessons from Other Democracies." In *Voter Turnout in Canada,* edited by Herman Bakvis. Toronto: Dundurn, 1991.

Blais, André, and Louis Massicotte. "Electoral Formulas: A Macroscopic Perspective." *European Journal of Political Research* 32 (August 1997): 107–129.

Franklin, Mark N. "Electoral Participation." In *Comparing Democracies: Elections and Voting in Global Perspective,* edited by Lawrence LeDuc, Richard G. Niemi, and Pippa Norris. Thousand Oaks, Calif.: Sage, 1996.

DEMOCRACY AND ELECTIONS

Elections are a necessary element of democracy but are not the only element. Even the most reductionist definition of democracy specifies the need for additional conditions. To be democratic, a country must have elections in which a multiplicity of parties can compete, votes are counted fairly, and the offices awarded give the winners control of government. Scholars offer contrasting definitions of democracy, according elections differing significance.

DEFINITIONS OF DEMOCRACY

The *minimalist* definition of democracy of Joseph Schumpeter characterizes it as involving elections "in which people acquire the power to decide by means of a competitive struggle for the people's vote." Schumpeter saw elections as a means of choosing a government, and not as a means of representing opinions and interests in proportion to their prevalence among the electorate. He viewed an election in terms of elite competition between two parties, or even two individuals, for the right to govern a country. Democracy gives the mass of the people the chance to determine the outcome rather than leaves it to palace intrigues, military coups, or other undemocratic means. As an economist, Schumpeter believed that competition between parties would lead them to produce what the consumers (that is, voters) wanted; elections were the means for deciding the "market share" that each won.

However, a minimalist definition is vulnerable to the "fallacy of electoralism," that is, to treating competitive elections as a sufficient condition of democracy. Elections can be unfair if they are held in countries that do not respect the rule of law, and they can be unfree if the ruling powers suppress criticism and institutions of civil society. The Freedom House classification of countries around the world finds that almost a third of countries holding elections are only partly free. Since the third wave of democratization began in the mid-1970s, the number of countries holding competitive elections has increased by 77 percent, whereas the number of countries recognizing the political and civil liberties of their citizens has increased by only 40 percent.

The most widely used definition of democracy today is Robert Dahl's concept of *polyarchy*, a term used to label the best system of government in the real world, because Dahl believes democracy to be an unattainable ideal. The definition emphasizes representation in the broad sense of institutions, procedures, and cultural norms that help make elections free and fair. The attributes of polyarchy include: constitutional vesting of control over government decisions in elected officials who are chosen in free and fair elections; universal suffrage; a right to organize political parties; and a free and uncensored media. Scholars often combine these criteria in a single quantitative index that is used to classify all countries in the United Nations as more or less polyarchical. Dahl's definition of democracy draws examples from countries that have succeeded in achieving uninterrupted evolutionary progress toward democracy, typically by expanding the franchise to every citizen, for example, England or the United States. But such a definition takes for granted the preexistence of many institutional requisites of democracy.

Institutional definitions of democracy include not only elections but also other institutions that are necessary to secure democracy. Juan J. Linz and Alfred Stepan emphasize that the rule of law is needed to ensure fair and free elections as well as to protect the civil liberties of individuals. It is also needed to protect the institutions of civil society, such as political parties, the press, and pressure groups, against repression or intimidation by the governing power. Democracy also requires institutions securing the accountability of governors to the governed, since in parliamentary systems a prime minister and cabinet are not popularly elected but depend for office on gaining and maintaining the confidence of parliament. An accountable government may be unable to produce what the voters want, for example, economic prosperity in the midst of a world recession, but the government's inability does not absolve it from the responsibility of giving an account of its economic policies to parliament and defending its economic record against competitors at an election.

Radical ideas of democracy often go far beyond the electoral process. *Egalitarian* theories extend the idea of the equality of citizens—expressed in one person, one vote, one value—to many spheres of social life. A familiar historical example is the campaign by suffragettes to secure full legal rights for women, for example, to hold property or enter the professions, as well as to vote. Concern for equality is reflected in equal opportunity legislation affecting employment, access to public facilities, and gender-related activities generally. The idea of "workplace democracy" introduces political issues into the evaluation of profit-making enterprises, and the idea of the "democratic school" or the "democratic family" extends the idea of equality to relations between adults and children. Proponents of a pervasive application of egalitarian principles throughout society claim that this may strengthen political democracy by making individuals better citizens or, in the case of economic relations, by providing the material basis for fair competition between rich and poor in election campaigns.

The idea of *deliberative* or *discursive* democracy is not concerned with elections. Marking ballots is a very crude way of determining what people want, and the oligopolistic reduction of choice to a few parties cannot represent the variety of ways in which individuals combine views on important issues of the day. Furthermore, an election campaign allows no opportunity for people to exchange ideas and information with one another. Deliberative democracy is defined by Jon Elster as "decision-making by discussion among free and equal citizens," an idea that can be traced back to classical Greece and is given modern currency by the German philosopher Jurgen

Habermas. In the process of discussion, people are expected to modify their views in the light of what they learn; the outcome is deemed to be different from and better than the result of asking people to vote in a "one-shot" referendum or parliamentary or presidential election. Although deliberative democracy can be applied to elected representatives, it is far better suited to a nonparty council meeting in a small town than to a congress or parliament elected by tens of millions of voters along party lines.

EARLY VERSUS LATE INTRODUCTION OF ELECTIONS

Every definition except the minimalist, "electoralist" one emphasizes that elections are not the only institution that needs to be established to complete the process of democratization. A new democracy with free elections is still an *incomplete democracy,* since it has yet to develop all of its attributes, however defined. Democratization is a dynamic process in which different political institutions and procedures that had been absent in an undemocratic regime are created. Rose and Doh Chull Shin emphasize that elections can be introduced either early or late in the process of democratization. In the first wave of progress toward democracy, begun in the nineteenth century, elections with universal suffrage tended to come after the establishment of the rule of law, institutions of civil society, and accountability to parliament. By contrast, in the third wave of democratization in the former Soviet Union, Africa, and Latin America, elections have often been introduced in the absence of strong institutions of civil society, accountability, and the rule of law.

In first-wave democracies, elections typically involved only a small fraction of the male electorate, and the representatives elected usually had limited influence on the way the country was governed. But other democratic institutions were present. By the time elections were held with universal suffrage to determine who would govern, all of the other elements of an established democracy were in place; thus, gaining the right to vote completed democracy. The dynamics are very different when elections with universal suffrage are introduced early, as in the third wave of democratization. Then, the priorities are to make sure the rule of law restrains the new governors and to create institutions of civil society independent of the government and strong enough to hold it accountable. If this fails to happen, then a new democracy may collapse and be replaced by an undemocratic regime. A third alternative is that, while some progress is made toward democracy, it is inadequate to complete democracy; the result is described by Rose and Shin as a "broken back" democracy, in which free elections with universal suffrage can decide who governs, but governors do not behave as in an established democracy, unrestrained by the rule of law and unaccountable to strong institutions of civil society.

While most scholars describe democracy in idealistic terms, Winston Churchill defended democracy as the lesser evil, noting: "It has been said that democracy is the worst form of government except all those other forms that have been tried from time to time." Richard Rose, William Mishler, and Christian Haerpfer have demonstrated the empirical strength of the Churchill hypothesis in a study of ten postcommunist countries of central and eastern Europe. Although many people there are critical of their new democracies, big majorities prefer an incomplete democracy to the totalitarian or dictatorial alternative that their countries experienced.

See also *Constitution and Elections; Downsian Model of Elections; Electoralism; Founding Elections: Democratization without Interruption; Franchise Expansion; Free and Fair Elections; Functions of Elections; Unfree Elections.*

RICHARD ROSE, UNIVERSITY OF STRATHCLYDE

BIBLIOGRAPHY

Dahl, Robert A. *Democracy and Its Critics.* New Haven, Conn.: Yale University Press, 1989.

Diamond, Larry. *Developing Democracy.* Baltimore, Md.: Johns Hopkins University Press, 1999.

Elster, Jon, ed. *Deliberative Democracy.* New York: Cambridge University Press, 1998.

Freedom House. *Freedom in the World: 1997–1998.* New York: Freedom House, 1998.

Katz, Richard S. *Democracy and Elections.* New York: Oxford University Press, 1997.

Linz, Juan J., and Alfred Stepan. *Problems of Democratic Transition and Consolidation: Southern Europe, South America and Post-Communist Europe.* Baltimore, Md.: Johns Hopkins University Press, 1996.

Rose, Richard, William Mishler, and Christian Haerpfer. *Democracy and Its Alternatives: Understanding Post-Communist Societies.* Oxford: Polity Press; and Baltimore, Md.: Johns Hopkins University Press, 1998.

Rose, Richard, and Doh Chull Shin. "Democratization Backwards: The Problem of Third-Wave Democracies." *British Journal of Political Science.* Forthcoming, 2000.

Schumpeter, Joseph A. *Capitalism, Socialism and Democracy.* 4th ed. London: George Allen and Unwin, 1952.

DEPOSIT

A sum of money paid as a precondition for a valid candidacy is called a *deposit.* Sometimes a deposit is nonrefundable, but typically a candidate will have his or her deposit returned on receiving a specified share of the vote or on being elected.

The requirement for a deposit is usually imposed to discourage frivolous candidacies. If no such mechanism is put in place, or if the one chosen proves ineffective, a balloting process may be undermined by a proliferation of candidates who have no serious desire for or prospects of election, and whose presence on the ballot can make the voting process daunting for the voters. On the other hand, if the deposit is too large, or if the share of the vote required for its return is too high, candidates from the poorer sectors of a society may be discouraged from contesting an election purely by the risk of losing their deposits, while frivolous but rich candidates may still be able to run.

The choice of an appropriate size for a deposit and of the share of the vote required to ensure its return is therefore a public policy decision affected by two conflicting objectives. There is no "correct" level at which these parameters should be set; rather, they have to be determined empirically, in light of the conditions prevailing in a particular society and its political culture.

The significance of a particular level of deposit is affected by the overall value of money in a country. From its introduction in 1918 until 1985, the deposit for British elections stood at 150 pounds. In 1918 this was a considerable sum, worth about 2,500 pounds at the current value. The 1985 increase in the deposit to 500 pounds, though on the face of it substantial, still took the deposit only to one-fifth of its real value at the time it was introduced. The threshold for return of the deposit was reduced in 1985, from 12.5 to 5 percent of the vote.

In some polities the discriminatory effects of requiring the payment of a deposit have led lawmakers to seek alternative ways of discouraging frivolous candidacies. One such approach is to require a candidate to be nominated by a significant number of nominators. If, however, the number of nominators so required is very substantial, such as the one million required for ballot access at the 1996 Russian elections, it may tend to discriminate even more strongly, since the organizational effort required to obtain so many signatures will be within the means of the entrenched parties and can be bought by the rich but will be beyond the resources of the poor.

See also *Administration of Elections; Candidates: Legal Requirements; Nomination Procedures; Parties: Qualification for Ballot.*

MICHAEL MALEY, AUSTRALIAN ELECTORAL COMMISSION

DESIGNING ELECTORAL SYSTEMS

The crafting of electoral systems is both an art and a science. As an example of the art of the possible, political elites agree to compromise upon a system that they believe will disadvantage them no more than any other player in the election. But design of electoral systems also rests upon the science of understanding how different systems give rise to different results and place varying incentives on both political leaders and their followers. The science is often tentative, as it involves predicting future party strength, voting behavior, and the unpredictable role of leadership.

Sometimes electoral systems are born of wide agreement; other times they are imposed by a dominant group. The evidence suggests that the most enduring and successful of electoral systems are those born of open, lengthy, and inclusive negotiations—when information is maximized and the electoral system's legitimacy is based upon the fact that its parents include all of the significant political forces contained within society.

IMPORTANCE

Electoral systems are tools of the people. They are the institutions used to select decision makers when societies have become too large for every citizen to be involved in each decision that affects the community. The electoral system is the method by which votes cast in an election are translated into the seats won in a legislature by parties and candidates. Some systems may give primacy to a close relationship between the votes cast overall and the seats won (proportionality), or they may funnel the votes (however distributed among parties) into a legislature that contains just a few broad parties. Another important function of an electoral system is to act as the conduit through which citizens can hold their elected representatives accountable. Finally, electoral systems help to structure the boundaries of acceptable political discourse by giving incentives to party leaders to couch their appeals to the electorate in distinct ways. In deeply divided societies, for example, where language, race, religion, or ethnicity represents a fundamental political cleavage, some electoral systems can reward candidates and parties who act in a cooperative, accommodating manner, while others reward those who appeal only to their own ethnic group.

The framework of political institutions used within a state combines to form the rules of the democracy game. But it is often argued that the easiest political institution to be manipulated, for good or for bad, is the electoral system, because in translating the votes cast in a general election into seats in the legislature, the choice of electoral system can effectively determine who is elected and which party gains power. With 40 percent of the votes, a party might assume absolute control of the legislature under one system, while it may be out of power in opposition under a different electoral system. Electoral systems may also encourage, or discourage, the forging of alliances between parties, which in turn will affect the broader political climate. Finally, if an electoral system gives rise to results that are not perceived to be fair, by both winners and losers, alienated groups may be encouraged to work outside the democratic boundaries, using confrontational and even violent tactics.

CONTEXT

Comparative evidence from around the world has highlighted the fact that electoral systems have different consequences from country to country, especially with regard to party fragmentation, seat shares, and ideological polarization. Although there are important shared experiences, the consequences of a particular electoral system depend heavily upon the historical, socioeconomic, and political context of the society in which it is used. For that reason, good electoral system design is rooted in an understanding of the broader historical and political picture—the cultural-political context and the framework of political institutions.

Socio-political context. The way proportional representation works in western Europe will be very different from the way that system works in West Africa, while the political consequences of the first-past-the-post system in India are clearly divergent from the consequences of that system in the United States. For these reasons the electoral system designer has to be, at the very least, anthropologist, historian, geographer, and political scientist. In fledgling democracies electoral system design is particularly dependent on the nature of the social plurality of the country. The first consideration is the basis of group identity: Do voters define themselves along the lines of race, ethnicity, religion, language, ethno-nationalism, regionalism, class or occupation, or a mixture of a number of these dimensions? Second, what is the level of hostility—that is, how intense are these social cleavages, both currently and historically? Third, if there is conflict, are people fighting over resources, cultural rights, or territory? Fourth, how many and how large are the various groups—are there a few large groups or many small ones? Finally, how are the groups distributed: are the members of communal groups dispersed or geographically concentrated?

Political institution context. The electoral system used to constitute parliaments is located within the broader constitutional framework of the state—or its democratic type. Political institutions that are important for the electoral system include the type of executive, the type of legislature, and the type of constitution. As for executive type, is there a presidential or a parliamentary system? If there is a parliamentary system, are there single-party governments, coalition governments, or constitutionally mandated governments of national unity? Is the parliament unicameral or bicameral? If bicameral, do the chambers have symmetrical or asymmetrical (that is, equal or unequal) powers? Are there reserved seats or quotas required for specific groups? Is the constitutional nature of the state unitary or federal (that is, centralized or decentralized)? If federal, is it a symmetrical or asymmetrical federa-

tion? Are the provinces polyethnic or ethnically homogeneous? If there is autonomy for certain groups within the state, is it territorial or nonterritorial? Is there cultural, functional, or personal legal autonomy? The answers to all these questions establish the framework for the electoral system.

THEORY

When electoral systems contribute to the failure or instability of a state, often it is because there is an inherent flaw in their design. Usually, the flaw stems from the way in which the system was chosen. When systems are too much the product of the desires of elites, or when the status quo is retained because it seems too troublesome to change, they are unlikely to endure as institutions respected by the people. It is best for designers of electoral systems to begin from first premises. What are the democratic needs of the nation? When it comes to the sphere of representation, what things are most important to the polity? What occurrences are most important to avoid? Ultimately, the question becomes, What do you want your parliament and government to look like?

These criteria need to be spelled out first and foremost by domestic actors and will vary from country to country. The chief problem facing electoral system designers is that trade-offs need to be made between competing desires and objectives. For example, a system that gives voters a wide degree of choice between candidates and parties may promote fragmentation and competition within parties. Conversely, a system that gives rise to a strong, coherent single-party government may alienate substantial political minorities. The key to choosing (or reforming) an electoral system is to prioritize which criteria are most important and then assess which electoral system, or combination of systems, best maximizes these objectives. The experience of fledgling and established democracies during the 1990s has highlighted at least six objectives that surface time and again in electoral system design processes; these are listed in no particular order in the paragraphs that follow.

The desire for stable, efficient, and enduring government. Academic research has highlighted that the endurance of a stable and efficient government is determined by a multitude of factors beyond political institutions. But the results a system produces can contribute to stability, or destabilize the political environment, in a number of important ways. The electoral system and democratic institutions lose legitimacy if (1) people perceive the system to be unfair, (2) governments appear to be unable to govern, and (3) the system overtly discriminates against certain parties or communal groups. Issues of fairness arise when one party wins more seats with fewer votes than its opponents or when a minority party wins a significant number of votes but no seats in parliament. The question of whether the government of the day can govern efficiently is partly linked to whether it has a working parliamentary majority or not, and this in turn is partly determined by the electoral system. Empirically, plurality-majority electoral systems are more likely to give rise to parliaments where one party can outvote the combined opposition, while proportional representation systems are more likely to give rise to coalition governments. Finally, the system should act in a neutral manner toward all parties and candidates. The public perception that electoral politics is an uneven playing field is often a precursor to more troubling social instability.

Making legislators, ministers, and governing parties accountable to the electorate. Representation is nothing without accountability. As scholars of presidentialism in Latin America have noted, elections without subsequent channels of holding the officeholder accountable lead to a form of democratic dictatorship. An accountable political system is one in which both the government and the elected members of parliament are responsible to their constituents to the highest degree possible. At one level voters can influence the shape of the government, either by altering the coalition of parties in power or by throwing out of office a single party that has failed in their eyes. Certain electoral systems can facilitate both of these objectives. Nevertheless, accountability involves more than the simple holding of regular national elections; it also depends on the degree of geographic accountability (which is largely dependent on the size and territorial nature of districts), as well as the freedom for voters to choose between candidates as opposed to parties.

Encouraging parties and voters to be conciliatory to their opponents. Increasingly, electoral systems are being recognized not only as ways to constitute governing bodies but also as tools of managing political conflict. Experience suggests that some systems, in the correct circumstances, can encourage parties to make appeals for electoral support outside their own core vote base. For example, even though a party may draw its support primarily from white voters, the electoral system may encourage the party to appeal also to black voters. For many electoral system designers the goal is to make parties less divisive and exclusionary in their appeals for support and more unifying and inclusive. In the multiethnic societies of the developing world electoral systems can make parties less ethnically, regionally, linguistically, or religiously homogeneous. The weight of evidence from both established and new democracies suggests that long-term democratic consolidation requires the growth and maintenance of parties that are based on broad political values and ideologies, rather than narrow ethnic, racial, or regional concerns.

Giving rise to parliaments and governments that are representative. The concept of representation may take on a number of forms. First, geographic representation, so important to the Westminster (Anglo-American) political system, states that each town, city, and province should have members of parliament whom its citizens choose and who are accountable to their community. Second, functional representation reflects the party-political situation that exists within the country. If a third of the voters vote for one political party but that party wins no seats, or hardly any seats, in parliament, the system has failed to adequately represent the will of the people. Third, descriptive representation implies that parliament should look, feel, think, and act in a way that reflects the people as a whole. A fully descriptive parliament would include both men and women, the young and old, the wealthy and poor, and it would reflect the different religious affiliations, linguistic communities, and ethnic groups within a society.

Facilitating a loyal opposition within democratic politics. Opposition parties in parliament have an important role to play in democratic consolidation and the maintenance of conflict resolution by nonviolent means. The opposition has the capacity to assess legislation critically, safeguard minority rights, and represent voters who did not support the party or coalition in power. If the electoral system itself makes opposition parties impotent, democratic governance is inherently weakened. In divided societies it has been argued that the electoral system should help to retard the development of a winner-take-all attitude, which leaves rulers blind to other views and to the needs and desires of opposition voters, and in which both elections and government itself are seen as zero-sum contests.

Ensuring that elections are affordable and manageable. In the developing world democratic consolidation is threatened by both the failure of elected governments and the inability of poor countries to afford the sophisticated administrative procedures that characterize free and fair elections. The wealthier nations covered the bulk of the costs for the first elections in fledgling democracies in the 1980s and 1990s, but as these fragile nations approach second- and third-generation elections the wealthy West has lost much of its interest in paying for democracy abroad. If a new democracy cannot sustain the running of elections on its own, the system is inherently flawed. Beyond the base issues of security and ease of voting, some electoral systems entail more costs than others. For example, a poor nation may not be able to afford the multiple elections required under a two-round system, nor may it be able to administer a complicated preferential vote count easily. Nevertheless, it is important to remember that simplicity in the short term may not always make for cost-effectiveness in the longer run. An electoral system may be cheap and easy to administer, but it may not answer the pressing needs of the nation. The best electoral system in any given case may at the outset appear a little more expensive to administer, but in the long run it might help to ensure the stability of the state and the positive direction of democratic consolidation.

Although choosing the best electoral system can be key to democratization, the meaningfulness of elections is determined by how powerful the elected parliament actually is. Hollow or choiceless elections in authoritarian systems, where parliaments have little real influence on the formation of governments or on government policy, are far less important than elections which constitute parliaments that actually have the power to determine central elements in people's everyday lives.

PROCESS

Like all political institutions, electoral systems come into existence through a wide array of circuitous routes. Sometimes they are consciously designed, other times they are imposed by powerful actors, and occasionally they emerge from widespread public consultation. The parents of electoral systems, however, are most often history and politicians. In general, four main process types can be identified.

Colonial inheritance. Inheriting an electoral system from their colonial history remains the most common way through which democratizing societies come to use a particular system. A full 70 percent of former British colonies, members of the Commonwealth of Nations, use classic first-past-the-post systems inherited from Westminster. Notably, the system is used in Canada and in the African nations Zambia, Kenya, Malawi, and Nigeria. In Jordan and the Palestinian Authority the block vote, which had been used during colonial times, was retained for multiparty elections in 1989 and 1994, respectively. Just under half of the francophone countries of the world use the French two-round system, while the majority of the remaining countries use list proportional representation, a system used by the French on and off since 1945 for parliamentary elections and widely used for municipal elections. All of the Spanish-speaking countries and territories use proportional representation in some form (as does Spain), while the six Portuguese-speaking countries use list proportional representation, as in Portugal. The influence of French constitutional design also played heavily on the institutional designers of the former Soviet Republics of the Commonwealth of Independent States. Eight of these new nations (all but Georgia, Kazakhstan, and Russia) use the two-round system in some form.

Conscious design. Increasingly, electoral systems are less the product of long-term evolution and history and more the result of conscious imposition or agreement. However, the nature of the process varies from case to case. Occasionally, a nondemocratic regime will impose the rules of the game under which future multiparty politics will be structured. This has happened repeatedly in Nigeria and occurred in Chile in 1989, when Gen. Augusto Pinochet's advisers crafted an electoral system they believed would advantage the con-

servative right. In Romania the opposition forces crafted the new electoral system after the collapse of the communist regime. The electoral systems in a number of countries (including Spain, Hungary, and Colombia) were born of negotiations between the agents of the regime and the powerful political or civil proponents of democracy. In South Africa, Zimbabwe, Cambodia, Liberia, Sierra Leone, Nicaragua, and Guatemala, choosing a new electoral system was an integral part of the peace process. Some countries (including South Africa and Mali) broadened the discussion of the electoral laws to take in the whole polity within national conventions or elected constituent assemblies. A new electoral system for democratic elections can be determined by international forces outside the country in question. In Germany in 1946, Japan in 1948, Namibia in 1989, and Bosnia in 1996 the electoral system was predominantly imposed by external actors. In Germany's case the external actors were the United States and the United Kingdom; in Japan, the United States; in Namibia, the United Nations and South Africa; and in Bosnia, the United States, the United Nations, and a number of consulting European governments.

Accidental adoption. In a surprising number of cases electoral systems have not been consciously designed at all but have evolved in part as the result of mistakes or as unintended consequences. By trying to limit the strength of the Muslim Brotherhood in Jordan in 1993, King Hussein transformed the Jordanian electoral system from the block vote to the single nontransferable vote. A switch in Papua New Guinea in 1975, for reasons of simplicity, changed the alternative vote into a first-past-the-post system—with serious implications for the nature of politics in the island state.

Evolution. Once a system is designed, it is not always rigidly fixed in place. In many cases, systems have evolved slowly to take into account new political dynamics and social realities. This was the case throughout the nineteenth and twentieth centuries in western Europe. But even in established democracies today, electoral systems are constantly changing in both small and large ways. Sweden introduced a more powerful form of preference voting to its proportional-representation system in 1998, while New Zealand switched completely from plurality to proportional representation in 1993. In the United Kingdom a referendum is planned to decide whether the classic first-past-the-post system should be retained in the twenty-first century. In Latin America many systems were altered in the 1990s at the request of both voters and politicians (as in Venezuela, Ecuador, and Brazil).

RANGE OF CHOICES

The range of electoral systems being used for national legislative elections around the globe is now greater than ever

ELECTORAL SYSTEMS

Alternative vote: Preference voting in single-member districts. If no candidate achieves an absolute majority of first preferences (that is, 50 percent plus one vote), votes are reallocated until one candidate has an absolute majority of votes cast.

Block vote: Plurality voting in multimember districts. Voters have as many votes as there are candidates to be elected. The candidates with the highest vote totals win the seats.

First past the post: Plurality voting in single-member districts. The winning candidate is the one who gains more votes than any other candidate but not necessarily a majority of votes.

Limited vote: Plurality voting in multimember districts. Voters have more than one vote but fewer votes than there are candidates to be elected. Candidates with the highest vote totals take the seats.

List proportional representation: Parties present lists of candidates to the electorate, voters vote for a party, and parties receive seats in proportion to their overall share of the national vote. Winning candidates are taken from the lists.

Mixed-member proportional representation: Combines both district and list proportional representation elections. The proportional-representation seats compensate for any disproportionality produced by the district seat results.

Parallel system: Combines district and list proportional representation elections. Unlike in mixed-member proportional representation, the proportional-representation seats do not compensate for any disproportionality arising from the district elections.

Single nontransferable vote: Plurality voting in multimember districts. Voters have only one vote. Candidates with the highest vote totals take the seats.

Single transferable vote: Preference voting in multimember districts. To win a seat, candidates must surpass a quota of first-preference votes. Voters' preferences are reallocated to other continuing candidates when an unsuccessful candidate is excluded or if an elected candidate has a surplus.

Two-round system: Plurality voting in a single-member district. A second election is held if no candidate achieves an absolute majority of votes (50 percent plus one vote) in the first election.

before. There are at least ten types of electoral systems in operation in 212 nations and related territories of the world, with many permutations of each form. In 1998 just over half (109, or 51 percent of the total) of the independent states and semiautonomous territories of the world that have direct parliamentary elections use plurality-majority systems (such as first past the post, the block vote, the alternative vote, or the two-round system). Another 74 (35 percent) use proportional representation–type systems (either list proportional representation, mixed-member proportional systems, or the single transferable vote); the remaining 29 (14 percent) use semi–proportional representation systems (such as the parallel system used by all but 4 of these, the single nontransferable vote, or the limited vote). Individually, first-past-the-post systems are the most popular, with 67 of 212 nation-states and related territories giving them 32 percent of the total, followed by the 66 cases of list proportional representation systems (31 percent). Next most popular are two-round systems (29, or 14 percent) and parallel systems that have both district and proportional-representation components (25, or 12 percent).

The most important decisions revolve around three basic mechanistic issues. (1) How many representatives are elected from each constituency or district (that is, what is the district magnitude)? (2) Is the formula used based on plurality, majority, or proportional representation? (3) What is the threshold (effective and imposed) for representation for parties and candidates? In combination, these three elements will be the chief determinants of the way votes cast are translated into seats won. They will affect the number of seats each party wins, the geographic distribution of party seats, and the nature of the individual candidates elected.

Up to the 1980s, it was argued that once an electoral system is in place in a country, it is very unlikely to change, as the power to change lay with those who had benefited from the system in the first place. However, this "freezing hypothesis" appears to be thawing. In the 1990s the pace of electoral system reform dramatically speeded up. Many unconsolidated, transitional, and fledgling democracies have radically altered their previous systems. For example, Fiji moved from first past the post to the alternative vote, Thailand moved from the block vote to a parallel system with proportional representation, and Ecuador switched from straight-list proportional representation to a parallel system with lists and the block vote. The constitutional discussions in Indonesia reformed that country's nationally based proportional-representation system, while in South Africa there is mounting pressure to build a district (geographic) link into the large-district, closed-list proportional representation system that the new democracy used in 1994 and 1999.

Not just new democracies grapple with electoral system reform: a number of established democracies have also reformed, or are looking to reform, their systems. Japan switched from the single nontransferable vote to a parallel system in 1993; New Zealand made a dramatic shift from first past the post to a mixed-member proportional system for its elections of 1996, and Italy moved to the same system, from list proportional representation, in the early 1990s. Furthermore, a number of other established democracies are considering change. The new Labour government in the United Kingdom set up a commission to recommend a proportional alternative to the British first-past-the-post system in 1997. Similarly, there are growing calls in Canada to change the first-past-the-post system to a more proportional system as a result of the fragmentation of the party system in that nation.

A survey of all these developments indicates that four main themes appear to be driving the calls for electoral system reform. First is the desire to increase the geographic representation of cities and villages and enhance the accountability of individual representatives within list proportional representation systems (such as those in Indonesia, Ecuador, and South Africa). Second is the unease with vote-seat anomalies inherent in first-past-the-post systems (as in New Zealand and the United Kingdom). Third is the desire to reduce party fragmentation in unstable political systems (including Indonesia and Italy). Fourth is the hope of encouraging interethnic accommodation in societies divided by communal identities (such as Fiji).

Oftentimes two or more of these competing objectives have existed at the same time in various nations, a circumstance that partly explains the greatly increased popularity and usage of mixed electoral systems that combine both district (geographic) representation and list (proportional) representation. Sometimes these mixed systems maintain overall proportionality (as in the mixed-member proportional systems of Germany and New Zealand), but more often parallel systems have been crafted that in effect run two separate elections for different parts of the legislature at the same time. The use of parallel systems has become particularly commonplace in the new democracies of Asia, eastern Europe, and West Africa.

The nature and specifics of the electoral system can be written in a number of places. Where the law finally sits will determine how easy it is to change the electoral system and how entrenched the details are. Some countries have put the principle of the electoral system in their national constitution. For example, South Africa, Namibia, and the Czech Republic entrenched proportional-representation electoral systems in their new democratic constitutions of the late 1980s and early 1990s; subsequently, they spelled out the details in a separate schedule to the act. Their constitutions, like most

others, require two-thirds of parliament for amendment. Some nations, like Norway, spell out the entire system (in that case, proportional representation) in their constitutions. Alternatively the system may not be embedded in the constitution but is entrenched in some other way. For example, in New Zealand the electoral law can be changed only through a two-thirds majority of the parliament or by referendum. Although entrenching the electoral system in the constitution may shield the system from needless manipulation for partisan advantage, it can make needed reform cumbersome and at risk of being blocked by powerful elites. Most nations put their electoral system in legislation passed by parliament. Such laws can be overturned by a simple majority in future legislative sessions. Finally, some countries (notably the United Kingdom) have simply evolved their electoral system over hundreds of years so that the law is based on a mishmash of various acts of Parliament and conventions.

ADVANTAGES OF PLURALITY-MAJORITY SYSTEMS

In the literature plurality-majority electoral systems have been favored on a number of theoretical and empirical grounds. Perhaps the most important is the way single-member districts retain the link between voters and their representative. Legislators represent defined areas of cities or regions rather than just party labels. Many supporters of plurality-majority systems argue that true representative accountability, and by implication true democracy, depends upon the voters knowing who their own representative is and having the ability to reelect, or throw her or him out, at election time.

The choice between individual candidates inherent within single-member district systems means that voters can assess the performance of candidates rather than just having to accept a list of candidates presented by a party, as happens under some list proportional representation electoral systems. The individual orientation also provides a chance for popular independent candidates to be elected. This characteristic may be particularly relevant in fledgling party systems, where politics revolves more around extended ties of family, clan, or kinship than strongly ideological party-political organizations.

Furthermore, plurality-majority systems are favored because of the way in which they funnel the party system of a country, and thus voter choice, into a competition between two broadly based political parties. The exclusion faced by fragmented minority parties under first-past-the-post systems causes the party system to gravitate toward a party of the left and a party of the right that, ideally, alternate in power. Thus this type of system makes "stable" single-party governments more common. Because of the seat bonus that large parties often receive under first past the post (where one party wins, for example, 45 percent of the national vote but 60 percent of the seats), coalition governments are the exception rather than the rule. The seat bonus for relatively large parties can also ensure that the opposition in the legislature earns enough seats to perform its role of reviewing legislation and safeguarding the rights of those outside of power.

In the fledgling democracies of the developing world it is sometimes argued that first past the post will encourage broadly based multiethnic political parties. Because the system gives incentives for political elites to coalesce into two broad organizations, these parties may encompass many elements of a diverse society. Stability in a divided society might also be engendered by excluding "extremist" parties from parliamentary representation: unless a minority party's electoral support is highly concentrated geographically, it is unlikely to win many seats under most single-member district systems. Under purely proportional systems a fraction of a percent of the national vote can sometimes lead to parliamentary representation. Finally, first-past-the-post systems are considered to be simple to use and understand. A valid vote usually requires only one mark beside the name or symbol of one candidate, and the count is easy to administer and conduct.

FLAWS OF PLURALITY-MAJORITY SYSTEMS

Despite their widespread use, plurality-majority electoral systems are criticized on a number of grounds; often they are considered particularly inappropriate for fledgling democracies. Chief among these criticisms is the charge that all single-member district systems are exclusionary in a number of important respects. These electoral systems may exclude smaller parties from fair representation. For example, in the 1983 British general election, the Liberal–Social Democratic Party Alliance won 25 percent of the votes but only 3 percent of the seats; in the 1981 New Zealand election the Social Credit Party won 21 percent of the vote but only 2 percent of the seats; and in the 1989 Botswana general election the Botswana National Front won 27 percent of the votes but only 9 percent of the seats.

Further, plurality-majority electoral systems exclude minorities from fair representation. If voting behavior dovetails with ethnic divisions, the majority group of a country or province will dominate the legislature. Under virtually all single-member district systems political parties put up the "lowest common denominator" candidate in a district to avoid alienating the majority of voters. Thus it is rare, for example, for a black candidate to be given a major party's nomination in a majority-white district, and there is strong evidence that ethnic and racial minorities across the world are far less likely to be represented in parliaments elected by plurality-majority systems. Likewise, the lowest common denominator candidate syndrome affects the ability of women to be elected, be-cause they are less likely to be selected as candidates by male-dominated party structures. Evidence across the world suggests that women are less likely to be elected to parliament under plurality-majority systems than under proportional-representation ones. In 1998 women constituted 13.7 percent of the members of legislatures elected by proportional-representation methods (seventy cases) and 8.4 percent of the legislatures elected by plurality-majority methods (eighty-four cases). For the twenty-four semi–proportional representation systems, the figure was 7.8 percent.

In divided societies plurality-majority systems are also criticized for encouraging the development of political parties based on clan, ethnicity, or region. Throughout much of Africa plurality-majority systems have encouraged parties to base their campaigns and policy platforms on conceptions of clan, ethnicity, race, or regionalism. This pattern is particularly apparent in Malawi, Zimbabwe, Zambia, and Nigeria. Politicized ethnicity is reinforced when "regional fiefdoms," where one party wins all the seats in a province or district, are exaggerated. Plurality-majority systems tend to create regions where one party, through winning a majority of votes in the region, wins all, or nearly all, of the parliamentary seats. This situation both excludes regional minorities from representation and reinforces the perception that politics is a battleground defined by who you are and where you live rather than what you believe in. And regional fiefdoms plague countries beyond the developing world: this tendency has long been put forward as an argument against first past the post in Canada. Regional fiefdoms also maximize wasted votes, which lead minority party supporters to feel that they have no realistic hope of ever electing a candidate of their choice. This discouragement poses a danger in nascent democracies, where alienation from the political system increases the likelihood that antidemocratic extremists will be able to mobilize antisystem movements.

In both established and fledgling democracies plurality-majority systems can be unresponsive to changes in public opinion. If each party's vote is territorially concentrated, one party can retain control of the government despite a substantial drop in popular support. A fall from 60 percent to 40 percent of a party's popular vote nationally may represent a fall from 80 percent to 60 percent in the number of seats held; this change does not affect the party's overall dominant position.

Finally, all single-member district systems are open to the manipulation of electoral boundaries, that is, the unfair gerrymandering or malapportionment of districts. This was particularly apparent in Kenya in 1993 and 1997, when huge disparities between the sizes of electoral districts—the largest had more than twenty times the number of voters as the smallest—allowed the ruling Kenyan African National Union Party to win a large parliamentary majority with less than a third of the popular vote.

ADVANTAGES OF PROPORTIONAL REPRESENTATION

In many new democracies proportional-representation systems are chosen precisely because they militate against the exclusionary tendencies of plurality-majority systems. By more faithfully translating votes cast into seats won, proportional representation is sometimes said to produce fairer results. Under proportional representation disproportionality and seat bonuses for the larger parties are constrained, and minority parties can gain access to parliament even if their vote is not geographically concentrated.

The bulk of the cited advantages of proportional representation revolve around this core principle of inclusion. Very few votes are wasted under proportional-representation systems. When the threshold for representation is low, almost all votes cast within proportional-representation elections go toward electing a party candidate of choice. It has been argued that participation increases as voters can be more confident that their vote will make a difference to electoral outcomes, however small. Because it takes fewer votes to win a seat under proportional representation, the system can facilitate minority parties' access to representation. Unless the threshold is unduly high, or the district magnitude is unusually low, any political party with even a few percent of electoral support should gain representation in the legislature.

Inclusion can also be engendered through the way in which some proportional-representation systems encourage parties to present inclusive and communally diverse lists of candidates. The incentive under national proportional-representation systems is to maximize the overall vote, regardless of where those votes might come from. Thus parties often strive to constitute lists of candidates which will appeal to a broad cross section of society. This, along with the increased chances for minority parties, means that under proportional representation, it is more likely that the representatives of minority cultures or groups will be elected. Similarly, it is more likely that women will be elected under proportional-representation systems. Parties can use the lists to promote the advancement of women politicians and allow the space for voters to elect women candidates without limiting their ability to vote on other ideological issues. Finally, inclusion of both minorities and majorities is fostered by the way in which proportional representation restricts the growth of regional fiefdoms. Proportional-representation systems reward minority parties with a minority of the seats, and thus provinces are unlikely to be represented nationally by representatives of a single party.

With reference to new democracies in Africa, it has been argued that proportional representation makes power sharing between majorities and minorities and powerful interest groups more visible. In many societies, power sharing between the numerical majority of the population who hold political power and a small minority who hold economic power is an unavoidable reality. Where the popular majority dominates parliament, negotiations between different power blocs are less visible, less transparent, and less accountable (as in Zimbabwe, for example). It has been argued, in particular in South Africa, that proportional representation, by including all interests in parliament, offers a better chance that decisions are made in the public eye—and by a more inclusive cross section of the society.

DISADVANTAGES OF PROPORTIONAL REPRESENTATION

Historically, the criticisms of proportional electoral systems have centered on two themes: the tendency of proportional-representation systems to give rise to coalition governments and the failure of some proportional-representation systems to provide a geographic linkage between a representative and her or his electorate.

The most often cited argument against using proportional representation is that it leads to a detachment of the representatives from their constituents. When seats are allocated in large multimember districts (as in Namibia, Israel, or South Africa), there is often no accountable link between voters and their member of parliament. Under closed-list proportional representation systems of this type, voters are unable to determine the identity of the persons who will represent them, and they do not have the ability to vote out a candidate if they feel he or she has failed in office. Thus national closed-list proportional representation is criticized for leaving too much power entrenched within party headquarters and wielded by senior party leadership. A candidate's position on the party list, and therefore his or her likelihood of success, is dependent on currying favor with party bosses, whose relationship with the electorate is of secondary importance.

Because proportional representation allows small parties to win representation, there are lessened incentives for parties to coalesce before elections. This situation then leads to a fragmentation of the party system that can be seen as destabilizing. The coalition governments born of fragmented party systems are cited as allowing tiny minority parties to hold larger parties to ransom in coalition negotiations. In Israel, for example, extremist religious parties are often crucial to government formation. Coalitions of incompatible parties can cause legislative gridlock and the subsequent inability to carry out coherent policies at a time of pressing need.

Under a proportional-representation system, it may be difficult to remove a reasonably sized party from power. When governments are coalitions, some political parties can be ever present in government, despite weak electoral performances from time to time. Finally, the use of a proportional-representation system presumes some kind of recognized party structure, since voters are expected to vote for parties rather than individuals or groups of individuals. This characteristic makes many types of proportional representation inappropriate for political systems that either do not have parties or have embryonic or loose party structures.

As can be seen by the previous discussions, both model types—first past the post and list proportional representation—can exhibit serious flaws for the workings of representative government in certain circumstances. This is partly why electoral system design has become such a growth industry and the scientific study of electoral systems gained so much ground in the 1990s. The pattern of electoral system design is increasingly one of innovation. Nations adopt new rules to reflect their own domestic desires and requirements. Mixed systems, of various forms, are rapidly becoming the norm; in these, designers try to combine the advantages of geographic representation with the benefits of proportionality or incentives for accommodation of minority interests.

See also *Alternative Vote; Binomial Electoral System; Duverger's Law; Functions of Elections; Limited Vote; List; Majority Systems; Mixed Electoral Systems; Plurality Systems; Preference Voting; Proportional Representation; Proportionality and Disproportionality; Second Ballot (or Runoff); Simultaneous Elections; Single Nontransferable Vote; Single Transferable Vote; Staggered Elections; Threshold of Exclusion.*

ANDREW REYNOLDS, UNIVERSITY OF NOTRE DAME

BIBLIOGRAPHY

Dummett, Michael. *The Principles of Electoral Reform.* Oxford: Oxford University Press, 1997.

Farrell, David M. *Comparing Electoral Systems.* London: Prentice Hall/Harvester Wheatsheaf, 1997.

Horowitz, Donald L. *A Democratic South Africa? Constitutional Engineering in a Divided Society.* Berkeley: University of California Press, 1991.

Katz, Richard S. *Democracy and Elections.* Oxford: Oxford University Press, 1997.

Lakeman, Enid. *How Democracies Vote.* London: Faber and Faber, 1974.

Lijphart, Arend. "Constitutional Choices for New Democracies." *Journal of Democracy* 2 (1991): 72–84.

———, and Bernard Grofman, eds. *Choosing an Electoral System: Issues and Alternatives.* New York: Praeger, 1984.

Mill, John Stuart. *Considerations on Representative Government.* Liberal Arts Press: New York, reprint 1958.

Reilly, Ben, and Andrew Reynolds. *Electoral Systems and Conflict in Divided Societies.* Washington, D.C.: National Research Council, 1999.

Reynolds, Andrew. *Electoral Systems and Democratization in Southern Africa.* Oxford: Oxford University Press, 1999.

Reynolds, Andrew, Ben Reilly, et al. *The International IDEA Handbook of Electoral System Design.* Stockholm: International IDEA, 1997.

Reynolds, Andrew, and Timothy D. Sisk. "Elections, Electoral Systems, and Conflict Management." In *Elections and Conflict Resolution in Africa,* ed. Timothy Sisk and Andrew Reynolds. Washington, D.C.: U.S. Institute of Peace, 1998.

Rule, Wilma, and Joseph Zimmerman, eds. *Electoral Systems in Comparative Perspective: Their Impact on Women and Minorities.* Westport, Conn.: Greenwood Press, 1994.

Sartori, Giovanni. *Comparative Constitutional Engineering: An Inquiry into Structures, Incentives, and Outcomes.* New York: Columbia University Press, 1994.

Taagepera, Rein, and Matthew S. Shugart. "Designing Electoral Systems." *Electoral Studies* 8 (1989): 49–58.

DISQUALIFICATION OF VOTERS, GROUNDS FOR

Electoral laws typically specify conditions that disqualify a person from voting. Some conditions, such as those that prohibit voting by persons of unsound mind, are generally regarded as reasonable in principle, though they may give rise to practical difficulties in implementation. Others, such as the disqualification of persons convicted of criminal offenses (or of particular categories of criminal offenses) or the disqualification of persons who are in prison may be more controversial; they often are perceived to discriminate against particular groups in society, especially where specific groups are over-represented in the prison population. In addition, some would see it as particularly inappropriate that a person who may have been wrongly convicted of a crime could be denied the opportunity to participate in a political process that might be his or her only avenue of redress.

In the past, qualifications of voters were used deliberately in many countries as a discriminatory mechanism, to exclude certain sections of society from political influence. The use of a property-based franchise in many countries was an example, as was the disenfranchisement of the majority of the South African population on racial grounds until the elections of 1994. Such mechanisms have become much less common as countries have sought to ensure that their electoral procedures meet, at least ostensibly, the standards set out in international human rights instruments such as the International Covenant on Civil and Political Rights and the Universal Declaration of Human Rights.

See also *Administration of Elections; Constitution and Elections; Franchise Expansion; Registration of Voters.*

MICHAEL MALEY, AUSTRALIAN ELECTORAL COMMISSION

DISTRICT MAGNITUDE

District magnitude is the number of seats allocated in a given district. Numerous studies have shown that the magnitude of districts is generally the most important factor in determining the degree of proportionality between party votes and seat shares.

Table 1. District Magnitude (M) and Deviation from Proportionality (D) for a Hypothetical Vote Distribution

	Percent votes by party					
M	37	31	19	9	4	D(%)
1	1	0	0	0	0	63.0
2	1	1	0	0	0	32.0
3	1	1	1	0	0	16.7
4	2	1	1	0	0	19.0
5	2	2	1	0	0	13.0
6	3	2	1	0	0	15.3
7	3	3	1	0	0	17.7
8	3	3	2	0	0	13.0
9	4	3	2	0	0	12.9
10	4	3	2	1	0	5.0
15	6	5	3	1	0	6.3
20	8	6	4	2	0	5.0
25	9	8	5	2	1	2.0
30	11	10	6	2	1	3.3
40	15	13	8	3	1	3.0
50	19	16	9	4	2	2.0

Note: Deviation from proportionality (D) is defined as:

$$D = \sum_{i=1}^{n} |\%v_i - \%s_i| / 2,$$

where v_i is the percentage of votes for the ith party, s_i is its percentage of the seats, and the summation is over all n parties.

The accompanying table shows the relation between magnitude and disproportionality for a hypothetical vote distribution and a proportional-representation formula. It is evident from the table that lower magnitudes tend to produce less proportional seat distributions than do higher magnitudes, although sometimes at lower magnitudes, a one-seat change in the magnitude produces a move in the opposite direction.

When magnitude is low, the magnitude exerts a very strong effect on the party system by underrepresenting smaller parties. When magnitude becomes larger than about twenty, vote and seat shares become very close to one another. Nearly perfect proportionality is obtained by very large districts. This example assumes that the seat-allocation formula is proportional representation. Under some non-proportional-representation systems, the effect can be different; in fact, under winner-take-all (at large) systems, higher magnitudes actually result in less proportionality than smaller magnitudes.

CALCULATING MAGNITUDE AND ITS COMPLICATIONS

Magnitude *(M)* may range from one to *S*, where *S* is the total number of seats in the legislative body, and is, for any given country, a function of both *S* and the number of electoral districts *(E)*. In systems like the United Kingdom and United States, in which all districts elect a single representative, $M = 1$ and $E = S$. On the other hand, in a few countries that employ proportional representation in a single nationwide district, such as Israel, Namibia, and the Netherlands, $M = S$ and $E = 1$. These two extremes represent the simplest relationships among the variables *M, S,* and *E*. However, most countries that use proportional representation employ districts of varying magnitudes, often using as districts the preexisting provinces or other administrative subunits and basing the *M* of any given district on its population. In these cases, there is no common magnitude across the country, but we may speak of average magnitude *(M')*, where $M' = S/E$.

For systems with varying magnitudes, the average magnitude of districts has been shown to approximate accurately a system with an identical uniform magnitude, as long as the picture is not clouded by such complicating features as legal thresholds and compensatory upper tiers and as long as the range of magnitudes is not excessively wide. For instance, in Costa Rica $S = 57$, $E = 7$, $M' = 57/7 = 8.1$, and the range of magnitudes is 4–21. Costa Rica's average magnitude is a good description of the overall system, and its degree of disproportionality is close to what it would be if all its districts were the same magnitude (8, in this case). For a country like Portugal, with one very large district, the average magnitude is a bit less valuable. Portugal has $S = 250$, $E = 20$, and $M' = 12.5$. However, the range is very large: from 3 to 56. The one very large district gives small parties a much greater opportunity to win seats than the average magnitude of 12.5 would imply.

FURTHER COMPLICATIONS

It gets still more complicated when the districts are not independent of one another, for instance when one or more of the districts is actually a compensatory upper tier. For example, Germany uses a districting structure much like Russia's, which would compute to an average magnitude of around 2. Because Germany's upper tier is fully compensatory, we can think of the country's magnitude as being "effectively" as large as its entire parliament.

The relationship between votes and seats can be further influenced by legal thresholds. In Germany a relatively small percentage of the total vote has been wasted on parties that fail to clear the 5 percent threshold, so the existence of the threshold makes very little difference to the actual seat allocation. Deviation from proportionality is only marginally greater than it would be without the threshold. However, in Poland in 1993, when over 28 percent of the votes were cast for parties that fell below the 5 percent threshold, the deviation from proportionality was much greater than would have been the case without the threshold. In such a case, the threshold, rather than the district magnitude per se, matters most.

For systems that combine thresholds, compensatory seats, and other complex features, there is no widely accepted means of determining their effective magnitude. What we can say with certainty is that compensatory seats effectively increase magnitude, while thresholds effectively decrease it.

For all the complexities raised here, in the end the effect of district magnitude is quite simple. As shown in the table, the smaller the magnitude, the greater the disproportionality when a proportional allocation formula is used. It is for this reason that complicating features like compensatory seats and thresholds are used. If a country has mostly districts of low magnitude, owing perhaps to a desire to provide geographically based representation, compensatory seats are sometimes included in electoral rules to increase proportionality. If, on the other hand, a country has mostly large districts, or a large compensatory district, in order to provide for a high degree of proportionality, then thresholds are often employed to prevent the high proportionality from encouraging too much fragmentation of the party system; thresholds inevitably reduce proportionality to some degree. Thus district magnitude—given its very predictable effects on proportionality—is the basic building block of any electoral system.

See also *Compensatory Seats; Designing Electoral Systems; Fused Votes; Gender Quotas; Proportional Representation; Proportionality and Disproportionality; Single Nontransferable Vote.*

MATTHEW SOBERG SHUGART,
UNIVERSITY OF CALIFORNIA, SAN DIEGO

BIBLIOGRAPHY

Cox, Gary W. *Making Votes Count: Strategic Coordination in the World's Electoral Systems.* New York: Cambridge University Press, 1997.

Lijphart, Arend. *Electoral Systems and Party Systems: A Study of Twenty-seven Democracies, 1945–1990.* Oxford: Oxford University Press, 1994.

Taagepera, Rein, and Matthew S. Shugart. *Seats and Votes: The Effects and Determinants of Electoral Systems.* New Haven, Conn.: Yale University Press, 1989.

DIVISOR

See *Quotas*

DONKEY VOTES

Donkey votes are valid votes cast by electors who mark their ballot straight down, straight across, or, less commonly, straight up or from right to left without regard to who the candidates might be or which parties they represent. These voters are thought to do so because they are functionally illiterate, lack information or motivation to make choices among candidates or parties, or regard attendance at the polls as an imposition from which to escape as speedily as possible.

Compulsory voting, complex ballots, and a highly competitive party system have given the phenomenon special prominence in Australia, where the term probably originated. In Australia and elsewhere there has been interest in the related "alphabetic advantage" that goes to the candidate who secures the advantageous place at the top of the ballot, and thereby secures the votes of voters who read no further.

Various forms of evidence to confirm the existence of the donkey vote have been put forward. One method compares surnames of different groups: successful candidates, all candidates, all voters, and the whole population. Another looks at voting patterns. Do second and subsequent preferences follow a politically rational path, or are they erratic? Do the votes for candidates of small parties vary significantly when those candidates are at the top of the ballot? If candidates with surnames beginning with the early letters of the alphabet are especially likely to be elected, it must be because some voters are more likely to vote for them, and the only plausible explanation is donkey voting. Most estimates place the donkey vote at 2-3 percent of the total valid vote.

Australian electoral law followed British practice, alphabetical order down the ballot, until 1937, when the Labor Party, then in opposition, nominated four candidates for the federal upper house from New South Wales whose surnames began with A. All won, and the government subsequently amended the law to group candidates of the same party and to determine each group's place by lot. In the 1950s a split in the Labor Party created the Democratic Labor Party, which sought to augment its 10-15 percent of the vote by selecting candidates high up the alphabet; it survived for twenty years. In 1961 the coalition federal government, comprising the Liberal and National Country Parties, retained office because a substantial proportion of one Communist candidate's votes went to an anticommunist Liberal because his was the next name on the ballot. Such incidents entering political folklore reinforced belief in the existence of the donkey vote.

Several remedies to reduce or eliminate donkey voting have been devised. Drawing lots for place on the ballot was enhanced in 1984 by double randomization of the draw. Probably the most advanced remedy is the "Robson rotation," introduced by a Tasmanian member of parliament for single transferable vote elections but capable of being used with any voting system. Ballots are printed with the names rotated, such that each candidate appears in every possible place on the ballot an equal number of times. Then no one can derive advantage by either birth or lot. Tasmanian electoral officials find it practicable. Showing party affiliations on the ballot assists under-informed voters, as does not requiring a complete set of preferences and "ticket voting," whereby a single mark adopts the full set of preferences of the party the voter wishes to support. Introduction of several such provisions in 1984 reduced interest in the donkey vote, and at the subsequent six elections, 1984 to 1998, those with A–D surnames, traditionally its beneficiaries, were no more successful than the whole population of candidates for the federal lower house.

See also *Alternative Vote.*

COLIN A. HUGHES, EMERITUS,
UNIVERSITY OF QUEENSLAND, BRISBANE

BIBLIOGRAPHY

Hughes, Colin A. "Alphabetic Advantage in the House of Representatives." *Australian Quarterly* 42 (September 1970): 24–29.

Mackerras, Malcolm. "The 'Donkey Vote.' " *Australian Quarterly* 40 (December 1968): 89–92.

Masterman, C. J. "The Effect of the 'Donkey Vote' on the House of Representatives." *Australian Journal of Politics and History* 10 (August 1964): 221–225.

DOUBLE SIMULTANEOUS VOTE

The double simultaneous vote is a method by which an intraparty election and general election take place at once. Since 1910 Uruguay has employed the double simultaneous vote to elect the president, national legislators, and subnational officials. Beginning in 1999, however, this system will not be utilized for the presidential election. Outside of Uruguay, the double simultaneous vote has been used only in Argentina and Honduras. Since 1987 eleven Argentine provinces have at one time or another employed the double simultaneous vote for provincial and municipal elections. Honduras utilized this method for its 1985 national and municipal elections.

Under the double simultaneous vote (often referred to as the Ley de Lemas [Law of Mottoes]) a party may present more than one candidate (such as for executive offices) or lists of candidates (such as for legislative offices). For example, in the 1971 Uruguayan presidential election, the Colorado Party had five presidential candidates; the National Party, two; and the Broad Front, one. The distribution of the vote percentages for the five Colorado Party candidates was Bordaberry (22.8), Battle (14.6), Vasconcellos (2.9), Pintos (0.3), and Ribas (0.2). For the National Party the distribution was Ferreira (26.4) and Aguerrondo (13.7), while for the Broad Front Seregni received 18.3. Combined, the candidates of the Colorado Party, National Party, and Broad Front respectively won 40.8 percent, 40.1 percent, and 18.3 percent of the vote. Since Uruguay uses the plurality formula to elect its president, the party with the plurality of the vote (the Colorado Party) won the presidency (the general election). The presidency was won by the Colorado Party candidate who received the most Colorado Party votes (the intraparty election): Bordaberry. Bordaberry, however, was not the individual candidate who received the most votes; Ferreira of the National Party received 3.6 percent more than him.

For party leaders, an advantage of the double simultaneous vote is that it reduces the incentives for disgruntled party members to form their own parties. It also avoids the costs associated with bitter preelection primaries. The double simultaneous vote was adopted in Uruguay due primarily to internal conflict within the country's two dominant parties (the Colorado Party and National Party) and the desire to maintain the parties' unity for reasons of electoral competition and governability. Similarly, the double simultaneous vote was adopted in Honduras in 1985 due to serious factionalism within the governing Liberal Party, and in the eleven Argentine provinces because of comparable problems within the Peronist Party (which occupied the governor's office everywhere the double simultaneous vote was adopted).

However, party leaders also have experienced the negative consequences of the double simultaneous vote, such as weak party discipline in the legislature and often severe intraparty conflict before, during, and after an election. The recognition of these and other negative factors has led several Argentine provinces to cease using the system.

See also *Fused Votes; List; Plurality Systems; Presidential Electoral Systems; Primary Elections; Proportional Representation.*

MARK P. JONES, MICHIGAN STATE UNIVERSITY

BIBLIOGRAPHY

Buquet, Daniel, Daniel Chasquetti, and Juan Andrés Moraes. *Fragmentación Política y Gobierno en Uruguay: ¿Un Enfermo Imaginario?* Montevideo: Facultad de Ciencias Sociales, Universidad de la República, 1998.

Jones, Mark P. "Federalism and the Number of Parties in Argentine Congressional Elections." *Journal of Politics* 59 (1997): 538–549.

González, Luis E. *Political Structures and Democracy in Uruguay.* Notre Dame, Ind.: University of Notre Dame Press, 1991.

Taylor, Philip B. "The Electoral System in Uruguay." *Journal of Politics* 17 (February 1955): 19–42.

Tula, María Inés. "La Reforma Electoral en los '90: Algunos Comentarios Sobre la Ley de Lemas en la Argentina." In *Política y Sociedad en los Años del Menemismo,* edited by Ricardo Sidicaro and Jorge Mayer. Buenos Aires: Universidad de Buenos Aires, 1995.

DOWNSIAN MODEL OF ELECTIONS

Anthony Downs's *An Economic Theory of Democracy* (1957), which was his doctoral dissertation in economics at Stanford University, is one of the seminal works on electoral behavior. Downs offers a model of voter choice and a model of candidate/party competition, and then he integrates these two models into a dynamic story about how candidates and parties devise platforms based on their anticipation of voter responses to the alternatives available to them, including the option of not voting at all. In addition, Downs offers insights into how voters decide when to seek information and into the role that information plays in voter choice.

The Downsian model of outcome-oriented voter choice is one of the three main approaches to understanding voting behavior. Unlike sociological models that see voter choice and the structure of the party system as rooted in underlying socio-demographic cleavages (for example, urban-rural, regional, class-based, ethnic, or religious conflicts), or the socio-psychological model that emphasizes partisan attachments formed at an early age (which, like choice of religion, are strongly conditioned by family and social environment), the Downsian approach emphasizes the volitional and prospective aspects of voter behavior.

Downs's model of party competition stresses the role of office-seeking politicians. Indeed, the Downsian model is almost schizophrenic in distinguishing the motivations of the voters from those of the politicians. The former wish to gain the election of candidates and parties who will implement policies as close as possible to those they prefer. The latter are seen as indifferent to policies except insofar as the policy platform they propose enables them to gain the support of a winning coalition of voters. Here, Downs's logic (inspired by the work of the economist Joseph Schumpeter) is directly analogous to Adam Smith's view of the "invisible hand." Smith's baker produces goods not out of a beneficent concern for the well-being of his customers but in order to sell them; for Downs, the link between voter desires for policy outputs and the candidates' desire for election is forged as candidates adopt policies that they think will "sell" with the voters. In the Hotelling-Smithies spatial model of economic competition, shops seek to locate where they can maximize their flow of customers; in the Downsian adaptation of this model, politicians compete to locate where (in policy terms) they can attract the most votes.

Another important contribution of *An Economic Theory of Democracy* is that it is the first work to recognize the problematicity of the decision to vote. In the basic Downsian calculus, voting is an instrumentally rational act only when the expected benefits of voting exceed the "opportunity costs" of alternative uses of one's time (including the time involved in deciding how best to vote). The outcome of a process of voting can be thought of as a collective good (as economists such as Mancur Olson use that term). Because any single voter's participation has only a minuscule chance of being decisive in changing the outcome of an election, voting raises the problem of "free riding." Even though a voter may very much want a particular candidate (or party) to win, the payoff he or she expects to get from having that candidate elected, rather than one of the opponents, must be discounted by the probability that the vote will be decisive (an "expected" benefit calculation). Thus, it would appear that a voter who can expect her preferred candidate to win is better off not voting, and a voter who can expect her preferred candidate to lose is also better off not voting. When rationality is judged in purely instrumental terms, only in the presence of electoral uncertainty is it possible for voting to be a rational act.

Of course, if we take Downs literally, then we cannot explain why so many people vote except by appealing to non-instrumental reasons such as a sense of citizen duty, but that does not mean that Downs's analysis is irrelevant. The Downsian approach to voter turnout allows us to appreciate turnout as a puzzle that needs to be explained, but it also identifies factors (for example, expected electoral closeness, magnitude of candidate differences, costs of electoral participation) that can help explain comparative variations in turnout across elections of different types or at different points in time. When judged by that test the Downsian approach does quite well.

Downs also makes important contributions to our understanding of the role that information plays in electoral choice. Just as Downs's approach to voter turnout emphasizes the need to take into account whether one's vote can be expected to make a difference in the election outcome, so his approach to political information emphasizes the need to take into account whether new information can be expected to make a difference in the choice voters make about which candidate or party to support or whether to vote at all. Similarly, just as Downs's approach to voter turnout emphasizes that voting has costs, so too his approach to information requires us to take into account the costs of gaining new information.

First and foremost, Downs offers what might be called a model of "rational ignorance." Only if new information can be expected to improve our decision making, so as to give us a higher expected payoff than before, and only if that expected gain exceeds the costs of pursuing the new information will it be instrumentally rational to seek additional political knowledge.

Second, although Downs would expect most voters to be relatively ignorant about politics, information useful to political choice may be gained at a relatively low cost as a "by-product" of other activities. For example, while voters may not know the values (or recent time path) of aggregate indicators such as GDP, inflation, or unemployment rates, they can use the information that comes to them when they buy things, and from their conversations with friends and neighbors, to assess inflation, unemployment, and the overall state of the economy.

Third, Downs highlights the "signaling" power of various types of informational cues, such as party labels, interest group endorsements, and professed ideology. To the extent that such cues are reliable predictors of the policy positions of the candidates and parties (or at least their positions relative to one another), such cues can dramatically reduce the costs of gathering information and make possible an informed vote, that is, a vote that matches the choice the voter would make if he or she were in possession of complete information about the options available.

While *An Economic Theory of Democracy* discusses political choices in multiparty settings, its principal focus is on two-party competition in a single election. The result most often associated with Downs is the "median voter theorem." This theorem asserts that, in two-party competition along a single ideological or policy dimension, the candidates of each party will converge toward the median voter in the electorate. This theorem leads us to expect tweedledum-tweedledee politics. However, it would be a mistake to identify the median-voter theorem as the Downsian model of two-party competition; and it would be an even greater mistake to think that spatial models of politics of the sort propounded by Downs are of no value just because in the United States (and in other countries using plurality-based elections) we do not observe the full convergence of party positions that the median voter theorem posits.

First, Downs's analysis does not confine itself to a single dimension. For example, he discusses the feasibility of putting together a winning coalition based on single-issue voting blocs. He also considers the role in voter choice of a candi-

date or party's previous performance, anticipating Morris Fiorina's notion of retrospective voting.

Second, and more important, even if we posit only a single dimension of political competition, that the election chooses a single candidate, and that the election is decided by a plurality vote, the median voter theorem holds only under very restrictive conditions. Eight assumptions of the basic Downsian model must be met for the median voter theorem to hold. The pure convergence result disappears if, contra Downs, we admit the possibility that other elections are taking place simultaneously in which candidates of each party are also running; or admit the possibility that voters or parties (or both) are looking beyond the outcome of this particular election to see its implications for future policies and future election chances; or recognize that candidates and parties care about more than simply winning, but also about what policies will be adopted (just as voters do); or admit the possibility that voters discount candidate platforms by taking into account the likelihood that the espoused positions will actually be implemented, then the pure convergence result disappears. In two-party contests, the Downsian spatial model of candidate and party competition gives us reasons why, in competition over a single issue dimension, there are pressures toward party convergence. But, within the Downsian framework there may also be strong countervailing, centrifugal pressures even when politics is one-dimensional. For example, if there are party primaries or nomination procedures in which party activists play a major role, then we would expect that candidates will locate somewhere between their party median and the overall voter median. In the United States there is strong empirical support for this prediction.

Downsian models of party competition and electoral choice (and so-called rational choice models of politics generally) have recently come under considerable attack because of alleged deficiencies in empirical performance. Most of that attack is misguided because it views Downs as the final word on election models, rather than as an important first start; takes Downs too literally; or takes too seriously the exaggerated claims of some modelers that game-theory and other mathematical tools allow them to "solve" for optimal electoral behavior, and that political actors will make the choices prescribed by their models. There is no such thing as *the* Downsian model of elections. Downs himself offered a richer and much more nuanced view of political competition than any of those who have sought to formalize Downsian insights. In general, the Downsian proximity model helps us understand how politicians develop strategies to attract votes. Only when we add institutional detail can we develop realistic models with predictive power. Moreover, we should see the Downsian approach as complementary to (rather than antithetical with) other approaches that help us understand the social embedding of political competition.

See also *Campaigning; Competitiveness of Elections; Democracy and Elections; Manifesto, Election; Paradox of Voting; Turnout; Unopposed Returns; Voting Behavior, Influences on; Wasted Votes.*

BERNARD GROFMAN,
UNIVERSITY OF CALIFORNIA, IRVINE

BIBLIOGRAPHY

Downs, Anthony. *An Economic Theory of Democracy.* New York: Harper and Row, 1957.

Grofman, Bernard. "The Neglected Role of the Status Quo in Models of Issue Voting." *Journal of Politics* 47 (1985): 231–237.

———. "Political Economy: Downsian Perspectives." In *New Handbook of Political Science,* edited by Robert Goodin and Hans-Dieter Klingemann, 691–701. New York: Oxford University Press, 1996.

———, ed. *Information, Participation and Choice: An "Economic Theory of Democracy" in Perspective.* Ann Arbor: University of Michigan Press, 1993.

Shapiro, Catherine R., David W. Brady, Richard A. Brody, and John A. Ferejohn. "Linking Constituency Opinion and Senate Voting Scores: A Hybrid Explanation." *Legislative Studies Quarterly* 15 (1990): 599–623.

DUVERGER'S LAW

First formulated by Maurice Duverger in the 1950s, Duverger's Law states that an electoral system in which legislative candidates are elected by plurality rule in single-member districts promotes the formation and maintenance of a two-party system. In part, Duverger's Law was an inductive generalization—based largely on the observation that the United States and United Kingdom, the world's most prominent examples of bipartism when Duverger wrote, both used single-member districts and plurality rule. But there was also a deductive argument underpinning Duverger's Law, concerning the likely reactions of voters and politicians to the exigencies of competing under plurality rule for a single seat.

The deductive argument has two parts, one pertaining to the process of election within the individual electoral districts and one pertaining to the process by which elected legislators from different districts join together. At the local (or district) level, politicians have strong incentives to form parties large enough to win a plurality, since that is what it takes to win a seat. But the only way to guarantee a plurality is to secure a majority, and so competition among politicians should lead to the formation of two big parties, both competing for majority support. In districts where politicians had for some reason formed more than two parties, voters would often face strong incentives to vote tactically. For example, if there were two left-of-center parties competing against a single right-of-center party, supporters of the weaker leftist party might be faced with the following choice: vote for the weaker leftist, split the left vote, and see the right-wing candidate elected; or vote for the stronger leftist (that is, vote tactically), thereby securing his or her election. The combination of politicians' desire to win, leading them to form or join large parties, and voters' desire to use their votes to achieve the best possible outcome, leading them to vote tactically, ensured what Duverger called *local bipartism:* in each district there would tend to be two viable parties.

Local bipartism, however, is no guarantee of national bipartism. In the plurality elections of Canada and India, for example, most districts have two viable parties, but the same two parties do not compete in all the districts. Instead, different pairs compete in different regions of the country, leading to multipartism in the national legislature despite local bipartism in the constituencies. The factors that promote linkage across districts, ensuring that the same two parties compete everywhere, are not spelled out in Duverger's analysis but appear to depend on the nature of the national executive (parliamentary or presidential), the presence or absence of national compensatory seats, and other factors that do not depend on the rules used to elect candidates within the districts.

See also *Coordination, Electoral; Fractionalization Index; Relevant Parties; Second Ballot; Single Nontransferable Vote; Single Transferable Vote; Tactical Voting; Wasted Votes; Winning an Election.*

GARY W. COX, UNIVERSITY OF CALIFORNIA, SAN DIEGO

BIBLIOGRAPHY

Cox, Gary W. *Making Votes Count.* Cambridge: Cambridge University Press, 1997.

Duverger, Maurice. *Political Parties.* Translated by Barbara and Robert North. New York: John Wiley and Sons, 1954.

Riker, William H. "The Two-Party System and Duverger's Law: An Essay on the History of Political Science." *American Political Science Review* 76 (June 1982): 753–766.

EFFECT OF ELECTIONS ON GOVERNMENT

Much is known about why voters in democracies vote the way they do and about what determines the outcomes of democratic elections. Much less is known about the consequences of elections for democratic governance itself. The emphasis in political science has been on what decides elections rather than on what elections decide. Nevertheless, a small body of relevant literature exists, and significant hypotheses and generalizations can be derived from it.

ELECTIONS AND GOVERNMENT FORMATION

Popular definitions of democracy frequently assert that the principal function of elections is to enable the people of a country to decide which individuals or parties shall form the country's government. There may be debates about who should constitute "the people" for these purposes or about which electoral system should be used, but the usual assumption on these definitions is that the connection between voting in democratic elections and the choice of governments is a close one—that, in choosing a new government in a democracy, the voice of the people is determinative.

In fact, that simple picture of the connection between electorates and governments, while not without validity, needs to be qualified in two important respects. In the first place, no people in any democratic country elects the entirety of its government. Judges are not normally elected by the voters (except in some American states), nor are civil servants and members of the armed forces. Direct democratic election of the head of government (president or prime minister) is somewhat more common but is still relatively rare, being confined largely to France, Israel, and some countries in the western hemisphere. Even in those countries, although the voters do choose the head of government, they do not choose the government's other leading members (the minister of finance,

the foreign minister, the justice minister, and so on). The only branch of government that is directly elected in every democracy is the main chamber of the national legislature.

In the second place, there are a number of countries in which the connection between the counting of ballots in a national election and the subsequent formation of a government is far from close. At one extreme, as in the United Kingdom, Germany, and Japan, the outcome of a national election normally leads to either the confirmation in office of the incumbent administration or the election of a new administration; but at the other extreme, notably in Italy and several of the smaller European democracies (Belgium, Denmark, Finland, the Netherlands, and Portugal), the holding of a national election normally leads merely to a prolonged process of interparty bargaining—and the outcome of that bargaining process need not accurately reflect the pattern of popular votes that have been cast. As a general rule, the more parties a country has, the more tenuous is likely to be the relationship between elections and the formation of governments.

It should also be noted that in parliamentary systems changes of government may take place without national elections being held at all. If an existing coalition government collapses for any reason, a new election need not be held; a new coalition can be formed out of political parties represented in the existing legislature. In France between 1945 and 1958 (to take an admittedly extreme case), only three national elections were held, but no fewer than seventeen separate governments held office.

ELECTIONS AND PUBLIC POLICY

The connection between the holding of elections and the formation of governments is thus more complicated than is often supposed. Even more complicated is the connection between the holding of elections and the content of public policy. Do elections affect not only the personnel of governments (as they usually do, if sometimes indirectly) but also governments' actual performance in office—the decisions they make, the policies they pursue? Putting the same question another way, does it make any difference which party or combination of parties is in power following a democratic election?

Three broad approaches to answering this question have been employed. All three rely on analysts' willingness, explicitly or implicitly (usually the latter), to construct "counterfactuals." That is, they rely on analysts' willingness to hypothesize that, if some party or combination of parties had been elected other than the one that was elected, then the content of the government's decisions and policies would, or would not, have been different from what it actually was.

The first approach may be dubbed "longitudinal." Using this approach, the analyst identifies one or more countries and one or more policy areas and asks whether, over a considerable period of time, it appears to have made any significant difference to the substance of policy which party or coalition of parties was in power. The most important recent examples of this approach are by Richard Rose and Phillip Davies *(Inheritance in Public Policy: Change without Choice in Britain,* 1994) and Hans-Dieter Klingemann, Richard Hofferbert, and Ian Budge *(Parties, Policies, and Democracy,* 1994).

Their conclusions do not directly contradict one another, but they differ significantly in emphasis. Rose and Davies, on the basis of an exhaustive study of government programs in the United Kingdom between 1945 and 1989, conclude that most British governments inherit the bulk of their programs from their predecessors in office and that the capacity of partisan administrations to effect major changes in policy, while not nonexistent, is severely restricted. The title and subtitle of their book capture the spirit of their analysis. By contrast, Klingemann, Hofferbert, and Budge, on the basis of a longitudinal study of party platforms and government performance in ten Western democracies since World War II, conclude that there is quite a close fit between the emphases of political parties' platforms and their subsequent conduct in office (whether on their own or in coalition with others). Left-wing parties, on the whole, govern in a left-wing manner, right-wing parties in a right-wing manner.

A second approach to studying the connection between election outcomes and the policies of governments may be dubbed the "promise/performance" approach. Using this approach, the analyst largely takes for granted that political parties' stated ideologies and policies will differ and asks whether the parties, once in power, do or do not fulfill their campaign promises. If the parties do fulfill their promises, then it does matter which party is in power (and the outcome of the prior election has been consequential). If not, not.

A rare example of the promise/performance approach being exploited in a sustained and rigorous manner is a study by Gerald Pomper and Susan Lederman *(Elections in America,* 1980). The authors analyzed in detail the platforms of the Democratic and Republican Parties in the United States between 1944 and 1978 and then compared the victorious party's platform pledges with its performance in office during the subsequent four years. Like Klingemann, Hofferbert, and Budge (whose study contains a promise/performance as well as a longitudinal element), Pomper and Lederman conclude that American parties in office do fulfill their campaign promises more often than not—and do so on important issues, not merely trivial ones.

A third approach may be dubbed the "correlational." Using this approach, the analyst typically takes a number of countries and a number of policy areas and sets out to identify which economic, political, demographic, or other attributes of the countries in question best account for (or "predict" in a statistical sense) the variations in policy that are observed.

Early examples of this approach (notably Phillips Cutright's "Political Structure, Economic Development, and National Social Security Programs," 1965), partly because they were based on large numbers of countries—democratic and undemocratic, advanced and backward, rich and poor—tended to suggest that economic and social factors were far more important than political factors in determining policy. However, most of these early studies not only covered extremely diverse countries (Bolivia as well as Belgium, Cuba as well as Canada), they also tended to focus on one policy area rather than others (chiefly social services and benefits) and to neglect issues of timing (so that a country that introduced, say, compulsory medical insurance in 1910 was treated exactly the same as one that did not introduce it until 1960).

However, other studies, many of them more recent, have found that politics—more specifically, the partisan coloration of the government in office—does make a difference to policy content. For example, Douglas Hibbs ("Political Parties and Macroeconomic Policy," 1977) analyzed data from twelve countries in western Europe and North America over the postwar period and found that labor and socialist governments, electorally dependent on working-class support, tended to pursue policies leading to relatively high inflation and relatively low unemployment, whereas center and conservative governments, more dependent on the middle classes, tended to pursue policies leading to lower inflation and higher unemployment. In a different policy context, Marilyn Field ("Determinants of Abortion Policy in the Developed Nations," 1979) found that, in democratic countries, there was a significant positive correlation between the presence or absence in government of leftist, noncommunist political parties and the liberality or otherwise of the countries' abortion policies.

DEFECTS OF CURRENT RESEARCH

Unfortunately, the research conducted so far on the policy effects of democratic elections has been patchy and limited in quantity. Taken as a whole, the existing work suffers from three principal defects.

The first is that a disproportionate amount of it relates to only two countries: the United States and the United Kingdom. Most of the work under the longitudinal and promise/performance headings deals with only one or the other of those two countries (though Klingemann, Hofferbert, and Budge is an exception). The correlational work is more encompassing, but, as in the case of Cutright, it suffers, if anything, from the opposite defect of taking in so many, and such different, countries that essential detail is lost. The effects of election outcomes are bound to be obscured if the comparison is between Germany and Burkina Faso or Chad. They are less likely to be obscured if the comparison is between Germany at different points in time or between Germany and other members of the European Union.

A second defect of the existing literature is that, with a few notable exceptions, like that of Field cited above, the focus is overwhelmingly on those policies of governments that can be measured in terms of public expenditure. The attractions of focusing on public expenditure are, of course, enormous. Government spending totals can be divided into different policy categories and then measured. Official data pertaining to them are usually available. Spending data can be fed with ease into analysts' equations. It is also the case that spending totals are frequently of great importance. The amount that a country's government spends on, say, retirement pensions or aid to families with dependent children is likely to affect, in the most intimate way, millions of individuals and their families (as well as providing a good indicator of past and present governmental priorities).

Nevertheless, no government's policies and decisions can be equated with the sum of its financial outlays. How much a government spends and on what it spends it are certainly important, but so are its policies on war and peace, crime and punishment, racial and gender equality, the treatment of ethnic minorities, the environment, the role of the church, abortion and contraception, civil rights, civil liberties, and, not least, constitutional issues such as the franchise and regional devolution. As it happens, issues like these have inflamed far greater political passions over the past one hundred years than issues of public expenditure. World War II certainly had vast implications for government spending, but to treat the war solely in terms of its impact on spending would be to miss the point.

A third defect of the existing literature, related to the second, is that analysts almost invariably consider the policy effects of elections—or the lack of them—without setting out their criteria for determining whether any specific effects are, or are not, to be regarded as important. They ask, for example, "Do elections matter?" without setting out the criteria by which it could be judged whether they mattered or not. A change in the level of a specific government benefit, resulting from the victory of one party over another at an election, might not loom large in the national public-expenditure totals, but it might have an enormous impact on the lives of those receiving the benefit. Judgments about the relative importance of different policies and policy areas are largely implicit in the literature. Ideally, they would be made explicit.

INERTIAL AND MALLEABLE POLICY AREAS

There seems to be a broad consensus that election outcomes may on occasion have significant policy effects, and the consensus is undoubtedly correct. In the United States the victories of Abraham Lincoln over Stephen Douglas (1860), of Franklin D. Roosevelt over Herbert Hoover (1932), and of Lyndon Johnson over Barry Goldwater (1964) were all highly consequential in policy terms. In the United Kingdom, the Liberal Party's victory in December 1910 and the Labour Party's victory in May 1997 both led to major constitutional upheavals—upheavals that would not have occurred had the Conservative Party won either election. More prosaically, Paul Pierson (*Dismantling the Welfare State?* 1994) has shown that although neither Ronald Reagan in the United States nor Margaret Thatcher in the United Kingdom succeeded in dismantling the welfare state (as both may have wished), they did succeed in scaling it back in significant ways—ways that their opponents would never have contemplated.

If it is conceded that elections may, at least on occasion, have important policy effects, the question then becomes: Under what circumstances, and in what policy areas, are elections likely to be important?

Somewhat surprisingly, political scientists have devoted little attention to trying to identify which kinds of elections are most likely to produce major policy changes (changes of the kind that would not have taken place had the other party won). It seems probable that major changes are most likely to follow elections in which the main parties' positions are polarized on one or more aspects of policy and in which one party or combination of parties succeeds in winning a decisive majority; but, since the subject has not been investigated in any systematic way, no one knows for sure. The attempt of David Brady, Charles Bullock, and Sandy Maisel ("The Electoral Antecedents of Policy Innovations," 1988) to link major changes in policy to "realigning" elections clearly succeeds in the cases of the Civil War period, the 1890s, and the Great Depression in the United States, but the authors are silent on the policy innovations of the Kennedy and Johnson eras, and they only partially succeed in extending their analysis to the United Kingdom and Ireland.

More has been written, but still not enough, about the policy fields that are most, and least, liable to radical change as a result of election outcomes. It seems reasonable to hypothesize that there are two broad types of policy area: those in which policy inertia predominates and those that are characterized by a greater degree of malleability or flexibility (that is, in which a victorious party or coalition is more likely to be able to make an immediate impact). The former area—the "zone of inertia"—seems likely to be inhabited by large spending programs that affect the well-being of large sections of the population, by much of foreign policy (with a country's vital national interests remaining more or less fixed), and by matters of constitutional policy, at least in countries like the United States where the written constitution is taken seriously. The latter area—the "zone of flexibility"—seems likely to be inhabited by matters not involving large sums of money and not threatening the personal interests of large numbers of citizens.

Unfortunately, notions like these have not been elaborated and expanded, and the impact of democratic elections on foreign policy, in particular, has been neglected. It is also true that the question of whether policy in a particular area can or cannot be changed radically—whether its character really is inertial or malleable—is a matter of judgment. A prominent British journalist asserted shortly before Thatcher was elected in May 1979 that "the balance of power in British society does not suddenly change because a new face appears in Downing Street. If the trade unions are strong now, so they will remain, whatever happens on May 3" (quoted in Richard Rose, *Do Parties Make a Difference?* 1984, p. 4). Most contemporary politicians and commentators agreed with this analysis. But they were wrong. Thatcher believed the British unions could be weakened, and she proceeded to weaken them. A seemingly inertial policy area turned out to be flexible after all.

One zone of policy that has been explored in more detail than others, but still deserves further exploration, concerns spending on major social welfare programs. Richard Rose and Terence Karran ("Inertia or Incrementalism?" 1984) maintain that, whichever party or coalition is in power, political leaders "inherit a set of commitments that have grown to their present size through the cumulative force of inertia" and that therefore governing "is principally about living with the consequences of past choices" (p. 44). Rose and Davies make the same point, specifically in connection with social welfare programs. There is no need to doubt the validity of this claim, and Klingemann, Hofferbert, and Budge, despite their general emphasis on the responsiveness of government policy to partisan control, acknowledge that there are signs in their ten-country data that policies relating to human services, such as health, education, and welfare, may be less subject to partisan

forces than policies in other domains. That said, even major human-services programs are not wholly predetermined, as Pierson has successfully shown.

What is clear is that, in a wide variety of democratic settings, election outcomes continue to have substantial effects on both the composition of governments and their substantive policies. What is less clear, and needs to be established, is the settings—in terms of both personnel and policy—in which the "reach," so to speak, of democratic election outcomes is more restricted. It may be that, in the future, a combination of international trade agreements, economic globalization, and the existence of multinational bodies like the European Union will severely limit the effective reach of democratic elections in many countries. If that were to happen, the claim that elections enabled citizens to control their governments would, in those countries, be seriously undermined.

See also *Functions of Elections; Government Formation and Election Outcomes; Second Ballot (or Runoff); Unfree Elections; Wasted Votes.*

ANTHONY KING, UNIVERSITY OF ESSEX

BIBLIOGRAPHY

Brady, David W., Charles S. Bullock III, and L. Sandy Maisel. "The Electoral Antecedents of Policy Innovations: A Comparative Analysis." *Comparative Political Studies* 20 (1988): 395–422.

Cutright, Phillips. "Political Structure, Economic Development, and National Social Security Programs." *American Journal of Sociology* 70 (1965): 537–550.

Field, Marilyn J. "Determinants of Abortion Policy in the Developed Nations." *Policy Studies Journal* 7 (1979): 771–781.

Hibbs, Douglas A., Jr. "Political Parties and Macroeconomic Policy." *American Political Science Review* 71 (1977): 1467–1487.

King, Anthony. "What Do Elections Decide?" In *Democracy at the Polls,* edited by David Butler, Howard R. Penniman, and Austin Ranney. Washington, D.C.: American Enterprise Institute, 1981.

Klingemann, Hans-Dieter, Richard I. Hofferbert, and Ian Budge. *Parties, Policies, and Democracy.* Boulder, Colo.: Westview Press, 1994.

Pierson, Paul. *Dismantling the Welfare State? Reagan, Thatcher and the Politics of Retrenchment.* Cambridge: Cambridge University Press, 1994.

Pomper, Gerald M., with Susan S. Lederman. *Elections in America: Control and Influence in Democratic Politics.* New York: Longman, 1980.

Rose, Richard. *Do Parties Make a Difference?* 2d ed. Chatham, N.J.: Chatham House, 1984.

Rose, Richard, and Terence Karran. "Inertia or Incrementalism? A Long-Term View of the Growth of Government." In *Comparative Resource Allocation: Politics, Performance, and Policy Priorities,* edited by Alexander J. Groth and Larry L. Wade. Berkeley, Calif.: Sage Publications, 1984.

Rose, Richard, and Phillip L. Davies. *Inheritance in Public Policy: Change without Choice in Britain.* New Haven, Conn.: Yale University Press, 1994.

Woldendorp, Jaap, Hans Keman, and Ian Budge. *Handbook of Democratic Government: Party Government in 20 Democracies, 1945–1990.* Dordrecht, Netherlands: Kluwer Academic, 1993.

ELECTION FINANCE

The structure of political finance and its regulation in democratic nations have undergone significant changes in the last several decades. Spurred in some cases by scandal, corruption, and the betrayal of public trust, and in others by the escalating costs of politics, many governments have enacted new laws to regulate or to alter the ways in which politics is financed. The topic has been the subject of national commissions—some public, some private—in Australia, Canada, France, Germany, Great Britain, Israel, Japan, Sweden, the United States, and other nations. Observers and participants are concerned about political financing in presidential as well as parliamentary systems, in both strong and weak party systems, and in mature as well as in developing democracies.

Scandals related to political money have led to governmental crises in countries such as Italy and Japan. In South Korea, political funding issues led to the imprisonment of two former presidents. To be sure, incredibly large monetary contributions and flagrant bribery have permeated the world of politics in most continents: Japan and South Korea in Asia; Brazil in South America; Mexico and the United States in North America; Italy, Germany, and Spain in Europe; and Israel in the Middle East.

Among the reforms that have been introduced in some countries are laws governing disclosure or transparency, expenditure and contribution limitations, and direct and indirect forms of public subsidies to political parties, candidates, and related organizations. Indirect forms of assistance include free or reduced-cost access for political broadcasting, free or reduced-cost mailings, free transportation, free space for billboards or posters, and free pamphlets carrying candidate or ballot-issue messages.

Concurrently, scholars have examined the effects of public money on political systems, the roles of both private and public funding, the relative merits of direct and indirect public funding, the effects of national election regulation on public participation, partisan alignments on the issue of public financing, high and rising campaign costs, the unanticipated consequences of legislative responses to campaign funding abuses and calls for political finance reform, the ambiguous interrelationships of local and national political financing, and the viability and stability of political systems in relation to political financing and public funding.

PRIVATE MONEY

The effort to understand the relationships between money and politics is as old as political theory. From Aristotle on, many political philosophers have regarded property or economic power as the fundamental element in politics. According to some, the attempt to reconcile economic inequalities lies at the base of the problem of money in politics. In this view, broadly based political power, such as that effected through universal suffrage, has helped mitigate the political effects of disparities in economic resources. The wealth of one small group may be matched by the human resources or voting power of a larger group.

In virtually all societies, money serves as a medium for commanding energies and resources, and it is transferable and convertible without necessarily revealing its original source. The convertibility of money is of particular advantage in politics. Money can buy goods, skills, and services. Other resources, in turn, can be converted into political money through a party's or an incumbent's advantages of public office (for example, in awarding contracts and jobs), in controlling the flow of information, and in making decisions. Skillful use of ideology, issues, and the perquisites or promises of office attracts financial support to political actors in legitimate forms as contributions or dues, or in unethical or illegitimate forms such as personal bribes.

Money is also symbolic. In this sense, money is instrumental in the deeper competition for power, prestige, or other values. Its importance lies in the ways people use it to gain influence, to convert it into other resources, or to combine it with other resources to achieve political power.

Power is distributed unequally in society. It does not vary directly with wealth, status, skill, or any other single characteristic; rather, an individual's power is determined by many such factors, no one of which stands alone and no one of which has meaning unless related to the purposes of the individual and the environment in which he or she acts. While money is only one element in the equation of political power, it is the common denominator shaping many of the factors comprising political power because it buys what is not or cannot be volunteered. Giving money permits citizens to share in the energy that must go into politics. In affluent societies, many individuals find it easier to show their support for a candidate or their loyalty to a party by writing a check than by devoting time to campaigning or other political work. Many citizens with no special talent or taste for politics will not give their time, so they use money as a substitute means of participation in a democracy.

Although money can be considered a substitute for service, it does not require so firm a commitment; for example, someone might give money to several parties, but that person is less likely to give time to more than one. Yet money has one advantage over service in that it is not loaded down with the personality or idiosyncrasies of the giver. Because of its universality, money is a tracer element in the study of political power.

GOVERNMENT MONEY

This conventional analysis of the role and impact of money, however, does not apply when its source is government or public funds. In this case the source is well known, and indirectly, the source is the taxpayers. Is money neutral when it comes from government sources? What influences are at work when the source is the government? How is government power utilized in the electoral and political arenas? Does government funding lead to more competition or less? Is equality of opportunity enhanced or diminished? To what extent is voter turnout or party participation enhanced or diminished by public funding? Although much has been written about the roles of money emanating from the private sector, little has been said about those of money derived from the public sector.

Both human and material resources are necessary to acquire, retain, and nurture political power. These resources can be purchased or volunteered, and to be used effectively, they must be organized, patterned, and channeled. When wealthy persons seek to translate their economic power into political power, one tool may be money. Individuals or groups use wealth to achieve policy goals by promoting the nomination or election of candidates and parties with views congenial to theirs. The great industrial, financial, labor, and other interests not only vie to dominate economic life but may also seek to master the political environment in many direct and indirect ways.

Government has the organization and resources. The government's power stems from the combination of the two; these elements distinguish government power from the private-sector elements that make for power. First, government sets the rules for election finance and can enforce them. When government imposes contribution or expenditure limitations, prohibits contributions from certain sources, or provides direct or indirect assistance, government is no longer a neutral factor but becomes a player affecting other players.

REGULATORY PATTERNS

Money is only one element in the equation of power. People, not dollars, vote. But money helps shape voter behavior and governmental decisions, and hence it is subject to various forms of regulation. Regulation seeks to achieve a system that

- Permits or provides enough money for vigorous, competitive campaigns

- Preserves opportunities for all citizens to participate equally

- Is open to emerging as well as established parties and to independent candidates

- Prevents corruption by freeing candidates, parties, and elected officials from undesirable or disproportionate influence of contributors;

- Frees citizens from pressure by candidates and parties to give financial support

The U.S. system has led scholars to recognize six basic forms of regulation that can be used to compare political systems around the world.

Limitations on expenditures. To meet the problems of disproportionate funding of candidates and parties and rising costs, the U.S. government has imposed limitations on expenditures. The Supreme Court, in *Buckley v. Valeo* (1976), found spending ceilings to be unconstitutional except when imposed as a condition of acceptance by the candidate of public funding. Elsewhere—except at the national level in Canada, Israel, South Korea, and a few other countries, and at the constituency level in Great Britain and Australia—spending ceilings are not favored. Where they are imposed, they often are neither observed nor easily enforced.

Restrictions on donations. To prevent candidates from obligating themselves to private interests, the United States has enacted prohibitions against accepting contributions from certain sources and has imposed ceilings on individual contributions. At the federal level, corporations, national banks, and labor unions are prohibited from contributing funds. Corporate executives and union officials, however, may contribute out of their own pockets. Labor unions, corporations, and trade associations may establish political action committees (PACs) to solicit and collect voluntary contributions from rank-and-file members and from corporate employees and stockholders, for political purposes.

PACs are organized by a corporation, labor union, trade association, or professional, agrarian, ideological, or issue group to support candidates for elective office and political parties. PACs raise funds for their activities by seeking voluntary contributions from the employees or members of their parent organization, which are pooled into larger, more meaningful amounts and then donated to favored candidates or political party committees. Essentially, PACs are a mechanism for individuals who desire to pool their contributions to support collective political activity at a level higher than any individual could achieve acting alone. The work place, professional associations, and single-issue groups have come to attract the loyalty of politically active citizens.

For certain purposes, such as registration and get-out-the-vote activities, which are considered nonpartisan in the United States, corporate and union treasury money can be used despite the ban on direct contributions; unions, in particular, spend considerable amounts from members' dues money on such activities. Moreover, federal law limits individuals from contributing more than $1,000, or political action committees from contributing more than $5,000, to any federal candidate per election. At the U.S. state level, prohibitions on individual, corporate, and labor contributions are not uniformly imposed.

In the United States, due to the relatively low contribution limits and the extent to which PACs have replaced parties as the focus of loyalty, the parties' need for financing has grown; this has led to the use of so-called soft money, given in unlimited amounts directly by corporations, labor unions, and wealthy individuals to the parties ostensibly for party-building expenses that do not affect campaigns for office and are therefore legal. Soft money has become controversial because it can be a means for subverting limitations and prohibitions.

Elsewhere in the world, prohibitions and limitations on the vested economic interests are fewer; business associations flourish as political givers; labor unions form the basis of socialist, communist, and leftist parties; and church and other groups participate directly in politics through parties they may control or influence. However, as multinational corporations grow, international trade expands, and immigration increases, countries have sought, with varying results, to restrict or prohibit contributions from foreign sources.

Prohibitions against government employee contributions. The United States has enacted laws to prevent government power from being used to solicit contributions from government employees. Individuals in all but the top policy-making positions are protected. With variations, this principle is widely followed in other countries.

Disclosure of contributions. The United States also has enacted laws requiring candidates and parties to disclose sources and amounts of campaign contributions and expenditures. The goals of such laws are to increase financial accountability by making secret funds illegal, to increase public confidence in the electoral processes, and to help curb excesses and abuses by increasing political risk for those who would undertake such practices.

In the United States, at the federal level and in most states, candidates and both party and nonparty political committees are required to disclose their funding sources on a periodic basis, before and after primary and general-election campaigns. The right of the voters to judge the candidates' sources of support, as well as their qualifications and programs, is considered essential to their choice on election day. Disclosure is the least controversial form of regulation. No country has as elaborate a disclosure agency, with administrative and enforcement functions, as the United States has in the Federal Election Commission (FEC) and certain state agencies.

Disclosure is used more sparingly or not at all in other democracies. A Swedish committee concluded in 1952 that the disclosure of the names of contributors violated the principle of secrecy of the ballot. That position continues to be widely held in Scandinavian countries. No country has put as great an emphasis on preelection reporting as has the United States, and disclosure in many democracies occurs annually or after elections, not before. In Canada, each candidate must appoint an auditor who reports to the candidate's official agent on the election expenses filed on behalf of the candidate. In Austria, Costa Rica, Israel, and Germany, the government audits the parties' use of public funds or validates expenses before additional public funds are provided. In the United States, the FEC's audits have been a subject of controversy, and the scope and tardiness of some audits have led to considerable criticism of the FEC. Some presidential candidates have had to return public funds when audits have disputed certain uses of monies.

Equality of media exposure. To prevent domination of the airwaves for partisan purposes, U.S. federal law regulating radio and television requires stations to make available equal amounts of time to rival candidates or parties. A provision was added in 1971, in an effort to control excessive charges to candidates, that broadcasters must sell political time at the lowest unit rate, the cost charged to any commercial or other favored advertiser.

Most nations with state control of television and radio provide free time to parties on government stations; most also broadcast simultaneously on all channels, including privately operated ones, and prohibit the private purchase of time by candidates or parties. These policies greatly reduce election expenditure. In Great Britain the parties voluntarily agree to air time allocations. In such systems it is mainly party leaders—cabinet officers or shadow cabinet prospects—who get on the air, not the back bencher members of parliament.

Public financing of campaigns. Historically, government financing of the political process has often been conducted in secret or indirectly to benefit the party or parties in power; use of state-controlled radio and television is just one example. Partly in response to abuses, many countries have attempted to formulate systems of public funding of elections that are open and fair. Public funding also has been instituted to give candidates or political parties alternative sources of funds and to reduce financial pressures upon them. The principle is well-established across the democratic world.

At least twenty-five countries have some form of public funding. Sweden pioneered the concept of provincial and local authorities providing subsidies to regional and local party organizations. Public funding is provided for the European Parliament elections. And in various countries, some subgovernments have established their own systems of public funding: states, cities, and localities in the United States; provinces in Canada; states in Australia; and länder in Germany and Austria, for example.

Where direct aid is not provided, some forms of indirect assistance may be made available, such as free television or radio time, free mailings, free poster space, free transportation for candidates, or tax incentives for political contributions. Since 1972 U.S. taxpayers have been able to contribute to the Presidential Election Campaign Fund (PECF) by checking a box on their federal income tax forms. In 1993 the checkoff amount was increased from $1 to $3. The rate at which taxpayers contributed through the checkoff declined from a high of 28.7 percent in 1981 to the 1996–1998 rate of about 12.5 percent. Twenty-one U.S. states enable taxpayers either to check off or add on limited political contributions through their tax payments.

In most nations with subsidies, governments fund the parties annually, not just at election time. At first, most subsidies were given in small amounts to supplement private resources already available to the political process. As the parties became large and permanent organizations, they needed constant support, and so fund raising to maintain the party organization became an ongoing concern. Government and parliamentary leaders now are involved day by day in helping sustain the parties. Permanent campaigning requires permanent fund raising, pressuring incumbents to work more and more for money for the party and to increase the amount of public funding.

Sometimes, public financing supplants individual contributions rather than those of large corporations and labor unions, whose giving is often the original target of such legislation. The reason is that individuals may feel that government has assumed primary responsibility for financing politics and therefore they need no longer give. Organized interests, whose donations are more closely tied to their lobbying activities and public policy objectives, usually continue to contribute.

The main difficulties in designing a public-funding program are who should receive the subsidy and how and when should it be made. The goal of government subsidization is to help serious contestants yet to permit challenges to those in power without supporting so many fringe candidates or parties that the electoral process is degraded. The most difficult problems in working out fair subsidies are definitional, that is, how to define major and minor parties and, in the U.S. system, how to distinguish serious from frivolous candidates seeking nomination. Any standards must be arbitrary, and certain protections should be provided to ensure that unpopular voices are heard.

DIFFERING REGULATORY CLIMATES

In some countries, such as Great Britain, spending controls are relatively effective in constituency campaigns but are nonexistent for the national parties' spending. In some countries— Canada, Germany, Israel, Japan, and Venezuela, for example— advanced campaign technology and professional management have brought high costs. Nowhere is money so available as to appear to be excessive, except in Israel and Venezuela. In part the high cost of campaigning in the United States reflects its decentralized federal system, with more popularly elected public offices per capita than any other country.

Politics is properly animated by the voluntary efforts of individuals, political parties, groups, and organizations. The new technologies and the professionalization of politics brought on in part by the laws themselves are having important consequences for voluntarism by requiring serious candidates to substitute paid experts for free, usually unskilled, help.

As campaigning has become more specialized technologically, skilled political consultants have supplanted or diminished the effectiveness of unskilled workers in an increasing number of countries, which has led to higher campaign costs. The professionalization of campaigning has led to competition in some democracies between private consultants and party operatives. Political consulting started and grew most rapidly in the United States, and U.S. consultants have been hired to run campaigns and teach their skills in countries as diverse as Canada, Great Britain, Israel, and Venezuela. The skills they offer include public opinion polls and survey work, preparing television broadcasts and spot announcements, direct mail fund raising, and, with the complexity of laws affecting campaigning, at least in the United States, election legal advice and political accountancy.

Laws regulating political finance require an agency to supervise compliance with the regulations. Most nations do not have elaborate election agencies. But the U.S. does. The FEC is a bipartisan agency consisting of six members. Commissioners serve staggered six-year terms, with a rotating one-year chairmanship. The commission receives campaign fund reports and makes them available for public inspection; makes rules and regulations (subject to congressional veto within thirty legislative days); maintains a cumulative index of reports filed and not filed; makes special and regular reports to Congress and the president; and serves as an election information clearinghouse. The commission also administers the public funding program for presidential and vice presidential elections. The commission has the power to render advisory opinions; conduct certain audits and investigations; subpoena witnesses and information; and go to court to seek civil injunctions. Criminal cases are referred by the commission to the attorney general for prosecution. Penalties vary in several sections of the law.

As the agency charged with administering and enforcing the Federal Election Campaign Act (FECA), the FEC has four major responsibilities: to provide disclosure of campaign finance information; to ensure that candidates, committees, and others comply with the limitations, prohibitions, and disclosure requirements of the FECA; to administer the public funding of presidential elections; and to serve as a clearinghouse for information on election administration.

To achieve the benefits of prompt filing of campaign information, Congress is considering requiring committees that meet a certain threshold of financial activity to file reports electronically. The FEC could receive, process, and disseminate the data from electronically filed reports more easily and efficiently than the data from hard copies, resulting in better use of commission resources. Moreover, information in the FEC's database would be standardized for committees at a certain threshold, thereby enhancing public disclosure of campaign finance information. In addition, committees participating in the electronic filing program would find it easier to complete and file reports. And opposing candidates, parties, and the public would be able to learn more rapidly the sources of funds and the expenditure allocations of the competitors.

Election commissions may be established by constitutional or statutory authority. In most cases the commissioners hold seats that are staggered by years, so that they do not all enter or leave office at once. They typically serve terms of five to seven years. In most countries with election authorities and disclosure provisions, parties but not candidates are required to file financial reports.

Levels of enforcement vary from country to country. Commissions and election officials have the responsibility to educate participants about the law and to induce compliance with the laws. In the United States, most infractions of election finance laws are civil matters, not criminal, and are considered as white-collar crime. But in some countries, such as South Korea, the sanctions can depose elected leaders and, upon conviction, imprison them.

CONCLUSION

Election finance is not neutral. Reforms are designed to minimize the effect of economic inequalities on politics by restricting the use of resources for political purposes and to maximize political equality by expanding resources to increase electoral competition. But election laws may be used by the party in power to gain advantages; the parties in opposition may accept the changes, hoping that when they are in power, they will reap the same benefits.

Even if scandal and financial stringency lie at the root of reform, belief in equality of opportunity can serve as a rationale legitimizing reform, even while the immediate beneficiaries of changes are the incumbents, their coalition partners, and the other major participants in the party system.

There can be no doubt that campaign finance regulation has brought increased probity, transparency, and a degree of equity to the monetary aspects of the campaign processes in most Western countries. The financial operations of parties are increasingly subject to public scrutiny and review. But significant reductions in the costs of campaigns and party operations have yet to be achieved, in part because of the inflation of the past decades and in part because of changes in campaign style, with the widening resort to costly professional communicators and to the electronic media. The legitimizing of public subventions also has made it easier for parties to resort to the state treasury when threatened with shortfalls.

However, little thought has been given to the secondary consequences of these reforms. Subsidy systems and their accompanying regulations may make it difficult for new groups and individuals to enter the competitive electoral struggle and may promote the ossification of the party system in certain countries. To the extent that these programs limit the entry of new competitors and parties, they may promote alienation or stimulate recourse to extraparliamentary tactics or even violent confrontation by those who may feel themselves, rightly or wrongly, excluded from the electoral process.

Many new democracies may lack a highly developed infrastructure of business federations, labor unions, and other advocacy groups from which private financing of campaigns can be drawn. But as associations and membership groups grow and a significant middle class emerges, some balance between private and public sources of funding for politics should become a reality.

See also *Administration of Elections; Campaigning; Public Aid to Parties and Candidates.*

HERBERT E. ALEXANDER, CITIZENS' RESEARCH FOUNDATION,
UNIVERSITY OF SOUTHERN CALIFORNIA EMERITUS

BIBLIOGRAPHY

Alexander, Herbert E. *Financing Politics: Money, Elections and Political Reform.* 4th ed. Washington, D.C.: CQ Press, 1992.

Alexander, Herbert E., and Rei Shiratori. *Comparative Political Finance Among the Democracies.* Boulder, Colo.: Westview Press, 1994.

Alexander, Herbert E., ed. *Comparative Political Finance in the 1980s.* Cambridge: Cambridge University Press, 1989.

Gunlicks, Arthur B., ed. *Campaign and Party Finance in North America and Western Europe.* Boulder, Colo.: Westview Press, 1993.

Lord Neil of Bladen, chair. *Standards in Public Life: Defunding of Political Parties in the United Kingdom.* London: The Stationery Office, cm 4057, 1998.

Sorauf, Frank J. *Inside Campaign Finance: Myths and Realities.* New Haven, Conn.: Yale University Press, 1992.

———. *Money in American Elections.* Boston: Scott, Foresman, 1988.

ELECTION FORECASTING

Any discussion of election forecasting must begin by asking: What is the purpose? Is election forecasting an end in itself, or a means of validating an analysis? Analysis focuses on general patterns and on understanding the broad, general causes that underlie them. It discounts the specific. For analysis, what matters is whether economic prosperity generally helps governments get reelected, rather than whether economic prosperity will determine the outcome of the next election in a particular country. When forecasting is the objective, what matters is the next election, not elections in general.

There is a place for long-, medium-, and short-term forecasts. Television networks want forecasts on election night, after the close of voting but before the votes have been counted. The press wants election-eve forecasts, even though voters may change their minds at the last minute. There is enormous interest in medium- to short-term forecasts all the way through the "horse-race" of an election campaign. And less widespread is elite interest in long-term forecasts; immediately after one election, politicians on all sides want to know whether it would be wise to plan for a "two-term" government. We might expect election-night forecasts to be more accurate than election-eve forecasts. And all of these short-term forecasts should be more accurate than long-term forecasts.

Long- and short-term forecasts differ in their nature as well as in their accuracy. Short-term forecasting is usually "black box" forecasting—in essence, persistence forecasting, possibly modified by unexplained (and possibly inexplicable) regional patterns or recurrent short-term trends. It is unconditional.

Long-term forecasting is usually based on a model of interrelationships between voting preferences and such factors as economic prosperity at home or peace abroad. It has a conditional rather than an unconditional character—forecasting the government's reelection "if and only if" these conditions hold. The perennial problem with such long-term forecasting is that these interrelationships are both weak and variable.

ELECTION-EVE FORECASTING

American political scientist William Buchanan noted in 1986 that pollsters had been publishing national election forecasts for fifty years. Pollsters typically took a sample of public opinion as near to the election as possible and predicted no change between their poll and the vote. Buchanan examined 155 such forecasts in 68 elections covering 10 countries. The pollsters had an 85 percent success rate in picking the winner, but their errors in predicting vote percentages were much larger than statistical theory would indicate, and there was no evidence of any improvement in accuracy over time. When they erred, they tended to err together. At the 1970 British general election, for example, four of the five main polls did not pick the winner.

Polls differ from textbook prescriptions for simple random sampling in many ways—heavily clustered random sampling, later superseded by quota sampling, and telephone sampling, all of which have their advantages but also their defects. Voters themselves are unable to predict accurately whether they will turn out to vote, and many change their mind shortly before voting—a phenomenon known as "late swing."

Election-eve forecasts at the British general election of 1992 were so bad that the Market Research Society commissioned a special inquiry, which concluded they were worse than in any previous election. On average, the four leading polls got the Conservative lead wrong by over 8 percent. The inquiry attributed the error to a combination of late swing, inaccurate target quotas, and a differential tendency of Conservatives to refuse to answer or to give a "don't know" response.

ELECTION-NIGHT FORECASTING

After the close of voting, forecasts can be based on "exit polls" taken as voters leave the voting stations. Exit-poll forecasts are usually available within minutes of the close of voting. In principle they should be very accurate, since nonvoters are excluded, votes once cast cannot be changed, and voters are conveniently accessible. Unfortunately, very large numbers refuse to disclose their vote.

As votes are counted and real but partial results become available, a forecast of the complete result can be based on a combination of the polling evidence and these incomplete results. In Britain the BBC-TV forecast has usually been based on a combination of exit polls and the declared constituency results, weighting the exit polls as equivalent to about three actual constituency results.

Complex election-night forecasting procedures allow for the possibility of regional and other variations in swing, both in the design of the exit poll and in the projection from constituency results already declared. In practice too, special allowance is usually made for constituencies with returns so unusual that no general prediction scheme could reasonably be projected either to or from them.

SHORT- AND MEDIUM-TERM FORECASTING

In the slightly longer term, opinion polls may be supplemented by second-order election results—by-elections, local elections, midterm U.S. congressional elections, or German *länder* elections, for example—which are more "real" tests of public opinion than polls. But these need careful interpretation, since voters are volatile. In anything other than election-eve polls or election-night forecasts, polls (and other indicators of public opinion) can never be used without some allowance of the possibility of change. Widespread industrial unrest during the 1979 "Winter of Discontent" led to a sudden and massive swing against the Labour government. The 1982 invasion of the Falklands provoked a surge of support for Prime Minister Margaret Thatcher. And after she had outstayed her welcome, her resignation turned a 16 percent Labour lead into a 20 percent Conservative lead between the second and last week of November 1990.

Such events are difficult to predict, though their consequences may be easy to foresee. But other short-term trends may be anticipated. During the last few weeks before a British election, the third party (currently Liberal Democrats) usually gains support as it receives more equal treatment by the media. Generally, governments gain ground during the year preceding an election. They can manipulate the real economy, the presentation of official statistics, tax rates, and even media coverage. This regular swing toward the government should be distinguished from any of its particular causes. Government activity is goal-directed, aiming to do whatever is required to win reelection. If one strategy fails, the government can try another. The true constant is not the influence of any particular factor on public opinion, but the government's constant aim to get reelected by whatever means lie within its power.

Consequently, a medium-term forecast would usually modify current indicators of public opinion by incorporating some estimate of the expected trend toward the government before election day. After the debacle of 1992, some British pollsters—notably ICM—incorporated adjustments into their raw figures, before publication, to allow for some swing back to the government before the next election. At certain points these adjustments reduced the published opposition lead by as much as 15 percent. Even so, ICM's heavily adjusted figures still revealed some trend back to the government as the 1997 election approached.

LONG-TERM FORECASTING

Long-term forecasting must inevitably be conditional. Most frequently, it has been based on the state of the economy, measured in a variety of ways. Many studies in different countries have found that incumbents of the left as well as the right are reelected when the economies are healthy. And fitting statistical models to sequences of elections or to trends in monthly opinion polls has provided useful insight into the connection between the economy and government popularity.

Unfortunately, such model-building has shown beyond doubt that the connection is neither very strong nor very sta-

ble. Models fitted to sequences of elections are based on so few data-points that the statistical "confidence intervals" around forecasts are large. The best known economic models of U.S. presidential outcomes not only failed in some cases to pick the 1992 winner but typically made forecasts with confidence intervals that included both a narrow victory for one side and a landslide for the other. With elections every four years, models fitted to sequences of monthly opinion polls can fit forty-seven out of every forty-eight data-points without getting any election-time poll—let alone the actual election—right. In essence, they are fitted to the wrong universe.

Bill Clinton's famous campaign reminder—"it's the economy, stupid"—is too simplistic by half. Something about the economy often seems relevant to the election outcome, but frequently it is something different from what had seemed so important in the past. "The economy" covers everything from taxes, inflation, unemployment, balance of payments, budget deficits, and levels and trends of prosperity to more elusive, psychological, and contestable variables like "confidence." Clinton himself defeated the incumbent in 1992 against a background of reasonably good economic conditions and a remarkably low-cost victory in the Gulf War. Seymour Martin Lipset (in "In Focus: The 1992 Election," p. 7) explains the failure of economy-based forecasts in 1992 by noting that "people thought conditions were worse than they were."

Yet even economic optimism is insufficient. In 1997 the British Conservative government was decisively defeated against a background of better economic conditions than when it won in 1992, and despite a resurgence of economic optimism prior to the election.

Of course, it is always possible after the event to explain the failure of economic models and to construct new ones that perform better at predicting all past elections, including the most recent. That may advance our knowledge and understanding of the past but it does not increase our confidence in forecasting the future.

FORECASTING IN MULTIPARTY AND FIRST-PAST-THE-POST SYSTEMS

It is at least plausible to suppose that voters reward governments for economic or other successes and punish them for failure. But there is no plausible reason why voters who wish to punish the government for its failures should switch to one opposition party rather than another. Economic models have little or nothing to say about which opposition party will benefit most from government failures. And yet the division of support between opposition parties in a first-past-the-post electoral system can mean the difference between the government suffering a humiliating defeat or being reelected by a landslide.

In a first-past-the-post system, *where* votes for a party are cast is important as well as how many. That affects the "gearing" between votes and seats, which was expressed in Britain for so long in the "cube law": the ratio of Conservative to Labour members of Parliament is the cube of the ratio of Conservative to Labour voters (though a "square law" would better approximate reality now). But where the votes are cast affects more than gearing: in Britain in 1951 and February 1974, the party with the most votes was not the one that got the most seats and formed the government. Gearing in U.S. presidential elections is even stronger, but the electoral college has not overturned the popular vote since 1888, when Benjamin Harrison lost the popular vote to Grover Cleveland but won a decisive 58.1 percent of the electoral vote. So although forecasts of the membership of the electoral college are particularly inaccurate, their inaccuracy is unimportant.

The cube law was replaced by the concept of "uniform national swing" (and later by "uniform within-region, or uniform within-category swings"). Uniform national swing assumes that the change in each party's percentage will be approximately constant across all types of constituency. The size of that change can be estimated by comparing a current national opinion poll with the previous national election result. Forecasts based on uniform swing preserve the idiosyncrasies of individual constituencies while taking account of trends. But swings are less uniform than they were. Despite an extremely accurate national exit poll in 1987, ITN forecast a Conservative majority of 68 MPs, when it turned out to be 102. Conversely, a uniform swing in 1992 would have given Prime Minister John Major a majority of 71, instead of the narrow margin of 21 that he received, which left him unable to discipline his maverick backbenchers and led to the indecisiveness that contributed to his landslide defeat in 1997.

First-past-the-post systems not only respond to the spatial distribution of votes but also influence that distribution. Many people do not vote their preferences. They switch from a "no hope" first preference to an "acceptable" second preference in hope of defeating an "unacceptable" third preference within their constituency. And they often make such tactical switches very close to election day or even on election day. Without changing the overall national party percentages, tactical switching between a pair of political allies can greatly improve the number of seats they jointly win in parliament. In 1997 the Conservatives lost as many as thirty-five seats through an intensification of Labour/Liberal tactical voting. Practical forecasting methods must distinguish the "tactical situation," for example, on the Conservative/Labour divide (where these are the top two parties), the Conservative/Liberal divide, and the Conservative/Scottish Nationalist divide.

CONCLUSION

The most accurate and reliable forecasts are short-term forecasts, essentially "black box" forecasts that do little more than convert a current opinion poll (updated perhaps by partial election results) into a forecast of the final and complete result of tomorrow's—or even yesterday's—election. In essence, they are based on little more than persistence forecasting. The most illuminating are long-term, conditional forecasts that are based on models of the relationship between events, economic conditions, foreign policy successes, and public opinion. These are less accurate because long-run tendencies are overlaid by powerful and unique short-term "disturbances" and because models that fit the past do not always fit the future, even when short-term disturbances are excluded. Voters "shift the goalposts" too much and too often. The epitaph of election forecasters must surely be the insight attributed to Joseph Stalin as he negotiated plans for the postwar order in Europe: "the trouble with democratic elections is that you can never be sure about the result."

See also *Bandwagon Effects; Cube Law; Exit Polls; Public Aid to Parties and Candidates; Public Opinion Polls: How They Work; Public Opinion Polls: Legal Regulations; Realigning Elections in the United States; Swing; Tactical Voting.*

WILLIAM L. MILLER, GLASGOW UNIVERSITY

BIBLIOGRAPHY

Buchanan, William. "Election Predictions: An Empirical Assessment." *Public Opinion Quarterly* 50 (summer 1986): 222–227.

Butler, David, and Dennis Kavanagh. *The British General Election of 1997.* London: Macmillan, 1997.

Crewe, Ivor. *Forecasting Election Results.* Manchester: Manchester Statistical Society, 1990.

Lipset, Seymour Martin, et al. "In Focus: The 1992 Election." *PS: Political Science and Politics* 26 (March 1993): 7–31.

Market Research Society Committee, chaired by David Butler. *The Opinion Polls and the 1992 General Election: A Report to the Market Research Society.* London: Market Research Society, 1994.

Mitofsky, Warren J. "A Short History of Exit Polls." In *Polling and Presidential Election Coverage,* edited by Paul J. Lavrakas and Jack K. Holley, 83–99. Newbury Park, Calif.: Sage, 1991.

Payne, Clive, Philip Brown, and Vincent Hanna. "By-Election Exit Polls." *Electoral Studies* 5, no. 3 (December 1986): 277–287.

Sanders, David. "Economic Performance, Management Competence and the Outcome of the Next General Election." *Political Studies* 44, no. 2 (June 1996): 203–231.

———. "The New Electoral Battleground." In *New Labour Triumphs: Britain at the Polls,* edited by Anthony King, 209–248. Chatham, N.J.: Chatham House, 1998.

ELECTION STUDIES, TYPES OF

The major topics covered under the heading of election studies are the conduct of election campaigns; analysis of aggregate election results; and the behavior of voters. Collectively, these are sometimes described as *psephology,* a term derived from the Greek word for pebble, as in ancient Greece pebbles were used instead of paper ballots. Election studies have been conducted on every continent about every kind of election, unfree as well as free, and have been undertaken by scholars in every branch of the social sciences and by historians.

THE CONDUCT OF ELECTION CAMPAIGNS

Election campaigns are public events, and therefore are easy to observe. There are written accounts of elections dating back to Greek and Roman times, and before society was literate, William Hogarth produced a scathing report on bribery, fraud, and violence in four engravings of a mid-eighteenth century English election. Prior to the introduction of the secret ballot, political organizers could keep records of how each person voted; analyses of these records are the oldest studies of voting behavior. The free press and, for the last half-century, television have provided day-to-day accounts of election campaigns. However, journalistic accounts do not paint a coherent portrait of a campaign as a whole, and they can be partisan or selective. Moreover, they tend to focus on personalities and "inside" stories and often fail to analyze election results and voting behavior. For example, Theodore White, in his breathless account of the 1960 election, *The Making of the President,* was so taken with John F. Kennedy's personality that he failed to explain why Kennedy failed to get half the popular vote.

The academic study of election campaigns as contemporary history was launched by R.B. McCallum at Nuffield College, Oxford University, with a study of the 1945 British general election. When McCallum sought a name to describe this type of election study, an Oxford classical scholar suggested psephology, as the ancient Athenians voted by dropping a pebble into an urn. The term has caught on, in Britain at least, as a phrase to describe or to satirize the analysis of elections. A Nuffield College study has appeared after every British election since, with David E. Butler a contributor or the senior author of each. Since 1959 each Nuffield study has contained chapters describing the preparations of the parties in the years leading up to the election, drawing on confidential interviews with major participants; a description of events

during the campaign; chapters reporting opinion polls, media coverage, and social characteristics of candidates; and an appendix with detailed statistical analysis of the results.

Scholars have applied the Nuffield approach across five continents, including studies of early elections in Africa, the Middle East, and Southeast Asia. They have also used it as a model for studying early twentieth-century elections, with the reading of private papers of politicians and party files substituted for personal interviews. The approach has not been applied in the United States due to the duration of the campaign; the dispersion of effort across a continent (as opposed to its concentration in London); and the fact that many offices—federal, state, and local—are at stake in a presidential election year.

In the early 1970s Howard Penniman at the American Enterprise Institute in Washington, D.C., developed a variant of the Nuffield approach in the "Democracy at the Polls" series of books. In fifteen years the institute produced more than two dozen books about elections in Europe, North America, South America, Latin America, Asia, and India. Each volume introduced readers to the party system of a country as well as described the events of a particular campaign—which was an advantage for Anglophone readers since the subjects were as varied as Greece, Israel, Japan, and Venezuela. Each volume had a number of authors; consistency within and among books was maintained by Penniman's editorship. The series also included cross-national analyses of different elements of the electoral process.

ANALYSIS OF AGGREGATE ELECTION RESULTS

The analysis of aggregate election results at the national level usually involves trend analysis. Scholars concentrate on changes in party votes between two successive elections or on the long-term stability or volatility in the vote for particular political parties, both of which are influenced by changes in socioeconomic conditions, alterations in electoral systems or franchise laws, or other factors. Cross-national comparison of national results can be used to test generic hypotheses or to see whether patterns in a single country reflect nation-specific or more general influences. The publication by Tom Mackie and Richard Rose of national election results for twenty-five countries from their first nationwide competitions has greatly facilitated such comparisons.

Because election results are invariably published at the constituency level or for smaller geographical subdivisions and show variations in voting, geographers were pioneers in relating election results to the aggregate socioeconomic conditions recorded in censuses. André Siegfried published a pioneering geographical analysis of voting in France in 1913, and his approach spread during the interwar period. Siegfried's approach was to produce maps showing how the votes of parties differed from place to place and to offer explanations for the observed geographical differences. German and American scholars began to undertake ecological analysis of voting in the 1920s, correlating statistically the social and economic characteristics of a district with its voting patterns. Electoral geography is particularly suitable to historical analysis, since census data about the socioeconomic characteristics of constituencies are available for elections held decades or even a century before surveys of individual voters were introduced. For example, William Miller used this method to analyze the transformation of the two-party British system of 1918 into a three-party system and back into a different two-party system by 1970. The development of high-speed computers and geo-coding to map statistical data onto small-scale geographical units, such as a census enumeration district or precinct, makes possible much more sophisticated analysis than approaches relying on simple maps.

The geographical approach has practical value to political parties. Parties can use data about the socioeconomic characteristics and voting history of a district to target specific campaign appeals. When constituencies are redistricted to adjust for population movement, parties can seek to maximize their electoral advantage by arguing for redrawing constituency boundaries to their partisan advantage.

Ecological analysis of voting is limited, however, since the data refer to a collection of voters, statements about individuals can only be inferences. In the classic example of the American deep South, the vote for white supremacist candidates correlated with a high percentage of blacks in a district, since blacks were not allowed to vote. In a more sophisticated use of ecological analysis, scholars emphasize that clustering people with particular individual characteristics in a constituency has a spatial effect above and beyond their individual characteristics. For example, two people similar in education, income, and other characteristics might vote differently if one lived in a racially mixed neighborhood while the other lived in an all-black or all-white district.

BEHAVIOR OF VOTERS

The infrastructure for studying individual voters by sample survey methods began to develop in the 1930s in market research companies and in a few university-based research institutes. The first scientific sample survey study of a major election was undertaken by Paul Lazarsfeld and his colleagues at Columbia University during the 1940 American presidential campaign. They repeated their study in the 1944 campaign, and their work was followed up in Britain in 1950. These studies were undertaken by sociologists and tended to emphasize the influence of social class on voting.

The second wave of voting studies started almost by accident; a 1948 University of Michigan survey on nonelectoral matters included a question about presidential voting that accurately predicted the outcome of the presidential race, which public opinion polls had failed to do. The survey team followed up with specially designed studies of the 1952 and 1956 elections, analyzed in a landmark book, *The American Voter*. The Michigan model of voting is social-psychological, emphasizing the party identification that individuals develop through a long-term process of intergenerational socialization. An individual's vote at a particular election will be consistent with the direction and strength of party identification, subject to modification by the short-term attraction of particular candidates and the salience of specific issues. Researchers have examined stability and change in party identification between elections through panel surveys of voters, interviewing the same individuals at two different elections to see what kind of voters change their behavior and why. Researchers also have studied, by means of cross-level surveys of congressional candidates and voters in the same district, the extent to which candidates and voters agree on issues. The match between voters' and candidates' views is usually significant but far from complete—if only because the thousands of people who vote for a candidate may disagree with each other on some issues.

The Michigan model has become dominant in studies of American voting, since most American studies rely heavily on the Michigan-based National Election Study for data about individual voters. Scholars in other countries have adopted the Michigan model for national election surveys, starting in Scandinavia and spreading throughout Europe and to Australia and Japan. The model has broad appeal and durability because of its generality; it focuses attention on survey data that concern long-term attachments as well as current issues. It asks individuals what their attitudes are, rather than just drawing inferences from their income, gender, class, or race. The Michigan model is not a theory for use in predicting how individuals vote. The relative importance of party identification, candidates, and issues is left for researchers to determine through the statistical analysis of empirical data.

The utility of the Michigan model in American elections has been challenged on many grounds. Although party identification has consistently favored the Democrats, the Republican candidate has won seven of twelve presidential elections since 1952, and Democratic presidential candidates have won half the vote in only two of thirteen elections since the end of World War II. The scale of split-ticket voting in American elections raises questions about whether a voter identifies with a local or a national party or has two different sets of identifications. Outside the United States, some scholars argue that party identification is tautological in a political system in which there are no party primaries requiring registration of a party affiliation and an individual has only one vote for a list in proportional representation or for a candidate in a single-member parliamentary constituency. Such conditions, they contend, make "identification" and "voting" virtually synonymous. Moreover, the Michigan model's downplaying of social-structure influences is inappropriate in countries where religion, language, or ethnicity are major cleavages influencing party formation and electoral choice.

The profusion of economic theories of voting and the accessibility of aggregate economic as well as political data have encouraged some social scientists to correlate monthly or quarterly economic data about inflation, unemployment, economic growth, and so forth with the results of monthly opinion polls of voter preferences. Strictly speaking, such efforts are studies not of elections but of fluctuations in the preferences of voters between elections.

CROSS-NATIONAL STUDIES

The systematic comparison of voting behavior across countries and continents emphasizes variations in features that are taken for granted within a particular national context. Elements that are constants within one country, such as the electoral laws or language, become variables in cross-national analysis. Seymour Martin Lipset pioneered the comparative analysis of electoral behavior in a series of journal articles collected in *Political Man*. Richard Rose published the first systematic cross-national comparison of voting behavior, across more than a dozen countries, with a single table showing the relative importance of class, religion, and region within a country and comparing the importance of these influences across fifteen countries.

The different approaches to electoral studies outlined above are not mutually exclusive. For example, academic studies following in the "Democracy at the Polls" tradition now appear from a multiplicity of authors who analyze parties and campaigning, election results, and voting behavior. In the case of elections in novel contexts—for example, postcommunist societies—a multimethod approach is essential in order to understand what is happening, as Stephen White, Richard Rose, and Ian McAllister illustrate in *How Russia Votes*.

See also *Campaigning; Founding Elections; Political Business Cycle; Public Opinion Polls; Swing; Unfree Elections; Volatility, Electoral; Voting Behavior, Influences on.*

RICHARD ROSE, UNIVERSITY OF STRATHCLYDE

BIBLIOGRAPHY

Bartolini, Stefano, and Peter Mair. *Identity, Competition and Electoral Availability: The Stabilisation of European Electorates, 1885–1985.* Cambridge: Cambridge University Press, 1990.

Budge, Ian, Ivor Crewe, and Dennis Farlie, eds. *Party Identification and Beyond.* New York: John Wiley, 1976.

Butler, D.E., Howard R. Penniman, and Austin Ranney. *Democracy at the Polls: A Comparative Study of Competitive National Elections.* Washington, D.C.: American Enterprise Institute, 1981.

Campbell, Angus, Philip E. Converse, Warren E. Miller, and Donald E. Stokes. *The American Voter.* New York: John Wiley, 1960.

Lazarsfeld, Paul, Bernard Berelson, and Hazel Gaudet. *The People's Choice.* New York: Duell, Sloan and Pearce, 1944.

LeDuc, Lawrence, Richard G. Niemi, and Pippa Norris, eds. *Comparing Democracies: Elections and Voting in Global Perspective.* Thousand Oaks, Calif.: Sage Publications, 1996.

Lipset, Seymour Martin. *Political Man.* New York: Doubleday, 1960.

Mackie, Tom, and Richard Rose. *The International Almanac of Electoral History.* 3d ed. London: Macmillan; and Washington, D.C.: CQ Press, 1991.

Miller, William L. *Electoral Dynamics in Britain since 1918.* London: Macmillan, 1977.

Rose, Richard, ed. *Electoral Behavior: A Comparative Analysis.* New York: Free Press, 1974.

Siegfried, André. *Tableau Politique de la France de l'Ouest.* Paris: Armand Colin, 1913.

Silbey, Joel H., Allan G. Bogue, and William H. Flanigan. *The History of American Electoral Behavior.* Princeton, N.J.: Princeton University Press, 1978.

Taylor, P.J., and R.J. Johnston. *Geography of Elections.* Harmondsworth, England: Penguin, 1979.

White, Stephen, Richard Rose, and Ian McAllister. *How Russia Votes.* Chatham, N.J.: Chatham House, 1997.

ELECTIONS IN DEVELOPING COUNTRIES

Elections in developing countries are distinguished from elections in established democracies in three fundamental ways. First, they usually (though not always) occur in new and fragile democracies where neither electoral practice nor democratic practice broadly defined are institutionalized features of national political life. Second, they occur in "low income" and "lower-middle income" countries—countries that the World Bank classifies as those where annual per capita income is under $785 and between $785 and $3,125, respectively. Slightly more than one-third of the world's six billion people live in low-income countries, while another third inhabit countries in the lower-middle category. Third, they occur within the context of agrarian societies and plural societies rather than in the context of industrial and postindustrial societies. Between 60 and 90 percent of the population in these countries reside in the rural areas; most of these people are poor farmers. The population is usually (though not always) divided among two or more ethnic, linguistic, and/or religious groups whose members inhabit a distinct homeland. The territorial space of these countries is consequently a cultural mosaic where most members of each group reside in different areas, maintain separate group identities, and rarely come into sustained contact with the members of other groups.

THE ELECTORAL EXPERIENCE IN EMERGING DEMOCRACIES

Compared with elections in the industrial democracies, elections in developing countries have yet to become an institutionalized and uninterrupted feature of political life. The experience with elections, however, varies greatly across the roughly eighty to one hundred countries that constitute the developing world. Since the mid-1970s, and especially during the last decade of the twentieth century, all but a handful of developing countries have held multiparty elections to choose their national governments—some for the third or fourth time.

Elections in most developing countries are not a new phenomenon. Rather, they are best understood as a frequently interrupted process that reflects the difficulties in establishing democratic polities in societies where the conditions for democracy are poor. In Latin America the experience with elections and elected government dates back to the nineteenth century, but it was not until the mid-1980s that the holding of "free and fair" elections at regular intervals became an institutionalized process. Prior to that time, elected governments alternated with military regimes that had seized power before elections could be repeated to sustain civilian rule. With the significant exceptions of Mexico and Costa Rica, every Latin American country has experienced an interruption in its electoral cycle by military coup. Yet while elections have been held in Mexico every six years since the 1920s, the domination of the process by the ruling party until the early 1990s meant that elections were exercises in ratifying the nominees of the Institutional Revolutionary Party (PRI) rather than contests that offered voters a real choice of government.

The electoral experience in Africa and Asia has been more varied. Virtually all of the countries on these two continents are former colonial territories that became independent states between 1947 and 1964. Multiparty elections were not held to determine the government of these countries until a few months before independence, as part of their transition to self-rule. However, the British introduced electoral practice into their colonies as early as the end of the nineteenth century and during the first years of the twentieth as a mechanism to facilitate colonial rule. This took the form of elections for a limited number of seats in a legislative council, a quasi-legislature consisting of members appointed by the colonial governor and elected members to advise the colonial government but which had no final authority to govern. The British also introduced electoral practice for the purpose of electing legislative councils at the provincial level as well as for councils at the district level. The electorate for these early elections was initially restricted to persons of property or education. For example, in India in 1919, only six million out of a total population of 245 million were granted the vote for legislative councils at the provincial level. In 1935 the franchise was extended to 35 million out of a total population of approximately 293 million, barely a quarter of the adult population. Universal suffrage did not come until independence. In some colonies, elections for some seats were carried out on an indirect basis to moderate the influence of the electorate.

The British also made use of communal rolls, which were separate registers for voters of different religious or racial communities to guarantee the election of a minimum number of representatives for each group. For example, in the 1930s in India, separate communal rolls were established for Hindu and Muslim voters. In Kenya the practice was used to guarantee representation for European and Asian communities in the 1950s. Separate voter rolls were established for African and European voters in Rhodesia during the 1960s, a practice that was continued for ten years after the country became the independent state of Zimbabwe in 1980. Although communal rolls were established to protect the rights of minorities, their use usually resulted in the overrepresentation of these groups; that is to say, their proportion of seats in the national legislature greatly exceeded their proportion of the total vote by all groups.

Electoral practice and experimentation were more extensive in Britain's former colonies than those of the other major colonial powers. Spain and Portugal, then under dictatorial rule, did not hold elections in their respective colonies. Belgium held no elections in the Congo prior to that country's independence in 1960. France did not hold elections in its African colonies until 1946, when elections were first held for twenty representatives to the French National Assembly. Elections within each colony for its own national legislature were not held until a short time before independence in 1960.

Whether a colony had a long, albeit restricted experience with elections or the electoral experience was limited to pre-independence polls, the design and structure of electoral systems in the former colonies continues to bear the imprint of the former colonial overlord. This is particularly true in the former British colonies; nearly all of these countries continue to elect their legislatures from single-member districts based on the "first-past-the-post" formula. The party or candidate gaining a plurality or more of the vote is elected. The present electoral systems of the former French colonies are more varied. Nearly two-fifths have adopted the current French practice of the "two-round" system, where legislators are elected from single-member districts but there is a second-round runoff election between the top two candidates if no candidate obtains a majority of votes in the first round. Only three former French colonies utilize some form of proportional representation, although five currently have parallel systems that combine PR and some form of district-based representation.

Electing representatives from single-member districts, either by plurality or majority vote, defines political accountability in reference to the residents of a particular geographic area and community. This is particularly true in the context of agrarian societies, as discussed later in this essay. Single-member districts also tend to inflate the proportion of seats won by the party wining the most votes overall. Because most countries in Africa and Asia are former British and French colonies, election from single-member districts is the most common practice on the two continents. In marked contrast, all but one Latin American country (Belize) elect their legislatures according to some form of list proportional representation, a practice that makes legislators accountable to the leadership of their political party rather than to the inhabitants of a particular region or community.

The elections held in Africa and Asia immediately before independence usually resulted in a large parliamentary majority for the political party that embodied the nationalist movement. Most former colonies therefore became independent as "one-party dominant" states, a situation that soon led to an inexorable drift into authoritarian rule. Small opposition parties were often pressured to merge into the ruling party or were suppressed. This tendency was particularly pronounced in Africa, where a number of countries amended their constitutions during the late 1960s and early 1970s to define the political system as a one-party state. Elections ceased to be held or became exercises to ratify the unopposed nominees of the ruling party. Not surprisingly, voter turnout in these elections declined over time, often to less than a quarter of the electorate.

In an interesting subset of one-party states, most notably Kenya, Tanzania, and the Ivory Coast, elections continued on a "semi-competitive" basis. Under this practice, elections were transformed into primary elections in which two or more candidates competed for the nomination of the ruling party. Primary elections maintained a measure of electoral accountability as approximately half of the incumbent legislators who stood for reelection typically lost. In these elections, voters exercised their option to change their representatives but could not change their government. Voter turnout in these countries was substantially higher than in one-party states where there were no contests, but it rarely exceeded 50 percent.

In a few countries, such as Nigeria and Uganda, the nationalist movement became divided between parties representing different regions and ethnic groups with the result that no single party won a commanding victory in the prein-

dependence elections. However, democratic practice fared no better in these countries than in those that became one-party states. Weak governments suppressed opposition parties, or civilian rule was terminated by military coup. In some countries, such as Ghana and Guinea, the drift into one-party rule was followed by military coup. In still others, for example Bangladesh, Pakistan, Ghana, and Nigeria, elected governments alternated with military regimes. Only in India, the world's most populous democracy, and in a handful of very small countries such as Botswana and Mauritius, has there been an uninterrupted series of multiparty elections since independence. Only in India have these elections resulted in an alternation of the party in power.

This tortuous experience with electoral politics and democratic governance in developing countries began to change during the 1980s as part of what is often referred to as the "third wave" of democratization—the worldwide transition from authoritarian to nominal democratic rule in approximately seventy countries since 1975. This process, which requires the introduction or reintroduction of multiparty elections, began in southern Europe, Argentina, and Brazil during the mid-1970s. It continued next in eastern Europe, most notably in Poland, and in South Korea, Taiwan, Thailand, and the Philippines in the mid-1980s. Although none of these countries were low-income countries, their transitions were soon replicated in the poorest countries of Latin America, across Africa (except in the Congo, Somalia, and Sudan), and among the remaining countries of Asia (except Afghanistan, Burma, China, Laos, North Korea, Vietnam, and Indonesia). By the end of the 1980s, every country in Latin America except Mexico had held multiparty elections at the national level. By the end of the 1990s, all African countries except Somalia and the Democratic Republic of the Congo (formerly Zaire) had held elections. Only in the Middle East has the introduction of multiparty elections occurred in no more than a handful of states (for example, Egypt, Lebanon, Jordan, Tunisia), and even in those countries on a restricted basis.

A fundamental lesson from these third-wave elections is that elections are a necessary but insufficient component of democracy. Whereas the establishment of democratic governance is impossible without the regular holding of multiparty elections in which voters are given a choice between leaders of alternative governments, the mere holding of such elections does not guarantee democracy. Students of democratic transitions therefore distinguish between democratic *transitions,* as marked by the holding of a "founding," or first, multiparty election, and the *consolidation* of democracy, as achieved by a more complex configuration of phenomena. Some scholars, such as Samuel P. Huntington, argue that democratic consolidation requires that a country pass what he calls the "two-turnover" electoral test—the regular holding of a series of elections in which the party that wins the first election and forms the government loses a later (though not necessarily the next) election and relinquishes power. The party that dislodged the winner of the first election is then in turn defeated in a later election. Passage of the two-turnover electoral test may take several decades. For example, in India this double alternation of government did not occur until 1980, thirty-three years after independence.

Most third-wave democratizers in Africa and Asia have yet to pass Huntington's test because it requires not only the holding of more than one election, but the holding of a series of elections that result in an alternation of government and, more fundamentally, in the willingness of the losers to play by the rules and accept defeat. Such willingness, however, requires that the electoral process be perceived by all contestants as "free and fair," that is, that all contestants believe that they had a genuine opportunity to compete for voter support and win the contest.

Whether a country passes the two-turnover test is closely linked to another dimension of democratic consolidation—what Juan Linz and Alfred Stepan argue is the establishment of a society-wide belief that democracy is "the only game in town." Elections become an institutionalized mechanism for determining who will rule once there is a popular consensus that there is no other legitimate procedure for doing so. Until such a consensus is reached, elections are likely to be marred by irregularities in procedure or to be exercises that produce outcomes that are not accepted by key political factions. The repeated attempts by authoritarian rulers in Africa to manipulate the electoral process to their advantage is an illustration of the problem. Thus, while forty countries on the continent held founding multiparty elections, and in some instances second elections, during the 1990s, incumbent parties "won" more than two-thirds of these contests. No African country can yet be classified as a consolidated democracy. This is not merely because an insufficient number of elections have been held to permit any country to pass the two-turnover test. Rather, the continued abuse of presidential power, the ineffectiveness of reconstituted legislatures, the persistence of human rights violations, and the absence of a level playing field during the run-up to many of these elections suggest that the commitment to democratic norms is limited to the *form* of democracy but not to its substance. It is for this reason that some observers argue that to equate the mere holding of multiparty elections in these countries with democracy is to commit the electoralist fallacy. Or, as argued by Fareed Zakaria, the holding of elections without the concomitant commitment to democratic values is to give rise to what he terms "ill-liberal democracy." Regrettably, elections

in many developing countries, particularly the poorest countries in Africa and Asia, have done just that.

A major reason for this outcome is that democratic elections cannot occur until there is a consensus among contesting parties on a corpus of rules and procedures that specify each aspect of the electoral process. These include the type of electoral system a country shall employ (that is, the electoral formula for translating votes into seats), who shall administer the election, how candidates and parties shall and shall not campaign for public support, who shall have access to the broadcast media and on what terms, rules regulating campaign finance, how the votes shall be counted, the maintenance of security, and so forth. Because each of these procedures affects each party differently, agreement on a single set of rules and adherence to the rules requires extensive bargaining between contesting parties prior to the election. No one party or candidate is likely to obtain all that it wants, but without agreement on the rules, the election cannot go forward. Arriving at this agreement is especially difficult in the run-up to founding and other early elections, the type of elections that occurs most frequently in developing countries, because an incumbent authoritarian regime usually has the power to shape the rules to its advantage. Early elections are thus marked by high levels of skepticism and distrust between an authoritarian regime seeking to introduce multiparty elections on its terms and opposition parties seeking to throw the incumbents out. Violations of the rules and outright fraud, especially by incumbents who usually control the electoral administration and security forces, are common.

A difficult question opposition parties therefore often face is whether to boycott the poll. On the one hand, they can withdraw from the contest in the hope of discrediting the incumbent authoritarian regime. However, by doing so they run the risk of shutting themselves out of the postelection political process. On the other, they can participate knowing that they will do so on an unlevel playing field with predictable results; they will either lose the election or be underrepresented relative to the proportion of votes they receive. Such outcomes illustrate another defining aspect of early elections in developing countries, namely, that they constitute an iterative process in which each successive election is potentially "fairer" and produces outcomes that are more representative of the popular will than its predecessor. What is a flawed process in its initial stages can, over time, evolve into the basis of a truly democratic system. Ghana, Kenya, and Mexico are current examples of this scenario at mid-stage. Improvement in the quality of elections also advances the overall process of democratization following the elections.

Notwithstanding these limitations, the international community has long placed great emphasis (perhaps excessive emphasis) on the holding of multiparty elections as the litmus test of democratization. Because elected government via competitive elections is the most fundamental component of democratic governance, the holding of a first or founding election has been regarded as the benchmark of transition from authoritarian to democratic rule. The international community, led by the United States, has therefore repeatedly pressured authoritarian governments to commit themselves to holding early elections on a multiparty basis. Since the mid-1980s the holding of multiparty elections has increasingly been a condition for assistance to developing countries. In addition to the United States, the United Kingdom, Germany, the Scandinavian countries, and the Netherlands now require some progress toward democratic governance before granting aid. The pressure on developing countries to hold elections rose dramatically following the end of the cold war. This was particularly true for those countries that were most dependent on foreign assistance and therefore most vulnerable to aid conditionality. African countries bear the greatest burden of conditionality. Stated simply, "no elections, no aid."

An interesting by-product of this renewed emphasis on elections has been the periodic involvement since the mid-1980s of international organizations such as the United Nations, the Commonwealth, and the Organization for Security and Cooperation in Europe. These organizations have provided substantial financial, technical, and material assistance to countries holding first and second elections. Bilateral aid agencies, especially the U.S. Agency for International Development, and nongovernmental organizations, such as the International Foundation for Election Systems, have also provided assistance. The provision of assistance to conduct elections has been complemented by efforts to certify that these early elections are "free and fair." These efforts have taken the form of sending teams of international observers to countries holding founding elections and of training domestic observers. The 1986 elections in the Philippines, the 1989 elections in Nicaragua and El Salvador, and the 1993 Cambodian elections illustrate the extent of international involvement.

ELECTIONS IN DEVELOPING COUNTRIES

Elections in developing countries have been an interrupted phenomena because conditions in these countries are far less supportive of democratic governance than in the middle-income countries and advanced industrial societies. Of the more than seventy countries that commenced democratic transitions by holding multiparty elections since 1975, roughly fifty are low-income countries. These include forty in sub-Saharan Africa, the poorest countries of Latin America, Bangladesh, Cambodia, Nepal, and Pakistan. The holding of first and second multiparty elections in such a large number

of low-income and culturally diverse societies suggests the following. First, that the desire for democratic governance is a universally held value found mainly in the West. Second, that it is technically feasible to conduct elections in remote rural areas where modern telecommunications and transportation are limited. (Founding elections have also been held in war-torn societies. This is particularly true where the international community provides assistance to implement the electoral process, such as in Angola in 1992 and in Mozambique and Cambodia in 1993.) Third, that turnout in these elections can be as high as 80 or 90 percent of the adult population, even though the average levels of income and education of the electorate—two predictors of turnout in industrial democracies—are low. The holding of elections and the initiation of democratic transitions does not appear to be determined by the level of a country's economic development.

The prospects for sustaining democratic practice, including multiparty elections, however, *is* highly correlated with the level of development as measured by average annual per capita income. The higher the average per capita income of a country, the longer democratic governance is likely to endure. In a monumental quantitative study of 135 countries between 1950 and 1990 (a period that does not capture the democratization in Africa), Adam Przeworski and colleagues argue that a democracy can be expected to last an average of only 8.5 years in a country where the annual per capita income is under $1,000. The "life expectancy" for democracy rises to sixteen years in countries where per capita income is between $1,000 and $2,000, to thirty-three years where per capita income is between $2,000 and $4,000, and to one hundred years where per capita income is between $4,000 and $6,000. If past experience is a predictor for the future, many of the most recent third-wave democratizers, most of which are in Africa, may fail. If they do, the holding of elections will once again be interrupted in these countries.

A major reason why both the electoral process and democracy as a system collapse in developing countries is that the state has insufficient resources to facilitate the types of bargaining and compromise on which the consolidation of democracy depends. Elections are usually perceived by the contesting parties as a zero-sum, or "winner-take-all," game. Winning becomes everything, while losing risks being totally shut out from the distribution of state resources, such as social welfare service, development projects, and patronage. Losers cannot accept defeat, with the result that they often allege that the entire process is rigged. It often is, but the cry of rigging also masks an unwillingness on the part of many losers to accept the fact that they were simply not popular with the voters. This unwillingness reflects the relative inexperience of candidates in countries holding elections for only the first or second time. In the absence of reliable surveys of public opinion, particularly of voters in the rural areas, candidates and parties frequently overestimate their appeal.

Given their respective fears of the consequences of losing, candidates and parties are often motivated to violate the rules. Elections in developing countries are thus highly divisive exercises in which trust often breaks down between competing parties during the run-up to aftermath of the election. The absence of trust, in turn, undermines the prospects for bargaining and tolerance between winners and losers and between government and opposition during the interelection period that follows. The level of animosity and mutual suspicion is especially high when an authoritarian incumbent regime is returned to power, as happened in Cameroon and Kenya following their return to multiparty elections in 1992 and in Cambodia following its founding multiparty election in 1993. This phenomenon poses an obvious dilemma: while there can be no democracy without elections, the electoral exercise itself may give rise to conflicts that undermine the democratic process.

ELECTIONS IN AGRARIAN AND PLURAL SOCIETIES

Because elections in developing countries occur mainly within the context of agrarian and plural societies, electoral behavior—and thus electoral outcomes—are shaped by different concerns than in the industrial democracies. More (sometimes most) citizens in developing countries define their political interests on the basis of where they live rather than in terms of what they do or their socioeconomic status or class. Their interests are shaped mainly by their affective ties to their local community and the specific needs of these communities. These needs are usually for various forms of collective goods such as the construction and staffing of a school, the establishment of a health clinic, the provision of water, adequate roads, and other infrastructure. Local issues are usually far more salient in the minds of most citizens than national issues. Ideological issues, especially when framed in terms of conventional left-right policy alternatives, are rarely the focus of political discourse.

A major consequence of this orientation toward politics is that citizens are most frequently motivated to participate in elections by political parties that mobilize and represent the interests of local communities within a particular region. Parties and voting patterns thus mirror the cultural-linguistic contours of society. The result is a "multiparty" electoral system that functions very differently from multiparty systems in the advanced industrial democracies. What looks like a multiparty system in terms of the number of parties that win seats in the national legislature or whose candidates compete for office is, upon closer inspection, a series of single-party or one-party dominant areas where one party has succeeded in persuading the local electorate that it will be more effective than its rivals at servicing local needs. It is not uncommon for the dominant party in an area to obtain between two-thirds and 90 percent of the vote. There is a high level of cultural homogeneity, and hence political homogeneity, as one moves from one constituency and region to another.

Given this tendency, major parties—those that win a plurality or majority of votes and seats nationwide and that form the government—are in fact coalitions of local or regional political organizations that appeal to local interests, while minor parties represent the people of only one region or a small number of regions. Both types of parties are found in the emerging democracies of Asia and Africa. For example, broad coalitions such as the Congress-I or the Bharatiya Janata Party (BJP) in India or the Kenya African National Union (KANU) in Kenya have typically formed the government in these countries, while minor parties such as the Dravidian Progressive Federation (DMK) in the Indian state of Tamil Nadu have repeatedly won seats in the national legislature by organizing a single regional constituency in successive elections. In a federal system such as India's, regional parties often control the government at the state level. In this context, elections are often referred to as an "ethnic census" because there is a high geographic concentration of the vote and because different parties emerge as the dominant party in areas inhabited by different ethnic or linguistic groups. In distinct contrast to voting patterns in the industrial democracies, only in a handful of areas—usually (though not always) in the urban areas—is there genuine interparty competition.

Another defining feature of elections in the context of agrarian and plural societies is that political mobilization invariably occurs via patron-client organizations that in turn give rise to "neo-patrimonial" patterns of political authority. Because most citizens are rural dwellers who have limited access to print media or to broadcasting directed to their local communities, the mobilization of rural electorates is done largely on a face-to-face and household-to-household basis by party agents working at the grass roots. However, the establishment of a party organization that is effective at mobilizing rural dwellers requires a large number of party cadres coordinated by party officials at the national and intermediary level. Party organizations are established territorially region by region, subregion by subregion, community by community, down to the household and individual voter. These organizations are held together over time by the steady flow of resources to meet both the collective needs of local communities and the personal needs of party agents. Leaders gain followers by dispensing patronage and largesse. Leaders maintain followings by continuously dispensing resources to supporters, who in turn dispense a portion of their resources to their own supporters or clients, who in turn dispense resources to their clients, and so on down the party hierarchy. Conversely, leaders lose supporters and organizations split into factions when they can no longer provide sufficient resources to their clients, who then withdraw their support. In agrarian society, politics is dominated by fights over the access to resources, because such resources are the glue that binds leaders and followers together.

The pressure to provide patronage frequently gives rise to corruption on the part of public officials, as leaders search for more and more patronage to service their clienteles. An unresolved question of democratization in developing countries, therefore, is whether the introduction (or reintroduction) of multiparty elections has increased corruption. Some observers argue that elections are a major impetus for corruption, because of the demands for patronage generated in the course of election campaigns. The need by candidates and parties for substantial sums of money to finance their campaigns is also cited as a source of corruption. In developing countries, where most candidates have limited resources, funds are often obtainable only from a small number of powerful private interests that expect favors following the election or (in the case of the ruling party) by a misappropriation of public funds. Other observers, however, argue that reports of rising corruption in countries holding elections are merely a consequence of a political process more open and transparent than in the past. The press now reports more incidents of corruption because they are free to do so, not because the level of corruption is actually higher than in the past.

These tendencies suggest the following rule to distinguish elections in developing countries from elections elsewhere: the more rural the society, as measured by the percentage of the population that resides in the rural areas or the percentage of the labor force engaged in agriculture, the more likely elections will be fought over local issues and result in high geographic concentrations of the vote and neopatrimonial forms of political authority. Conversely, the greater the percentage of the population that resides in the urban areas, and the greater the percentage of the labor force engaged in nonagricultural occupations, the more likely that elections will be fought over questions of national policy and ideological issues. There will also be a greater geographic dispersion of the vote among competing parties. Because election campaigns in developed countries are mainly media campaigns or campaigns conducted by direct mail, campaigns are not as labor intensive as in agrarian societies. Party organizations are thus smaller relative to the size of the electorate, which in turn means that the demands for patronage are more modest than in developing countries. Demands for patronage are also less because public-sector employment in the advanced in-

dustrial democracies is no longer as attractive as it once was, compared with employment in the private sector. In developing countries, especially the poorest, public-sector employment is the only source of significant income.

THE FUTURE OF ELECTORAL POLITICS IN DEVELOPING COUNTRIES

An underlying argument in this essay is that while elections are an essential component of democracy, they are not its cause but its effect. The future of elections in developing countries is therefore a function of the overall process of democratization and the propensity to sustain this process by key political elites and, to a much lessor extent, by society at large. This is particularly true given that the economic and social conditions for democratization in these countries are far from optimal. In the context of poor, agrarian, and plural societies, political leadership matters much more for the future of electoral politics than in societies with higher per capita income and a more homogeneous social structure. Democratization, including the successful iteration of the electoral process, requires either that leaders previously supportive of authoritarian rule recognize that it is now in their interest to guide their country toward democracy, or that the preponderance of political elites be democrats. Democratic transitions are usually initiated by the former. Democratic consolidation, however, cannot occur without the latter. The spread of democratic values must also occur across society at large. But if these are the requisites for democratic consolidation, including the institutionalization of elections, how might democratic elites and values become dominant forces in the political system?

The answer lies largely in the continuous process of political liberalization and the enlargement of political space in nascent democracies. Critical to this process is the expansion and strengthening of civil society, especially in the rural areas. An important variable in the improvement of elections in democratizing countries has been the emergence of civil society organizations that have performed the role of watchdogs of the state. Human rights organizations, legal aid organizations, constitutional reform groups, and, especially, organizations for the observation of elections have raised the quality of early elections *and* changed the composition of national political elites. Where domestic observer organizations have developed the capacity to follow the run-up to an election, including the appointment of the electoral commission, voter registration, the delimitation of constituency boundaries, and campaigns by candidates in the field, early elections have become "freer" and "fairer." Where domestic monitoring organizations have succeeded in posting observers to most if not all polling stations on election day and conducted parallel tabulations of the vote, the improvement in the quality of early elections has been especially high. The impact of NAMPHREL in the Philippines in 1986, of the Zambian Election Monitoring Committee in Zambia in 1991, and of the Catholic and Protestant Church organizations in Kenya in 1997 are all examples of early elections being improved by civil society organizations. The emergence of civil society, however, is dependent on the willingness of incumbent elites—often authoritarian rulers seeking to retain power—to permit civil society to function. The suppression of civil society in Nigeria by the military regime of Sani Abacha from 1993 to 1998 is a case in point. Yet in June 1998 a change in military leadership ended the suppression of civil society and set the stage for the founding elections held between February and April 1999 and Nigeria's return to democratic rule in May.

Democratic consolidation and the sustaining of elections may also turn on adjusting a country's constitutional framework, including the electoral formula via which the country translates votes into seats in the national legislature and other legislative bodies. In the context of plural societies, it is increasingly apparent that the prospects for democratic consolidation are greatest when the following three constitutional mechanisms are established to accommodate regional and ethno-linguistic interests, particularly the interests of minorities: parliamentary forms of government or other provisions that limit the power of the executive; some form of political decentralization or federalism; and an electoral system that produces highly proportional results in terms of the distribution of seats among competing parties in the legislature. This does not necessarily mean that proportional representation should be adopted by emergent democracies seeking to consolidate democratic rule. In agrarian societies, where most people define their interests largely in terms of where they live, district-based representation assures a greater measure of governmental accountability to rural populations than is possible under party-list proportional representation. Where there is a high geographic concentration of the vote, it is also possible to design district-based electoral systems or mixed-member proportional systems that produce highly proportional results. Tinkering with the design of a country's electoral system is part of a larger process of constitutional adjustment. While the immediate objective is to enhance and sustain democratic electoral practice, it is unlikely that this goal can be achieved in isolation from the consideration of other constitutional issues.

A final, and yet unknown, component of enhancing and sustaining early elections in developing countries is the role of the international community. Although democratization is fundamentally an internal process, the extent of international involvement in the electoral experience of developing countries since the mid-1980s demands that more thought be given to the future role of the international community in this area. At what point does continued international financial and technical support become counterproductive with respect to the establishment of a self-sustaining electoral process? Should not countries that regard themselves as emergent democracies finance their own elections and establish efficient organizations for election administration that can be reactivated prior to each election? What will be the future of domestic observer organizations that have heretofore been dependent on foreign donors for up to 90 percent of their budgets? These questions are particularly difficult to answer with respect to the poorest democratizers. The role of the international community in supporting early elections in countries where the commitment by political elites to democratization has been weak also raises the issue of "premature closure." In some contexts, particularly in war-torn societies, the early holding of elections may actually delay the transition to democratic rule by exacerbating the conflict between the principal contestants. The 1992 elections in Angola and Ethiopia, the 1993 elections in Cambodia, and the 1996 elections in Sierra Leone are four examples.

The quality, shape, and outcome of elections in developing countries are very different from those in the established democracies because of the inherent nature of these societies. The quality of these elections is also largely derivative of the overall process of democratization. One can best understand the dynamics of these elections and the likelihood that they will evolve into sustainable components of democratic life by remembering these two fundamental constraints.

See also *Boycott of Elections; Colonial Elections; Electoralism; Founding Elections: Africa; Founding Elections: Latin America; Free and Fair Elections; Observation of Elections; Postconflict Elections; Premature Closure; Technical Assistance in Elections.*

JOEL D. BARKAN, UNIVERSITY OF IOWA

BIBLIOGRAPHY

Barkan, Joel D. "Elections in Agrarian Societies." *Journal of Democracy* 6, no. 4 (October 1995): 105–116.

———. "Kenya: Lessons from a Flawed Election." *Journal of Democracy* 4, no. 3 (July 1993): 85–99.

Huntington, Samuel P. *The Third Wave: Democratization at the End of the Twentieth Century.* Norman: University of Oklahoma Press, 1991.

Karl, Terry. "Imposing Consent? Electoralism vs. Democratization in El Salvador." In *Elections and Democratization in Latin America, 1980–85,* edited by Paul W. Drake and Eduardo Silva. San Diego: Center for Iberian and Latin American Studies, University of California, San Diego, 1986.

Kumar, Krishna, ed. *Postconflict Elections, Democratization and International Assistance.* Boulder, Colo.: Lynne Rienner, 1998.

Linz, Juan, and Alfred Stepan. *Problems in Democratic Transition and Consolidation.* Baltimore: Johns Hopkins University Press, 1996.

Przeworski, Adam, et al. "What Makes Democracy Endure?" *Journal of Democracy* 7, no. 1 (January 1996): 39–55.

Zakaria, Fareed. "The Rise of Illiberal Democracy." *Foreign Affairs,* 76, no. 6 (November–December 1997): 22–43.

ELECTORAL COLLEGES

See *Indirect Elections*

ELECTORALISM

Elections are necessary for achieving successful democracy and normally herald the presence of some form of democratization, but they are in themselves insufficient for reaching that goal. Under some circumstances, elections may even impede democratization. This is especially the case when they

- serve as rituals of symbolic participation to ratify existing authoritarian rule (the Soviet Union; Indonesia under Suharto);

- involve so much coercion and patronage that legal opposition parties are denied a fair chance to compete for power (Mexico prior to 1994);

- are employed prematurely to arrest liberalization by blocking negotiations (El Salvador 1982);

- exacerbate ethnic, religious, or other basic cleavages (Burundi 1993);

- are staged "demonstrations" to legitimate intervention by a foreign power or to please foreign donors (Vietnam 1967; Bosnia 1996).

Under these circumstances, elections are likely to be characterized by degrees of repressiveness that limit organizational pluralism as well as individual dissent. Elections can also be held for other reasons that, however laudable, should not be confused with democratization, for example when they are used as the crowning moment in bringing about peace in a civil war (Liberia in 1997).

EQUATING DEMOCRACY AND ELECTIONS

Many policy makers and scholars engaged in promoting democracy abroad equate elections with democratization. They argue that "free and fair" elections are central in crafting new democracies. In keeping with these beliefs, a worldwide industry of election assistance has arisen. Such assistance can be traced to the turn of the century in the Caribbean but has become increasingly sophisticated in the post–cold war era. Many people—in government, international organizations, academia, and nonprofit assistance organizations—see elections as mechanisms for transplanting democracy, and

they rely almost reflexively on competitive contests. This is "electoralism."

Electoralism is the faith, widely held by U.S. policy makers and some scholars, that merely holding elections will channel political action into peaceful contests among elites and accord public legitimacy to the winners in these contests. As an ideology, it elevates elections over all other dimensions of democracy. In doing so, it makes two key assumptions. First, it presumes that contested campaigns, or what Robert Dahl has called the "chaff" of a democratic polity, will produce a *process* in which purposeful political parties will arise in order to compete, alliances and coalitions will form depending on the relative strengths of these parties, parliamentary or presidentialist systems will emerge, fair electoral administrations will take shape, and representative legislatures will result. Second, it presumes that some minimum form of "electoralist" democracy will be the *outcome* of this process. Although such regimes may still be a far cry from liberal democracies—insofar as their militaries are not subordinate to elected civilian officials, their executive power is not constrained by other autonomous government institutions, or civil and political rights are not recognized—electoralists hold that democratic "goods" are likely to follow from the very fact that their legislative and executive offices are filled through regular competitive elections.

Critics of electoralism take issue with these assumptions. While most critics accept that the introduction of elections will almost always have significant political meaning, at a minimum forcing contending forces to change their strategies and strengthening some actors vis-à-vis others, they believe that even competitive party elections may downplay or even exclude significant parts of the population from contesting power. Competitive elections may also obfuscate the way in which critical arenas of decision making are beyond the control of elected officials. Furthermore, there is no guarantee that introducing elections will produce other institutions of democracy, such as political parties, representative legislatures, or fair electoral administrations. Nor will electoralist democracies necessarily become liberal democracies. Finally, critics note that electoralism can lead to unintended consequences, including igniting or perpetuating civil war.

ASSESSING THE IMPACT OF ELECTORALISM

The impact of electoralism is mixed. Larry Diamond has shown that, although the number of electoral democracies has increased strikingly, especially in the 1990s, there is a growing gap between these "formal" electoral polities and liberal democracies. In many recent cases (Colombia, Pakistan, Paraguay, Russia, Sri Lanka, Turkey, and Ukraine, among them), elections have contributed to increases in violence and violations of civil and political rights. Yet there are also signs that electoral democracies have positive effects on civil and political rights and may evolve into more liberal democracies. Where there is electoral competition, there are also demands for government accountability, the airing of opposing viewpoints, and debate over public policy. Freedom House surveys over the past twenty years suggest that the emergence of electoral democracy is the best indicator of subsequent progress in the area of civil liberties and human rights, and there is some evidence of this in Africa as well.

Thus, electoralism may or may not lead to full democratization. What matters is whether accidental or opportunistic arrangements aimed at guaranteeing stability or even legitimizing nondemocratic rule through elections can be translated into more durable and reliable agreements regarding the dispersion of power and the respect for a broad range of civil and political rights. Whether they can be depends first on the extent to which elections are "free and fair," in the broadest meaning of these terms. Although outside observers may deem an election free and fair based on the voting procedures and their observations on election day (for example, the secrecy of the ballot, access to all polling stations, proper ballot boxes, proper counting procedures, and the like), a more effective measure of free and fair is the degree to which crucial freedoms are present *prior* to election day, especially freedom of movement, speech, assembly, and association as well as freedom from fear in connection with the election and the election campaign. If the months before an election are characterized by a pronounced lack of transparency, the failure to establish an independent and impartial electoral commission, a disorderly electoral campaign, overly partial access to media or to public funds, prejudicial treatment of candidates by police, the army, and the courts, and so on, then prospects are poor for ongoing democratization following the vote.

Furthermore, if the interested parties have not negotiated how elections should be conducted, who gets to vote, what kind of electoral system is used, what constitutes free and fair, and what issues are subject to democratic vote, then elections will not serve the purpose of democratization. But if these contexts are founded on a "democratic bargain," that is, a common set of rules that all participants have agreed upon, then they are more likely to produce the outcome that electoralists assume.

Why does the concept of electoralism matter? Since elections cannot be equated with democracy and may actually impede democratization in some cases, an ideology that suggests otherwise may lead to serious foreign policy errors in the name of democracy. If the mere holding of elections is taken as *the* central indicator of democratization, the political legitimacy conferred by such contests may be used to ratify existing concentrations of power rather than change them. In

the process, not only might countries and people suffer, the very notion of democracy might be devalued.

See also *Democracy and Elections; Founding Elections; Free and Fair Elections; Functions of Elections; Observation of Elections; Postconflict Elections; Premature Closure; Technical Assistance in Elections; Unfree Elections.*

TERRY LYNN KARL, STANFORD UNIVERSITY

BIBLIOGRAPHY

Carothers, Tom. *In the Name of Democracy: U.S. Foreign Policy During the Reagan Years.* Berkeley: University of California Press, 1991.

Dahl, Robert. *A Preface to Democratic Theory.* Chicago: University of Chicago Press, 1956.

Diamond, Larry. *Developing Democracy: Towards Consolidation.* Baltimore, Md.: Johns Hopkins University Press, 1999.

Herman, Edward S., and Frank Brodhead. *Demonstration Elections: U.S. Staged Elections in the Dominican Republic, Vietnam and El Salvador.* Boston: South End Press, 1984.

Karl, Terry Lynn. "Imposing Consent? Electoralism vs. Democratization in El Salvador." In *Elections and Democratization in Latin America, 1980–1985,* edited by Paul W. Drake and Eduardo Silva. San Diego: University of California, San Diego, Center for Iberian and Latin American Studies, 1986.

Karantnycky, Adrian. "The Decline of Illiberal Democracy." *Journal of Democracy* 10, no. 1 (January 1999): 112–123.

Sisk, Timothy D., and Andrew Reynolds, eds. *Elections and Conflict Management in Africa.* Washington, D.C.: U.S. Institute for Peace, 1998.

ENTRENCHED (OR RESERVED) REPRESENTATION

See *Elections in Developing Countries*

ESTATE AND CURIA CONSTITUENCIES

From the thirteenth century to the French Revolution of 1789 representation in European countries typically was based not on linkages between deputies and individual voters voting in territorial constituencies, but on the functional representation of social groups or organizations, commonly called estates or curiae. This form of representation was so generic across continental Europe that German historians coined the word *standestaat*—the state of the corporations and estates—to describe it. In the decades after the French Revolution, this type of representation ended in most of western Europe, but it continued to a significant extent in central and eastern Europe until the early twentieth century. In Sweden and Finland the national parliaments continued to comprise multiple bodies elected by separate estates until 1866 and 1907, respectively. In Austria, and in Russia during its brief experiments with parliamentary elections before the First

World War, separate estates elected members of the national parliaments, although their deputies sat together in a single body. In some European monarchies, for example, Hungary before the First World War and France from 1815 to 1848, remnants of estate representation were retained by the creation of upper houses composed largely of the hereditary peerage. The one relic that remained into the late twentieth century was the British House of Lords. The decision by the Labour government in 1998 to abolish the right of hereditary peers to sit in the Lords marked the end of the seven-hundred-year history of estate representation in Europe.

Estate parliaments almost always comprised three estates. The first estate comprised the clergy, the second the nobility, and the third the representatives of the towns and cities. In some countries the peasantry was also represented in a separate estate. Members of the noble and clerical estates sometimes sat by virtue of their office or position, for instance the heads of noble families sat by hereditary right, and bishops and abbots sat ex officio or sometimes by election of their colleagues. The representatives of the third estate were typically chosen by the ruling bodies of the cities and towns, which themselves usually were a tiny oligarchy of rich merchants. Guilds of craftsmen, lawyers, and doctors were sometimes represented as well. Representation by social group reflected a pre-Enlightenment, organic view of society as consisting of social groups rather than of individuals. The powers of the estates varied widely among countries and over time, but they usually included the right to present grievances and sometimes the power to legislate and tax.

THE ESTATES OF WESTERN EUROPE

As the power of the monarchy grew during the seventeenth and eighteenth centuries, the power of the estates usually dwindled. The formerly powerful estates of Prussia disappeared in the seventeenth century. The Portuguese Cortes held its last meeting in 1697. The French Estates General was not summoned between 1614 and 1789. But there were exceptions: in some German principalities, such as Württemberg and Mecklenburg, the estates continued to be vigorous defenders of corporate privilege against royal power, and during Sweden's brief Age of Liberty, from 1720 to 1772, the Riksdag dominated the monarchy. In Poland the Sejm developed into a single-chamber estate representing only the nobility, to whom the cities, the peasantry, and the crown were effectively subject. In the British Parliament the House of Lords combined the estates of the clergy and the nobility in the upper house; the boroughs and the counties were represented in the House of Commons, the lower house. Great Britain was unusual in that Parliament played a central role in government continuously from 1688 and that the House of Commons,

comprising all the counties and many of the boroughs, was closer to a territorial than a functional form of representation.

The democratic revolution of the late eighteenth century was symbolized by the decision of the members of the three French estates meeting in 1789 to sit as a single parliament rather than as three separate bodies. The principle that sovereignty rested with the nation and was exercised indirectly through a parliament chosen to represent individual citizens became the norm across most of western Europe over the next generation. Estate representation retained a place in many European monarchies, as estates formed part or all of the membership of the upper house of the national legislature. This was the case in Austria, Hungary, Portugal, Prussia and other states within the German Empire, Spain, and the United Kingdom. In most cases the membership consisted of nominees of the Crown as well as members of the hereditary aristocracy and representatives of the clergy. Only in Hungary and the United Kingdom was the membership confined largely to the hereditary aristocracy.

The membership of the British House of Lords reflected the long and complex process of state building in the United Kingdom. The Protestant Reformation of the sixteenth century resulted in the removal of most of the clerical estate. At the beginning of the twentieth century the House of Lords comprised 596 hereditary peers, the 26 senior bishops of the Church of England, and the 5 law lords (senior members of the judiciary). English peers, peers of Great Britain (created after 1603), and peers of the United Kingdom (created after 1707) sat as of right. After the union of the English and Scottish parliaments in 1707 and the union with Ireland in 1801, the Scottish and Irish peers elected representatives to the House of Lords from among themselves.

THE ESTATES OUTSIDE OF WESTERN EUROPE

The estate system was more resilient in parts of northern, central, and eastern Europe. Sweden retained a four-estate parliament until 1866. The Finnish parliament was modeled on Sweden's, reflecting Finland's heritage as a part of that country prior to its annexation by Russia in 1809. It was replaced by a single-chamber parliament in 1907.

In the Austrian Empire the first direct elections to an imperial parliament, the Reichsrat, took place only in 1873. The Austrian curia system reflected the medieval tradition of the empire's provincial assemblies. The four Austrian estates represented major feudal landowners; members or chambers of commerce and trade; the cities; and the countryside. For the city and rural estates, only voters paying a minimum tax could vote. The number of seats allocated to each curia reflected the balance of power in the empire. Of the 353 members of the Reichsrat in 1891, 85 were elected by 5,000 large landowners; 129 were elected by 1,388,000 peasants; 118 were elected by 339,000 citizens of cities and towns; and 21 were elected by 583 chambers of commerce and industry. In 1897 a fifth curia, based on universal male suffrage, was added. The estate system was abolished in 1907.

The complex system of elections to the Duma during the Russian Empire's brief experiment with an elected parliament between 1906 and 1912 was essentially a version of estate representation. The tsarist regime copied the Austrian system and manipulated it in order to protect its power in the four Duma elections held between 1906 and 1912. The 1905 electoral law provided for indirect representation. Members of the Duma were to be chosen by electoral colleges; the members of the colleges were divided into five curia, representing towns, landowners, peasants, cossacks, and workers. The peasants, with 42 percent of the seats, were the largest group. Workers elected only 2.5 percent. The large landowners formed part of the landowners' curia, together with representatives elected by the minor landowners, the Orthodox clergy, and local monasteries. The peasants and cossacks were elected in two stages: first at the level of the household, where every ten households chose one voter, and then at the village level. Industrial workers were elected by a meeting of the representatives of individual factories. Every factory employing more than fifty workers was entitled to one delegate and received one additional delegate for every thousand workers employed. Thus the largest factories, where the workers were most easily organized by radicals, were greatly under-represented. Despite the efforts of the regime to maintain control, the members of the first two Dumas proved troublesome, and in 1907 the regime revised the electoral law to halve the representation of the peasantry, to the advantage of the landowners. After 1907 the tsar nominated half the membership of the upper house; the other half was elected on an estate principle by the Orthodox Church, the chambers of commerce, the assemblies of the nobility, Polish landowners, and the provincial councils (zemstva).

TWENTIETH-CENTURY REVIVAL

Under the influence of Catholic social teaching, estate representation enjoyed a brief revival in Europe during the 1930s under the guise of corporatism. In Ireland the 1937 constitution provided for a Senate representing functional interests. Forty-three of the sixty senators were elected from panels representing culture and education, agriculture, labor, industry and commerce, and public administration and social services. Six Irish senators were elected by the universities. The authoritarian regimes of Engelbert Dollfuss in Austria (1932–1934), António de Oliveira Salazar in Portugal (1932–1968), and Gen. Francisco Franco in Spain (1939–1975) all established

legislatures partially or entirely incorporating contemporary versions of estate representation.

See also *Choice, Elections as a Method of; Colonial Elections; Franchise Expansion; Functions of Elections; Plural Voters, Second-Chamber Elections.*

TOM MACKIE, UNIVERSITY OF STRATHCLYDE

BIBLIOGRAPHY

Anderson, Eugene N., and Pauline R. Anderson. *Political Institutions and Social Change in Continental Europe in the Nineteenth Century.* Berkeley: University of California Press, 1967.

Carsten, Francis L. *Princes and Parliaments in Germany from the Fifteenth to the Eighteenth Century.* Oxford: Clarendon Press, 1959.

Koenigsberger, Hans G. *Estates and Revolutions: Essays in Early Modern European History.* Ithaca, N.Y.: Cornell University Press, 1971.

Myers, Alec R. *Parliaments and Estates in Europe to 1789.* London: Thames and Hudson, 1975.

Palmer, Robert R. *The Age of the Democratic Revolution: A Political History of Europe and America, 1760–1800.* Princeton, N.J.: Princeton University Press, 1959.

Rokkan, Stein, and Jean Meyriat. *International Guide to Electoral Statistics.* Vol. 1, *National Elections in Western Europe.* The Hague: Mouton, 1969.

Temperley, Harold. *Senates and Upper Chambers: Their Use and Function in the Modern State, with a Chapter on the Reform of the House of Lords.* London: Chapman and Hall, 1910.

EXIT POLLS

It took a messenger five days to reach George Washington with the news that he had been elected the nation's first president. It was weeks before the people of the country were made aware of Washington's unanimous election. That was election reporting circa February 1789. Today, exit polling—the statistical sampling and interviewing of voters as they leave polling stations—permits not only accurate election-day forecasting but also election-day analysis of results.

In the early days of television, following World War II, news executives wanted to report elections more extensively than radio had been doing it. They wanted their election news reporters to be the first to tell the nation who won, who next would control their democracy. Their first attempt at projecting winners was in the Dwight D. Eisenhower/Adlai Stevenson contest in 1952. They projected odds of victory for each candidate. The national winner was the candidate with the best odds. It was not a complete success. They did not report state-by-state results.

In 1962 CBS, in partnership with Louis Harris Associates and IBM, projected winners for thirteen senatorial and gubernatorial contests in seven states. These election estimates were based on actual vote returns in a representative sample of precincts throughout each state. Sampling of polling places and the rapid transmitting of results to a central computer were innovations that gave rise to the term "quick counts."

By 1964 NBC and ABC joined CBS in making state-by-state projections. All three networks gave names to their innovations. CBS called it "vote profile analysis" (VPA), NBC had "election vote analysis" (EVA), and ABC called its system "research selected voter profile" (RSVP).

Until the mid-1970s, state projections were based solely on actual vote counts. The winner of an election, therefore, could not be known until after the polls had closed and the votes had been counted.

EXIT POLLS AS PREDICTIVE TOOLS

The networks developed a second method for estimating the final vote in the late 1960s, but they did not all use it to make projections until 1982. Instead of relying on actual vote counts, the networks queried voters about their vote as they left their polling places. This approach, widely known today as exit polling, enabled election reporters to know the vote before the polls closed. The technique has been referred to as "election-day polling" and "street polling" in the United States and "same-day polling" by the British. Exit polls are widely used in democracies around the world to project elections. In the 1990s exit polls were used for the first time for national elections in Japan, Mexico, Palestine, and Russia.

In November 1967 CBS conducted research in preparation for its first in-house presidential election projections. An exit poll was done in the Kentucky gubernatorial election, and same-day telephone polls were attempted in three cities having mayoral contests. The exit polling technique was suggested by George Fine, who headed the research firm that conducted the interviewing and data collection for CBS News's election coverage from 1967 through 1988. Fine previously had used a similar approach to interview movie patrons about what they had seen as they left the theater.

In 1968 CBS conducted exit polls in presidential primaries in six states. It also used them in twenty-one states for the general election. The network's motivation for using exit polls was to corroborate the projections it obtained using quick counts. No one at CBS was satisfied with a projection based solely on these vote counts, since they trickled in over several hours. Those that arrived earliest were not necessarily a representative sample of the state. Preelection polls were not deemed reliable enough to corroborate the quick counts. Preelection polls include reports from people who may not vote and who may change their minds about which candidate to vote for. Exit polls do not have these problems; they include only people who have already voted. News executives saw exit polls as a safer second source of information about the outcome, and they provided an estimate that was available at poll closing time. At the start, news executives never thought of making a projection based solely on an exit poll.

Election forecasters use probability samples of precincts for their projections. These are not bellwether precincts. Each precinct's chance of selection is proportionate to the number of people who voted there at a recent election. There is nothing particularly meaningful about any one polling place. Separately, they are not predictive of a state's vote, but collectively they represent all voters in a state. The only difference between the two methods of estimating the final vote is the source of the vote information. In the quick counts (VPA, EVA, and RSVP), election forecasters use the vote reported by polling place officials. In exit polls they rely on the self-reports of a probability sample of voters. All three networks abide by two unwritten rules: they will not project a winner in a state race until the polls in the state are closed; and presidential winners will be announced only after one candidate has won the 270 electoral votes required for victory in states that have concluded their voting.

EXIT POLLS AS ANALYTICAL TOOLS

Exit polls make it possible to say not only who won but how and why they won. CBS began to use them in analyzing elections in 1970. The year before, Earl Ubell, the science reporter for WCBS-TV, developed a long exit poll questionnaire for his station's coverage of the New York City mayoral race. That was the first time that a detailed analysis of an election based on an exit poll was available on election night.

Before 1982 exit polls were used to analyze the national presidential vote, and in midterm elections they focused on the House of Representatives. In these pre-1982 exit polls, most national samples included data from enough precincts to provide exit-poll analysis for state-level races in only California and New York. Since 1982 such analysis has been available for most state contests.

See also *Election Forecasting; Public Opinion Polls: How They Work; Public Opinion Polls: Legal Regulations.*

WARREN J. MITOFSKY, MITOFSKY INTERNATIONAL

BIBLIOGRAPHY

Draper, A.F. "UNIVAC on Election Night." *Electrical Engineering* (April 1953): 291–293.

Kihss, Peter. "Poor and Rich, Not Middle-Class, the Key to Lindsay Re-Election." *New York Times,* November 6, 1969, 30. [The first article to use an exit poll to analyze an election.]

Levy, Mark R. "The Methodology and Performance of Election Day Polls." *Public Opinion Quarterly* 47 (spring 1983): 54–67.

Lavrakas, Paul J., and Jack K. Holley, eds. *Polling and Presidential Election Coverage.* Newsbury Park, Calif.: Sage Publications, 1991.

Lavrakas, Paul J., Michael W. Traugott, and Peter V. Miller, eds. *Presidential Polls and the News Media.* Boulder, Colo.: Westview Press, 1995.

Russo, Michael. "CBS and the American Political Experience: A History of the CBS News Special Events and Election Units, 1952–1968." Ph.D. diss., New York University, 1983.

Woodbury, Max A., and Herbert F. Mitchell Jr. *How UNIVAC Predicted the Election for CBS-TV.* Philadelphia: Remington Rand, December 15, 1952.

F

FEDERAL COUNTRIES, ELECTIONS IN

Of about 190 sovereign countries in the world, 23 are federations. Although some federations have little or no experience with free elections (for example, the United Arab Emirates) or have a chaotic electoral history (Pakistan, Nigeria), many are mature democracies. For the year 1997, Freedom House rated no less than ten federations "1" on a scale of political rights ranging from 1 (very democratic) to 7 (not democratic at all).

Federalism implies the existence of two levels of government, each having sovereign jurisdiction within its own constitutionally delimited sphere. When it comes to elections, this division of sovereignty has several consequences.

Federalism fragments "the popular will" into a multiplicity of arenas, a feature that greatly enriches the documentation on voting behavior available to psephologists. It is also a major constraint on the mode of enactment, the substance, and the implementation of electoral rules.

The Canadian literature on federalism offers two useful concepts for examining this topic. *Intrastate federalism* (otherwise known as representational federalism) refers to those arrangements whereby the interests of the smaller states and various minorities are protected within central institutions. *Interstate federalism* (also called jurisdictional federalism) refers to the jurisdictional rivalry between the two levels of government. Elections in federal countries can be analyzed through these two dimensions.

INTRASTATE FEDERALISM

Federalism influences the structure of the central government, usually by inflating the weight of voters who reside in smaller units at the expense of those who reside in larger ones. This weighting is typically achieved by imposing equal representation of states in the second chamber, irrespective of their population; about half of existing federations follow that

model. It is less widely appreciated that federalism also affects representation in the first chamber as well. In federations with proportional systems, federal electoral districts usually correspond to state boundaries. The number of seats in each state has to be readjusted periodically in order to reflect population shifts. In federal parliaments with single-member districts, district boundaries never cross state boundaries, and the reapportionment of seats among states leads to a new delimitation of electoral boundaries (redistricting) within each. In Canada and Australia, redistricting is performed by independent boundary commissions, one per state, whereas in the United States each state legislature redraws the district maps. In Germany and India there is a single boundary commission for the whole country. In official reports on elections in federal countries, district results are often arranged state-by-state rather than alphabetically by district name.

Another concession to federalism is the allotment of a minimum number of seats in the first chamber to the least populous units of the federation. For example, each U.S. state and Swiss canton or half-canton is entitled to at least one seat in the first chamber, irrespective of its population. The number of seats a Canadian province has in the House of Commons cannot be less than the number of its senators. None of the "original states" of Australia can have less than five seats in the House of Representatives. Among mature federations, Canada is the most prone to deviating from strict representation by population, insofar as the present formula has a subtle equalization effect favoring the provinces with below-average population increases, a feature that can be explained by the weakness of the executive-appointed Senate.

The influence of federalism is generally weaker when it comes to popularly elected presidents. Each state has a number of votes in the U.S. electoral college equal to its number of representatives and senators in Congress. As a result, the voting power of smaller states is slightly inflated: under the 1990 census figures, the four smallest states, together with the District of Columbia, had in the aggregate 1.14 percent of the U.S. population but controlled 2.79 percent of the votes in the electoral college. At the other end of the scale, California and New York together had 19.2 percent of the population but only 16.2 percent of the presidential vote. Supporters of the electoral college argue that it incites candidates to campaign in small states as well, instead of focusing on vote-rich metropolitan areas. Opponents point out that the college makes it possible for a candidate to win the election with fewer popular votes than his or her main opponent, a puzzling event that occurred twice (1876, 1888) in American history.

While consistent with the spirit of federalism, the rationale for an electoral college that inflates the weight of smaller states has been ignored in all other federations where presidents are elected by the people. In Argentina, Austria, Brazil, Mexico, Russia, and Venezuela presidents are directly elected on a one person, one vote basis, with no consideration of their performance in individual states. Indeed, Argentina was, until 1994, the only federation outside the United States that had an electoral college for presidential elections.

INTERSTATE FEDERALISM

Holding elections at two levels of government raises issues of congruence and uniformity of electoral legislation.

There is *congruence* when elections for both federal and state offices within an individual state are conducted under the same legislation. Congruence occurs if the national law is used for electing state legislators (as in Brazil and South Africa) or if state laws apply to the election of federal legislators (as in the United States), or if the two governments, in the absence of constitutional constraints, happen to select the same rules.

Uniformity is said to exist when the same body of rules applies across the states for the election of the same category of officials. Federalism threatens the uniformity of national legislative elections insofar as local conditions in some areas of the national territory may be held to justify special electoral arrangements. An example of nonuniformity is the Swiss practice of electing federal legislators by plurality in single-member districts in five small states and by proportional representation in all others.

One of the most fascinating issues for psephologists studying federations is the congruence between national and subnational electoral formulas. Some federal constitutions specifically demand congruence. This is the case, for example, in Austria, Brazil, Mexico, and South Africa, and it was the case in Germany under the Weimar constitution. Malaysia imposes single-member districts at both levels.

Most federal constitutions leave that issue open, which makes wide discrepancies between the national electoral system and various subnational systems possible. Too little systematic research has been performed on subnational electoral systems to allow categorical generalizations. It appears that in practice, even in those federations where congruence is not constitutionally mandated, the same electoral formula tends to predominate at both levels, whether it be plurality (Canada, India, the United States), the alternative vote (Australia), list systems of proportional representation (Argentina, Austria, South Africa, Switzerland), or a mixed corrective electoral system (Germany). This observation suggests that congruence has a major advantage: congruence makes it easier for individual citizens and political actors to understand and master the rules of the political game.

However, the power of state governments to regulate their own elections makes it possible for some states to hold elections under an electoral formula that differs from that prevailing federally and in other states. Indeed, state governments may be laboratories for testing new formulas. In the United States the cumulative voting system was used for electing state legislators in Illinois from 1870 to 1980. From the 1920s to the 1950s, the Canadian provinces of Alberta and Manitoba elected their legislative assemblies under a mixed system based on the coexistence of the single transferable vote in major cities and the alternative vote in rural single-member districts, and British Columbia had a brief experience with the alternative vote provincewide from 1951 to 1953. These still remain the only experimentations in Canada with formulas other than first past the post, at least at higher levels of government. Since 1907 Tasmania has deviated from the Australian pattern by electing its state legislators by proportional representation and single transferable vote, as New South Wales did during the 1920s, while Queensland returned to plurality from 1942 to 1962. In Switzerland five cantons or half-cantons (Graubünden, Uri, Obwald, and the two half-cantons of Appenzell) use a majoritarian system for state-level elections, whereas Glaris uses a mixed electoral system.

Before 1918 Imperial Germany was an extreme example of noncongruence. Reichstag elections were direct, with a secret ballot and universal male suffrage. However, for elections to the Landtag of the Kingdom of Prussia, which then included some 60 percent of the population of the Reich, voting was public and elections were indirect and conducted on the basis of the three-class system. Voters were divided into three classes, depending on the amount of taxes they paid. The highest class included 4 percent of the population, the intermediate class 16 percent, and the lower class 80 percent. Each class elected an equal number of grand electors, who in turn elected members of the Prussian Landtag. The electoral rules then in force in the other states for their *landtag* elections differed on basic points from federal legislation and from one another.

Still today, *länder* elections offer less dramatic but interesting variations from the federal model. Three of the sixteen *länder* use straight list proportional representation. Three others, while emulating the federal mixed corrective system, require voters to cast a single vote (which is counted as a vote for both the local candidate sponsored by a party and the list sponsored by that party) rather than two distinct votes, as in Bundestag elections.

In Austria voting is compulsory for *landtag* elections in three *bundesländer* (Styria, Tyrol, and Vorarlberg), which together comprise about one-quarter of the population. For federal legislative and presidential elections, voting is compulsory only in those three states. This incongruity might have consequences on the outcome of elections if turnout were appreciably lower in the other six states. In practice, however, turnout is uniformly high in all states.

WHO CONTROLS THE RULES? THREE MODELS

Congruence, or the lack of it, depends in part on which government has control over the enactment of electoral rules and the management of elections. On this point, there is much diversity among federations. For analytical purposes, three basic models can be identified.

Under the "watertight-compartment" model, each level of government is more or less fully in charge of regulating its own elections. Argentina, Australia, Austria, Canada, Germany, Mexico, and Russia lean in that direction. Under the "centralist" model, found in Belgium, Brazil, Malaysia, Nigeria, Pakistan, South Africa, and Venezuela, the federal legislature has exclusive jurisdiction over elections at both levels. In other words, these federations operate like unitary states in the matter of electoral rules. The opposed extreme is the "confederate" model, exemplified by the European Union (but not practiced in any federation). Not only national legislators, but members of the European Parliament as well are elected under laws enacted by every member state, with European Union legislation simply stipulating the number of members that each country is to return.

The choice that a state makes among those three models is largely a matter of circumstances. The centralist model appears to be appropriate to many of the contexts where it is used: developing countries with a spotty democratic record, where electoral politics at the state level are too chaotic to allow state authorities jurisdiction in that area. Some unitary states that are in the process of transforming themselves into federations, like Belgium, also find it necessary to follow, at least temporarily, the centralist model, since there are initially no state authorities to enact legislation for state elections, so perforce central authorities must fill that void.

The confederate model and patterns canting in that direction are typical of federations composed of units that were formerly distinct, at least at their beginnings, when there was no federal electoral law because no federal parliament existed in the first place (Argentina, Australia, and Canada started that way). The watertight-compartment model is the most respectful of the canons of federalist orthodoxy and is in force in many mature democratic federations, but it can be costly if federal and state electoral administrations do not cooperate, and it can be confusing for citizens if state and federal electoral rules differ markedly.

Not all federations fit squarely in those three models. The United States is located somewhere between the watertight-compartment and confederate models. The franchise for federal elections is determined within each state by the state legislature and must be the same as for the most numerous branch of the state legislature. However, successive constitutional amendments have stipulated that the right to vote could not be denied or abridged by any state on account of race, color, or previous condition of servitude (1870), sex (1920), failure to pay a poll or other tax (1964), or age for people age eighteen and over (1971). The times, places, and manner of holding elections for senators and representatives are also prescribed in each state by the state legislature, although Congress may at any time by law make or alter such regulations. Theoretically, Congress could enact a full-fledged national election law. In practice, Congress has refrained from using its power, except with regard to the use of single-member districts, voting rights, and federal campaign legislation, with the result that election rules vary from state to state even when it comes to electing federal legislators and the president.

The Swiss pattern is akin to that of the United States. For elections to the second chamber (the Council of States), each state determines how its two delegates will be appointed; all now provide for direct election by the people by a majoritarian system. For elections to the first chamber (the National Council), state legislation applies, but only in the absence of federal legislation. In practice, the federal legislation governs the distribution of seats among states and the details of the proportional-representation system as well as other general points of electoral procedure, while state laws apply in all unprovided cases.

In India the Union Parliament has exclusive jurisdiction with regard to federal elections, while state elections are an area of shared jurisdiction but are subject to federal paramountcy. Theoretically, this regime stands between the centralist and the watertight-compartment models. In practice, it has worked like the former, since federal legislation governs state assembly elections as well. The fact that a single, federally appointed election commission manages elections at both levels is supplementary evidence that India leans heavily toward the centralist model.

THE DRIVE FOR UNIFORMITY AND INTERGOVERNMENTAL COLLABORATION

Even in countries that follow the watertight-compartment model, various factors may push toward greater uniformity. National constitutions normally protect some basic rights like freedom of expression and the right to vote or to be a candidate. Those provisions, as interpreted by the judiciary, have curbed the ability of both central and state legislatures to legislate as they wish. In the United States the Supreme Court struck down spending limits for legislative elections in 1976. Earlier, the power of the states to draw federal or state electoral district boundaries had been severely curtailed by judicial decisions imposing a strict understanding of the "one person, one vote" doctrine. In Canada the Charter of Rights and Freedoms (1982) has been successfully invoked against federal provisions forbidding independent spending as well as against provincial apportionment schemes and referendum spending limits.

In Australia a desire to reduce the cost of elections led the states to use the federally prepared permanent register of voters for state elections. The federal and state governments concluded intergovernmental agreements to that effect, as provided for by the commonwealth and state electoral laws. Some federal governments may also be induced to rely partly on provincial lists to prepare their own registers, as in Canada.

This article has focused on the influence of federalism on electoral machinery. This is not to suggest that federalism has no impact on other dimensions of the electoral process. Some, among them Mark Franklin, have suggested for example that federalism drives turnout down because it leads to a multiplication of elections, generating boredom among voters. Others, including Frank Sorauf, have contended that federalism weakens the national leadership of parties, although others disagree.

Although important, national elections are often less decisive in federations than in unitary countries, for the simple reason that central governments dominated by one party or coalition may have to deal with state governments dominated by other parties. Germany is a good example of this phenomenon. Chancellor Helmut Kohl and his allies won the 1994 election. However, his Social Democratic opponents still had a majority of the seats in the Bundesrat, the second house of the German parliament, which is composed of delegates from the *länder* governments. Opposition control of the Bundesrat was an important qualification to Kohl's victory, since the Bundesrat has an absolute veto over legislation affecting the interests of the *länder* (more than half of the total legislative output), as well as a suspensive veto over other legislation.

See also *Administration of Elections; Offices Filled by Direct Election; Second-Order Elections; Simultaneous Elections; Staggered Elections; Ticket Splitting; Ticket Splitting in the United States.*

LOUIS MASSICOTTE, UNIVERSITY OF MONTREAL

BIBLIOGRAPHY

Burnham, Walter Dean. "The United States: The Politics of Heterogeneity." In *Electoral Behavior: A Comparative Handbook,* edited by Richard Rose. New York: The Free Press, 1974.

Franklin, Mark N. "Electoral Participation." In *Comparing Democracies: Elections and Voting in Global Perspective,* edited by Lawrence LeDuc, Richard G. Niemi, and Pippa Norris. Thousand Oaks, Calif.: Sage Publications, 1996.

Sorauf, Frank J. *Party Politics in America.* 2d ed. Boston: Little, Brown, 1972.

Truman, David B. "Federalism and the Party System." In *American Federalism in Perspective,* edited by Aaron Wildavsky. Boston: Little, Brown, 1967.

FIRST-PAST-THE-POST SYSTEM

See *Majority Systems; Plurality Systems*

FOUNDING ELECTIONS (DEFINITION)

A founding election is the starting point in a process that may or may not lead to a country becoming an established democracy. It introduces an electoral system, encourages political elites to organize parties to compete for votes, and reveals what could previously only be guessed at: how much support different elites have among those eligible to vote. The institutions of a founding election tend to persist, since those who have done best have an incentive to keep the rules the same in subsequent elections.

First elections of one sort or another have now been held in more than one hundred countries around the globe, and in very different historical, political, social, and economic contexts. Thus, no standard sequence of events follows after a founding election. It can lead to the gradual evolution into an established democracy or to the collapse of the regime holding it and that regime's replacement by undemocratic, unelected rule. Hence, this encyclopedia devotes five different entries to the subject.

In the simplest case, a founding election is followed by *uninterrupted democratization,* in which one election follows another until sooner or later the country becomes an established democracy. Britain is a familiar example of this process. Alternatively, a founding election can be followed by the repudiation of the regime that held it, a period of undemocratic rule, and then the introduction of a new set of democratic institutions in a *refounding* election. In the German Third

Reich (1933–1945), Adolf Hitler suspended elections for twelve years, and the Federal Republic of Germany held refounding elections after World War II, leading to it becoming an established democracy. But there is no guarantee that a refounding election will always lead to the secure institutionalization of democracy. Since the French Revolution of 1789 France has had a series of refounding elections, each of which collapsed before the Fifth Republic, founded in 1958, became secure. Latin American countries have often had founding elections that failed to establish democracy securely.

The global third wave of democratization was launched in the mid-1970s by an explosion of founding elections in new democracies lacking any democratic tradition, as in Africa after decolonization and in eastern Europe after the collapse of the Soviet-led communist bloc. The very different contexts in which founding elections have been held have led to major differences in the sequence of events thereafter. In some cases the regime calling the election could not be considered democratic; in Turkmenistan elections are unfree and uncompetitive. In central Europe, countries such as the Czech Republic and Hungary have held at least three free elections and changed control of government, evidence of progress toward becoming established democracies. In some African countries, the regime calling a founding election was subsequently repudiated.

See also *Founding Elections: Africa; Founding Elections: Democratization without Interruption; Founding Elections: Latin America; Founding Elections: Postcommunist; Founding Elections: Refounding after Breakdown; Unfree Elections.*

RICHARD ROSE, UNIVERSITY OF STRATHCLYDE

BIBLIOGRAPHY

Anderson, Eugene N., and Pauline R. Anderson. *Political Institutions and Social Change in Continental Europe in the Nineteenth Century.* Berkeley: University of California Press, 1967.

Diamond, Larry. "Is The Third Wave Over?" *Journal of Democracy* 7, no. 3 (1996): 20–37.

Huntington, Samuel P. *The Third Wave: Democratization in the Late Twentieth Century.* Norman: University of Oklahoma Press, 1991.

Markoff, John. *Waves of Democracy: Social Movements and Political Change.* Thousand Oaks, Calif.: Pine Forge Press, 1996.

Rose, Richard, and Doh Chull Shin. "Democratization Backwards: The Problem of Third-Wave Democracies." *British Journal of Political Science.* Forthcoming, 2000.

Seymour, Charles H., and Donald Paige Frary, eds. *How the World Votes: The Story of Democratic Development in Elections.* 2 vols. Springfield, Mass.: C.A. Nichols, 1918.

FOUNDING ELECTIONS: AFRICA

A founding election occurs when, for the first time after a prolonged period of authoritarian rule, citizens choose top state leaders through a popular vote conducted under competitive conditions. Such elections are watersheds in a country's political history because they mark the end of an *ancien régime* and the introduction of a liberalized alternative. Ideally, founding elections give birth to democracy, but, as African experience shows, such effects may be partial or short-lived.

THREE WAVES

The waves of election in sub-Saharan Africa differ from Huntington's three waves. The first wave swept the western, central, and eastern parts of the continent between the mid-1950s and the mid-1960s, heralding independence from European colonial rule. It featured a universal expansion of the franchise as, for the first time, African adults gained the right of political participation. In countries where the mass nationalist movement was unified, independence elections usually were won by a dominant political party that later went on to declare a single-party state. Where the nationalist movement was fragmented, often along ethnic lines, minority governments found difficulty in consolidating power, and civilian leaders tended soon to succumb to military coup. Indeed, only three African countries (Botswana, Gambia, and Mauritius) sustained systems of multiparty competition from independence onward.

A smaller, second swell of founding elections arose in the late 1970s. In independent Africa, this round of elections represented an effort to find an alternative formula to military rule. In countries like Ghana and Nigeria, military leaders became disillusioned with the frustrations of governing and convened elections as a means of turning political responsibility back to civilians; elsewhere, elections were called after military dictators had been driven from office by their own citizens (for example, Sudan) or by neighboring armies (as in Uganda). During the same period, some form of independence election was held in several countries in southern Africa (like Angola, Mozambique, and Zimbabwe) whose decolonization had been delayed by the intransigence of white settler governments. The interlude of democratic practice that followed this round of founding elections was either cut short by new coups or compromised by the centralizing drive of victorious liberation movements.

By the early 1990s political ferment had prompted a third round of founding elections. Unlike in other world regions, where elite reformers took the initiative for democratization, in Africa the transitions were more commonly led by mass protest. At issue was political competition, expressed in the demand for the replacement of entrenched autocrats. Rulers such as Mathieu Kérékou in Benin and Kenneth Kaunda in Zambia—who had routinely chosen to turn elections into single-party plebiscites—were forced to dismantle their self-serving monopolies of political power and permit electoral contests between multiple political parties. By the end of 1997, only four countries in sub-Saharan Africa had failed to complete a multiparty election during the 1990s: Nigeria, Somalia, Swaziland, and Zaire. All others had either held regular competitive polls (in five cases) or were swept along in the third wave of founding elections (about forty cases). The fact that, for the first time in a generation, Africans again were able to exercise a measure of choice in selecting national leaders was hailed by optimists as a sign of a new democratic impulse on the continent.

DISMANTLING MONOPOLIES

Why did African strongmen permit elections that threatened their own hold on power? By 1990 they faced an unusual—and ultimately irresistible—conjunction of pressures from within and without their countries' borders. In the international arena, the superpowers suddenly withdrew support from their African proxies in the cold war, cutting off much-needed military and developmental aid. Western donors and lenders also began to attach new political conditions to their assistance, including good governance and multiparty elections. At the same time, three decades of mismanagement had created an economic crisis in many countries that took the form of negative growth rates, the trickling up of poverty, and massive official corruption. Cash-strapped governments had little choice but to accept painful and unpopular austerity measures in order to stabilize their economies and set them on a path to growth.

Against this background, weakened authoritarian governments faced a rising chorus of protest at home. Building on economic grievances, students, workers and civil servants began to demand basic political rights and the ejection of corrupt leaders. Sensing a rare opportunity, out-of-power politicians grabbed the leadership of mass protest movements, crafting popular demands into a program of political reforms under the banner of democracy. In every African country where mass protests occurred, the ruling party without exception conceded a package of political liberalization reforms. These typically included constitutional amendments to lift restrictions on the activities of political parties and to impose term limits on the presidency. In most countries, the reforms also included an announcement of a date for the convocation of a competitive election, though some leaders prevaricated and stalled.

The founding elections of the 1990s obviously were not the first elections to be held in postcolonial Africa. But they broke with established practice in important respects. At the end of the 1980s, the model form of political regime in Africa had been a civilian one-party system that featured ritualistic ballots in which the president and his cronies were the only candidates. These plebiscitary regimes encouraged mass participation but denied meaningful competition, characteristics that ultimately could be turned against the incumbent government. Accustomed to popular participation in mass political rituals but frustrated by the absence of real political choice, African citizens were primed to rebel. Initially they did so through unconventional means of strikes, riots, and demonstrations, but, once the opportunity became available, they readily channeled their urge to participate into competitive elections.

National elections are generally exciting events; founding elections are moments of especially high drama. By allowing long-denied choice, they create uncertainty, not only for the political careers of long-standing leaders, but potentially also for entire modes of governance. With such high stakes, the campaigns for Africa's founding elections of the 1990s were hard-fought, with each side struggling to control key resources. Sitting presidents used the power of incumbency to control election timing and to write the rules for conducting the poll. They took full advantage of the fusion of party and state to allocate public funds and media time to their own campaigns and to deny the same to their opponents. Opposition forces enjoyed certain strengths of their own, offering appealing messages of anticorruption and prodemocracy that captured the giddy aspirations of the moment. And the emergence of a lively and critical print press during the run-up to founding elections helped offset incumbent advantages in many places.

Founding elections have been described as a heroic moment for political parties. Re-entering the political arena after years of being banned, exiled, or marginalized, parties are assumed to steal center stage from protest movements by aggregating opposition interests for electoral purposes. In practice, the opposition parties that emerged in Africa in the 1990s were not always united and effective. For every country like Zambia, where a grand coalition of class and regional groupings combined under a unified party umbrella, there was a country like Kenya, where the opposition never came together, fragmenting into myriad minor parties. A strong and cohesive opposition party was a force for regime transition: it helped compel leaders to convene elections, countered any manipulation of the electoral process, and, finally, made possible the ejection of sitting presidents. Another major influence on these outcomes was the presence of delegations of international election observers, who scrutinized Africa's high-profile founding contests more closely than any round of elections before or since.

FOUNDING ELECTIONS OF 1990–1994

Were these elections "free and fair"? This important question casts light on the quality of the foundation laid for a new democracy. It is best answered for sub-Saharan Africa by distinguishing between "early" (1990–1994) and "late" (1995–

1997) founding elections. Of the fifty-four presidential and legislative elections conducted in the first period, more than half were endorsed as "free and fair" by international and domestic monitors.

Early founding elections also introduced an innovation into African politics: the electoral rotation of leaders. Prior to 1990, a chief political executive had been replaced at the polls on only one occasion in sub-Saharan Africa, in Mauritius in 1982. Between 1990 and 1994, however, incumbent rulers were replaced in fourteen of twenty-nine presidential contests. Included in this group were sweeping leadership and regime transitions in which the loser peacefully accepted the verdict of the electorate. The significance of such events should not be underestimated: in Zambia in October 1991, an African nationalist founder was defeated for the first time ever, and in South Africa the hateful apartheid regime was terminated. Incumbent rulers routinely miscalculated the extent of their political support: they permitted elections because they thought they could win, but they subsequently fell to stunning losses. Because leadership turnover was associated with a "free and fair" verdict, early founding elections demonstrated that the postcolonial generation of African leaders could not survive a truly competitive contest. As such, elections were as much a solvent to authoritarianism as a foundational institution of democracy.

FOUNDING ELECTIONS OF 1995–1997

By contrast, late founding elections did not displace leaders or introduce regime change. Election observers were unable to endorse any of the founding elections held after 1994 as meeting international standards. This trend of declining electoral quality can be explained in terms of political learning by incumbent elites about the costs of open leadership contests and with reference to the nature of the previous regime. Late founding elections were held in countries (like Sudan, Chad, and Liberia) where the leader had come to power by military means and where he tightly supervised a phony ballot with himself as a candidate. Not surprisingly, the slowest and most reluctant political reformers departed furthest from the democratic ideal. Moreover, the rotation of top leaders in founding elections became much less common after 1994, occurring only once, in Sierra Leone in February 1996. While incumbent rulers could not resist domestic and international demands to hold elections, they learned how to manage and manipulate these events to their own ends.

The meaning of Africa's recent founding elections is therefore mixed. To the extent that elections were flawed, they lost their "founding" effects. Instead of resolving the old regime's crisis of political legitimacy, flawed elections led to deepening political conflicts which, in countries like Kenya and Cameroon, took the form of escalating ethnic violence. Far from founding democracy, flawed elections led at best to liberalized

autocracy and at worst to a hardening of the old regime. Generally speaking, the later in the 1990s that founding elections were held, the more likely were these outcomes.

Successful competitive elections, however, founded fledgling democratic regimes. Successful elections were the culminating events of regime transitions in the early 1990s in Benin, Mali, South Africa, Zambia, and a dozen other countries. At a minimum, the conduct and broad acceptance of competitive polls created institutional and cultural precedents that will be difficult for rulers to ignore in the future. This is not to say that founding elections are the be-all and end-all of democracy. Far from it. Their successful completion marks a transition to democracy but it does not guarantee democracy's consolidation. The briefness, imperfection, and ultimate demise of previous multiparty interludes following earlier rounds of founding elections in Africa should serve as a sharp reminder that the consolidation of democracy is an extremely difficult project in the contemporary subcontinent. But the promise of founding elections—already achieved in a handful of African countries—is that citizens can change top political leaders without having to resort to violence.

See also *Colonial Elections; Elections in Developing Countries; Electoralism; Founding Elections (Definition); Free and Fair Elections; Premature Closure.*

MICHAEL BRATTON, MICHIGAN STATE UNIVERSITY

BIBLIOGRAPHY

Ake, Claude. "The Unique Case of African Democracy." *International Affairs* 69 (winter 1993): 239–244.

Bratton, Michael, and Nicolas van de Walle. *Democratic Experiments in Africa: Regime Transitions in Comparative Perspective.* New York: Cambridge University Press, 1997.

Huntington, Samuel. *The Third Wave: Democratization in the Late Twentieth Century.* Norman: University of Oklahoma Press, 1991.

Joseph, Richard. "Africa: The Rebirth of Political Freedom." *Journal of Democracy* 2, no. 1 (fall 1991): 11–25.

O'Donnell, Guillermo, and Philippe Schmitter. *Transitions from Authoritarian Rule: Tentative Conclusions about Uncertain Democracies.* Baltimore, Md.: Johns Hopkins University Press, 1986.

Wiseman, John A., ed. *Democracy and Political Change in Sub-Saharan Africa.* New York: Routledge, 1995.

Young, Crawford. "The Third Wave of Democratization in Africa: Ambiguities and Contradictions." In *State, Conflict, and Democracy in Africa,* edited by Richard Joseph. Boulder, Colo.: Lynne Rienner Publishers, 1998.

FOUNDING ELECTIONS: DEMOCRATIZATION WITHOUT INTERRUPTION

In an established democracy it is easy to see the end result of a founding election, since for an extended period of time democratization has been uninterrupted by undemocratic rule. However, extended periods of unbroken democratization characterize only a small minority of the countries that hold free elections today. Within Europe, where democratic governance is today the norm, many countries of the continent alternated between democratic and undemocratic regimes throughout the twentieth century. Less than half of the established democracies of Europe made uninterrupted progress through the century, among them Belgium, the Netherlands, Switzerland, three Scandinavian countries, and the United Kingdom. Even in those countries, qualifications must be made. Within the United Kingdom democratization has proceeded differently in Britain than in Ireland. Although the United States has an uninterrupted history of competitive elections, the American Civil War and the conduct of elections in the Deep South for a century thereafter question the claim that the United States established a democracy two centuries ago.

PREMODERN ELECTIONS

Although the earliest elections in countries that experienced uninterrupted democratization featured voting for representatives, they followed traditional practices and were not intended to lay the foundations of democracy. Yet in these societies, the earliest elections provided foundations on which subsequent practices were built. For example, the debate about representation in the British House of Commons at the start of the twenty-first century takes for granted the principle that members of Parliament ought to represent compact and recognizable geographical constituencies, a basis of membership that can be traced back to the House of Commons in the thirteenth century.

Early elections were first distinctive in that the right to vote was very restricted; it could depend on inheritance, property or land ownership, a church office, or educational qualifications. Since most of a monarch's subjects had no property and were illiterate, franchise laws disqualified the great majority of adult males and all women. Since well-to-do individuals could be aristocratic, rich, and educated, it was possible for an individual to have more than one vote. In England individuals could buy the right to vote attached to a particular piece of property, and thus control what became known as "rotten boroughs." Moreover, in the absence of a secret ballot, voters who were economically dependent on landlords or elite patronage were not free to vote as they wished but followed the dictates of others.

Second, the few who had opportunities to vote were often divided into constituencies very unequal in population and voters. For example, an 1873 Austrian law divided members of parliament into four curiae, representing large landowners; cities and towns; chambers of commerce and industry; and rural communities. Although this law created an electorate of more than a million males, their votes were very unequal. The votes of landowners counted for more than 30 times as much as the votes of city residents, and more than 150 times as much as the votes of rural communities. The German Empire established after 1870 was a federal system, and its different parts displayed a great variety of systems of representation and claims to vote, most of which were traditional rather than making votes equal.

Third, the representative bodies of the earlier era lacked the constitutional powers of today's bodies. A parliament was usually a talking shop, where elected representatives could raise issues of concern with an absolute monarch, and the king's advisers could take heed of what was said or dismiss it. Where a monarch was absent, as in the Republic of Venice, a representative council could have a real influence on government. For the most part, though, elected representatives were confined to voicing concerns of large landowners, aristocrats, church officials, urban merchants, and an educated elite.

The rules for traditional elections reflected customs that sometimes dated from medieval times and usually lacked a modern rationale. The modern states that arose in Prussia and France in the late seventeenth and early eighteenth century were concerned not with elections but with increasing the capacity of the king's servants to act effectively by institutionalizing the rule of law, bureaucracy, and, incidentally, recognizing limited rights of association in civil society. The increased complexity of society stimulated these institutions to express diverse political opinions, some at variance with the established autocratic powers. The eighteenth-century Enlightenment encouraged intellectuals to examine political institutions from fundamental principles and to challenge institutions. In Europe these challenges eventually cracked the "cake of custom" on which traditional forms of undemocratic rule rested. In the United States the need to write a constitution from scratch forced the Founders to reason from basic principles; in France it led to the Revolution of 1789 and an undemocratic dictatorship under Napoleon.

MODERN ELECTIONS

The modernization of the state was the starting point for elections in today's sense. In England the 1832 Reform Act created a founding election by making sweeping changes in the right to vote and representation. Although the act added only three hundred thousand voters, it did start to rationalize claims to vote. Subjects with a stipulated amount of property or education had the right to vote, and the right to vote was subsequently broadened. This process occurred in different ways throughout Europe. In federal systems, such as Switzerland and Germany as well as the United States, franchise reform tended to be decided by partners to the federal compact rather than at the national level.

The introduction of modern elections also required fundamental changes in the established system of representation, in which traditional elites were dominant and any parties were loose groupings, cliques, or cabals of notables in parliament, who did not claim to represent interests and values outside the parliamentary "club." In the absence of nationwide party competition, a "general" election was not general, that is to say, each constituency elected its own representative without regard to national issues or to the choice of government. Without nationwide parties, there was no contest in many constituencies, and local notables were returned unopposed. The organization of political parties reflected the multiplicity of cleavages in society, including religion versus anticlerical interests; urban versus rural interests; industrial manufacturers versus industrial workers; and language or ethnic divisions. By the latter half of the nineteenth century, nationwide parties began to appear in western Europe, and the expansion of suffrage stimulated party organization on a nationwide basis. Yet in some countries, such as France, even though the right to vote was granted to a majority of males early on, nationwide party organization did not effectively commence until the beginning of the twentieth century.

FROM FOUNDING ELECTION TO DEMOCRACY

The uninterrupted progress from a founding election to an established democracy was everywhere a lengthy journey, requiring generations to accomplish. The first step was the creation of the institutions of a modern state, in which bureaucratization strengthened the executive, and the rationalization of representation—extending the vote to new groups of subjects, such as the urban and educated middle class and peasants—strengthened assemblies formerly consisting of elites and traditional notables. A second step was the organization of political parties to contest elections nationwide for offices in a national parliament that was free to criticize the government of the day and eventually to hold it to account in the name of the people. Founding elections could be held before the accountability of the government to the electorate was fully established. In the United States, for example, elections for the House of Representatives were direct and competitive at a time when the electoral college still had some importance in the presidential ballot and more than a century before the direct election of the Senate. In Britain competitive elections were introduced while the hereditary upper chamber of Parliament, the House of Lords, retained major powers.

In the long-established democracies, founding elections invariably were held before there was universal suffrage for men and long before women gained the right to vote. In Britain all men and women did not gain the right to vote until 1918, and the franchise was not made uniform by the abolition of traditional claims to extra votes until 1949. In Switzerland women did not gain the right to vote until 1971. In the United States the right to vote was not effectively guaranteed to African Americans or to whites until the federal Voting Rights Act of 1965, which became law more than a century and a half after the first competitive election.

Evolution is the central characteristic of an uninterrupted process of democratization; hence, in many countries it is not reasonable to select a single election as the first founding election. In the west European countries that have had uninterrupted democratic progress, elections in the modern sense became the norm only in the late nineteenth century. In Norway elections were initiated while the country was under the Swedish crown; the achievement of Norwegian independence in 1905 did not disrupt the electoral system. Ireland held competitive elections while it was part of the United Kingdom, when the basic cleavage was between Irish nationalists and pro-British unionists. After Ireland gained independence in 1921 it introduced a new electoral system, and a new set of cleavages emerged between exclusively Irish parties.

An uninterrupted series of free elections does not guarantee that a country is a stable democracy. Whereas free elections are indicative of democracy in Scandinavia, the introduction of free, competitive elections in Northern Ireland has been accompanied by continuing violent as well as nonviolent protest because of the diametrically opposite voting patterns of Catholic nationalists and pro-British unionists. In the United States a civil war followed the election of Abraham Lincoln in 1860, and the war's outcome sustained for a century a "dual" system of voting and other rights in the Deep South and the North.

Nor does an uninterrupted series of elections result in governments that can deal with all of a country's political, economic, and social problems. Elections simply offer citizens the opportunity to reward with their vote a government that performs satisfactorily or to express dissatisfaction by voting the government of the day out of office. India, to take an extreme case, has held an uninterrupted series of elections since its achievement of independence in 1947, but its government has been marked by chronic corruption, intermittent and substantial communal riots and violence, and the two-year emergency suspension of political rights beginning in 1975.

See also *Democracy and Elections; Estate and Curia Constituencies; Franchise Expansion; Unopposed Returns.*

RICHARD ROSE, UNIVERSITY OF STRATHCLYDE

BIBLIOGRAPHY

Daalder, Hans. "Paths Toward State Formation in Europe." In *Politics, Society and Democracy: Comparative Studies in Honor of Juan J. Linz,* edited by H.E. Chehabi and Alfred Stepan, 113–130. Boulder, Colo.: Westview Press, 1995.

Lipset, Seymour Martin, and Stein Rokkan, eds. *Party Systems and Voter Alignments.* New York: Free Press, 1967.

Mackie, Tom T., and Richard Rose. *The International Almanac of Electoral History.* 3d ed. London: Macmillan, 1991.

Rokkan, Stein. *Citizens, Elections, Parties.* Oslo: Universitetsforlaget, 1970.

Rose, Richard. "Dynamics of Democratic Regimes." In *Governing the New Europe,* edited by Jack Hayward and Edward Page, 67–92. Oxford: Polity Press, 1995.

FOUNDING ELECTIONS: LATIN AMERICA

Throughout the twentieth century many Latin American countries have oscillated between democracy and dictatorship. Argentina for example has arguably held five founding elections: in 1916, 1946, 1958, 1973, and 1983.

According to Samuel Huntington, four Latin American countries (Argentina, Chile, Colombia, Uruguay) took part in the first wave of democratization (1828–1926). All but Chile broke down with the first reverse wave of democratization (1922–1942). Ten Latin American countries (Argentina, Bolivia, Brazil, Chile, Colombia, Costa Rica, Ecuador, Peru, Uruguay, Venezuela) participated in the second wave of democratization (1943–1962). By the end of the second reverse wave of democratization (1958–1975), only three democracies/semidemocracies (Colombia, Costa Rica, Venezuela) were left standing. During the third wave of democratization (1975–) the Latin American experience with democracy has been quite positive. As of late 1999, eighteen of the nineteen Latin American countries are democracies (employing a minimalist definition of the term), with Cuba the sole dictatorship.

The Latin American democracies can be divided into four rough categories in terms of the founding election that initiated their current democratic period. In the first category are countries that did not succumb to the second reverse wave of democratization, and whose founding election dates to the second wave of democratization. In the second are countries in which the transition to democracy involved a series of elections whose competitiveness increased gradually over time. For these countries, while we can identify a single election as the beginning of the "democratic" period, the contrast between the regimes governing before and after this election is not nearly as stark as in the other categories. The third category comprises countries where the transition from dictatorial to democratic rule was preceded by the direct election of a constituent assembly to draft a new constitution. Once the constitution was completed, new constitutional officers were chosen in democratic elections. Finally, there are countries where the first democratic election of constitutional officers was held without a prior constituent assembly election.

SECOND-WAVE DEMOCRACIES

Colombia, Costa Rica, and Venezuela were second-wave democracies that did not break down during the second reverse wave.

The founding election for Colombia's current democratic period took place in 1958, following a twelve-year civil war. In 1957 the two dominant political parties (Liberal and Conservative) agreed to the creation of a coalition to end the violence and restore stability to Colombia. This regime (the National Front) reigned from 1958 to 1974. Under it, the Conservatives and Liberals engaged in power-sharing practices such as alternating the presidency every four years and dividing all seats in collegial bodies equally. Colombia held its first post–National Front competitive democratic election in 1974.

Costa Rica's current democratic period began following a brief civil war in 1948 caused by President Rafael Angel Calderón Guardia's attempt to remain in power through electoral fraud. The anti-Calderón forces were victorious, and following a year and a half of rule by a National Liberation junta, the junta turned power over to the winner of the 1948 elections. The National Liberation forces then formed the National Liberation Party, whose candidate, José Figueres Ferrer, won the 1953 presidential election. Since then, Costa Rica has maintained a strong and vibrant democratic system.

Venezuela's first experience with democracy was short-lived (1945–1948). Its present democratic period began in 1958, following the end of the Marcos Pérez Jiménez dictatorship. Intent on avoiding another breakdown, political elites made several agreements designed to safeguard the nascent democracy. The 1958 presidential election was won by Rómulo Betancourt of Democratic Action. From that point onward, Venezuela experienced continuous democratic governance.

COUNTRIES OF GRADUAL DEMOCRATIZATION

It is more difficult to identify the founding election in countries whose democratization process involved increasingly competitive elections, culminating in an election that most observers judged as free and fair. Countries in this category are Brazil, the Dominican Republic, Mexico, Nicaragua, Panama, and Paraguay.

Throughout most of the 1964–1985 Brazilian military dictatorship, restricted democratic elections for national legislators and subnational officials took place. These elections became increasingly democratic over time and contributed to the gradual nature of the Brazilian transition. The country's founding election occurred in 1986, when the Chamber of Deputies and two-thirds of the Senate were elected. The Chamber and Senate then jointly drafted Brazil's 1988 constitution. The first direct presidential election took place in 1989.

Following U.S. military intervention in 1965, the Dominican Republic experienced a series of manipulated elections in which the victor was always Joaquín Balaguer. The current democratic period began in 1978, when Dominican Revolutionary Party candidate Antonio Guzmán defeated Balaguer (after the U.S. government placed intense pressure on Balaguer to prevent him from employing fraud to prevent his defeat). Since 1978 the Dominican democracy has been relatively successful, despite Balaguer's return to office in 1986 and his use of electoral fraud in 1990 and 1994, which finally led to the premature end of his presidency in 1996 through a negotiated constitutional reform.

Since the 1930s regular periodic elections have been held in Mexico. Until recently, however, the governing Institutional Revolutionary Party always employed fraud when necessary to insure its electoral victory. During the 1980s elections in Mexico became increasingly competitive, culminating in 1994 with the first presidential election widely accepted as free and fair. In 1994 the Institutional Revolutionary Party maintained its hold on the presidency and won absolute majorities in the Chamber of Deputies and Senate. In the midterm elections of 1997, however, the Institutional Revolutionary Party, while remaining the largest party, lost its absolute majority in the Chamber of Deputies, signaling a new era in Mexican politics.

Nicaragua does not fit as easily into this category as the other countries. The Sandinista National Liberation Front overthrew the sultanistic dictatorship of Anastasio Somoza Debayle in 1979. The Sandinistas then ruled via a revolutionary junta until 1985. In late 1984 Sandinista leader Daniel Ortega was elected president, assuming office early the following year. Although the 1984 elections are generally regarded as free and fair, the withdrawal of a few prominent anti-Sandinista parties and candidates tarnished the election. In the next presidential election, held in 1990, the principal opposition candidate, Violeta Barrios de Chamorro, surprised the Sandinistas by defeating Ortega.

Following the 1981 death of strongman Omar Torrijos, Panama reformed its constitution and began holding elections in which Torrijos's Democratic Revolutionary Party employed fraud to guarantee its victory. In December 1989 the United States invaded Panama, overthrew the government of Manuel Noriega, and installed as president the opposition candidate (Guillermo Endara), who was considered to have won the 1989 election. The first free and fair election was held in 1994, in which the Democratic Revolutionary Party's presidential candidate, Ernesto Pérez Balladares, was victorious.

Between 1954 and 1989 Gen. Alfredo Stroessner and his Colorado Party governed Paraguay. In 1988 Stroessner was elected to his eighth consecutive term as president. In February 1989 Gen. Andrés Rodríguez overthrew him in a coup. Rodríguez immediately called for new elections, which were held less than three months after the coup. Rodríguez, the Colorado Party presidential candidate, won the election handily. In 1991 Paraguay held a constituent assembly election, and one year later the country promulgated a new constitution. In 1993 Paraguayans elected the Colorado Party candidate (Juan Carlos Wasmosy) president in the country's first democratic presidential election.

DEMOCRATIZATION VIA CONSTITUENT ASSEMBLIES

The democratic transitions in El Salvador, Guatemala, Honduras, and Peru involved an electoral cycle in which a democratic constituent assembly election first took place. Once an assembly drafted a new constitution, democratic elections were held to elect a new government.

Anxious to avoid a Sandinista-style revolution, El Salvador's military dictatorship held a constituent assembly election in 1982. In 1984 the Christian Democratic Party candidate, José Napoleón Duarte, won the first democratic presidential election. The Farabundo Martí National Liberation Front (FMLN), which was engaged in a guerrilla war against the government, did not participate in the electoral process. The FMLN did not fully participate in the electoral process until 1994, when its presidential candidate placed second to the victorious Nationalist Republican Alliance candidate, Armando Calderón Sol.

In 1984 Guatemala held a constituent assembly election. The country celebrated national elections in 1985. Vinicio Cerezo of the Christian Democratic Party won the presidential contest, with his party obtaining a bare absolute majority of the seats in the unicameral legislature. Throughout his five-year term Cerezo was constrained in his ability to govern by the military's considerable veto power as well as its outright autonomy in many key areas.

Under increasing U.S. pressure and mindful of the recent civil war in Nicaragua, the Honduran military called a constituent assembly election in 1980. In 1981 Honduras held its first democratic presidential, legislative, and municipal elections. Roberto Suazo Córdova won the presidency, and his Liberal Party obtained an absolute majority in the unicameral congress. The Liberal Party's traditional rival, the National Party, won all but four of the remaining congressional seats. Despite a moderate constitutional crisis, in 1986 Suazo Córdova successfully transferred power to his elected successor, fellow Liberal José Azcona Hoya.

Peru began its participation in the third wave of democratization in 1978 by holding a constituent assembly election. The country proclaimed a new constitution in 1979, and in

1980 Popular Action's presidential candidate, Fernando Belaúnde, was elected. In 1992 President Alberto Fujimori carried out a self-coup. A new constituent assembly was elected in 1992 and drafted a new constitution. The constituent assembly, under the 1993 constitution, served as the national legislature until 1995. Fujimori handily won the 1995 presidential contest with 64 percent of the vote.

DEMOCRATIZATION WITHOUT CONSTITUENT ASSEMBLIES

In Argentina, Bolivia, Chile, Ecuador, and Uruguay military rule yielded to democratic elections without the mediating presence of either semicompetitive elections or a constituent assembly.

During the 1976–1983 military dictatorship between 10,000 and 20,000 Argentines disappeared or were killed by the military, with many more tortured or imprisoned. The United Kingdom defeated Argentina militarily following the 1982 Argentine invasion of the Malvinas (Falkland) Islands, and the country experienced serious economic crisis. In 1982 the military began a gradual withdrawal from power, culminating in 1983 when Raúl Alfonsín of the Radical Civic Union won election as president.

Following a chaotic four-year transition from military rule, in 1982 Bolivians elected the Popular and Democratic Union candidate, Hernán Siles Zuazo, to a four-year term as president. However, he served for only three years due to the growing ungovernability of Bolivia under his stewardship. In 1985 the people elected Revolutionary Nationalist Movement leader Victor Paz Estenssoro as president.

Chile's most recent democratic period began with the defeat of a 1988 plebiscite, which, if successful, would have granted Gen. Augusto Pinochet eight more years as president (a post he had held since the 1973 military coup). In 1989 democratic elections were held to choose the president and congress. Christian Democrat Patricio Aylwin, the candidate of the anti-Pinochet coalition (the Concertación), won the presidency. The Concertación won a majority of the seats in the Chamber of Deputies and Senate, although the presence of nine institutional senators appointed by the outgoing Pinochet government gave the center-right/right opposition an overall Senate majority.

In 1976 the Ecuadoran military government, in consultation with the political parties, commissioned the drafting of a new constitution. In 1978, following a plebiscite in which the electorate ratified the new constitution, the first round of the presidential election was held. In 1979 a run-off election took place (concurrent with the election of most of the congress), with the presidential candidate of the Concentration of Popular Forces, Jaime Roldós, emerging victorious.

In 1984, after a period of bargaining between party leaders and the military government (which included the 1980 popular rejection, in a referendum, of a new constitution drafted by the military), Uruguay held democratic elections for national and departmental offices. The vote distribution was remarkably similar to that in the 1971 election, which immediately preceded the 1973 breakdown of Uruguayan democracy. The Colorado Party received a plurality of the vote, with the party's Julio María Sanguinetti winning the presidency. The National Party finished second, and the Broad Front garnered most of the remaining votes.

See also *Colonial Elections; Elections in Developing Countries; Electoralism; Founding Elections (Definition); Free and Fair Elections; Premature Closure.*

MARK P. JONES, MICHIGAN STATE UNIVERSITY

BIBLIOGRAPHY

Casper, Gretchen, and Michelle M. Taylor. *Negotiating Democracy: Transitions From Authoritarian Rule.* Pittsburgh, Penn.: University of Pittsburgh Press, 1996.

Diamond, Larry, Marc F. Plattner, Yun-han Chu, and Hung-mao Tien, eds. *Consolidating the Third Wave Democracies: Themes and Perspectives.* Baltimore, Md.: Johns Hopkins University Press, 1997.

Domínguez, Jorge I., and Abraham F. Lowenthal, eds. *Constructing Democratic Governance: Latin America and the Caribbean in the 1990s.* Baltimore, Md.: Johns Hopkins University Press, 1996.

Huntington, Samuel P. *The Third Wave: Democratization in the Late Twentieth Century.* Norman: University of Oklahoma Press, 1991.

Levine, Daniel H. "Paradigm Lost: Dependence to Democracy." *World Politics* 40 (April 1988): 377–394.

Linz, Juan, and Alfred Stepan. *Problems of Democratic Transition and Consolidation: Southern Europe, South America, and Post-Communist Europe.* Baltimore, Md.: Johns Hopkins University Press, 1996.

O'Donnell, Guillermo, Philippe C. Schmitter, and Laurence Whitehead, eds. *Transitions from Authoritarian Rule: Latin America.* Baltimore, Md.: Johns Hopkins University Press, 1986.

Pastor, Robert A., ed. *Democracy in the Americas: Stopping the Pendulum.* New York: Homes and Meier, 1989.

FOUNDING ELECTIONS: POSTCOMMUNIST

Elections were central to the transition from communist to postcommunist rule in the Soviet Union and eastern Europe. There were elections in communist systems; but they were elections without choice. Formally, as in a Western democracy, sovereignty in the communist systems derived from the people, and the people exercised their sovereignty by choosing their representatives to parliaments and lawmaking bodies at various levels. Some individuals, however, were excluded from "the people," including those who had been connected with the former regime, and others were deliberately over-represented. More important, voters had no choice of candidate; the right to nominate was restricted to the communist party and other bodies that it controlled, and they nominated a single candidate for each of the seats available. People found it difficult not to vote, although voting was not a legal requirement; and they found it still more difficult to vote against the candidate, although this option was open to voters. The ballot instructed voters to "cross out the names of all the candidates other than the one you are voting for"; but since there was just a single name, a vote in favor could be cast by putting the ballot, unmarked or even unread, into the box. To vote against the candidate, voters had to use the screened-off booth in the polling station, which was clearly a disincentive. Not surprisingly, the last elections conducted under this system in the USSR, in 1984, produced impressive results, with a turnout of 99.99 percent and a vote in favor of the single list of candidates of 99.95 percent.

Elections without choice were not without political significance. For the regime, they were held to symbolize the "moral-political unity" of the working people. Elections gave the party authorities an opportunity to check their ability to mobilize millions of voters. They also provided a way for career-minded party activists to make themselves known and secure political advancement. And for the population, they had elements that were more than ritual. Voters, for instance, could write comments on their ballots, which were gathered after the election and sent to party officials. (In Alexander Solzhenitsyn's *First Circle,* an engineer just after the war had "given vent to his feelings and on his ballot paper had applied an obscene epithet to the Genius of Geniuses himself"; detectives spent a month examining the handwriting of local residents before the offender was identified and arrested.) Voters also found it possible to engage the authorities in a gentle game of tactics by threatening not to vote if, for instance, a leaky roof was left unattended. But even from the regime's point of view, elections of this kind began to lose their value at an early stage because the population refused to take them seriously and because they helped officials escape scrutiny of their honesty and competence. From the 1960s onward, accordingly, most of the communist-ruled states were cautiously widening the scope of candidate choice, if not yet of political party or philosophy.

A GLIMMER OF POLITICAL CHOICE

The first elections that reflected at least elements of political choice were held in Poland in the late 1950s. Throughout the 1960s and 1970s Poland employed a "list" system that imparted a heavy bias toward the candidates who were listed first but that also allowed more candidates to be nominated than there were seats to be filled. In local and national elections in 1984 and 1985 a different system was used that, for the first time, provided for the nomination of two candidates for each of the seats available. In 1985 two candidates contested each of the 410 popularly elected seats; an additional 50 seats were filled from a 50-candidate national list that faced no competition.

In Romania the 1975 elections were the first to take place with more candidates than seats available: 139 of the 349 constituencies offered two candidates, and in several cases, Central Committee members ran against each other. In the 1980 and 1985 general elections these principles were taken further, and in 1985, 145 constituencies had two candidates and 40 constituencies had three.

In Hungary, where the most remarkable developments took place, the practice of multiple candidacies, first introduced in 1967, was made mandatory for elections at the national level from 1985 onward; in 1985, twenty-five of the seventy-one independent candidates put forward by citizens were elected in place of candidates sponsored by the authorities.

These were partly reformed elections, with a widening choice of candidates and, in Hungary, the first independently nominated contenders. And they offered voters some opportunity to influence policy on minor issues, and sometimes even on larger ones: in Poland, for instance, a referendum that the government intended to demonstrate support for official policies in 1987 was defeated because voters failed to support it in sufficient numbers. On the other hand, voters had no opportunity to choose among organized political alternatives, and until the late 1980s only Czechoslovakia (during its short-lived Prague Spring) had even suggested that electoral contests allow a variety of parties to put genuinely different programs to the electorate. And in several of the communist-ruled countries, the government had not widened candidate choice at all: not in the USSR, although some reform-minded scholars had discussed doing so in the 1960s; not in Bulgaria, where the opportunity nominally existed after 1973; not in Czechoslovakia, where the liberal electoral law of 1967 was rescinded in 1971 before it had been put into effect. Albania was one of a very few states worldwide that claimed 100 percent turnout, and in the 1987 election only a single ballot detracted from what would otherwise have been unanimous support for the regime.

REFORM FROM ABOVE IN THE USSR

The decisive change came, as it so often did in the communist-ruled states, from above, and from the state whose policies defined the scope for political innovation throughout most of eastern Europe. Mikhail Gorbachev, elected general secretary of the Soviet Communist Party in March 1985, attached little importance at first to political reform for its own sake. But in his speech to the party congress in 1986 he suggested that the party needed to make "correctives" in the electoral system, and this became an explicit objective of the new leadership from the start of the following year. The USSR adopted a new electoral law in December 1988, which allowed citizens to nominate candidates and required all voters to use the booth, whether or not there was a single candidate. The elections that took place under the new law in March 1989 were not simply different, but were a decisive moment in shifting power from the party authorities to ordinary citizens. More of the successful candidates than ever before, in fact, were members of the Communist Party; but the defeats suffered by party officials at all levels were more striking—thirty-eight regional and district party secretaries were defeated, including a member of the ruling Politburo, and Boris Yeltsin enjoyed a runaway victory in Moscow with nearly 90 percent of the vote. These national elections were followed by contests in all fifteen republics in the course of 1990, in several of which nationalist groupings won majorities; and then in 1991 the first Russian presidential election took place, with a choice of six candidates, although voters still had no choice of organized party.

There was a clearer founding election in 1993, which was the first to take place after the collapse of the USSR and the first to allow a choice of party as well as a choice of candidate. The electoral law was devised so that nationally organized parties or movements would compete for half the seats in a newly formed State Duma, subject to a 5 percent threshold, while the other half would comprise deputies elected in single-member constituencies on a first-past-the-post basis. Thirteen parties took part in the election, most of them hastily formed, and eight of them won more than 5 percent of the vote to secure parliamentary representation. To the surprise and concern of many observers, right-wing nationalist Vladimir Zhirinovsky's Liberal Democratic Party won the party-list contest, with 22.9 percent of the vote, although the most successful party overall was Russia's Choice, led by former acting prime minister Yegor Gaidar. The largest bloc of seats went to independent candidates, who won two-thirds of the single-member constituencies. The new constitution, adopted in a referendum on the same day as the State Duma voting, committed the new regime to "ideological diversity" and "multiparty politics," and in this sense the constitution concluded the postcommunist transition; in a disappointment for the authorities, only 54.8 percent of the electorate had bothered to cast their vote.

FOUNDING ELECTIONS IN EASTERN EUROPE

Most countries of eastern Europe had held founding elections by 1993. The most important, arguably, was in Poland in June 1989, when a newly legalized Solidarity movement won all the seats available to it in the lower house and won ninety-nine of the possible one hundred seats in the Senate. The Sejm elected the former communist leader, Wojciech Jaruzelski, to the newly created executive presidency by a single vote, but his attempts to form a communist administration were unsuccessful and the job was eventually entrusted to Tadeusz Mazowiecki, the editor of Solidarity's weekly newspaper and a former political prisoner. He was eastern Europe's first noncommunist prime minister in more than forty years.

In Hungary the center-right Democratic Forum won elections in March and April 1990 and formed a coalition government with two other parties under József Antall. The German Democratic Republic disappeared entirely as a result of its decisive vote for the prounification Christian Democrats in March 1990, a vote that led to reunification the following October. In Czechoslovakia, elections in June 1990 led to an overwhelming success for Civic Forum and Public against Violence, the anticommunist alliance that had headed the Velvet Revolution. Former communists did better in Romania, where a communist-influenced National Salvation Front won two-thirds of the vote at parliamentary elections in May; in Bulgaria, where they won a majority in the election that was held in June 1990; and in Mongolia in July 1990.

DISTINCTIVE TRAITS

Postcommunist founding elections had a number of distinctive characteristics. For a start, the countries of the region usually held more than one founding election: a first one that broke the party's political monopoly, and at least one other that was conducted on a more competitive basis with a choice of parties (in Russia in 1989 and 1993; in Poland in 1989 and 1991; in Bulgaria in 1990, 1991, and 1994; and in Romania in 1990, 1992, and 1996). Equally distinctive, postcommunist founding elections were often won by the postcommunists themselves, particularly in the second round of fully competitive elections, as in Lithuania in 1992, Poland in 1993, and Hungary in 1994. The first postcommunist elections in eastern Europe did little to clarify the party system: Russia, for instance, had thirteen competing parties in 1993 but forty-three in the elections of December 1995; and independents rather than organized parties won the largest share of the vote in several elections, including Russia in 1993 and Ukraine in 1994.

Competitive elections led to parliaments that were much less socially representative of their respective societies, with a particularly sharp fall in the proportion of women deputies. And sometimes, as in Russia and Poland, the combination of an elected parliament and a directly elected president introduced a new source of tension; that combination led in Russia, in late 1993, to what was in effect a presidential coup.

Postcommunist founding elections, however, appeared to mark a decisive move toward elections themselves, and toward the general principle that the only legitimate basis for government is the freely given consent of the governed.

See also *Electoralism; Founding Elections (Definition); Free and Fair Elections; Premature Closure.*

STEPHEN WHITE, GLASGOW UNIVERSITY

BIBLIOGRAPHY

"Elections in Eastern Europe." Special issue of *Electoral Studies* 9, no. 4 (December 1990).

Gabal, Ivan, ed. *The 1990 Election to the Czechoslovakian Federal Assembly.* Berlin: Sigma, 1996.

Hermet, Guy, Richard Rose, and Alain Rouquié, eds. *Elections without Choice.* London: Macmillan, 1978.

Karasimeonov, Georgi, ed. *The 1990 Election to the Bulgarian Grand National Assembly and the 1991 Election to the Bulgarian Grand National Assembly.* Berlin: Sigma, 1997.

Stokes, Gale. *The Walls Came Tumbling Down: The Collapse of Communism in Eastern Europe.* New York: Oxford University Press, 1993.

Toka, Gabor, ed. *The 1990 Election to the Hungarian National Assembly.* Berlin: Sigma, 1995.

White, Stephen, Richard Rose, and Ian McAllister. *How Russia Votes.* Chatham, N.J.: Chatham House, 1997.

FOUNDING ELECTIONS: REFOUNDING AFTER BREAKDOWN

A majority of countries introduced free elections and then turned to an undemocratic system of government that abolished competitive elections and introduced unfree elections. Some, but not all, of these countries subsequently introduced refounding elections in a second attempt at democratization. Refounding elections can have several different outcomes. In some instances, most notably Germany, "second chance" elections led to the creation of an established democracy. In other instances, they failed and were followed by yet another turn to undemocratic rule, as in Argentina.

A refounding election is an ambiguous starting point for a new regime. The country's past history shows that free elections can be held, thus differentiating it from completely new democracies without any tradition of free elections under communist or colonial rule. However, past history also shows that undemocratic forces were strong enough to subvert a fledgling new democracy and to establish government without free elections.

The specific circumstances of the reintroduction of elections are of primary importance, for they set the terms under which old and new politicians compete for office, under rules

that may be familiar but circumstances that are novel. If the period of undemocratic rule was relatively brief, then a refounding election may be little more than a return to the preexisting status quo. This was the case in France in 1946, as the transition from the Third to the Fourth Republics was interrupted for six years by wartime defeat and occupation. In Finland also, which like France was occupied in World War II, there was continuity between prewar and postwar electoral institutions.

Germany, Austria, and Italy had each held competitive elections before establishing undemocratic systems of rule between the two world wars. Following their victory in World War II, the Allied occupation powers encouraged refounding competitive elections while their forces were still in place and could step in if another breakdown occurred. The parties participating in the refounding elections were led by politicians who had had experience of democratic party competition prior to Nazi and fascist takeovers. The continuity of parties was particularly marked in Austria. In Germany the electoral system was substantially altered in reaction against the failure of the democratic Weimar republic, and the parties reacted against the Nazi experience too. In Italy left-wing groups that had opposed Mussolini's dictatorship formed parties, and the Catholic Church sponsored a Christian Democratic alternative. In Japan elections with a secret ballot had been introduced in 1900 and had been suspended during the war. From the refounding election of 1946 Japan has evolved into an established democracy.

In the Mediterranean region, refounding elections were held in Greece in 1974 after the fall of a military regime, in Spain in 1977 after the death of Gen. Francisco Franco, and in Portugal in 1975 after a military uprising against an undemocratic regime. Among the postcommunist countries of Europe, Czechoslovakia is exceptional in having consistently held democratic elections between the two world wars. Other postcommunist countries had at best a brief experiment with competitive elections after the First World War, followed by dictatorship, or had a history of undemocratic rule followed by founding elections in 1990.

Refounding elections can demonstrate continuities only if significant party identification existed prior to the initial collapse of democracy and if the same parties come forward to contest the new elections. When a country had little prior experience of free elections and then experienced a lengthy period of undemocratic rule, as in Portugal, a refounding election was to all intents and purposes a new start. When a country had significant experience of democracy, and democratic parties continued clandestine underground activity or were maintained in exile, then they could reemerge at a refounding election. This happened on the left in Austria, Germany, and Italy after the collapse of fascism and in Spain after the death of Franco.

New parties often emerge to fill the gap left by the collapse of parties associated with a discredited undemocratic regime, such as the communist parties in the postcommunist countries of central and eastern Europe. Thus, a refounding election often involves competition among old and new parties.

Refounding elections are not the product of evolution but of the more or less abrupt collapse of an undemocratic regime. The proponents of some theories of democratization argue that it depends on the gradual development of democratic cultural norms; their argument implies that the chances of democracy taking root are low when transitions are abrupt. But the empirical evidence in Europe rejects this hypothesis; the countries that had refounding elections between 1945 and 1975 are now established democracies. One explanation for their success is that the experience of undemocratic rule under Hitler or some other dictator made citizens more appreciative of democratic institutions. Another theory is that the spread of affluence after 1945 gave individuals a material incentive to support a refounded democracy.

See also *Colonial Elections; Elections in Developing Countries; Electoralism; Founding Elections (Definition); Founding Elections: Africa; Founding Elections: Democratization without Interruption; Founding Elections: Latin America; Founding Elections: Postcommunist; Free and Fair Elections; Premature Closure; Unfree Elections.*

RICHARD ROSE, UNIVERSITY OF STRATHCLYDE

BIBLIOGRAPHY

Baker, Kendall, Russell Dalton, and Kai Hildebrandt. *Germany Transformed: Political Culture and the New Politics.* Cambridge, Mass.: Harvard University Press, 1981.

Gunther, Richard, P. Nikiforos Diamandouros, and Hansjürgen Puhle, eds. *The Politics of Democratic Consolidation: Southern Europe in Comparative Perspective.* Baltimore: Johns Hopkins University Press, 1995.

Linz, Juan J., and Alfred Stepan, eds. *The Breakdown of Democratic Regimes.* Baltimore, Md.: Johns Hopkins University Press, 1978.

McDonough, Peter, Samuel H. Barnes, and Antonio Lopez-Pina. *The Cultural Dynamics of Democratization in Spain.* Ithaca, N.Y.: Cornell University Press, 1999.

Weil, Frederick D. "The Sources and Structure of Legitimation in Western Democracies." *American Sociological Review* 54, no. 4 (1989): 682–706.

FRACTIONALIZATION INDEX

Fractionalization is the extent to which a set of groups is divided. A fractionalization index is a formula for summarizing in a single number how fractionalized some set of groups is. Fractionalization indices are used in the study of elections primarily to characterize party systems. They have also been used, in electoral studies and more broadly in political science, to characterize such concepts as the ethnic fractionalization of a country.

ORIGINS AND VARIETY OF INDICES

The most commonly used fractionalization index originated in economics, where a converse concept—industrial concentration—is of considerable importance. The Hirschman-Herfindahl concentration index, H, is defined as $1/\Sigma(p_i^2)$, where p_i is the share of the "population" that is in group i. In economics, these populations might be any theoretically relevant measure of size. Market share is typical, but others—such as patient admissions in a study of hospital concentration—are possible. Similar indices have appeared in many disciplines, including sociology, where they have been used to measure consensus, and biology, where they have been used to measure diversity.

In the party system case, the populations are shares of the vote or legislative seats held by each party. Douglas Rae adapted H into a converse fractionalization index: $F = 1 - H$. Political scientists have used the index F widely as an index of ethnic fractionalization, with the relevant populations being the shares of total population in a given ethnic group.

F is often characterized as the probability that any two individuals drawn from the population are in different groups. This is true only if the population is very large or if individuals are drawn with replacement. One should then be careful about this interpretation when characterizing how fractionalized a small population, such as a legislature or coalition, is.

Scholars have proposed many different fractionalization indices, especially if we include under that rubric the many concentration indices discussed in the economics literature. The differences between them are often subtle and may be significant only in particular types of cases. The key feature of an appropriate index is that it responds to both the absolute number of groups under consideration and the equality of the shares of those groups. The first criterion requires that for N groups of equal size, the value of a fractionalization index should increase as N increases. The second criterion requires that for a given number of groups, the value of a fractionalization index should increase as shares are transferred from a larger group to a smaller one (the "principle of transfers"). Virtually all of the indices widely used are rescaled, if necessary, to produce values between zero and one. The various indices differ implicitly in how they meet these criteria. For most empirical applications, however, the indices are highly correlated and offer similar answers. F meets all of these criteria, and its simplicity is undoubtedly a source of its popularity.

APPLICATION OF INDICES

Another cautionary warning about the application of fractionalization indices concerns the difficulty of defining appropriate groups and group sizes. If parties make alliances, or even different alliances in different electoral districts, as they do under *apparentement* in Switzerland, do we count the parties or alliances as separate groups? How do we define "vote share" in systems such as the single transferable vote or the additional member system? Where do we draw the lines between groups when individuals have partial membership in multiple groups, as with racial groups? To which group do we attribute individuals with multiple full memberships, as with multilingual individuals and linguistic groups? In what circumstances do we consider two subgroups to be a single group, as with Protestants and Catholics? The answers to such questions generally will affect our results as much as the choice of index.

Fractionalization indices have other important applications as well. For example, Duverger's Law is central to election studies, suggesting relationships between electoral systems and party systems and, in particular, suggesting the number of parties that will compete or win seats under a given electoral system. Empirical investigation of Duverger's Law requires some measure of the number of parties. Simple counting often will not work, since there may be many small or even trivial parties that we would not want to count as equivalent to major parties.

The fractionalization index F leads to one possible alternative. In particular, note that if there are two equally sized groups, then $H = 1/2$; if there are three equally sized groups, then $H = 1/3$; and so on. This feature provides a natural measure of the "effective number of parties": $N_{eff} = 1/H = 1/(1-F)$. For unequal distributions, N_{eff} provides some sense of how many important parties are in a system. For example, if there are three parties with 44 percent, 44 percent, and 12 percent of the vote, $N_{eff} = 2.5$, suggesting a "two-and-a-half party" system, which is in line with our intuitive sense of the distribution. Several major contemporary studies of electoral systems and party systems—notably those of Rein Taagepera and Matthew Shugart; Arend Lijphart; and Gary Cox—use this measure, although it has important detractors (including Giovanni Sartori and Richard Katz). Some scholars have also used this method to measure the "effective number" of ethnic groups in a country. N_{eff} does not always match our intuitions, however, so other measures of effective parties have been suggested. These alternative measures, in turn, imply different fractionalization indices.

See also *Additional Member System; Apparentement; Cube Law; Duverger's Law; Single Transferable Vote.*

BURT L. MONROE, INDIANA UNIVERSITY

BIBLIOGRAPHY

Cox, Gary W. *Making Votes Count: Strategic Coordination in the World's Electoral Systems.* Cambridge: Cambridge University Press, 1997.

Curry, B., and K.D. George. "Industrial Concentration: A Survey." *Journal of Industrial Economics* 31, no. 3 (1983): 203–255.

Katz, Richard. *Democracy and Elections.* New York: Oxford University Press, 1997.

Laakso, Markku, and Rein Taagepera. "Effective Number of Parties: A Measure with Application to West Europe." *Comparative Political Studies* 12, no. 1 (1979): 3–27.

Lijphart, Arend. *Electoral Systems and Party Systems: A Study of Twenty-Seven Democracies, 1945–90.* Oxford: Oxford University Press, 1994.

Molinar, Juan. "Counting the Number of Parties: An Alternative Index." *American Political Science Review* 85, no. 4 (1991): 1383–1391.

Rae, Douglas W. *The Political Consequences of Electoral Laws.* 2d ed. New Haven, Conn.: Yale University Press, 1971.

Rae, Douglas W., and Michael Taylor. *The Analysis of Political Cleavages.* New Haven, Conn.: Yale University Press, 1970.

Sartori, Giovanni. "The Influence of Electoral Systems: Faulty Laws or Faulty Method?" In *Electoral Laws and Their Political Consequences,* edited by Bernard Grofman and Arend Lijphart, 43–68. New York: Agathon, 1986.

Taagepera, Rein, and Matthew Soberg Shugart. *Seats and Votes: The Effects and Determinants of Electoral Systems.* New Haven, Conn.: Yale University Press, 1989.

FRANCHISE EXPANSION

The "franchise" refers to the right of suffrage, that is, to the legal definition of who is eligible to cast a ballot in a state.

FRANCHISE DIMENSIONS AND PROBLEMS OF ANALYSIS

The development of political rights, and in particular that of voting, was the result of a long historical process going back to the eighteenth century and rooted in the development of civil rights. Civil rights developed primarily in relation to the market—rights of property, contract, free residence, and workplace choice—and in relation to societal associability—as freedom of faith, thought, and speech and freedom to assemble and associate. The development of political rights added the decisive element necessary for political mobilization, by providing the legal basis for the development of interest groups and political parties. However, voting rights should not be seen as a linear development from the preceding and prerequisite civil rights. As late as the second half of the nineteenth century there were cases where voting rights were not accompanied by firmly established rights to association and expression, as well as the reverse. Moreover, the legal conferral of the right to vote is insufficient to extend suffrage, since historically the problem of the franchise goes beyond the strict definition of who is eligible. Even after voting rights were formally extended, barriers—such as poll taxes and literacy tests—made the actual expansion and equalization of the franchise a long and complex process on both sides of the Atlantic.

There are, therefore, four fundamental dimensions to be considered in analyzing expansion of the franchise.

The quantitative level of the enfranchised population. Various estimates of the percentage of the population enfranchised exist for many countries and many eras, but these data are not standardized. The enfranchised electorate is sometimes calculated as a percentage of the total or male population; sometimes as a percentage of the "adult" population, as defined by the legal standard of the country for adulthood; and sometimes as a percentage of the population above the legal age for voting (which often is higher than the age of legal adulthood for civil rights, since voting was regarded as an especially demanding activity). I have adopted the definition of enfranchised electorate used by Peter Flora (in *State Economy in Western Europe,* 1983): those people who are legally eligible to vote as a percentage of the total population (male and female) age twenty and older. In this way we have a cross-country and cross-era reference point to evaluate the size of the enfranchised portion of the population.

The suffrage qualifications that defined eligibility. The history of western electoral development presents a bewildering variety of criteria by which people qualify for suffrage rights. Prior to the French Revolution, membership in a corporate estate—as the nobility, the clergy, or city corporations—was a condition for access to the vote. After the American and French Revolutions, individual wealth requirements supplanted the early corporate requirements, and suffrage qualifications were usually based on property, income, or tax contribution; education or other cultural skills; and sex and age. The history of franchise expansion is the history of the progressive lowering of these qualification barriers and thresholds, frequently characterized by important "reversals," that is, by the disenfranchisement of previously enfranchised people.

The electoral equalization of suffrage. In many countries a vast inequality in the vote persisted long after the formal right to vote was granted. Curia and estate systems persisted in several countries into the early twentieth century, by which the eligible population voted for different curiae/estates as the nobility, the clergy, the freeholders, or the city dwellers, each of which was endowed with a number of seats normally inversely related to the eligible number of voters. The right of some "special" voters to cast more than one vote also persisted in several cases. These franchise inequalities circumvented the formal principle of "one person, one vote" by giving certain votes more value than others.

Politico-administrative abuses and harassment of voters. Finally, the history of the franchise is also the history of the abuses and harassment that prevented citizens legally entitled to vote from doing so. These included tricky rules and tests for voter registration, manipulation of residential requirements, choice of voting days, violations of the secrecy of the vote, district malapportionment and gerrymandering, and other artifices. Strictly speaking, these devices did not violate the legal entitlement to vote of certain citizens, but only made their actual participation in the vote more difficult. De facto, however, these measures disenfranchised certain social groups.

THE HISTORICAL DEVELOPMENT OF THE FRANCHISE

A direct comparison of the United States and Europe is difficult. This is due first to the considerable historical variation among U.S. states in suffrage legislation and practices. In many respects, there has been as much, if not more, variation among U.S. states as among European countries. The second difficulty lies with the concept of the "electorate." In European countries the definition of citizenship includes the right to vote and automatic voter registration. Citizens may or may not vote, but the state does not require any other action of them to do so. In the United States there is a sharp distinction between legal eligibility to vote and actual voter registration, and only the combination of the two allows citizens to cast their vote if they want to do so. The "electorate" in Europe, therefore, does not closely correspond either to the American electorate—which defines a necessary but insufficient prerequisite for voting—or to the American registered voters—who are eligible citizens having performed the positive action of registering to vote, an action that many European citizens might not be able or willing to do if required. With this caveat in mind, some comparative treatment of these experiences is possible.

France and Great Britain are often discussed as two polar examples of historical franchise development. The British franchise is regarded as the prototype of slow and gradual enlargement. Although it lacks reversals, it is characterized by long periods of formal recognition of profound inequalities. The French pattern—oscillating from 1789 to 1848 between recognition of the universality of (male) suffrage and a tightly restricted franchise—is regarded as the prototype of early and sudden enlargement, but it is characterized by frequent reversals and by a tendency toward plebiscitarian manipulation of mass support.

To these two extreme cases one should contrast that of the United States. The early colonial governments, even those based on joint stock companies, royal charters, or proprietary fiat, had representative assemblies. Even though voting rights were based almost exclusively on property qualifications, in the colonies a popular-base principle was an early cultural feature, enhanced by the Revolutionary War and captured in the opening words of the United States Constitution. However, in the United States the franchise expanded slowly, grudgingly, and by compromising steps, and despite the early start of franchise expansion in America, it took much longer than in Europe to complete. Administrative and legal obstacles were fully removed only in the 1960s. Enormous energies were spent for almost two centuries debating and fighting over which Americans were "the people" the Constitution was speaking of, and franchise development was not lacking in reversals in certain periods.

The differences among these three extreme models indicate that it is difficult to find a common dimension along which to evaluate national cases. We may distinguish an early versus late dimension in terms of the timing of the expansion pattern, a sudden versus gradual dimension in terms of the tempo of such expansion, and a continuity/reversal dimension with respect to the presence or absence of significant reversals in the process of expansion. Moreover, questions of inequality and violation of the "one-person, one-vote, one-value" principle must be considered to avoid drawing false inferences from gross levels of enfranchised population.

EARLY VERSUS LATE FRANCHISE

Table 1 provides the figures for individuals allowed to vote as a percentage of the population (male and female) age twenty and older during the last two centuries in thirteen European countries. Due to the considerable variations among U.S. states in both institutional qualifications and quantitative levels, it proves difficult to obtain reliable aggregate, national figures of enfranchised people as a percentage of the population age twenty or older. In this case we must rely on a more qualitative analysis.

Before 1850 four countries were far along in enfranchising their people: the United States, France, Denmark, and Switzerland. The American Revolution, notwithstanding its democratic and anti-British rhetoric, did not affect the development of suffrage to any considerable extent. Only in a few states were suffrage reforms advanced, while in others there were no changes or even negative changes with respect to the previous colonial property tests. For sure, across most colonies the Revolution increased the number of those able to meet the property freehold tests, but this increase was in itself less significant than the fact that the Revolution made explicit the basic idea that voting had little to do with real property. The Constitutional Convention and the U.S. Constitution that it drafted did not intervene in the matter of suffrage qualifications, which were left entirely to the states. Article 1, section 2 stipulated only that those individuals who could vote for the "most numerous Branch of the State Legislature" could also vote for their representative in the Congress.

Yet, property requirements were a less formidable barrier in pre- or postrevolutionary America than in Europe at the same time, given the relatively wide diffusion of landed property. Scholars have estimated that more than 50 percent of the adult white males could vote in the late colonial period if they wanted to do so, and in many states between 80 and 90 percent could vote by the time of the ratification of the Constitution (1789). These estimates conceal considerable variation. While in Massachusetts the revolutionary turmoil caused a reaction and a stiffening of the property requirement, Vermont in 1781 adopted a constitution with no formal property qualification at all. In the first half of the nineteenth century the United States progressively eliminated property and taxpaying qualifications. New states like Vermont (admitted to the Union in 1791), Kentucky (1792), and Indiana (1816) entered the Union without property or tax qualifications, and after Mississippi (1817) no new state came in with property or tax qualifications. So, between the 1850s and the Civil War (1861–1865) the Union had universal white manhood suffrage. (See Figure 1.)

Between 1815 and 1848 France was torn between reactionary attempts to restrict suffrage and radical-plebiscitarian tendencies pressuring for universal and egalitarian elections. However, the French direct franchise remained limited on property grounds to a small stratum of about 100,000 voters out of more than seven million adult males, until France suddenly introduced in 1848 universal, equal male suffrage for citizens over twenty-one years. This turning point led to a remarkable jump in the franchise, from about 1–2 percent of the adult population to 36 percent.

In Switzerland universal male suffrage for citizens twenty years or above was introduced with the constitutional reform that followed the military confrontation between Protestant and Catholic cantons (the Sonderbund) of the autumn 1847. However, Switzerland had never really known any franchise requirement based on wealth, income, or taxation (regime censitaire) and had a long tradition of general voting in the mountain cantons. Electoral inequalities arose through the electoral privileges of the cities (of the plateau), against which had been directed the 1830 and 1833 revolutions, which had enlarged and equalized the suffrage. Estimates place the Swiss electorate of 1848 at about 30 percent of the adult male population, but in Switzerland this was less of a break with the past than in France.

Denmark, too, introduced universal male suffrage in the wake of the 1848 revolution, which produced in the kingdom a radical jump from autocracy to proto-democracy. The principle, however, was applied to men over thirty and was tempered by many more restrictions than in France or Switzerland (voters had to reside in the electoral district for one year prior to the election; dependent people without a family were excluded, as were those who received poor relief and those whose patrimony was under bankruptcy proceedings). These stipulations resulted in an enfranchised electorate smaller than in the other two cases, of about 25 percent.

Table 1. The Electorate as a Percentage of the Population Age Twenty and Older in Select Countries, 1830–1975

Year	Austria	Belgium	Denmark	Finland	France	Germany	Ireland	Italy	Neth	Norway	Sweden	Switz	UK
1831		1.9			0.8		1.7						3.8
1832										9.9			
1833		1.9					2						5.9
1834					0.8								
1835							2.1			9.8			6
1837					0.9								
1838										10			
1839					0.9								
1841										9.7			
1842					1								
1844										9.4			
1846					1.1		2.7						6.8
1847		1.8								9.4			
1848		3.1			36.3							~30	
1849			25.7		43.4								
1850										9.3			
1852			25.6		42								
1853			25.1						4.6	9			
1854			25.7										
1856										8.9			
1857		3.3			40.8								
1858			25										
1859										8.9			
1860													
1861			25.3					3.4					
1862										8.8			
1863					41.2								
1864		3.6	24.6										
1865								3.5		8.8			
1866			25.3				6.7						8.3
1866			25.5										
1867						(35)							
1868										8.6			
1869			25.8		42		7.4						14.5
1870		3.7						3.5	5	8.5			
1871					43.7	33	7.7						14.9
1872			26								9.8		
1873	10.3[1]		26.5							8.4			
1874						36.2		3.6					
1875											10.2		
1876			26.7		42			3.8		8.3			
1877					41.8	36.9							
1878						37.4					10.5		
1879	10.4[1]		26.9							8.3			
1880								3.8	5.4				
1881			27.1		41.6	36.2	8.2				10.7	38.7	16.4
1882								12.1		9.4			

Table 1. *(Continued)*

Year	Austria	Belgium	Denmark	Finland	France	Germany	Ireland	Italy	Neth	Norway	Sweden	Switz	UK
1883													16.5
1884		3.9	27.8			36.8					10.9	38	
1885	13[1]				41.3					11.4			29.3
1886							27.4	14.1					29.0
1886/87									5.7				
1887			28.3			37.3					10.1	38.1	
1888									11.8	11.8			
1889					41.8		28.9						
1890			29.4			37.4		15.2			10.4	38.3	
1891	12.9[1]								11.5	12.6			
1892		3.9	29.3			37.8		16.6			10.7		29.3
1893					41.8								
1894		37.3							11.3	16.4			
1895			29.5					11.8					28.9
1896	13.4/35.7[2]										10.8	38.2	
1897								11.7	20.9	16.6			
1898			30.0	42.0		37.8							
1899											11.5	38.0	
1900		37.7						12.3		34.8			28.5
1900/01	14.2/34.1[2]												
1901			29.0	8.3					21.2				
1902					43.2						12.7	37.9	
1903			29.1			38.3				34.4			
1904				9				13.5	24.4				
1905											14.0	37.4	
1906					43.7					35.2			28.5
1907	37.9			76.2		38.3							
1908				75.9							15.8	37.5	
1909			29.8	75.6				15.0	25.7	58.5			
1910			30.1	75.5	43.4								28.7
1911	38.0			75.7							32.5	37.0	
1912		38.2				38.7				60.2			
1913			30.1	77.8				42.0	27.6				
1914					42.8						32.8	36.3	
1915										77.1			
1916				75.4									
1917				74.5							32.3	38.6	
1918			69.1				74.2		39.3	80.4			74.8
1918							74.1						
1919	85.9	43.8		74.1	43.4	97.9		48.8				40.1	
1920	90.1		74.0			95.1					33.0		
1921		45.5						52.5		86.9	87.9		
1922				73.4			77.5		80.7			40.3	74.5
1923	90.0						97						75.1
1924			79.6	73.5	39.9	98.5					87.4	88.2	75.6
1925		45.2						81.8				40.4	

(continued)

Table 1. *(Continued)*

Year	Austria	Belgium	Denmark	Finland	France	Germany	Ireland	Italy	Neth	Norway	Sweden	Switz	UK
1926			82.0										
1927	92.6			74.8			95.4			88.4			
1928					40.0	97.9					88.5	40.7	
1929		45.3	80.6	76.5					82.1				95.5
1930	89.9			75.5		98.5				89.6			
1931												41.0	97.0
1932		54.0	82.0		39.6	98.4	93.7				89.0		
1933				75.9		97.6	94.9		82.9	91.0			
1934													
1935			83.9									42.4	97.4
1936		45.6		77.1	40.1					92.6	90.1		
1937							95.0		85.2				
1938							95.0						
1939		45.1	84.6	77.8								42.3	
1940										90.6			
1941													
1942													
1943			85.4				96.9					43.4	
1944							97.2				91.8		
1945	69.4		86.7	96.5	88.3					91.2			99.6
1946		45.5			88.0			95.0	90.0				
1947			87.0									43.7	
1948				98.9			95.4	95.0	89.2		96.3		
1949	89.3	91.5				95.6				96.0			
1950		91.4	88.2										96.0
1951				97.3	83.0		95.7					42.9	97.6
1952									89.7		95.6		
1953	93.6		90.5			97.3		98.0		97.8			
1954				97.4		96.3							
1955		94.1										42.3	97.0
1956	94.1				87.9					90.5	95.3		
1957			93.1			97.5	97.9			97.3			
1958		93.9		96.7	88.2				96.6		96.0		
1959	95.2									91.3		40.8	97.5
1960			93.2								94.9		
1961		94.4				97.2	97.9			96.9			
1962	96.4			97.3	86.4								
1963								98.7	90.2			38.4	
1964			97.0								93.5		95.7
1965		92.9				95.6	98.2			96.0			
1966	96.4		97.1	95.4									95.3
1967										93.6		38.2	
1968		92.8	96.2		85.5			98.9			95.7		
1969						93.8	99.5			99.0			
1970	98.7			99.8							97.1		99.8
1971	97.3	94.3	97.0							94.7		80.8	
1972				99.8		98.8		98.9	99.8				

Table 1. (Continued)

Year	Austria	Belgium	Denmark	Finland	France	Germany	Ireland	Italy	Neth	Norway	Sweden	Switz	UK
1973			99.0		87.5		98.1			99.4	96.3		
1974		94.3											99.8
1975	98.0		98.5	99.8								83.5	

Note: In some countries, two elections were held in the same year with different electorates (for example, Denmark, 1866).
1. The percentage refers to the combined electorate of the second and fourth curiae, which represented, respectively, the urban and rural male electorate and can therefore be added together. The electorates of the first and third curiae, representing, respectively, the large landowners and the chambers of commerce and trade, were only about 5,000 and 550 and can therefore be omitted without major distortion.
2. The first figure corresponds to the third and fourth curiae, as indicated in note 1. The second figure corresponds to the electorate of the fifth curia, which was added by the 1896 reform. In this curia there was universal and equal suffrage for male citizens over age twenty-four. However, citizens of the first four curiae gained a second vote in the fifth curia; the two figures cannot be summed. Rather, they should be subtracted. The total electorate for the population age twenty and older should be between the first and the second figures but is much nearer to the second than to the first.

Another early achiever of high levels of male suffrage was Germany. Before 1867 Germany was not unified, and no "German" parliament existed. However, the short-lived Frankfurt Assembly of 1848 was elected by universal male suffrage, and many German states had a fairly large male electorate at that time (in particular the Kingdom of Prussia). The two elections held in 1867 for the new parliament of the North Confederation were conducted with universal male

(twenty-five years of age and older) suffrage, and the electorate was about 35 percent of the adult population. After the foundation of the *Reich* in 1871, all elections were direct and equal and featured universal male suffrage.

All other countries had in the middle of the nineteenth century very restricted suffrage requirements based on property, income, taxpaying, educational qualifications, wealth tests, or some combination of the foregoing, with electorates rang-

Figure 1. Duration of Property and Taxpaying Qualifications in the United States

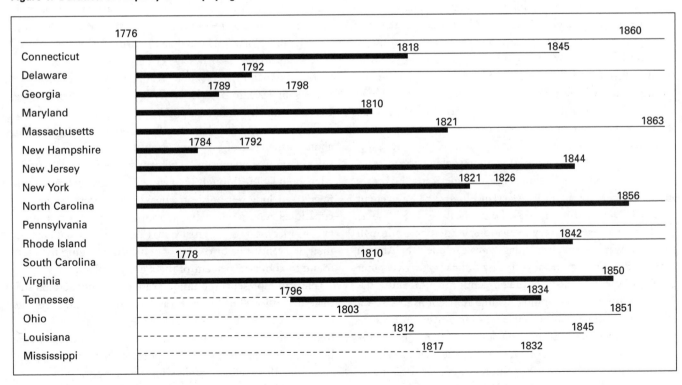

Notes: Heavy lines indicate the duration of property qualifications. Fine lines indicate the duration of taxpaying qualifications. Broken lines represent the period prior to the states entering the Union.
Vermont and Kentucky came into the Union in 1791 and 1792, respectively, and Indiana in 1816 without property or taxpaying qualifications. After Mississippi, in 1817, no state came in with a property or taxpaying qualification.
Source: K.H. Porter, *A History of Suffrage in the United States.* New York: AMS Press, 1971. Originally published in 1918.

ing between 3 and 8 percent of the population age twenty or older. Norway is a case to be singled out. The 1814 Norwegian constitution enfranchised 25 percent of all men (roughly 10 percent of the population age twenty or older) and introduced the most liberal voting qualifications of the time in Europe. However, 1848 passed unnoticed in Norway, and the electorate kept stable at around 9 percent or even declined to 8 percent in the 1870s.

Apart from the American, French, German, Danish, and Swiss forerunners, only in Austria, Sweden, and the United Kingdom did the electorate surpass 10 percent of the adult population in the 1870s–1880s. In Austria at the time of the first direct elections to the lower house, in 1873, the enfranchised electorate was about 10 percent. In Sweden the establishment of a second chamber and of centrally recorded elections came after 1866, and through the 1870s the electorate ranged around 10 percent. Finally, in Britain the electoral reforms of 1867–1872 brought the electorate to about 15 percent of the population age twenty and older.

Between 1840 and 1880 the American peculiarities emerged more clearly. As property and tax requirements were progressively removed, two other problems came to the fore that were absent in Europe: immigration and race. The increasingly complex ethnic and racial composition of the country, coupled with the high immigration rate, renewed the issue of who was eligible to vote. The battle over the voting rights of immigrants, triggered in the 1850s mainly by Irish Catholic immigration, resulted in attempts to restrict the franchise via more stringent residential requirements. The voting rights of African Americans were highly differentiated among the states of the Union before the Civil War. Some states had never excluded the African American population from voting (Maine, Massachusetts, New Hampshire, New York, Rhode Island, Vermont). Others deliberately altered their constitutions to exclude African Americans (Delaware in 1792; Kentucky in 1799; Maryland in 1800; Connecticut in 1818; New Jersey in 1820; Pennsylvania in 1838). The southern states kept slavery legislation on the books through the Civil War, and the remaining states excluded the African American population from voting by ordinary law. Even after the Civil War and passage of the Fifteenth Amendment to the Constitution (1870) banning voting restrictions based on race, the constitutional principle was circumvented by state legislation that reintroduced old voting requirements and invented new ones not based on race but meant to adversely affect African Americans. Only through long decades of agitation and political pressure was the process completed with the Civil Rights Acts of 1957 and 1960; the Voting Rights Acts of 1965, 1970, 1975, and 1985; and several crucial Supreme Court decisions.

A second American peculiarity—absent or marginal in Europe—was that the necessary act of voter registration allowed a variety of administrative barriers to remain in place after legal restrictions on the right to vote had been removed. Strictly speaking, these registration barriers concerned not the franchise but electoral turnout. Often, however, these barriers were so high, systematic, and deliberately targeted at certain social groups that they can be regarded as resulting in *actual* disenfranchisement. The combination of these problems makes it difficult to compare the American franchise level with the European ones, even if there is little question that at the end of the nineteenth century the United States remained, comparatively speaking, a relatively high-franchise system.

The period 1880–1920 is the crucial phase in the expansion of suffrage for all other European countries. The first to see substantial electoral enlargement were Ireland and the United Kingdom, with the reforms of the mid-1880s that introduced a uniform household franchise, a uniform lodger franchise, and a uniform 10 £ occupation franchise in every borough and county of the country, while leaving ownership franchise differentiated. The electorate was increased by 80 percent through these measures and reached the level of about 30 percent of the adult population.

Three other countries enlarged their electorates to one-third of the adult population, corresponding roughly to universal male suffrage, before the turn of the century: Belgium, Austria, and Norway. The Belgian reform of 1893 introduced universal suffrage for males age twenty-five and older for the National Assembly, suddenly increasing by ten times (from 3.9 percent in 1892 to 37.3 in 1894) its very restricted suffrage. In Austria the 1896 reform of the lower house (the Abgeordnethous) brought the electorate from about 12–13 percent to about 36 percent of the adult population. Finally, in Norway suffrage grew slowly from 10 percent to 16–17 percent of the adult population through gradual reforms that extended suffrage to include not only citizens who met property and occupational requirements but citizens who paid a minimum tax on income (1885). Finally, in 1898 universal suffrage for men of twenty-five or older was achieved, bringing the electorate to about 35 percent of the adult population.

Finland represents the unique case of late but sudden suffrage expansion (but Finland was early in extending the vote to females). Between 1809 and 1904 the franchise was extremely restricted. In 1904 an increase in the electorate brought the enfranchised adult population to about 9 percent. The 1906 reform—following the temporary loosening of the Russian hold on Finnish political affairs—introduced universal suffrage for males and females over twenty-four years, direct and secret elections, and proportional representation. In a single and relatively unopposed reform, the new unicameral Finnish parliament (Eduskunta) was elected by 76 percent of the adult electorate, the largest franchise of all western countries at that time.

Italy, Sweden, and the Netherlands were the last to adopt universal male suffrage. Italy had the largest electorate of the three in the 1880s. The Zanardelli Reform Act of 1882 significantly increased the electorate, to about 13 percent of the adult population, by lowering the male voting age from twenty-five to twenty-one and by reducing the minimum tax, equivalent wealth requirement, and educational qualifications. The latter became the dominant requirement: before the Zanardelli reform, 80 percent of the enfranchised population received the right to vote by virtue of meeting the tax and property qualifications; after the reform this percentage dropped to 34.7 percent, while 63.5 percent were inscribed thanks to intellectual and educational capacities. However, in the period of antisocialist legislation starting in 1894, voter registration rolls were revised and educational tests were made more stringent, with the result of disenfranchising almost 5 percent of the adult population. The electorate again reached 15 percent of the adult population on the eve of the 1912 electoral reform that introduced near-universal male suffrage. The 1912 reform enfranchised all males over age thirty, bringing the electorate to 42 percent of the adult population (citizens between the ages of twenty-one and thirty had the right to vote if they paid a minimum tax or had completed military service, finished primary school, or exercised official functions). The number of voters suddenly rose from 2,930,000 to 8,443,000, an increase of 251 percent.

The Swedish pattern of franchise development resembles the Italian one, but no disenfranchisement occurred in Sweden in the 1890s; rather, the electorate remained fairly stable throughout the 1880s and 1890s, at around 10 percent of the adult population, and rose to about 15 percent in the first decade of the twentieth century. In 1909, only a couple of years before Italy, near-universal male suffrage was introduced for citizens age twenty-four and older, doubling the Swedish electorate from 15.8 to 32.8 percent of the population over age twenty.

The Netherlands' pattern differs from those of Italy and Sweden, as the first steps of the enlargement came earlier and the whole process was more gradual. The first reform of the 1880s (1887) doubled the electorate from 5.7 to almost 12 percent of the adult population through a lowering of economic requirements. A second doubling of the electorate, from 11 to 20 percent, took place with the reform of 1896, which, although not introducing universal suffrage, enfranchised many workers, large parts of the lower middle classes, and sections of the rural proletariat and small farmers and tenants. Universal male suffrage was introduced only after

Word War I, in 1918, but this final enlargement (to 39.3 percent) was relatively minor since the electorate had already grown to almost 28 percent of the adult population in the last prewar election (1913).

The final stage of enfranchisement concerned the female electorate, and in this case the sequence of countries is far easier to describe, since in most cases it was a sudden decision. Only two countries enfranchised women before World War I: Finland in 1907, together with males; and Norway between 1909 (for women whose income or husband's income exceeded a minimum) and 1915. In Austria, Denmark, and Germany female enfranchisement took place in a single shot immediately after the war. In the United States women's enfranchisement is normally associated with passage of the Nineteenth Amendment to the Constitution (1920), which prohibited states from denying the right to vote "on account of sex." However, and contrary to the European national experiences, the process had started much earlier at the state level: Wyoming had granted the right to vote to women in 1869, while still a territory; Colorado followed in 1893; and between 1896 and 1918 twelve other states granted this right. The United Kingdom and Ireland enfranchised women of thirty years or more (with certain minimal limitations) in 1918 and completed the process in 1928 and 1923, respectively. In both cases the age limit was brought down to twenty-one years, as for men. The Netherlands and Sweden extended suffrage to women at the beginning of the 1920s (1922 and 1921, respectively). Finally, Italy, France, and Belgium did so only in the aftermath of Word War II, between 1945 and 1948. Last was Switzerland, which gave women the vote at the national level only in 1971, 123 years after the same right was granted to men. In Switzerland, as in the United States, women's suffrage was granted much earlier in certain cantons.

SUDDEN VERSUS GRADUAL ENFRANCHISEMENT

Similar levels of franchise in different countries at a given time may be the result of a gradual growth of the electorate or of sudden expansions of it. Sudden increases in the franchise exposed democratizing regimes to more pronounced strains than did gradual developments. It is therefore important to assess comparatively the tempo of enfranchisement—that is, the rapidity with which the suffrage was extended—in order to relate it to other politico-institutional developments.

In the vast majority of cases, the enlargement of the electorate proceeded by relatively big jumps (see Table 1). Gradualism did not characterize any of the considered countries.

Sudden and big changes were always the case for female enfranchisement, with the single possible exception of the

United States if we consider state differences as an element of gradualism. In Europe, only in Norway, Ireland, and the United Kingdom did female enfranchisement proceed in two (but almost consecutive) steps: 1909–1915, 1918–1923, and 1918–1929, respectively.

Male enfranchisement was more differentiated. If we define a "jump" as an increase of more than 10 percent of the electorate, jumps predominate over gradual evolution. The early-comers—France, Germany, Switzerland, and Denmark—brought their electorates to an almost universal male level suddenly, and thereafter the electorates remained at the same level until after World War I, when they were enlarged to include females. The United States could be considered a case of very early, gradual enlargement only if we regard as gradual the inclusion of immigrants, women, and African Americans in the electorate as a result of diverging state legislation.

In every other country, a jump of at least 10 percent in the male electorate occurred. Going from the earlier jumps to the later, the cases are the following: the United Kingdom produced the first important jump, of about 13 percentage points, in 1885, and of about 13 points in 1918; Ireland also jumped 18–19 percentage points in 1918; Belgium, 33.4 points in 1894; Austria, 22 points in 1896; Norway, 18.2 points in 1900; Finland, 30 points in 1907; Sweden, 16.7 points in 1911; Italy, 27.0 points in 1913; the Netherlands, almost 12 points in 1918. The biggest and most frequent jumps occurred before World War I (except in the Netherlands). In the United States, after the end of property and tax requirements, the major jump in the eligible male electorate occurred after the Civil War, with the enfranchisement of the African American population in a large number of states. However, once again, the peculiarity of the United States, with its different state electoral legislation and the sharp gap between legal eligibility and actual voter registration, makes a precise calculation of electorate changes both difficult and misleading. Consider that, as a result of the 1965 Voting Rights Act and other national actions, African American voter registration in the eleven states of the old Confederacy more than doubled between 1960 and 1990 (1960, 29 percent; 1992, 65 percent). These African Americans had been eligible to vote for a century, but their lack of voter registration was a result not of their unwillingness to register but of state regulations and even administrative harassment. It is indeed difficult to judge whether the historical jumps in African American voter registration should be judged as increases in electoral participation or as de facto, if not de jure, enlargement of the franchise.

The most sudden increases, on the order of one-third of the adult population, were experienced by Belgium, at an early stage, and by Finland and Italy later. Austria had a sudden increase of about one-fifth of the adult population in 1896. Ireland (1886), Norway (1900), and Sweden (1911) had smaller jumps of around 18 percent of the adult population. Finally, the Netherlands had only one jump—very late, after World War I—and it also was the smallest in magnitude, at just above 10 percent, like the two British increases. All the other states not mentioned here experienced gradual expansion of suffrage by means of small modifications in economic or wealth requirements and in revisions of the voter registration rolls.

A "gradual" development implies not only the absence of sudden major increases but also a constant (even if minor) increase in each decade. The Netherlands is the most clear-cut west European case of gradual enlargement. The average increase per decade is considerably higher than in the other countries, pointing to a progressive enlargement of the electorate. In the three decades preceding the final granting of universal male suffrage after World War I, the electorate of the Netherlands increased by about 6, 10, and 6 percent, for a total of 22 percent. In Norway very gradual development was the characteristic of the pre-1890 and post-1900 periods. Overall, the Norwegian pattern is gradual and progressive, but in the 1890s the Norwegian male electorate increased by about 20 percent of the adult male population. Britain, despite its famed gradual development, presents two peaks, and in other decades the rate of growth is near zero.

A comparative classification of the Western enfranchisement process along its two dimensions—timing and tempo—is provided in Table 2. This is as far as one can go in comparing the quantitative development of the franchise.

CONTINUITY VERSUS REVERSALS IN FRANCHISE ENLARGEMENT

A third dimension of suffrage enlargement is the existence or absence of reversals; that is, the more or less linear nature of the enlargement itself. In most cases the development of the electorate was a fairly linear process, and only in a few cases did significant reversals occur. France is the classic historical case for which the label "early, sudden, and followed by re-

Table 2. Comparative Enfranchisement: Timing and Tempo

		TIMING		
		Early	Intermediate	Late
TEMPO	Sudden	France, Denmark, Germany, Switzerland	Belgium	Finland, Italy
	Intermediate		Austria, Ireland	Sweden
	Gradual	United States	United Kingdom, Netherlands, Norway	

versal" was originally forged. However, the reversals in France occurred with respect to the high promises of revolutionary times. After the restoration of the monarchy in 1815, France kept a very restricted franchise but readopted universal male suffrage in 1848, to have at that time the largest franchise in the whole of Europe. After 1848 a revision of the voter registration lists (1850), meant to restrict the franchise, demanded as a prerequisite three years' residence in the voting place. However, this reform had only minor effects: the electorate decreased from 9,837,000 in 1849, to 9,836,000 in 1852, to 9,490,000 in 1857. The reform reduced the electorate by about 3 percent.

In Denmark the very democratic promise of the 1848 revolution was somehow muted in the following decades. In 1866 suffrage was restricted, but the changes concerned mainly the First Chamber (the Landsthing), for which higher property qualifications were introduced. The confrontation between the king and the conservatives, with their stronghold in the First Chamber, on one side, and the rural-supported liberals in the Second Chamber on the other, manifested itself in the stagnation—albeit at a relatively high but not yet universal level—of male suffrage throughout the 1850s and 1860s. No evidence of significant disenfranchisement exists post-1849 (see Table 1).

The major case of franchise reversal occurred in Italy in the 1890s. The revision of the voter registration lists in 1894 reduced the electorate from 2,934,000 in 1892 to 2,121,000 in 1895: almost a third of the electorate of 1892 lost its right to vote in 1895. This disenfranchisement was a clear break in the growth initiated by the reform law of 1882, and it was seventeen years and five elections before, in 1909, the electorate returned to the level of 1892. The Italian disenfranchisement policy was the only one directly linked to and relevant for the history of mass party formation and regime consolidation.

Significant franchise reversals cannot be identified in the United States if we stick to the definition of the electorate as those citizens eligible to vote. However, as stated before, the peculiarity and differentiation of state registration laws can be regarded as barriers that functionally corresponded to formal franchise requirements, even if, strictly speaking, they depressed turnout rather than the electorate. This was particularly true for the wave of more-demanding registration laws that spread after the Civil War in almost all American states. Before the Civil War the main thrust of registration laws and practices came from a "nativist" impulse toward restricting access to the ballot box of new immigrant groups. After the Civil War, and in particular at the end of the nineteenth century, the changes made to the registration laws and the imposition of more stringent tests were clearly designed to prevent the voting of "noncompetent" and "dangerous" people, and they actually impeded or discouraged poor urban voters in the North and Midwest and excluded the African American population in the South.

INEQUALITIES

In a less than strictly legal definition of the franchise, actual access to the vote and equality of the vote are important, as well as legal eligibility. The "one-person, one-vote, one-value" principle requires that the vote of each citizen have the same weight and the same value. Institutional inequalities in voting rights normally represented the lesser importance of certain people or social groups or their "danger" to the established order. In defending the class-weighted voting system in Prussia, a minister argued that classes of people had to vote on the basis "of their actual importance in the life of the state." Three of these institutionalized inequalities persisted throughout the nineteenth century and into the early twentieth: curia/estate voting, indirect voting, and plural voting. These mechanisms were absent in U.S. House elections, where the battle was about who could vote, not about his or her vote's value.

Indirect Voting. Indirect voting means that the ballot is cast not for legislative candidates but for "grand electors," who in turn select representatives to parliament. This double step introduced an additional barrier to nonelites, particularly at the local level, and obviously offered a weightier vote to the "grand electors" than to the rest of the population. The mechanism was conceived as a filter against "dangerous" candidates. France (1815–1817), the Netherlands (1815–1831), and Switzerland (1815–1848) used indirect voting in the early part of the nineteenth century. Austria, Finland, Norway, and Sweden kept some form of indirect voting well into the twentieth century. In Austria voting was indirect from 1861 until 1901 in the fourth curia, and since 1897 also in the fifth curia, so that the bulk of the enfranchised electorate was subject to it. In Finland voting was indirect until 1906 for the estate of peasants, which obviously constituted the overwhelming majority of the adult population. Norway and Sweden kept indirect voting to 1906 and 1908, respectively, even though in Sweden after 1866 the vote was only partly indirect. Indirect voting was retained in Prussia until 1918, and Prussia had an overwhelming importance for German Reich politics.

Curia and Estate Systems. These systems divide the population into separate social groups called "curiae" or "estates." By assigning a disproportionate number of seats to the upper estates—generally representing aristocratic and wealthy families and the clergy—these mechanisms made the vote of some citizens count more than that of others. Prussia, Austria, and Finland retained curia-estate systems throughout the nineteenth century, and Sweden until 1866. In Prussia primary electors (the vote was indirect) were divided into three classes on the basis of the tax they paid, all three classes electing a similar number of deputies. In 1893 the proportion of the electorate in the three classes was 3 percent, 11 percent, and 86 percent, respectively. To give an extreme example of the resulting inequalities of the vote, one can look at the Essen and Frankfurt constituencies, where respectively the Krupp and the Rothschild families were the only members of the first class. In Austria, from the first direct election of the lower house in 1873 to the electoral reform of 1907 the system was based on four curiae of electors. The first curia (85 seats) was made up of male landowners who paid at least 50 florins of taxes per year; the second (21 seats) comprised members of the chambers of commerce and trade; the third (118 seats) included all male urban dwellers twenty-four years or older who paid 10 florins or more; the fourth curia (129 seats indirectly elected) comprised male rural commune residents who paid at least 10 florins. The Finnish and Swedish curia systems were similar in the first half of the nineteenth century. The four estates—of the noble families, the clergy, the burghers, and the peasants (excluding tenants and agricultural laborers)—elected the usual disproportionate number of representatives. In addition, other complex aspects increased the inequality. This mechanism yielded four houses formally endowed with the same powers in which, in 1900, the roughly 150 noble families had the same weight as the 1,083 enfranchised clericals, the 23,469 eligible burghers (representing all those living in urban areas), and the 10,184 enfranchised peasants (representing the whole rural population).

Plural Voting. Finally, throughout the nineteenth century in Europe the practice of attributing extra votes to the wealthy, well educated, or representatives of special institutions (churches, universities) persisted in Finland, Austria, Belgium, and the United Kingdom.

The Finnish system continued to use plural voting based on professional and income qualifications in the estate of burghers until 1906. In Austria plural voting practices were relatively minor before 1897, but they became a large factor in the context of the enlargement of the franchise. When an additional fifth curia was added in 1897, in which universal and equal suffrage existed for male citizens over age twenty-four, the electors of the first four curiae all gained a second vote. Between 1896 and 1907, therefore, about 40 percent of Austrian males cast two votes.

In Belgium between 1831 and 1892 suffrage was very restricted but was equal. In 1894 the introduction of universal male suffrage was counterbalanced with plural voting procedures: one additional vote was granted to married male citizens older than thirty-five, widows paying more than five Fr

of taxes, and citizens older than twenty-five who owned real estate above a certain value; two additional votes were granted to citizens having a higher or mid-level education or holding a public office requiring such level of education. Combining the two qualifications, one could get to a maximum of three extra votes. The result was that in 1899–1900 there were 901,000 voters with one vote; 313,000 with two votes (making 626,000 votes), and 237,000 with three votes (711,000 votes). The half-million citizens with more than one vote greatly outweighed electorally the 900,000 with a single vote.

In the United Kingdom and Ireland plural voting remained in vigor well into the twentieth century, when each citizen had to meet the economic requirements of different constituencies (counties and boroughs) and extra seats were reserved for election by university graduates. In 1924 plural voting was restricted to a maximum of two votes, and in 1948 all plural voting was abolished. In Ireland plural voting was maintained for university graduates and occupiers of business premises (maximum two votes); it was abolished in 1923. In these countries, however, the weight of the extra voting was never overwhelming, and by the 1880s inequalities had become minor.

Among the remaining countries, France resorted to plural voting only in the 1820s for a very few highly restricted franchise elections. Sweden eliminated plural voting in the 1866 reform. No plural voting inequalities existed in Denmark, Germany, Switzerland, Italy, the Netherlands, or Norway, which in their electoral development always kept to the principle of equal vote.

We can conclude that institutional franchise inequalities were numerous, important, and protracted in Austria and Finland; relatively minor and gradually removed in Britain and Ireland; multiple but also early removed in Sweden; limited to one device but protracted in Norway (indirect voting) and Belgium (plural voting); and fundamentally absent in Denmark, France, Germany (with the important exception of the Prussian state), Italy, the Netherlands, Switzerland, and the United States.

THE POLITICAL MEANING OF THE FRANCHISE

This article has documented the historical and cross-country variation in the enfranchisement process of Western states. The historical process was analyzed comparatively across four main dimensions: timing, tempo, linearity, and inequalities in voting rights. The straightforward characterization that often leads from a few exemplary cases (typically France versus Britain) proves unsatisfactory. A far more complex and differentiated picture emerges, which is not easy to simplify in idealtypes.

Any discussion of the expansion of the franchise requires a concluding reflection on the political meaning and role of the franchise in the broader political system. The differences that were documented indicate that the process of enfranchisement played an ambivalent and often ambiguous role in the eyes of the ruling elite. Expansion and equalization of the franchise resulted from pressure from below by social movements and political organizations. However, the resistance that they met and the way in which they were dealt with largely depended on the nature of the state, the political regime, and the principle of legitimation of its political elite. Indeed, from the American and French Revolutions to the First World War, the expansion of suffrage indicates two quite different situations and prevalent motivations: suffrage as a device for integrating social groups into the state, and as a device for political representation of the same groups.

In autocratic and nonliberal regimes, the franchise was often granted from above to incorporate social groups into the state and to make them loyal to the dynastic rulers and their bureaucracies, but the franchise was blocked as an instrument of representation by high inequalities and by the fact that the resulting elective assemblies were not recognized as the source of political legitimacy, executive control, or legislative production. Dynastic autocracies like Denmark, Prussia (later Germany), and Austria often granted more extensive voting rights than liberal regimes like Britain, Belgium, and the Netherlands, probably because their rulers required some measure of plebiscitary legitimation in the absence of effective channels of representation. The goal of the electoral process was to offer symbolic participation without making an impact on the selection and recruitment of the ruling elite, which continued to be co-opted and selected from dominant social and bureaucratic groups and continued to be sheltered from electoral pressures from below.

In liberal regimes, where responsible government was consolidated and legislatures were powerful bodies and sources of political legitimacy, suffrage built upon already established opposition and association rights and grounded their representational expression. Since suffrage was an instrument of interelite recruitment and competition and the main tool for selecting the ruling political elite, it was extended more cautiously. Political elites that were elective and legitimated by a restricted but effective franchise and interelite competition could then better resist the pressures for enlargement and equalization of the franchise.

The nature of the state was also important. Persistent traditions of premodern representative bodies and relatively weak central state bureaucratic and dynastic structures caused suffrage to develop slowly as the result of conflicts and compromises among established social hierarchies, corporate institutions, and local government. On the contrary, strong absolutist traditions and bureaucratic central rule made it easier to standardize franchise decisions and strategies at the center. The difference can be appreciated by contrasting the experiences of the Dutch and British with those of Germany, Austria, and France. However, the clearest distinctions concern the American versus the European experience. The republican identity of the United States rested on the "rule of the people" principle, but the weakness of the central authority made impossible an early standardization of franchise rights and procedures. Local resistance and geographical inequalities persisted longer in the United States than in the European nation states. It is not surprising, therefore, that a crucial role was played in the United States by the court system, and in particular by the Supreme Court, while in Europe the courts played no role and franchise expansion was left entirely in the hands of the central decision makers. The U.S. Supreme Court did not interfere with state franchise legislation until the Civil War; moved hesitantly until the beginning of the century, learning its potential to intervene on the basis of the Fifteenth Amendment; and became the crucial actor in the franchise equalization process in the twentieth century, with its outlawing of discriminatory clauses and intervention on the disenfranchising effects of voter registration rules. A similar role for the judicial system was impossible in Europe, not only because of its weakness with respect to the central political authorities (even in England), but also because it was not necessary. The European inequalities, when they existed and persisted, were highly institutionalized and as such could not be challenged even by the most active judiciary. Once they were abolished by the center, however, their dismantling at the local level was much easier.

See also *Administration of Elections; Age of Voting; Compulsory Voting; Democracy and Elections; Estate and Curia Constituencies; Functions of Elections; Open Voting; Registration of Voters in the United States; Secret Ballot; Women: Enfranchisement.*

STEFANO BARTOLINI, EUROPEAN UNIVERSITY INSTITUTE, FLORENCE, ITALY

BIBLIOGRAPHY

Bendix, Reinhard. *Nation-Building and Citizenship: Studies of Our Changing Social Order.* New York: John Wiley and Sons, 1964.

Campbell, Peter. *French Electoral Systems and Elections 1789–1957.* London: Faber, 1958.

Carstairs, Andrew. *A Short History of Electoral Systems in Western Europe.* London: Allen and Unwin, 1980.

Flora, Peter, et al. *State Economy and Society in Western Europe: A Data Handbook in Two Volumes.* Vol. 1, *The Growth of Mass Democracies and Welfare State,* 181–197. Frankfurt: Campus Verlag; London: Macmillan Press; Chicago: St. James Press, 1983.

Marshall, Thomas Humphrey. *Class, Citizenship and Social Development.* New York: Anchor Books Edition, 1965.

Meyriat, Jean, and Stein Rokkan, eds. *International Guide to Electoral Statistics.* Vol. 1, *National Elections.* The Hague: Mouton, 1969.

Noiret, Serge, ed. *Political Strategies and Electoral Reforms: Origins of Voting Systems in Europe in the 19th and 20th Centuries.* Baden-Baden: Nomos Verlagsgesellschaft, 1990.

Porter, Kirk Harold. *A History of Suffrage in the United States.* New York: AMS Press, 1971. Originally published in 1918.

Rogers, Donald Wayne, ed. *Voting and the Spirit of American Democracy: Essays on the History of Voting and Voting Rights in America.* Urbana: University of Illinois Press, 1992.

Rokkan, Stein. "Mass Suffrage, Secret Voting and Political Participation." In *Political Sociology,* edited by L.A. Coser, 101–131. New York: Harper and Row, 1966.

Rokkan, Stein. *Citizens, Elections, Parties.* Oslo: Universitetsforlaget, 1970.

Romanelli, Raffaele, ed. *How Did They Become Voters? The History of Franchise in Modern European Representation.* The Hague, London, Boston: Kluwer Law International, 1998.

Williamson, Chilton. *American Suffrage from Property to Democracy, 1760–1860.* Princeton, N.J.: Princeton University Press, 1960.

FRAUD AND FALSIFICATION OF VOTES

See *Administration of Elections; Tendered Ballots*

FREE AND FAIR ELECTIONS

Free and fair is a catchphrase that is often used—in spite of its vagueness and multidimensionality—to characterize elections of a certain quality. For reasons of political sensitivity, the United Nations and other international organizations were at first cautious in wording their declarations and conventions on the criteria for evaluating elections. Now, however, they are more outspoken, as in the 1990 Copenhagen Document of the Conference on Security and Cooperation in Europe (now the Organization for Security and Cooperation in Europe). The concept of free and fair elections is particularly important in two different, yet related, respects: election observation and monitoring, and theories of democracy.

THEORIES OF DEMOCRACY

Most modern theorists of democracy consider electoral competition as a necessary element of democracy. An influential example is American political scientist Robert A. Dahl. Dahl sees polyarchy—his preferred term for the real-life approximation to the democratic ideal, used to avoid confusing what is normally called democracy with full-scale, absolute democracy—as a political order characterized by high levels of liberalization (or public contestation) and participation (or inclusiveness). He defines a polyarchic political order through the existence of seven institutions, all of which must be present for a government to be classified as a democracy/polyarchy. One of these institutions is free and fair elections, that is to say, elected officials are chosen in frequent and fairly conducted elections in which coercion is comparatively uncommon.

Like most theorists of democracy, Dahl does not give a detailed account of what he means by "free and fair elections." However, he emphasizes that elections cannot contribute to democratic development unless other important democratic rights and liberties—such as the right of access to alternative sources of information, freedom of expression, and freedom to organize—have been established first. This is consistent with Dahl's claim that development toward democracy/polyarchy will generally be more steady and certain if contestation develops in advance of participation, such as suffrage expansion or a substantive broadening of the rights to stand for election. In this view, the holding of free and fair elections presupposes that some of Dahl's other required institutions for polyarchy/democracy are firmly established and protected, before such elections can themselves contribute to the consolidation of a polyarchic political order. As Dahl himself did put it in 1992: Free and fair elections are the culmination of the democratization process, not the beginning.

ELECTION OBSERVATION AND MONITORING

The use of the expression "free and fair" in connection with international and domestic election monitoring and observation is the other main field that interests us here. After its supposed first appearance in a report on Togoland's 1956 referendum on independence, "free and fair" became the verdict by which the UN recognized as legitimate the plebiscites conducted during the late 1950s in former colonies and trust territories.

Could it be that we are dealing with a terminological problem, with "free and fair" being used primarily as a synonym for "acceptable" or "passed"? In fact, no organization made a discernible effort to establish a clear-cut definition or a set of practicable guidelines to judge whether a particular election can be characterized as free and fair. This negligence violates standard methodological procedures and is surprising, especially given the heightened interest of international and national groups and organizations since 1989 in providing election assistance, monitoring, and observation.

Many groups and organizations have produced useful manuals and guidelines on election observation and monitoring, but there is still no good methodology for summarizing the many—often conflicting—observations from an electoral process into one overall, reliable, valid, and precise conclusion. As will soon become apparent, however, it is not surprising that no organization has yet developed a full-fledged methodology for arriving at incontestable conclusions about the freedom and fairness of elections.

The two constituent elements, "free" and "fair," may be seen as two independent dimensions that must be clearly defined and distinguished from each other as well as from the other elements of democracy. They must also be "operationalized," so that they can be measured and used not only to evaluate elections but also to determine an election's potential for contributing to democratic development.

The freedom dimension will be considered first because if its requirements are not fulfilled, then fairness is moot. To be free is to have the right and the opportunity to choose, that is to say, a person is constrained neither de jure nor de facto in his or her choice of action. A particularly odious kind of coercion is that which occurs when certain choices are expected to have negative consequences for one's safety, welfare, or dignity.

The freedom dimension consists of basic political rights and liberties, as enshrined in the Universal Declaration of Human Rights (1948), the Covenant on Civil and Political Rights (1966), and a number of similar regional documents, such as the African Charter on Human and Peoples' Rights (1981) and the Charter of Paris for a New Europe (1990). These basic rights include freedom of movement; freedom of speech (for voters, candidates, media, and others); freedom of assembly and association; freedom from fear related to the electoral process; and freedom to participate in the electoral process, be it as a voter, a candidate, or a campaign worker for a political party or a candidate of one's own choice.

These rights and liberties correspond closely to Dahl's other institutional characteristics that a government must have to be classified as a polyarchy/democracy. However, they are also preconditions for free and fair elections, the last of Dahl's institutional elements of a democracy.

One manifest element in the development of election monitoring and observation has been an increased concern for the early phases of the electoral process, which must be subdivided for analytical purposes. The concern for what goes on in the weeks and months before election day is partly to be explained by observers' concern for the status of political rights and liberties, which must be ensured before other aspects of the election attract our attention.

The fairness dimension reflects the various aspects of the impartiality of the electoral process. The fairness of an electoral process is infringed every time one of the political actors—be it voters or supporters of a particular party, a group of voters, a candidate or group of candidates, or political party or group of parties—is treated differently, directly or indirectly, from other political actors in a way that might have implications for the electoral outcome.

The concept of fairness thus subsumes the concept of regularity, which implies that rules and regulations are applied in a regular way, that is, unbiased and according to the book. It also subsumes the concept of reasonableness, which implies that all political competitors are treated in a reasonable way, for example, that resources relevant for the political contest (such as media access) are allocated to them in an equal scheme. Scholars and election observers disagree over whether fairness should also include the type of electoral system, that is, the seat-allocation system. Seat-allocation systems using proportional-representation formulas produce a distribution of party strength in the elected body that is "fairer" (meaning more directly proportional) than the distribution produced by a majoritarian-allocation system. However, considerations other than proportionality might be given more weight in evaluating fairness, and therefore it has become the accepted norm not to include the seat-allocation system in the "free and fair" discussion.

It is not easy to distinguish between the two aspects of fairness—regularity and reasonableness—since they both reflect the level of impartiality, or the degree to which a level playing field has been established and the various players have accepted it as level. Yet, for analytical reasons, the two aspects should be separated to the extent possible. Regularity—the routine and impartial application of constitutional provisions, electoral law, various supporting regulations and manuals, and so forth—is a definite concept. Reasonableness is broader and more general, covering the provision by officials and securing by participants of equitable—and ideally equal—resources for participation in the electoral process.

It is also necessary to distinguish between the entire electoral system as established by formal electoral legislation and accompanying administrative regulations, on the one hand, and the application thereof by the electoral administration (and others) during specific electoral processes, on the other hand. If the formal system is, by and large, acceptable but the actual application is open to legitimate criticism, then the situation is different from one where the overall electoral system is somewhat flawed, in which case administration of the system may be less important. The distinction between the formal system and its application is important because basic election observation and monitoring doctrine has long considered it more important to monitor and observe the application of existing electoral legislation than to assess the legislation as such. Electoral observation has thus traditionally been very much concerned with the regularity aspect of the fairness dimension.

The traditional emphasis on regularity differs from Dahl's approach, which focuses on the functioning of all elements of the entire electoral system, not just the formal rules as they are articulated in the legislation *or* the application of the rules. However, international observers have gradually come to accept Dahl's approach. If a country's electoral legislation states that the candidates' nomination papers must be handed in at the election official's premises on a specific date between 9 a.m. and 12 noon and those offices actually were open for this purpose, traditional election observation would not see a problem. But if the effect of the legislation was to deny one or more serious contestants the opportunity to submit their nomination papers, and consequently their nominations were declined, then the legislation suddenly becomes a serious matter, even though the behavior of the election administration was formally correct.

Observers also must make a distinction between three main phases of the electoral process, since elections are not simply election-day activities. The electoral process in its entirety is what matters, and the process should be judged on the basis of a full scrutiny of all elements, including early voter registration, possible biases during the registration campaign, intimidation and harassment of the opposition during the election campaign, unequal media access, misuse of government resources by the incumbent party, the voter education campaign, and so forth. The pre-election-day phase will often be more important for the overall level of freedom and fairness of an election than what goes on at election day. A major reason for this is that the voters' general attitude toward the electoral process, and maybe the politicians' attitude as well, is strongly influenced by what goes on prior to election day. If voters are not free to assemble as they want, or if parties and candidates encounter bureaucratic difficulties when trying to register for election, it augurs badly for the quality of the election.

Theorists long ago recognized the importance of considering the pre-election-day phase in assessing the character of an election process. Individuals and organizations working as practitioners in this field are increasingly coming to the same conclusion.

Similarly, the period after election day is also important, and not only for the obvious reason that fraud might occur during the transportation of ballots, counting, and reporting. Furthermore, the electoral outcome is not always accepted by all political actors, which means that they sometimes will not take office or will revert to political violence.

A CHECKLIST FOR ELECTION ASSESSMENT

Most organizations involved in election observation and monitoring have felt a need to develop election-observation manuals or checklists, so as to make the data collection more systematic and reliable than would otherwise be the case. These guidelines also would be instrumental in producing a better-founded and more easily defended conclusion at the end of the day.

A considerable overlap between the efforts of the various organizations has been unavoidable, since the organizations are concerned with the same types of problems. It is also no surprise that they have been affected by the situation in the country where the list was first to be used.

The checklist in Table 1 lists the elements that should be included in a final assessment of the freedom and fairness of a particular election. The placement of some of the elements under one of the two dimensions and in one of the three phases is not indisputable; the purpose of the list is to point to the need for some kind of systematic arrangement.

The checklist demonstrates that many factors are relevant for evaluating elections, even though the list does not claim to be exhaustive, just as it cannot claim to be a manual or list of instructions for election observers and monitors.

PROBLEMS OF METHODOLOGY

This brings us to two central methodological problems. First, election observers—individuals as well as organizations—might in an election-observation mission disagree on the extent to which the various criteria have been fulfilled. The disagreement may or may not be explained in part by ordinary data collection and sampling problems, which arise often due to the difficult circumstances. Second, observers have not yet agreed upon the relative importance of the different assessment criteria—are they all equally important? If not, which are more important? Are some of the criteria of such paramount importance that they must be fulfilled for an election to be rated as free and fair, and which criteria would have this sine qua non character? Could such weighting schemes be the same for all observers and all elections?

As mentioned above, the criteria of the freedom dimension are generally more important than those of the fairness dimension since they provide the necessary framework of rights and liberties. Observance of these political freedoms is a prerequisite for an election's acceptability, so the election cannot be declared "acceptable"—much less free and fair—if these rights and rules are not established and adhered to. This observation highlights the importance of the pre-election-day phase. It can probably even be argued that fulfillment of most of the criteria of the earliest phase is more important than a handful of scattered irregularities on election day, even though the irregularities are usually more heavily publicized by the media because of the particular interest of partisan opposition representatives and election observers on election day.

The assessment of a particular election as free and fair—or less so—is marred by problems of social science methodology, such as problems of multidimensionality, problems caused

Table 1. The Three Phases and Two Dimensions of Election Observation

Phase	Dimensions	
	Free	**Fair**
Prior to election day	• Freedom of speech for all political actors: voters, candidates, media, and others • Freedom of assembly • Freedom of association • Equal and universal suffrage • Right to stand for election for political parties as well as for independent candidates	• Transparency in the electoral process (including provisions for making all relevant information public) • Absence of special privileges for any political party or social group in the electoral act and the electoral system • Impartial and independent electoral commission (or other election administration body) • Constituency delimitation (if relevant) • No impediments to inclusion in the electoral register • Impartial voter registration and voter education campaigns • Impartial treatment of political parties and candidates by police, army, courts of law, and other government institutions • Equal access for parties and candidates to publicly controlled media • Equitable access for voters to political and voter information • No misuse of government facilities for campaign purposes • Impartial and transparent allotment of public funds to political parties and candidates (if relevant)
On election day	• Opportunity to participate in the election • Secrecy of the ballot (not as an option, but as an indispensable duty for all polling station personnel) • Absence of intimidation of voters	• Access to all polling stations for accredited representatives of the political parties and independent candidates, domestic and international election observers, and the media but not for others • Effective and impartial design of ballots • Ballot boxes that can resist tampering attempts • Impartial assistance to voters (where necessary) • Suitable and transparent counting procedures and procedures for establishing a full ballot account • Suitable and transparent procedures for the treatment of invalid ballot papers • Suitable precautionary measures when transporting election material • Suitable protection of polling stations
After election day	• Legal possibilities of complaint	• Impartial and prompt treatment of election complaints • Official and expeditious announcement of election results • Unbiased reports by the media of election results • Acceptance of election results by all involved • Installation in office of those who were duly elected

by unclear weighting schemes, data collection problems, sampling problems, and measurement problems. There also appears to be a terminological, maybe even conceptual, problem: "Free and fair" has become a catchphrase for the media and for many politicians. The words indicate something of high quality; they connote the best quality one can think of. But everybody knows that many first or second elections in democratizing countries are not particularly free and not particularly fair. So the unreflecting use of this term to condemn elections that might, under the circumstances and everything considered, be "good enough," "acceptable," or at least "a small step in the right direction" is unduly harsh and unhelpful. The concept of free and fair has probably been stretched too far, and it might help to illustrate this point by looking at Figure 1.

The figure builds on three assumptions: that it is possible to work with the two main dimensions (freedom and fairness) without reference to the complex discussion of subdimensions; that most measurement problems have miraculously been solved; and that a usable measurement scale has been developed, which means that we can indicate comparable low and high (negative and positive) values on the two dimensions by using standard scores. To assess an election as free and fair is to place it close to the upper right corner. However, in most cases, especially when the "democraticness" of such elections is the basic issue, that would not be possible (even forgetting inherent real-life methodological problems). Elections that by all standards are not free and fair would be in the lower left corner, which leaves us with the shaded area as the most interesting for the discussion of free and fair elections.

Figure 1. Graphical Representation of the Free and Fair Dimensions

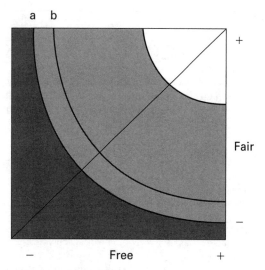

Note: White represents elections that are free and fair; dark gray represents elections that are clearly *not* free and fair; light gray represents elections that fall between the two extremes.

Elections in the shaded area are neither free and fair beyond discussion nor clearly *not* free and fair. They might, however, be considered acceptable, given the technical-administrative limitations in the country in question, given that we might be dealing with a first election, and assuming that the prospects for further progress toward democracy are bright. In addition to the criteria listed in Table 1, observers must consider how demanding to be in evaluating the fulfillment of the criteria and in assessing the general situation in the country. The inclusion of such considerations demonstrates that election quality assessment is not always a simple mixture of technical assessment and political considerations.

A stricter application of the criteria in the checklist will move the dividing line between the acceptable (shaded zone) and the unacceptable, not free and fair area (curve *a*), in a northeastern direction (to curve *b*). Because it is sometimes difficult to separate the two main dimensions to everybody's satisfaction, it might be helpful to consider the diagonal connecting the two extreme points. The point at which the line crosses curve *a* is the nadir, which separates "acceptable" and "not acceptable" elections. This point can be approximated in a real election assessment situation only if two additional considerations are included in the observers' deliberations: Did the election (or referendum) result reflect the will of the people, and what are the chances that the election, in spite of its shortcomings, will stimulate further democratization, will strengthen adherence to the entire body of constitutional and electoral legislation, and will involve more people and more groups in society in the future political process? Still, ob-

servers and others passing judgment on electoral processes should remember that their first obligation is to carry out a technical assessment, which also might help avoid accusations of politically motivated interference in a country's internal affairs. However, it should be stressed that the two considerations just mentioned can be seen as primarily technical, even though complicated.

It is a good idea to admit that the application of any assessment criteria is not an easy task. That was the solution chosen by South African legislators in connection with the April 1994 parliamentary and provincial elections, where the Independent Electoral Commission was entitled to approve the elections only if they could officially be declared "substantially free and fair." "Substantially" is not a precise term, but it makes clear that "free and fair" should not be seen as "either-or." The South African formulation interprets "free and fair" as equivalent to "acceptable," as suggested here.

CONCLUSION

For elections to be classified as free and fair, fairness and impartiality must prevail in all aspects of the official treatment of the political contestants (voters, candidates, political parties, and others). Even more important, no political contestants should be constrained (apart from nondiscriminatory economic constraints) in their politically relevant activities. In assessing an election, observers must strike a delicate balance between technical and nontechnical considerations and must simultaneously balance all the positive and negative individual elements. An important question in this regard is whether the "wrong" done had any impact on the election result. The predominance of this question in the halls of many departments of foreign affairs and international organizations probably explains why they appear to be more permissive than the individuals and election monitoring organizations more directly involved when it comes to issuing the verdict that a particular election was "free and fair."

See also *Colonial Elections; Elections in Developing Countries; Electoralism; Founding Elections (Definition); Founding Elections: Africa; Founding Elections: Latin America; Founding Elections: Postcommunist; Premature Closure; Unfree Elections.*

JØRGEN ELKLIT, UNIVERSITY OF AARHUS

BIBLIOGRAPHY

Beetham, David, ed. *Defining and Measuring Democracy.* London: Sage, 1994.
Code of Conduct for the Ethical and Professional Observation of Elections. Stockholm: International IDEA, 1997.
Dahl, Robert A. *Democracy and Its Critics.* New Haven, Conn.: Yale University Press, 1989.
Dahl, Robert A. "Democracy and Human Rights under Different Conditions of Development." In *Human Rights in Perspective. A Global Assessment,* edited by Asbjørn Eide and Bernt Hagtvet, 235–251. Oxford: Blackwell, 1992.

Diamond, Larry. "Promoting Democracy in the 1990s: Actors, Instruments, and Issues." In *Democracy's Victory and Crisis*, edited by Axel Hadenius, 311–370. Cambridge: Cambridge University Press, 1997.

Dundas, Carl W. *Dimensions of Free and Fair Elections: Frameworks, Integrity, Transparency, Attributes, Monitoring.* London: Commonwealth Secretariat, 1994.

Elklit, Jørgen, and Palle Svensson. "What Makes Elections Free and Fair?" *Journal of Democracy* 8 (July 1997): 32–46.

Geisler, Gisela. "Fair? What Has Fairness Got to Do with It? Vagaries of Election Observation and Democratic Standards." *Journal of Modern African Studies* 31 (December 1993): 613–637.

Goodwin-Gill, Guy S. *Free and Fair Elections. International Law and Practice.* Geneva: Inter-Parliamentary Union, 1994.

The OSCE/ODIHR Election Observation Handbook. 2d ed. Warsaw: ODIHR Election Unit, 1997.

FUNCTIONS OF ELECTIONS

Elections are the central institution in both the normative and empirical theories of modern democracy. On the normative side, elections are supposed to be instrumental in realizing the values that make democracy attractive (or unattractive, from the perspective of opponents of democracy); elections are supposed to create incentives for political actors to behave in particular ways and to define an institutional framework from which particular outcomes will emanate. On the empirical side, the questions are how and how much those normative expectations are realized. How, and how much, do elections shape behavior and determine the outputs of the political system, and to what degree do the empirical effects of elections correspond to the normative demands of democratic theory? Whether from the perspective of formal systems theory or from the more common use of the word "functions," the things that elections are supposed to do, or allow to be done, or cause to be done may be identified as the functions of elections. What are these functions?

This question can be answered in at least four ways, depending on for whom or for what the functions are performed. At root, these four ways of categorizing the functions of elections refer to many of the same behaviors, and so the four naturally involve some overlap and repetition. Nonetheless, because the four categorizing schemes focus attention on the functions of elections from different perspectives, they may give quite different interpretations of the same phenomenon. Two of these perspectives might be described as systemic and the other two as personal. From the point of view of the system, what are the functions of elections in the realization of democracy? And beyond the normative questions of democratic theory, what do elections contribute to the functioning of the political systems in which they figure? Indeed, what functions might elections perform for systems that are not, or perhaps do not even aspire to be, democratic?

From the personal point of view, what are the functions of elections for citizens? And what are the functions of elections for those who hold, or seek to hold, public office? In each category, one can distinguish the functions of elections in a generic sense (consequences of holding elections) from the functions of specific electoral systems (consequences of holding elections in particular ways).

ELECTIONS AND DEMOCRACY

From the perspective of democratic theory, the function of elections is to assure, or at least to promote, achievement of the values that make democracy desirable. At least five such values have direct bearing on the democratic functions of elections. These are popular sovereignty, liberalism, personal development, community, and equality. How elections can contribute to their achievement is affected by the nature of the society in which they are to be achieved, and consequently assumptions about society have an impact on both the place of elections in democratic theory and the particular electoral arrangements that would be appropriate.

Popular sovereignty refers to the idea that "the will of the people" ought to determine public policy. In representative democracies, elections are expected to contribute to this aim in two ways. On one hand, elections are the central part of the institutional mechanism for discovering what the popular will is, that is, for aggregating the individual preferences and opinions of citizens into a single collective decision or for selecting one interpretation of the popular will from among many competing views. On the other hand, elections—in particular, the desire for reelection—provide an incentive for officials to implement the decisions to which election results point. How elections are supposed to do these things depends on the assumptions made about the structure of the views that are to be aggregated into a single popular will.

If there are only two combinations of opinions on the specific questions to be decided, or only two viable conceptions of the popular will, then the alternative that wins a contest decided by simple majority rule has the best claim to be regarded as the true popular will. Alternatively, if the ideological space in which individual preferences or conceptions of the popular will can be located is unidimensional—in the sense that the voters' preference rankings are single-peaked—then two candidates, whether individuals or parties, strategically picking policy proposals so as to win election (that is, using policy as a means to win election rather than seeking election as a means to implement policy) should tend to converge on the first preference of the median voter. This point of convergence is the alternative that can defeat every other alternative in a straight contest, and thus the alternative that has the best claim to be called the popular will. In either case, the function of the electoral system is to allow the people to decide between exactly two alternatives. On one hand, this means restricting the choice presented to the voters to a simple dichotomy, and on the other hand assuring that the alternative that receives the greater number of votes is the one that wins. It is not essential that the members of a representative body who support each of the alternatives be proportional in number to their popular support, only that the supporters of the alternative that wins a majority of the votes have sufficient representation to control government decisions.

If the structure of the political space is more complex, however, so that there is not a unidimensional policy space, binary competition will not, even in theory, guarantee convergence on a Condorcet preferred outcome, because in general none exists. In this case, the best definition of the popular will in a representative democracy is that decision that would have been made had the whole people been able to participate directly in the decision. For this to emerge requires a representative body that reproduces in microcosm the full distribution of opinions found in society at large. Only in such a body can the pattern of compromises and vote trades that might occur in a full assembly of the citizens be reproduced in the representative body. Thus under this scenario, rather than restricting popular choice to two alternatives, the electoral system must provide opportunities for many competitors, and rather than being concerned only with which competitor wins a majority, the system must assure that each competitor wins representation proportional to its popular support.

Liberalism focuses on the ability of the people to protect themselves against attempts by the government to deprive them of their fundamental rights and on the ability of minorities among the people to protect themselves against attempts by majorities to use the power of the government to deprive them of their rights. Rather than allowing the people affirmatively to determine the direction of government decisions, elections are supposed to allow groups to set limits beyond which the government may not, or because of the fear of electoral defeat will not, go. How elections are to do this depends on the presumed structure of divisions among groups in society and on whether one assumes that those who govern comprise a separate group with their own group interest or are merely the leaders of some or all of the other groups that make up the society as a whole.

One view of society assumes that it is not divided into stable groups with mutually opposed interests; although differences of interest will arise on particular questions, these divisions will not be coincident across questions. Electoral competition, in this view, is not about conflicting interests but about differences in the ability and judgment of the candidates—about choosing the "best" candidate for the job, not about choosing the candidate whose views the voter prefers. Permanent majorities with an interest in exploiting permanent minorities will not form. In this case, the only problem is the venality of the governors themselves, and frequent elections will be adequate to allow the people to eject those who would use public power to advance their private interests before they have had a chance to do permanent harm.

In a second, pluralist, view, society is made up of many interests that have a capacity for enduring organization and structure. In this case, it is possible that a stable majority will form and oppress the minority. The problem, then, is to prevent such a majority from seizing control of the government, while at the same time retaining the majoritarian defense of the people as a whole against their governors. Two key institutional devices to achieve this aim are the separation and division of powers. The electoral system can contribute to the effectiveness of these devices if officials in the different branches and levels of government are chosen by different electorates, at different times, and by methods that advantage different types of interests. In this case, any of several majorities will have the ability to block potentially oppressive actions by the governors, while a potentially oppressive majority would have to be stable over time and extend to many different arenas before it would be able to seize effective control of government. Moreover, an electoral system that encourages candidates to appeal to, and hence depend on and be attentive to, a broad range of interests ought also to diminish the likelihood of oppressive government.

The pluralist argument is plausible only if one ignores the problem of elected officials as a class (who always control all the elected offices) and only to the extent that groups (including elected officials) are understood to be cross-cutting and fluid in their composition. If, however, society is deeply segmented, there is every reason to assume that a stable and potentially oppressive majority will form, and no reason to suppose that politicians will feel a need to restrain this tendency in order to make electoral appeals that cross segmental lines. This segmentation then leads to a class of "veto-group" models that suggest that liberal democracy can nonetheless be maintained if each of the potentially threatened social groupings is allowed a veto. In the consociational democracy subtype, the veto-group concept is coupled with the ideas of subgroup autonomy and proportional sharing. In this case, rather than helping bridge intergroup divisions, as in the pluralist model, elections operate independently within each segment, on one hand allowing the members of each group to choose their own leaders (presumably in accordance with one of the other models of democracy), and on the other hand demonstrating the group's size and thus its appropriate share of the benefits that are to be divided proportionately.

Personal development reflects concern with the effects of democracy on the growth of citizens as individuals, rather than concern with the content of the policies decided. The claim is that active participation in making the decisions that affect one's life is essential to the full development of human capacities and to meaningful, as opposed to merely juridical, citizenship. Given the impossibility of direct democracy in mass societies, elections are expected to provide one of the primary venues for participation by citizens—not just in the act of voting but as candidates, as campaign workers and contributors, and even as officeholders. For elections to be effective in allowing citizens to take responsibility for managing their own lives, however, the connection between these forms of participation and the political outcome must be direct and transparent. Elections must also be structured so as to give candidates and other political activists an opportunity and an incentive to educate and inform the citizens, rather than to appeal to their emotions and prejudices.

Community implies both a unity of fundamental interest and a common will to make decisions based on that mutuality of interest rather than on individual advantage. In some theories of democracy, such a community is presumed already to exist (for example, "guided democracy") or to be a precondition for the existence of democracy (as in Rousseau's social contract). In other theories, the objective of democracy is the creation of such a community.

If a true political community already exists, then the purpose of elections is only to give it powerful reinforcement and institutional expression. Elections are not contests between competing opinions or interests but rather rituals of affirmation. Thus, although elections may involve choice among alternative candidates, it is not necessary that elections be contested in order to perform their central function. Indeed, the communitarian ideal would be like the spontaneous unanimity that medieval scholars saw as the ideal for elections by monastic communities. While competition is not central, high (ideally universal) participation is.

If the objective instead is to foster the development of community, then communication, "political talk," plays a central role. It is through discussion that citizens come to empathize with one another and to learn their common interest. The campaign that precedes an election is at least as important as the final choice. Electoral institutions should encourage and facilitate both vigorous debate and extensive participation in political discussion. Moreover, in contrast with the private voting decisions of popular sovereignty and liberal theories ("thin" theories) of democracy, elections in this view involve public decisions made in public; not only officials, but individual citizens as well should be prepared to justify their political decisions to one another. Thus one might question whether the secret ballot undermines the fulfillment of an important function of elections. (Suggesting a return to open balloting, of course, requires that one ignore the real-world problems that led to the introduction of secret voting in the first place—bribery and intimidation of the poor and weak by the rich and strong.)

The preceding paragraphs concerning personal development and community have tacitly assumed that elections are capable of performing the functions required by these theories of democracy. Some theorists argue, however, that they are not capable of this, and thus that elections may be an obstacle, not a route, to democracy. Does choosing officials constitute real participation in the making of important decisions, or is it merely choosing individuals to whom real responsibility will be ceded? Can the "general will" be presented to the people for ratification, or must they construct it for themselves? Can people who are confined to a subordinate role in their economic relationships be convinced to take electoral participation seriously, or would a more thoroughgoing social reformation be required before electoral participation could become meaningful? In each case, an affirmative answer to the second question would suggest that the contemporary equation of democracy with the holding of free elections is in error, and that overreliance on elections will produce at best a shadow of real democracy.

Equality is supposed to be both reflected and promoted by elections. The fundamental reflection of the equality of citizens is in the equality of the ballot; every citizen has the same number of votes as every other citizen. This may also be said to promote the overall equality of citizens, in contrast to their inequality with regard to such resources as wealth and social status. (Historically, the ballot has not always been equal, but departures from equality are failures to perform this democratic function of elections.) Equality may also be reflected in equal ratios between the number of citizens and number of representatives per constituency.

Some people argue, however, that this attention to numbers misconstrues the real meaning of democratic equality. For example, if attention is focused on equality of the capacity of a vote to change an outcome, then it appears clear that the influence of voters in marginal constituencies is vastly greater than that of voters in safe constituencies, and one might expect politicians to be more solicitous of the interests of the marginal areas. If attention is focused on equality of result, then majorities are going to be more equal than minorities; a cohesive majority of 55 percent may well get its way 100 percent of the time. If attention is focused on the political influence of each citizen, then the numerical equality of the vote may be swamped by other societal inequalities. In each case, the democratic function of the electoral system would involve redressing the inequalities that would be entailed or ignored by strict application of numerical criteria. Similarly, if attention is focused on the likelihood that members of particular social groups will be able to win election (either as a means to the legislative representation of their particular experiences and viewpoints or as a symbol of their full and effective citizenship), so that descriptive representation is the indicator of equality, minorities and members of socially stigmatized groups may require special advantages in the electoral arena in order to overcome their disadvantages and achieve real equality.

ELECTIONS AND THE POLITICAL SYSTEM

Although Aristotle, arguably Rousseau, and some contemporary personal development- and community-oriented theorists have regarded elections as antidemocratic, free elections are now regarded by most people as the defining characteristic of democracy, and so it makes sense to begin with the functions of elections in the democratic process. Beyond those functions that are specifically related to the achievement or maintenance of democracy, however, elections also have a number of functions that would contribute to the maintenance of any political system. These are functions that might be performed by unfree elections in nondemocratic systems as well as by free elections in democracies.

The most obvious function of elections is to fill offices. On one hand, this means that there must be an adequate number of candidates for the positions to be filled. Thus electoral rules must set procedures for candidacy that allow enough candidates to qualify and that allow for replacement of candidates or elected officials who die, resign, or become ineligible between elections. Indeed, one advantage of partisan elections is that they enlist the parties as recruitment organizations for minor offices that might go unfilled without someone to encourage candidates to come forward. On the other hand, elections must have winners. Thus there must be a way to resolve ties (for example, a coin toss or giving precedence to the older candidate) or to deal with the situation in which no candidate meets the formal threshold for election (such as the use of a run-off election in single-member majority systems).

Associated with the function of filling offices is that of choosing governments. In presidential systems, the choice of president is equivalent to the choice of government. Similarly, in a parliamentary system with two cohesive parties, the choice of members of parliament necessarily gives one party or the other a majority, and thus nearly as directly entails the choice of that party's nominee to form the government. When a coalition must be formed in order for a government to be installed, however, it is possible that a parliamentary election will produce deadlock, from which no government

can be formed. In this case, unless a fresh election can resolve the deadlock, the result is likely to be the collapse of democracy. (In this respect, it is essential to distinguish between contemporary British usage of the term *hung parliament* to indicate a parliament in which no single party has an overall majority and a truly hung parliament in which no combination of parties with an overall majority is prepared to allow a government to be installed.) More generally, however, elections can be said to have failed, at least partially, in the function of government choice whenever postelection negotiations among party leaders, rather than the electoral decisions of voters, determine what coalition is formed.

In filling offices, election also serves, along with swearing-in ceremonies, as a social ritual confirming the transformation of a mere citizen into a public official. In this respect, elections symbolize deference to the norms of popular government, and in accordance with those norms, election conveys legitimacy to the new official.

At a more practical level, elections also contribute to the feedback process in the political system. This is most obvious when there is a real electoral choice; even if they are not defeated, incumbents can discern from a loss of votes that all is not well and can adapt before popular discontent reaches crisis proportions. Even when there is no substantial choice, changes in the rates of abstention or the casting of spoiled ballots can be warning signs of popular restiveness.

Some scholars also argue that elections are an effective way to reach decisions that are good in some objective sense. Historically, the use of elections to choose bishops and abbots was based on faith that the will of God would be expressed through the consciences of the voters. In more modern terms, if the probability that an individual will make the correct choice (assuming that such a choice can be defined) is greater than 0.5, then decisions made by majority voting have the maximum probability of being correct. On prudential grounds, if voluntary obedience to law is more likely when government decisions are in conformity with popular desires or prejudices, then elections may be the most efficient means to achieving the goal of political stability and civil peace.

FUNCTIONS FOR CITIZENS

There are a number of functions that elections either perform for the voters or allow the voters to perform for themselves. While some of these closely parallel functions already cited with regard to democracy or system maintenance, addressing them from the perspective of the voters rather than the system highlights some of the complexities involved.

The most obvious function of elections from the voters' perspective is that elections allow the voters to elect, that is, to make a *choice*. But what kind of choices are they making?

The first choice voters make in an election is whether to vote at all—and if they vote, whether to cast intentionally spoiled ballots. At the individual level, each voter has the opportunity to decide whether he or she wants to participate in the electoral process, and thus become implicated in it, or wants to stand aside, accepting the consequences of the political process but not accepting personal responsibility for them. Collectively, these individual choices allow the voters to undermine the claim to democratic legitimacy that is supposed to flow from electoral success; thus a campaign to encourage abstention or the casting of spoiled ballots may be an effective political tactic of a regime's opponents.

If the voter intends to cast a valid ballot, a number of further questions have an impact on the meaning of that vote. The first question is whether the vote is to be directly instrumental (that is, to contribute to the immediate electoral decision) or expressive (to "send a message"). If it is to be instrumental, then toward what ends, among what type of alternatives, and according to what criteria is the voter choosing?

A first dichotomy concerns the connection between elections and the choice of government. On the one hand, the people may directly choose their government, even if it is from a very restricted set of options and with a high likelihood that the government actually will be chosen by a minority of voters. On the other hand, the people may choose parties to negotiate for them in the formation of a government, with a high likelihood that the government will have the support of parties that among them have the support of a majority of the voters, but with little popular input into which of the several possible governments that might be formed actually will be. This distinction between choice of government and choice of negotiators to choose a government is most relevant for parliamentary systems but may be significant for questions of coalition formation in any multiparty legislative body. If the voters are directly choosing a government, a coalition that is formed in advance of an election gains a privileged position if its constituent parties collectively win a majority in that election; recombinations of parties to form an alternative majority during the legislative term do not have the same legitimacy, because they were not chosen by the people. If, on the other hand, the voters were choosing negotiators to act for them in the choice of government, then any majority coalition is as legitimate as any other.

A related dichotomy concerns the constituency orientation of the voters (whether constituency is defined geographically or in some other way). Are they choosing representatives on the basis of constituency-specific criteria (the quality of the particular candidates, the interests of a particular set of citizens, and the strategic situation within that constituency), or do they see the constituency choice primarily as a contribution to a national decision? While the first orientation lets the citizens advance their particular interests and may generate a more diverse legislature, it undermines the credibility of claims about an overall majority or direct popular choice of any particular alternative, since in general the election within each constituency will have been decided on different grounds.

A third dichotomy concerns the nature of the alternatives among which voters are choosing. Are they choosing among candidates as autonomous individuals or among candidates as representatives of political parties? The dilemma is that the focus on the individual responsibility of the representative to his or her constituents—implied by the first alternative—is incompatible with the collective responsibility of the party to the electorate as a whole that is implied by the second alternative and that, moreover, is required if there is to be a direct connection between popular choice and overall government policy. As with the dichotomy between constituency and national orientations, the more flexibility and specificity in the decisions of individual voters, the less the clarity of the decision by the electorate as a whole.

Whether the criteria of choice are constituency-based or national, are the voters choosing among candidates as people or supporters of particular leaders, or as supporters of particular policies? If the choice is conceived as a choice of policies, then the victors clearly have a strong democratic mandate to enact the policies they promised in their campaigns; as circumstances change or new problems arise for which they want to pursue other policies, however, they have a far weaker claim to a popular mandate for those changes. (Although this is true of one "package" of policies versus the other, if there are several relevant but imperfectly aligned issues, even policy-oriented electoral choice may leave the majoritarian legitimacy of any one of the winning party's proposals in doubt.) On the other hand, while officials chosen for their ability to inspire confidence rather than their specific proposals have a stronger claim to change course as conditions change, they never can claim popular endorsement of any particular course of action. Moreover, choice based on personality may be interpreted from some perspectives as an abdication of responsibility on the part of the voters; in effect, they are electing someone to relieve them of their democratic responsibility of self-government.

Finally, are the voters' choices made retrospectively or prospectively? Are they judging the performance of current officeholders either favorably (vote for them) or unfavorably (vote for someone else), or are they trying to pick the most desirable future, albeit, perhaps, by using prior performance as one indication of how particular candidates might perform if elected? As with the choice between candidate-oriented and policy-oriented voting, prospective voting represents an endorsement (or rejection) of particular promises, while retrospective voting represents only a more general endorsement of past performance. Further, retrospective voting has the danger of both encouraging officeholders to give priority to the short-run over more enduring interests and, to the degree that officeholders view themselves as the captives of events beyond their control, weakening their incentive to value the interests of their constituents over their own short-run interests.

All of this has assumed that the purpose of voting is to have an impact on the immediate outcome of the election. But in addition to this instrumental function, elections also serve an expressive function; they allow the voters to "send a message" to the government, or simply to let off steam. If the primary function of elections is to allow voters to express themselves, then the idea of strategic voting either dissolves or, in a more sophisticated analysis, is fundamentally altered. Simply put, if the value of voting for the voters comes from the opportunity to express their opinions, this goal cannot be achieved by disguising those opinions; any strategy except sincerity distorts the message the voters intend to send. More subtly, however, the message the voter wants to send may not be his or her true opinion, but rather an opinion that the voter hopes will inspire the desired reaction in officeholders. In this case, the strategic problem for voters is to anticipate the reactions of politicians rather than the outcomes of elections; this might dictate voting for a party that is unlikely to win (possibly voting for the party only *because* it is unlikely to win) rather than voting for a party that is both more preferred and more competitive. Whether the votes are sincere or strategic, the ability of elections to facilitate popular expression is limited by the poverty of the vocabulary they offer to voters (one candidate or another) in comparison with the complexity of the messages potentially to be sent. With many voters trying to say many things, it might be impossible to look at the aggregate returns and know just what the people were saying.

Elections give the voters power over officeholders. In doing so, elections give officeholders an incentive to treat the voters with respect, and so to help redress the natural imbalance of power between the rulers and the ruled. Most significantly, elections give voters the power to "turn the scoundrels out," even if only to replace them with a new group of scoundrels. Moreover, election constitutes officeholders as the representatives of specific constituents, thus giving each citizen a point of access to the government establishment and a person with official status whose job it is to protect his or her interests and to intercede on his or her behalf.

Even if elections fail in their function of empowering citizens, they may contribute to the psychological contentment of the citizens by giving them the feeling that they are empowered. A feeling of self-respect may be more likely to result if the citizens have real power, but it does not depend upon it. In fact, the actual power that a citizen would have in a large society in which every individual had equal power is so small as to suggest that a sense of personal political efficacy can only be an illusion. Nonetheless, real benefits of both a material and a psychological nature can accrue to voters from having that illusion widely accepted.

The educative function also can be served if citizens believe their votes to be effective, whether or not they are effective in reality. On one side, belief that their votes will be effective gives the voters an incentive to become informed. On the other side, belief in the power of the voters, or even a cynical desire to maintain the illusion of power in the minds of the voters, gives politicians an incentive to inform the voters. Indeed, even when elections are generally recognized to be of ritual rather than substantive importance, that ritual demands an electoral campaign in which the rulers explain and justify their policies to the ruled.

Elections also help integrate voters into a community. Participation in the mass activity of voting provides a common experience as well as symbolizing community membership. Often citizens are addressed by candidates as members of a single community rather than as members of isolated subgroups. Moreover, an electoral campaign itself, like other forms of political activity, provides a forum for social interaction that extends the range of connections among citizens.

ELECTIONS AND OFFICIALS

Although it is generally understood that the primary function of elections is to do things for the citizens, and thus in some respects to do things *to* government officials (direct them, constrain them, reward or punish them), they also can perform a number of valuable functions *for* officials.

The most important thing that elections do for officials is give them legitimacy. Rule can, of course, be maintained by force, but rule by force is far more expensive and far less effective than rule maintained by right. This realization gives politicians a powerful incentive to abide by the norms of democratic electoral practice as well as to contribute to maintenance of the popular idea that elections are effective means of controlling and directing the government.

All governing involves building and maintaining coalitions, and elections provide politicians with a focal point for this activity. The publicity and excitement of a campaign aid in motivating potential supporters and in committing them to a party or candidate. The periodic and synoptic nature of electoral choice makes elections particularly well suited to the building of durable coalitions, as opposed to coalitions built to resolve a single question. In particular, the idea of a "blackmail" party that forces a candidate or party to accept policies it does not want by threatening withdrawal of support and likely electoral defeat can be adapted in reverse by candidates or parties. Because the consequence of defeat is loss of influence over all issues for a significant period of time, candidates can "force" their wavering supporters to accept or even to advance positions on specific issues that they ordinarily would oppose by claiming general electoral necessity.

A third function of elections for officials is to provide a "reality check." Most simply, elections provide information regarding popular acceptance of the policies and performance of government that cannot be ignored; no matter how strong the temptation toward self-delusion, and no matter how ambiguous and amenable to self-serving reinterpretation electoral returns may be, the possibility of defeat has a strong capacity to focus the minds of politicians. Moreover, the need to defend their policies in electoral campaigns forces politicians to ask themselves whether those policies are, in fact, defensible.

Ironically, elections also may help insulate officials from the public. Although the threshold of ire that must be crossed for discontented citizens to vote against the current government is far lower than the threshold for civil disobedience, riot, or insurrection, the consequences for the government also are far less severe. What is an expressive function from the perspective of the voters may be a safety valve function from the perspective of the rulers—an opportunity for the voters to let off steam before their discontent becomes harder to control. Indeed, recognition that workers with votes could be less dangerous than workers without was an important contributing factor to the decision of conservative forces in the 1860s in both Germany and Britain to extend the right of suffrage to the working class.

Going further, elections may even become an instrument of rule. Especially if electoral competition is effectively restricted to representatives of a hegemonic or dominant class, or if all competitive parties effectively form a cartel, substantial challenges to the ruling elite may never appear on the ballot even if there is effective electoral competition within that elite. Nonetheless, the fact that they participated in making a choice among the candidates with whom they were presented implicates the voters in that choice.

See also *Democracy and Elections; Effects of Elections on Government; Offices Filled by Direct Election.*

RICHARD S. KATZ, JOHNS HOPKINS UNIVERSITY

BIBLIOGRAPHY

Barber, Benjamin. *Strong Democracy: Participatory Politics for a New Age.* Berkeley: University of California Press, 1984.

Bentham, Jeremy. "Radical Reform Bill with Extracts from the Reasons." In *The Works of Jeremy Bentham,* vol. 3. New York: Russell and Russell, 1962.

Dahl, Robert A. *A Preface to Democratic Theory.* Chicago: University of Chicago Press, 1956.

Downs, Anthony. *An Economic Theory of Democracy.* New York: Harper and Row, 1957.

Duverger, Maurice. *Political Parties.* New York: John Wiley, 1959.

Katz, Richard S. *Democracy and Elections.* New York: Oxford University Press, 1997.

Lijphart, Arend. *The Politics of Accommodation.* Berkeley: University of California Press, 1968.

Rose, Richard, and Harve Mossawir. "Voting and Elections: A Functional Analysis." *Political Studies* 15, no. 2 (June 1967): 173-201.

FUSED VOTES

Fused votes occur where a citizen casts a single ballot for the election of more than one political office. Citizens are unable to divide their votes (for example, for the president, senate, and house) among the candidates or lists of different parties. Split-ticket voting of any type is expressly prohibited.

Fused votes are most common in presidential systems in which presidential and legislative elections are held simultaneously. Over the past decade the number of countries employing fused votes has gradually declined.

It is important to distinguish between two variants of fused votes. The first is the rigid variant. Bolivia, the Dominican Republic, Guatemala, Guyana, Honduras, and Venezuela currently employ or have employed fused votes without any possibility of intraparty choice or fusion candidacy.

Prior to 1997 Bolivians cast a single ballot for the president, senate, and house. Since 1997 Bolivia has employed fused votes for the election of the president, the senate, and the one-half of the house chosen from party lists. Until 1993 Hondurans cast a single ballot to elect the president, unicameral legislature, delegation to the Central American Parliament (since 1989), and mayors/municipal councils. In 1993 Honduras separated the three national elections from the municipal elections, and in 1997 it eliminated fused voting altogether. The Dominican Republic employs a fused ballot to elect the senate and house. Prior to 1995 Guatemala employed fused votes for the election of the president and the one-quarter of the unicameral legislature chosen from a country-wide list. In Guyana the candidate of the party that wins a plurality of the vote in the legislative election is elected president. Prior to 1993 Venezuela used fused votes for the election of its senate and house.

A less rigid variant of the fused vote is employed in Uruguay, where voters cast a single ballot to elect the president, senate, and house. However, because the same presidential candidate is often on the ballot of several distinct senate and house subparty lists, voters normally possess some intraparty (although no interparty) choice. Similarly, in the few instances (most recently in 1986) where the Dominican Republic employed fused votes for the presidential, legislative, and municipal elections, it allowed a presidential candidate to appear on the same ballot with the legislative and municipal candidate lists of more than one party (a type of fusion candidacy). Thus voters possessed some limited interparty choice.

An advantage of fused votes for electing the president and national legislature is they eliminate split-ticket voting, thereby increasing the likelihood that the president's party will have a majority of the legislative seats. A legislative majority in turn enhances governability.

A disadvantage of fused votes is they severely restrict voter choice. For example, a Bolivian must simultaneously vote in a presidential election in which the second ballot method is used, a senate election in which three-member districts and the limited vote are employed, and a house election in which multimember districts and proportional representation are utilized.

Fused votes also are used for the direct election of the president and vice president. In virtually all presidential systems that have an office of vice president, a citizen casts a single vote for president and vice president (the Philippines is a notable exception).

See also *District Magnitude; Double Simultaneous Vote; Limited Vote; List; Presidential Electoral Systems; Second Ballot (or Runoff); Ticket Splitting; Ticket Splitting in the United States.*

MARK P. JONES, MICHIGAN STATE UNIVERSITY

BIBLIOGRAPHY

Cox, Gary W. *Making Votes Count: Strategic Coordination in the World's Electoral Systems.* New York: Cambridge University Press, 1997.

González, Luis E. *Political Structures and Democracy in Uruguay.* Notre Dame, Ind.: University of Notre Dame Press, 1991.

Nohlen, Dieter. "Sistemas Electorales y Gobernabilidad." In *Elecciones y Sistemas de Partidos en Americá Latina,* edited by Dieter Nohlen, 391–424. San José de Costa Rica: IIDH/CAPEL, 1993.

Shugart, Matthew. "The Two Effects of District Magnitude: Venezuela as a Crucial Experiment." *European Journal of Political Research* 13 (1985): 353–364.

Taylor, Michelle M. "When Electoral and Party Institutions Interact to Produce Caudillo Politics: The Case of Honduras." *Electoral Studies* 15 (1996): 327–337.

FUSION CANDIDATES

See *Cross-Filing*

G

GENDER QUOTAS

Gender quotas mandate the presence of a minimum percentage of women (or a maximum percentage of either sex) on the party lists used for legislative elections. There are two distinct types of gender quotas: national quota laws and political party quota rules. National quota laws are generally more effective than party quota rules for two reasons: they apply to all parties, not a select few; and the bureaucracy or judiciary enforces a quota law, whereas the party leadership enforces an internal party quota rule.

In addition to gender quotas, some countries (for example, Bangladesh, Nepal, Tanzania) reserve a very small proportion of the legislative seats for women. Reserved seats are substantively distinct from quotas and are not discussed here.

QUOTAS IN PRACTICE

Since 1991 several countries (Argentina, Belgium, Bolivia, Brazil, Costa Rica, the Dominican Republic, Ecuador, Italy, Panama, Paraguay, Peru, and Venezuela) have adopted national quota legislation (the Italian quota law was declared unconstitutional in 1995). These laws specify minimum percentages for women on the legislative lists that range from 20 percent (Ecuador) to 40 percent (Costa Rica). Also since 1992, Taiwan, which employs a quota–reserved seat hybrid, began holding its first democratic elections.

Since the late 1970s many political parties have adopted quotas for the representation of women on their legislative lists. Quotas are currently employed by a large number of major political parties throughout the world. These include the Social Democrats in Denmark, the Social Democratic Party in Germany, Labour in Norway, the Sandinista National Liberation Front in Nicaragua, the Party of the Democratic Revolution in Mexico, the African National Congress in South Africa, and the Spanish Socialist Party.

Party quotas are especially attractive in countries that elect their legislators solely from single-member districts. (The Labour Party in Great Britain used quotas for the 1997 parliamentary election, prior to their being declared illegal.) In

these countries the implementation of national quota legislation, mandating a minimum percentage of women candidates, is not very feasible (although such a proposal is under consideration in India).

In 1991 Argentina was the first country to adopt a national quota law. The law was first applied in 1993. It mandates that women account for a minimum of 30 percent of the candidates on each party list, and that the women be placed in electable positions on the list. The latter requirement has been interpreted by the executive and judicial branches as meaning that, at a minimum, every third candidate on the party list must be a women, except in districts where a party is renewing two seats, where the second candidate, at a minimum, must be a woman. The Ley de Cupos [Law of Quotas] increased the percentage of women elected to the Argentine Chamber of Deputies from an average of 4 percent between 1983 and 1991 to 21 percent in 1993, 28 percent in 1995, and 27 percent in 1997.

The Argentine case highlights two vital elements that condition the effectiveness of any quota law: presence and placement. In Argentina the political party controls access to the party list (presence) and the location of candidates on the rank-ordered list (placement). This is not the case in countries such as Brazil and Peru that employ pure preference voting (where the party cannot rank order the candidates) or in closed-list countries, such as the Dominican Republic and Venezuela, that have quota laws (or party quota rules) that do not mandate the location of women on the party list. For example, in Argentina the quota law guarantees that if a party wins six seats in a district, a minimum of two of the winning candidates will be women. In a similar district using preference voting (or where the quota law or party quota rule does not refer to placement), employment of a quota law provides no such guarantee. In the absence of a placement requirement, a quota law or rule ensures a substantial percentage of women candidates but provides no guarantee that a substantial percentage of women will be elected.

Unlike other factors identified as influencing the level of women's legislative representation, such as a country's political culture and level of economic development, gender quotas represent the only viable route by which to significantly increase the percentage of women legislators in the short to medium term. Nevertheless, three major critiques are generally lodged against quotas.

CRITICISM OF QUOTAS

Many critics contend that quotas will create a ceiling for women's legislative representation. Although this phenomenon should be closely monitored, in the absence of quotas the percentage of women in a large majority of the world's legislatures is unlikely to reach the level of most proposed ceilings (on the order of 30 percent) during the next twenty years.

Critics also claim that quotas stigmatize some women legislators by bringing them to power by special treatment. This may not be as serious as is often claimed. First, evidence from Argentina suggests that women legislators have not been overly stigmatized by the use of quotas. Second, in a large majority of democracies, the candidate lists for legislative elections are constructed through a process of elite negotiation, where candidates from different groups and factions are integrated into the party lists. Gender quotas are merely one of many determinants of the composition of the lists and should not be seen as stigmatizing their beneficiaries more than other, informal, quotas do.

That quotas discriminate against men is another common criticism of quotas. While this statement is correct, discrimination against women continues to occur in a large majority of the world's political parties. Quotas are simply a corrective remedy to address this discrimination.

CONCLUSION

Gender quotas represent the only option in most countries to significantly increase the percentage of women elected in the short to medium term. However, quota advocates must consider the manner in which quotas will interact with existing electoral legislation. The efficacy of quotas is seriously affected by the type of party list used (closed, open), district magnitude, degree of party centralization, rules governing campaign finance, and other factors. The interaction between these factors and the quota legislation can significantly enhance or diminish the ability of quotas to influence the percentage of women elected.

See also *Candidates: Selection; District Magnitude; Preference Voting; Women: Representation and Electoral Systems.*

MARK P. JONES, MICHIGAN STATE UNIVERSITY

BIBLIOGRAPHY

Camacho Granados, Rosalía, Ester Serrano Madrigal, and Silvia Lara. *Las Cuotas Mínimas de Participación de las Mujeres: Un Mecanismo de Acción Afirmativa.* San José, Costa Rica: Centro Nacional para el Desarrollo de la Mujer y Familia, 1996.

Dahlerup, Drude. "Using Quotas to Increase Women's Political Representation." In *Women in Parliament: Beyond the Numbers,* edited by Azza Karam, 91–106. Stockholm, Sweden: International IDEA, 1998.

Inter-Parliamentary Union. *Men and Women in Politics, Democracy Still in the Making: A World Comparative Study.* Reports and Documents Series, no. 28. Geneva: Inter-Parliamentary Union, 1997.

Jones, Mark P. "Gender Quotas, Electoral Laws, and the Election of Women: Lessons from the Argentine Provinces." *Comparative Political Studies* 31 (February 1998): 3–21.

———. "Increasing Women's Representation Via Gender Quotas: The Argentine Ley de Cupos." *Women & Politics* 16, no. 4 (1996): 75–98.

Lovenduski, Joni, and Pippa Norris, eds. *Gender and Party Politics.* Thousand Oaks, Calif.: Sage, 1993.

Phillips, Anne. *The Politics of Presence.* Oxford: Oxford University Press, 1995.

Rule, Wilma, and Joseph F. Zimmerman, eds. *Electoral Systems in Comparative Perspective: Their Impact on Women and Minorities.* Westport, Conn.: Greenwood, 1994.

GERRYMANDERING

Gerrymandering is the drawing of district boundaries so as to favor a particular group or individual. This can be achieved either by diluting votes, distributing them among several districts in order to reduce their impact, or by concentrating votes in one district, thereby conceding that district to benefit surrounding districts. The term owes its origin to a salamander-shaped district created by the Massachusetts legislature in 1812 when Elbridge Gerry was governor. Gerrymandering may be used to advantage a political party; to protect incumbent legislators regardless of party; to discriminate against groups, for instance, ethnic minorities in the United States until the 1970s or communist voters in the Fifth French Republic; or to ensure representation of minority groups, for instance, "majority minority" districts in the United States today.

Opportunities to gerrymander arise when boundaries are set or altered. For instance, legislation providing for redistricting after a census, or constitutional provisions requiring equality of population among districts, may necessitate redistricting to reflect population change. Gerrymandering is facilitated if the governing party controls the districting system, but it is hindered if redistricting is in the hands of an independent commission. If control over redistricting is shared—for instance, if different parties control the two houses of a bicameral legislature, or if redistricting is the responsibility of a commission controlled by all parties in the legislature—opportunities for partisan gerrymandering are restricted, although redistricting to protect incumbents may still occur. Judicial review of district boundaries, as in the United States, may also inhibit gerrymandering. Gerrymandering is unlikely in proportional-representation electoral systems because districts typically are very large and almost always use local or regional boundaries (for example, *länder* in Germany or regions in Italy), which are difficult to alter. Conversely, gerrymandering is likely in single-member districts, which are smaller.

PARTISAN GERRYMANDERING

In the United States partisan gerrymandering has been widely used to protect the interests of the governing party. In congressional elections from 1946 to 1964, the party with the power to redistrict a state won more seats in relation to votes than parties that lacked this power. In France gerrymandering has also been very common. During the Second Empire (1852 to 1870) and much of the Fifth Republic (1958–   ), conservative governments diluted the weight of left-wing urban voters by combining parts of urban areas with larger, rural, more conservative areas.

In the Republic of Ireland the governing party or parties have sometimes changed the number of deputies elected in a district in an effort to translate votes into the maximum number of seats, although not always effectively, according to Peter Mair. In 1973 the ruling coalition's strategy backfired, leading to the coinage of another variant on the gerrymander, the "Tullymander," or failed gerrymander, after the Irish minister James Tully, who was responsible for the redistricting. Up to 1969 in Londonderry, Northern Ireland, a majority of voters were Catholics and Irish Nationalists, but gerrymandering gave Protestant Unionists a majority of seats on the city council.

In recent decades gerrymandering has become less common in many countries. Its decline is reflected in the increasing use of independent boundary commissions, as in Canada at both the federal and provincial levels since 1964 and in Ireland since 1979, and in the abolition of the pro-rural bias in the terms of reference of the Australian and New Zealand boundary commissions. In the United States gerrymandering remains common. The Supreme Court decisions in *Baker v. Carr* (1962) and *Wesberry v. Sanders* (1964) established the justiciability of redistricting. But until *Bandemer v. Davis* in 1982, the Court refused to involve itself in the political thicket of partisan gerrymandering, and it has never struck down a redistricting decision on the grounds of partisan bias.

RACIAL GERRYMANDERING

The Court has been active, however, in cases involving allegations of racial gerrymandering. After Congress banned the use of poll taxes and literacy tests in the Voting Rights Act of 1965, many southern legislatures sought to dilute the impact of African American voters by creating at-large districts or by gerrymandering strictly defined. Congress amended the Voting Rights Act in 1982, making illegal any voting practice or law that had the effect of discriminating against minorities, regardless of intent. The Court decided in *Thornburg v. Gingles* (1986) to uphold the 1982 revision to the Voting Rights Act. Following the 1990 census and redistricting, a number of irregularly shaped majority-minority districts were drawn so as to ensure a solid majority of either African Americans or Hispanics. Subsequent Court rulings have put limits to the pursuit of "affirmative action gerrymandering." The Supreme Court in *Shaw v. Reno* (1993) struck down a proposed redistricting in North Carolina on the grounds it had no justification other than to create a black majority district. *Shaw* was the first in a series of cases in which the Court overturned such proposals, although the Court has refrained from ruling that ethnic criteria can form no part of the redistricting process.

See also *At-Large Elections; Positive Discrimination in Redistricting in the United States; Reapportionment and Redistricting; Rotten Borough; Safe Seat.*

TOM MACKIE, UNIVERSITY OF STRATHCLYDE

BIBLIOGRAPHY

Butler, David, and Bruce Cain. "Reapportionment: A Study in Comparative Government." *Electoral Studies* 4 (December 1985): 197–214.
———. *Congressional Redistricting.* New York: Macmillan, 1992.
Cain, B. *The Reapportionment Puzzle.* Berkeley: University of California Press, 1984.
Cotteret, Jean, Claude Èmeri, and Pierre Lalumiére. *Lois Èlectorales et Inègalitès de Rèprèsentation en France, 1936–1960.* Paris: Armand Colin, 1960.
Gudgin, Graham, and Peter Taylor. *Seats, Votes and the Spatial Organisation of Elections.* London: Pion, 1978.
Jaensch, D. "Under-Representation and the Gerrymander in the Playford Era." *Australian Journal of Politics and History* 17 (1971): 82–95.
Mair, Peter. "Districting Choice under the Single-Transferable Vote." In *Electoral Laws and Their Political Consequences,* edited by Bernard Grofman and Arend Lijphart, 289–307. New York: Agathon Press, 1986.

GOVERNMENT FORMATION AND ELECTION OUTCOMES

Governments in parliamentary democracies, by definition, must command majority support in the lower house of parliament to gain and retain power. Even if a parliamentary vote of investiture is not formally needed in order to put a new government into place after an election, any incumbent government can be thrown out of office if it loses a parliamentary vote of confidence or no-confidence. (The former is typically proposed by the government itself in an attempt to face down opposition; the latter is typically proposed by the opposition in an attempt to bring down the government.) Therefore, governments will not form in the first place if they do not expect to be able to win key legislative votes.

TYPES OF GOVERNMENTS

The relationship between government formation and election outcomes in Western parliamentary democracies depends very much on the electoral system. Since few Western parties win 50 percent of the votes cast at an election, in a proportional electoral system only rarely will a single party win a majority of the seats in a legislature. Most single-party parliamentary majorities, including the "landslide" majorities won by Margaret Thatcher and Tony Blair in Britain, for example, are in fact "manufactured" by disproportional electoral systems (such as the single-member plurality, or "first-past-the-post" system) that give parties a far higher share of seats in the parliament than the share of votes they won in the election.

If a single party does win a legislative majority, then government formation is often seen as a trivial process, resulting in a *single-party majority government*. But it is trivial only if parliamentary members of the majority party are united behind leaders who want to take office. A party split can, in theory, prevent a majority party from taking power. In practice, however, the types of electoral systems that manufacture legislative majorities also punish party splits so severely that parties with legislative majorities almost invariably take over the government in a relatively straightforward manner.

Michael Gallagher and colleagues reviewed evidence on the formation of 383 governments in fourteen west European countries with a long postwar tradition of parliamentary democracy. Of these governments, 13 percent were single-party majority cabinets, most of them in Britain.

When no single party wins a legislative majority—almost always the case under a proportional-representation electoral system—then negotiations between parties are necessary to ensure that the government taking office can win key legislative votes. The result of these negotiations may take a number of forms.

Negotiations may lead to the creation of a *majority coalition* of parties that go into government together. Gallagher et al. found that majority coalitions formed in 54 percent of the 383 cases that they surveyed. Alternatively, negotiations may lead to a *single-party "minority" government,* in which a single party takes control of the government but depends on "outside" support from other parties when it needs to win key legislative votes. Single-party minority governments made up 20 percent of the postwar European total. Outside support may be explicitly negotiated between parties in a deal that underpins the government, or it may arise on a more informal, even issue-by-issue, basis. Finally, rather than consisting of a single party, a minority government may involve a coalition of parties that do not themselves command a majority but rely on outside support. *Minority coalitions* are less common than other minority governments, but they still comprise about 10 percent of all postwar governments in European parliamentary democracies.

"OFFICE-SEEKING" AND GOVERNMENT FORMATION

There is a long tradition in political science of scholarship on government formation in parliamentary democracies after elections in which no single party wins a majority. Early accounts assumed that senior politicians, when negotiating over government formation, were concerned above all else with the desire to get into office. This "office-seeking" assumption led scholars to predict "minimal winning" coalitions—winning coalitions such that the departure of any party would deprive the government of its majority. The logic behind the assumption is that any "surplus" party, over and above the winning threshold, would be consuming some of the spoils of office while not being an essential part of the legislative majority that makes the capture of those spoils possible. Minority governments are almost impossible to accommodate in an office-seeking approach, since a minority government faces a majority opposition, the members of which, by assumption, have both the ability and the incentive to take office for themselves.

Political scientists, in the office-seeking approach to analyzing government formation, take the distribution of seats in the legislature produced by an election and identify all of the possible minimal winning coalitions—those with no surplus members. This set of minimal winning coalitions determines the power structure in the legislature that is generated by the election. A striking feature of this power structure is that it can sometimes bear very little relationship to the proportional allocation of seats among parties. For example, in a ninety-nine-seat legislature in which two parties win forty-nine seats each and another party wins one seat, the party winning one seat is theoretically as powerful as either of the parties winning forty-nine seats. Each of the three parties is a vital member of two minimal winning coalitions. The support of each party is equally vital to any government that might form, so that the parties have equal bargaining power despite their very unequal electoral success. For similar reasons, it is possible for a party to lose seats in an election yet gain bargaining power. This phenomenon is one of the main arguments used by those who oppose proportional-representation electoral systems as begetting the politics of coalition.

POLICY PLATFORMS AND GOVERNMENT FORMATION

In more recent accounts of government formation, political scientists have moved beyond the office-seeking approach to assume that the policy positions of political parties are also important. Senior politicians may take policy seriously because they really care about policy or, more instrumentally, because they fear electoral retribution if they renege on policy promises made to voters at election time.

Taking policy into account has a huge impact on political science accounts of government formation. First, it opens up the possibility of minority governments, which as we have seen are common in parliamentary democracies. They are common because policy differences between members of a divided majority opposition may prevent them from agreeing on any single alternative to an incumbent minority government. Policy-seeking models of government formation do not, therefore, treat minority governments as anomalies.

Second, policy-seeking accounts open up at least the theoretical possibility that no stable government can be formed from among the parties. Instability can arise if each party holds a different dimension of policy to be most important (perhaps economic policy, on the one hand, and policy on social and moral issues, on the other). In these circumstances, it is possible for a legislative "voting cycle" over government formation to take place, in which Government B beats Government C in a majority vote, Government A beats Government B, but Government C beats Government A to start the whole cycle again.

Examples of chaotic instability in government formation are in practice rare, however. They are rare because the institutional and constitutional structures within which governments are formed and defeated create an orderly environment, which tends to result in a stable government-formation process. The effectiveness of these structures at stabilizing the process of government formation has led political scientists to locate recent models of policy-driven government formation within the "new institutionalist" approach to political science, which sets out to investigate rigorously the impact of particular institutions on political outcomes.

THE "NEW INSTITUTIONALISM"

Scholars have explored several institutional features of the government-formation process within this tradition. These features include the fact that real-world cabinets comprise ministers who each have jurisdiction over a particular policy area. Also of potential importance are the constitutional constraints that may influence the order in which parties are allowed to attempt to form a government; the largest party after the election or the incumbent government is often given the first chance to form a new administration. Research has also shown the vote-of-confidence procedure to be important, since it allows an incumbent prime minister to attempt to face down the opposition by staking his or her government's future on a vote on a single policy issue.

Parties with policy positions close to the center of the political spectrum typically find themselves at an advantage in the government-formation process. In this way, the politics of coalition tend to exert a centripetal pressure on government policy. The distribution of party policy positions, by the same token, is thus an aspect of any election outcome, and it has an important bearing on government formation.

The new institutional account of government formation thus moves away from the idea that there can be a universal model of government formation that can be applied to every parliamentary democracy, toward the idea that it is important to model the specific institutional features of any given democracy when analyzing the making and breaking of its governments. The institutional approach, while still in its infancy, offers a potentially fruitful way of combining the power of a theoretical model with detailed local knowledge in order to broaden and deepen our understanding of the relationship between election outcomes and government formation.

See also *Effect of Elections on Government; Manufactured Majorities; Winning an Election.*

MICHAEL LAVER, TRINITY COLLEGE, UNIVERSITY OF DUBLIN

BIBLIOGRAPHY

Blondel, Jean, and Ferdinand Müller-Rommel, eds. *Governing Together: The Extent and Limits of Joint Decision-Making in Western European Cabinets.* London: Macmillan, 1983.

Gallagher, Michael, Michael Laver, and Peter Mair. *Representative Government in Modern Europe.* New York: McGraw-Hill, 1995.

Huber, John. *Rationalizing Parliament: Legislative Institutions and Party Politics in France.* New York: Cambridge University Press, 1996.

Laver, Michael, and Norman Schofield. *Multiparty Government: the Politics of Coalition in Europe.* Oxford: Oxford University Press, 1990.

Laver, Michael, and Kenneth A. Shepsle. *Making and Breaking Governments.* New York: Cambridge University Press, 1996.

Luebbert, Gregory. *Comparative Democracy: Policy Making and Government Coalitions in Europe and Israel.* New York: Columbia University Press, 1986.

Strom, Kaare. *Minority Government and Majority Rule.* Cambridge: Cambridge University Press, 1990.

Warwick, Paul. *Government Survival in Parliamentary Democracies.* Cambridge: Cambridge University Press, 1994.

I

See *Administration of Elections; Open Voting*

ILLITERATE VOTERS, PROVISIONS FOR

See *Administration of Elections; Open Voting*

INDIRECT ELECTION

Indirect election is a process by which the executive or legislators are elected by other elected officials, rather than directly by the voters. The head of state in many democracies, especially parliamentary democracies, is indirectly elected, as is the president of the United States. In a few federal systems, upper-house legislators—often called senators—are indirectly elected. Wherever indirect elections are held, the selection of the officeholder in question is left to intermediaries who stand between voters and the office or offices being filled. These intermediaries may comprise an electoral college or the national legislature, in the case of executives, or subnational executives, in the case of senators.

An electoral college is a body that serves the purpose of carrying out an indirect election; it does not also sit as a legislative body. However, in some countries legislators may be among the members of the electoral college, and in some countries the same body that sits as the electoral college may also perform the function of a constituent assembly, meaning a body with the authority to amend the constitution.

PARLIAMENTARY SYSTEMS

In parliamentary republics (that is, those that are not constitutional monarchies), the head of state is typically elected indirectly. The head of state, called *president,* is usually a separate person from the head of government (prime minister). Generally, these presidents are elected by the legislature or by an electoral college composed primarily of legislators. The prime minister, rather than being formally elected by parliament, is usually appointed by the president after consulting with the leaders of parties represented in parliament to determine which potential prime minister is most likely to command the confidence of a majority of parliament. This is often the only formal power that presidents in parliamentary systems can wield without the consent of the prime minister or other actor, although sometimes they have some discretion over when to dissolve parliament and hold an early election.

Presidents in parliamentary republics are usually elected by parliament itself, but the German and Italian presidents are elected by electoral colleges that consist of parliamentarians and delegates from state or regional legislatures. Often, as in Greece, Hungary, Italy, Slovakia, and Turkey, the constitution prescribes an extraordinary majority—at least at the first ballot—to elect a president. If the initial balloting fails to produce the requisite majority for any contender, usually a second ballot is held with new candidates, but if there is still no winner with the required majority, the necessary majority is reduced. For example, a relative majority among the two highest placed candidates from the second ballot can elect the president in Germany and Hungary. Presidents in most parliamentary systems serve longer terms than does parliament (Latvia is an exception). Thus the majority that elected the president will not always be the majority that controls parliament.

PRESIDENTIAL SYSTEMS

In presidential systems nowadays, the president—who is both head of government and head of state—is with only one exception (the United States) elected directly. The U.S. president is elected by an electoral college. The members of this body are known as electors. Voters in most states mark their ballots next to the presidential and vice-presidential ticket that they prefer, as if the election were direct, but in reality they are voting for a slate of electors selected by the party of their preferred ticket before the election. These electors are constitutionally barred from serving simultaneously as legislators or other federal officials. The United States is unusual among countries that use an electoral college in that the electoral college never actually meets as a body to deliberate on a choice for president. Rather, the electors chosen in each state assemble and transmit their votes to Congress, which determines if there is a majority of the total number of electors nationwide for one presidential and vice-presidential candidate. In nearly every state, the winner of a plurality of the vote in that state takes all of the state's electors. In the rare case that no presidential candidate wins a majority of electors, the U.S. House selects from among the top three finishers in the electoral college. (In the event of such an indirect election in the House, each state delegation has only one vote.) The Senate selects the vice president from among the top two finishers in the electoral college balloting. The U.S. House has not used this variant of the indirect election procedure to select the president since 1824, and the Senate has not decided a vice-presidential race since the election of 1836. Because the electoral college is not a deliberative body, and because it is generally taken for granted that the presidential selection will be completed in the electoral college rather than referred to Congress, the only real practical effect of the electoral college on the U.S. presidential election is to encourage each contender for the presidency to allocate resources on a state-by-state basis, taking account of which of the larger states are within the candidate's reach. It is thus possible for the winner of a majority of the electoral vote not to have won the most popular votes, although this has happened only twice, in 1876 and 1888.

Until a 1994 constitutional amendment, Argentina elected its president in a manner very similar to that of the United States, but now a direct procedure is used. There remains one Latin American presidential system in which a partially indirect procedure is used to elect the president. In Bolivia a direct election is held, but in the event that no candidate receives more than 50 percent of the popular vote, a joint session of congress selects the president from among the top two (prior to 1993, top three) finishers in the popular vote. Chile, before 1973, used a similar procedure.

Finland, which uses a hybrid form of government that more closely resembles parliamentarism than presidentialism, is another country that formerly used an electoral college to elect its president. Unlike the U.S. or Argentine electoral colleges, the Finnish, which was elected on a partisan basis much like the parliament, was empowered to deliberate and take multiple ballots until it produced a winner. In 1988 a direct vote was adopted and was decisive if one candidate received a majority. Otherwise, the electoral college, which was still elected separately, made the selection. In 1994 the electoral college was abolished entirely.

Indonesia and Taiwan are two countries that have long used an electoral college that also serves as a constituent assembly. Indonesia has a combination electoral college–constituent assembly, of which legislators comprise about half the membership. During the long reign of Suharto (1965–1998), the non-legislative members of this assembly were presidential appointees, and a large number of the appointive seats were reserved for senior military officials. With the fall of Suharto, a smaller share of seats remains reserved for the military, and many seats are held by delegates from provincial governments. In Taiwan the National Assembly, which is a directly elected body that is separate from the legislature, formerly elected the president and served as a constituent assembly. Since 1996, however, the president has been elected directly.

LEGISLATURES

In contemporary democracies, the lower houses are universally elected directly. So are most upper houses, but some are elected indirectly. The French and Dutch senates, as well as a portion of the Belgian senate, are elected by regional assemblies. Irish senators are elected by functional groups in a corporatist arrangement.

Indirect election of senators is sometimes found in federal systems, on the theory that if the senate represents states (or provinces), it should be left to the legislators or executives of these subnational units to determine who represents them in the federal legislature. In Germany the prime ministers of the states (länder) appoint their representatives to the upper house (Bundesrat). Because the German states all have parliamentary forms of government, appointment by the prime minister is essentially the same as election by the legislature that selected the prime minister. It is worth noting, however, that should a state government lose its majority and resign, the state's delegates to the Bundesrat are also subject to recall at the wish of the new prime minister.

The U.S. Constitution originally provided for election of senators by state legislatures, although direct election has been mandated since the passage of a constitutional amendment in 1913. Argentina had a similar indirect procedure until a constitutional amendment in 1994 changed to direct election. Switzerland also formerly had nearly all its upper-house legislators indirectly elected (by cantonal legislatures), but now most cantons use direct election. Austria and India are two federal systems in which the upper house continues to be elected by the legislatures of the federal units.

Critics often brand indirect election as less than fully democratic. However, as long as the representatives who make the selection are themselves democratically elected and accountable through subsequent election, through political parties, or both, indirect election arguably is no less democratic than direct election, and it may be especially consistent with principles of federalism (that is, the sovereignty of subnational units). Nonetheless, there is a general trend away from indirect election of executives and legislators, with the exception of relatively powerless presidents in parliamentary republics.

See also *Offices Filled by Direct Election; Papal Elections; Presidential Electoral Systems.*

Matthew Soberg Shugart,
University of California, San Diego

BIBLIOGRAPHY

Lijphart, Arend. *Patterns of Democracies.* New Haven, Conn.: Yale University Press, 1999.

Mackie, Thomas T., and Richard Rose. *The International Almanac of Electoral History.* Washington, D.C.: Congressional Quarterly, 1991.

INITIATIVE: EUROPE

Any definition of *popular initiative* has to be elaborated with regard to the referendum, since the two phenomena of direct democratic decision making are closely related. The referendum is a process through which political authorities formulate a legal text or question of principle and submit it to a popular vote. The initiative is a process through which a certain number of citizens formulate a legal text or question of principle and submit it to a popular vote. The main difference between the referendum and the initiative process is the author of the legal text or the question of principle.

In Europe no less than twenty-one countries give their citizens some kind of initiating power. Since the forms of initiative vary greatly between countries, it is useful to elaborate categories.

TYPOLOGY

There are two types of popular initiative. The first includes those initiatives that are binding on the political authorities. In other words, these initiatives either become law directly (if the authorities approve them) or have to be put on the ballot (if the authorities disagree with them or alter their content or if the constitution requires it). From the point of view of the people, this form of popular initiative, sometimes called a *direct initiative,* is the most powerful.

In Europe this first type of popular initiative exists in only seven countries. In Switzerland, cradle of the popular initiative on the national level, 100,000 citizens may formulate an initiative either as a precisely worded amendment to the constitution or as a general statement. Although the procedure between the two forms varies, the outcome of the popular verdict is, in either case, binding on the political authorities. Switzerland's smallest neighbor, the principality of Liechtenstein, provides its electorate with two types of initiative: the constitutional and the legislative. Whereas the first type requires the signatures of fifteen hundred voters to get on the ballot, the second needs only one thousand. The result of the popular vote is binding, and the text becomes law, unless the prince refuses it. As in Switzerland—with the exception of the prince's veto—the initiative process in Liechtenstein is very much controlled by the people. Parliament is unable to alter the text of a valid initiative.

Since achieving independence in 1991, Latvia has allowed one-tenth of its voters to launch a constitutional initiative, which may be precisely worded. If accepted by parliament, the initiative becomes law, unless it concerns parts of the constitution that demand a compulsory referendum. If the initiative is amended by parliament, a referendum has to be held. The constitution of Belarus provides for a general initiative through which 450,000 citizens who have the right to vote, including no less than 30,000 of each region and the city of Minsk, may oblige the president to hold a national referendum. (Latvia and Belarus also provide for indirect initiatives.)

The fifth European country that provides its citizens with a direct initiative is Hungary (which, like Latvia and Belarus, also provides for an indirect initiative). A referendum has to be called if a popular initiative gathers 200,000 signatures. Slovakia provides its electorate with a general initiative, which can be launched by at least 350,000 voters and obliges the president of the republic to call a referendum. Its outcome is binding on parliament. Finally, in 1994 San Marino introduced a legislative initiative. For such an initiative, upon which the electorate must vote if parliament rejects the proposal, the signatures of 1.5 percent of the electorate (about 450 voters) are necessary.

Initiatives in the second category provide the people with the right to initiate a legislative process or to address a petition to the political authorities. Initiatives in this category do not assure the people that the authorities will follow the proposal or that a popular vote will be held. Thus, in order to have a political impact, these initiatives, sometimes called *indirect initiatives,* must have the support of parliament. The vast majority of countries that have indirect initiatives are in eastern Europe and introduced the initiative process along with their new political order after the Berlin Wall fell in 1989 *(see Table 1).*

INITIATIVES IN PRACTICE

Switzerland dominates the other states of Europe by far in the use of the initiative. No fewer than 127 initiatives have been put on a Swiss ballot since the institution originated in 1891. Only 12 were successful, though. This rather low rate of success should not be interpreted as a weakness of the initiative process. As different observers have pointed out, the Swiss popular initiative has many indirect effects on the legislative process and on the political arena in general. Voters in Liechtenstein have decided 29 popular initiatives, of which 9 were

Table 1. Indirect Initiatives in Europe

Country	Legislative level	Number of signatures required	Required signatures as a percentage of electorate
Albania	legislative level	20,000	0.9
Andorra	legislative	10% of the electorate	10.0
Austria	legislative	100,000 or one-sixth of the voters in each of three länder	1.7
Belarus	constitutional legislative	150,000 50,000	2.0 0.7
Georgia	constitutional legislative	200,000 30,000	6.4 1.0
Germany	constitutional, limited to special territorial issues of the länder	10% of the electorate	10.0
Hungary	general petition	100,000 50,000	1.2 0.6
Latvia	legislative	10% of the electorate	10.0
Lithuania	constitutional legislative	300,000 50,000	11.4 1.9
Macedonia	constitutional legislative	150,000 10,000	11.0 0.7
Moldova	constitutional	200,000, to which at least half of the districts and municipalities must each contribute 5,000	8.2
Poland	legislative	100,000	0.4
Romania	constitutional legislative	500,000, of which at least 20,000 have to be collected in at least half of the counties and the city of Bucharest 10,000 have to be collected in at least one-quarter of the counties and the city of Bucharest	2.9 1.5
Slovenia	constitutional legislative	30,000 5,000	1.9 0.3
Spain	legislative	500,000	1.4
Ukraine	general	3,000,000	7.8
Yugoslavia	constitutional legislative	100,000 30,000	1.4 0.4

Note: "General" indicates that an indirect initiative may pertain to any level: constitutional (language that would amend or require the amending of the constitution); legislative (abstract, impersonal language undelimited in time that would affect a legal text at the legislative level); or other (for example, language on a local issue).

accepted. The legislative initiative process in San Marino resulted in popular votes on five occasions. All five proposals were accepted.

Among the countries with an indirect initiative process, only three have had initiatives that had to be decided at the polls: Hungary (one in 1990, which was endorsed by voters but without the necessary turnout of 50 percent), Slovenia (one in 1996, which was refused), and Lithuania (one in 1992, one in 1994 that was split into eight different questions, and one in 1996; all of these initiatives, although accepted by the voters, could not become law since the necessary turnout of 50 percent was never reached).

The general trend in Europe, and especially in eastern Europe, points toward an increased use of direct democracy in general and of the initiative process specifically.

See also *Initiative: United States; Referendums: Europe; Referendums: Latin America; Referendums: United States.*

ALEXANDER H. TRECHSEL, UNIVERSITY OF GENEVA

BIBLIOGRAPHY

Butler, David, and Austin Ranney, eds. *Referendums around the World: The Growing Use of Direct Democracy.* Washington, D.C.: AEI Press, 1994.

Gallagher, Michael, and Pier Vincenzo Uleri, eds. *The Referendum Experience in Europe.* London: Macmillan, 1996.

Suksi, Markku. *Bringing in the People: A Comparison of Constitutional Forms and Practices of the Referendum.* Dordrecht: Martinus Nijhoff, 1993.

Trechsel, Alexander H., and Nicolas von Arx. "Wo die Welt noch stimmt. Die weltweite Ausbreitung von Volksabstimmungen." *Neue Zürcher Zeitung,* Nr. 187, August 14, 1999, p. 79.

Trechsel, Alexander H., and Pascal Sciarini. "Direct Democracy in Switzerland: Do Elites Matter?" *European Journal of Political Research* 33, no. 1 (1998): 99–124.

Wili, Hans-Urs. "Volksrechte in den Staaten der Welt." *Sondernummer zu Gesetzgebung heute* 1 (1997): 11–64.

INITIATIVE: UNITED STATES

The initiative process permits citizens to petition to place on the ballot statutes (statutory initiative) or constitutional amendments (constitutional initiative). These ballot questions may be submitted to the legislature or local governing body before going to the ballot (indirect initiative) or they may go directly to the ballot (direct initiative). In all cases, ballot qualification for the initiative is the result if proponents meet a threshold number of signatures—usually determined by a percentage of the vote for governor in the preceding gubernatorial election for statewide measures, or a similar threshold at the local level.

Proponents of the initiative at both the turn of the twentieth century and the turn of the twenty-first century have made strikingly similar arguments. They contend that adopting the initiative will reduce the power of political parties and party bosses, reduce the power of special interests, lead to a more educated and participatory public, and provide a means of avoiding legislative gridlock. Opponents counter that the initiative will actually benefit special interests, lead to a long and complicated ballot, and frustrate voters because of ballot complexity and confusing election campaigns. The two sides see legislatures in starkly different terms: one distrusts elected representatives and the other sees them as more able to make public policy.

STATE AND LOCAL REGULATIONS

Twenty-four states have some form of initiative process; most of these states provide the direct initiative. Hundreds of local governments permit the initiative, many in states that do not permit the process at the state level. In states that provide both the direct and indirect initiatives, proponents of the initiative usually take the direct initiative option, even if it means obtaining more petition signatures. In states that provide both the statutory and constitutional initiatives, proponents usually take the constitutional route, again, even if it means obtaining more valid signatures.

States show substantial variation in the stringency of signature requirements. The range of the number of signatures for statutory initiatives is from a low of 2 percent of the vote for governor in the last gubernatorial election in North Dakota to a high of 15 percent of the gubernatorial vote in Wyoming. For constitutional initiatives the range is from 4 percent, again in North Dakota, to 15 percent in Illinois. The median threshold for statutory initiatives is 8 percent, and for constitutional initiatives it is 10 percent.

Roughly half of the states also impose a geographic distribution requirement on petitioners, mandating that a minimum number of signatures be gathered in a specified number of counties. The intent behind a geographic distribution requirement is that initiative proponents show some minimal level of support across much of the state. The political scientist David B. Magleby has found the stringency of a state's signature requirements is correlated with the number of initiatives and popular referendums on the ballot.

Figure 1. Provisions for Initiative and Popular Referendum in the United States

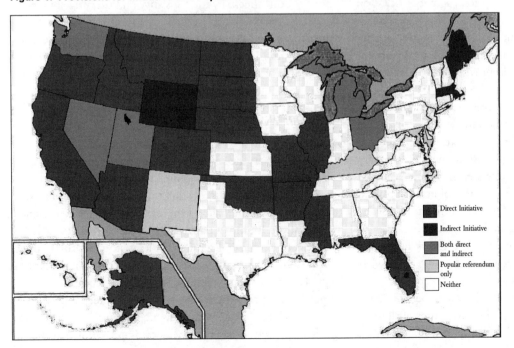

Direct Initiative

Indirect Initiative

Both direct and indirect

Popular referendum only

Neither

State provisions for initiative also often limit the subject matter of initiatives by either excluding some subjects from the process or requiring that each measure be limited to a single subject. Specific budget amounts and designation of specific individuals to offices are examples of excluded subjects. The single-subject rule arose to prevent initiative proponents from logrolling issues together to expand their electoral coalition across several issues into a single referendum. In practice, applying the single-subject rule to initiatives is difficult because of the length and complexity of initiatives. In preelection judicial considerations of initiatives, courts are often called on to decide if initiatives violate the single-subject rule. States also define differently the percentage of the vote needed for passage; some states require a majority of those voting on the measure, others a majority voting in the election. Nevada requires a majority vote in two consecutive elections for a constitutional initiative to pass.

HISTORICAL BACKGROUND OF THE INITIATIVE PROCESS

The region of the United States most identified with the process is the West; most states with the process adopted it during the Progressive era. Within the West, California has often been a leader in initiative politics, and in the late twentieth century the California initiative process propelled issues like property taxes, affirmative action, and illegal immigration onto the national stage. The prominent role that political consultants play in the California process is becoming more a part of the process in other states as well.

During the 1990s the number of measures going before voters set new records. Before the surge in activity that began in the mid-1970s, the 1910–1939 period was the time of greatest initiative use. The recent growth in initiative activity has been even greater for measures that failed to qualify for the ballot. Use of the initiative dropped off in the 1940s and reached a low point in the 1960s.

Only California permits initiatives on primary election ballots. This has encouraged some strategic behavior on the part of initiative proponents who attempt to identify settings in which support is likely to be greatest. In the 1978 primary election, when there were no contested statewide races for Democrats although there were for Republicans, Howard Jarvis's proposition 13 was timed to benefit from this lower-than-normal Democratic turnout. Voting on initiatives in closed primary states means nonpartisan voters have only ballot questions to vote on; at such times they are usually less likely to vote.

Most—roughly two-thirds—of all statewide initiatives have been defeated; in contrast, roughly two-thirds of all measures put on the ballot by state legislatures since adoption of the initiative in 1898 have passed. Voter rejection of initiatives appears to stem from voters being uncertain about the costs and consequences of most initiatives. Opponents of initiatives often heighten confusion about initiatives in an effort to tap into this voter distrust of initiatives.

OTHER PARTICIPANTS—THE PROFESSIONALS AND THE COURTS

Initiative politics has become professionalized on both sides by media consultants, pollsters, and campaign managers. Proponents generally retain petition-circulation firms and lawyers trained in drafting initiatives to combat the frequent legal challenges that arise during campaigns and, if the measure is approved by voters, challenges to the constitutionality of the measure.

Courts also play an active role in overseeing the process, adjudicating such matters as ballot-question titling and wording and signature verification. Courts have often declared unconstitutional, in whole or in part, the comparatively few initiatives that win voter approval. Two notable U.S. Supreme Court decisions on initiatives include the 1912 decision in *Pacific States Telephone and Telegraph v. Oregon,* which ruled that the initiative did not violate the clause of the U.S. Constitution that requires each state have a republican form of government, and the landmark 1967 case *Reitman v. Mulkey,* which overturned a 1964 California initiative that reversed California's open housing law. Federal and state courts have often followed the lead in this case and reversed a vote of the people when that vote affected constitutional rights or guarantees.

Proponents of the initiative effectively have insulated the process from checks by the legislative and executive branches, but the judiciary has played an important role in overseeing the process and deciding on the constitutionality of successful measures. In some states this appears to have politicized the judiciary and might have been an element in voters not retaining some state supreme court justices.

VOTER PARTICIPATION AND VOLATILITY

Participation in the initiative process ranges from writing or sponsoring measures, to signing or circulating petitions to place an initiative on the ballot, to voting on those measures that qualify for the ballot. One of the most frequently cited justifications for the initiative is that it acts as a safety valve for citizens to get around recalcitrant legislators. Yet the number of citizens who actually participate in writing initiatives or circulating them is small. The limited data we have on petition signing, primarily from signature gatherers, indicate that few individuals read what they are signing. The signature-gathering process has become increasingly professionalized, and many solicitors gather signatures for multiple petitions at the same time.

Voting on initiatives lacks the simplifying devices of candidate characteristics in the campaign and party cues on the ballot, but voters often have endorsements from political elites and the media to help them. Research demonstrates that the credibility of the communicator as well as the believability of the message is important for initiative campaigns. Voting intentions on initiatives are volatile, often exhibiting a shift from support for the measure in early polls to defeat on election day. For those who vote, the average rate of nonvoting—the drop-off—for initiatives in states like California and Washington is roughly three to four times higher for ballot initiatives than for contests like governor or president and is approximately the same as for offices like treasurer or auditor. Average voter drop-off for initiatives, however, is 6 to 7 percent less than for legislative referendums. Voters pick and choose which ballot measures they will vote on, and as many as one-quarter of all voters skip voting on some propositions.

ISSUE DEFINITION

With the exception of a few issues on which voters have strong and stable opinions, most initiative campaigns are battles waged on television over issue definition. Both sides seek to define the issue or question in terms intended to motivate voters. These campaigns often involve contested claims and emotional appeals on one or both sides. There are few sources of impartial information. Some states provide a voter guide or handbook with official summaries, budget implications, and arguments and replies from the two sides. One problem with many of these voter guides is that they are too long and not written clearly.

Opponents of initiatives sometimes place on the ballot counterinitiatives that address the same policy concerns but are more acceptable to the opponents of the initial initiative. This tactic can be successful because in some states when two or more initiatives on the same subject pass, whichever measure receives the most votes takes effect. In one California election, voters could choose among four pairs of initiatives and counterinitiatives on subjects like the environment and petroleum taxes, and in a different election, they could choose among five separate initiatives all having to do with insurance reform. In the first case, voters reacted to the spate of initiatives and counterinitiatives by rejecting them all. Such an outcome was likely the preferred result for the sponsors of the counterinitiatives. The result for voters is a long ballot and a difficult task of sorting through the claims and counterclaims on many similar measures.

Voter confusion also often arises from the wording of the question or the official title of the measure. Some initiatives have a reverse wording—"yes" effectively means "no" on the issue, or vice versa. For example, voters might understand the measure to deal with nuclear power, but a "yes" vote could be a vote to limit nuclear power. An example of a misleading title is the so-called civil rights initiative, which was really a vote to overturn affirmative action. Proponents of initiatives seek to define the initiative from the very beginning of the campaign; they use positive titles as "paycheck protection," "victims' bill of rights," or "three strikes and you're out."

INFLUENCE ON ISSUES

The issues put before voters reflect all ideological perspectives and often narrow interests. In a canvass of all initiatives between 1978 and 1992, three-quarters of all initiatives fell into four issue categories: revenues, taxes, and bonds; government or political reform; regulation of business or labor; and public morality. Issue categories like civil rights, civil liberties, health, welfare, housing, environment or land use, and education or national policy were voted on much less frequently. Some issues, like tax reduction, immigration, or gun limitation, are of widespread interest, whereas others represent only narrow interests. Examples of the latter include votes on gambling on Indian reservations or standards for dental hygienists.

Even if the initiative is defeated, it can shape the election agenda. For candidates, identification with an initiative can help mobilize voters committed to that issue to turn out to vote for both the candidate and the initiative. Other issues might divide the opposing candidate's supporters while unifying the sponsoring candidate's base; such issues might include wedge issues like illegal immigration or affirmative action. Use of the initiative by candidates is one reason the process has expanded in recent years. The process has also been a means of promoting a particular reform like term limitation, property tax reduction, medicinal marijuana, or "clean money" campaign finance reforms. On these kinds of issues, interest groups form to promote their agendas and look for allied groups in the state to help carry the issue.

The initiative helped set the agenda of American politics during the final decades of the twentieth century, not only in initiative states but in other states and at the national level as well. The Reagan tax cuts of the early 1980s drew from the tax revolt of California's proposition 13 and the tax cutting and spending limiting measures that followed it. Other examples of public policy questions that have been linked to initiatives include the nuclear freeze, legislative term limitation, immigration, and affirmative action. The agenda-setting nature of the initiative is one reason interest groups and even political parties have become active participants in initiative politics.

See also *Choice, Elections as a Method of; Initiative: Europe; Plebiscites and Plebiscitary Politics; Recall Elections; Referendums: Europe; Referendums: Latin America; Referendums: United States.*

DAVID B. MAGLEBY, BRIGHAM YOUNG UNIVERSITY

BIBLIOGRAPHY

Bowler, Shaun, Todd Donovan, and Caroline J. Tolbert, eds. *Citizens as Legislators: Direct Democracy in the United States.* Columbus: Ohio State University Press, 1998.

Bowler, Shaun, and Todd Donovan. *Demanding Choices: Opinion, Voting and Direct Democracy.* Ann Arbor: University of Michigan Press, 1998.

Cronin, Thomas E. *Direct Democracy: The Politics of Initiative, Referendum, and Recall.* Cambridge: Harvard University Press, 1989.

Gerber, Elizabeth. "Legislative Responsiveness to the Threat of Popular Initiatives." *American Journal of Political Science* 40 (February 1996): 99–128.

Lupia, Arthur. "Shortcuts Versus Encyclopedias: Information and Voting Behavior in California Insurance Reform Elections." *American Political Science Review* 88 (March 1994): 63–76.

Magleby, David B. *Direct Legislation: Voting on Ballot Propositions in the United States.* Baltimore: Johns Hopkins University Press, 1984.

Magleby, David B., and James D. Gordon. "Pre-election Judicial Review of Initiatives and Referendums." *Notre Dame Law Review* 64, no. 3 (1989): 298–320.

Magleby, David B., and Kelly D. Patterson. "Consultants and Direct Democracy." *PS: Political Science and Politics* (June 1998): 160–169.

Schrag, Peter. *Paradise Lost: California's Experience, America's Future.* Berkeley: University of California Press, 1998.

Wolfinger, Raymond E., and Fred Greenstein. "The Repeal of Fair Housing in California: An Analysis of Referendum Voting." *American Political Science Review* 62 (September 1968): 753–770.

INVALIDATING VOTES, PROCEDURES FOR

See *Administration of Elections; Tendered Ballots*

LANDSLIDE RESULT

See *Winning an Election*

LIMITED VOTE

When voters in a multimember district can vote only for candidates (not lists) and have fewer votes to cast than there are seats to be filled, they are said to have a limited vote. In contrast, if they have as many votes to cast as there are seats to be filled (and cannot cumulate these votes), they are said to have a block vote.

A limited-vote system in which voters had two votes in three-seat districts was used in a handful of British parliamentary constituencies between 1867 and 1884. The Spanish senate is currently elected by a similar system: in most provinces, citizens cast three votes in districts returning four members. The most limited of limited-vote systems—in which voters cast only a single vote in multimember districts—is currently used in Taiwan and was formerly used in Japan and South Korea.

Both the limited vote and the block vote are typically combined with plurality rule, under which the victors in an M-seat district are the M candidates garnering the most votes. In systems that combine the block vote with plurality rule, it is possible for the largest party to win all the seats: it need only get its supporters to the polls and ensure that they each cast all their votes. The limited vote, as does the cumulative vote, allows for a more proportional outcome, hence for the representation of minority viewpoints. When voters have only a single vote in an M-seat district, for example, any group of citizens constituting more than $1/(M+1)$ of the voting population can guarantee themselves a seat.

In addition to allowing for better minority representation, limited-vote systems also pose coordination problems for parties at nomination time. Whereas parties in a block-vote sys-

tem can simply nominate as many candidates as there are seats to be had, in a limited-vote system this strategy can lead to poor results. In the single-vote case, for example, suppose there are 100 voters, three representatives to be elected, and three parties—party A with 54 supporters, party B with 24, and party C with 22. B and C nominate one candidate each. A has the choice of nominating two or three candidates. If A nominates two candidates and A's supporters split equally between the two, then both will win (topping the poll with 27 votes each). However, if A nominates three candidates and A's supporters split equally, then the order of finish is B first (24), C second (22), and a three-way tie for third among A's nominees (with 17 votes each). Thus, only one of A's three nominees can win, and A will win only one seat due to "over-nominating."

See also *Coordination, Electoral; Cumulative Voting; Fused Votes; Plurality Systems; Single Nontransferable Vote.*

Gary W. Cox, University of California, San Diego

BIBLIOGRAPHY

Cox, Gary W., and Frances Rosenbluth. "Reducing Nomination Errors: Factional Competition and Party Strategy in Japan." *Electoral Studies* 13 (March 1994): 4–16.

LIST

A list is a legally defined set of candidates, nominated by a party or other group, to whom seats can be awarded collectively. In some cases, such as elections to Spain's lower house, citizens vote directly for lists rather than for candidates. In other cases, such as elections to Finland's parliament, citizens vote for individual candidates, but these votes are pooled by list for purposes of allocating seats to lists.

Lists can differ in the number of parties endorsing the candidates. Single-party lists comprise candidates of a single party, while joint lists comprise candidates of more than one party.

Lists can also differ in terms of how seats allocated to the list are distributed among its candidates. The seats allocated to a *closed* list are allocated to the candidates in order of their appearance on the list (so if the list wins three seats, the first three names on the list are declared elected). The seats allocated to an *open* list are allocated to the candidates on the list in accordance with the number of votes each candidate wins (so if the list wins, for example, three seats, then the three candidates on that list winning the most votes are declared elected). Some lists consider both the number of votes each candidate garners and the order of the candidates on the list, variously weighing these two factors in determining which candidates get the list's seats. These lists are sometimes called *flexible*.

See also *Apparentement; Coordination, Electoral; Designing Electoral Systems; Double Simultaneous Vote; Fused Votes; Pooling Votes; Preference Voting; Proportional Representation.*

GARY W. COX, UNIVERSITY OF CALIFORNIA, SAN DIEGO

LOT

In the modern era, selection of officials through popular election is regarded as the *sine qua non* of democracy. In democracy's classical origins, however, election was regarded as less democratic than selection by lot. Indeed, although the most important Athenian officials (especially the military commanders) were chosen by voting, and some argue that their ultimate political primacy stemmed from the fact that they were elected, the hallmark of Athenian democracy was not election by vote, but rather selection by lot.

Decision by lot plays three roles in the history of elections. In probably its first, but now least important, usage, decision by lot was believed to allow the gods (or later the one God) to manifest their/His will through the supernatural manipulation of the physical world. In Athens, the Treasurers of Athena and of the other gods always were selected by lot. Similarly, the first recorded appointment of an official of the Christian church, the choice by the eleven surviving apostles of Matthias to succeed Judas Iscariot, was made by lot from two candidates previously nominated by vote.

The combination of lot and vote, or lot alone, was used to select most secular officials in Athens. This second role, as an alternative to voting in the filling of secular positions, appears to have had four justifications or functions. First, it was intended to prevent the entrenchment of a ruling faction, no matter how popular and no matter how efficient. Second, because the officials being selected generally were to serve as members of large boards rather than as holders of individual offices, selection by lot guaranteed a representative balance among the tribes, and other groups, into which the Athenian citizenry was divided. Third, it enshrined the equality of citizens (or at least the equality of citizens within the various census classes, since in the early days of the democracy some offices were restricted to members of the upper classes). Lot was considered to be more consistent than election with democracy because the latter undermined the presumed equality of the citizens. Coupled with short terms and prohibitions against serving in the same office more than once, selection by lot guaranteed that every citizen would have the opportunity to govern as well as be governed. Fourth, selection by lot provided a way of apportioning the duties and responsibilities of running the *polis,* that is, a method for conscripting officeholders and jurors. The last three of these functions, in particular, continue to justify the use of lot in the selection of modern juries.

The third role of the lot is to break ties. The electoral laws of most American states and many other countries provide that whenever "a tie vote makes it impossible to determine which of two or more candidates has been elected" (California Election Code, section 10551), the tie will be broken by lot. Similar provisions may be used when two or more candidates are tied at the bottom of the poll in the single-transferable-vote system or the alternative-vote system in order to determine which candidate will be eliminated. Other possibilities to avoid the unacceptable outcome of having no result include calling a fresh election (for example, Maryland for some offices), allowing the returning officer or some other official to cast the deciding vote (as in Canada), or giving preference to the older candidate (as in Italy). The lot can also be used to resolve ties in legislative chambers. The usual practice is that a motion producing a tie vote, having failed to achieve an absolute majority, is defeated. But in Sweden, with an even number of seats in the Riksdag until 1976, the rule was that tie votes would be decided by lot, with the proviso that the government could never lose a vote of confidence by lot.

See also *Choice, Elections as a Method of; Secret Ballot.*

RICHARD S. KATZ, JOHNS HOPKINS UNIVERSITY

MAJORITY SYSTEMS

A majority system is one in which a candidate is required to win at least 50 percent plus one of the valid votes cast to be elected. The majority rule is used in twenty-three countries for legislative elections and in sixty-five countries for presidential elections. There is the possibility that none of the candidates will meet the required threshold of a majority of votes. This problem is solved though the use of multiple rounds or ranked votes.

MULTIPLE-ROUND SYSTEMS

There are many variants of the multiple-round system. The simplest is the majority runoff, in which a second round is held between the top two candidates of the first round. One of the two candidates is bound to get a majority of the votes in the second round and to be elected. This procedure is used for the election of the president in fifty-five countries.

A second approach, the majority-plurality system, consists of substituting the plurality rule in the second round. This procedure is utilized in French legislative elections, in which candidates must have obtained the support of at least 12.5 percent of registered voters in the first round to be eligible to stand in the second round. This procedure is not used for any presidential election.

It is also possible to have more than two rounds. There are two possibilities here, depending on the presence or absence of an automatic elimination rule. We can first distinguish repeated ballots without any elimination rule. Such a system is used for the election of the president in Namibia and Seychelles. The other option is to resort to multiple ballots but with an elimination rule. The standard elimination rule is that the candidate with the fewest votes on the last ballot must withdraw from the race. This procedure is followed for the selection of party leaders in Canadian party leadership conventions.

RANK-ORDER SYSTEMS

The second method of ensuring that one candidate obtains a majority of the votes is to take into account the whole rank order of preferences among voters. Under the alternative vote, voters are asked to indicate not only which candidate they prefer the most but to rank all candidates from first to last. If a candidate gets a majority of first preferences, he or she is elected. If no candidate secures a majority, the candidate with the fewest first preferences is eliminated and the second preferences of those voters who ranked that candidate first are counted and transferred to these candidates. If this transfer confers a majority to a candidate, he or she is elected. Otherwise, the weakest remaining candidate is eliminated and subsequent preferences (which means third preferences for those who ranked the two eliminated candidates first and second) are similarly transferred, and so on until one candidate gets a majority of the votes.

The alternative vote is similar in its logic to repeated ballots with automatic elimination of the weakest candidate. The difference is that in the former, voters vote only once, indicating their whole range of preferences on the same ballot, whereas in the latter, voters are asked to vote many times, each time indicating only their first preference after having been informed about the outcome of the previous ballot. The alternative vote prevails for the election of the president in Ireland and Sri Lanka and for the election of the House of Representatives in Australia and the legislature in Nauru.

CONSEQUENCES OF MAJORITY RULE

The consequences of the majority rule are easier to assess in the case of presidential elections, where majority systems are predominant. Table 1 shows the number of candidates and the percentages of the votes obtained by the two leading candidates in the first round and the runoff in democratic countries that scored 1 or 2 on political rights in 1996, according to Freedom House, and that have a presidential election under the majority rule.

These presidential elections average nine candidates, almost twice as many as plurality elections. The winner typically obtains 42 percent of the vote in the first round, and the runner-up 29 percent. These outcomes are not very different from those observed in plurality elections. In six cases out of sixteen, the leading candidate got a majority of the votes in

Table 1. Illustrative Results of Presidential Elections in Majority Systems with Runoff

Country	Date of election	Percent of first-round votes for the winner	Percent of first-round votes for the runner-up	Percent of second-round votes for the winner	Percent of second-round votes for the runner-up	Total number of candidates
Austria	4/19/98	64	14	—	—	5
Benin	3/3/96 and 3/18/96	34	37	53	48	7
Brazil	10/3/94	54	27	—	—	8
Bulgaria	10/27/96 and 11/3/96	44	27	60	40	14
Chile	12/11/93	58	24	—	—	6
Cyprus	2/8/98 and 2/15/98	40	41	51	49	7
Ecuador	5/19/96 and 7/7/96	26	27	55	46	9
Finland	1/16/94 and 2/6/94	26	22	54	46	11
France	4/23/95 and 5/7/95	21	23	53	47	9
Madagascar	11/3/96 and 12/29/96	37	23	51	49	15
Mongolia	5/18/97	61	30	—	—	?
Poland	11/5/95 and 11/19/95	35	33	52	48	13
Portugal	1/14/96	54	46	—	—	2
Romania	11/3/96 and 11/17/96	28	32	54	46	16
São Tomé and Principe	6/30/96 and 7/21/96	41	37	53	47	5
Slovenia	11/23/97	56	18	—	—	8

Note: Cape Verde was excluded because the winner was unopposed; Mali was excluded because opposition parties boycotted the election (turnout was 28 percent); and Uruguay was excluded because it has not yet conducted a presidential election under the majority system.

the first round and was elected. Among the ten cases where a second round took place, the candidate who was ahead on the first round lost five times. And in the eight elections where the gap between the first two candidates was less than five points, the leading candidate in the first round won only three times.

The debate over electoral systems has focused on the virtues and vices of plurality versus proportional representation. The arguments for and against the majority rule have not been systematically articulated. Often, majority and plurality systems are collapsed into a "majoritarian" category, a dubious practice since the consequences of the majority rule can be quite different from those of a plurality formula.

There are four major arguments in support of the majority rule. First, the majority principle is at the heart of democracy. In referenda, the majority wins, and in legislatures, laws (except constitutional amendments) are adopted through the majority rule. It would seem natural to apply the same logic in legislative elections. Second, those elected in a majority system must have the support of more than half the voters, which ensures that they are acceptable to a great number of people.

Third, the majority rule makes it difficult for "extremist" parties to thrive, unless they have wide support. In a two-round system, for instance, parties have to make alliances after the first round if they wish to do well in the second. But, as the case of the Front National in France shows, a party that is perceived to be extremist may find that no other party is willing to make a deal with it. The consequence is that the "extremist" party finds it almost impossible to get the majority required to be elected. The same logic applies in the alternative vote, as "responsible" parties will refrain from any deal with the "extremist" option and will encourage their supporters not to cast their second or third preferences for that party. Fourth, the majority rule, like plurality, is usually based on single-member districts, which are deemed to promote closer links between legislators and their constituents.

The majority rule has its drawbacks. Perhaps the most important one, in the view of its critics, is that it fails to produce either one-party majority governments or a broadly representative legislature. It usually allows the presence of many parties and leads to the formation of coalition governments. Electoral contests in France are typically fought by two coalitions, the left and the right. Voters have a more direct say under the majority rule than under proportional representation about which coalition will form the government, but those who believe in the great virtues of one-party majority governments are bound to prefer the plurality rule.

The majority rule is also bound to dissatisfy those who insist on the necessity of broad and fair representation. Since many parties usually run in the election, voters are offered a wide range of options. Since the threshold for being elected is very stringent, however, it is in majority systems that disproportionality between seat and vote shares can be the greatest (this is so only if first ballot or preference votes are taken into account).

In this regard, the debate about whether the Front National should be represented in the French National Assembly is revealing. Those who defend the majority system, which makes it almost impossible for a radical party with 15 percent of the vote to elect its candidates, argue that a party that is completely unacceptable to the great majority of French voters should not be in the Assembly. Those who would like a proportional-representation system contend that the perspective of the Front National, whether the majority of people like it or not, is part of the political landscape, and that it is important that its views be expressed—and criticized—in the Assembly.

Responsiveness and accountability are generally considered to be the top two criteria for assessing electoral formulas. Because proportional representation is the best guarantor of the former and the plurality rule of the latter (through one-party governments), the majority rule has not been widely adopted in legislative elections. We should note, however, that the institutions of the Fifth Republic, which include the use of the majority rule in both presidential and legislative elections, are deemed to be a great success in France. Similarly, the Australians seem to be quite satisfied with the alternative vote for the election of their lower house.

The majority rule is, however, widespread for presidential elections. The main reason seems to be the concern that the elected president, who is supposed to represent the whole country, have strong popular endorsement. It seems, for instance, that a number of Latin American countries decided to move to a majority-runoff formula for the election of their presidents after the breakdown of democracy in Chile in 1973 following the election of Salvador Allende on a weak plurality of the vote.

Mark Jones makes a case against the runoff (and in favor of the plurality rule) in presidential elections. His main argument is that the formula for presidential elections has a strong impact on the number of parties that participate in legislative elections. More specifically, run-off presidential elections produce more parties in the legislative arena, make it very unlikely that the party of the elected president will have a majority in the legislature, and are thus prone to produce stand-offs between the president and the legislature. In order to obtain an effective government, Jones contends, countries ought to elect their president under the plurality rule.

In presidential elections, therefore, the debate between the majority and the plurality rules boils down to whether it is more important to avoid electing presidents with very weak support or to avoid electing presidents who have very little control over the legislature.

See also *Alternative Vote; Designing Electoral Systems; Manufactured Majorities; Plurality Systems; Presidential Electoral Systems.*

ANDRÉ BLAIS, UNIVERSITY OF MONTREAL

BIBLIOGRAPHY

Blais, André, Louis Massicotte, and Agniezka Dobrzynska. "Direct Presidential Elections: A World Summary." *Electoral Studies* 4 (December 1997): 441–455.

Jones, Mark. *Electoral Laws and the Survival of Presidential Democracies.* Notre Dame: University of Notre Dame Press, 1995.

MALAPPORTIONMENT

See *Gerrymandering*

MANIFESTO, ELECTION

*M*anifesto is the British and Italian term for the official program published by a political party at the start of its election campaign. The American term is *platform*. Practice and terminology differ widely across countries, however. Parties in many continental European countries have a "basic program," which they modify only at twenty-year intervals. For an election campaign, they issue "action" or "economic" programs or sometimes different booklets for women, youth, workers, and other constituencies. In Australasia the program may not even be officially printed. Instead, it may be presented in an hour-long televised address by the party leader.

As a result of these variations, statements of party policy for an election may reach greater or lesser numbers of voters. Extremes are Sweden, where party workers deliver party documents to every household, and Britain, where the manifesto is distributed (and sold!) through bookshops. Nevertheless, even with limited circulation, a manifesto's launch at a press conference and dissection in newspapers and on radio and television ensure that its leading themes are widely known to the public. Almost all parties issue statements of election policy, and all such statements have two elements in common: a unique status as the only official policy program approved by the whole party, and an effect on opinion makers who read them to discover which policies and priorities the party is advocating for government.

The term *election program* is generally used to cover such statements, in whatever particular form they appear.

IMPORTANCE TO THE PARTY MANDATE

As the only official statements of party policy in an election, election programs are central to mandate theories of democracy, which explain how popular preferences get transformed into government action. Mandate theory assumes that:

1. Voters choose between parties largely on the basis of which program appeals most to them

2. The party or parties with a majority of votes forms the government

3. Once in government, the party or parties carry through the program they presented in the election

Unless programs are effected in this way, voters will not have much prospective influence over what governments do, however much they may vote "retrospectively" (that is, in terms of the government's past record). If mandate theory does not work, democracy loses much of its justification as a uniquely responsive form of government.

A crucial question for democratic theory, therefore, is whether mandate theory *does* work. The extent to which parties in government carry through their program can be checked in two ways. Specific pledges of action made in the election program can be identified and the extent of their fulfillment checked. Research in Britain and North America, by Richard Rose and Colin Rallings, respectively, finds that around 70 percent of specific election pledges are carried out—a relatively high figure. However, such pledges are more commonly made in peripheral areas than in central matters of policy, and there is only a limited number of them in each manifesto. An alternative approach is to assume that the emphases of an election program are indicative of a party's policy priorities. If a program gives a lot of space to "youth," for example, the party is trying to convince voters that it will devote a major effort in government to youth. Scholars Ian Budge, David Robertson, and Derek J. Hearl measured emphases by attributing the sentences of election programs to specified policy areas and calculating percentages to control for the length of the statements. H-D. Klingemann et al., in one study, and Michael J. Laver and Budge, in another, related these percentages to government expenditures and legislative programs in corresponding policy areas in about fifteen postwar democracies. They found a relationship between election emphases, on the one hand, and government plans and expenditures in most areas, on the other, although the relationship is affected by institutional arrangements.

The link assumed by mandate theory between party promises and government action is upheld by research on election programs. In this crucial respect, democracy does work.

Underpinning the link between election promises and government action is the fact that party leaders often have no other plan for what to do in office. The parties of a coalition government may devise a policy program after the election to guide action for the next three or four years, but the programs of the individual parties feed into the coalition's policy program. Single-party governments have to rely on their party program, and some coalition governments on the dominant party's program, for a rough indication of priorities over their term in office. Election programs are the only medium-term programs for socioeconomic development regularly produced by any organization in a democracy. Thus they have a special status as "democratic five-year plans," even if they are more illuminating on priorities and targets than on specific strategies to achieve them.

PRESENTATION AND STYLE

Although election programs may serve, in the absence of an alternative, as a basis for government action, their status as a campaign document shapes their presentation and style. This is one factor limiting the number of specific pledges made by parties and confining them, generally, to peripheral policy areas. Parties do not want to be pinned down to specific proposals on central matters, which can then be criticized and which could be hard to fulfill in government.

For the same reason, parties tend to steer clear of issues that might favor rival parties and tend to emphasize issues that favor themselves. Naturally, they do not want to publicize issues that are to their own electoral disadvantage. Moreover, a party would lack credibility if it tried to claim that it would do better than its rivals on their preferred issues. For example, rather than promising to cut taxes more than Liberals or Conservatives, a socialist party might not mention them, but concentrate instead on its plans for welfare. The result of such different focuses is that the programs of rival parties may seem to refer to totally different situations, even when issued for the same election. According to one program, the country will be in a state of collapse, while another will claim that good times are here or just around the corner.

TRACING PARTY IDEOLOGY THROUGH PROGRAMS

Because a party's credibility on issues is linked to its long-standing preoccupations and record in government, what a party says in a particular program is closely linked to its underlying ideology—socialist, liberal, conservative, new politics, and so on. In turn, these ideologies "place" parties in a

Figure 1. Left-Right Orientation of American Parties, 1952–1992

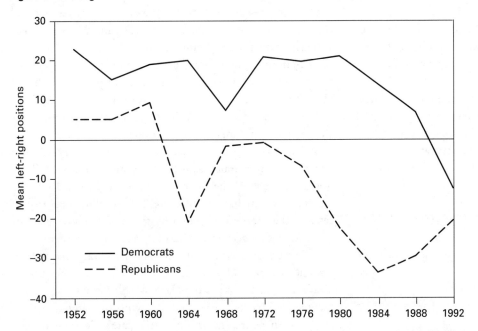

ables them to "appropriate" some issues but not others, and find it hard to change this fact. In turn, this finding casts doubt on Anthony Downs's hypothesis that two-party competition leads to policy convergence on the position of the average voter. American parties converge (but never entirely) in some elections, such as 1968 *(see Figure 1)*. In other elections they are far apart, as in the elections of the 1980s.

The substantive nature of left-right contrasts can also be traced from analysis of election programs. Core left-wing positions are support for welfare, government intervention, and peace. The right believes in political and economic freedom, traditional morality, and military alliances abroad. There is no logical reason why such positions should be put together by parties. It is just that parties on each extreme tend to endorse all of them. Centrist parties, on the other hand, support welfare as well as tradition and may favor government intervention in support of both.

particular position on a left-right ideological spectrum. Not all of the text of a program relates to this underlying division, but about 30–50 percent of it does. By identifying clusters of "left" and "right" policies in a program and subtracting the percentage of text mentioning "right" themes from the percentage mentioning "left" ones, each program can be scored as –100 (totally right), +100 (totally left), or somewhere in between. About half the content of programs is unrelated to left-right contrasts, so in practice parties rarely take positions beyond the –30 to +40 range.

The left-right positions taken by American and German parties in their election programs since the end of World War II in 1945 are illustrated in Figures 1 and 2. American parties do not seem to be more or less ideological than the German parties by this measure. Another interesting feature of the figures is the high degree of stability in party ideological positions regardless of what is going on in the world around them. The American parties always stay on the top or bottom of the figure and never cross each other. German parties rarely do so.

This finding supports the ideas advanced above that parties are tied into their long-standing record, which en-

CONCLUSION

Party manifestos (election programs) thus have practical uses for the actual operation of democracy and research uses for

Figure 2. Left-Right Orientation of German Parties, 1953–1990

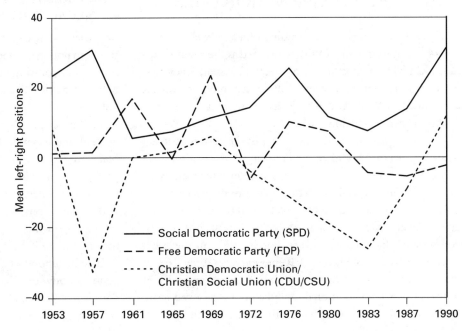

those interested in studying democracy. The manifesto tells the public what a party's policies and priorities are and thus enables them to vote in a policy-oriented way for the ones they favor. The written program forms an input, or even a blueprint, for government, which parties put into effect because they believe in it ideologically.

Election programs, therefore, can be studied by political scientists to check on the extent to which party policy and ideology are changing. They can also be related to what the party actually does in government. Comparative research shows that the priorities and pledges of election programs are actually implemented in government.

See also *Campaigning; Downsian Model of Elections; Regulation of Television at Elections.*

IAN BUDGE, UNIVERSITY OF ESSEX

BIBLIOGRAPHY

Budge, Ian. "A New Spatial Theory of Party Competition." *British Journal of Political Science* 23 (May 1994): 443–467.

Budge, Ian, David Robertson, and Derek J. Hearl, eds. *Ideology, Strategy and Party Change.* Cambridge: Cambridge University Press, 1987.

Klingemann, H-D, Richard I. Hofferbert, and Ian Budge. *Parties, Policies and Democracy.* Boulder, Colo.: Westview, 1994.

Laver, Michael J., and Ian Budge, eds. *Party Policy and Government Coalitions.* London: Macmillan, 1992.

Rallings, Colin. "The Influence of Election Programmes: Britain and Canada, 1956–1979." In *Ideology, Strategy and Party Change,* edited by Ian Budge, David Robertson, and Derek J. Hearl. Cambridge: Cambridge University Press, 1987.

Rose, Richard. *Do Parties Make a Difference?* London: Macmillan, 1980.

MANUFACTURED MAJORITIES

An election is about awarding offices as well as about counting votes. Office is awarded as the result of applying a specific set of electoral system rules to a particular distribution of votes. If the system tends to convert a minority of votes into a majority of seats, it can be described as manufacturing a majority.

The first-past-the-post electoral system awards seats in parliament to the candidate with the largest share of the vote in a constituency. The only circumstance in which the winning candidate is certain to have a majority of the votes is if only two candidates contest the seat. Even when two parties take virtually every seat, it is not necessarily true that each constituency has two candidates. For example, in the 1998 election of the U.S. House of Representatives, only 168 of the 435 districts had just two candidates; in the majority of districts there were additional candidates who received more or less trivial numbers of votes. In voting for the British

House of Commons, at least three significant parties normally contest each seat—the Conservatives, New Labour, and the Liberal Democrats—and in Scotland and Wales nationalist parties add a fourth contender.

When three or more parties compete nationwide for votes, there is a higher probability that no party will win an absolute majority of the national vote. This is the case not only in Britain, Canada, and Australia but also in contests for the American presidency, where third-party candidates intervened in 1948, 1968, 1980, 1992, and 1996. In Britain, no party has won as much as half the popular vote since 1935. Yet in fourteen of the fifteen elections held since 1945, the electoral system has manufactured an absolute majority of seats in the House of Commons, for parties whose share of the vote has ranged from 39.2 percent to 49.7 percent.

In American presidential elections the winner requires an absolute majority of votes in the electoral college but not an absolute majority of the popular vote. Electoral college votes are awarded by state; the candidate with the largest share of the vote in a state gains all of the state's electoral college votes. The effect of this system is to manufacture a large majority in the electoral college for the leading candidate, whatever his or her share of the popular vote. For example, in 1992 Bill Clinton won only 43 percent of the popular vote but 69 percent of the electoral college vote. In 1984 Ronald Reagan won 59 percent of the popular vote and 98 percent of the electoral college vote. In a four-candidate race for the presidency in 1860, Abraham Lincoln won a big majority in the electoral college—180 of 303 votes—with 39.8 percent of the popular vote.

THE LIKELIHOOD OF MANUFACTURING A MAJORITY

Whether a first-past-the-post electoral system can manufacture a majority depends on the number of parties contesting seats at the constituency level and on the division of the vote between parties. It is easier to manufacture a majority if the vote is fairly evenly divided between the second- and third-place finishers. In Britain in 1997, the Labour Party won 63 percent of the seats in Parliament with 43 percent of the popular vote, because its Conservative opponents took only 30 percent of the vote. In elections in which the Labour and Conservative Parties took more than nine-tenths of the total vote, Labour sometimes lost despite having a larger share of the vote than the 43 percent that manufactured its landslide majority in 1997.

The likelihood of a majority being manufactured also depends on how the leading party's votes are distributed at the constituency level. The more seats won by a relatively narrow vote, the fewer surplus votes (votes in excess of a winning plurality) are wasted. In a complementary way, if a party loses a seat, the worse the local result, the fewer votes wasted there. In Britain the Labour Party has wasted far fewer votes than the Conservatives in recent elections. Because of the geographic concentration of the Labour vote, if the two parties received equal shares of the national vote, Labour could win eighty seats more than the Conservatives and an absolute majority in the House of Commons and achieve this outcome with less than two-fifths of the popular vote.

Proportional-representation systems are designed to give one party a majority of seats only if that party wins half the popular vote. This rarely happens. But the requirement that a party pass a threshold of votes to qualify for any seats normally causes a few percent of votes to be wasted and benefits the largest parties; however, only in exceptional circumstances are the wasted votes sufficient to manufacture a majority of seats for a party with less than half the popular vote. In Sweden, where the Social Democratic Party has been dominant for generations, it has won half or more of the seats in a proportional-representation election on three occasions. Twice it did so by winning more than half the vote; in 1944 it won 50.0 percent of seats with 46.5 percent of the vote.

THE CASES FOR AND AGAINST MAJORITY GOVERNMENT

The argument in favor of an electoral system that manufactures a majority is that government by a single party fixes responsibility clearly on that party in government. The electorate can then know how to vote in order to return the governing party to power or to turn it out of office, depending on their assessment of its record. Defenders of the existing British system use this argument. The advocates of manufactured majorities also cite the experience of New Zealand coalition government after proportional representation replaced a system that regularly manufactured majorities for one party. But none of the advocates of manufactured majorities goes so far as to argue that the leading party should be awarded an absolute majority of seats even if its vote falls to a third or less of the popular vote. A few countries, including the Republic of Korea and Malta, have awarded bonus seats to the party with the most votes to give it an absolute majority that it did not win in the initial allocation of seats.

Advocates of proportional representation view the purpose of elections as giving representation to diverse views in the electorate, and they do not think it appropriate to abandon this goal for the sake of manufacturing a majority of seats for a party that won only a plurality of votes. In many countries with proportional representation, the government of the day need not represent parties with a majority of seats in parliament. If its opponents are divided, and especially if its minor-

ity of seats is close to a majority, then through "log rolling" the government can gain majority support, albeit from different coalitions on different measures. Arend Lijphart goes further, arguing in favor of coalition government and against one party having an absolute majority of seats, because coalition governments have a broader base of electoral support than single-party governments with a manufactured majority. For this reason, they are more likely to arrive at consensual policies.

See also *Alternative Vote; Bonus Seats; Government Formation and Election Outcomes; Majority Systems; Plurality Systems; Winning an Election.*

RICHARD ROSE, UNIVERSITY OF STRATHCLYDE

BIBLIOGRAPHY

Curtice, John, and Michael Steed. "The Results Analyzed." In *The British General Election of 1997,* edited by David Butler and Dennis Kavanagh, 295–325. London: Macmillan, 1997.

Jenkins, Lord. *The Report of the Independent Commission on the Voting System.* London: Stationery Office, Cm. 4090-I, 1998.

Lijphart, Arend. *Democracies: Patterns of Majoritarian and Consensus Government in Twenty-One Countries.* New Haven, Conn.: Yale University Press, 1984.

Strom, Kaare. *Minority Government and Majority Rule.* New York: Cambridge University Press, 1990.

Schumpeter, Joseph. *Capitalism, Socialism, and Democracy.* 4th ed. London: George Allen and Unwin, 1952.

MINORITY REPRESENTATION

See *Colonial Elections; Elections in Developing Countries; Positive Discrimination in Redistricting in the United States; Proportional Representation*

MIXED ELECTORAL SYSTEMS

An electoral system is mixed if its mechanics involve the combination of different electoral formulas (plurality and proportional representation; or majority and proportional representation) for an election to a single body. This definition excludes the cumulative vote, the limited vote, and the single nontransferable vote, which are variants of the plurality formula. We also agree with the vast majority of the literature, which views the single transferable vote as a form of proportional representation rather than as a mixed system, because reaching a quota is the precondition for winning a seat.

Applying this definition, we find mixed systems currently in force for electing the first (or only) chamber in no less than thirty countries with working, directly elected parliaments.

Those countries include one-fifth of the world's population. In addition, mixed electoral systems are used for electing the second chamber in France, Italy, Japan, Mexico, and Taiwan and for the Scottish Parliament and Welsh National Assembly. Mixed systems can be found in countries of all sizes and on all continents. Many of these countries are democratic and are major industrial powers (see Table 1).

TYPES OF MIXED SYSTEMS

All mixed systems entail the combination of proportional representation and plurality or majority. It follows that mixed systems can be distinguished one from another on the basis of the combination that is involved. The most basic distinction is between those systems in which the two formulas are used independently of each other and those in which the application of one formula is dependent on the outcome produced by the other formula.

Let us start with independent combinations. There are three possible independent combinations. In the first two types, there are two kinds of districts: the majority or plurality districts and the proportional representation ones. In the first type, the territory is divided into two parts, one consisting of majority or plurality and another of proportional representation districts. In such a system some voters vote under one formula and others under another. We call such a system a *coexistence* system. In the second type, there are again two kinds of districts, but the two formulas apply throughout the territory to all voters, and each voter has two sets of representatives, one elected in a majority or plurality district and one elected in a proportional representation district. We call such a combination a *superposition* combination.

In the third type of independent combination, the two formulas are mixed *within* each district. In this case, within each district some seats are allocated under the plurality or majority rule and others under proportional representation. We call such a system a *fusion* system.

Among dependent combinations, we distinguish *conditional* and *unconditional* systems. In conditional systems, whether one formula applies hinges on the outcome produced by the other formula. The law specifies that after the first formula is used, the second formula comes into play only if the outcome resulting from the first formula does not meet a certain condition. In unconditional combinations the two formulas always apply, but how one formula will be applied depends on the outcome produced by the other formula. Unconditional systems take different forms. The best known is *correction,* whereby proportional representation seats are distributed so as to correct the distortions created by the plurality or majority rule.

Coexistence. The simplest independent combination is coexistence, in which one part of the territory is subject to the plurality or majority rule and the other part to proportional representation. This system is typified by the French Senate.

French senators are elected in each department by a 145,000-member electoral college composed of members of the National Assembly, regional and departmental councillors, and delegates from municipal councils. In departments with four seats or less (numbering 85 and having a total of 206 seats), candidates need a majority of the vote to be elected at the first ballot. If there is no winner, a second ballot is held and the leading candidates are elected (a majority-plurality system). However, in departments with five seats or more (numbering 15 and having a total of 98 seats), senators are elected by proportional representation using the D'Hondt formula.

In addition to the French Senate, the parliaments of Panama and Niger also use such hybrids. Historical instances of such hybrids at the national level include Greece (1955–1958) and Zimbabwe (1980–1985), and at the subnational level include the Canadian provinces of Alberta and Manitoba from the 1920s to the 1950s.

Superposition. The second type of independent combination is superposition, in which all voters are subject to the two formulas, and independent sets of districts are established for each formula. Under such a system, each voter has two sets of representatives, one elected in a plurality or majority district and one elected in a larger proportional representation one.

A superposition procedure was adopted in 1994 for the five-hundred-seat Japanese house of representatives. Three hundred members are elected by plurality in single-member districts, and the other two hundred are elected by proportional representation in eleven districts. Thus, there are two sets of deputies, each elected under different rules. Both plurality and proportional representation apply throughout the country. Each voter has two sets of representatives: one elected in a district, others elected for a wider region. Each system operates independently of the other. Notably, proportional representation seats are filled without any consideration of the results in single-member districts.

Superpositions are the most popular type of mixed system today. They can be found in sixteen countries, ranging in size and population from Russia to Andorra. Different formulas are used for electing the majoritarian component. In some places, straight plurality is used in single- or multimember districts (as in Andorra, Croatia, Guinea, Japan, Russia, Senegal, Seychelles, South Korea, Thailand, Ukraine, and the Mexican Senate), whereas in others the single nontransferable vote prevails (as in Taiwan and in the Japanese House of Councillors).

Majority runoff remains popular in former communist countries (Armenia, Azerbaijan, Georgia, Lithuania). In most

Table 1. Existing Mixed Systems In Sovereign Countries

Country (Year introduced)	Type	Majoritarian component	Proportional-representation component	Percent proportional representation	Two votes?	Dual candidacy allowed?
Albania (1997)	Correction	115 members; majority runoff	40 members; 1 district; first 10 seats to two stronger parties, and remaining 30 to other parties	26	Yes	Yes
Andorra (1993)	Superposition	14 members; 7 (2-member) districts; FPTP	14 members; 1 district; LR-Hare	50	Yes	UK
Armenia (1995)	Superposition	150 members; SMD; Majority-runoff	40 members; 1 district; LR-Hare	21	Yes	Yes
Azerbaijan (1995)	Superposition	100 members; SMD; majority runoff	25 members; 1 district; LR-Hare	20	Yes	No
Bolivia (1996)	Correction	68 members; FPTP; SMD	62 members; 9 districts; D'Hondt	48	Yes	Yes
Cameroon (1988)	Supermixed	21 members; FPTP; SMD	159 members; 52 districts; if leading party has a majority, winner-take-all. Otherwise, half of seats to leading list, other half distributed among other parties by PR			NA
Chad (1997)	Supermixed	25 members; SMD; majority	100 members; 34 districts; if leading party has a majority, winner-take-all. Otherwise, PR-D'Hondt			NA
Croatia (1995)	Superposition	47 members; 34 districts; FPTP	80 members; 1 district; D'Hondt	63	Yes	UK
Ecuador (1979)	Supermixed	8 members; 4 districts; plurality with minority representation	**a**. 52 members; LR-Hare **b**. 12 national seats; LR-Hare	90	Yes	No
France, Senate (staggered) (1948)	Coexistence	206 members; 85 districts; majority-plurality	98 members; 15 districts; D'Hondt	31	NA	NA
France, municipal elections (cities with a population of 3,500+) (1982)	Fusion	Half of the seats; winner-take-all; 2 ballots	Half of the seats; D'Hondt; 2 ballots	50	NA	NA
Georgia (1992)	Superposition	84 members; SMD; majority runoff	150 members; 10 reg. districts; 1 nat. district	64	Yes	Yes
Germany (1949)	Correction	328 members; FPTP; SMD	328 members; 1 district; LR-Hare	50	Yes	Yes
Guinea (1991)	Superposition	38 members; FPTP; SMD	76 members; 1 district; LR-Hare	67	Yes	No
Hungary (1990)	Supermixed	176 members; SMD; majority-plurality	**a**. 152 members; 20 districts; PR D'Hondt **b**. 58 national corrective seats	54	Yes	Yes
Italy, Chamber of Deputies (1993)	Correction	475 members; FPTP; SMD	155 members; 1 district; LR-Hare	25	Yes	Yes
Italy, Senate (1993)	Correction	232 members; FPTP; SMD	83 members; 18 districts; D'Hondt	26	No	Yes
Japan, House of Representatives (1994)	Superposition	300 members; FPTP; SMD	200 members; 11 districts; D'Hondt	40	Yes	Yes

Table 1. Existing Mixed Systems in Sovereign Countries *(Continued)*

Country (Year introduced)	Type	Majoritarian component	Proportional-representation component	Percent proportional representation	Two votes?	Dual candidacy allowed?
Japan, House of Councillors (staggered) (1982)	Superposition	152 members; 47 districts; SNTV	100 members; 1 district; D'Hondt	40	Yes	Yes
Lithuania (1992)	Superposition	71 members; SMD; majority runoff	70 members; 1 district; LR-Hare	50	Yes	Yes
Mexico, Chamber of Deputies (1963)	Correction	300 members; FPTP; SMD	200 members; 1 district; LR-Hare	40	Yes	Yes
Mexico, Senate (1996)	Superposition	96 members; 32 districts; FPTP with minority representation	32 members; 1 district; PR	25	Yes	UK
New Zealand (1993)	Correction	67 members; FPTP; SMD	53 members; 1 district; St. Laguë	46	Yes	Yes
Niger (1993)	Coexistence	8 members; FPTP; SMD	75 members; 8 districts; LR-Hare	90	NA	NA
Panama (1983)	Coexistence	26 members; FPTP; SMD	45 members; 4 districts; LR-Hare	63	NA	NA
Philippines (1995)	Correction	208 members; FPTP; SMD	52 members; 1 district	20	Yes	No
Russia (1993)	Superposition	225 members; FPTP; SMD	225 members; 1 district; LR-Hare	50	Yes	No
Senegal (1992)	Superposition	50 members; 30 districts; FPTP	70 members; 1 district; D'Hondt	58	No	UK
Seychelles (1993)	Superposition	25 members FPTP SMD	9 members; 1 district; LR-Hare	26	No	UK
South Korea (1994)	Superposition	253 members; FPTP; SMD	46 members; 1 district; LR-Hare; 1 seat to each party with 3–5% of national vote	15	No	No
Taiwan, National Assembly (1991)	Superposition	234 members; 27 districts; SNTV	100 members; 2 districts; LR-Hare	30	No	No
Taiwan, Legislative Yuan (1992)	Superposition	128 members; 27 districts; SNTV	36 members; 2 districts; LR-Hare	24	No	No
Thailand (1997)	Superposition	400 members; FPTP; SMD	100 members; 1 district; PR	20	Yes	No
Tunisia (1993)	Correction	144 members; 25 districts; FPTP	19 members; 1 district; D'Hondt	12	No	Yes
Ukraine (1997)	Superposition	225 members; FPTP; SMD	225 members; 1 district; LR-Hare	50	Yes	Yes
Venezuela, Chamber of Deputies (1993)	Correction	100 members; FPTP; SMD	99 members; 22 districts; D'Hondt	50	Yes	Yes

Abbreviations: AV: alternative vote. UK: unknown. FPTP: first-past-the-post. LR: largest remainder. NA: not applicable. PR: proportional representation. SMD: single-member district. SNTV: single nontransferable vote. STV: single transferable vote.

cases, proportional representation members are elected in a single national constituency, sometimes with the specific objective of overcoming ethnic divisions. Mixed systems based on the principle of superposition also existed in Iceland (1915–1920) and Bulgaria (1990–1991).

Fusion. In superposition, two types of districts are established. It is possible, however, to combine the two formulas within one district. We call such a system a fusion system. For now, such a system exists only for French municipal elections.

Each French municipality with a population above 3,500 is an electoral district (the largest cities—Paris, Lyon, and Marseille—are subdivided into electoral districts). The party list that obtains a majority of the valid votes on the first round gets half of the seats. The other half is distributed by proportional representation (using the D'Hondt formula) among all parties, including the leading party. If no list secures a majority of the valid votes in the first round, a second round is held between lists that obtained at least 10 percent of the vote. Provision is made for amalgamating competing lists between the two rounds, so that the weakest parties can conclude agreements with the strongest in order to get some representation. In the second round, a mere plurality of the vote entitles the leading list to half of the seats, and the other half is distributed among all parties (again, including the leading party) by proportional representation using D'Hondt. There is a 5 percent threshold at both rounds. This is a case of independent combination, since the application of proportional representation does not hinge on the outcome produced by the plurality or majority rule. Contrary to coexistence and superposition, however, the two formulas are used within the same district.

Correction. Coexistence, superposition, and fusion are independent combinations. But in some systems, the application of one formula depends on the outcome produced by the other formula. The best-known type is *correction* (or *compensation),* whereby proportional representation seats are distributed so as to correct the distortions created by the plurality or majority rule. This system is in place in Germany.

The Bundestag includes 328 members elected by plurality in single-member districts, plus 328 members elected by proportional representation. The two systems, however, do not operate independently of each other. Proportional representation seats are distributed so as to correct the distortions created by first-past-the-post and to produce an overall distribution of seats that mirrors the percentage of votes cast for each party: they are corrective (or compensatory) seats. In contrast with the so-called direct seats, most of which go to the strongest parties, most proportional representation seats go to the weakest parties.

Correction can be achieved in many ways. In Germany all 656 seats are first distributed by proportional representation on the basis of the second (or "party") votes cast by voters. The results of this computation are compared with the distribution among parties of the 328 constituency seats. The other 328 seats are then awarded so as to make the final distribution of 656 seats proportional.

Italy attempts to achieve the same objective by a different technique. There is no notional computation involving all seats. Instead, proportional representation seats are distributed on the basis of votes cast only for defeated candidates, rather than for all candidates, a feature that produces a topping-up effect similar to the German procedure. (For the Italian Chamber of Deputies, the successful candidates' winning margin of votes is added to the votes cast for defeated candidates, thus reducing the corrective effect of proportional representation seats. This is not the case for the Senate.) In the Philippines the forty-six national seats are corrective because no party may get more than three; in addition, the top five parties were precluded from obtaining any party-list seats in the 1998 election, in order to better represent weaker parties.

Corrective systems can be found at present in Bolivia, Germany, Italy, Mexico, New Zealand, the Philippines, Tunisia, and Venezuela, as well as in thirteen of the sixteen German *länder.* The Germans call their corrective system "personalized proportional representation"; New Zealanders speak of theirs as a "mixed member proportional representation" system; whereas in Scotland and Wales, this kind of mixture is officially referred to as an "additional member system of proportional representation."

Conditional. Correction is not the only way the two formulas can be used in a "dependent" fashion. Conditional systems are those in which the use of one formula hinges on the outcome produced by the other. In corrective systems, proportional representation always applies, but how it is applied depends on the results of the plurality or majority component. In conditional systems, a given formula may or may not be used, depending on some conditions provided by the law. For now, we have only historical (and short-lived) instances of this type.

A 1923 Italian law specified that two-thirds of the seats be awarded to the party obtaining a plurality of the national vote, provided that party received at least 25 percent of the vote. The remaining seats were to be distributed among the other parties by proportional representation. Under such a system, the plurality rule may or may not apply, depending on the share of the vote the leading party secures. The same principle was embodied, subject to variations in detail, in a 1926 Romanian law, in French laws of 1919 and 1951, and in the Italian 1953 election law.

Supermixed. A few mixed systems cannot be forced into one of the five basic types, because proportional representation and plurality or majority are combined in more than one of the five basic ways identified above. These "supermixed" systems use more than one type of combination.

The Hungarian system is chiefly a superposition system: 176 members are elected by majority-plurality in single-member districts, and 152 are elected by proportional representation (using the D'Hondt formula) in twenty regional districts. The two sets of legislators are elected independently. It is also a corrective system, since there are fifty-eight national compensatory seats.

Ecuador's single-chamber parliament also has two sets of members. In 1996 12 members were elected by straight proportional representation in a single national district for a term of four years. In addition, 60 members were elected in provincial districts for a shorter term: 8 in two-member districts by the plurality rule, with some possible representation for minorities, and 52 by proportional representation in districts having three members or more. In 1998 the numbers of national and provincial members were raised to 20 and 101, respectively. This complex system combines coexistence and superposition.

Cameroon and Chad blend condition and coexistence. The Cameroonian Assembly includes 180 members. Plurality prevails in the 21 single-member districts. In the 52 multi-member districts, all seats go to the leading list if it has a majority of the vote. Otherwise, the leading list gets one-half of the seats, and the other half is distributed among other parties by proportional representation. In Chad all 100 seats in the multimember districts go to the leading list if that list secures a majority of the vote; otherwise, they are distributed by proportional representation. These 100 members "coexist" with another 25 who are elected by double ballot in single-member districts.

PROPORTIONALITY OF VARIOUS FORMULAS

Judging by the results of the most recent election held under each system, the degree of proportionality among mixed electoral systems varies widely. Mixed systems as a group lean toward plurality and majority rather than proportional representation. Corrective systems most closely approximate full proportionality, whereas superposition and coexistence systems produce much less proportional outcomes. Outcomes under conditional systems are disproportional when the condition is fulfilled and the majority premium granted, but they are quite proportional when the condition is not fulfilled and when proportional representation prevails. The degree of proportionality of the various formulas is affected not simply by the type of blend but also by the ratio of proportional representation to majoritarian seats, the threshold, the number of parties that do not cross the threshold at a given election, and the number of votes they receive.

SOME CHALLENGES
CONFRONTING MIXED SYSTEMS

Complexity. Not all mixed systems are as complex as those that exist in Hungary or Italy, yet they tend to be more difficult to understand than a straight proportional-representation system because the intricacies often found in the latter are compounded by its hyphenation with a plurality or majority formula. Plurality systems can be explained and understood in ten seconds and majority systems in less than a minute, whereas proportional-representation systems (especially those that involve multiple tiers or ballot transfers) necessitate more

time, but most experts are aware that the mechanics of mixed systems stretch their teaching capacities as well as the learning abilities of their students. If excessive complexity in electoral arrangements is a vice, mixed systems are certainly defective. Supermixed, fusion, conditional, and corrective systems are more vulnerable to this criticism than simpler blends like superposition or coexistence systems.

Fairness. In much of the literature arguing for proportional representation, fairness is equated with proportionality. We take the view that a fair system is a system that does not grant a built-in advantage to a specific political party.

The issue of fairness is most relevant for coexistence and conditional systems. In countries where electoral behavior varies sharply among regions, imposing different formulas in different regions may appear as a manipulation. The system used at the 1956 Greek election resulted in the governing party winning a majority of seats even though it had been outpolled by the opposing coalition. Where the line should be drawn between the "proportional representation" and "majoritarian" areas will always be a topic of contention. Any decision made by the ruling party or coalition is likely to be self-interested, or at least to be branded as such.

Conditional mixed systems have an especially poor reputation. The French law of 1951–1958 is still cited as an example of electoral engineering at its worst, although its results were less disproportional than those a plurality or majority system would have produced. The Italian law of 1953 was nicknamed by its opponents the "swindle law," and its similarity to Mussolini's infamous law of 1923 was loudly pointed out. Its adoption after stormy sittings of parliament provoked a small group within the government to depart the coalition. Ultimately, the ruling cartel headed by the Christian Democrats failed by a hair's breadth (54,000 votes out of 27 million cast) from winning the required 50 percent majority, and all seats were distributed by proportional representation, leading to the repeal of the law two years later.

Stability. It is difficult to ascertain how durable mixed systems are, since the vast majority of those now in existence have been in operation for less than ten years. However, many now-defunct mixed systems did not last more than one or two elections. Three mixed systems lasted at least a generation: in Iceland (1915–1959), in Alberta (1924–1956), and in Manitoba (1920–1955). Only three current systems have been in existence for long: since 1948 for the French second chamber, since 1949 in Germany, and since 1963 in Mexico. Most of them underwent important and repeated alterations.

The historical trend over the past century and a half has been from plurality or majority toward proportional representation, and it is therefore tempting to assume that mixed systems are an intermediate step in a historical continuum that will end in proportional representation. This pattern holds for a few countries, like Denmark and Iceland. However, many other countries, especially former communist countries, moved from plurality or majority to mixed systems but have not moved to proportional representation. Others (like France) moved from majority or plurality to a mixed system but returned to plurality or majority thereafter. In Bolivia, Germany, Italy, and Venezuela mixed systems constituted a move away from straight proportional representation.

SOME FEATURES OF MIXED SYSTEMS

Should voters have two votes? Mixed electoral systems are sometimes referred to as "two-vote systems" because Germany, the best-known of them, so provides, at least since 1953. Looking at existing superposition, corrective, and supermixed systems (the only mixed systems in which two votes can be granted to each voter) in sovereign nations, we find seventeen (including Germany and New Zealand) that grant two votes to each voter and seven that grant a single vote. Italian voters have two votes for electing deputies, but a single one for electing senators. Providing for a second vote may reinforce the popular legitimacy of proportional representation members, since they appear to be elected on their own merits rather than on the basis of votes cast for other candidates.

The existence of two votes offers interesting research opportunities for psephologists. A comparison of first and second votes in a specific area may indicate the degree of personal support enjoyed by some star candidates. In Germany, where split voting increased from 6.4 percent of the votes cast in 1953 to 15.6 percent in 1990 (for more recent elections, such figures have not been computed), the two-vote system has fostered strategic voting by voters who support large as well as small parties. Some Social Democratic Party (until 1980) and Christian Democratic Union (since 1983) voters chose to give their second vote to the Free Democrats in order to ensure the latter would overcome the 5 percent threshold. Some Free Democrat supporters give their first vote to the local candidate sponsored by their larger allies. At the 1996 Italian chamber election, where some 37.5 million votes were cast, it has been estimated that at least 2 million voters split their ticket.

Is it possible to be a candidate at both levels? A few countries specifically rule out the possibility that a candidate stand in an individual district while having his or her name on the party's regional or national list. This is now the case in Azerbaijan, Guinea, the Philippines, Russia, South Korea, and Thailand. The general trend, however, exemplified by Armenia, Bolivia,

Georgia, Germany, Hungary, Italy, Japan, Lithuania, Mexico, New Zealand, Ukraine, and Venezuela, is to allow an individual to be a candidate at both levels (in Hungary, at all three levels). Georgia initially prohibited this possibility but now allows for it, whereas Russia went the other way in its 1993 and 1995 laws. Mexico allows dual candidacies for only sixty (only thirty prior to 1994) of the candidates sponsored by a party. In all cases where dual candidacies are authorized (except Mexico), the law establishes a pecking order: if a candidate is elected in an individual district, his or her name is deleted from the national list.

This possibility offers a distinct advantage to politicians over a straight plurality or majority system, since it amounts to an insurance policy against defeat. It appears to be used widely in Germany.

Two classes of members? Both superposition and correction involve two sets of members for the whole country. Plurality or majority elections tend to take place in single-member districts, whereas proportional representation members are invariably elected from larger districts and frequently from the nation as a whole. Are proportional representation members perceived as less legitimate than their plurality or majority colleagues? Are there conflicts between the two categories of members? The Mexican constitutional amendment of 1963, which introduced the new category of proportional representation "party members," specifically stated that all plurality and proportional representation members are representatives of the nation, belong to the same category, and have equal rights and obligations. That the Mexican government felt it necessary to add such language is revealing.

Although opponents of such hybrids often charge that they would create "two classes of members," there is little evidence, except in New Zealand, that such a perception exists.

See also *Additional Member System; Compensatory Seats; Designing Electoral Systems; Plurality Systems; Proportional Representation; Second-Chamber Elections; Ticket Splitting.*

LOUIS MASSICOTTE AND ANDRÉ BLAIS, UNIVERSITY OF MONTREAL

BIBLIOGRAPHY

Blais, André. "The Classification of Electoral Systems." *European Journal of Political Research* 16 (1988): 99–110.

Blais, André, and Louis Massicotte. "Electoral Systems." In *Comparing Democracies: Elections and Voting in Global Perspective*, edited by Lawrence LeDuc, Richard G. Niemi, and Pippa Norris, 49–81. Thousand Oaks, Calif.: Sage Publications, 1996.

———. "Mixed Electoral Systems: An Overview." *Representation* 33, no. 4 (1996): 115–118.

Massicotte, Louis, and André Blais. "Mixed Electoral Systems: A Conceptual and Empirical Survey." *Electoral Studies* 18 (September 1999): 341–366.

NOMINATION PROCEDURES

Nomination procedures are those procedures in accordance with which candidates establish their eligibility to be included on the ballot. Under party list systems of election, endorsement by a political party is frequently a precondition for candidacy, although individual candidates are still sometimes shown on the ballot. Under other systems, while there may be no particular reason why candidates should not be able to put themselves forward for election, the electoral law often reflects a tradition of candidates being nominated by someone else.

The number of nominators may be merely nominal or may be designed to provide a real obstacle to the nomination of candidates who do not have a significant level of support in the community. Nominators themselves may be required to have certain qualifications; for example, to be registered voters. Sometimes there is also a requirement that nominators be geographically dispersed; a certain minimum number of nominators may be required from each province or constituency, a mechanism designed to exclude candidates whose appeal is territorially limited and who may be thought likely to pursue parochial interests.

In some cases, for example Australian federal elections, streamlined nomination procedures are made available to candidates of registered parties. Nomination procedures frequently include a requirement for the payment of a deposit.

Proper election administration requires that the deadline for receipt of nominations, and the place or places at which nominations may be made, be defined with complete precision. The role played by the electoral administration in examining and validating nominations also requires clear definition. Two issues arise. The first is whether the formal requirements for nomination have been met: whether the nomination was lodged before the deadline, whether the required number of nominators have signed the form, whether the correct deposit has been paid, and so on. Such questions can normally be answered objectively by the officer responsible for receiving the nominations, and it is normally the duty of such an officer to decide them.

A second issue that may arise is whether a particular candidate meets the prescribed qualifications for candidacy or is subject to any disqualifications. Questions of this type are much more problematical: an electoral official or administration may, for example, be in no position to determine, or to determine expeditiously, whether a candidate suffers from unsoundness of mind, meets language requirements, or is a citizen of another country. Difficulties may arise because pertinent information is not available or because the law specifying qualifications and disqualifications is unclear.

Nevertheless, in many jurisdictions it is thought desirable to have questions of qualifications and disqualifications resolved definitively prior to election day. Sometimes this may be approached by involving the courts directly in the processing of nominations or by empowering the electoral administration to make final and definitive rulings. Difficulties may arise with such an approach, however, if rejected candidates have avenues of appeal available. Such candidates could have their campaigns severely disrupted by the need to go to court to overturn an initial ruling rejecting their nominations, which was ultimately held to be incorrect. In the meantime, the preparations for the election, such as the printing of ballots, could be seriously disrupted (since they would depend on the outcome of the challenge), and voters would certainly face a confusing state of affairs.

An alternative approach to the problem is to limit the role of the electoral administration to rejecting a nomination that has not met the formal requirements, but to permit challenges to an election to proceed after the polling, with the option of holding a fresh election if a candidate is found to have been unqualified for nomination.

The final stage of the nomination process is normally a public declaration of the names of all candidates who will appear on the ballot. In some countries this event is immediately followed by a prescribed process, often involving a random draw, for determining the order in which candidates will appear on the ballot.

See also *Administration of Elections; Candidates: Legal Requirements and Disqualifications; Candidates: Selection; Coordination, Electoral; Cross-Filing; Deposit; Parties: Qualification for Ballot; Primary Elections.*

MICHAEL MALEY, AUSTRALIAN ELECTORAL COMMISSION

BIBLIOGRAPHY

Administration and Cost of Elections Project website: *www.aceproject.org*
Blackburn, Robert. *The Electoral System in Britain.* London: Macmillan Press, 1995.
Mackenzie, W.J.M. *Free Elections: An Elementary Textbook.* London: George Allen and Unwin, 1958.

NONCITIZENS AND THE RIGHT TO VOTE

Formal citizenship, as a legal indicator of membership in the political community, often is assumed to be the first and universal requirement for voting in the election of public officials. In fact, there have been and are many exceptions to this principle.

One set of exceptions is based on recognition of a political community wider than the individual national state. The Maastricht Treaty, which established the European Union, grants to all citizens of an EU member state who are resident in another the right to vote for municipal officials and members of the European Parliament for the place of their residence. Although the Fourth French Republic (1946–1958) did not recognize them as citizens of France, residents of the French *Territoires d'Outre-Mer* and *Territoires sous Tutelle* were allowed to elect representatives to the French parliament. In a reflection of Britain's imperial past, citizens of Commonwealth countries or the Irish Republic who are resident in the United Kingdom on the day the electoral register is compiled each year are registered as if they were British subjects. Conversely, British subjects are allowed to vote in Ireland, and until 1984 British subjects resident in Australia were allowed (in fact required, given compulsory voting) to vote in that country's elections. Most other Commonwealth countries do not give special voting rights either to Britons or to citizens of the rest of the Commonwealth, although Mauritius allows any Commonwealth citizen resident in the country on the prescribed day to vote. Citizens of Brazil residing in Portugal may obtain "special equal rights," in which case they may vote in Portuguese elections.

A second set of exceptions takes lengthy residence within the country or declared intention to become a citizen as adequate evidence of community membership, in the absence of formal citizenship. During the nineteenth and early twentieth centuries, at least twenty-two American states or territories allowed aliens to vote either immediately upon declaring their intentions to become citizens or after postdeclaration residence of between six months and two years; the last such provision was eliminated in 1926. On the other hand, Uruguay grants suffrage to aliens who have resided in the country for at least fifteen years. Far more liberal is the New Zealand provision allowing noncitizens to vote in national elections after only one year. Originally applied only to British subjects, this provision has applied since 1975 to all legal residents.

Noncitizens frequently are granted voting rights in local elections, even when they are excluded from national elections. Although Britain had excluded non-British subjects from the parliamentary franchise by the end of the seventeenth century, those who met the necessary property requirement were eligible to vote in local elections until the 1880s. In the latter decades of the twentieth century, the Netherlands permitted noncitizens to vote in municipal elections after five years of uninterrupted residence, and Sweden permitted noncitizens to participate in local elections after they had been residents of Sweden for three years. By the end of the century Denmark required only one year's residence before noncitizens could vote in local elections. Venezuela also grants voting rights in local elections to noncitizens but requires that they have resided in the country for more than ten years. Within the United States, aliens are permitted to vote in school board elections in Chicago and New York City and to vote in the local elections of Takoma Park, Maryland.

See also *Compulsory Voting; Constitution and Elections.*

RICHARD S. KATZ, JOHNS HOPKINS UNIVERSITY

BIBLIOGRAPHY

Aylsworth, Leon E. "The Passing of Alien Suffrage." *American Political Science Review* 25 (February 1931): 114–116.
New Zealand Royal Commission on the Electoral System. *Report of the Royal Commission on the Electoral System: "Towards a Better Democracy."* Wellington: V. R. Ward, Government Printer, 1986.

NONPARTISAN ELECTIONS

Nonpartisan elections are elections in which party labels are absent from the ballot. In a nonpartisan electoral system, a voter cannot determine a candidate's party affiliation based solely on the information in the voting booth. Nonpartisan elections are common in the United States. The state of Virginia prohibits the names of political parties from appearing on the ballot for the election of all offices except the U.S. president and vice president. Nebraska has used nonpartisan elections for its state legislature since 1934, and the Minnesota state legislature used nonpartisan elections from 1913 to 1973. Twenty-one of the fifty U.S. states select some judges using nonpartisan elections. However, the largest number of nonpartisan elections in the United States occur at the local level. A survey of cities and towns conducted by the International City/County Management Association found that 73 percent of municipalities of 10,000 or more residents used nonpartisan elections. The survey results also suggest that municipalities with populations under 10,000 are more likely than larger cities to use nonpartisan elections. Additionally, elections for school boards and offices in special districts are often nonpartisan.

The use of nonpartisan elections in America came out of the Progressive movement of the early twentieth century. For judicial posts, the reformers argued that judges should be neutral, rather than partisan, arbitrators. At the municipal level, the stated goal of reformers was to make local government more business-like and less corrupt by weakening the political party machines that dominated city politics. The use of nonpartisan municipal elections was part of a larger reform plan to destroy political parties that included replacing elected mayors with appointed city-managers and switching from ward or district representation to citywide or at-large elections. Although the reformers stated that nonpartisan elections would make city government more efficient, a revisionist interpretation of their efforts claims that reformers wanted to diminish the power that workers and ethnic minorities had under the party machines. Revisionists believe that nonpartisan elections were part of the Progressive-era reformers' plan to replace party politics with government by an upper-middle-class elite.

TYPOLOGY

The simple definition of nonpartisan elections conceals the great variety of electoral systems that may arise when governments remove party labels from the ballot. In particular, American political scientist Charles Adrian noted that "nonpartisan elections do not guarantee nonpartisanship." Parties play an active role in some nonpartisan electoral systems but are absent from others. Simplifying a typology first suggested by Adrian, nonpartisan elections fall into three main categories. In a Type I nonpartisan system, political parties play an active role in elections. Parties nominate candidates, and the party affiliations of candidates are widely known even though they are not on the ballot. In this type of system, as under partisan elections, it is difficult for an independent candidate to win election.

A Type II nonpartisan system is characterized by a lack of activity by traditional political parties and by the strength of other interest groups, which often endorse slates of candidates and sometimes even recruit potential officeholders.

One example of these interest groups is the "good government" slating group, which often comprises members of the white business class. Other examples include neighborhood groups and local factions organized around popular community leaders or elected officials.

The Type III nonpartisan system has neither political parties nor nominating groups. This type of system is the ideal, or pure, nonpartisan election, in which the candidates themselves, rather than any group affiliation, are the focus of the election and the campaign.

CASE STUDIES

Rory Austin, in a study of representation in six American cities, found nonpartisan electoral systems that fell into each of the three categories. Elections in Alexandria, Virginia, typify a Type I nonpartisan electoral system, in which political parties are strong despite the nonpartisan ballot. The city council comprises seven representatives—six legislators and a mayor. Every three years the entire body is up for citywide election. The two major political parties (Democrats and Republicans) nominate a mayoral candidate and a slate of legislators in a party caucus held several months before the general election. This partisan activity occurs despite the Virginia state law mandating nonpartisan ballots. Furthermore, the law does not appear to weaken political parties in Alexandria: in the four municipal elections from 1988 to 1997, only one independent candidate ran for mayor and four ran for other council seats. All five independent candidates received fewer votes than the Democratic and Republican nominees. The independent candidate for mayor polled less than 2 percent of the vote. In both 1991 and 1997 the two independent candidates for council seats came in last and second-to-last. Part of the difficulty that independent candidates face in Alexandria is that Virginia uses a party-column ballot even though the columns do not identify the party. Getting a nomination from a major party remains a key to winning a seat in Alexandria's nonpartisan election.

Springfield, Massachusetts, is an example of a Type II nonpartisan electoral system. The city has a legislature of nine citywide representatives whom voters elect every two years. Unlike Alexandria, there are no party nominations, and most candidates do not mention party activities in their biographies that appear in the local newspaper. In the absence of party competition, community leaders often support slates of candidates. In the 1993 election, an African American community leader worked for the election of a mayoral candidate and three council members whose issue stances and voting records were consistent with his organization's goals. He urged his supporters to "bullet vote" (or to "plump" their votes) by casting ballots for only three candidates rather than a full slate of nine. The mayoral candidate and two of the three endorsed council members won election due in part to bullet voting in predominantly African American precincts. In this same election, a member of the U.S. House of Representatives and former mayor of Springfield used his political organization to campaign for people who earlier had supported his personal political aspirations, including the winning mayoral candidate and three successful city council challengers. In the absence of partisan activities, other political organizations fill the void. In Springfield, one organization worked for the interests of the African American community while the other organization based its nominations on whether the candidate had supported the former mayor's election to the U.S. House.

Huntsville, Alabama, has a Type III nonpartisan system. The city council has five legislators elected from single-member districts. Local newspaper accounts of council elections do not mention activities by political parties or other political organizations. Instead, politics in Huntsville are candidate-centered and individualistic. Campaigns focus on what the incumbents have done and what the challengers intend to do for their districts. Likewise, newspaper coverage of council politics in Huntsville stresses the "personal agendas" and "self-interests" of the legislators.

Nonpartisan electoral systems can change over time. During the 1980s, Raleigh, North Carolina, was a Type II system. Active groups included business associations, such as the Home Builders Association, neighborhood organizations, and groups representing the interests of African Americans. In 1985 a candidate for the council tried to mobilize Republican voters in a run-off election. At the time, the city was heavily Democratic and the three other candidates in the election were registered Democrats. The Republican's opponents chastised him for trying to bring partisanship into a nonpartisan election. By the 1990s the growth of the Republican Party in the American South, which had once been dominated by the Democratic Party, extended down to the local level in Raleigh. The neighborhood and racial minority groups continue to back candidates, but these candidates now campaign as Democrats. Also, the business and prodevelopment groups began successfully to back Republican candidates for the city council. The system currently is in a transition from Type II to Type I. The party affiliation of candidates has become important in the city council races due to changes in the political environment, even though the ballot remains nonpartisan.

INFLUENCE ON ELECTION OUTCOMES

Given the variety of political systems that can occur under nonpartisan elections, one may wonder whether nonpartisanship makes a difference for political outcomes. Numerous studies have investigated the effect of nonpartisan elections on who wins office. Several of these studies have found that nonpartisan elections produce elected officials who are of a higher income and occupational status than partisan elections produce. A study of American cities by political scientists Susan Welch and Timothy Bledsoe found that nonpartisan elections, especially when they are citywide or at-large, benefit Republican candidates.

Studies of the electoral success of African Americans and females under nonpartisan elections have produced mixed results. Most research has found that nonpartisan elections have a slight tendency to reduce African American officeholding. Austin discovered that cities that hold partisan elections and are controlled by Democrats have significantly higher levels of African American officeholding than cities that conduct nonpartisan elections. Unlike the studies of African American officeholding, studies of the effect of nonpartisan elections on female officeholding have found no relationship.

Three other lines of research on the political effects of nonpartisan elections have not received as much attention but deserve further examination. The first is determining the relationship between nonpartisan elections and voting behavior. Some studies have shown that voters are more likely to use ethnic name as a voting cue under nonpartisan than partisan elections. However, this literature does not address whether nonpartisan elections tend to be more candidate-oriented, with voters basing their decisions on factors such as the race or ethnicity of the candidate, and less issue-oriented than partisan elections.

The second area is measuring the effects of nonpartisan elections on policy outcomes or substantive representation. A few studies have examined the consequences of nonpartisan elections for overall municipal expenditures, but this research has failed to answer definitively whether nonpartisan elections lead to a more efficient government, as urban reformers claim.

The third area, which is related to the second, is analyzing the effect of nonpartisan elections on legislative behavior and coalition formation. Of particular concern are whether nonpartisan elections lead to less pork-barrel politics and whether they foster the exclusion of minority representatives from legislative coalitions. Austin, in attempting to answer the latter question, found that the dominant legislative faction is more likely to include African American representatives in partisan cities controlled by Democrats than in cities with nonpartisan elections.

See also *Offices Filled by Direct Election; Parties: Qualification for Ballot; Ticket Splitting.*

RORY AUSTIN, GEORGE WASHINGTON UNIVERSITY

BIBLIOGRAPHY

Adrian, Charles R. "A Typology for Nonpartisan Elections." *Western Political Quarterly* 12 (June 1959): 449–458.

Austin, Rory A. "Testing the Impact of Electoral Structures on Minority Office-holding and Policy Representation." Ph.D. diss. University of Rochester, 1998.

Book of the States, 1998–99 Edition. Lexington, Ky.: Council of State Governments, 1998.

Cassel, Carol A. "The Nonpartisan Ballot in the United States." In *Electoral Laws and Their Political Consequences,* edited by Bernard Grofman and Arend Lijphart. New York: Agathon, 1986.

Davidson, Chandler, and Luis Ricardo Fraga. "Slating Groups as Parties in a 'Nonpartisan' Setting." *Western Political Quarterly* 41 (June 1988): 373–390.

Renner, Tari, and Victor S. DeSantis. "Contemporary Patterns and Trends in Municipal Government Structures." In *Municipal Year Book 1993.* Washington, D.C.: International City/County Management Association, 1993.

Welch, Susan, and Timothy Bledsoe. *Urban Reform and Its Consequences.* Chicago: University of Chicago Press, 1988.

NORMAL ELECTIONS

See *Realigning Elections in the United States*

OBSERVATION OF ELECTIONS

The International Institute for Democracy and Electoral Assistance (IDEA) defines electoral observation as the purposeful gathering of information regarding an electoral process and the making of informed judgments about the process on the basis of the information collected.

IDEA's process-oriented definition highlights one of the most common purposes of electoral observation: to legitimize an electoral process. "Informed judgment" refers to whether the electoral process has been entirely, partially, or reasonably "free and fair," to use the popular cliché, or has represented the wishes of the people, to use the less demanding wording of the Commonwealth. The need for legitimacy might be internal, in places where an electorate's distrust of the process renders a respected external judgment useful. But the need might also be external. In some cases free and fair elections are an indispensable requirement for international acceptance and recognition of a regime (for example, for admission to the Council of Europe). Or the evaluation might affect the allocation of assistance (for countries whose external aid is linked to human rights and democracy).

Apart from governing regimes, international political organizations, and international aid organizations, other actors might have different purposes for observation. Opposition parties are not particularly interested in legitimization. After all, the best proof that an election has been properly conducted is the triumph of the opposition. From the opposition's point of view, confidence building is one of the main purposes behind the request for observers. This is particularly true in founding elections, when opposition parties are weak, inexperienced, and distrustful of the intentions of the regime. The participation of international actors in the electoral process has proven extremely useful in fostering the confidence and ensuring the participation of opposition parties. The opposition parties usually expect that observation will help deter fraud. The argument is valid, although frequently exaggerated in the case of smaller missions. In most cases, only long-term missions with significant resources can effectively reduce fraud and manipulation. Electoral observation might also help build and reinforce democratic practices and institutions, which is referred to as capacity building. In many cases specific observation activities might put in motion changes that will outlast the electoral process. If previously nonexistent freedoms are allowed to flourish during an electoral process, a regime might find it difficult to withdraw them at a later stage.

Election observation has other possible purposes for which there is less agreement. Observation might contribute to the resolution of conflict or to the solution of technical problems. Organizations in place for observation may also mediate or provide assistance if called upon to do so during the election process, since observation, mediation, and assistance fulfill a common set of objectives. However, the three roles might engender a conflict of interest. How can an organization impartially evaluate an electoral process to which it has provided technical assistance? IDEA copes with the problem by restricting its involvement in mediation and technical assistance such that they do not jeopardize the main observation responsibilities.

INTERNATIONAL ELECTORAL OBSERVATION: HISTORY AND ACTORS

The first elections to occur under international observation were the general elections in Moldavia and Wallachia in 1857, organized under the supervision of a European commission composed of Austrian, British, French, Prussian, Russian, and Turkish representatives. However, observation of elections has been an instrument of the international community mainly since the First World War. The countries of central Europe held a large number of plebiscites regarding statehood under international auspices following the treaties of Versailles and Saint Germain and the Venice Protocol.

The United Nations (UN). UN involvement in electoral observation can be traced to the 1948 elections in Korea but did not acquire significance until the 1950s and 1960s (the so-called decolonization era). UN operations during that period followed a common pattern. The first step was generally to determine when and under what circumstances the election, plebiscite, or referendum (often referred to at the time as "a consultation") should be held. This determination to consult the people of a particular territory on its future status was made, in most cases, by the administering authority, which subsequently communicated the decision to the UN and invited the organization to render its assistance in supervising or observing the process. The first mission of the Trusteeship Council (the UN body with oversight of trust territories) to include an electoral component took place in the Trust Territory of Togoland under British administration in 1956. The UN undertook approximately thirty missions in the context of decolonization between 1956 and 1990. One characteristic of observation missions in the decolonization era was their comparatively small size. The number of observers rarely exceeded thirty, even where there was deep mutual distrust among electoral participants or open or latent conflict with neighboring countries.

Although in a formal sense the Namibian election of November 1989 comes under the category of decolonization, the scale, scope, and duration of the operation there make it an important watershed and a category in itself. At its maximum deployment, the United Nations Transition Assistance Group (UNTAG) in Namibia was almost 8,000-strong, including just under 2,000 civilians, 1,500 civilian police, and approximately 4,500 military personnel. Almost 1,800 UNTAG electoral personnel supervised 2,500 counterparts and 358 polling stations. The UNTAG ratio of five international observers per polling station has not been matched since nor is it likely to be aimed at in the future.

Three aspects of UNTAG are rarely noted. First, it was the earliest mission to have confidence building built into its mandate, since its task included the creation of conditions for a free and fair election. In order to create such conditions, UNTAG organized a massive public information campaign using radio, television, and visual materials and prints, as well as a people-to-people campaign of voter education. Its political offices also developed extensive contacts with all relevant actors. Second, UNTAG was the first UN electoral mission undertaken as part of a broad political settlement, which was later to become the standard for large-scale missions. Third, the success, visibility, and size of the operation were instrumental in creating the myth that the success of electoral observation is related to the number of observers. Although UNTAG's success in Namibia may be explained better by the political willingness of the two sides to cooperate than by the sheer number of observers, the magic of numbers resulted in a variety of oversized operations in other countries of the region (South Africa, Mozambique) or was used as an explanation for the failure of others (Angola).

The same year that UNTAG observed the elections that led to an independent Namibia, the UN began observing elections in Nicaragua. The Nicaraguan elections were the first that the UN would observe in an independent country. The number of polling stations and the context of the mission made it impossible to use the intensive approach of Namibia; that would have required the deployment of more than twenty thousand observers on election day. The reduced scale of operations led to the systematic use of statistically based verification methods that have since become a standard approach, used in large-scale observation missions in such places as Angola, El Salvador, Eritrea, Haiti, Mozambique, and South Africa. (The 1993 Cambodian election is not included in this description, since the UN's work there involved the organization, rather than the observation, of an electoral process.)

The Organization of American States (OAS). The OAS has observed elections since the early 1960s. Following the assassination of Gen. Rafael Leonidas Trujillo Molina, president of the Dominican Republic, in 1961, his successor started introducing democratic reforms and appealing to the OAS for assistance. Between 1962 and 1990 the OAS participated in more than twenty operations in the region. However, these were small operations of short duration. The 1990 elections in Nicaragua were the first in which the OAS undertook operations on a significant scale for a substantial length of time. As it was for the UN, Nicaragua was a testing ground for the OAS of new methodologies and approaches that it used in subsequent cases. In contrast to the UN charter (which makes no reference to democracy), the OAS charter and later resolutions (particularly the Santiago Commitment to Democracy of June 1991) take a firm and explicit stand for representative democracy. The OAS created a Unit for the Promotion of Democracy in 1991, and it has been quite active since.

The Commonwealth. Another organization that has contributed significantly to observation is the Commonwealth Secretariat, a body created in 1965 to coordinate relations among the nations and dependencies that once formed the British Empire. Like the OAS, the Commonwealth is committed to promoting democracy. The 1991 Declaration of Harare establishes the support of the organization for "democratic processes and institutions which reflect national circumstances, the rule of law and the independence of the judiciary, and just and honest government." The Commonwealth's earliest observations took place in Guyana in 1964 and in Gibraltar in 1967. However, its first major mission was observing the elections that resulted in the independence of Zimbabwe in 1980. Its success in Zimbabwe was followed later the same year by a heavily criticized operation in Uganda, after which the Commonwealth discontinued observation operations for almost ten years. In the 1990s they resumed again, fostered by the

Declaration of Harare. The Commonwealth has been present since then in most relevant elections in its member-states.

European institutions. In Europe, the Council of Europe, the European Union, and the Organization for Security and Co-operation in Europe (OSCE) have for years supported democratic values. They began observing elections in the early 1990s. The Council of Europe, defined by Ives Beigbeder, who has written extensively on international organizations, as "an exclusive club of European democracies," requires that its members hold free elections at reasonable intervals by secret ballot, in order to ensure the free expression of the people in the choice of the legislature. As a consequence, the Council's involvement in observation is usually related to requests for membership or observer status on the Council. After the breakdown of the Soviet empire, the Council of Europe observed elections in the German Democratic Republic, Hungary, Romania, the Czech and Slovak Federal Republic, Bulgaria, Albania, Poland, Croatia, Estonia, Lithuania, and Slovenia.

In 1991 the European Council, which comprises the elected heads of government or heads of state of European Union member-countries, made a policy decision to encourage vigorously human rights and democracy. Starting with their observation—through the International Commission of Jurists—of the Madagascar constitutional referendum of 1992, the European Parliament and other institutions of the European Union have observed the most important elections: South Africa, Mozambique, Nicaragua. They have assumed an increasingly important role, including massive involvement in the 1998 Cambodian elections.

The OSCE, created in 1973, recognized democracy as the only valid system of government for its member countries in 1990. After the Copenhagen meeting of the Conference on the Human Dimension of the OSCE, in which the main prerequisites for democratic governance were defined in detail, the organization established an Office for Democratic Institutions and Human Rights (ODIHR), with headquarters in Warsaw. This office has become increasingly involved in electoral assistance and observation and took a leading role in eastern Europe and in countries of the Commonwealth of Independent States. Another branch of the OSCE, the Parliamentary Assembly, whose Secretariat is based in Copenhagen, has also frequently participated in elections throughout the region.

International nongovernmental organizations. Nongovernmental organizations have been active in electoral observation and in the wider field of democracy assistance. The oldest group is probably the International Human Rights Law Group, which started an Election Observer Project in 1983 and published in 1984 the pioneering "Guidelines for International Election Observing," by Larry Garber. Two institutions set up in the early 1980s by the U.S. National Endowment for Democracy—the National Democratic Institute for International Affairs and the International Republican Institute—have been very active in the field of electoral observation and have organized a large number of observer missions. The International Foundation for Election Systems is probably the largest organization that provides electoral assistance. It has organized a number of missions to observe elections, usually with a limited number of observers. The Carter Center has been another important participant, through the so-called Council of Freely Elected Heads of Government. The special characteristic of the Center/Council missions is the renown of their observers, who usually include former president Jimmy Carter and other elected heads or former heads of government. In Latin America, the Center for Electoral Advice and Promotion (CAPEL, after the Spanish acronym for Centro de Asistencia y Promoción Electoral) of the Inter-American Institute of Human Rights usually organizes observation missions involving high-level electoral officers from the countries of the region. The collaboration of these organizations has helped create a functioning network of electoral organizations and helped transfer lessons and experiences among countries of the region.

The above list of organizations involved in observation is just the tip of the iceberg and does not do full justice to the many important organizations. Popular elections might attract a large number of organizations. A good example of observer crowding might be the Nicaraguan elections of 1996, to which seven of the major players described above sent missions: the Organization of American States (117 observers), the European Union (94), Carter Center (56), International Republican Institute (27), International Foundation for Election Systems (25), National Democratic Institute (9), and CAPEL (23). There were also observers accredited by twenty-two embassies, nineteen parliaments or local governments, ten political parties, five religious institutions, six electoral organizations, and forty-eight other organizations. They were complemented by approximately 5,000 observers from nonpartisan domestic observation groups and some 30,000 to 50,000 party poll-watchers representing twenty-three parties, four alliances, and fifty-five "Grupos de Participación Popular."

NATIONAL ELECTORAL OBSERVATION: A SHORT AND RICH HISTORY

Domestic observation of elections probably emerged simultaneously with competitive elections. The presence of political party "observers" (or "poll-watchers," or "party agents") is common even in countries with long democratic traditions.

The reasons for their involvement go beyond the "making of informed judgments." They serve to discourage electoral manipulation, demonstrate their party's organizational strength to voters, and provide their parties with information on voter turnout and election results. Another usual participant is the press, which may be involved in activities usually performed by observers, ranging from the investigation of abuse to the conduct of preelection, exit, and postelection polls. In spite of the importance of party agents and the press, a new type of observer has emerged: the nonpartisan domestic observer.

Although there might be earlier examples, the operation organized by the National Citizens Movement for Free Elections to monitor the 1986 presidential elections in the Philippines might be considered the starting point of nonpartisan domestic observation. Both the scale and the impact of the monitoring effort were impressive. The movement recruited, trained, and mobilized approximately 500,000 volunteers to monitor polling sites throughout the Philippine archipelago on election day. Its report challenged the official results favoring President Ferdinand Marcos and put in motion a series of events that concluded with his exile three weeks after the election. Another early case was the domestic observation of the Chilean plebiscite of October 1988. The observers' early publication of two separate projections of the results, based on large statistical samples (quick counts), helped convince the incumbent to acknowledge defeat. Another example was the Panamanian national elections of 1989, in which the information gathered and the results projected by an independent monitoring group allowed former U.S. president Carter to denounce the fraud committed by the government of President Manuel Noriega.

Domestic observation also took place in Europe and Africa following the end of the cold war. In eastern Europe domestic election observers play an important role in Albania (Society for Free Elections and Democratic Culture); Bulgaria (through the Bulgarian Association for Fair Elections); and Romania (Pro Democracy Association). In Africa observer groups can be found in Benin (Study and Research Group on Democracy and Economic and Social Development in Africa, better known by its French acronym—GERDDES—Groupe d'Etude et de Recherche sur la Démocratie et le Développement Economique et Social en Afrique); Burundi (Group of Independent Observers); Kenya (National Election Monitoring Unit); Malawi (Public Affairs Committee); Namibia (Council of Churches); and Zambia (Zambia Election Monitoring Committee), among others.

In the overwhelming majority of cases, domestic observers do not have the authority to intervene if they detect irregularities. They may transmit information to the electoral authorities and publicly denounce the authorities if no action is taken, but their ability to correct wrongdoing is limited to the moral authority they have been able to achieve. One exception is South Africa, where the Independent Electoral Commission created an independent directorate for the sole purpose of monitoring and evaluating the 1994 elections. The monitors of the commission, most of them recruited from nongovernmental organizations, could investigate violations of the campaign Code of Conduct and of prescribed procedures and had some effective enforcement powers.

The National Democratic Institute has been especially active in helping set up and support domestic observers. Most of the operations described in the previous paragraphs owe much to the contributions of the institute. The institute has also worked extensively with political parties on the training of their poll-watchers and has published a handbook, "How Domestic Organizations Monitor Elections: An A to Z Guide."

In most cases, domestic observers are close to the opposition, which might be their main limitation. But they frequently have proven their impartiality by helping a winning incumbent reaffirm the legitimacy of his or her victory. A well-known case is the confirmation of the victory of the ruling party in Bulgaria by the Bulgarian Association for Fair Elections. On the other hand, domestic observers too close to the government are usually suspect. There is little reason to expect that the opposition will manipulate elections.

FORMATION OF OBSERVER GROUPS

Domestic observer organizations may emerge from an existing organization, be created from scratch, or result from the coalition of several organizations. The advantage of established organizations is their availability of already existing structures, which might command significant resources. The National Teachers Union in Mexico could count on the participation of teachers throughout the country as well as on its central and regional offices to support its organizational efforts. The disadvantage, though, is that existing organizations come with a history. Despite the purity of their intentions, or the impartiality of their efforts, their observation can be tainted with allegations of past partisanship.

Forming an entirely new organization can be time-consuming, and the infancy of an organization is likely to be a period of uncertainty. Unless the organization develops well in advance of the elections, teething problems will affect the observation of the prepoll electoral process. In the Philippines, the National Citizens Movement for Free Elections began activities thirty months before the elections, and thus had time to recruit a large number of volunteers. But sometimes it is possible to start working only a few months before the elections. In those cases the leadership concentrates on fund raising, setting up an adequate board or steering committee, and organizing the observation network. The result might be an excessive concentration on polling operations. The advantage, though, is that a new organization finds it easier to create an image of and a reputation for impartiality.

The establishment of coalitions of several groups is another frequent organizational approach. In Zambia six non-governmental organizations formed the Zambian Election Monitoring Committee. In Malawi church organizations from different denominations formed the Public Affairs Committee. In Bangladesh several organizations coalesced in the Fair Elections Monitoring Alliance. Coalitions simplify the recruitment of observers, since they use their existing networks. Coalitions might also facilitate the image of neutrality by allowing a "balanced" mix of participating organizations. However, reconciling different management styles might take some time. Although it is essential that a coalition use democratic methods for decision-making, strong leadership is usually an important ingredient.

Domestic observers have several advantages over international observers. First, they know the country and the political environment well. They have information networks that would be difficult or impossible for foreigners to access. They speak the languages, know the customs, and belong to the community. It is easier for external electoral experts to educate domestic observers about the electoral process than for domestic observers to teach the external experts about the country's culture and political environment.

Second, a domestic observer costs a fraction of an international observer. National observers require minimal transportation, since they live close to observation targets. In Mozambique the cost of an ambitious plan for deploying political party observers was about US$30 per observer, including recruitment, training, and internal transportation. International observers usually require international travel, per diem, and other expensive arrangements, frequently including interpretation. The average cost could be two hundred times higher than that of national observers. The cost differential affects the number of observers that can be deployed. An international operation involving fifty observers would be considered large, and a Namibian-type effort with two thousand observers would be a freak occurrence. However, numbers in the thousands are normal in domestic observation. The number of observers has a profound impact on the accuracy of the observation and on the methodological approach, as will be discussed below.

Finally, international observers have more external than internal impact. For example, the European Union mission to the 1996 Nicaraguan elections did not include well-known figures, and its report did not receive massive attention from the Nicaraguan press. Although the mission's report was probably influential in Brussels, it did not provide significant internal legitimacy to the electoral process. An international observation mission needs a very well known figure—like former president Carter—to have an effective internal impact. On the other hand, domestic observers can include in their organizational set-up a council, board, or steering committee of respected national personalities and have a significant impact on the internal perception of the electoral process. But national observers never attract as much attention outside their country as the more flamboyant international observers do.

There are problems, however, to national observation. Frequently, national observer groups are loose coalitions of small regional organizations, and they have difficulty achieving uniformity of criteria. They also suffer from some of the biases of international observation and tend to concentrate too heavily on election day. Furthermore, they more frequently preach than practice impartiality. In most cases national observers are somewhat partial to the opposition, although governments have learned to organize national observation groups closer to their own positions.

A more detailed analysis of the comparative advantages of different approaches to observation is provided below. However, even a superficial comparison suggests that national observation has substantive advantages over international observation. The latter should be redefined in a way that complements and reinforces national efforts. Large-scale international missions should be reserved for thoroughly justified special cases.

OBSERVATION AS PREACHED: "IDEAL" APPROACHES

IDEA's *Code of Conduct for the Ethical and Professional Observation of Elections* sets out some of the basic principles that observers should respect in conducting observation. Observation should be respectful of the target countries' sovereignty and culture and should be comprehensive and accurate. Many different organizations employ distinct approaches. But most of them can be classified within three main types, which attempt to respect the basic principles of comprehensiveness, accuracy, and respect for national sovereignty in different ways.

The first approach (see Figure 1) is what might be called the "ideal" long-term observation model and corresponds roughly to the practices employed in important cases by the UN, the OAS, the European Union, and the Organization for Security and Cooperation in Europe. It is a large-scale, expensive approach that requires the permanent presence of a significant number of observers throughout the electoral process, including their deployment to the main regions of the country. This approach aims at the direct observation of

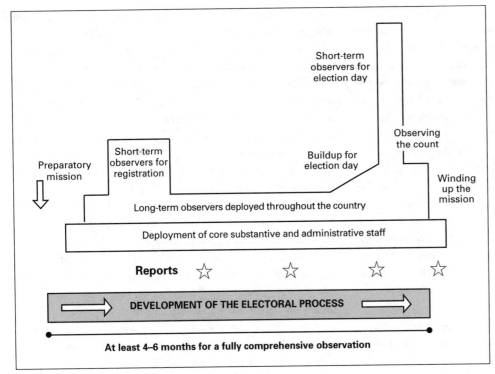

Figure 1. The "Ideal" Long-term Observation Model

the Commonwealth, the Carter Center, the Center for Democracy, and other nongovernmental organizations. It requires far fewer resources than the previous approach, since it aims only to observe the last stages of the electoral campaign, the events of election day, the counting of votes, and, in some cases, the registration of voters. Information concerning other aspects of the electoral process is indirectly gathered through detailed fact-finding visits involving contacts with electoral authorities, the government, political parties, and relevant personalities. Some organizations establish a small permanent office to carry out these functions, to keep headquarters informed of developments, and to make arrangements for the visits of the fact-finding missions.

events and aims to achieve comprehensive chronological and geographical coverage. In most cases, the observation should begin three to four months before election day. After a short preparatory mission, a small group of substantive and administrative staff is deployed, followed as soon as possible by a group of long-term observers deployed throughout the country. It takes time to make the presence of long-term observers well known in their assigned regions and to develop a network of relevant contacts. In most cases, the registration of voters requires a short-term increase in the number of observers. Many more short-term observers arrive a week or so before the election, so that a representative number of polling stations can be visited and a quick count can be conducted. After the elections, a smaller number of observers should remain to observe the counting of votes, allocation of seats, and other post-electoral activities. Whereas long-term personnel might require electoral knowledge and the ability to develop an effective network of contacts, the observation of polling or registration is simple, and requirements for short-term observers are minimal.

The second approach, in Figure 2, is the "ideal" short-term observation model, and corresponds roughly to the practice of

This approach requires considerable political and electoral experience in fact-finding missions. In most cases, organizations following this approach also deploy persons with substantial experience in election day observation. The Commonwealth, for instance, relies on parliamentarians, members of electoral commissions, and the like. Since the emphasis is more on qualitative than quantitative observation, the size of missions tends to depend on the availability of resources.

The third approach is the "election day observation," in which observers conduct a short visit, arriving a few days before election day and usually leaving the day after the elec-

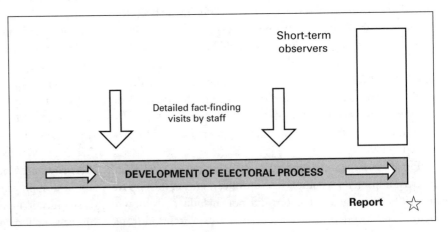

Figure 2. The "Ideal" Short-term Model

tions. Although much vilified, this approach can be effective when conducted by individuals or organizations who have in-depth knowledge of the country and follow the evolution of the electoral process through indirect channels. If the election-day observers are academics and professionals who specialize in the country, keep informed of events, and have substantive political and electoral knowledge, they might be effective judges of the adequacy of the electoral process. Unfortunately, this is rarely the case, and practice is far different from the ideal descriptions above.

OBSERVATION AS PRACTICED: TOO LITTLE, TOO LATE

Although most organizations involved in observation vehemently defend their commitment to the principles of comprehensiveness and accuracy, they do not live up to those high standards. They always have explanations for shortfalls in specific cases: invitations arrive too late; obtaining resources takes additional time; administrative requirements complicate the setting up of missions; recruitment takes longer than expected; and so on. No matter how reasonable the excuses, in many cases the outcome is a parody of the "ideal" approaches.

Long-term observers sometimes arrive only six-to-eight weeks before the election. Their late arrival deprives them of the opportunity to observe crucial aspects, like the registration of voters and candidates. Installation and deployment takes a good part of the initial period. Long-term observers do not have time to develop a network of contacts. The typical result is that long-term observers spend most of their time making logistical arrangements and planning observation routes for short-term observers. In the case of short-term missions, a usual consequence of limited time and resources is the elimination of the fact-finding missions, which are a necessary element for ensuring comprehensiveness of the short-term model. Fact-finding missions are usually replaced by a mission to prepare the ground and make logistical arrangements for the short-term observers.

THE CHALLENGES OF COORDINATION

Most writing on observation discusses the subject from the perspective of a single organization conducting an integrated observation exercise, from data gathering through analysis, evaluation, and reporting. However, the number of organizations conducting observations can be very large in important or interesting cases, as in Nicaragua in 1996.

Coordination is especially important if observation is conceived as a set of information-gathering activities. Although information gathering is the aspect of observation that requires the largest share of resources, the subsequent analysis of the raw data is essential for making an informed judgment on the adequacy of the electoral process. Analysts require skill at extracting conclusions from raw data, identifying trends from a large number of isolated facts, differentiating between irregularities and systematic attempts to manipulate some aspect of the electoral process, identifying underlying problems, and relating the electoral information to its social and political context. Analysis is less resource intensive than data gathering, but it requires definite skills. Evaluation—the next activity—is even less resource intensive but requires the use of standards that are, in most cases, nonexistent, fuzzy, or difficult to apply. The last, but by far the most important, activity involved in observation is reporting. Who issues the report, and how and when the "message" of the mission is voiced, count at least as much as the comprehensiveness and accuracy of the information on which the report is based.

Achieving effective coordination becomes increasingly difficult as we move from data gathering to reporting. There are practical and theoretical arguments for cooperation among nonpartisan observers, whether international or national, in the gathering of information. Some people even argue that there are strong incentives for close cooperation. Working together facilitates larger samples and more adequate coverage in areas like registration or voting, and it also leads to significant labor and cost savings in the collection of raw data concerning the remaining components of the electoral process. Better retrieval of media information becomes possible, events can be witnessed at more public meetings, and more people can follow the processing and adjudication of complaints.

Cooperation in analysis is significantly more difficult. The first problem is that not much analysis is done, given the pressure of time. The second is that different analysts might reach different conclusions from the same data, since there are no standards of "normality." Is 5 percent inconsistency in an electoral roll acceptable? Some might claim that it is too high, while others might think it quite normal under the circumstances.

Evaluation is inherently difficult because it involves multiple dimensions. Even the standard concept of "free and fair" elections involves a bidimensional judgment. The issues are further complicated by the fact that each of the two dimensions involves several "components." For example, the dimension "free" involves the freedoms of speech, assembly, association, and movement; equal and universal suffrage; the absence of impediments to standing as a candidate; freedom from fear and intimidation; the opportunity to participate in the poll; and legal possibilities of impartial treatment of complaints and petitions. It is thus entirely possible and legitimate that different organizations employ dissimilar criteria for their final evaluation. An organization that gives considerable weight to malfunctioning aspects will have a poorer opinion of the elections than one that attaches priority to aspects that performed normally.

The last activity of the observation cycle—reporting—is by far the most difficult to coordinate. Unless organizations are in full agreement in analysis and evaluation, they will find it difficult to issue joint reports. But even if there is full agreement, most organizations have a strong interest in separate reporting, since that allows them to reinforce their organizational identity. The pressure for separate reporting is far stronger in the case of post–election day statements and press conferences. There is much less interest in the publications issued two or three months after the elections—they rarely make the best sellers' list.

One could expect that cooperation and coordination would be easier to achieve in data gathering. Two organizations have made efforts to improve coordination among observers. The United Nations has developed the so-called coordination and support approach, as a limited response to the dispersion of efforts and the trend to concentrate international observation on election day. The approach is based on the establishment of an "electoral assistance secretariat" to identify organizations and countries sending observers; to convince donors to send more long-term observers and fewer short-term observers; and to provide effective logistic and technical support to arriving observers. When successfully implemented, an electoral assistance secretariat develops a core network of long-term observers and organizes a "joint international observer group" to standardize and coordinate approaches and share information. The secretariat usually makes an effort to recruit volunteer observers among international residents, including the diplomatic community. The UN's initial design foresaw the participants in the group sharing information and performing joint analysis, while having the freedom to evaluate and report individually. The approach included joint discussion after the elections among the different observer organizations included in the Joint International Observer Group concerning the approach they would take to reporting. Although such meetings might help in achieving independent but consistent reporting, the UN's aim was not to force consensus.

While the UN considers its approach as better employed in cases that do not receive excessive international attention, International IDEA concentrated on cases like Russia, where a plethora of observer organizations was expected. IDEA's approach involves providing a neutral ground where different organizations can meet in advance, discuss their operational plans, and establish arrangements to increase the efficiency of their operation, like coordination of observers' routes, employment of compatible forms for the observation of events on election day, joint debriefing, and so on. IDEA has complemented these meetings with two international gatherings for an overall discussion of coordination problems.

However, it has been difficult to achieve effective coordination. The UN has encountered situations where diplomatic representatives have pressed for a joint report with a favorable evaluation. IDEA's cooperation arrangements have concentrated on the deployment of observers on election day. Experience shows that observer organizations are reluctant to lose their identity, which tends to be a side effect of coordination.

HOW TO DO IT: APPROACHES TO SPECIFIC OBSERVATION TARGETS

As discussed above, organizations involved in electoral observation might differ substantially in their approaches, but all would probably agree that coverage should be comprehensive. Comprehensiveness might be defined in chronological and geographical terms as the coverage of the entire electoral process throughout the country. The long-term approach involves fielding and regionally deploying observers early in the process. In the short-term approach, comprehensiveness is achieved through periodic visits and extensive interviewing.

However, comprehensiveness can also be functionally defined as the activities that are part of the electoral process. These activities can be conceived as the targets of the observation efforts. The functional deconstruction of the observation process makes possible a more nuanced analysis of methodological approaches and resource requirements. Table 1 describes possible approaches and resource requirements for fifteen common targets of observation.

INTERNATIONAL AND NATIONAL OBSERVATION: STRENGTHS AND WEAKNESSES

The deconstruction of the electoral process into its components, and the analysis of effective approaches to observing each one, suggest that most components of the electoral process can be adequately covered with qualitative assessments by small teams of experts. The two main exceptions—requiring large numbers of observers—are the observation of freedom of assembly, movement, nonexistence of fear and intimidation, and observation of the events on election day, including counting at polling stations. Although present techniques of observing voter registration also require large numbers of observers, there are alternative and more efficient approaches based on expert analysis. Given these different resource requirements, what are the relative advantages of international and domestic observation for the different observation targets?

One almost obvious conclusion is that international observers are not particularly cost-effective for information

Table 1. Approaches and Resource Requirements for Observing Different Stages of the Electoral Process

Observation targets	Suggested approaches and resource requirements
Existence of an enabling environment	Qualitative assessment by a small team of persons deeply familiar with the political and the security situation. An understanding of the environment is necessary not only for making the decision on involvement but for providing a framework for defining reasonable benchmarks in relation to the remaining electoral activities.
Legal framework of electoral process	Qualitative assessment by a small team of experts, which might include suggestions on potential improvements. Analysis should include the credibility of the electoral institutions, their acceptance by opposition parties, organizational arrangements, and the selection of authorities at all relevant levels. Occasionally, an inadequate and biased legal framework might lead to discontinuation of observation efforts.
Delimitation of constituencies	Qualitative assessment by a small team of experts on the compatibility of the existing delimitation with the principle of equal suffrage.
Registration of voters	Traditional approach has been for observer teams to visit registration sites, as is done on election day. However, a preferred approach would be to conduct expert analysis of registration procedures and regional allocation of resources; to evaluate political party participation in identification of registration stations; to perform statistical analyses, including sample analysis of consistency of electoral rolls; to follow up specific complaints concerning registration; to visit randomly registration stations. (Comments are based on the construction of ad hoc rolls; the approach would be different if enumeration or other approaches were used.)
Registration of political parties, alliances, and candidates	Qualitative assessment of legal requirements for inscription. Follow-up of specific complaints concerning intimidation and pressures on candidates and attempts to constitute new parties.
Impartial complaint procedures during the prepolling period	Qualitative assessment of procedures by small team of experts, follow-up of relevant complaints, analysis of contested decisions.
Voter information and education	Qualitative analysis by small expert team. Content analysis of educational materials. Analysis of allocation of resources to regions and sectors. Analysis of civil society involvement.
Freedom of assembly and movement	Two possible approaches: direct observation of campaign events by extensive regional deployment of international observers; or direct observation by effective networks of national observers throughout the country.
Freedom from fear and intimidation	Follow-up of specific complaints by affected individuals and parties by small, specialized teams, frequently traveling to the regions.
Freedom of expression and equitable access to the media	Qualitative/quantitative assessment by specialized team, including evaluation of procedures for distribution of time in public media and conditions of access to other media. Content analysis and evaluation of media. Follow-up of specific complaints.
Funding of campaigns and use of public resources	Procedures to be followed depend on the situation and regulation of specific countries. In all cases, evaluation should include follow-up of complaints concerning misappropriation of public resources.
Electoral preparations	Expert analysis of electoral preparations. Incompetence and mismanagement of the electoral process might exist even in a generally free and fair election. A thorough knowledge and understanding of the adequacy of electoral preparations will help distinguish irregularities from fraud and manipulation during the evaluation stage.
Voting	The two standard approaches are: 1. Mobile observation, where teams of observers with adequate transportation each observe the opening of a polling station, visit a variable number of polling places during the day, and observe the closing and counting in another polling station. With this approach, which is typical of international observer missions, observers perform two different types of observation. There is "direct" observation when the observers are at a polling station. There is also "indirect" observation, because the observers will ask the authorities of the polling station as well as party poll-watchers about problems and irregularities that might have taken place before the observers' arrival. The coverage of indirect observation varies with the moment of arrival of the observers. At polling stations visited early in the

Table 1. Approaches and Resource Requirements for Observing Different Stages of the Electoral Process *(continued)*

Observation targets	Suggested approaches and resource requirements
	day, the coverage will be minimal. If the visit takes place toward the end of the day, it will cover the entire voting process at that station. An obvious requirement for the reliability of "indirect" observation is the presence of poll-watchers of opposition parties. 2. Static observation, where one or two observers stay for the whole day in a polling station. This approach is typical of domestic observers and is rarely practiced by international missions (Namibia being an exception). All the observation is direct, and it enables the collection of quantitative information on a number of relevant phenomena. If one prominent issue is that many duly registered voters cannot find their names in the electoral rolls, this approach allows the preparation of reliable statistics.
Vote counting and compilation of results	Parallel vote tabulations or quick counts at polling stations. Direct observation at polling centers. (A polling center is a site, such as a school building, that has multiple polling stations.) Analysis and random checks of procedures for transmission and compilation of results.
Adequate processing of postelectoral complaints and petitions	Qualitative assessment of procedures by small team of experts, follow-up of relevant complaints, analysis of contested decisions.

gathering, with the exception of certain areas where expertise is important, as discussed in the previous sections. The observation of the respect for basic freedoms is the typical focus of long-term, regionally deployed international observers. However, success in information gathering depends on the ability of observers to establish effective networks of contact with their national counterparts. The main impact of long-term observers, regionally deployed, is that their presence will probably have a deterrent effect and significantly contribute to confidence building. This aspect is more appreciated by opposition parties than by the government and cannot be easily replaced by national observers.

The differences between international and domestic observation concerning information gathering are particularly evident on election day. The typical mobile international operation has the advantage of an element of surprise, which can deter fraud and abuse. International observation is based on sample observation, and well-designed samples might be a reliable representation of the universe. However, the data collected during the short visits to polling stations during the day are largely impressionistic and provide reliable quantitative data for only a very limited number of variables. The typical national static observation allows collection of complete information on events in the polling station being observed. Since domestic organizations are usually able to cover all or most of the polling stations, their presence results in both accurate data and widespread deterrence. Although international observation missions—particularly the UN—adequately conduct "quick counts," national observers also conduct them efficiently.

Differences between domestic and international observation of targets requiring expert knowledge depend on the

characteristics of the country where the observation is being conducted. In developed countries like Mexico or South Africa, most of the expertise required for specialized analysis exists and can be part of the national observation methodology. On the other hand, there are countries where national expertise does not exist, making the expertise provided by international observers necessary.

Another important difference between domestic and international observation concerns the impact of their reporting. Domestic observers are listened to mostly inside the country, while the opposite is true of international observers. It is important to remember that the impact on legitimization is not always achieved by carefully thought out reports, based on the information collected by the observers and carefully analyzed and chronicled by the media. Nor should it be assumed that the higher the quality and accuracy of the information on which the report is based, the greater will be its impact on public opinion. In far too many cases, opinions are shaped by mission statements issued shortly after polls close and based more on an overall political evaluation of the after-poll situation than on a careful and detailed analysis of the information collected by the mission. Media coverage frequently is based on the timing of the statement and the name recognition of the head of the mission, rather than on the quality of the information on which it is based. These aspects should be as much an integral part of the planning of the mission as the technical requirements.

Observation, whether international or national, will continue to be an important feature of democratization processes in the near future. However, observer organizations must review carefully their observation approaches, selecting those that best fit the situation on the ground. This is particularly true in relation to those observation targets that are best covered by small teams of experts rather than by large numbers of observers. Reviewing observation approaches is also necessary in order to achieve a better integration of international and domestic observation, establishing links between the two levels that increase the overall synergy.

International observation is costly, and its use should be carefully evaluated on a case-by-case basis. It began as a demand phenomenon: a response to pressing needs in difficult situations. As time went by, it has developed some of the distinguishing features of a supply phenomenon: the existence of a request is the main consideration, and not much attention is paid to either the situation on the ground or the effective need for a costly tool like international observation.

See also *Administration of Elections; Elections in Developing Countries; Electoralism; Founding Elections; Free and Fair Elections; Premature Closure; Technical Assistance in Elections; Unfree Elections.*

HORACIO BONEO

BIBLIOGRAPHY

Beigbeder, Ives. *International Monitoring of Plebiscites, Referenda and National Elections.* Dordrecht: Martinus Nijhoff, 1994.

Carothers, Thomas. "The Observers Observed." *Journal of Democracy* 8, no. 3 (1997).

Commonwealth Secretariat. *Election Observation: The Commonwealth Experience.* London: Commonwealth Secretariat, 1996.

Council of Europe. *Handbook for Observers of Elections.* Strasbourg: Council of Europe, 1992.

Ebersole, Jon M. "The United Nations Response to Requests for Assistance in Electoral Matters." *Virginia Journal of International Law* 33, no. 91 (1992).

Elklit, Jorgen, and Palle Svenssonn. "What Makes Elections Free and Fair?" *Journal of Democracy* 8, no. 3 (1997).

Garber, Larry. *Guidelines for International Election Observation.* Washington, D.C.: International Human Rights Law Group, 1990.

Geisler, Gisela. "Fair? What Has Fairness Got to Do with It? Vagaries of Election Observation and Democratic Standards." *The Journal of Modern African Studies* 31, no. 4 (1993).

Goodwin-Gill, Guy. *Free and Fair Elections: International Law and Practice.* Geneva: Inter-Parliamentary Union, 1994.

Gould, Ron. *Reference Guide for Election Observers.* London: Commonwealth Parliamentary Association, 1994.

Gould, Ron, and Christine Jackson. *A Guide for Election Observers.* Aldershot, England: Dartmouth, 1995.

Hanf, Theodore, et al. *Observing Democratic Elections: A European Approach.* Freiburg: Arnold Bergstraesser Institute, 1995.

International Foundation for Election Systems. *How to Organize and Conduct an Election Observation Mission.* Washington, D.C.: IFES, 1992.

International Institute for Democracy and Electoral Assistance. *Lessons Learnt—International Election Observation.* Stockholm: UN and IDEA, 1995.

———. *Code of Conduct for International Observers.* Stockholm: IDEA, 1997.

Kumar, Krishna, and Marina Ottaway. *From Bullets to Ballots: Electoral Assistance to Post-Conflict Societies.* Washington, D.C.: U.S. Agency for International Development, 1997.

Mair, Stefan. *International Election Observation: One Form of Democratization Assistance.* Ebenhausen: Research Institute for International Politics and Security, 1994.

McCoy, Jennifer, et al. "Poll-Watching and Peace-Making." *Journal of Democracy* 2, no. 4 (1991).

National Democratic Institute. *NDI Handbook: How Domestic Organizations Monitor Elections.* Washington, D.C.: NDI, 1995.

Nevitte, Neil, and Santiago Canton. "The Role of Domestic Observers." *Journal of Democracy* 8, no. 3 (1997).

Organization for Security and Cooperation in Europe. *The OSCE/ODIHR Election Observation Handbook.* Warsaw: ODIHR, 1997.

Rigby, Vincent. *Les organismes qui parraient les equipes chargees de l'observation international des elections.* Ottawa: Bibliotheque du Parliament, 1992.

Tomasevski, Katarina. *Between Sanctions and Elections: Aid Donors and Their Human Rights Performance.* London: Pinter, 1997.

OFFICES FILLED BY DIRECT ELECTION

The right to vote is politically important insofar as the offices filled by election are politically significant in terms of the constitutional and statutory powers of the officeholders. Democratic political systems confer political authority and legitimacy on popularly elected officials, thus making them far more important than their numbers imply. In a democratic election, voters invariably choose popular representatives for the nation's highest lawmaking body. But in parliamentary democracies the head of the executive branch of government, the prime minister, is not elected, and the judiciary is usually headed by officials who are appointed, not elected. The great majority of public offices are filled not by elected individuals but by civil servants who remain in place whoever wins an election; they qualify for their position on merit, by having specialist professional qualifications and by examination. Public offices can also be filled in a variety of other ways: patronage, purchase, or heredity.

NATIONAL ASSEMBLY ELECTIONS

The national assembly, whether a congress or a parliament, is the national body most commonly filled by popular election. Election of its members by popular vote makes the national assembly a representative body, and the fact that the assembly has hundreds of members makes it representative of a diversity of parties, interests, and opinions. In contemporary assemblies, members normally represent a party. In constitutional terms, a national assembly is a legislature; its approval is required for the enactment of major legislation and the budget. However, in the strict sense, it is rarely a lawmaking body; laws are normally drafted by the sponsoring department in the executive branch of government. Members of the assembly examine proposals and criticize and amend them. When votes are taken, they are usually along party lines, thus disciplining the way in which individual representatives voice personal or constituent opinions.

Most assemblies have two houses: a lower house representing the electorate on the basis of one person, one vote, one value, and an upper house chosen differently. The upper house provides representation for groups other than the national electorate. In federal systems, the upper house is often representative of the states and is chosen by state governments, as is the case in Germany and Austria today and was common in the United States until the Seventeenth Amendment, ratified in 1913, mandated that all senators be popularly elected. The Canadian senate, whose members sit until seventy-five years old, is filled by appointment on the advice of the prime minister. In the Netherlands the upper chamber consists of representatives elected by local government. In Ireland most members of the upper chamber are elected by vocational constituencies representing farming, business, labor, and so forth. Britain is unusual in that for seven centuries a substantial proportion of the upper chamber of its Parliament, the House of Lords, was filled by hereditary peers; in 1999 the new Labour government of Tony Blair abolished the right of all hereditary peers to sit in the upper house of Parliament.

EXECUTIVE-LEGISLATIVE RELATIONS

In addition to approving legislation, a parliament has a second important power: it grants or withholds confidence in the executive branch of government. The prime minister and cabinet are not required to win popular election; they must win a vote of confidence in parliament. In countries such as Britain, where the first-past-the-post electoral system usually gives the party with a plurality of votes an absolute majority of seats in parliament, it is reasonable to say that the electorate chooses the government of the day. However, elections under proportional representation usually produce a parliament in which no party has an absolute majority of seats, leading to haggling between parties before a coalition government is chosen. In such circumstances, it is more accurate to say that a popularly elected parliament chooses the government of the day.

Popularly elected presidents may or may not have substantial political powers. In Austria and Ireland their job is primarily to be head of state. But the United States, France, and many Latin American countries popularly elect a president with substantial executive powers. The French constitution is distinctive in having a prime minister accountable to parliament as well as a popularly elected president with executive powers. If the two offices—which are filled by the same electorate, although at different times and by different rules—are filled by politicians of different parties, they must live together, in a relationship the French call "cohabitation." This cannot happen in a parliamentary system in which the head of state has no electoral mandate and the prime minister is accountable to a popularly elected parliament. Where the chief executive is a separately elected president, elected representatives can criticize the president and reject legislative proposals but may remove him or her from office only through impeachment. Israel is atypical in having a parliamentary system of government in which, since 1996, the prime minister has been popularly elected.

The judges in the highest national courts are invariably appointed rather than subject to popular election. In many European countries a judicial career is a civil service job, filled by examination, with promotion by merit. In the United States, Supreme Court justices are appointed through a political process: nominated by the president and confirmed by the Senate. In Canada the prime minister appoints federal judges without the need for confirmation by parliament. In England the highest judges are chosen by the prime minister or the lord chancellor, the latter being a member of the government of the day.

SUBNATIONAL ELECTIONS

Some offices below the national level of government are also filled by election. In a democratic federal system, elections for offices with substantial political power are held at what is called the state level in the United States, the *land* level in Germany, and the national level in the newly devolved assemblies of Scotland and Wales. The forms of subnational election vary along the same lines as elections for national government. In some countries the state elects a governor or president, whereas in others the head of the executive is chosen by the state's parliament. The outcomes of subnational elections can differ from those of national elections, first because the constituency of a state can differ substantially from that of the nation as a whole. For example, neither Minnesota nor Mississippi is a microcosm of the United States. Second, elections at the state or *land* level often occur at a different time than national-level elections. Third, the parties competing at the lower level can differ from their national counterparts; this is especially true in Quebec and in Scotland, where nationalist parties are important.

In local government, councilors are elected, usually with powers restricted by the national government in unitary systems and sometimes by the *land* or state government in federal systems. The definition of "local" varies too, from an American county that can take an hour or more to drive across, to a small French commune that can be traversed on foot in fifteen minutes. Population varies as well. France has tens of thousands of communes; the median has less than five thousand inhabitants, so that a typical commune's councilors are very close to their voters. England, by contrast, has only a few hundred local authorities, and the median council is responsible for more than one hundred thousand people. As a general rule, the smaller the population of a local government, the weaker it is, because it lacks the financial resources to do much, whereas the bigger it is in population, the greater its resources but the lesser the contact between councilors and individual voters. The American practice of electing a mayor as the head of the executive branch of government is not common internationally, but it is gaining increasing interest.

LIMITS ON ELECTION

A committed democrat, the American political scientist Robert Dahl has stressed that election is not always the best grounds for filling an office. Technical competence—for example, a medical degree—is necessary for some jobs, such as being a surgeon or a public health official. Economy and efficiency are also criteria: it can be cheaper for a public agency to buy catering services from a restaurant than to hire cooks for a staff lunchroom through a civil service exam or to fill the posts by election. Appointment by patronage or by bipartisan board can be endorsed as a way to ensure representativeness in a multicultural environment, for example, of minorities unlikely to secure votes in a city or statewide election. Historically, use of the civil service criterion of technical expertise has been the standard prescription for reforming abuses of office by elected officials. Today, new public management theories often apply economic analysis, stressing that buying services from nongovernmental agencies can be more flexible and cheaper than appointing or electing public officials.

The number of offices filled by popular election is not an indication of the degree to which a political system is democratic. The British system minimizes opportunities to elect officials: many English voters can vote only for one member of Parliament and a local ward councilor. By contrast, the American system allows a person to vote for four offices at the national level—the president, two senators, and one representative—and dozens of officials in long ballots listing executive, legislative, and, sometimes, even judicial offices, at the state, county, and local level. The great majority of European democracies are more like Britain in restricting the number of offices filled by election.

The fewer the number of offices filled by popular election, the clearer the lines of accountability between voters and popularly elected officials. A unitary state in which only the lower house of parliament is popularly elected by the first-past-the-post gives the clearest answer: the party that has a majority in Parliament is responsible. But this arrangement also gives voters the minimum of choice. If the upper house of the assembly is also elected, it too can claim popular representative status. If a president is elected by a nationwide ballot, and representatives by geographically small districts, then the president may have a stronger claim to represent "all the people" (or, at least, all who voted for him), whereas the representative can claim to represent his or her district, and collectively representatives can claim to represent everyone too. In a unitary state, officeholders at the national level are normally assumed to have a better claim to represent all the people than are councilors who represent a single city or town, and the constitution normally vests superior authority in officeholders elected nationally. But in a federal system, state and local officials can claim to be more representative of voters, because their constituency is smaller and may be homogeneous and distinctive. Nationalists in places such as Quebec or Scotland use this claim to superior status to justify the right to secession.

See also *Appendix; Choice, Elections as a Method of; Federal Countries, Elections in; Nonpartisan Elections; Presidential Electoral Systems.*

RICHARD ROSE, UNIVERSITY OF STRATHCLYDE

BIBLIOGRAPHY

Dahl, Robert A. *After the Revolution? Authority in a Good Society.* New Haven, Conn.: Yale University Press, 1970.

Inter-Parliamentary Union. *Parliaments of the World.* 2 vols. Aldershot, England: Gower, 1986.

Maddex, Robert L. *Constitutions of the World.* Washington, D.C.: Congressional Quarterly, 1995.

OPEN VOTING

Open voting is voting at public elections (including referendums and plebiscites) in which no deliberate effort is made to conceal the choice made by individual voters from other voters or from their fellow citizens. The openness of such voting is intentional, and so open voting is the antithesis of secret voting.

Oral voting, a form of open voting, was the norm into the nineteenth century, partly because the issue of open-versus-secret voting was only rarely raised, and partly for practical reasons: Only a relatively small number of voters came together to vote, and an easily administered secret ballot had not yet been invented. Much political thinking during this period, conservative as well as liberal, held that only socially and intellectually independent citizens should have the vote and that such voters would not mind letting their fellow citizens know their political opinions and actions—and would be willing and able to defend their opinions publicly, if necessary.

FORMS OF OPEN VOTING

Open voting takes several forms: voting by acclamation at a public meeting, where the individual's behavior is discernible to bystanders; oral voting, in which the voter states his or her preference in front of a poll clerk who, after eligibility checks, enters the vote in an electoral register or a manuscript poll book that may later appear in printed form; voting in which the voter has the option of voting openly or of using whatever secrecy provisions are available; and voting for a particular candidate (or policy option) by joining the queue of people supporting that choice, who are subsequently counted. A variant of this last form of open voting is the use of separate ballot boxes for the various candidates or parties, a practice that has sometimes been used in countries with a low level of literacy. There may be other forms of open voting, but the above-mentioned are the most important.

The various forms can be combined. In Denmark between 1848 and 1900 voting was by acclamation in the first round of parliamentary elections and, after eligibility checks, oral in the second round (if a second round took place). In a subvariant of oral voting, intended to simplify an otherwise lengthy and complicated oral-voting process, a voter handed in an (unofficial) ballot paper provided by the political parties (or others); the color of the paper or other marking nevertheless made the voter's choice identifiable. Similarly, the provisions for assistance to illiterate voters in some countries prescribe that they vote with the help of an election official and that their vote be read aloud and checked by party agents in order to avoid fraud by the assisting official. This is also de facto open voting and can be required of voters who have few resources to resist attempted influence. The first form of open voting mentioned above, voting by acclamation at a public meeting, is still often used in elections, for example, in trade unions, political parties, and university departments.

THE NINETEENTH CENTURY

During the nineteenth century voting was open in many countries where public offices at the national or local level were filled through public elections: Britain before the Ballot Act (1872); Prussia (for the Second Chamber), 1849–1918; Denmark, 1848–1900; Iceland before 1906; Hungary, more or less, before 1938; most U.S. states until 1896; Belgium before the 1870s. The situation was more fluid in France before 1913, partly because of shifts between open and secret voting and partly because of inadequate implementation of secrecy regulations during the periods when secrecy was in force.

Open voting—whether by acclamation or by individuals indicating their choices to poll officials—is more easily managed with small electorates. It is also easier to implement when the vote choice is simple (for example, when selecting one or two candidates out of five or six) and when the election is for only one public office, not for a number of offices (as is often the case in the United States).

Open voting came under attack when suffrage was enlarged and more offices were contested during the late nineteenth and early twentieth century. The sequence of changes in suffrage requirements and other institutional electoral arrangements is intriguing and complicated. The growth of contestation between political parties following the political mobilization that took place in the wake of industrialization and urbanization, particularly in Europe, also contributed to a decline in support for open voting, since most parties became aware of the need to protect their followers from undue political influence.

STUDYING OPEN VOTING

The study of electoral behavior under open voting has taken two main routes: studies and analyses based on aggregate voting statistics; and studies and analyses based on the information on individual voting behavior contained in poll books, manuscript poll lists, voting lists, and so on. The former suffer from the same methodological problems as all studies based on aggregate electoral statistics, but also (precisely because of the openness of these elections) from the frequent lack of statistics on partisan division, due to elections not being seriously contested—if contested at all—in all localities, and from low turnout figures since the electoral outcome is almost self-evident. The latter suffer from problems related primarily to the random occurrence of the source material (printed and manuscript poll books and lists) as well as the amount of work that such studies require.

Poll books—printed books in which voters' partisan choices are clearly indicated—exist in considerable numbers (above all from Britain, but also a few from other places, including Denmark). But the spread and length of coverage is accidental, and in any case it is not conditioned by research interests. Hence, the extant poll books and other kinds of manuscript poll lists are not necessarily from the most interesting or the most representative elections and locations. However, the lists that do exist often contain valuable additional information about the individual voter—not only a name but also some or all of the following: address, occupation, age, tax payment, value of property, religious affiliation, even previous voting record. This information can be used to establish social categories for the analysis of voting behavior, but it is also of value for nominal record linkage (computerized, manual, or semicomputerized) of voters from more than one election when relevant material exists for successive elections. High-probability links of individual voters over successive elections can produce panel data on electoral behavior for the historical psephologist as well as useful information on possible explanatory social variables.

The situation is different in the United States, where most surviving voting lists contain just the voters' names and their partisan choices. The scattered nature of this material and the difficulties connected with the use of supporting material—such as ordinary population registers—because of population turnover and the differences between regions probably explain why American historians and political scientists have been less attracted by this material than their European colleagues.

Norwegian political scientist and sociologist Stein Rokkan repeatedly underlined how, under open-voting systems, the individual voters were firmly constrained by their roles in the subordinate systems of the household, the neighborhood, work, the church, the civil association, and so on when voting. Voters are not cut off from these other roles when acting as citizens in the political system, and they must therefore take responsibility for what they do as voters in their everyday interaction within the regular environment. Rokkan's point about the importance of the social context of electoral behavior under open voting is confirmed by many empirical analyses and also by the changes that accompanied the transition to secret voting. Similarly, D.C. Moore's concept of "deference community" has also proved helpful outside its original application to English county politics in the mid-nineteenth century.

Open voting remains a fascinating field of study because of the insights the field provides about electoral behavior under conditions that are different from those studied in recent elections as well as the light it sheds on the development of the political institutions themselves. However, open voting is not just a historical phenomenon; in some countries, educationally disadvantaged voters may still have to reveal their vote choice to others, and secrecy provisions in some elections and some countries are still so inadequate that voting is really more open than secret.

See also *Acclamation, Election by; Australian Ballot; Franchise Expansion; Free and Fair Elections; Registration of Voters; Secret Ballot.*

JØRGEN ELKLIT, UNIVERSITY OF AARHUS

BIBLIOGRAPHY

Bourke, Paul, and Donald DeBats. "Identifiable Voting in Nineteenth-Century America: Toward a Comparison of Britain and the United States before the Secret Ballot." *Perspectives in American History* 11 (1978): 259–288.

Drake, Michael, and Jeremy Mitchell. *Introduction to Historical Psephology.* Milton Keynes: Open University Press, 1982.

Elklit, Jørgen. "Nominal Record Linkage and the Study of Non-Secret Voting: A Danish Case." *Journal of Interdisciplinary History* 15 (winter 1985): 419–443.

Hanham, H.J. *The Reformed Electoral System in Great Britain 1832–1914.* London: The Historical Association, 1971.

Mitchell, Jeremy C., and James Cornford. "The Political Demography of Cambridge, 1832–1868." *Albion* 9 (1977): 242–272.

Moore, D.C. *The Politics of Deference: A Study of the Mid-Nineteenth Century English Political System.* Hassocks: Harvester Press, 1976.

Rokkan, Stein. "Mass Suffrage, Secret Voting and Political Participation." *Archives européennes de Sociologie* 2 (1961): 132–152.

Rokkan, Stein. *Citizens. Elections. Parties.* Oslo: Scandinavian University Books, 1970.

Rusk, Jerrold G. "The Effect of the Australian Ballot Reform on Split Ticket Voting: 1876–1908." *American Political Science Review* 64 (1970): 1220–1238.

Sternberger, Dolf, Bernhard Vogel, and Dieter Nohlen, eds. *Die Wahlen der Parlamente und anderer Staatsorgane. Ein Handbuch.* Vol. 1, *Europa.* Berlin: Walter de Gruyter, 1969.

Vincent, J.R. *Poll-books: How Victorians Voted.* Cambridge: Cambridge University Press, 1967.

OVERSEAS VOTING

Voting by persons outside the country in relation to which their votes are cast is called *overseas voting.* Overseas voting is a special case of absentee voting and tends, like absentee voting within a country, to involve either a tendered balloting process or a special procedure to identify those eligible for an overseas vote.

Overseas voting arises in three distinct circumstances. It is most simply implemented to provide voting facilities for persons who are only temporarily absent from a country, such as tourists or persons on short-term work postings. It may, however, also be extended to expatriates who, while retaining citizenship, are for all practical purposes permanently resident in another country. Finally, it has been found increasingly necessary at elections held in the immediate aftermath of conflict or societal breakdown to provide voting facilities for people who have left a country as refugees or forced migrants. For example, at the 1996 elections for Bosnia-Herzegovina, and at the 1997 Liberian elections, extensive resources were devoted to enabling voting by people who had been displaced from those countries.

These three categories of overseas voting give rise to different challenges. The decision on whether or not tourists and expatriates should be enfranchised is usually a domestic political one, and countries are not generally thought to be under a special obligation to provide such facilities. In the case of refugees and forced migrants, on the other hand, international human rights law becomes important, and the enfranchisement of forced migrants may be a fundamental element of the political reconciliation to which elections are expected to contribute.

The system of representation used for an election may become a significant implementation issue for overseas voting. Where constituency-based systems are used, it is necessary not just to register voters but also to define the constituency in which they should vote. This can be straightforward in relation to tourists but is potentially much more complex in relation to expatriates, forced migrants, and refugees, some of whom may have been out of their country for many years and may have only a tenuous connection with a particular constituency.

Overseas voting is a particular issue for countries that have military forces deployed overseas. Even countries that do not normally arrange external voting often feel a strong imperative to enfranchise those who are putting their lives at risk.

The mechanisms for external voting by the military are likely to be different from those applying at "normal" elections, since postal services and diplomatic missions may not be able to function normally in war zones; typically, recourse will be had to the military's own methods of communication.

See also *Absentee Voting; Administration of Elections; Tendered Ballots.*

Michael Maley, Australian Electoral Commission

P

PANACHAGE

See *Proportional Representation*

PAPAL ELECTIONS

The election of the bishop of Rome, the head of the Catholic Church, is unquestionably the oldest and the longest-functioning election on the planet. The electoral process has gone through many changes and developments since the time of Peter the Fisherman. It has, however, always been a political process, sometimes a corrupt one, and pregnant with drama and fascination. One dimension of it has not changed. The pope is elected by the clergy of Rome, as all bishops in the early days of the Catholic Church were selected by the clergy and laity of their own dioceses. The current legal fiction is that each of the cardinals (maximum 120) is a parish priest of Rome with a parish church under his care. In fact, the parish is run by a vicar, and the cardinal's responsibilities are an occasional visit and perhaps a financial contribution. Nonetheless the custom keeps alive the tradition that a diocese should select its own leader—"he who presides over all should be chosen by all," as Pope Leo I wrote. The cardinals' role as electors was definitively established only in the eleventh century.

EARLY PAPAL ELECTIONS

The first several papal elections (the winning candidates of which were almost certainly married men) were, it seems, to select the chairman of the ruling collegium, since at that time Rome apparently was governed by a committee and not by a monarchical bishop.

The custom of appointing cardinals who were not parish priests of Rome or its suburbs began only in the thirteenth century. For most of the first thousand years of the papacy, the laity of Rome and especially their political and civic leaders played an important role in ratifying the papal election (as did the emperors, first Byzantine, then German—indeed in 1903 the Austrian emperor vetoed the election of a cardinal, albeit before the fact of his election). At times in the early middle ages, the cardinals (and other clergy) would select a pope and then bring him out on the balcony. If the people cheered, he was crowned. If they booed, the electors tried again.

In the tenth century important Roman families had de facto control of the outcome of the elections through a skilled combination of bribery and force. The most notorious of these families was the Theophylact family, whose legendary matron Marozia appointed and then deposed Pope John X and then appointed Popes Leo VI and Stephen VII. She was the mistress of Pope Sergius III, whom she also appointed pope, and after his death she deputed their son as John XI, a young man not out of his teens. This was not a good time to be pope; a third of the popes elected between 872 and 1012 died violent deaths, often because they resisted the schemes of the Roman nobility.

ELECTORAL REFORMS

There have been repeated attempts at reform, some more successful than others. In 1059 Nicholas II decreed that the popes should be elected by only the six cardinal bishops of the suburban sees. Several centuries after the German emperors had weakened the Roman nobility's hold on the papacy, Aeneas Sylvio Piccolomini, who was elected Pius II in 1464, left an account of the buying and selling of the papacy, which had become routine. Deals were made in the latrines by some of the (eleven) cardinals to block his election, deals that, according to Piccolomini, a renaissance humanist, smelled of their place of origin. Perhaps the most corrupt of all the elections was that in 1492, when Rodrigo Borgia became Alexander VI in a conclave in which it was said that only five of the twenty-two cardinals could not be bought.

Gradually, the present form of the conclave (from the Latin word for *key*, because the cardinals were under "lock and key") emerged. In 1179 Alexander III ruled that the winning candidate must receive two-thirds of the vote. Pius XII in 1945 added the requirement of two-thirds plus one, so that a man could not guarantee his own election. John Paul II revoked the requirement for the extra vote and decreed that after thirty-three ballots a pope might be elected by a simple majority (a change of an eight-hundred-year-old custom that, according to some, was a way to insure that his conservative policies survived his death). Alexander III also excluded all but the three orders of cardinals—bishops, deacons, and priests—from voting, thus ending lay participation.

At the second Council of Lyons (1274) it was decreed that the electors should be locked up in a secure place, that they should sleep in a communal dormitory, and that their food supplies should be cut in half after three days if they had not elected a pope. After five more days they were to receive only bread, wine, and water. In 1345 Clement VI permitted a curtain or a wall between beds. Only at the end of the nineteenth century did Leo XIII permit each cardinal to have his own room.

In 1505 Pope Julius II decreed that simoniacal elections were invalid and that anyone whose election had been bought should be considered an apostate. His own election, however, was simoniacal. Pope Pius XII in 1945 revoked the apostasy label, and Pope Paul VI, to preserve the validity of a papal election, revoked the invalidity of such an election. Since the end of the papal states in 1870, however, there is perhaps less grounds to worry about anyone wanting to buy an election.

The requirement of secrecy during and after the conclave was treated lightly until the twentieth century. In the nineteenth century the cardinal electors, often living in the Lateran Palace, would chat happily with the crowds while walking down the street to St. John Lateran's Cathedral where they would vote. Only after the veto of the candidacy of Cardinal Rampola by the Austrian emperor Franz Joseph in 1903 did the rules against campaigning before the conclave and talking about it afterward become strict, indeed attached to the most solemn of excommunications by Pope Paul VI and Pope John Paul II. Nonetheless, campaigning goes on while a pope is still alive, and more overtly after his death. It is, however, called "consulting." Moreover, the pattern of voting and indeed the votes of each of the electors are eventually known after an election, sometimes immediately after.

ELECTIONS IN THE TWENTIETH CENTURY

During the twentieth century the cardinal electors were locked in extremely uncomfortable quarters in the Sistine chapel. However, John Paul II ordered that henceforth the electors would live in the new, motel-like St. Martha's house at the other side of Vatican City and vote in the Sistine chapel. Whether this arrangement will lead to further leaks while the conclave is in process remains to be seen. Pope John Paul's rules also require a careful screening of the Sistine for bugs, which might betray that secrecy. Whether such precautions can outwit modern electronic eavesdropping also remains to be seen. It is alleged that at the election in 1958, Cardinal Francis Spellman of New York sent a message from inside the chapel to the Central Intelligence Agency station in Rome.

Pius XII eliminated the provision for a "servant" or "valet" or "secretary" to accompany the cardinals into the conclave, though at his election in 1939, he was accompanied by his housekeeper (Madre Pasquelina, later called "LaPapessa"). While this fact was a secret at the time and for many years thereafter, she was the first woman (that we know of) who was permitted inside a conclave.

The cardinals may go into conclave fifteen days after the death of the pope and must begin after twenty days. They enter late in the afternoon and begin voting the next morning, after having taken the most solemn oaths of secrecy and responsibility under Michelangelo's painting of the Last Judgment. There are two "scrutinies" each day, one in the morning and one in the afternoon, and two ballots in each scrutiny. Each cardinal writes on a ballot the name of his candidate and deposits it in a chalice on the chapel's altar. Three cardinals count the ballots. If no one is elected, the ballots together with straw are burned in a stove with a chimney that reaches to the roof of the chapel. Black smoke appears from the chimney, and those outside mutter, " 'e nero." However, if someone is elected, the straw is omitted and (sometimes) a tiny trickle of white smoke appears to exultant shouts of " 'e bianco!" In the two elections of 1978 the Vatican had a hard time producing white smoke. Shortly thereafter, the cardinal dean appears with full solemnity on the balcony of St. Peter's and announces, "I have joyous news for you! (cheers). We have a pope! (more cheers). Charles Cardinal of the Holy Roman Church Wojtyla! (Yet more cheers). Who chooses for himself the name of John Paul!" (most cheers of all).

Inside the most recent conclaves some men are called *great electors,* the men who have influence, power, intelligence, and a clear notion of what they want for the church (such as Leo Suenens in the 1963 conclave and Franz Koenig in the second 1978 conclave, both to their later regret). Others, perhaps not so gifted, are content to follow along with the dynamics of the voting, dynamics they attribute (rather at odds with traditional Catholic teaching) to the influence of the Holy Spirit (and thus deny that the conclave is a human political event). It is most important to an elector to be able to go home and claim that he voted for the winner even before it became clear that he would be the winner.

The election of a pope is an event of high drama and great theater. While it is filled with traditional splendor, the process has been and is in constant transition (as illustrated by Pope John Paul's dramatic change in the requirement for two-thirds majority). Catholics debate whether it is the best way to elect the most important religious leader in the world, the spiritual ruler of more than a billion people. Some wonder whether the democracy of the first thousand years (and especially of the early centuries) might not be both more suitable for the modern world and more traditional.

See also *Acclamation, Election by; Qualified Majority Voting.*

ANDREW GREELEY, UNIVERSITY OF CHICAGO

BIBLIOGRAPHY

Duffy, Eamon. *Saints and Sinners: A History of the Popes.* New Haven, Conn.: Yale University Press, 1997.

Greeley, Andrew. *The Making of the Popes 1978: The Politics of Intrigue in the Vatican.* Kansas City, Kan.: Andrews and McMeel, 1979.

McBrien, Richard P. *Lives of the Popes: The Pontiffs from St. Peter to John Paul II.* San Francisco: Harper, 1997.

PARADOX OF VOTING

Two quite different things have been called "the paradox of voting." Neither of them is a paradox in the strict philosopher's sense. Rather, they are both surprising facts.

SURPRISING FACT NUMBER 1: PEOPLE SOMETIMES VOTE

In his highly influential *An Economic Theory of Democracy* (1957), Anthony Downs proposed that rational voters would vote if and only if the discounted benefit to them of voting exceeds the cost of voting. The benefit is modeled as the utility income they would get between this election and the next if their favorite party wins, minus what they would get if their less preferred party wins. This benefit must be discounted by the probability of being decisive. If my favorite party would win without my vote, or would lose even with my vote, then there is no point in my voting. Voting is worthwhile only if my vote turns a loss for my side into a tie, or a tie into a victory. These two possibilities are rare even in small elections; they almost never happen in large-scale city, state, or national elections. The cost of voting, at least in time, is not trivial. Therefore a Downsian rational actor would almost never vote.

Many scholars from within the rational-choice tradition have attempted to avoid this conclusion. They all fail. Therefore, voting cannot be regarded as a strategically rational thing to do. It must be regarded as an altruistic, or solidaristic, or community-building act. However, once a voter has gone to the trouble of going to the poll, it costs no more for that voter to cast a ballot for his or her favorite candidate than to do anything else. So the other part of Downs's analysis, which holds that the dynamics of democracy favor the policies preferred by the median voter, survives the failure of his prediction of rational abstention.

This "paradox of voting" can, however, explain many of the observed variations in turnout. Turnout is lower in bad weather than in good weather, and lower when voting is on a weekday than when it is on a holiday or a Sunday—as predicted by Downs's model. It is also generally lower in safe districts than in marginal ones. Although Downs's model implies that the discounted value of voting is infinitesimal even in close elections, the observation that people are even less likely to vote in safe districts is consistent with the spirit of his analysis.

SURPRISING FACT NUMBER 2: SOMETIMES EVERY POSSIBLE OUTCOME IS A LOSER

This surprising fact was discovered by the Marquis de Condorcet in 1785. Whenever there are at least three options and at least three voters, there may be no majority winner. Suppose that there are three voters—P, Q, and R—and three options—a, b, and c. P prefers a to b and b to c. Q prefers b to c and c to a. R prefers c to a and a to b. Then a beats b by 2 votes to 1 *(P and R voting for a, Q voting for b)*. Similarly, b beats c by 2 to 1. We would expect group decisions to be transitive. My decisions are transitive if, given that I prefer a to b and b to c, I also prefer a to c. If that were not so, it would be hard for me ever to choose anything. But in this case, the group chooses c over a by 2 votes to 1.

This is not a true paradox: it is simply a possibility that does not occur to people until it is demonstrated to them. The individual preferences are transitive but the group choice is not. Therefore, whatever the group chooses, there is something else it would rather have chosen. This "majority-rule cycle" or "Condorcet effect" (both terms being better than "paradox of voting") has wide ramifications for the study of elections and democratic theory. Kenneth Arrow uses it in the proof of his General (Im)possibility Theorem, which shows that no method of deriving a social ordering from individual orderings satisfies some minimal requirements of fairness and logicality. (A "social ordering" is a ranking of possible states of affairs.) Arrow's theorem may thus be regarded as a generalization of the Condorcet effect. Corollaries of Arrow's theorem in turn show that all reasonable electoral systems are manipulable by voters, or by politicians, or by both; and that cycles are much more likely when there are multiple issue dimensions than when there is only one.

The main practical implications of this so-called paradox of voting concern the design of electoral systems and the study of two-dimensional politics. For over a century, electoral reformers who have not known the underlying mathematics of voting have made unsustainable claims that this or the other is "the best" or even "a perfect" electoral system. By Arrow's theorem, no such claim can be made. However, some electoral systems are better than others for specific purposes. The best system for electing a legislature differs from the best system for choosing an executive, or for deciding the outcome of a referendum, or for jury decisions, or for ranking candidates for academic positions.

Normal politics, in most countries most of the time, run along one principal issue dimension—often, it is distributive politics, balancing the claims of the poor and the rich. When another issue dimension becomes salient, the prevalence of cycles makes the outcomes much less predictable. William Riker (in *Liberalism against Populism,* 1982) applied this line of reasoning to U.S. national politics in 1860. Abraham Lincoln was elected president with less than 40 percent of the popular vote, in a campaign where the candidates and parties deliberately introduced the issue of slavery to crosscut the normal distributive politics of the time. Electoral systems other than that in use at the time might have delivered the 1860 election to either of two other candidates. Similar claims may be made about dramatic political upsets in other countries, such as the paradoxical repeal of the Corn Laws in Britain, in 1846, by a government representing agriculture, which was the principal loser from repeal.

See also *Condorcet Theorems; Downsian Model of Elections; Second-Order Elections; Wasted Votes.*

IAIN MCLEAN, NUFFIELD COLLEGE, OXFORD UNIVERSITY

BIBLIOGRAPHY

Arrow, Kenneth J. *Social Choice and Individual Values.* 2d ed. New Haven, Conn.: Yale University Press, 1963.

Black, Duncan. *The Theory of Committees and Elections,* 2d ed., edited by Iain McLean, Alistair McMillan, and Burt L. Monroe. Norwell, Mass.: Kluwer Academic, 1998.

Downs, Anthony. *An Economic Theory of Democracy.* New York: Harper and Row, 1957.

Green, Donald P., and Ian Shapiro. *Pathologies of Rational Choice Theory.* New Haven, Conn.: Yale University Press, 1994.

McLean, Iain, and Fiona Hewitt, eds. *Condorcet: Foundations of Social Choice and Political Theory.* Brookfield, Vt.: Edward Elgar, 1994.

McLean, Iain, and Arnold B. Urken, eds. *Classics of Social Choice.* Ann Arbor: University of Michigan Press, 1995.

Riker, William H. *Liberalism against Populism.* San Francisco: W.H. Freeman, 1982.

PARALLEL VOTE COUNT

See *Administration of Elections*

PARTIES: QUALIFICATION FOR BALLOT

Parties may be included on a ballot as the primary entities for which votes are to be cast. Even where votes are cast for individual candidates, however, it is often thought desirable to indicate on the ballot the party affiliations of some or all of the candidates.

There is great variety around the world in the legal regimes governing the listing of parties on the ballot. The most common approach, however, involves some form of registration of the parties. Registration can serve several purposes. On the one hand, it can provide a structured mechanism for determining whether a party meets prescribed qualifications. Just as important, however, registration can provide a clear mechanism for determining who is entitled to speak for the party in dealings with the election administration. This is important for avoiding misunderstandings, particularly of the type that can arise when a party splits or is affected by internal schisms.

Under some electoral regimes, qualifications that apply to individual candidates may also be applicable to parties; for example, a disqualification of candidates who advocate racial hatred can also be applied to parties that advance such views. Frequently, however, there will also be qualifications that are specific to parties. Typically, parties are required to have a constitution or articles of association that define their structures and internal lines of authority. They may also be required to demonstrate their viability by proving that they have a prescribed minimum membership, or alternatively that they enjoy the support of a specified number of people, whether or not those people are members of the party. For example, at the elections organized in Cambodia by the United Nations in 1993, applications for party registration had to be supported by five thousand registered voters. As a precondition for party registration, a party often will have to agree to adhere to legal requirements relating to the disclosure of its financial arrangements. Finally, parties may be required to apply for approval of the symbols, or abbreviations of names, that they wish to use on the ballots.

This last requirement often gives rise to controversial issues. From time to time parties may attempt to register names, abbreviations, or symbols that are deceptively similar to those of other parties. Where party registration is being introduced for the first time, parties may try to (mis)appropriate the names, abbreviations, or symbols traditionally associated with other parties. When a party splits, there often are disputes as to which of a number of factions is entitled to continue using the established name, abbreviation, or symbol of the party. Parties may also be constrained from adopting names or symbols that are obscene, offensive, or frivolous.

A scheme of party registration will normally specify by whom, to whom, and by what mechanism an application for registration may be made; the limitations on party names, abbreviations, or symbols; a process by which objections can be lodged to the proposed registration of a party, and the way in which such objections will be resolved; the rights that accrue to registered parties; and the way in which parties may be deregistered if they go out of existence or fail to meet their legal obligations.

See also *Administration of Elections; Coordination, Electoral; Cross-Filing; Deposit; Nomination Procedures; Nonpartisan Elections; Ticket Splitting; Ticket Splitting in the United States.*

MICHAEL MALEY, AUSTRALIAN ELECTORAL COMMISSION

BIBLIOGRAPHY

Administration and Cost of Elections Project website: www.aceproject.org

PARTY PLATFORM

See *Manifesto, Election*

PLEBISCITES AND PLEBISCITARY POLITICS

The term *plebiscite* and the expression "plebiscitary politics" are used to encompass a variety of types of popular votes. In English and in German, *plebiscite* is often used generically as a synonym for any kind of referendum-type vote. This is not the case in French, where the distinction between *plebiscite* and *referendum* is the subject of endless political debates on constitutional theory and political science. The connotation of *plebiscite* is mainly negative: the term is most often used to mean an unfair, unfree, and noncompetitive vote of confidence for a leader and regime. *Referendum,* by contrast, generally means a free, fair, and competitive vote on a specific question.

Many scholars and opinion makers use *plebiscite* to refer to any popular competitive poll (whether an election or a referendum-type vote) with a result that strongly favors one of the candidates or one of the questions posed to the voters. In international law *plebiscite* denotes popular votes concerning the international and legal status of territories. The expression "plebiscitary politics" as synonymous with "direct democracy" is used—mainly with a negative connotation—to refer

both to selecting political leadership by means of a direct popular vote and to referring political decisions directly to the voters, bypassing parliaments and parties. Most of these meanings originate in relevant historical experiences.

Considered in a comparative perspective and across time, *plebiscite* and "plebiscitary politics" are loosely defined and not accurately used. Strictly defined, a plebiscite is any kind of popular vote (election-type or referendum-type) that takes place in a political context where there is no real competition and no opportunity to choose in a free and fair way. Thus the term *plebiscite* should be used only for unfree popular votes in nondemocratic regimes.

Nonetheless, the line between plebiscite and referendum can be blurred. A few democracies use referendums regularly and according to constitutional provisions; others use them only in exceptional circumstances and may not have constitutional provisions. Therefore, many popular votes in democratic states occur in exceptional circumstances and are subject to manipulation by those who initiated the referendum. It is not clear that there can be full and complete compatibility between democratic government based on political representation and popular votes of the referendum type. Some scholars and politicians evoke the danger of a plebiscitary drift—that is, of a threat to democracy—whenever popular votes of the referendum type can be initiated by individuals or institutions or tend to become frequent or regular.

All this considered, it is not surprising that the use of *plebiscite* and "plebiscitary politics" is subject to considerable conceptual stretching. The following aims to sketch out a chronological intellectual history of the meanings and uses of the word *plebiscite*.

ORIGIN OF THE TERM

Plebiscite originates from the Latin expression *plebis scitum* (*plebs,* "common people," and *sciscere,* "to establish, to order"), which means "decree of the common people." In the government of the republic of ancient Rome (third to first century B.C.) the plebe voted at times on questions presented by the tribunes. Here we find the seeds of an important element in the history of the concept of plebiscite: a politician who holds a public office directly appeals to the people for a vote of confidence.

The modern concept of plebiscite, as well as the distinction between plebiscite and referendum, goes back first to the experiences of popular "votes" (in town meetings) on constitutions in Britain's former colonies in North America—specifically, in Massachusetts in 1778 and 1780; in New Hampshire in 1778, 1781, and 1784; in Connecticut in 1816; in Maine in 1819; and in New York in 1821. France conducted popular votes on national constitutions in 1793, 1795, and 1799. Voters in Switzerland had approval of federal constitutions through national referendum in 1802 (in a vote promoted by Napoléon Bonaparte), 1872, and 1874; cantonal referendums were held to ratify the first federal constitution of 1848. At the roots of the modern constitutional and representative governments of these three political systems are their earliest experiences of citizen votes on constitutions. The differing experiences of the three systems have resulted in diverse political combinations of representative government and direct participation through popular votes.

We can trace the origins of the referendum phenomenon and the terms for the main types of popular votes (veto, referendum, popular initiative, recall) back to the American and Swiss experiences; the modern origins of the phenomenon and the concept of plebiscite and "plebiscitary politics" stem from the French experience. All of the voting traditions originate in the political ideas and experiences of liberalism and democratic constitutional government.

Although nine French popular votes were called between 1793 (approval of the constitution) and 1852 (establishment of the Second Empire), they were not termed plebiscites. By 1869 one French dictionary applied the term to the decision submitted to popular approval during the First Republic (1793, 1795) and to the conferring of a ten-year presidency on Louis Napoleon and the establishment of the Second Empire (1851, 1852).

Eventually French-language authorities distinguished between plebiscite and referendum. *Plébiscite,* defined as the contents of a decision, was used to indicate the decrees that emanated from popular sovereignty; popular votes concerning the annexation of territory or a political regime change were also to be considered plebiscites. *Référendum* was identified as a word used by the Swiss to denote the popular ratification of laws approved by parliament; the term was also used to describe votes on constitutions in the American states. Another crucial difference developed through the nineteenth and twentieth centuries between the French experience and the Swiss and American experiences: whereas Swiss and American citizens may sign a petition asking for a popular vote, in France the decision to hold a popular vote always comes from the top of the political structure.

NINETEENTH-CENTURY FRANCE

According to the German social theorist Max Weber (1864–1920), the plebiscite "is the profession of 'faith' in the vocation as leader of the person who demands this acclamation." For Weber, who refers explicitly to the nineteenth-century French experience, the notion of plebiscite is associated with the experiences of political regimes characterized by the presence of a charismatic leader who establishes direct emotional contact with the masses, in part by means of popular votes. In this way, the concept of plebiscite is identified with caesaristic and bonapartist regimes under an individual charismatic leadership. They tend to be transitory regimes and therefore temporary and unstable, although they often precede the establishment of a more permanent and stable authoritarian regime. Here we find the origins of the idea that the plebiscite is—by definition—a phenomenon that concerns only undemocratic politics.

The French experience illustrates in a paradigmatic way the tension between representative government, plebiscites and referendums, and plebiscitary politics. One of the characteristics of the regimes of Napoléon Bonaparte (1799–1814) and Louis Napoleon (1852–1870) was the legitimization of their leadership and their regimes through unfair and noncompetitive popular votes held to mobilize mass consensus. The popular votes promoted by Napoléon Bonaparte (1800, 1802, 1804, 1815), by Louis Napoleon (1851, 1852, and 1870), and a century later by Charles de Gaulle can all be classified as plebiscites; yet there are significant differences between them. The plebiscites promoted by Napoléon Bonaparte and Louis Napoleon were, no doubt, unfair and unfree votes that took place in a noncompetitive political regime. Indeed, the last plebiscite of Louis Napoleon was already defined as a post-bonapartist plebiscite, to be distinguished from the preceding experiences by its greater electoral freedom and the presence of an opposition.

More than a century after the original bonapartist plebiscites, the crisis of the Fourth Republic and the transition to the Fifth Republic were characterized by the politics of General de Gaulle and his charismatic leadership. The gaullist regime from 1958 to 1962 can be classified as a pure caesaristic regime (characterized by a strong one-person leadership, emotional links between the leader and his followers, and its nature as a provisional transition regime). De Gaulle applied the principle and practice of plebiscitary politics by including a provision for the referendum in the new constitution and using it in a discretionary way. As a result, citizens were asked to vote on the following questions: approval of the new constitution (1958), the right to self-determination for Algeria (1961), the Évian agreement (April 1962), and above all the constitutional amendment concerning the direct election of the president (October 1962). De Gaulle's political career was concluded in 1969 with his defeat on the popular vote he promoted on amending the constitution, in part to create new regional councils.

The French experience has led to attempts to distinguish between caesaristic plebiscites on the one hand and constituent or republican plebiscites on the other. From this point of view, the popular votes promoted by de Gaulle offered greater guarantees of a free, fair, and competitive vote than had their bonapartist predecessors. The presence of competing political parties, the control exerted by a critical and influential press, a well-educated electorate, the close votes in some cases, the resignation of de Gaulle after the negative result of 1969—all these indicate profound differences between bonapartist and gaullist plebiscites.

During the twentieth century the connotation of plebiscite as an undemocratic phenomenon was strongly reinforced by the experiences of popular votes called in Italy (1929 and 1934) by Benito Mussolini during the fascist regime and in Germany (1933, 1934, 1936, 1938) by Adolf Hitler during the National Socialist regime. This type of vote, as mentioned earlier, aims at confirming apparent consensus and conferring popular legitimacy on leaders and regimes that are anything but democratic. These examples emphasize why any kind of referendum-type votes may have negative connotations among political scientists, particularly since World War II.

TERRITORIAL AND SOVEREIGNTY ISSUES

The term *plebiscite* has also been applied to popular votes on territorial issues, specifically the annexations and secessions that have punctuated the history of Europe from the French Revolution on, and during the twentieth century, the histories of many other regions as well. Here the term *plebiscite* is mainly used to denote popular votes concerning a specific matter, namely conflicts and decisions over territories and sovereignty.

In some cases this kind of vote is the result of a crisis preceding or following a military conflict; sometimes the result achieves international relevance and at other times it remains of only national relevance. The purpose of such votes is to legitimize political decisions that imply the annexation by a state of a territory and its resident population or that involve self-determination and secession. These votes may take place after the fall of regimes whose wide territories comprise internal cleavages of an ethnic, linguistic, religious, or economic nature. That kind of vote embraces experiences over three centuries and many different political contexts. Here again plebiscites have encompassed a broad spectrum of experiences, from unfair, unfree, and noncompetitive votes to fair, free, and competitive votes, as the following examples show.

The first plebiscites on territorial matters occurred during the period of the French Revolution. There were some cases from 1790 to 1798 concerning the annexation to France of Avignon and a few hundred nearby communes, which had been ceded to the Catholic Church four centuries earlier; other annexations considered were those of Belgium, Geneva,

the German Rhineland, Nice, and Savoy. The city of Nice and the region of Savoy were definitively annexed to France after a second vote, held in 1860. Popular votes on territorial annexations, officially designated plebiscites, took place in some Italian cities and regions from 1848 to 1870, marking a crucial phase in the nation-building process of modern Italy. Popular votes on questions of territory and sovereignty include the plebiscites in the Danubian principalities of Moldavia and Wallachia, which endorsed the birth of Romania as a nation (in 1864). In 1905 a popular vote ratified the decision of the Norwegian parliament to break away from the union with Sweden.

After World War I, under the auspices of U.S. president Woodrow Wilson and of the League of Nations, a number of plebiscites were held concerning the self-determination of certain regions and European populations involved in the agreements sanctioned by the peace treaties. Such was not the case after World War II except for the vote on the Saar region (1955). In the postwar era the balance of power resulting from the cold war evidently took precedence over the principle of self-determination.

Nowadays, democratic regimes still hold a number of popular votes concerning conflicts and crucial decisions dealing with territories and sovereignty. However, these generally are called referendums rather than plebiscites.

REGIME CRISES AND CHANGES

Regime crisis and change lend themselves to popular votes to decide and solve crucial political matters such as the institutional form of the state ("monarchy or republic?") or to legitimize a new regime by approving a new constitution. Here again, some situations are characterized by more or less free and fair votes, others by more or less unfree and unfair votes.

In France after World War II, decisions concerning the end of the Third Republic and the constitution of the Fourth Republic were submitted to popular votes (1945–1946). The later gaullist experience, mentioned earlier, is a good example of the practice of plebiscitary politics during a change of regime. In Greece, nine popular votes concerning institutional and regime change were held from 1862 to 1974, most of them undemocratic. In Italy in 1946, after the fall of the fascist regime, the choice between monarchy and republic was decided by a popular vote.

A significant number of such popular votes have occurred in Latin America as well. Two of these are particularly worth mentioning: the 1980 vote in Uruguay and the 1988 vote in Chile. These experiences demonstrate the difficulties even undemocratic regimes have in controlling the outcomes of plebiscites. In both cases, the options proposed by the two authoritarian regimes were defeated, and political maneuvers that had been expected to demonstrate consensus and reinforce the legitimacy of the regimes had the opposite effect and became important turning points in the transition to democracy. An important step toward democracy was made in Argentina after the fall of the military regime, when President Raul Alfonsín decided to put the Peace and Friendship Treaty between Argentina and Chile to popular vote and then to parliament. The signing of the treaty put an end to a century-old territorial conflict. In Brazil (1993) voters were called upon to choose between a monarchy and a republic and between presidential and parliamentary systems.

In Africa in the course of the 1990s decisions to adopt democratic constitutions and to establish multiparty competitive regimes were often ratified by popular votes. In South Africa (1992) President F. W. de Klerk resorted to a plebiscite to gain a popular mandate to end apartheid.

The crisis and collapse of the communist regimes in the former Soviet Union and in central and eastern Europe were marked by dozens of both electoral and plebiscite-type votes. The popular vote of March 1991—the first and last plebiscite of the Soviet Union—and then the popular vote of April 1993 in the Russian Federation were characterized by a context of political and institutional crisis, a conflict between the two charismatic personalities of President Mikhail Gorbachev and President Boris Yeltsin, and a conflict with the parliamentary assemblies. These circumstances made the votes reminiscent of bonapartist and gaullist plebiscites.

The political crises caused by the fall of the Soviet Union and the other communist regimes in Europe have created a favorable climate for numerous plebiscites. For example, the vote that determined the dismemberment of the Federal Republic of Yugoslavia can be considered a plebiscite of secession.

PLEBISCITARY POLITICS AND DEMOCRACIES

At the beginning of the twentieth century some social scientists pointed out the emergence in modern democracies of plebiscitary politics—that is, of charismatic political leadership linked to the organization of mass parties. The British historian and diplomat James Bryce stated, "What is common to all these cases is the disposition to trust one man or a few led by one rather than an elected assembly."

Max Weber formulated a theory of plebiscitary democracy centered on the figure of a charismatic leader; he saw confirmation of his theory in the emergence of strong personalized leadership in Britain and the United States. An essential element of plebiscitary democracy is the popular election of the head of government (formally or de facto). Weber foresaw a presidential republic for Germany where the president could be recalled by means of a popular vote promoted by a quali-

fied majority of the parliament. He also considered the possibility (by law or de facto) for the head of government to appeal directly to the people as a further characteristic of a plebiscitary democracy. Weber maintained a distinction between the innovation of using the plebiscite to elect a head of the executive branch and the conservative effects of legislation by referendum.

See also *Acclamation, Election by; Initiative: Europe; Initiative: United States; Recall Elections; Referendums: Europe; Referendums: Latin America; Referendums: United States.*

PIER VINCENZO ULERI, UNIVERSITY OF FLORENCE

BIBLIOGRAPHY

Abromeit, Heidrun. *Democracy in Europe: Legitimising Politics in a Non-State Polity.* Oxford: Berghahn Books, 1998.

Bowler, Shaun, Todd Donovan, and Caroline Tolbert, eds. *Citizens as Legislators: Direct Democracy in the United States.* Columbus: Ohio State University Press, 1998.

Budge, Ian. *The New Challenge of Direct Democracy.* Cambridge: Polity Press, 1996.

Butler, David, and Austin Ranney. *Referendums around the World: The Growing Use of Direct Democracy.* Basingstoke, England: Macmillan, 1994.

Denquin, Jean-Marie. *Référendum et Plébiscite.* Paris: LGDJ, Pichon et Durand-Auzias, 1976.

Farley, Lawrence T. *Plebiscites and Sovereignty: The Crisis of Political Illegitimacy.* Boulder, Colo.: Westview Press; London: Mansell Publishing, 1986.

Fraenkel, Ernst. *Die repräsentative und die plebiszitäre Komponenten im demokratischen Verfassungsstaat.* Tübingen: J.C.B. Mohr, 1958.

Gerber, Elisabeth R. *The Populist Paradox: Interest Group Influence and the Promise of Direct Legislation.* Princeton: Princeton University Press, 1999.

Ranney, Austin, and Howard R. Penniman. *Democracy in the Islands: The Micronesian Plebiscites of 1983.* Washington, D.C.: American Enterprise Institute for Public Policy Research, 1985.

Rourke, John T., Richard P. Hiskes, and Cyrus Zirakzadeh. *Direct Democracy and International Politics: Deciding International Issues through Referendum.* Boulder, Colo., and London: Lynne Rienner, 1992.

Smith, Daniel A. *Tax Crusaders and the Politics of Direct Democracy.* New York: Routledge, 1998.

Suksi, Markku. *Bringing in the People: A Comparison of Constitutional Forms and Practices of the Referendum.* Boston: Nijhoff, 1993.

Wambaugh, Sarah. *Plebiscites since the World War, with a Collection of Official Documents.* Vols. 1–2. Washington, D.C.: Carnegie Endowment for International Peace, 1933.

White, Stephen, Richard Rose, and Ian McAllister. *How Russia Votes.* Chatham, N.J.: Chatham House, 1997.

Zimmerman, Joseph F. *The Recall: Tribunal of the People.* New York: Praeger, 1998.

PLURAL VOTERS

Plural voters are individuals who are entitled to cast more than one vote in any one election on the basis of more than one qualification. Plural voting was important in some European countries and in some British colonies in the nineteenth and early twentieth centuries. Plural voting continued in the United Kingdom until 1948.

Plural voting originated in the extreme diversity of franchise requirements in many European countries. Citizens meeting the criteria of property, income, education, or membership in social groups were often entitled to cast a vote in respect of each of them. As franchise laws were standardized and liberalized, some of these ancient plural voting rights were retained, and in a few cases, new plural voting rights were created, in part to counteract the electoral weight of the newly enfranchised citizens, who tended to be poorer and less educated.

Belgium, for example, used plural voting to protect the interests of the "respectable" in society when they faced a widening electorate. The franchise in Belgium was on a very restrictive taxpaying basis until 1893, when changes to the electoral law introduced universal male suffrage, increasing the electorate from 137,000 to 1,370,000, and introduced plural voting. Married men age thirty-five and older who were householders received an extra vote, as did all owners of property above a specified minimum. A university degree was another entitlement to vote. In the newly enlarged electorate, 290,000 voters had two votes, and 220,000 had three votes, so that plural voters, although fewer in number than those with only one vote, cast more ballots in aggregate.

In nineteenth-century Austria, voters cast ballots in four separate curiae, representing the aristocracy, the towns, the peasantry, and the chambers of commerce. The introduction of a fifth curia in 1897, based on universal male suffrage, in effect created a second vote for all voters who already had a vote in one of the other curiae.

In the United Kingdom plural voting rights were common before the First World War. In 1910 there were 500,000 plural voters in an electorate of nearly 8,000,000. After 1918 there were only 230,000 plural voters in an electorate of more than 21 million; their entitlement was based on the possession of either a university degree or a business.

University graduates were entitled to a second vote, which was cast in special university constituencies. From 1918 until 1948, when they were abolished, there were twelve university seats: graduates of Oxford, Cambridge, and London Universities and Queen's University in Belfast each had their own constituency, and graduates of the Scottish, Welsh, and English "provincial" universities shared eight. The British tradition of university representation continues in the Republic of Ireland, where a second vote is given to all Irish university graduates, who elect six of the sixty members of the Irish senate.

Plural voting on the basis of ownership of a business also continued in the United Kingdom until 1948. Business owners were entitled to a vote in the constituency in which their business was located, provided that they did not already have a vote in that constituency based on residence. In principle, therefore, a businessman would be entitled to cast a vote in the constituency in which he lived and in every other constituency in which he owned a business. The business vote comprised only about 1 percent of the national electorate and, although probably heavily Conservative, had only a marginal effect on election outcomes. However, had the business vote still been in existence in 1950, some believe that the Conservative Party, not Labour, might have won the 1950 general election.

Plural voting was also a feature of the franchises in some British colonies prior to the introduction of universal suffrage. For instance, the 1956 electoral law in Kenya provided for seven qualifications for the vote, including completing secondary education, higher education, property ownership, and lengthy government service. A voter could obtain a maximum of three votes on the basis of the various categories.

See also *Colonial Elections; Estate and Curia Constituencies; Franchise Expansion; Weighted Voting.*

TOM MACKIE, UNIVERSITY OF STRATHCLYDE

BIBLIOGRAPHY

Blewett, Neil. "The Franchise in the United Kingdom, 1885–1918." *Past and Present* 45 (1965): 27–56.

Butler, David. *The Electoral System in Britain since 1918.* 2d ed. Oxford: Clarendon Press, 1963.

Mackenzie, William. *Free Elections: An Elementary Textbook.* London: Allen and Unwin, 1958.

Mackenzie, William, and K. Robinson, eds. *Five Elections in Africa.* Oxford: Oxford University Press, 1960.

Mill, John Stuart. *Utilitarianism, Liberty and Representative Government.* London: Dent; New York: Dutton, 1964. First published 1861.

PLURALITY SYSTEMS

Plurality systems are those systems in which the winning candidate is the one who receives more votes than any other candidate. The only plurality formula currently in use is the first past the post, in which only one candidate is to be elected, voters are asked which candidate they prefer, and the candidate with the most votes wins. This system is used for the election of the president in eighteen countries, including Iceland, Mexico, the Philippines, South Korea, and Taiwan. The first-past-the-post formula is also used in legislative elections in fifty-five countries, among them Bangladesh, Britain, Canada, India, Kenya, Morocco, and the United States. The system is widespread in former British colonies and prevailed in Sweden and Denmark until 1908 and 1915, respectively.

THE PLURALITY DECISION RULE

Prior to 1997 Uruguay utilized a plurality formula other than first past the post to elect its president. Under that system, known as the double simultaneous vote, the plurality rule was applied sequentially, first among the parties, and then among the candidates within the leading party. In Uruguayan elections, each faction *(sublema)* within a party *(lema)* presented its own candidate. Each voter was asked to indicate which candidate he or she preferred. The votes for all candidates within each *lema* were added, and the leading *lema* was proclaimed the "winner." Then the candidate with the most votes within the winning *lema* was elected.

Other systems that rely on the plurality rule to elect one person, but with different ballot structures, have been devised, but they have not been utilized in national political elections. Under approval voting, voters are asked to indicate not which candidate they prefer but which one(s) they support or approve. Winners are determined as in first past the post: the candidate with the most votes is elected. (Approval voting could be used under majority or even proportional-representation systems.)

The plurality rule may also be applied to elect more than one person. This is the case in multimember districts. There are many possibilities, depending on the type and number of votes that voters are allowed to cast.

One possibility is that voters have only one vote. Two subtypes can be distinguished here. Under the block vote, voters cast their single ballot for a party list, and the party that gets the most votes wins all the seats. This system is used in U.S. presidential elections to elect the members of the electoral college within each state. In the other subtype,

known as the single nontransferable vote, voters cast their ballot for one candidate. If five members are to be elected, the five candidates who receive the most votes win the five seats. This procedure is used for legislative elections in Jordan and Vanuatu.

The second possibility is that voters have as many votes as there are members to be elected. The best-known example is the two-member constituency, in which each voter is allowed to vote for two candidates, and the two candidates with the most votes are elected. This system prevailed in Britain until the Reform Bill of 1832. A few two-member constituencies remained in Britain until 1945 and in Canada until 1965. Another variant is the cumulative vote, whereby voters are allowed to give more than one vote to a given candidate. The system was used in Illinois until 1980.

The third possibility is the limited vote: voters have more than one vote but fewer than the number of members to be elected. This procedure is still used for elections to the Spanish senate.

PLURALITY AND THE TWO-PARTY SYSTEM

Maurice Duverger claimed that the plurality rule leads to a two-party system. Table 1 shows the proportion of votes and seats obtained by the two leading parties in sixteen democratic countries (those with a score of 1 or 2 on political

Table 1. Results of Legislative Elections in Plurality Systems

Country	Date of election	Percent of votes of first party	Percent of votes of second party	Percent of seats of first party	Percent of seats of second party
Bahamas	3/14/97	58	42	85	15
Barbados	9/6/94	49	39	68	29
Belize	6/30/93	51	49	45	55
Botswana	10/15/94	53	38	68	33
Canada	6/2/97	38	19	52	20
Dominica	6/12/95	36	34	24	52
Grenada	6/20/95	33	31	53	33
India	Feb–Mar '98	26	25	26	33
Jamaica	12/18/97	56	39	83	17
Malawi	5/17/94	46	34	48	32
Mongolia	6/30/96	47	41	66	33
St. Lucia	5/23/97	61	37	94	6
St. Vincent & the Grenadines	6/15/98	54	46	47	53
Trinidad & Tobago	11/6/95	49	46	47	47
United Kingdom	5/1/97	43	31	63	25
United States	11/5/96	50	48	52	47

Note: Bangladesh, St. Kitts and Nevis, and Solomon Islands were excluded for lack of data; Micronesia and Palau were excluded because no political parties exist; Papua New Guinea was excluded because its legislature has two tiers of seats.

Table 2. Results of Presidential Elections in Plurality Systems

Country	Date of election	Percent of votes of first candidate	Percent of votes of second candidate	Total number of candidates
Iceland	6/29/96	41	29	5
Kiribati	10/1/94	51	18	4
Korea, South	12/18/97	40	39	7
Malawi	5/17/94	47	34	4
Palau	11/5/96	62	38	2
Panama	5/8/94	33	29	7
Philippines	5/11/98	46	17	10
Taiwan	3/23/96	54	21	4
Venezuela	12/5/93	31	24	n.a.

Note: Guyana was excluded, since the results in presidential elections depend on the results in legislative elections.

rights in 1996, according to Freedom House) that use the plurality rule in single-member districts.

The mean share of the vote for the first and second parties is 47 percent and 37 percent, respectively. Although the two leading parties obtain 84 percent of the votes, on average about 16 percent of voters support "third" parties, and in three countries—Canada, Grenada, and India—the two leading parties together failed to get 65 percent of the votes.

Although the plurality rule does not seem to lead to a two-party split of the vote, it does seem to promote a two-party split of seats. The leading party (in terms of votes) gets, on average, 58 percent of the seats, a bonus of 11 percentage points over its share of votes, and the top two parties combined win an average of 91 percent of the seats. But again there are some exceptions: in Canada, Dominica, and India the two leading parties failed to win 80 percent of the seats.

Nine democratic countries use the plurality rule to select their president. Typically, five candidates run in a presidential election (see Table 2). The average percentage of votes obtained by the winner is 45 percent. Only in three elections did the winner obtain a majority of the votes, and in two cases no candidate secured 40 percent of the votes. The two leading candidates total, on average, 73 percent of the votes. The vote is more fractionalized in presidential than in legislative elections (the average vote for the two leading parties in the latter is 81 percent).

The objective of an election is to determine who will govern. Whether there is a one-party majority government matters a lot. In the elections represented in Table 1, a party won enough seats to form a majority government in thirteen countries out of sixteen. André Blais and Ken Carty found a similar pattern. Most of the time, these majorities are "manufactured," since the leading party does not obtain a majority of the votes.

PROS AND CONS OF ONE-PARTY MAJORITY GOVERNMENTS

The basic argument in favor of the plurality rule (at least its first-past-the-post variant) is that it produces one-party majority governments. This is indeed true in most (but not all) cases. But why are one-party majority governments construed to be such a good thing by proponents of the plurality rule? There are two main reasons. First, one-party majority governments are more stable, and government stability is perceived to enhance political stability. Whether the plurality rule promotes political stability is an open question, since the evidence is ambiguous.

The second reason is that one-party majority governments are more directly accountable to voters. It is easy for voters in a plurality election to get rid of a government they do not like; they just throw the rascals out and replace them with a new government. Responsibility is not as clear and straightforward in the case of coalition governments; each of the parties forming the government can blame its coalition partners, and voters may find it difficult to sort out each party's responsibility.

An additional argument in favor of a plurality system is that it produces close links between the member of parliament who represents a given constituency and his or her voters at the same time it enhances the accountability of individual members, who can be held responsible for defending constituency interests.

A final virtue of the plurality rule, in the eyes of its proponents, is its great simplicity. The plurality rule can be explained in a few seconds, whereas the intricacies of various proportional-representation formulas can be opaque.

Plurality elections are criticized, on the other hand, for their lack of fairness and responsiveness. The plurality rule is considered by many to be unfair because it systematically overrepresents large parties and under-represents small ones. This is illustrated in Table 1. The average vote for the leading party in these legislative elections held under the plurality rule is 47 percent, and that party's average share of the seats is 58 percent.

Plurality elections are also criticized for their incapacity to allow a great diversity of viewpoints to be expressed in the legislature. Few women, in particular, get elected in plurality elections. It can be argued, finally, that the plurality rule is not very effective at producing what it is supposed to achieve. In approximately one case out of five, plurality elections do not lead to the formation of a one-party majority government. Furthermore, in some cases the government is formed by a party other than that which received the largest share of the vote. For instance, in two successive elections in New Zealand (1978 and 1981), the National Party formed the government even though it had obtained fewer votes throughout the country than the Labour Party. The outcome of the 1995 election in Dominica is even more stunning. The Dominica United Workers' Party, which finished second with 34 percent of the votes, won 52 percent of the seats and formed a majority government.

Proponents of the plurality rule believe that it is good because it has built-in incentives to make the governing party attentive to public opinion; the party in power knows that its best interests lie in doing what the majority wants it to do; otherwise, it will be kicked out of office. Critics of the plurality rule, however, do not trust a procedure that is bound to produce a legislature and a government that do not accurately reflect the wide variety of interests and values in society.

See also *Approval Voting; Cube Law; Cumulative Voting; Designing Electoral Systems; Double Simultaneous Vote; Limited Vote; Manufactured Majorities; Single Nontransferable Vote.*

ANDRÉ BLAIS, UNIVERSITY OF MONTREAL

BIBLIOGRAPHY

Blais, André. "The Debate Over Electoral Systems." *International Political Science Review* 12 (July 1991): 239–260.

Blais, André, and Ken Carty. "The Impact of Electoral Formulae on the Creation of Majority Governments." *Electoral Studies* 5 (December 1987): 209–218.

———. "The Effectiveness of the Plurality Rule." *British Journal of Political Science* 18 (October 1988): 550–553.

Blais, André, and Stéphane Dion. "Electoral Systems and the Consolidation of New Democracies." In *Democratic Transition and Consolidation in Southern Europe, Latin America and Southeast Asia,* edited by Diane Éthier. London: Macmillan, 1990.

Blais, André, and Louis Massicotte. "Electoral Systems." In *Comparing Democracies: Elections and Voting in Global Perspective,* edited by Lawrence LeDuc, Richard Niemi, and Pippa Norris. Sage: Beverly Hills, 1996.

———. "Electoral Formulas: A Macroscopic Perspective." *European Journal of Political Research* 32 (August 1997): 107–129.

Blais, André, Louis Massicotte, and Agnieszka Dobrzynska. "Direct Presidential Elections: A World Summary." *Electoral Studies* 4 (December 1997): 441–455.

Duverger, Maurice. *Political Parties.* London: Methuen, 1954.

Norris, Pippa. "Legislative Recruitment." In *Comparing Democracies: Elections and Voting in Global Perspective,* edited by Lawrence LeDuc, Richard Niemi, and Pippa Norris. Sage: Beverly Hills, 1996.

Powell, G. Bingham, Jr. *Contemporary Democracies: Participation, Stability and Violence.* Cambridge: Harvard University Press, 1982.

POLITICAL BUSINESS CYCLE

Analysis based on the political business cycle depends on the notion that a government's economic policy is driven more by the need to remain in power than by intrinsically economic considerations. Accordingly, economies boom or expand in the periods immediately before and after elections and stagnate or even contract in the intervals between them.

It is often regarded as a fact of economic life that economic activity is subject to periodic booms and slumps. Economic growth over the long term is rarely smooth; on the contrary, periods of relatively rapid economic expansion are likely to be followed by stagnation or even by periods of contraction. In the nineteenth century, economists became familiar with the idea of business cycles as a way of describing these economic fluctuations. Several different sorts of cycle, varying in length from five to sixty years, were subsequently identified and a wide variety of explanations offered for them—including the weather, wars, the effects of new technologies, and the differential expectations of producers in capital and consumer goods markets.

With the steady expansion of democracy—and voting—in the twentieth century, political scientists began to notice an equally common phenomenon: that the condition of the domestic economy in the months before an election was often a factor in determining the incumbent government's electoral success. Indeed, over the years a considerable amount of evidence has been assembled to suggest that voters are more favorably disposed toward the incumbent party or parties when the economy is thriving than when it is in trouble. The simple corollary to this sort of "economic voting" is that rational governments will try to engineer favorable economic conditions in preelection periods. The suspicion that this practice is widespread among democratic governments is what underpins political business cycle analysis.

Politicians themselves are reluctant to admit publicly that such manipulations are even considered, let alone implemented. Their public statements invariably assert that they are acting purely in the best interests of the economy and the public, that they are not just pursuing policies that work to their own party-political benefit. Government officials frequently point out that the management of the economy, aimed at securing stable growth, is difficult enough without engaging in the sort of manipulative fine-tuning that would be implied calculating political business cycles.

TESTING FOR CYCLES

Notwithstanding politicians' disclaimers, however, there are various ways of testing for the existence of political business cycles. These include examining whether certain macroeconomic indexes such as unemployment and inflation follow a cyclical pattern in the periods between elections; estimating statistical models of unemployment and inflation to assess whether these variables fall to an unusual degree during preelection periods; and analyzing data on government expenditure to see whether it increases in preelection or election years.

There are two main variants of the political business cycle model. The best-known study is by William Nordhaus; his work follows the logic of Keynesian demand management. The English economist John Maynard Keynes (1883–1946) argued that governments can stimulate the economy into increased activity at any time either by reducing taxes or by increasing government spending. Either of these expedients is likely to have the beneficial short-run consequence of reducing unemployment, followed some time later by an undesirable increase in inflation. Nordhaus held that an opportunistic government could take advantage of these tendencies. An increase in public spending just before an election might well increase employment in the short term, which would be good for votes. Sometimes, inflation might rise after the election. This increase would weaken popular support of the government, but at a time when support would matter less.

Nordhaus's seminal analysis has been criticized on both theoretical and empirical grounds. The main theoretical critique derives from rational expectations theory. This approach in part follows the logic of "once bitten, twice shy." It suggests that rational voters will adjust their expectations and behavior to counteract any opportunistic manipulations that governments might attempt. Thus, if a government does increase spending in a preelection period, voters will simply discount any consequent reductions in unemployment—and, as a result, the government will fail to derive any electoral benefit from it. Empirically, analyses conducted across a number of advanced industrial countries have failed to find evidence for the existence of a consistent political business cycle in either unemployment or inflation. Put simply, movements in unemployment and inflation over time fail to follow the sort of cyclical pattern, punctuated by elections, implied by Nordhaus's opportunistic political business cycle.

The second main variant of the political business cycle model is the partisan cycle. The logic of the partisan cycle model is that governments adjust the economy primarily to improve the economic position of their own "natural" sup-porters. Thus different sorts of government will behave differently in terms of their efforts to manipulate the economy. Left-wing governments, whose support base is traditionally stronger among the unemployment-vulnerable working class, will seek to reduce unemployment before elections. Right-wing governments, whose support is traditionally stronger among the more employment-secure middle class, will attempt to reduce inflation in preelection periods.

The partisan cycle model is subject to the same rational expectations critique as its opportunistic counterpart: even if governments of different political hues target different macroeconomic indicators in search of electoral advantage, rational voters will still discount such targeting to the point that it is ineffectual. From an empirical point of view, the partisan cycle model has had mixed success. Douglas Hibbs (1987) found some supporting evidence for such a cycle in a number of countries, including the United States and the United Kingdom, in the years immediately after World War II. However, studies covering other countries and more recent time periods have found less support for the general existence of such partisan cycles.

ASSESSING ALTERNATIVE MEASURES

If the evidence for the existence of political business cycles is mixed, do governing parties then not attempt to use macroeconomic policy to maximize their own electoral advantage? A major limitation of political business cycle models is that they focus too closely on a limited set of macroeconomic indicators. Models that focus primarily on variations in government expenditure over time are, for reasons of data availability, invariably restricted to using annual data. Yet elections are held in particular months, and party popularity can vary substantially during the course of a year. In electoral politics, timing counts for a great deal. Models based on annual data are simply too crude to pick up the ways in which governments might vary public expenditure in order to improve their own electoral chances.

Political business cycle models that employ either quarterly or monthly data, however, exhibit an equally serious limitation: in search of political business cycles, they focus almost exclusively on variations in unemployment and inflation. Although these two variables are undoubtedly important indicators of the general health of the national economy, they are by no means the only indicators available. Moreover, there may well be other variables—such as interest rates and tax rates— that have a more direct bearing on the likely electoral decision making of the average (or even the party's target) voter.

Data from the United Kingdom in the 1980s and 1990s provide a simple test for the idea that governments consistently try to engineer some sort of political business cycle that works to their own electoral advantage. General elections were held in Britain in 1983, 1987, 1992, and 1997. Examination of the relevant data on unemployment and inflation shows that neither unemployment nor inflation systematically rose or fell in advance of, or in the aftermath of, each of these elections. In short, in terms of the two conventional macroeconomic measures used to detect political business cycles, the Conservative Party governments of the 1980s and 1990s did not seek to manage the economy to their own electoral advantage.

Such a conclusion is not supported, however, by the evidence relating to interest rates and taxes. In advance of the general elections of 1983, 1987, 1992, and 1997, interest rates and tax rates both fell noticeably. This trend does not constitute conclusive evidence of a political business cycle as such. Nonetheless, given the impact of interest rate changes on consumer confidence in the United Kingdom and the impact of consumer confidence and tax rates on government support, the reductions in the two measures suggest a considerable measure of electoral calculation on the part of successive Conservative chancellors. In short, the evidence from Britain for the 1979–1997 period supports the notion that governments do seek to improve their electoral position by securing favorable movements—at electorally appropriate times—in those macroeconomic variables that they believe are most likely to seduce voters into lending them their support.

It is likely that the macroeconomic variables governments choose to concentrate upon will vary according to context. And it is also likely, given the difficulties associated with macroeconomic fine-tuning, that many of the self-aggrandizing economic stratagems of governments will fail to achieve their desired objectives or else go unnoticed by voters, as the Conservative government's massive defeat in 1997 shows.

See also *Election Studies, Types of; Voting Behavior, Influences on.*

DAVID SANDERS, UNIVERSITY OF ESSEX

BIBLIOGRAPHY

Alesina, Alberto. "Politics and Business Cycles in Industrial Democracies." *Economic Policy* 8 (1989): 55–98.

Alt, James E., and K. Alec Chrystal. *Political Economics.* Brighton, England: Wheatsheaf, 1983.

Hibbs, Douglas A. *The American Political Economy: Macroeconomics and Electoral Politics.* Cambridge: Harvard University Press, 1987.

Lewis-Beck, Michael S. *Economics and Elections: The Major Western Democracies.* Ann Arbor: University of Michigan Press, 1988.

Nordhaus, William D. "The Political Business Cycle." *Review of Economic Studies* 42 (1975): 169–190.

Rogoff, Kenneth, and A. Siebert. "Elections and Macroeconomic Policy Cycles." *Review of Economic Studies* 65 (1988): 1–16.

Sanders, David. "Conservative Incompetence, Labour Responsibility and the Feelgood Factor: Why the Economy Failed to Save the Conservatives in 1997." *Electoral Studies* 18 (1999): 251–270.

———. "Economic Performance, Management Competence, and the Outcome of the Next General Election." *Political Studies* 64 (1996): 203–231.

POLL TAX

The poll or capitation (head) tax in the United States was a lump-sum tax levied by state and local governments on individuals, who often had to pay the tax in order to vote. Although the device is popularly associated with racial and class restrictions on suffrage in the South, it actually expanded the suffrage when it was introduced shortly after the American Revolution; it unintentionally discouraged voting by newly enfranchised white women after 1920; it was excessively blamed for many of the South's ills in the 1930s and 1940s; and after a long crusade against it, it was banned in the mid-1960s as a mere footnote to the civil rights movement.

In the colonial era, men had to own a certain amount of property in order to vote. (Women were almost always disfranchised.) But between 1775 and 1791, New Hampshire, Delaware, Georgia, and North Carolina adopted constitutions allowing men to vote if they paid any state tax, and all began to levy a poll tax. Thus, by 1791 the poll tax made possible virtually universal white male suffrage in four states, half of them in the South, giving those states the broadest suffrage in the world at the time.

During and after Reconstruction, however, the poll tax constricted rather than enlarged the ranks of voters. By 1904 all eleven southern states that had formed the Confederacy during the Civil War made payment of a poll tax a prerequisite to voting. Although the tax was sometimes defended as a source of revenue for schools, it was an effective disfranchising device precisely because the upper-class white Democrats who framed it usually designed it not to be paid by those they did not want to vote. Poll tax delinquents were almost never prosecuted. In some states, only property owners received notice of poll taxes due, while in others, it was not even included on property tax bills. Seven of the eleven states made the poll tax due six to nine months before the November election, long before people were thinking of elections. To vote, one often had to keep one's poll tax receipts for months or years and bring them to the polls. In five states the tax could accumulate for more than one year—in Georgia after 1877 and Alabama after 1901, indefinitely. One knowledgeable observer termed Georgia's cumulative poll tax "the most effective bar to Negro suffrage ever devised."

The poll tax was effective, too, because southerners, especially black southerners, had very little cash income. In 1880 the average southern income, including noncash income, was $86 in contemporary dollars; in 1900, $100. But because the income distribution was extremely skewed, most people received much less than the average. And because sharecroppers, small farmers, factory workers, miners, and others bought most of their necessities on credit, they might not see more than a few dollars in cash during a year. To such men, who composed majorities or near-majorities of the adult male populations of every southern state at the turn of the century, a levy of a dollar or two might seem enormous. A cumulated poll tax was impossibly high.

How restrictive was the poll tax? Contemporary southern experts on disfranchisement thought it the best device to keep people they called "the dispossessed" from voting. Unlike literacy or property tests, which often included "grandfather" or "understanding" clause loopholes for whites, the poll tax applied to everyone, regardless of race, in general elections, and only South Carolina allowed citizens to vote in primaries without paying. Overall turnout in presidential elections in the 1880s in Georgia, the only southern state with a poll tax in force at the time, was less than two-thirds as high as in the rest of the South. Estimated black turnout in Georgia was less than half of that in Florida, a state with the same percentage of African Americans, in the same elections. No one has suggested any variable or combination of variables other than the poll tax that can account for such stark differences. These figures cast considerable doubt on the assertions of political scientist V. O. Key Jr. and his student Frederic Ogden that "the poll tax has had little or no bearing on Negro disfranchisement" and that "the poll tax helped in a minor way to achieve disfranchisement."

Key and Ogden underestimated the effect of the poll tax for two reasons. First, they concentrated on a later period, after the establishment of the white primary early in the twentieth century. By the 1940s and 1950s, when Key and Ogden were writing, blacks had been altogether cut out of the region's most important elections for generations, suffrage restrictions had produced a culture of political inaction, and decades of economic growth had made the poll tax seem economically less consequential. Without the poll tax, the establishment of which preceded the legalized white primary in nearly every southern state, Republicans and Populists or their successors would have remained a threat even if blacks had been excluded from Democratic primaries.

Second, Key and Ogden neglected the indirect effect of the poll tax on politicians' strategies and the heightened effect of the tax when it was adopted at the same time as other restrictive laws, such as literacy tests or restrictive registration laws. Many anti-Democratic southern politicians, realizing that disfranchisement laws would decimate their potential supporters, ceased to run, concentrated on local rather than statewide elections, or even joined the hated Democratic Party. The resultant decline in structured competition between political parties further dampened turnout, especially among those who shared political interests with the disfran-

chised. In sum, legal changes caused behavioral changes, which produced a solidly apathetic South.

A coalition led by the leftist Southern Conference on Human Welfare and later joined by labor unions, black activists, and liberals throughout the country organized state and national moves against the poll tax from 1938 through 1950. In response, Georgia, Florida, Arkansas, and Tennessee repealed the tax, joining North Carolina and Louisiana, which had done so in 1920 and 1934, respectively. The U.S. House of Representatives passed bills repealing the poll tax five times during the 1940s, but southern filibusters prevented any Senate action. White women's organizations led the campaign to reduce the period of accumulation of the poll tax to two years in Alabama; race- and gender-segregated registration figures available from Louisiana and Alabama show that white women were the main immediate beneficiaries of poll tax liberalization.

Although constitutional qualms, Senate rules, and a concentration on other means of disfranchisement stalled national action on poll tax repeal during the 1950s, the administration of John F. Kennedy pushed the Twenty-fourth Amendment, which abolished the poll tax in national elections, through Congress in 1962, and the necessary number of states ratified it by 1964. Two years later, in *Harper v. Virginia Board of Elections,* the U.S. Supreme Court ruled state poll taxes in violation of the Equal Protection Clause of the Fourteenth Amendment on the grounds—by that time widely accepted by the public—that wealth was not a valid reason to burden citizens' fundamental right to vote.

See also *Franchise Expansion; Registration of Voters in the United States.*

J. Morgan Kousser, California Institute of Technology

BIBLIOGRAPHY

Key, V. O., Jr. *Southern Politics in State and Nation.* New York: Alfred A. Knopf, 1949.

Kousser, J. Morgan. *The Shaping of Southern Politics: Suffrage Restriction and the Establishment of the One-Party South, 1880–1910.* New Haven, Conn.: Yale University Press, 1974.

Lawson, Steven F. *Black Ballots: Voting Rights in the South, 1944–1969.* New York: Columbia University Press, 1976.

Ogden, Frederic D. *The Poll Tax in the South.* Tuscaloosa: University of Alabama Press, 1958.

Williamson, Chilton. *American Suffrage: From Property to Democracy, 1760–1860.* Princeton, N.J.: Princeton University Press, 1960.

POOLING VOTES

In some electoral systems, votes cast for a candidate count not just for that candidate but also for the list to which the candidate belongs. In other systems, votes cast for a list count not just for that list but also for a cartel (or alliance) to which the list belongs. Whenever a vote is formally cast for an individual or group but is also counted in favor of a larger group to which the individual or group belongs, the vote is said to pool or to be a pooling vote.

In Chile, for example, citizens formally vote for individual candidates. But a vote for candidate X pools to the list level—that is, it is counted in the first instance as a vote for the list to which candidate X belongs. Votes for the other candidate on X's list (there are two candidates per list in Chile) also pool to the list level, after which the list vote total is established; the list vote total is simply the sum of the votes cast for X and for X's list mate. Seats are then allocated in two steps. First, lists win seats on the basis of their respective vote totals (using the d'Hondt method of proportional representation). Second, the seats awarded to each list are reallocated to the list's candidates (by plurality rule).

In Poland candidate votes can pool both within lists and within cartels. A citizen's vote for candidate X is counted as a vote for that candidate's list and also for any cartel or alliance to which the list belongs. Seats are allocated first to cartels, on the basis of cartel vote totals arrived at by summing the votes of all lists within the cartel, then to lists within each cartel on the basis of list vote totals, then finally to candidates on each list.

Pooling votes are one means by which candidates can contribute to the electoral success of larger entities—parties or alliances—and at the same time document their personal contribution very clearly. In other multimember systems, candidates of the same party may be unable to cooperate (as in the single-nontransferable-vote system) or unable to document their contribution to the collective cause (as in closed-list systems). In part because of this ability to observe the contribution of each candidate to the overall list vote, the pooling vote can promote personalism and factionalism within parties.

In addition to Chile and Poland, pooling votes are also cast in, for example, Brazil, Finland, Hungary, and Liechtenstein.

See also *Apparentement; Binomial Electoral System; List; Proportional Representation; Single Nontransferable Vote.*

GARY W. COX, UNIVERSITY OF CALIFORNIA, SAN DIEGO

POSITIVE DISCRIMINATION IN REDISTRICTING IN THE UNITED STATES

Positive discrimination seeks to remedy a situation of chronic under-representation of minorities by devising new electoral boundaries in order to give racial

and ethnic minorities a greater opportunity to elect representatives of their own choice. District lines can be drawn to enhance or diminish the electoral prospects of targeted groups. When the purpose of a redistricting is to increase the representation of legally protected racial and ethnic groups, it is referred to as positive discrimination or, alternatively, affirmative action gerrymandering.

U.S. courts have made it quite clear that the goal of this kind of remedial action is not to achieve proportional representation nor to elect a person of a particular race or ethnicity. Rather, it is to further the right of a particular community to determine its duly elected district representative regardless of the winning candidate's race or ethnicity. It does not matter whether a majority-black district elects a white or black representative as long as he or she is the person who is truly chosen by the community. Critics have argued that the implicit goal of positive electoral discrimination is descriptive representation (that is, African Americans should represent African Americans, Latinos should represent Latinos, and so on) on a proportional basis. Nonetheless, the U.S. courts have held firm to the distinction.

ORIGINS AND EARLY APPLICATIONS

The origins of this line of reasoning lie in the Fourteenth and Fifteenth Amendments to the U.S. Constitution and the Voting Rights Act of 1965. The Fourteenth Amendment, passed in 1868, extends an equal protection guarantee to the right to vote (ensuring that the right to vote cannot be denied to any individual on the basis of race). The Fifteenth Amendment, passed two years later, explicitly prohibits abridgment of the right to vote on the basis of "race, color or previous condition of servitude."

Initially, these constitutional protections were applied to the voting franchise itself, but with the passage of the Voting Rights Act in 1965, the courts began to review all voting rules and procedures that diluted a person's vote. Such dilutions came in several forms. The two most prevalent were at-large voting systems and discriminatory districting. In the former, a racial and ethnic minority could be consistently outvoted by a white majority if candidate support was polarized along racial lines and if elections were held at large rather than in districts. But even when jurisdictions were divided into districts, the lines could exclude or limit minority representation if they "cracked" or "packed" a minority population. *Cracking* means dividing a population that is large enough to control the outcome of a district into smaller parts; *packing* means concentrating a group that might control two seats into one. Thus, preventing unfair discrimination in redistricting amounted to having the courts review whether district lines cracked or packed a protected minority group (that is, a group covered under the 1965 Voting Rights Act).

TOWARD POSITIVE DISCRIMINATION

The transformation from an emphasis on negative to positive discrimination came with the 1982 amendments to the Voting Rights Act. These amendments altered the burden of proof: instead of showing that lines were drawn intentionally to dilute the voting strength of minority groups, redistricting's challengers were limited to a results test that examined the effects boundaries had on a group's opportunity to elect a representative of its own choice.

In a defining 1986 Supreme Court decision, *Thornburg v. Gingles,* the Court interpreted the amended Voting Rights Act to require a three-prong test that came to be known as the *Gingles* criteria. When a group was sufficiently large in a reasonably compact area to constitute a district majority, when there was evidence of racially polarized voting, and when it could be shown that a minority group voted as a cohesive bloc, the Court would consider possible remedies—single-member districts if there were none or redrawn lines if districts existed—that would enhance the community's opportunity to elect a representative of its choice. What this meant practically was that jurisdictions that met the conditions of the *Gingles* criteria and had the population to draw additional majority-minority districts (that is, districts in which the minority population was in the majority) were obligated to do so; otherwise, they faced a potential lawsuit from outside groups or the Justice Department.

The Court in the period from 1986 to 1992 left many unanswered questions. How far did the obligations to create majority-minority districts extend? How bizarrely shaped could the districts be? If a minority group already had some elected minority officials, was the political jurisdiction in question required to create additional seats? What happened if the additional seat for one protected minority group diminished the share of representation for another protected group? The 1991 round of redistrictings thrust many of these questions upon the courts. They were particularly problematic in the rural South, where there was a well-documented history of discrimination and exclusion but where the minority black population was dispersed over wide areas. Pressured externally by the Justice Department's vigorous enforcement of the Voting Rights Act and internally by the usual partisan and incumbent demands, the 1991 redistrictings produced some incredibly contorted districts in the name of enhanced minority representation.

Legal challenges to these districts led to another round of important decisions that limit the extent of affirmative action

gerrymandering. In *Shaw v. Reno* (1993) and subsequent cases, the Court ruled that while it was permissible for line drawers to take race and ethnicity into account when deciding boundaries for seats, race or ethnicity could not be the primary consideration. Using race as the primary criterion for drawing lines potentially violates the Fourteenth Amendment. Under the equal protection doctrine, state actions that employ racial categories are suspect and therefore subject to strict scrutiny by the courts.

How could a court know whether race was the primary criterion in a redistricting plan? First and foremost, evidence could be found in a district's shape. If the lines followed a noncompact pattern and the only plausible explanation for the shape was that it demarcated neighborhoods of racial and ethnic concentration, the court could assume that race was a primary consideration. Also the court would look at whether other conventional criteria, such as observing communities of interest and the boundaries of city and county jurisdictions, were obviously subsumed in the quest for putting racially similar areas in the same district.

LEGAL RETREAT

As with affirmative action policies generally, there was a legal retreat in the mid-1990s from the more aggressive policies of the earlier period. Protection against negative discrimination continued to exist, but it became possible for well-intentioned communities to go too far in remedying past under-representation. Still, the impact of the Voting Rights Act has been significant. Black and Latino representation at the federal, state, and local levels has increased dramatically since 1982, and most of the minority officeholders have been elected in majority-minority districts. The same is not true for Asian representatives. Although technically protected by the Voting Rights Act, the Asian community has benefited far less from it than have blacks and Latinos, for two reasons. First, the Asian population is rarely concentrated in large enough numbers to qualify under the *Gingles* criteria, and second, Asians have been very successful in winning white support and hence have had a harder time showing that special protections are necessary.

As the racial mixture in U.S. urban areas has become more complex, it is unclear how the traditional voting rights framework will sort out the various claims to representation that the competing protected groups might make. This has led some voting rights proponents to look to other kinds of electoral systems as more practical solutions to the problems posed by single-member, winner-take-all systems. A few southern jurisdictions have adopted semiproportional rules under the pressure of federal action to remedy under-representation, and proportional representation discussions have become more common in the United States. There is a growing recognition that the United States has been trying to achieve racial proportionality with rules that do not lend themselves naturally to such results. Because there is no constitutional basis for requiring proportionality, it will be up to the political system to adopt structural changes if they are called for, and the forces of resistance are considerable.

See also *At-Large Elections; Gerrymandering; Reapportionment and Redistricting.*

BRUCE E. CAIN, UNIVERSITY OF CALIFORNIA, BERKELEY

BIBLIOGRAPHY

Cain, Bruce. "Voting Rights and Democratic Theory: Toward a Color-Blind Society?" In *Controversies in Minority Voting: A Twenty-five Year Perspective of the Voting Rights Act of 1965,* edited by Bernard Grofman and Chandler Davidson. Washington, D.C.: Brookings Institution, 1992.

Cain, Bruce, and Ken Miller. "The Fragile Logic of Voting Rights: Extending the VRA to 'Other Minorities.' " In *Voting Rights and Redistricting in the United States,* edited by Mark E. Rush. Westport, Conn.: Greenwood, 1998.

Davidson, Chandler, and Bernard Grofman, eds. *Quiet Revolution in the South.* Princeton: Princeton University Press, 1994.

Grofman, Bernard, Lisa Handley, and Richard G. Niemi. *Minority Representation and the Quest for Voter Equality.* Cambridge: Cambridge University Press, 1992.

Kousser, J. Morgan. "The Voting Rights Act and the Two Reconstructions." In *Controversies in Minority Voting: A Twenty-five Year Perspective on the Voting Rights Act of 1965,* edited by Bernard Grofman and Chandler Davidson. Washington, D.C.: Brookings Institution, 1992.

Thurnstrom, Abigail M. *Whose Votes Count?* Cambridge: Harvard University Press, 1989.

POSTCONFLICT ELECTIONS

Postconflict elections are elections held in the immediate aftermath of a civil conflict, when a country remains divided and the system of government is still open to question. Such elections are a phenomenon of the post–cold war era. They are usually held at the insistence of the international donor community, which is increasingly reluctant to recognize the legitimacy of governments that have not been democratically elected. They are also held under the supervision of and with considerable support from the international community. Postconflict elections are thus not purely domestic processes and cannot be understood without reference to the donor community.

The goals of postconflict elections are complex, with domestic and foreign actors often seeking to achieve conflicting objectives. For the major domestic actors—the parties that fought the civil conflict—the goal is usually to consolidate their military victory or, conversely, to achieve electorally the victory that eluded them on the battlefield. The international community and domestic prodemocracy organizations have

multiple goals: to facilitate the transfer of power from those holding it through force to those that receive a popular mandate in the elections; to promote reconciliation; and to further encourage the consolidation of a democratic political system.

MAJOR POSTCONFLICT ELECTIONS

Some information about the nature, timing, and outcome of the major postconflict elections held since the end of the cold war is given below.

Nicaragua, presidential and parliamentary elections, February 1990. The elections resulted in the transfer of power from the Sandinistas to the Opposition National Union. Under pressure from the international community, the Sandinistas accepted the defeat. The country has followed a reasonably democratic path ever since, holding a second general election in 1997.

Ethiopia, regional and local elections, June 1992. Organized hurriedly and before the demobilization of competing armies was completed, the elections were boycotted by all major opposition parties and were followed by a period of renewed conflict. Nevertheless, the government went on to organize elections for a constituent assembly in 1994 and elections for the new National Assembly in 1995. These elections were also boycotted by the main opposition parties. Respect for democratic norms in general remained weak.

Angola, presidential and parliamentary elections, September 1992. The Popular Liberation Movement of Angola (MPLA), the incumbent party, narrowly won the elections. After waging a seventeen-year war, the National Union for the Total Independence of Angola (UNITA), the only significant opposition party, refused to acknowledge its electoral defeat. War resumed immediately. Despite endless negotiations and repeated agreements, peace still eluded the country seven years later.

Cambodia, parliamentary elections, May 1993. No party received an absolute majority. Funcinpec, the opposition party that received the greatest number of votes, was forced to form a coalition with the incumbent Cambodian People's Party (CPP), led by Hun Sen, which still controlled the military and much of the administrative apparatus. This coalition broke down in 1997 when Hun Sen staged a military coup d'etat. In new elections, held in August 1998 at the insistence of the international community, Hun Sen won a narrow victory, but they were not recognized as fair by the opposition.

El Salvador, presidential and parliamentary elections, March–April 1994. These were among the most successful postconflict elections and were followed by continuing progress toward reconciliation and democratic consolidation, despite the serious economic problems the country faced.

Mozambique, presidential and parliamentary elections, October 1994. Massive international assistance in demobilizing combatants and organizing the elections, international financing of the opposition parties in order to level the playing field, and a one-year postponement to complete preparations enabled successful elections that reconfirmed the incumbent Frelimo and were accepted by the opposition. A fragile democracy has survived since then.

Haiti, parliamentary and presidential elections, June–November 1995. After the United States and the international community forced the military to accept the return to power of deposed president Jean-Bertrand Aristide in 1994, new elections were held at the end of his mandate. The elections were very troubled and had to be held again in many areas. Eventually, all sides accepted the election results, but the situation remains volatile, with extreme poverty compounding the political problems.

Bosnia and Herzegovina, parliamentary and presidential elections, September 1996. In pursuance of the Dayton Peace Accord, signed by the governments of Bosnia-Herzegovina, Croatia, and Serbia in December 1995, elections were held for the parliament and rotating presidency of the Republic of Bosnia and Herzegovina. Elections were also held in the two component "entities" of the republic, as follows: presidential and parliamentary elections in the Republic of Srpska, and parliamentary elections in the Croat-Muslim federation. Voting took place along ethnic lines, with the more militant nationalist parties prevailing everywhere. Elections in 1998 reconfirmed this trend.

Liberia, presidential and parliamentary elections, July 1997. The elections returned to power Charles Taylor, the warlord who already controlled the country militarily. His election was apparently the result of a conscious decision by the voters that peace was more important than democracy and that only Taylor's victory would prevent more violence.

POLITICAL IMPEDIMENTS TO POSTCONFLICT ELECTIONS

Political conditions in countries emerging from civil conflict are not favorable to the holding of free and fair competitive elections. Invariably, such countries lack political institutions, technical capabilities, economic resources, social and political stability, and, in many cases, a commitment to democracy. There were major impediments to free and fair elections in all recent cases—and it is a tribute to the resourcefulness, technical capability, and commitment of the international donor agencies that elections could be held at all.

Despite the signing of peace accords, war-torn societies remain highly fragmented, polarized, and prone to violence. In most cases, the extremist sections of the warring parties are not reconciled to the peace accords. Law enforcement agencies are demoralized, understaffed, and lack adequate resources. For example, in Angola, Bosnia and Herzegovina, Cambodia,

Ethiopia, and Liberia, security was precarious. The process of demobilizing warring armies was not complete in all countries. Moreover, as a result of the prolonged conflicts, the social fabric had been destroyed, creating a climate in which sensible political debate and dialog were not always possible.

Elections in war-torn societies are also hampered by the absence of viable electoral institutions and of trained personnel capable of handling the job even-handedly. Even when the composition of the national election commission is balanced, members may lack the necessary experience. At the national level, donors are usually able to provide adequate technical support, but at local levels assistance is usually much more limited. Inexperienced polling station officials can create havoc. In Ethiopia, for example, confused polling station officials in good faith advised voters to write their name on the ballot papers. In Angola, polling station officials used their own criteria in deciding which ballots were spoiled, leading to a recount of the vote—and inevitably to accusations of fraud.

War-torn societies often lack political parties—as opposed to armed movements—and lack a free press, civil society institutions, and an independent judiciary. For example, in Angola, Ethiopia, Cambodia, and Liberia, politico-military groups that had recently fought in their respective wars had not fully transformed themselves into political parties prior to the elections. In all countries broadcast media were state monopolies or were tightly controlled by the government, and the independent press was at best in its infancy. Civil society organizations capable of participating in a democratic process were just emerging in most countries—Nicaragua and El Salvador were partial exceptions.

LOGISTICAL OBSTACLES TO POSTCONFLICT ELECTIONS

War-torn societies invariably face major logistical obstacles that make the elections extremely expensive to conduct and even minimum standards of freedom and fairness difficult to maintain.

The physical infrastructure of war-torn societies has usually been severely damaged. The severity of the problem varies widely, depending on the duration of the conflict, the extent to which the combatants have pursued a scorched-earth policy, and conditions before the war. The size of the country also has an impact. In small countries with fair prewar infrastructure, such as El Salvador or Bosnia, for example, war damage impeded the organization of elections less than in a large, underpopulated, and extremely underdeveloped country such as Angola. Poor infrastructure affects the electoral process at all stages: voter registration, campaigning by the candidates, the setting up of polling stations, the collection of ballot boxes, and even the counting of the votes. In rural Angola, for example, the counting of the ballots in most stations did not start until the day after the polls closed, because poll officials had no electricity and could not see to count the ballots. This logistical problem and others led to such a delay in the vote count that the war had resumed before the results were announced.

Poor security compounds the difficulty in holding a fair election, particularly in the countryside. Conflict often continues in some pockets even after a peace agreement has been signed. Furthermore, simple banditry is a common problem in the aftermath of war, when weapons are plentiful but jobs scarce. Improved programs to demobilize combatants and reintegrate them into civilian life can alleviate the problem but cannot eliminate it completely in the short run. The sooner after the end of hostilities elections are held, the more likely it is that they will be hampered by poor security.

War-torn societies invariably have a significant population of internally displaced persons and refugees. Their participation in the elections entails additional logistical challenges, even when the parties agree that they should be allowed to vote. They are difficult to register, because many have no identification papers and have been separated from those who can vouch for their identity. When voting is organized by electoral districts, rather than nationally, organizers must decide whether refugees should vote in the place they came from and hope to return to, or where they are residing temporarily. They must also decide whether refugees should be allowed to vote only if they return or whether polling stations should be set up in refugee camps. These problems must be addressed adequately, because nonparticipation by refugees can severely distort election results—refugees were over 25 percent of the population in Liberia and Eritrea, for example.

THE ELECTION PROCESS

Because of the numerous political and logistical obstacles, elections held in the aftermath of a war usually entail a particularly complex process, which most often has to be carried out within an unrealistically short time-frame. Between the signing of the peace agreement and election day, most countries typically have to demobilize the combatants and reintegrate them into civilian life, amend the constitution or adopt a new one, enact laws on the registration of political parties and election laws, set up electoral institutions all the way down to the level of the polling stations, register voters, and register candidates. It is also desirable to provide access to the media for all parties and to conduct civil education. These steps invariably take much longer to accomplish than envisaged, and many are not completed or are poorly carried out.

One of the most difficult tasks is the demobilization of combatants, which is rarely completed. Typically, the number of combatants is unknown, allowing both sides to hold back units. Soldiers do not always surrender all their weapons—a suspiciously high percentage of those they do surrender is very old or in poor condition. Even after soldiers are assembled, delays in processing them often lead some to rejoin armed units, frustrating the process.

In many cases, such as in Cambodia or Angola, elections are held even though demobilization has only partially been accomplished and problems remain in other areas, such as voter registration, access of all parties to the media, or freedom of movement throughout the country. Elections often cannot be postponed, for two reasons. One is peace agreements that lock in the election date. In Angola, for example, the election date had been set after difficult negotiations, and it was feared that a postponement would lead to a resumption of hostilities. (In any event, the holding of elections when both sides remained armed had the same effect.) Another factor that often prevents postponement is the desire of the international donors to disengage, or at least reduce their exposure, as soon as possible, because the international presence is very expensive. Additionally, elections are considered the capstone of the international peacekeeping efforts, after which donors can start reducing their presence. As a result of these pressures, elections are sometimes held too soon, leading to the premature closure of the democratization process.

THE ROLE OF THE INTERNATIONAL COMMUNITY

Elections in war-torn societies are heavily dependent on the assistance of the international community. Multilateral and bilateral donors, as well as international nongovernmental organizations, provide financial support, help keep the parties engaged in the election process, and support the technical tasks of demobilizing combatants and preparing the elections. Many elections could not be held without international assistance. Others would have to be postponed for long periods. Although international intervention is helpful, it also raises many dilemmas and entails considerable risk.

Financial support in the aftermath of a conflict is crucial, because few postconflict states would otherwise have the resources to demobilize soldiers and facilitate their reintegration into civilian life as well as to organize elections that are particularly costly because of the many logistical problems. International assistance, however, introduces practices that the country will not in the future be able to afford on its own and yet that come to be expected. In Cambodia, where the international community spent about $2 billion on the two-year process leading from the peace agreement to the elections, domestic election monitors were not only paid but paid at a daily rate that exceeded the monthly salary of a schoolteacher. In many countries, much of the election material was imported, with ballots and educational material printed elsewhere. The use of air transport, justifiable under postconflict conditions, also set unrealistic expectations for the future. In Mozambique, the international community financed opposition political parties, particularly the former rebel movement Renamo, to make it possible for them to compete against the much better organized incumbent party Frelimo. While this was a well-intentioned effort to ensure a fair electoral competition, it also raises the question of how far international donors should intervene in the domestic political process of other countries.

Another important issue is whether the international workers transferred skills and know-how to the national election officials, or whether they ended up doing the job themselves. Elections are a recurrent event, and the countries need to learn to handle them routinely, at low cost, and on their own. Studies in several countries found that a few years after the initial elections there was no trace of the electoral institutions that had been put in place earlier, that no effort had been made to keep up and update the skills acquired by those who had served as polling station officials and monitors, and that it would be difficult even to find these individuals again. The next elections would thus probably require an almost completely new training process. At the national level, the problem was a political one, namely that most governments were not interested in allowing a permanent, independent election commission to develop.

The international community's ability to solve the logistical and technical problems of holding elections in war-torn societies is impressive. Experts can tackle almost any difficulty. Air transport makes balloting possible even in remote regions where the infrastructure has been almost totally destroyed. Demobilization and reintegration of combatants, even when incomplete, usually helps create a less tense climate.

But technical and financial support cannot remove all the political obstacles, such as disagreement on basic issues among the political parties. Furthermore, international support in many cases covers up the real extent of the political problems, with the result that some elections are held even when political conditions should dictate otherwise. In Angola and Cambodia the major parties were not willing to abide by the election results and would not have cooperated sufficiently to allow elections to be held if left to their own devices. Nevertheless, international assistance made it possible to hold elections and even hid the extent of the disagreement. The result was evident immediately in Angola, where civil war resumed, and somewhat less immediately in Cambodia, where a political compromise that owed little to election results was eventually reversed in a coup d'etat. What the two countries needed

was negotiations among the parties, but instead the international community intervened and superimposed elections that inevitably failed. The case of Liberia provides a different example of how international support can lead to the holding of elections that do not address the underlying political problems. Despite all the international expenditure, Liberians elected Charles Taylor, not because they believed in his leadership or program, but because he was better armed and could restart the war if he did not win. A war-weary population simply opted for peace instead of democracy.

TRANSFER OF POWER, RECONCILIATION, AND DEMOCRATIZATION

The international community makes a substantial investment in postconflict elections. This investment is based on the assumption that they will lead, not only to the transfer of power to a democratic government that enjoys national and international legitimacy, but also to a long-term process of democratic consolidation and to national reconciliation. Experience to date suggests that the assumption is overly optimistic and that few postconflict elections fulfill such ambitious expectations.

Most postconflict elections have resulted in the transfer of power to the party that received the most votes, although considerable international pressure had to be exercised at times to convince the losers to accept the election results. The major exceptions were Cambodia, where the majority party was forced to enter into a coalition with the ruling minority party, and Angola, where UNITA refused to accept election results and the country returned to war.

Fewer elections have initiated a sustainable process of democratic consolidation. While democratization has continued in El Salvador, Nicaragua, and possibly Haiti, it has halted in Angola, and the prognosis for Bosnia, Cambodia, Ethiopia, and Liberia is extremely uncertain. As a result, there is now general recognition that postconflict elections are an essential, though insufficient, condition for democratization. Further progress toward democratization depends upon a complex and not clearly understood set of conditions, involving both internal conditions and external influences.

Reconciliation among the parties that were formerly at war often remains problematic. Postconflict elections are expected to transform a violent conflict into a nonviolent one, enabling the former warring parties to pursue their conflicting goals relying on ballots rather than bullets. Elections give all sides an opportunity to capture political power by presenting their agendas to the citizens, debating with their opponents, and mobilizing public opinion. Conflict-resolution mechanisms will thereby be institutionalized in the body politic. But this objective has been only partially realized. In Angola, elections led to war despite high levels of international intervention. In Ethiopia, the major opposition parties boycotted the elections and remain unwilling to engage with the government. In Cambodia, the military has intervened again. However, in other countries the adoption of a democratic system of government has started healing the wounds of war and has increased positive interactions among the political actors.

RETHINKING POSTCONFLICT ELECTIONS

International intervention has allowed countries emerging from a civil conflict to form new governments through elections. These postconflict elections have met with mixed success, however, suggesting that there is a limit to what international assistance can accomplish and that the best programs fail if minimal internal conditions are not met.

At least four conditions are needed for successful elections: 1) the existence of a state capable of performing basic functions; 2) a working consensus among warring parties about national boundaries, the structure and functioning of government, and the relations between national and subnational units; 3) a demonstrable commitment on the part of the major parties to abide by the clauses of the peace agreement and by the election results; and 4) significant progress toward the demobilization and reintegration of ex-combatants.

When these conditions are not met initially, elections should be preceded by protracted negotiations. The successful elections in South Africa that put an end to apartheid were preceded by almost four years of negotiations. This example underlines the time needed for parties emerging from a bitter conflict to build even a minimum of trust and a consensus. The failure of elections in Angola, where no negotiations took place beyond those leading to a very incomplete peace agreement, strengthens this conclusion. The bargaining among political parties also should continue after the elections: in both Nicaragua and Cambodia, the danger of renewed conflict was averted by talks among the parties, while in Angola, where no talks were held either before or after elections, war resumed.

See also *Administration of Elections; Colonial Elections; Elections in Developing Countries; Electoralism; Founding Elections; Free and Fair Elections; Observation of Elections; Premature Closure.*

MARINA OTTAWAY AND KRISHNA KUMAR,
CARNEGIE ENDOWMENT FOR INTERNATIONAL PEACE

BIBLIOGRAPHY

Diamond, Larry, ed. *Consolidating the Third Wave Democracies.* Baltimore: Johns Hopkins University Press, 1997.
———. *Promoting Democracy in the 1990s: Actors and Instruments, Issues and Imperatives.* Washington, D.C.: Carnegie Commission for Preventing Deadly Conflict, 1995.

Huntington, Samuel. *The Third Wave: Democratization in the Late Twentieth Century.* Norman and London: University of Oklahoma Press, 1993.
Kumar, Krishna, ed. *Post-conflict Elections, Democratization and International Assistance.* Boulder, Colo.: Lynne Rienner Publishers, 1998.
Lijphart, Arend, and Carlos Waisman, eds. *Institutional Design in New Democracies: Eastern Europe and Latin America.* Boulder, Colo.: Westview Press, 1996.
O'Donnell, Guillermo, and Philippe Schmitter. *Transitions from Authoritarian Rule: Tentative Conclusions about Uncertain Democracies.* Baltimore: Johns Hopkins University Press, 1986.
Ottaway, Marina. *South Africa: The Struggle for a New Order.* Washington, D.C.: Brookings Institution, 1993.

PREFERENCE VOTING

Although modern elections are understood primarily as contests among political parties, they are also contests among individual candidates. In some cases, the two are inextricably linked; if a party has only one candidate for a single seat, the election of (or a vote for) that candidate is indistinguishable from the election of (or a vote for) that candidate's party. Whenever a party has more candidates than the number of seats that it wins in a constituency, however, the distribution of seats among parties and the allocation of each party's seats among particular individuals become separable, in that the same seat or seats could be filled by different individuals without changing the outcome with respect to parties.

The decision regarding which individuals will fill their party's legislative seats (or other positions) can be made by the party in advance of the election, can be made by the voters as part of the election itself, or can be made through some combination of party-organizational and voter choice. Although the first possibility may involve choice by the voters in a public election (as with the direct primary in the United States) or the expression of preferences by party members, and potentially by nonmembers as well, in a poll conducted by the party, the term *preference voting* refers specifically to the second and third possibilities. That is, the use of preference voting in an election means that the voters are forced or allowed to choose not only among parties, but also among individuals within the group of candidates nominated by the party or parties for which they are voting. In the most extreme case, voters may even be allowed to substitute the names of other individuals for those who had received the party's official sanction.

The first question with regard to preference voting is whether voters are forced to choose among the candidates of their party or are merely allowed to do so. The clearest examples of the first situation are the single transferable vote (and its single-member-district equivalent, the alternative vote) and the single nontransferable vote. In both cases, no votes are cast for parties—the partisan totals produced in official statistical reports are merely the sum of the individual votes (generally first preferences in the case of the single transferable vote system) cast for each party's candidates, but the votes are never aggregated by party in determining the winners. If a party has more than one candidate, the act of voting *requires* that the voter either choose one from among the party's candidates or rank one candidate above the others. Similarly, if a party has more than one candidate in the first round of a two-ballot majority system (as often happens in the Louisiana congressional "primary" election), a voter is forced to choose among them in order to be able to vote at all; this was also the case in the French presidential election of 1995, in which Rally for the Republic (Rassemblement pour la République; RPR) voters were forced to choose between two candidates—Edouard Balladur and Jacques Chirac—in the first round of a two-ballot majority election. Voters may even be forced to choose among candidates in a list proportional representation system; in Finland, for example, a voter selects a candidate rather than a party, although the first step in determining the result is to compute party totals, which serve as the basis for allocating seats among parties.

Alternatively, the expression of an intraparty preference may be simply an option available to the voter. For example, in the pre-1994 Italian system for elections to the Chamber of Deputies, the party and intraparty votes were separate. Having first cast a party vote, the voter had the option of voting for up to three or four (after 1992, the option of voting for one) of its candidates. In this case, the allocation of seats among parties was determined entirely by the distribution of party votes, while the selection of the particular candidates to fill each party's share of the seats was determined entirely by the distribution of personal preference votes cast (except that the party's list order would be used to resolve exact numerical ties). The Swiss and Luxembourg systems of proportional representation, with panachage and cumulation, allow the voter to give two votes to some candidates and one or none to others, but they also permit each of a party's candidates to receive an equal number of votes, in which case no relative preference is expressed. Similarly, whenever a party has more than one candidate, cumulative voting in a multimember plurality election gives each voter the possibility, but not the necessity, of giving more votes to one of the party's candidates than to another.

In each of these examples, the choice among a party's candidates is based entirely on explicitly cast preference votes—whether optional or required. It is also possible to give the party a significant role in the ordering of candidates while still giving voters the option of casting individual preference votes. The methods by which this can be done are virtually limitless. In Austria and Norway it is done by counting simple party votes as if they were preference votes for the party list as submitted by the party. In Belgium party votes are counted as votes for the first candidate on the list, but if any candidate, in particular the first candidate on the list, has more personal votes than the required quota (the number of party votes divided by the number of seats won by the party in that district), the surplus is transferred to the first candidate in the party's list order who has not yet been elected. In Slovakia the party's list order prevails unless a candidate receives personal votes equal to at least 10 percent of his or her party's vote; these candidates jump to the head of the list, in the order of their individual voting strength. In the single-transferable-vote system for elections to the Australian Senate, parties can give their voters the option of marking a single preference (voting "above the line"), which is counted as a ranking of all of the party's candidates in the order submitted by the party; a voter who does not use this option must instead number all of the candidates of all parties on the ballot in order to cast a valid vote.

In those cases in which explicitly cast preference votes are the sole determinants of the order of election, intrapartisan defeats (the defeat of an incumbent while a new candidate of the same party is elected) often are among the primary sources of parliamentary turnover, generally exceeding interpartisan turnover of seats. One result is that candidates are forced to develop campaign organizations and bases of support independent of their party, in order to compete effectively with other candidates of the same party. This tends to undermine party cohesion and to encourage "pork-barrel" politics and personal service over a politics of principle and policy, since it is easier for an individual to claim credit for the former than the latter. In Italy and Japan, which recently reformed their electoral systems to eliminate preference voting, the need for candidates to campaign for personal preference votes was also assumed to stimulate political corruption.

In cases where a single party is dominant, and even more so in single-party systems, an intraparty preference vote can introduce an effective electoral choice where there otherwise would be none. Even when the system is heavily biased in favor of the party's list order, the personal preference vote may force party managers to take the personal popularity of candidates into account in determining that order, if only to avoid the embarrassment of having the order overturned by the voters. Moreover, the preference vote can provide an effective means for candidates to demonstrate their personal appeal, which then can be used as evidence that they deserve better list placement next time.

See also *Alternative Vote; Cumulative Vote; Gender Quotas; List; Proportional Representation; Single Nontransferable Vote; Single Transferable Vote.*

RICHARD S. KATZ, JOHNS HOPKINS UNIVERSITY

BIBLIOGRAPHY

Katz, Richard S. "Intraparty Preference Voting." In *Electoral Laws and Their Political Consequences,* edited by Bernard Grofman and Arend Lijphart. New York: Agathon, 1986.

Ortega Villodres, Carmen. "Strategic Dilemmas under the STV: Malta, Ireland and Australia." Paper presented at the 1998 Joint Sessions of Workshops, European Consortium for Political Research, University of Warwick, March 23–28, 1998.

PREMATURE CLOSURE OF DEMOCRACY

Multiparty, competitive elections held at regular intervals are a central feature of democratic systems. The holding of such elections is usually a milestone in the process of transforming authoritarian countries into democracies. However, elections held under the wrong conditions can lead to a premature closure of the process of democratization and to the reconsolidation of authoritarian governments. Rather than being a step toward democracy, premature elections are an obstacle to further change.

Democratization is often represented as a three-step process: 1) a period of liberalization or political opening, during which the authoritarian regime relaxes its hold and allows some political opposition activity; 2) a transition, represented by the holding of free and fair multiparty elections (transitional elections); and 3) a protracted period of democratic consolidation, during which democratic institutions are strengthened, political parties and organizations of civil society become better implanted, and elections become routinized. At the end of the third period, the country has a democratic, open political system.

An open political system is one that allows the entry of new participants. There are two types of open political systems: those that are open by design, that is, democratic political systems; and those that are open by necessity. A political system open by design possesses institutions designed to ensure access for all organizations and individuals. Although some actors will be more powerful than others, some degree of access, guaranteed by law and protected by institutions, exists for everybody. A political system open by necessity does not recognize the right of individuals and groups to participate freely in political activities, nor does it possess institutions that protect such rights. Rather, such a system is essentially authoritarian, but the incumbent government decides pragmatically that it needs to allow some political activity by organizations it can no longer suppress.

The attainment of a political system open by design is the end goal of a process of democratization. The initial opening, however, is most often dictated by necessity, when the government no longer has the power to exclude or co-opt all new claimants and is forced to implement some reforms. Such openings are uncertain and cannot be sustained unless the government continues to feel the pressure from a growing opposition.

Historically, the transition from a system open by necessity to one open by design has been long and characterized by conflict, as incumbent regimes struggled to retain their power and previously excluded groups fought to gain a role. In the United States and Western Europe, for example, it took many decades for the franchise to be extended to the entire population. In many countries, violence and civil war were part of the process.

Post–World War II transitions to democratic governments have been much shorter, particularly those in the former socialist countries of Eastern Europe. In the late 1980s the collapse of communist parties under a wave of popular mobilization led to the formation of new political parties and to genuinely competitive elections. The period of liberalization preceding the elections was very short. For example, in Czechoslovakia multi-party elections followed within six months of the popular insurrection that caused the downfall of the communist government; Czechoslovakia also moved quickly toward democratic consolidation, going from the lowest Freedom House rating for political and civil liberties in 1988–1989 to the highest (for the Czech Republic) by 1993–1994. The rapid progress of socialist countries from a political opening forced by popular agitation to multiparty elections, and in some cases even to the consolidation of a political system open by design, became the model all countries were expected to follow.

INTERNATIONAL ASSISTANCE, ELECTIONS, AND PREMATURE CLOSURE

During the 1990s a new factor was introduced in democratization processes around the world: democracy assistance programs launched by donor countries to facilitate and in some cases even to force change in authoritarian countries. Democratization thus was no longer a purely internal process, pushed forward only by the mounting strength of domestic organized groups. Domestic demands for change were supplemented by the donors' efforts to promote democracy through a mixture of pressure on reluctant governments (including the suspension of aid), technical and financial assistance for the organization of transitional elections, and a variety of programs that sought to strengthen government institutions and organizations of civil society.

A major focus of democracy assistance programs has been support for transitional elections. Even though donors agreed that "elections do not a democracy make," they assumed that elections were always a necessary step in the direction of democracy and should thus be organized as soon as possible. The experience of the 1990s shows that the assumption is unwarranted and that transitional elections may lead to a premature closure of the process of democratization. Although reversals of democratization are bound to occur in some cases—few countries follow a linear path from initial opening to consolidation without setbacks—some of the failures of the 1990s can be traced directly to the premature holding of elections, when political conditions were unfavorable, because of international pressure.

Successful elections require at a minimum two conditions: the existence of one or more opposition parties with sufficient support and sufficient organizational capacity to win a substantial number of votes; and a commitment by all sides to abide by the election results, either because of genuine commitment to democracy or because the price of noncompliance could be high. Without such conditions, elections are likely to lead to a relapse into authoritarianism.

A very poor showing by opposition parties in transitional elections sends a signal to the incumbent government that the opposition is not dangerous. Without international pressure and support, opposition parties usually do not succeed in forcing the government to hold elections until they have acquired considerable strength and constitute a threat to it. Donor pressure, however, can force a government to hold elections even if the opposition is weak, divided, or disorganized. Elections held under such circumstances set up the opposition for failure. The government may then conclude that its position is secure and that it does not need to make further concessions. Easy victories in a succession of weakly contested elections in 1992, 1994, and 1995 led the Ethiopian government to proclaim simultaneously that the country had become fully democratic and that there would not be a viable opposition for at least ten or fifteen years. The government's confidence, encouraged by the weakness of the opposition, led to closure of the process of democratization.

Premature closure can also occur when all parties do not accept the rules of the game. In Cambodia the 1991 peace settlement called for the holding of multiparty elections, a solution favored by the international community but not fully upheld by the Cambodian parties. Elections were held under UN supervision in 1993, although conditions were unfavorable. The competing parties remained armed, the demobilization efforts undertaken under UN supervision having largely failed. Moreover, the former government party still controlled the country's administrative apparatus, so that no other party could have governed effectively even had it won the elections. Finally, there was no commitment to democracy on the part of the major players. After the election, they agreed to form a government with two prime ministers, a nonconstitutional arrangement. In July 1997 a military coup d'etat brought this ill-fated experiment to a nondemocratic closure.

An even more dramatic example of how elections can cause a premature closure is offered by Angola. The 1992 election, which followed fifteen years of civil war and a very shaky peace agreement, directly caused a resumption of the conflict, when the losing party went back to war rather than accept its electoral defeat. Despite a new peace agreement, six years later the conflict was not resolved, and democracy remained a much more distant prospect than it had been in 1992.

AVOIDING PREMATURE CLOSURE

Avoiding the premature closure of democratization processes emerged as a challenge for international donors in the late 1990s. The donor community proposed two major approaches to minimizing the danger of premature closure. One approach called for donors to help establish institutions that encourage power-sharing and thus give all parties a stake in furthering democratization. The second suggested lengthening the liberalization period preceding elections in order to create more favorable conditions. The two approaches are complementary rather than mutually exclusive.

The transition in South Africa is an example of a successful attempt to avoid premature closure based on both a lengthy process and institutions. The country experienced a political opening in 1990, when Nelson Mandela was released from prison and negotiations started between the government and the African National Congress (ANC). The situation was extremely tense. The ruling National Party feared a complete transfer of power to the ANC. The ANC feared violence by extremist white organizations, and above all by the army, that would lead the government to revert to repression, closing the window of opportunity then open. Smaller political parties, black and white, feared complete marginalization. Four years of difficult negotiations led to an agreement on an interim constitution and a transitional power-sharing government. When elections were finally held, all parties accepted the results. Universal acceptance could not have been achieved without the prolonged negotiations and the agreement to form a government of national reconciliation.

The experience of many other countries that narrowly avoided premature closure in the 1990s confirms the importance of preelection agreements or pacts in reducing the possibility that elections will result in closure. After the 1990 elections in Nicaragua, the defeated Sandinistas came close to rejecting the outcome. Their eventual acceptance was aided by an agreement that the new government would put a Sandinista former minister in charge of restructuring the military and demobilizing the redundant personnel, assuaging the losers' fears of massive purges. In Cambodia postelection negotiations between the supposed winner and the former ruling party led to a joint government with two prime ministers. Although the agreement eventually failed, as shown by the 1997 coup d'etat, it safeguarded peace for several years.

The fact that elections can precipitate a premature closure of political openings, whereas negotiations, pacts, and power-sharing arrangements often avoid such closures, suggests the danger of the transition model that became dominant during the 1990s and the necessity of a longer period of liberalization, negotiations, and pact-making before transitional elections are held.

See also *Electoralism; Founding Elections; Free and Fair Elections; Observation of Elections; Postconflict Elections; Unfree Elections.*

MARINA OTTAWAY,
CARNEGIE ENDOWMENT FOR INTERNATIONAL PEACE

BIBLIOGRAPHY

Diamond, Larry, ed. *Consolidating the Third Wave Democracies.* Baltimore: Johns Hopkins University Press, 1997.

———. *Promoting Democracy in the 1990s: Actors and Instruments, Issues and Imperatives.* Washington, D.C.: Carnegie Commission for Preventing Deadly Conflict, 1995.

Huntington, Samuel. *The Third Wave: Democratization in the Late Twentieth Century.* Norman and London: University of Oklahoma Press, 1993.

Kumar, Krishna, ed. *Post-conflict Elections, Democratization and International Assistance.* Boulder, Colo.: Lynne Rienner Publishers, 1998.

Lijphart, Arend, and Carlos Waisman, eds. *Institutional Design in New Democracies: Eastern Europe and Latin America.* Boulder, Colo.: Westview Press, 1996.

O'Donnell, Guillermo, and Philippe Schmitter. *Transitions from Authoritarian Rule: Tentative Conclusions about Uncertain Democracies.* Baltimore: Johns Hopkins University Press, 1986.

Ottaway, Marina. *South Africa: The Struggle for a New Order.* Washington, D.C.: Brookings Institution, 1993.

PRESIDENTIAL ELECTORAL SYSTEMS

One of the defining characteristics of presidential government is the popular election of the chief executive. Most of the academic literature on electoral systems, however, focuses on methods to elect legislatures. One reason is that electoral rules to fill collective offices, like legislatures, are more varied and complex than rules to fill a single-member office, such as a presidency. Another reason is that there are many more long-standing parliamentary democracies than presidential democracies. In parliamentary systems each voter's single ballot for the assembly is inherently also a vote for who will lead the executive. Therefore, assembly elections are what have mattered most in a majority of democracies, until recently. The situation changed dramatically in the 1980s and 1990s, however, when most of the reestablished democracies, new democracies, and protodemocracies founded in Latin America, postcommunist Europe, Africa, and Asia incorporated directly elected presidents. The method by which these presidents are elected is critical. Electoral rules can influence who competes for executive office and who wins it. In addition, the presidential electoral system has an indirect effect on the party system in the legislature, which, in turn, affects the level of partisan support or opposition that presidents can expect in congress and the nature of legislative-executive relations.

HOW PRESIDENTS ARE ELECTED

The most immediate questions with respect to presidential elections are who votes, how, and how are the votes translated into a decision. With respect to the first question, most presidents are directly elected, meaning that citizens' votes are the immediate currency by which the office is won. There are, of course, important exceptions. Most prominent is the United States, where citizens formally vote for members of an electoral college, who in turn select the president. (In the twentieth century, however, the electoral college has never failed to select the candidate who won the most popular votes.) A similar electoral college system was used in Argentina prior to 1989. In a number of countries, presidents are *indirectly* selected by the legislature. Despite their titles, however, most of these presidents (for example, in the Czech Republic, Germany, Israel, and Italy) have quite limited formal powers, serving a largely symbolic role as head of state while the prime minister exercises the power of chief executive. Bolivia combines direct and indirect election, such that if no candidate wins a majority of the popular vote, the president is selected by a joint session of Congress. These exceptional cases aside, presidential elections tend to be direct, so that the important issue is how votes are cast and tallied.

Two types of formulas account for most presidential elections: plurality and majority runoff. Under plurality rule, the candidate with the most votes is elected. Under majority runoff, a majority of votes is required for election in the first round. If no candidate secures a majority, then the top two candidates compete in a run-off election. In recent decades, majority runoff has been increasingly popular among electoral reformers, replacing plurality systems in Brazil, Colombia, the Dominican Republic, Ecuador, El Salvador, Guatemala, South Korea, and Peru; replacing congressional selection in Chile and Taiwan; and being enshrined in the postcommunist constitutions of Bulgaria, Lithuania, Moldova, Poland, Romania, Russia, and Ukraine. One prominent argument for adopting majority runoff is to avoid the "plurality trap," by which a candidate who may be vehemently opposed by a majority of voters can win the presidency by securing the most votes in a divided field. (The election of Salvador Allende to the Chilean presidency in 1970 is frequently cited as an example of the dangers of plurality election. Allende won only 36 percent of the popular vote in 1970. It is worthwhile to note, however, that the Chilean electoral system was not plurality rule; rather, Congress chose the president in lieu of any candidate winning an outright majority. The congressional norm was to respect the plurality result.) An important rationale for majority runoff elections is to ensure that presidential elections produce a majority mandate for the chief executive.

First, consider plurality rule, where the threshold for success in the general election is high—one must win first place. The best strategy for a presidential aspirant who cannot reasonably expect to win the most votes is to enter a preelectoral coalition with a viable candidate, in exchange for whatever concessions can be negotiated. There is a gamble involved in plurality elections, however. If preelection coalitions do not form, or if voters do not cluster around a couple of leading candidates they regard as viable, then plurality elections can yield presidential winners with the support of only minorities of the electorate. The Philippines in 1992 and Venezuela in 1993 both elected presidents with less than 30 percent of the popular vote using plurality rule. The recent trend in the reform of presidential electoral systems has been toward majority runoff, which provides insurance against the election of weak plurality winners by requiring a second-round election if no candidate wins a first-round majority.

The second round under majority runoff can encourage the formation of coalitions of parties, candidates, and voters around the remaining two candidates. However, an important irony of majority runoff is that it simultaneously creates disincentives to coalition formation in the *first* round of election. This is because under majority runoff, the threshold for initial electoral success is lower than under plurality. One need finish only second in the first round to survive. Moreover, given that electoral coalitions can be renegotiated after the first round in anticipation of the run-off election, even nonviable candidates must compete in the first round in order to establish their electoral strength and the value of their second-round endorsement. These two effects are reinforcing. The more candidates enter in the first round (perhaps to establish their "bargaining currency"), the greater the expected fragmentation of the vote among candidates. The greater the vote fragmentation, in turn, the lower the hurdle is to winning second place, and thus entry into the second round of competition. Majority runoff, then, encourages competition and occasional success by outsider candidates, who

would have difficulty putting together credible campaigns under plurality competition.

Three cautionary examples of this phenomenon are the elections of Fernando Collor in Brazil in 1989, Alberto Fujimori in Peru in 1990, and Jorge Serrano in Guatemala, also in 1990. Each of these politicians:

- campaigned as a political outsider, running explicitly *against* the traditional party system;

- ran under the banner of a new political party that was initially little more than a vehicle for its candidate's presidential campaign;

- survived to the second round of a majority runoff election by winning less than one-third of the first-round vote in a divided field of candidates;

- confronted intransigent opposition from the legislature that evolved into a constitutional crisis.

Collor was impeached by Congress in 1992 on corruption charges, although his conviction was later overturned by Brazil's supreme court on the grounds that the congressional investigation violated norms of due process. Fujimori ended his deadlock with the Peruvian Congress in 1992 with a self-coup, in which he ordered the military to close the legislature and arrest his opponents. Under international pressure, Fujimori later agreed to hold elections for a new assembly, which also drafted a revised constitution in 1994. Serrano attempted a self-coup in the style of Fujimori but was abandoned by the military and removed from office in 1994.

It is not the case, of course, that all majority runoff presidential elections generate victories by outsider candidates, or even that viable outsider candidacies are necessarily undesirable. The extent to which majority runoff encourages and rewards outsider candidacies depends on the strength of the existing party system. In each of the cases cited above, voter disillusionment with the traditional parties preceded the rapid rise of outsider candidates. One could also argue that the permeability of majority runoff elections to new parties and outsider candidates is an attractive feature in that it discourages the ossification of the party system and increases competitiveness. At the very least, however, it is important to recognize that majority runoff achieves these ends by encouraging candidate entry into presidential contests and correspondingly by decreasing the incentives for preelectoral coalitions among presidential aspirants and their parties.

The tendency toward a more fragmented vote among first-round presidential candidates has an important indirect effect on the party system in the legislature. Many countries hold executive and legislative elections concurrently. Where legislative elections are held concurrently with majority runoff presidential elections, they are always concurrent with the *first round*. Moreover, presidential elections tend to weigh more heavily in the minds of voters than legislative elections—perhaps because of the prominence of the office or the amount of money spent on the campaign. For whatever reason, voters' choices in executive elections tend to spill over into legislative elections. Notwithstanding the prevalence of ticket-splitting in some systems, most voters in most countries cast their votes for the same party at the presidential and legislative level. As a result, the fragmentation of the legislative party system tends to mirror that of the presidential competition where elections to the two branches are concurrent. Because majority runoff encourages the proliferation of presidential candidates, legislative party systems are more fragmented than in plurality systems, even where legislative elections are held under proportional representation.

ALTERNATIVE ELECTORAL FORMULAS FOR PRESIDENTS

There is no reason for those designing rules of electoral competition to regard plurality or majority runoff presidential elections as the only viable alternatives. Plurality elections may be attractive in that they encourage broad preelectoral coalitions, but there is the risk that if such coalitions fail to materialize or to hold, the winner of the presidential contest may be opposed by a clear majority. The chief advantage of a two-round system is to avoid such an outcome; however, it does not necessarily follow that the requisite vote share for a first-round victory must be 50 percent.

For example, since 1949 Costa Rican presidential elections have required that the first-place candidate win at least 40 percent of the vote in the first round or a run-off election ensues. This first-round threshold has been perceived as attainable and so has encouraged broad first-round coalitions, with the result that Costa Rica has had a first-round winner in all twelve presidential elections under this system. Perhaps more strikingly, these coalitions have depressed electoral fragmentation sufficiently that nine of the twelve presidential victors won absolute majorities. Thus, Costa Rica has insured itself against a first-round victory by a plurality winner with an excessively low vote share, but without encouraging the level of electoral fragmentation associated with a standard majority runoff system.

In 1994 Argentina replaced its electoral college for the presidency with a system similar to Costa Rica's, although somewhat more complex. A first-place candidate with:

- more than 45 percent of the vote, *or* with

- more than 40 percent of the vote *and* at least 10 percent more of the vote than the second-place candidate

wins in the first round; otherwise there is a run-off election. In the first election held under this rule, in 1995, Carlos Saúl Menem won reelection to the presidency with an absolute majority.

In both Costa Rica and Argentina, lowering the first-round threshold for victory suggests a compromise between plurality and majority runoff formats. Nevertheless, such systems do not completely preclude the possibility of narrow victories by minority candidates. Moreover, the level of the threshold is essentially arbitrary. An election in which the top two candidates won 40 percent and 39 percent of the vote, for example, would produce a first-round winner in Costa Rica but not in Argentina. In Argentina, an election with vote shares of 45 percent–44 percent–11 percent *would* produce a winner; whereas 44 percent–35 percent–9 percent–7 percent–5 percent would not, even though the first-place candidate's claim to a resounding victory would appear more plausible in the latter election.

The basic intuition behind alternative formulas for presidential elections appears to be that both a higher absolute share for the first-place candidate and a larger relative victory over other candidates ought to count toward first-round victory. These two criteria are incorporated into a formula known as the double complement rule, which has been proposed by political scientists but has yet to be adopted in practice. Under the double complement rule, the leading candidate (v_1) wins in the first round if the extent by which he or she falls short of a majority is less than half the extent by which the second place candidate (v_2) falls short. Arithmetically, the first place candidate wins if:

$$50\% - v_2 > 2\ (50\% - v_1)$$

Under this rule, a minority candidate wins in the first round only if he or she is significantly stronger than the competitors. Thus, the double complement rule would prevent the plurality trap, but because it holds open the possibility of first-round victory, it encourages coalition building to block highly objectionable candidates from eking out a victory in the first round against a divided field.

THE ELECTORAL CYCLE

In addition to the formula by which presidential election winners are determined, the relative timing of presidential and legislative elections—the electoral cycle—is critical in shaping the nature of the party system and the likely level of support for the president in the legislature. In many countries, presidential and assembly elections are always concurrent, with members of both branches serving simultaneous terms. Examples are Bolivia, Costa Rica, Honduras, Nicaragua, Peru,

Uruguay, Venezuela, and, in the wake of recent reforms, Brazil. In a few countries (among them Colombia, the Dominican Republic, Ukraine), the branches serve terms of equal length but elections are held on different calendars, and thus their terms are nonconcurrent. In others, there is an alternating pattern of concurrent elections and legislative midterm elections (for example, the United States, the Philippines, Argentina). In still others, presidential and legislative terms are asynchronous, leading to irregular patterns, with legislative elections occurring sometimes early in presidential terms and sometimes later (Chile since 1993, Ecuador, El Salvador, France, Korea since 1987, Poland, and Russia are examples).

The critical point here is that the spillover effects of the presidential electoral system on the legislative party system are greater when elections are concurrent than when they are nonconcurrent. In plurality systems, broader coalitions behind presidential candidates translate into less fragmentation of the vote among legislative parties. Thus, fragmentation of the legislative party system is lowest under the plurality/concurrent format, even with proportional representation elections to the legislature. Under the plurality/nonconcurrent format, the tendency toward broad coalitions is present in presidential elections but is naturally mitigated for legislative elections, which are held at different times and on their own terms. In contrast to both plurality formats, highly fragmented presidential contests under majority runoff generate highly fragmented legislative party systems, under concurrent and nonconcurrent formats alike.

Through spillover effects, the electoral cycle affects prospects for support of the president in the legislature. In the first place, the more fragmented the legislative party system, the lower the expected share of legislative seats held by the president's—or any other single—party. Second, presidents tend to enjoy their greatest popularity at the time of their election and immediately thereafter, during their "honeymoon" period, and to experience decreasing levels of popular support thereafter. Thus, under concurrent elections, the party of the winning presidential candidate generally increases its share of legislative seats, as does the party of an incumbent president if legislative elections are held early in the presidential term. By the middle of the term, however, a president's party tends to lose seats—in increasing proportions the later in the president's term the legislative elections are held.

The temporal effect is particularly important with regard to asynchronous electoral cycles, where presidential and legislative terms are of different lengths. In France, for example, the seven-year presidential term and five-year parliamentary term have been critical in determining the nature of relations between the president and parliament. President François Mitterrand (elected in 1981 and reelected in 1988) used his authority to dissolve parliament and call elections during both of his honeymoon periods, securing large gains for the Socialists in each case. But five years into both of his terms, the Socialists endured significant losses in parliament, ushering in two-year periods of cohabitation marked by strained relations between the president, on the one hand, and the cabinet and parliament, on the other. President Jacques Chirac, who upon election in 1995 inherited a secure legislative majority as a result of Mitterrand's late-term losses in 1993, did not call for honeymoon elections. By spring 1997, however, with support for the parties that backed him steadily eroding, Chirac called parliamentary elections for May, a year before the constitution required. The move came too late, the president's supporters lost their legislative majority, and Chirac was forced to name a premier from the left.

When the terms of the chief executive and the legislature are constitutionally fixed, such that early elections cannot be called, the effects of an asynchronous electoral cycle could be even more important. Russia, for example, has a five-year presidential term and a four-year term for members of the lower house of the legislature, the Duma. (Under the Russian constitution of 1993, the president may dissolve the Duma and call new elections if the Duma rejects three consecutive presidential nominees for the post of prime minister.) The president was first popularly elected in 1991. The first Duma was elected in 1993 to a special two-year term; the next was elected in 1995, followed by a second presidential election in 1996. Assuming both branches always fulfill their constitutional terms, there are prospects for concurrent elections every twenty years, with intervening legislative elections held sometimes during presidential honeymoons, sometimes around the midterm, and in other instances late in the presidential term. This electoral cycle suggests that the prospects for partisan support in the Duma will vary for future Russian presidents, but the difference is completely arbitrary—the result of an asynchronous electoral cycle.

PUTTING THE PIECES TOGETHER

The elements of presidential electoral systems discussed above are almost invariably subjects of fierce bargaining at the creation of political institutions. The method for electing the president, the term length of the president and legislators, and the sequence by which these offices are filled all have implications for the immediate political fortunes of the leaders who establish new regimes. Decisions about the shape of these institutions, therefore, are frequently driven by the career interests of incumbent politicians and aspirants to office; however, the implications of these choices are long-lasting and pervasive.

The choice of electoral formula in presidential elections affects the likely fragmentation of the vote, which, in turn, has direct effects on the viability of outsider candidacies and on the fragmentation of the legislative party system. Both of these, in turn, affect the prospects for conflict between executives and legislatures. Majority runoff presidential elections are increasingly popular among electoral reformers, and they provide insurance against narrow victories by candidates with minority support. But majority runoff reduces the threshold for success in the first round of presidential elections, discouraging broad preelectoral coalitions relative to plurality systems. Various alternative electoral formulas, including the double complement rule, encourage broad electoral coalitions while also safeguarding against the plurality trap.

The electoral cycle also has long-term implications for the relations between the executive and legislative branches. Either a concurrent or a honeymoon electoral format is more likely to generate strong partisan support for the executive in the legislature than a format with regular mid- or late-term elections. Midterm elections are more likely to provide an effective check on executive power by favoring the president's opponents in the legislature. The ubiquity of asynchronous electoral cycles is testament to how little concerns about the long-term effects of institutional design enter the calculus of those who craft presidential electoral systems. Asynchronous systems generally represent compromises on the term lengths and electoral calendars for various offices, with the side effect of creating arbitrarily distinct prospects for the partisan support of different presidents.

Presidential government allows voters to express separate preferences for leadership of the legislature and the executive, but it also requires choices about the system for electing presidents and the interaction between this system and that for electing legislators. Separate elections mean that voters' collective decisions may yield dissimilar, and even conflicting, choices for the two elected branches of government. The performance of any regime depends critically on who occupies the executive and on the relations between the branches. Under presidentialism, the potential for cooperation and conflict between branches depends in large part on how and when presidential elections are conducted.

See also *Appendix; Majority Systems; Offices Filled by Direct Election; Plurality Systems; Second Ballot.*

JOHN M. CAREY, WASHINGTON UNIVERSITY, ST. LOUIS

BIBLIOGRAPHY

Shugart, Matthew S. "The Electoral Cycle and Institutional Sources of Divided Government." *American Political Science Review* 89, no. 2 (June 1995): 327–343.

Shugart, Matthew S., and John M. Carey. *Presidents and Assemblies: Constitutional Design and Electoral Dynamics.* New York: Cambridge University Press, 1992.

Taagepera, Rein, and Matthew S. Shugart. "Plurality Versus Majority Election of Presidents: A Proposal for a 'Double Complement Rule.'" *Comparative Political Studies* 27, no. 3 (April 1994): 323–348.

PRIMARY ELECTIONS

The direct primary election, usually referred to simply as a primary election, is a process for nominating a political party's candidates that is regulated and usually mandated by the government and that enables voters to directly choose the nominees of parties.

In theory, one of the major functions of a political party in a democratic system is the nomination of candidates. In practice, political parties in most countries may use a small group or committee of leaders or activists at the national, state, or local level to choose the candidates. Or the selections may be made by a convention of delegates from local units of the party. Sometimes the party opens the process to all of its members who choose to attend a caucus or cast their vote for a nominee at a poll.

The United States is the only country in which almost all party nominations are made directly or indirectly by the voters rather than by the leaders or groups of persons who are active in the party. Therefore, this study of primary elections refers only to the nominating process followed in the United States.

Two characteristics distinguish the direct primary from other forms of nomination: it is an election open to all voters who, in one way or another, decide to participate in a party's nomination of candidates; and the election is operated by the government, which may require some or all political parties to use this method of nomination, specify how voters may become eligible to participate, and determine the rules and procedures for operation of the primary election.

Political parties in the United States nominate by direct primary as a result of laws passed not by Congress but by states, and for that reason there are some important differences from state to state in the operation of primaries, such as open and closed primaries and run-off primaries.

At the national level in the United States, presidential candidates are nominated by national conventions, but a series of state-by-state primary elections held over a period of several months largely determines how much delegate support each candidate will have at the national party convention. In recent years, by the time the convention meets, one candidate has usually won enough support in state primaries to have the majority of delegate votes needed for nomination.

Party candidates for statewide office (such as governor), for seats in Congress and in state legislatures, and for partisan elections to local offices are chosen by the voters in direct primary elections. In a few states, particularly in the South, the major parties have the option of nominating by convention; some states also give this choice to minor parties. In some localities, some or all officials are elected in nonpartisan elections; in this case there is usually a two-stage election, with a runoff between the two top candidates if no one has a majority in the first stage. This first stage is often called a primary election.

HISTORICAL BACKGROUND OF STATE PRIMARIES

The primary election system in American states was a direct result of the Progressive movement in the late nineteenth and early twentieth centuries. It was a reaction against the strong party organizations in northern states that were often boss-dominated and were usually able to control party nominations. Progressive leaders favored the direct primary for theoretical and practical reasons. In theory they believed in direct democracy; in practice they wanted the primary election as a vehicle for wresting party control from the conservative organizations that dominated the Republican Party in most northern states. The argument for primary elections was particularly strong in states that were dominated by one party, Republicans in the North and Democrats in the South, because in most elections winning the nomination of the dominant party was tantamount to being elected. The first comprehensive, compulsory primary law was adopted by Wisconsin in 1903, and by 1917 almost all northern states had such primaries. The holdouts were a few northern states with particularly strong party organizations.

In the South the direct primary was adopted in a number of states beginning in the late 1870s, first by Democratic Party rule and then by state law. The major reason for enabling voters to choose party nominees was to legitimize Democratic control over southern politics and to block efforts by Populists and some Republicans to challenge effectively the Democratic Party. Some southern states made primaries optional or gave the parties considerable control over rules and procedures for the primary. In most southern states African Americans were banned from primaries from the early 1900s until 1944, when court decisions overruled this practice.

STATE RULES FOR PRIMARIES AND THEIR CONSEQUENCES

State laws determine the requirements that voters must meet to vote in a particular party's primary election. The terms "closed" and "open" are often used to describe who can vote in a party primary, but the variations are somewhat more complicated. Sixteen states have completely closed primaries where you must be registered with a party prior to the primary election to vote in that party's primary. Ten other states also have closed primaries but permit some persons (such as independents), or in some states any person, to shift registra-

tion to a party on the day of the primary. Twenty states do not require any party registration, and eleven of these do not even require the voter to say in which party primary he or she wishes to vote. Three states have a so-called blanket primary, where a person can vote in one party's primary for some offices and in the other party's primary for others. Some state parties have gone to court to challenge the use of open primaries, with mixed success.

What difference does it make how closed or open a primary is? Very little research exists to show what proportion of voters in more-open states shift back and forth frequently from one party primary to the other. There is some evidence that, in states where primaries are closed, voters are more likely to identify with a party than to think of themselves as independents. In open primary states, voters are more likely to cross over from their own party's primary to the other party's if their primary has less competition, and to vote for a candidate who shares their viewpoints. A Republican, for example, in the absence of a compelling contest in the Republican primary, would probably vote for the most conservative candidate in the Democratic primary.

Most southern states require run-off primaries; if no candidate gets a majority in the first primary, a runoff is held between the top two candidates. When the Democratic Party dominated southern state politics, it often had multicandidate primaries and needed a runoff to get a candidate who could command majority support. There is some evidence that run-off primary elections reduce the chance of an African American candidate being nominated. Louisiana has what is, in reality, a nonpartisan election with a runoff for state officials. There is a single primary for all candidates and registered voters. Anyone winning a majority in the first stage is elected; if a runoff is required, the top two candidates, regardless of party, run in the election. The courts have required that, if this system is used in congressional elections, the first stage, rather than the runoff, be scheduled for the date on which congressional elections are held in all other states.

TURNOUT IN PRIMARIES

Voter turnout is usually lower in primaries than in general elections. The majority party in a state usually has a larger number of voters in its primary election than does the minority party. Voters are more likely to vote in the primary that has the larger number of candidates running and the prospect of a closer election. The majority party is likely to attract more candidates to the primary because the winner would have a good chance to win the general election. The minority party sometimes has difficulty finding one serious candidate to run and may have little or no primary competition. The major exception to this rule is that the majority party is more likely to have an incumbent running, and a strong incumbent may scare away primary competition.

THE EFFECT OF PRIMARIES ON STATE GENERAL ELECTIONS

The pattern of turnout and voting in state primary elections affects the outcome of general elections in various ways. The candidate chosen by voters in a primary may not be the one who has the best chance of winning in the general election. If turnout is low in the minority party primary, those who do vote may not be representative of the larger group of potential voters for the party in the general election. This would be true, for example, if most of those voting in the primary were traditional supporters of the party. If a primary campaign is bitterly divisive, those who supported the losing candidate may fail to turn out and vote for the primary winner in the general election.

Until recently, Democrats usually won elections in most southern states. Therefore, turnout in the Democratic primary was very heavy and included many conservative voters; the result was often the nomination of a conservative Democrat. Turnout in the Republican Party was light, and often there was only one candidate running. In recent years, many conservative voters have shifted from the Democratic to the Republican primary, which has become more competitive. Southern Democrats are now more likely to nominate a more liberal candidate; a larger and more representative group of Republicans nominate a conservative; and therefore the Republicans have a better chance of winning the general election in a conservative state.

PREPRIMARY ENDORSEMENTS BY STATE PARTIES

Some of the state party organizations that are relatively strong try to exert some influence over the nominating process by making preprimary endorsements of candidates. Some state parties adopted the practice when their state first established the mandatory primary, and some have adopted it more recently. As of 1999, seven states had laws that provided for party endorsements; in four more states, one or both parties made endorsements under party rules; and in five more states, the state or county leaders of one or both parties often made endorsements. Only one of these states (Louisiana) is in the South, but Virginia state law permits parties to use primaries or conventions for nomination, and both major parties sometimes use conventions. In the eleven states where parties regularly endorse candidates under state law or party rules, the statewide endorsements are made in public either by a convention or by the state committee. Convention delegates may be elected by local caucuses or appointed by local party committees.

In the states that by law permit preprimary endorsements, candidates who win support from the convention gain some advantage in getting on the primary ballot. Candidates may have to get a certain percentage of the convention vote (such as 20 percent or 25 percent) to get on the primary ballot at all or to get on the ballot without having to get petitions signed (which in some states is a considerable advantage). The candidate with the largest convention vote may gain top position on the primary ballot, which should help get votes. Normally, when parties are making endorsements under just their own rules, the top vote-getters gain no ballot advantage.

In theory, the party will endorse the strongest candidate, the one with the best chance of being elected. The endorsement process may help unify the party and minimize the divisiveness of primaries. It may also reduce the impact of campaign financing on the outcome of the primary. These benefits will occur only if the party endorsee succeeds in winning the primary, because other contestants either drop out or are defeated by the endorsee. The proportion of endorsees who win nomination has dropped from nine-tenths in the 1960–1978 period to three-fourths in the 1980–1998 period.

THE EFFECT OF PRIMARIES ON THE PRESIDENTIAL NOMINATING PROCESS

Democratic and Republican presidential candidates are formally nominated by national conventions, but in recent years the choice has actually been made in presidential primaries held in the various states. Presidential primaries were established in the early twentieth century by some of the states that were mandating primaries for nominating other officials. In the 1930s and 1940s only about a dozen states had primaries, presidential candidates seldom campaigned in them, and few of these primaries were direct contests between major candidates. Most state parties chose their national convention delegates in caucuses and state conventions, often controlled by party organizations. From 1948 through 1968 presidential candidates campaigned selectively in the fifteen or so primaries, and in some campaigns primaries played a key role, including Dwight Eisenhower's defeat of Robert Taft at the 1952 Republican convention and John Kennedy's victory in a few primaries that were critical to his Democratic nomination in 1960. But as late as 1968 Hubert Humphrey won the Democratic nomination against Eugene McCarthy without entering any primaries.

Starting in 1972, state primaries began to assume a dominant role in the presidential nominating system. Within a few years a large majority of states held primaries, the results of which were binding on convention delegates. Voter turnout in these primaries increased rapidly, especially in years when there was a serious contest for a party's nomination. Presidential candidates had to change their tactics, from picking and choosing primaries where they could gain a tactical advantage to entering almost all of them. The growing importance of primaries has led to the decline in influence of state party organizations and their leaders, such as governors, over the state delegation to the convention.

Now most states hold presidential primaries, and their impact is far greater than the conventions held in a minority of states. The early primaries and a few early caucuses, even in smaller states like New Hampshire and Iowa, have assumed great importance because of intensive coverage by the media. Because the early primaries have so much impact on the outcome, in the 1996 and 2000 elections many states have been moving their primaries to earlier dates, a process referred to as "front-loading." As recently as 1976, only about one-fifth of the delegates selected in the Republican primaries were chosen in the first six weeks of the primary season. In 1996 the primaries ran from New Hampshire in late February to four states in early June, but two-thirds of the state primaries occurred in the first five weeks after New Hampshire, through March 26, and half occurred in the first three weeks. The schedule for the 2000 primaries was similar, but California—with 10 percent of the electoral vote—moved its primary up three weeks to March 7, and some other states were considering joining the front-loading trend.

The political effect of this trend is to increase the advantage of a front-running candidate who can win most of the early primaries and gain momentum so quickly that most other candidates drop out, assuring the front-runner's nomination within a few weeks. The compressed early primary schedule makes it more difficult for an underdog candidate to become a serious contender by doing better than expected and maintaining momentum in the early primaries.

The growing importance of the presidential primaries and the frequent ability of one candidate to gain a majority of delegate votes during the primary campaign have reduced the importance of the national convention. It has become largely a showcase for the nominee and the party and an arena where the party strives to rebuild unity, particularly after a divisive primary campaign. The mechanics of the primary process, as it has evolved in recent years, do not necessarily guarantee that a party will nominate the candidate with the best chance of winning the general election.

See also *Candidates: Selection; Double Simultaneous Vote; Nomination Procedures; Presidential Electoral Systems; Second Ballot; Tactical Voting; Turnout.*

MALCOLM E. JEWELL, UNIVERSITY OF KENTUCKY

BIBLIOGRAPHY

Bartels, Larry M. *Presidential Primaries and the Dynamics of Public Choice.* Princeton, N.J.: Princeton University Press, 1988.

Epstein, Leon. *Political Parties in the American Mold.* Madison: University of Wisconsin Press, 1986.

Jewell, Malcolm E. *Parties and Primaries: Nominating State Governors.* New York: Praeger, 1984.

Key, V.O., Jr. *American State Politics: An Introduction.* New York: Alfred A. Knopf, 1956.

Merriam, Charles E., and Louise Overacker. *Primary Elections.* Chicago: University of Chicago Press, 1928.

Morehouse, Sarah M. *The Governor as Party Leader: Campaigning and Governing.* Ann Arbor: University of Michigan Press, 1998.

Norrander, Barbara. *Super Tuesday: Regional Politics and Presidential Primaries.* Lexington: University Press of Kentucky, 1992.

PROPORTIONAL REPRESENTATION

Proportional-representation systems are those in which seats are allocated to political parties in proportion to the votes they receive at election. How proportional seat shares are to vote shares is, however, a matter of degree and not an all-or-nothing proposition. At one extreme are the decidedly nonproportional winner-take-all systems in which a plurality of a constituency's votes confers 100 percent of its seats. At the other extreme is the ideal case of "perfect PR" in which a party's seat share exactly equals its vote share. In between are systems in which a bare majority of votes does not guarantee all the seats, but in which seat shares still diverge to some degree from vote shares, usually in favor of the parties winning larger vote shares.

Constitutional designers in most countries have not sought to achieve exact proportionality between votes and seats above all other goals. Moreover, they have had available to them an increasing array of technical methods for achieving any degree of proportionality that they might desire. Given the diversity of ends and means, one can begin to appreciate the diversity of PR systems in operation. One metaphor for the more complicated systems would be Ptolemaic astronomy: where the astronomers added epicycles upon cycles to make planetary orbits come out right, the constitutional engineers have in some cases added tiers upon thresholds upon formulas to make various political orbits come out right.

This essay surveys the electoral features that appear in the universe of proportional-representation systems. The key issue in all systems, proportional or not, is how votes cast in an election ultimately turn into seats awarded to individual candidates. Electoral engineers have three broad areas with which to tinker in translating votes to seats. First, they can alter the votes themselves, by adjusting the ballot structure (that is, the options that voters are given on the ballot). Second, they can define the geographic relationship between votes and seats, by adjusting the district structure (that is, the variously interrelated constituencies within which votes are counted and seats awarded). Third, they can alter the formulaic structure (the mathematical formulas by which specific vote totals are converted into intermediate or final seat allocations at various stages in the process).

Although proportional representation can in principle be used in executive elections, to do so requires executive arrangements different from those found in presidential countries such as the United States. Electing a single person as president unavoidably entails use of a winner-take-all rule at some point in the process. To introduce an element of proportional representation, the executive would either have to be plural (as, for example, in Switzerland and formerly in Uruguay) or subject to rotation in office (also used in Switzerland for the chairmanship of the executive council). This essay focuses on legislative rather than executive elections, where proportional representation is easier to introduce.

BALLOT STRUCTURE

Voting in proportional-representation systems can take a variety of forms: checking a box next to a party's name or symbol, pulling a lever, punching a hole in a computer punchcard, writing a sequence of numerals in boxes next to candidates' names, and so forth. These different physical actions become abstractly similar when they are counted and thereby reduced to various numerical vote totals. Not all vote totals are created equal, of course. Some totals, such as the sum of all votes cast for candidates whose last names begin with the letter "S," are irrelevant to any further operation of the electoral system. Other vote totals, however, form the basis upon which seats are awarded to candidates, lists, or cartels. Those vote totals that figure in the mathematical operations by which seats are allocated are *seat-relevant*.

Three questions are fundamental in sorting through the voting methods in use, or proposed for use, in proportional-representation elections:

1. For what entities does the voter vote? Sometimes citizens can vote only for individual candidates, sometimes they can vote only for whole lists of candidates nominated by parties (or alliances of parties), and sometimes they have the option to do either or both.

2. How many votes may each voter cast? The number of *candidate* votes (that is, votes cast for individual candidates) each voter possesses can range from one to the total number of candidates competing. Similarly, the number of *list* votes each voter possesses can range from one to the total number of lists competing.

3. How do votes contribute to seat-relevant vote totals? If each voter casts one vote, then a basic distinction is made

between votes that affect only a single seat-relevant vote total (*exclusive* votes) and those that affect more than one seat-relevant vote total (*nonexclusive*). If each voter casts more than one vote, then how those votes affect seat-relevant vote totals can be described in terms of whether cumulation, plumping, or panachage are allowed.

Further discussion will clarify the meaning of the terms—exclusive vote, cumulative vote, and others—introduced above. Consider first those systems in which voters cast a single vote for a candidate. An *exclusive* candidate vote is one that benefits only the candidate for whom it is cast. Such a vote increases the vote total of the candidate for whom it is cast and never transfers to, or otherwise appears in, any other vote total that is used for purposes of seat allocation. Exclusive candidate votes are mostly a feature of first-past-the-post systems but also appear in the more proportional system known as the single nontransferable vote.

A *nonexclusive* candidate vote, in addition to appearing in the vote total of the candidate for whom it is cast, also affects other vote totals relevant to the allocation of legislative seats. There are three main types of nonexclusive vote in current use: votes that transfer to the vote total of another individual candidate (who may or may not be politically allied with the candidate originally receiving the vote); votes that transfer to the vote total of the party list to which the candidate originally voted for belongs; and votes that simultaneously affect the vote totals of candidates running for two or more different offices.

Nonexclusive candidate votes that transfer to the vote totals of other candidates are cast in Australia, Ireland, Malta, and Nepal (in the senate) under the name of the single transferable vote. The single transferable vote has also been used at the local level in the Anglo-American democracies, where it is frequently advocated as the method of choice in implementing the proportional representation ideal.

Nonexclusive candidate votes that transfer to *list* vote totals are cast in, for example, Belgium, Brazil, Chile, Denmark, Finland, Hungary, Liechtenstein, and Poland. These votes are called *pooling* votes (see box, "The Pooling Vote in Finland and Poland").

Nonexclusive candidate votes that transfer to vote totals relevant to other offices are known as *fused* votes. Fused votes appear in several Latin American countries that combine presidentialism with proportional representation in their legislative races. For example, in Uruguay, voters cast a single vote for a slate that includes a candidate for the presidency as well as candidates for the senate and the lower house. The Uruguayan fused vote simultaneously affects three separate vote totals: one relevant to determining who the president will be, one relevant to filling senate seats, and one relevant to

THE POOLING VOTE IN FINLAND AND POLAND

Voters in Finland and Poland cast their votes for individual candidates. Once cast, however, these votes can pool at two different levels. First, candidates join together in lists (known as "electoral alliances" in Finland). Seats are allocated to lists before they are allocated to candidates, on the basis of *list* vote totals arrived at by summing the votes of all candidates within the list. This is the first kind of pooling that can occur. In Poland, *apparentement* (or "blocking") of lists is allowed: lists can join together in cartels for the purpose of seat distributions. Seats are allocated to cartels before they are allocated to the lists within the cartel, on the basis of *cartel* vote totals arrived at by summing the votes of all lists within the cartel. Thus, in Poland, candidate votes can pool at two levels: within lists and within cartels. The closest approximation to the second kind of pooling in Finland does not entail further vote pooling in a strict sense. Finnish parties can run joint lists, with candidates from more than one party on the list. This has some of the same political consequences for small parties as does allowing *apparentement* in Poland.

filling lower house seats. Split-ticket voting, in the sense of supporting one party's presidential candidate while voting for another's congressional candidates, is not technically possible. Bolivia and Honduras also currently have fused votes, while Venezuela and the Dominican Republic have used such votes in the past.

Consider now the possibility that voters cast *multiple* candidate votes. Rules regulating how these votes can be cast arise under the headings of plumping, panachage, and cumulation. *Plumping* means voters need not use all of their votes; they can partially abstain. *Panachage* means voters need not vote for candidates of only a single party; they can split their votes. *Cumulation* means voters who cast M votes need not vote for M candidates: they can give more than one of their votes to a single candidate.

To illustrate these terms, suppose voters can cast as many votes as there are seats to be filled, with panachage, plumping, and cumulation allowed. Such a system was used in Illinois state legislative elections from 1870 until 1980 and is still used in Switzerland (where the candidate votes also pool to the list

level and voters have the shorthand option of casting a list vote as well). Alternatively, suppose voters can cast as many votes as there are seats to be filled, with plumping and panachage (but not cumulation) allowed. Such a system was used, for example, in U.K. parliamentary elections before the third Reform Act (1884), in many state elections in the nineteenth- and early twentieth-century United States, and in India from 1952 to 1957 (in about a third of the districts). Finally, suppose voters can cast as many votes as there are seats to be filled, with panachage (but neither plumping nor cumulation) allowed. This system has been employed in Mauritius since its independence in 1968. In principle, one could prohibit panachage in a system with multiple candidate votes (which would then make it similar to an open-list system), but in practice no country appears to do this.

The terms just reviewed are used similarly when speaking of list, rather than candidate, votes. Suppose, for example, that voters possess a single list vote. If this vote affects only the vote total of the list for which it is cast, then it is exclusive. If it affects other vote totals used in the allocation of seats, then it is nonexclusive. The only nonexclusive list vote in current use is of a pooling variety: the vote cast for list X may pool with the votes cast for other lists—Y and Z, say—that are allied with X in a cartel. Pooling list votes are used in Israel, the Netherlands, and Switzerland (where they pool across parties) and in Sweden and Uruguay (where they pool within parties). In addition, the candidate vote in Poland, as previously noted, pools not just to the list but also to the cartel level.

There currently are no systems that give voters multiple list votes. Such systems are theoretically possible and might provide slightly different ways of facilitating alliances between parties than is available through the techniques of joint lists and *apparentement,* but in practice no country appears to have explored such possibilities.

Having reviewed the technical possibilities in constructing ballots, one can ask how they affect the proportionality of a system. The proportionality of systems using a single list vote is greater when that vote is nonexclusive—that is, when the system allows *apparentement* of lists. A few rules of thumb can also be offered for systems that use candidate votes. Consider a multimember district in which the seats are awarded in order to the candidates winning the most votes. The least proportional ballot structure for this district would be one in which voters were each given as many votes as there were seats to be filled and prohibited from splitting or cumulating their votes. Under such a system, which would be similar to a list system operating under a winner-take-all rule, any party with majority support in the electorate could win all the seats. Although there are no systems that use this particular ballot scheme, there have been so-called bloc-vote systems, identical to that just described except that panachage is al-

PLUMPING AND PANACHAGE (SPLIT VOTING) IN NINETEENTH-CENTURY ENGLAND

Many English constituencies before passage of the third Reform Act in 1884 returned two members to the House of Commons. Each voter possessed two votes that he (the suffrage was restricted to men) could cast in any way he wished, short of cumulation. An example of the possibilities is given in the returns from the election of 1874 in Pontefract. Two Conservative candidates, Waterhouse and Pollington, faced a single Liberal, Childers. 699 voters plumped for Childers: that is, they gave one of their votes to Childers and abstained from using the other. Sixty voters plumped for Waterhouse, and 37 plumped for Pollington, indicating that some Conservative voters saw significant distinctions between the two Conservative candidates. Some 619 voters cast a partisan double vote: giving one vote to each of the two Conservative candidates. Another 235 voters took advantage of the possibility of panachage, or splitting their votes across party lines: 182 gave one vote to each of Childers and Waterhouse, while 53 gave one vote to each of Childers and Pollington. The Liberal Childers and the more moderate Conservative, Waterhouse, both won seats, Waterhouse benefiting in particular from the large number of split votes that the two shared.

lowed. These systems also make it possible for a party with majority support to win all the seats, although they must make sure that their supporters do not exercise their splitting option too much.

A more proportional ballot structure for a multimember district in which seats go to the top vote-getters could be arranged by either reducing the number of votes per voter (the limited vote) or allowing cumulation (the cumulative vote). The extreme case of the limited vote gives each citizen a single vote, yielding the so-called single-nontransferable-vote system. Under the single nontransferable vote, in an M-seat district, any group of citizens constituting more than $1/(M+1)$ of the voting population can guarantee themselves a seat. Thus, a bare majority cannot guarantee themselves all the seats (they can guarantee themselves at most half), and the

system thus qualifies as proportional by the definition given at the outset of this essay. Indeed, if the parties can marshal their supporters to the polls in a sufficiently disciplined fashion, the outcomes under the single nontransferable vote will be equivalent to those under the d'Hondt method of proportional representation.

DISTRICT STRUCTURE

Most countries conduct national legislative elections by carving their national territory into a number of geographically defined electoral districts (or constituencies); apportioning a certain number of seats to each district; and then holding separate elections in each district to fill the available seats. In these countries, the election of the legislature is decentralized in the sense that the votes cast and seats awarded in one district neither affect nor are affected by the votes cast and seats awarded in other districts. Other countries complicate the picture by lessening the independence of the districts in various ways: by requiring that votes "wasted" in one district cumulate to some "higher" district in the system, there potentially to fetch seats; by requiring that parties meet a certain vote threshold throughout the country before they are eligible to receive votes in any constituency; and in many other ways. In these more complex systems, the election cannot be neatly decentralized; who gets how many seats in a given district may depend on vote totals or seat allocations in other districts. Still other countries complicate the picture in another way, by apportioning seats not just to geographically defined groups of voters but also to non-geographically defined groups—for example, the long-standing Maori seats in New Zealand or the seats reserved for the Italian and Hungarian minorities in Slovenia.

This section considers the range of possible district structures that a proportional-representation system might employ, focusing on geographic districts. The district structure of an electoral system refers to the number, magnitude, and interrelationships of its electoral districts. The number of districts can range from one, in countries such as Israel and Namibia that elect from the nation at large, to several hundred, in countries such as the U.K. and France that use single-member districts. The magnitude of a district is the number of representatives it is entitled to elect. Some systems use districts that are all of the same or similar magnitude, while others mix small-magnitude and large-magnitude districts. Finally, the interrelationships of districts can be described by classifying districts as primary, secondary, or tertiary.

If a district cannot be partitioned into smaller districts within which votes are aggregated and seats allocated, it is called *primary*. Thus, for example, the 435 districts used in U.S. House elections are all primary. Although these districts are divided into smaller subdistricts for purposes of vote administration and counting (aggregation), no seats are attached to or allocated within the subdistricts—thus, they do not count as "electoral districts" as defined here. Systems possessing only primary electoral districts are typically called *single-tier.*

A secondary electoral district is one that can be partitioned into two or more primary electoral districts. Usually, seats are allocated first within primary districts, then—if any remain to be allocated—within secondary districts. An example is Belgium, where the primary districts *(arrondissements)* are grouped into secondary districts (provinces), with a second round of seat allocation at the provincial level. The initial allocation of seats occurs as follows. The total number of valid votes cast in an *arrondissement* is divided by the number of seats in the chamber to which the *arrondissement* is entitled, yielding the Hare quota. Each party then acquires as many seats as there are whole quotas contained in its vote. After this allocation, certain parties qualify for participation in the provincial allocation of seats (those garnering at least 66 percent of the quota in at least one *arrondissement* in the province and having formed in advance of the election a same-party, different-constituency cartel by formally affiliating the various *arrondissement* lists within the province). Each party's total vote in the province is divided by the number of seats it has won in the *arrondissement* allocations, plus one. The party with the largest quotient (the "highest average") wins the next available seat. Its quotient is then recalculated, and the d'Hondt allocation process continues until all seats are allocated. In the final stages of allocation, further electoral rules dictate how the seats won by the party at the provincial level should be distributed to its *arrondissement* lists, and thence to the candidates on those lists.

As the Belgian example suggests, primary and secondary electoral districts are hierarchically ordered—not just in the sense that secondary districts comprise several primary districts but also in the sense that votes or seats transfer from the primary to the secondary level for purposes of seat allocation. It is also possible for a system to have geographically overlapping districts that are not hierarchically ordered. In Ecuador the whole nation serves as a district for the election of *diputados nacionales,* while the provinces serve as districts for the election of *diputados provinciales.* But Ecuadorians have two votes, one for each kind of deputy, and there are no vote transfers between the provinces and the national district. Thus Ecuador has two different kinds of primary district, rather than a hierarchical structure of districts.

Even tertiary districts can exist. In Greece, for example, seat allocations are made to district-based deputies in three stages: in primary districts *(nomoi),* secondary districts ("major districts"), and a single tertiary district (the nation).

Tertiary districts, along with secondary districts, are sometimes called *upper tiers* in the literature. Systems possessing them are called *multitier* or are said to feature complex districting.

Having reviewed the technical possibilities in constructing districts, one can ask how they affect the proportionality of a system. The rules of thumb here are simple. First, increasing the magnitudes of the districts used in a system usually increases its proportionality. Second, adding upper tiers, especially if a significant share of the total seats are allocated in those upper tiers, also usually increases its proportionality. The reason that these techniques are qualified as "usually" increasing proportionality is simply that their effectiveness depends on other features of the electoral system. In particular, if a system uses nothing but winner-take-all formulas, then increasing the district magnitudes or adding upper tiers will decrease proportionality rather than increase it. Few systems, however, combine winner-take-all formulas with larger magnitudes or upper tiers, so the effect is usually to boost proportionality.

FORMULAIC STRUCTURE

Once one understands the ballot and district structures of an electoral system, one knows how voters vote and in which districts their votes are aggregated into seat-relevant totals. The next step is translating these vote totals into seat allocations. This votes-to-seats translation is the domain of electoral formulas. In simple systems, such as that of the United States, just one electoral formula is in operation. Many systems, however, employ more than one electoral formula. Brazil, for example, uses two. One electoral formula (d'Hondt) converts list-vote totals into an allocation of seats among lists. Another formula (plurality rule) converts the votes cast for candidates on a given list into an allocation of the list's seats (awarded in the first stage) among its candidates.

In order to trace the votes-to-seats translation in complex systems to its final outcome—an allocation of seats among candidates—one must navigate through an entire subsystem of electoral formulas: the formulaic structure. The basic elements of the formulaic structure are the electoral formulas themselves, where an "electoral formula" is a method for translating vote totals into an allocation of seats. These formulas can be classified in terms of *to whom or what* they award seats (candidates, lists, or cartels) and in terms of *where* they award seats (in primary, secondary, or tertiary districts).

Formulas for candidates, lists, and cartels. Mathematically, an electoral formula is just a function that takes various vote totals as input and produces a distribution of seats as output. In terms of input vote totals and output seat allocations, there are three basic kinds of formulas: those that take candidate vote totals as inputs and produce allocations of seats among candidates as outputs (candidate formulas); those that take list vote totals as inputs and produce allocations of seats among lists as outputs (list formulas); and those that take cartel vote totals as inputs and produce allocations of seats among cartels as outputs (cartel formulas).

In addition to electoral formulas (functions mapping votes into seats), some electoral systems also employ other rules in allocating seats. For example, in closed-list systems, if a list wins N seats, then the first N candidates on the list are awarded seats. These rules, too, are elements of the formulaic structure.

There is a definite sequence in which cartel formulas, list formulas, candidate formulas, and other rules for seat allocation are used. Seats are always allocated first to cartels (if any), then to lists (if any), and finally to candidates.

In some systems, of course, there are neither cartels nor lists. This is the case in Taiwan and Australia, for example, and in both countries there is only one kind of seat allocation—directly to candidates.

In other systems, lists but not cartels exist as entities to which intermediate seat allocations can be made. Usually, this means that voters can vote directly for lists, but this is not always the case (for example, Poland). When intermediate seat allocations are made to lists, the question arises as to how the list's seats are to be allocated among the candidates on the list. One method is to have the party establish the order of candidates on the list, with the first candidate on the list getting the first seat to which the party is entitled, the second on the list getting the second seat, and so on. This is the *closed*-list system (used, for example, in Spain's lower house). Another method is to let the party's voters decide which of its candidates will win the seats allocated to the party's list. This is the *open*-list system (used, for example, in Finland). Finally, there are also intermediate methods, which give both party leaders and voters some say in the allocation of a list's seats among its candidates. These are the *flexible*-list systems (used, for example, in Greece). A necessary condition for voters to have any influence on list allocations, of course, is that they have the ability to vote for individual candidates (possibly in addition to the ability to vote for lists). Candidate votes that influence seat allocations among the members of a given list are generally referred to as *preference votes*.

In yet other systems, intermediate seat allocations are made both to lists and to cartels. A cartel is a group of lists that are legally allied for purposes of seat allocation. The cartel vote is determined by summing the votes of all lists participating in the cartel. The initial allocation of seats is to the cartel, based on the cartel vote (although at this same stage, allocations to unallied parties, if any, will also be made). The cartel's seats are then allocated among its component lists in proportion to the various lists' vote shares. In practice, citizens

vote only for lists, not for cartels. Thus, there are no closed or flexible cartels; they are all open.

Sweden from 1911 to 1952 is an example of a polity in which *apparentement*—that is, the formation of list cartels—was legal. On the ballot, both the name of the party and the name of the cartel to which it belonged (if any) would appear. *Apparentement* was important in that it allowed the nonsocialist parties to overcome the underrepresentation of small parties that was built into the method of proportional representation used in Sweden at that time, without going through the difficulties of an actual merger.

In the example just given, the cartels were composed of lists from different parties but the same constituency. Two other possibilities—*apparentement* between lists from the same party and constituency, and between lists from the same party but different constituencies—have also arisen in practice.

Sweden's contemporary electoral system provides an example of the first possibility: Swedish law allows multiple lists with the same party label in a given constituency, the votes for all these lists being summed for purposes of the initial seat allocation to parties. Which candidates from which lists secure the seats allocated to the party is determined by the number of votes cast for the various lists within the party.

Belgium provides an example of *apparentement* of lists from the same party but different constituencies. Parties must formally affiliate their various *arrondissement* lists within each province if they wish to participate in the provincial seat distribution. This creates a cartel of same-party, different-constituency lists. Allocation of the seats awarded to the provincial cartel among the cartel's component *arrondissement* lists is by d'Hondt.

Locating formulas in the district structure. The various electoral formulas and other rules used to allocate seats in a proportional-representation system can also differ in terms of the type of district within which they are used: primary, secondary, or tertiary. Usually, there is a sequence of allocations, starting in the primary districts and proceeding to the secondary and tertiary districts (if there are any). Cross-tabulating the sequence of allocations in primary, secondary, and tertiary districts with the sequence of allocations to cartels, lists, and candidates produces a table or matrix within which each of the separate acts of seat allocation in an electoral system can be located. Before looking at how this cross-tabulation works, consider the formulas themselves.

Proportional-representation formulas. Proportional-representation formulas are traditionally divided into two chief families, one based on quotas and largest remainders, one based on divisors and largest averages. The first kind of proportional-representation formula operates as follows. An electoral quota, Q, is established and each list first receives as many seats as there are whole quotas contained in its vote total. Any remaining seats are then allocated, in order, to the parties with the largest remainders, where a party's remainder equals its vote total less the product of the number of quota seats it won in the first round of allocations and the quota Q. One can think of Q as the "price" of a seat, denominated in votes. If a party wins 5 seats, it must "pay" 5Q to acquire them, leaving it with a remainder of v-5Q (where v is the party's total vote).

The electoral quota can be calculated in a number of different ways, usually dependent on the district magnitude, M, and the total number of valid votes cast, V. Common quotas include the Hare (or simple) quota,

$$Q_{Hare} = V/M;$$

the Droop quota,

$$Q_{Droop} = 1 + \text{the greatest integer} \\ \text{less than or equal to } V/(M+1),$$

and the Hagenbach-Bischoff quota,

$$Q_{HB} = V/(M+1)$$

Note that with any quota less than or equal to $V/(M+1)$ it is theoretically possible for each of M+1 parties to amass a quota, hence to allocate more seats than are available in the district. In practice, therefore, quotas at or below the Hagenbach-Bischoff level need auxiliary rules to decide how seats are to be allocated, in case more lists garner quotas than can be given seats.

If seats remain unallocated after each list gets its "quota seats," then the remaining seats are distributed in order to the lists with the largest remainders. Thus, the first unallocated seat goes to the list with the largest remainder, the second unallocated seat goes to the list with the second-largest remainder, and so on until all seats are allocated.

The second main family of proportional-representation methods, known as divisor systems, involves calculating "averages" that reflect how much each party has paid in votes for its seats. Each method establishes a sequence of divisors. To begin with, all parties' vote totals are divided by the first divisor in the sequence, with the party owning the highest average thus produced winning the first seat. The winning party's vote total is then divided by the second divisor in the sequence to produce a new average for it. The second seat is awarded to the party that now owns the highest average, and so on iteratively until all the seats are allocated. A frequently used divisor method was invented by Viktor d'Hondt and uses the sequence of numbers 1, 2, 3, and so on as the divisors. Thus, at any given stage a party's average is $A = V/(S + 1)$, where V is the party's vote total and S is the number of seats already awarded to the party. Other divisor or highest-average methods are reviewed in the article on quotas.

In addition to these two traditional families of proportional-representation formulas, both applicable in systems that allow citizens to cast a single list vote or a single pooling vote, one must also consider a formula operating in systems that give citizens one or more nonpooling candidate votes. The typical rule used in such systems is that the top M vote-getters in an M-seat district win the seats. This rule is often called "plurality rule," because when M = 1 it reduces to what we ordinarily call plurality rule. But whereas plurality rule in a single-member district is a winner-take-all system and clearly fails the minimal standard for a proportional-representation system (that it not be possible for a party with a bare majority of votes to guarantee itself all the seats), plurality rule in multimember districts—as used for example with a single nontransferable vote (Taiwan)—clearly meets this standard. Whether the rule "award the seats in an M-seat district to the M candidates with the most votes" is called plurality or not, it can form part of a proportional system when combined with multimember districts (and certain ballot structures), and so ought to be included under the heading of proportional-representation formulas. That this rule produces a winner-take-all outcome when M = 1 is not a decisive objection, since the same is true of all the list proportional representation formulas mentioned above as well. This essay shall continue to use the term *plurality rule* for the first-M-past-the-post rule, reserving the term "winner-take-all" for formulas that award all the seats to the largest single vote-getting candidate or list.

Thresholds and bonus seats. Another important wrinkle in discussing electoral formulas concerns the existence of thresholds and bonus seats. Pure electoral formulas can be hedged by various thresholds that a candidate or list must satisfy before being eligible to receive any seats. Such thresholds are part of the mathematical translation process that converts votes into seats, and thus properly are a part of the electoral formula as defined here.

Thresholds can be defined at the level of the primary, secondary, or tertiary district. Examples of the first are as follows:

- Argentina: Only lists whose vote exceeds 3 percent of the registered electorate in the district can receive seats

- Israel: Only lists whose vote exceeds 1.5 percent of the vote in the district (which in this case coincides with the nation) are eligible to receive seats (the 1.5 percent threshold came in with the June 1992 election, replacing the older 1 percent threshold)

- Japan: Only candidates whose vote exceeds one-fourth of the Hare quota are eligible to receive a seat

- Lithuania: In the first round of a dual-ballot contest (in single-member districts), only candidates whose vote exceeds 50 percent of the total vote are eligible to receive a seat, and then only if turnout in the district exceeds 40 percent of the registered electorate

Examples of thresholds that operate at the level of the secondary electoral district are:

- Austria: Only lists associated with parties that have won at least one seat in a primary district contained in the secondary district are eligible to receive a seat

- Belgium: Only partisan cartels associated with parties that have won at least 0.66 of a Hare quota in at least one of the primary districts within the secondary district are eligible to receive seats

- Germany 1949: Only lists associated with parties that either had won at least one seat in a primary district contained in the secondary district or had won at least 5 percent of the total vote in the secondary district were eligible to receive seats

- Greece 1974–1981: Only lists associated with parties that had won at least 17 percent of the national vote, or two-party joint lists whose component parties had won at least 25 percent of the national vote, or multiparty joint lists whose component parties had won at least 30 percent of the national vote were eligible to receive seats

It is conceptually possible, of course, to have threshold requirements both at the primary- and at the secondary-district level. An example is Iceland, where a party must win at least ⅔ of a Hare quota to win seats in a district, and must win at least one constituency seat in order to be eligible for the national distribution of seats.

Whenever there are threshold requirements that some parties fail to meet, the rest of the parties will divide 100 percent of the seats based on less than 100 percent of the total votes. The qualifying parties may divide the resulting "surplus" seats more or less proportionally, or the surplus may be used to create bonus seats for some parties (typically the largest). Even without threshold requirements, a polity may see fit to create bonus seats.

Three countries where bonus seats are in use are South Korea, Malta, and Turkey. In South Korea, if the party winning the most seats in the primary electoral districts does not win a majority of such seats, then it is given a bare majority of seventy-five nationally allocated seats (which can in principle be well above what its proportionate share would have been). In Malta, if a party wins a majority of first-preference

votes but fails to win a majority of seats in the legislature, then it is given a sufficient number of adjustment seats to ensure it a parliamentary majority. In Turkey, the largest party in districts returning five or more members is entitled to a bonus seat, with the remaining seats distributed among all parties in proportion to their votes (by the d'Hondt method).

Formulas and proportionality. In order to construct a system in which it is not possible for a party with a bare majority of support in a given district to guarantee itself all the seats—that is, in order to construct a proportional-representation system as here defined—what sort of formulaic structure is needed? The answer depends not just on the formulas but also on the ballots and districts, but here one can take the existence of multimember districts for granted and concentrate on the formulas. If the system employs only candidate formulas, then it is sufficient that plurality rule be combined with a limited or cumulative vote in order to produce proportionality. If the system has both candidate and list formulas, then it is sufficient that the list formulas be proportional. Finally, if the system uses candidate, list, and cartel formulas, then it is sufficient that the cartel formulas be proportional. If the cartel formula is proportional, then even if the list formulas used to reallocate each cartel's seats to its constituent lists were winner-take-all (which they never are in practice), it will not be possible for a bare majority of votes to guarantee all the seats.

SOME EXAMPLES

The previous sections have described the ballots, districts, and formulas that together make up proportional-representation electoral systems in the abstract. This section provides a few examples of concrete systems illustrating the abstract possibilities.

Consider a simple system first. In Spain, the Congress of Deputies is elected as follows. Each voter can cast a single list vote (with no option to cast candidate votes). Deputies are elected from fifty-two separate primary districts, ranging in magnitude from one to thirty-three, with no upper tiers. The formula used in each district is the d'Hondt divisor formula, subject to a 3 percent threshold. Seats awarded to each list are reallocated to the candidates on those lists in accordance with the order of their names on the list. In this system, there are only two stages at which seat allocations are made (first to lists, then to candidates), both occurring in the primary districts of the system.

Consider next a somewhat more complicated system. In South Korea, each voter can cast a single candidate vote. Deputies are elected from 224 single-member districts by plurality rule. In addition, 75 seats are awarded in a national secondary district, as follows. If no party wins a majority of the 224 district seats, then the largest party gets a bare majority (38) of the national seats, the rest being distributed proportionally to district seats won (subject to a 5-seat threshold). If there is a party with a majority of the 224 district seats, then each party gets a share of the national seats proportionate to the share of district seats that it has won. Finally, seats allocated to national lists are reallocated to the candidates on those lists by list order. All told, the South Korean system has three stages at which seats are allocated, one occurring in the primary districts and two in the single secondary district.

Consider, finally, an even more complicated system: Belgium. In working through fairly complicated systems such as Belgium's, it is useful to employ a table or matrix, the rows of which are defined by the various entities to which seat allocations are made (partisan cartels, lists, joint lists, independent candidates, and so on), and the columns of which are defined by the electoral district within which the allocation is made (primary, secondary, tertiary). The i–j cell in this formulaic matrix, corresponding to the intersection of the i–th row (or entity) and j–th column (or level), provides a description of the formula or other rule governing the allocation of seats to the i–th entity at the j–th level.

As can be seen from the row and column headings of the matrix in Figure 1, seat allocations in Belgium are made to three different kinds of entity (candidates, lists, and partisan cartels) at two different levels (*arrondissements* and provinces). As can be seen from the cells within the matrix, allocations are not made in every possible cell. Partisan cartels, for example, are not awarded seats at the *arrondissement* level; they take receipt of seats only at the provincial level. Turning now to the nonempty cells, the numerals in parentheses indicate the sequence of seat allocations. The first allocation of seats is to lists within primary districts—and thus corresponds to

the cell at the intersection of the "lists" row and the "primary districts" column. The second allocation of seats is to partisan cartels at the provincial level. The third allocation of seats is to *arrondissement* lists at the provincial level (corresponding, as explained in the cell, to the reallocation to the cartel's component *arrondissement* lists of the seats awarded in step 2 to each partisan cartel). Finally, the fourth step is the reallocation of seats won by lists in steps 1 and 3 to the candidates on those lists. Each step has its own formula or rule of allocation.

Proportionality of results. An idealized proportional-representation system allocates seats in exact proportion to votes. In order for a real-world system to approximate this ideal, however, two things are necessary. First, constitutional designers of the system must want to achieve a proportional outcome. Second, they must ensure that the full range of features in the system—from ballot structure to district structure and formulaic structure—work together to produce that end. In particular, it is crucial that both the district and formulaic structures facilitate proportionality. To see this, consider a pair of examples. In example 1, party A is given the right to choose the ballot and district structures of a polity, but party B gets to choose the formulaic structure. If party A wished to create a proportional system, it could choose a closed-list system of voting with each district returning, say, one hundred members. But party B could thwart this design by choosing a winner-take-all formula (the list with the most votes wins all the seats). In example 2, party A chooses the ballots and formulas, while B chooses the districts. If A seeks to create a proportional system by combining a closed-list system of vot-

Figure 1. A Formulaic Matrix for Belgium

	Primary districts *(arrondissements)*	Secondary districts (provinces)
Partisan cartels	—	(2) Seats unallocated in step 1 are aggregated within each province and distributed by proportional representation—using the d'Hondt method. A cartel must obtain 66 percent of a Hare quota in one of the *arrondissements* contained in the province and must also have formally affiliated its various *arrondissement* lists in the province in order to participate in the secondary seat allocation.
Lists	(1) Each list receives as many seats as its vote contains full Hare quotas.	(3) Seats awarded to partisan cartels in step 2 are reallocated to each cartel's component *arrondissement* lists by proportional representation—using the d'Hondt method.
Candidates	(4) Seats awarded to lists in steps 1 and 3 are reallocated to each list's candidates, by a transferable vote system that puts most of the emphasis on list order.	

ing with (say) the d'Hondt proportional-representation formula, B can counter by choosing single-member districts.

The proportionality of a system depends jointly on the formulas and the districts. It is not really meaningful to classify electoral systems as winner-take-all or proportional representation solely on the basis of the formula, as is sometimes done. One must combine a proportional formula with large district magnitudes (or important upper tiers) to attain high levels of proportionality. And one can force a winner-take-all system by choosing either single-member districts or a winner-take-all formula.

Given the diversity of constitutional designers' goals around the world and the potential sensitivity of an electoral system's proportionality to a combination of factors—thresholds, bonus seats, formulas, district magnitudes, upper tiers, and so on—the question arises as to how proportional real-world systems are in practice. In order to answer this question, one needs to *measure* proportionality.

A number of methods have been proposed for doing this, all based on the observed discrepancies between the vote shares and seat shares earned by parties, variously weighted and counted. Without going into the details of these different methods (on which see the article "Proportionality and Disproportionality"), one can note that in practice systems that are more disproportional (by any measure) are also those in which the largest parties in terms of vote share are more heavily overrepresented. Thus, although the measures themselves are not designed explicitly to measure how overrepresented the larger parties are, practically speaking that is what they do.

Other consequences of proportional representation. While increasing district magnitude, allowing cumulative voting, or otherwise tinkering with electoral law can in certain circumstances increase the proportionality of a system, changes toward (or away from) the proportional-representation ideal can also affect other important aspects of political performance. Students of elections have in particular stressed three sorts of consequences that a move toward proportional representation (away from winner-take-all) can have: first, it can increase the number of parties operating in the system, thus producing multiparty coalition governments as the typical executive arrangement, as opposed to single-party majority governments; second, it can increase the dispersion of parties across the ideological spectrum, as more parties seek out an electoral niche, again with possible consequences for government formation; third, it can increase the rate of turnout in elections, because parties have more consistent incentives to mobilize their supporters in multimember proportional-representation districts (in which the last-allocated seat is typically up for grabs) than in single-member plurality districts (in which the outcome may be foregone).

Arguments pro and con. Debate over the relative merits of single-member plurality and proportional representation has flowed and ebbed for over a century. Much of the time, participants in this debate seem to talk past one another, but there are some points of agreement, too. This section first reviews some areas where the debate quickly reaches differences of interpretation that have not been resolved; then considers an area where points are conceded; and finally turns to a relatively neglected but important point having to do with the structure of governance with which a single-member plurality or proportional-representation electoral system is combined.

Unresolved differences. Some examples of unresolved differences can be seen in the opposing interpretations that proponents of single-member plurality and proportional representation put on four central distinctions between these two electoral systems. The differences of opinion arise not because the "facts" are in dispute but because each side evaluates the same facts differently.

For example, there is broad agreement that single-member plurality is associated with bipartism, while proportional representation is associated with multipartism. Proponents of single-member plurality emphasize that two-party systems give rise to stable single-party governments that can be held clearly accountable at the next election for government policy, whereas multiparty systems give rise to unstable multiparty governments in which it is not clear whom to blame or credit. Proponents of proportional representation, in contrast, emphasize that the single-party governments of single-member plurality are artificially manufactured by the electoral system and that the two major parties often conspire to exclude further competitors from entering the fray, producing a two-party "monopoly" over politics. Proportional representation, they argue, produces real competition between parties and real governing majorities—constructed through the hard work of compromise rather than by the automatic overrepresentation of large parties under single-member plurality.

To take a second example, there is broad agreement that the (typically two) candidates competing under single-member plurality face strong electoral incentives to adopt centrist positions, while the (typically many) candidates or lists competing under proportional representation face incentives to disperse across the ideological spectrum in their country. Proponents of single-member plurality interpret the centrist incentives of single-member plurality as producing candidates who make broad, inclusive, and moderate appeals, while arguing that the dispersive incentives of proportional representation will produce candidates who pander to extremists and special interests. Proponents of proportional representation, in contrast, interpret the centrist incentives of single-member plurality as leading to a "no choice" election for voters (between Tweedledee and Tweedledum), while arguing that the dispersive incentives of proportional representation lead to elections with real choices in which varieties of opinion can be articulated clearly and approved or disapproved at the polls.

To take a third example, there is broad agreement that turnout is higher under proportional representation than single-member plurality. But there is no agreement over whether higher rates of turnout are good. Proponents of single-member plurality tend to argue that they are not (or at least that they are not worth sacrificing the other benefits of single-member plurality), while proponents of proportional representation put greater stock in high turnout.

As a final example, everyone agrees that some voters will cast votes for candidates or lists who do not win seats under either single-member plurality or proportional representation, but that this is much more frequent under single-member plurality. Proponents of single-member plurality tend to view voting for a loser as a bit of bad luck, compensated by the fact that a voter's party will win elsewhere, so that his or her views will still be represented in the legislature. Proponents of proportional representation call votes cast for losing candidates wasted votes and typically reject any notion of "virtual representation" by legislators from other districts.

Although each of the four arguments reviewed above has been developed further than can be indicated here, it is fair to say that they are all unresolved in the following sense: none of them have been framed in terms of values that all parties to the debate hold. No one has been able to state a few simple normative precepts and argue from them to the superiority of one or the other system. Instead, each side invokes a fair number of competing normative judgments pitched at a fairly high level of specificity.

Point conceded: Engineering wasted votes through gerrymandering. Perhaps the only point that is generally evaluated in the same way by both sides concerns gerrymandering. Gerrymandering, which entails the redrawing of district lines by one party in order to maximize the number of wasted votes of others, is an endemic feature of some single-member plurality systems (particularly those in the United States). No one argues in favor of partisan gerrymandering. Everyone agrees that it would be nice to get rid of it. And everyone agrees that proportional-representation systems are substantially less prone to this sort of manipulation. Thus, there is at least one argument that holds sway across the debate—but proponents of single-member plurality are not willing to give up what they see as the benefits of single-member plurality or incur what they see as the costs of proportional representation in order to eradicate gerrymandering.

Point conceded: Minority representation. Another point on which the opponents agree upon the facts concerns the representation of women and minorities. Various studies show that more proportional systems do tend to elect more women and more minorities (whether ethnic, linguistic, or religious) as representatives. Proponents of proportional representation typically put a high value on this ability of more proportional systems to produce a legislature that better mirrors the composition of the electorate, arguing that it enhances regime legitimacy and citizen satisfaction with democratic governance. Proponents of single-member plurality are more likely to put relatively little value on "descriptive representation," arguing instead in favor of the representation of ideas or values (and defending the notion that such representation is, at least in principle, disconnected from the identity of representatives).

The neglected interaction between electoral rules and governmental structure. One point relevant to the debate between single-member plurality and proportional representation that has rarely been stressed is that one's view on the matter should depend on whether the government is presidential or parliamentary. In particular, in presidential regimes there is reason to limit the move to proportional representation. The argument goes as follows: first, proportional representation tends to promote multipartism; second, multiparty presidential regimes have in practice performed poorly.

That multiparty presidential regimes have performed poorly is evident from the Latin American record. Chile (1932–1973) is the only case of a multiparty presidential system lasting more than a quarter century. All the other examples of long-lived presidential democracy—Colombia, Costa Rica, pre-1973 Uruguay, Venezuela, and the United States—come from two-party systems. The gist of the problem with multiparty presidential regimes is that they have typically operated under divided government, the president lacking a workable legislative majority. This has led to a syndrome of bargaining failures with bad systemic consequences.

Given the record of multiparty presidentialism, it seems prudent to choose a moderate form of proportional representation, one that will not produce many parties. There are a variety of techniques that might be employed to moderate the influence of proportional representation—including fused votes, concurrent elections, and small-magnitude legislative districts.

A FINAL COMMENT

The potential proportionality of an electoral system can be affected by changing any of an array of electoral rules governing the ballots, districts, and formulas used in the system. At the same time, it is important to remember that the actual proportionality of a system depends not just on the rules but also on the actions that politicians and voters take under and in light of those rules. Thus, for example, the Chilean electoral system imposed by Augusto Pinochet (and first used in 1989) would have produced markedly more disproportional results had the Chilean parties not responded swiftly to the incentives the system put in train to form coalitions. More generally, the outcomes of elections—whether described in terms of proportionality or other normative or performance criteria—generically depend on a similar mix of rules and political behavior in light of the rules. Much of the difficulty in coming to closure on the normative debate over proportional representation stems from the difficulty of forecasting the responses of politicians and voters, and hence outcomes, based solely on knowledge of the varying rules.

See also *Additional Member System; Apparentement; Bonus Seats; Compensatory Seats; Coordination, Electoral; Cumulative Voting; District Magnitude; Duverger's Law; Limited Vote; List; Pooling Votes; Preference Voting; Proportionality and Disproportionality; Quotas and Divisors; Single Nontransferable Vote; Single Transferable Vote.*

GARY W. COX, UNIVERSITY OF CALIFORNIA, SAN DIEGO

BIBLIOGRAPHY

Cox, Gary W. *Making Votes Count.* Cambridge: Cambridge University Press, 1997.

Duverger, Maurice. *Political Parties.* New York: Wiley, 1954.

Katz, Richard. "Intraparty Preference Voting." In *Electoral Laws and Their Political Consequences,* edited by Bernard Grofman and Arend Lijphart. New York: Agathon, 1986.

Lakeman, Enid. *How Democracies Vote.* London: Faber and Faber, 1970.

Lijphart, Arend. *Electoral Systems and Party Systems: A Study of Twenty-Seven Democracies, 1945–1990.* Oxford: Oxford University Press, 1994.

Nohlen, Dieter. *Sistemas Electorales Del Mundo.* Translated by Ramon Garcia Cotarelo. Madrid: Centro de Estudios Constitucionales, 1981.

Rae, Douglas. *The Political Consequences of Electoral Laws.* Rev. ed. New Haven, Conn.: Yale University Press, 1971.

Reed, Steven R. "Structure and Behaviour: Extending Duverger's Law to the Japanese Case." *British Journal of Political Science* 29 (1991): 335–356.

Riker, William H. "The Two-Party System and Duverger's Law: An Essay on the History of Political Science." *American Political Science Review* 76 (1982): 753–766.

Sartori, Giovanni. *Parties and Party Systems: A Framework for Analysis.* Cambridge: Cambridge University Press, 1976.

Taagepera, Rein, and Matthew Soberg Shugart. *Seats and Votes: The Effects and Determinants of Electoral Systems.* New Haven, Conn.: Yale University Press, 1989.

PROPORTIONALITY AND DISPROPORTIONALITY

Many elections are conducted under one or another variant of proportional representation, a principle according to which parties receive more or less the same share of the seats as they win of the votes; if a party wins 20 percent of the votes, then, under a proportional-representation system, it should receive close to 20 percent of the seats. Indeed, in a completely proportional outcome, every party wins exactly its "fair share" of the seats, a situation referred to as full proportionality. In practice, though, this never happens. For a variety of reasons some parties receive more than their fair share, while others receive less. The discrepancy between the parties' vote shares and seat shares is referred to as disproportionality. The same issues arise in the United States, although here proportional representation is employed not to award seats to parties but to apportion representatives among the states.

It is worth entering the caveat that virtually all attempts to measure the degree of proportionality produced by an election compare parties' shares of the votes with their shares of the seats, even though a party's share of the votes is an imperfect measure of its "true" support. For one thing, some voters may cast their vote for one of a party's candidates on personal grounds and may not regard their vote as support for the party per se. For another, a party that receives 30 percent of the votes but is hated by the other 70 percent of voters is, in reality, less popular than one that receives 30 percent of the votes and is the second choice of the other 70 percent of voters, yet most measures of disproportionality treat these parties as having equal support. Some electoral systems, such as the single transferable vote and the Borda system, allow voters to rank order candidates or parties, but most do not. A further note of caution is that some electoral systems give voters an incentive not to vote for the party they most strongly support; for example, when single-member constituencies are used, the fear of wasting a vote by casting it for a doomed third-party candidate will lead some electors to vote instead for whichever major-party candidate they dislike less. The result might be a close correspondence between parties' vote shares and seat shares, but this proportionality will be somewhat artificial, since vote shares are an inaccurate measure of genuine support. In this article we shall make the simplifying assumption that the share of votes won by a party adequately measures its support, while acknowledging that the real world is not so simple.

MEASURING DISPROPORTIONALITY

Every competitive election produces some disproportionality. The question that arises, then, is: given two election outcomes, each of which is somewhat disproportional, how do we decide which one is the more disproportional? Clearly, some measure of disproportionality is needed, and it is here that complications arise. The problem is not that a suitable measure has not been devised—far from it. There are many measures of disproportionality in use in political science, each with its own logic, and these measures are but a small set of a much larger set of approaches employed in other disciplines, for example by economists to measure the inequality of a given distribution of income. There is no universal consensus as to which measure should be preferred, although some have advantages over others.

Disproportionality can be conceived of in many different ways, and for each way, a method of proportional representation exists to minimize disproportionality so defined. We might conceive of disproportionality as the degree of over-representation of the most over-represented party; the d'Hondt method of proportional representation, known in the United States as the Jefferson method, minimizes disproportionality thus defined. Alternatively, we could conceive of the minimization of disproportionality as minimizing the under-representation of the most under-represented party; the method of smallest divisors, also known as the Adams method, is the most proportional according to this perspective. The aim might be to try to ensure that the number of votes that every party has to "pay" for each of its seats is as equal as possible, which is the rationale behind the "equal proportions" method used to apportion representatives to states in the United States. Or we might wish to ensure that all voters' shares of a member of parliament are as equal as possible, the thinking behind the Sainte-Laguë method (known in the United States as the Webster method). Needless to say, the meaning of "as equal as possible" is itself subject to argument. There are many other ways of looking at disproportionality and at what a proportional-representation system should try to do. The result is that there are many methods of proportional representation, each of which maximizes proportionality according to its own conception of proportionality, and each of which therefore generates a measure (or sometimes several measures) of disproportionality, which we can employ to determine which of two election outcomes is the more proportional.

Compared with the highly sophisticated and mathematically complex indices employed by economists to measure income inequality, the indices used by political scientists to measure disproportionality are rudimentary. This does not reflect simply a lower degree of mathematical sophistication; it springs also from the belief that among the desirable properties of any index of disproportionality are that its result is easy to interpret and that it is reasonably simple to compute. In addition, the number of cases is far smaller; few elections are contested by as many as twenty parties, whereas the units in a measurement of income inequality may run into millions.

Accordingly, the two most widely used measures of the disproportionality generated by elections are straightforward. The Loosemore-Hanby measure sums the differences between vote share and seat share for each party, and divides this by two. The least squares measure squares the vote–seat difference for each party, sums these values, divides the result by two, and takes the square root of this value. Compared with the Loosemore-Hanby measure, the least squares is slightly more complicated to compute but has the advantage that it registers a few large vote–seat differences more strongly than a lot of small vote–seat differences. In addition, it satisfies Dalton's

principle of transfers, which states that if a seat is transferred from an over-represented party to a party that is less over-represented, without thereby making the party receiving the seat more over-represented than the party from which the seat is transferred, a satisfactory measure of disproportionality should record that the amount of disproportionality has declined. Both measures have the attraction that they run from 0 (perfect proportionality) to 100 (complete disproportionality).

These measures can be illustrated by a simple example. Take two cases, where four parties win vote shares of 40, 20, 20, and 20, as shown in Table 1. In election 1, party A is over-represented by 10 percentage points, while D is under-represented by the same amount; in election 2, parties A and B are over-represented by 6 percentage points, while C and D are under-represented by the same amount. The indices differ in their assessment of the proportionality of the outcome; according to the Loosemore-Hanby measure, election 1 is "fairer," while according to the least squares measure, election 2 produces less disproportionality, because the least squares index registers two large vote–seat differences more than it registers four moderate differences. This example makes it clear that these two widely used indices are by no means identical, yet it is true to say that these indices, and most of the rest, are strongly correlated with one another; an outcome rated highly disproportional by one index will be rated as highly disproportional by all the other indices as well, and the differences between them could be seen as mainly a matter of nuance. Whether such nuances are important depends on the uses being made of the indices.

INFLUENCES ON DISPROPORTIONALITY

However disproportionality is measured, certain factors will work to increase or decrease it. Three in particular stand out: district magnitude, thresholds, and electoral formula.

District magnitude refers to the number of representatives elected from a district, or constituency. One very robust finding from a wealth of research is that under any system of proportional representation, the greater the district magnitude, the higher the degree of proportionality. The reason is not hard to

Table 1. Measures of Disproportionality Applied to Two Election Outcomes

	Election 1		Election 2	
	% votes	% seats	% votes	% seats
A	40	50	40	46
B	20	20	20	26
C	20	20	20	14
D	20	10	20	14

Disproportionality according to two indices:
Loosemore-Hanby: Election 1, 10 percent; Election 2, 12 percent.
Least squares: Election 1, 10 percent; Election 2, 8.5 percent.

see. With more seats to share, the discrepancies between vote shares and seat shares become smaller. For example, given the configuration in Table 1, where four parties divide the votes 40-20-20-20, in a district with five seats it would be possible to give every party exactly its fair share, by allocating the seats 2-1-1-1. With more than five seats, it will not always be possible to give the parties exactly their fair shares, but there will be no great disparities. With fewer than five seats, in contrast, it is impossible to avoid such disparities. In the worst case, there is only one seat to be allocated, party A will take it, and the outcome is a good deal of disproportionality: a party with 40 percent of the votes has won 100 percent of the seats, and three parties with 60 percent of the votes between them have received 0 percent of the seats. If this result were replicated nationwide, the parliament elected would not accurately reflect the wishes of the voters. Even though in practice some of the disproportionalities from individual constituencies are likely to even themselves out across the country, the national outcome is likely to be quite disproportional. Empirically, the amount of disproportionality tends to be highest in countries that use single-member constituencies and lowest where parliament is elected under proportional representation using large districts (such as Denmark and the Netherlands).

Thus, if a state holds elections for, say, a two-hundred-member parliament, disproportionality is likely to be lowest if the entire country is treated as one two-hundred-member district, and highest if it is divided into two hundred single-member districts. If it is divided into forty five-member districts, the outcome will be much more proportional than if it is divided into two hundred single-member districts. Proportionality increases as average district magnitude increases, with the rate of increase being greatest at the lower end of the scale; an increase in average district magnitude from one to five will have more impact than an increase from eleven to fifteen. It should be noted that this "law" works only in the case of proportional-representation elections; when an election is conducted under non–proportional representation rules, such as the block vote or at-large elections, large district magnitude actually makes the result even more disproportional than when single-member districts are used.

A second factor affecting the degree of disproportionality is the use of thresholds. In many countries that use proportional representation, parties do not qualify for any seats unless they exceed a certain level of voting support. The rationale for thresholds is that they prevent an excessively fragmented parliament, and, by encouraging small parties to merge, help bring about a stable party system.

A third influence is the electoral formula. The different methods of achieving proportional representation all, as noted above, aim to maximize proportionality, according to their own definition of proportionality. However, we are not forced to the relativist conclusion that all formulae must thus be judged equally proportional. In any one election, it is true, such a relativist conclusion would be perfectly justified. However, in the long term certain formulae, by tending to favor larger parties over smaller ones when one or the other must be favored, will lead to the over-representation of larger parties; the d'Hondt formula, which is widely used in Europe to award seats to parties, has this effect. Other formulae tend to favor smaller parties over larger ones; an example of such a formula is the equal proportions method, which is used in the United States to apportion representatives among the states and will in the long run give smaller states more than their fair share. The Sainte-Laguë method comes closest, in the long term, to giving every party its fair share of seats, because it does not favor either smaller or larger parties—one reason, perhaps, why it is so rarely used in practice.

CONSEQUENCES OF DISPROPORTIONALITY

When disproportionality exists, who benefits? The answer, almost everywhere, is larger parties. In some countries the electoral laws are deliberately tailored to benefit the larger parties, that is, to ensure that the share of seats they receive is greater than their share of the votes. This is commonly done by the imposition of thresholds, which ensure that small parties win no seats while the larger ones take up their unclaimed share. There have been cases in postcommunist Europe where the combination of even modest thresholds (5 percent of the votes) and a very fragmented party system has led to over 30 percent of votes being cast for unrepresented parties, with the consequent marked over-representation of those parties that overcome the threshold.

The fact that thresholds are used to create disproportionality shows that disproportionality is not universally regarded as an evil. Quite a few countries employ a scrupulously fair formula to apportion seats to different parts of the country but, when it comes to awarding seats to parties based on the votes they win at an election, employ a formula that favors larger parties. The rationale for this, apart from simply being based on the self-interest of the parties that are in a position to set the electoral rules, is that if every party, no matter how small, receives the same share of the seats as it wins of the votes, the result might be a very fragmented parliament from which no stable government can emerge. The deliberate creation of a degree of disproportionality, then, can be a method of "electoral engineering," designed to promote stability at the expense of completely accurate representation.

See also *Compensatory Seats; Cube Law; District Magnitude; Proportional Representation; Quotas and Divisors; Reapportionment and Redistricting; Single Transferable Vote; Threshold of Exclusion; Winning an Election.*

MICHAEL GALLAGHER, TRINITY COLLEGE, UNIVERSITY OF DUBLIN

BIBLIOGRAPHY

Balinski, Michel L., and H. Peyton Young. *Fair Representation: Meeting the Ideal of One Man, One Vote.* New Haven, Conn.: Yale University Press, 1982.

Cowell, Frank. *Measuring Inequality.* 2d ed. New York: Prentice Hall, 1995.

Fry, Vanessa, and Iain McLean. "A Note on Rose's Proportionality Index." *Electoral Studies* 10, no. 1 (March 1991): 52–59.

Gallagher, Michael. "Proportionality, Disproportionality and Electoral Systems." *Electoral Studies* 10, no. 1 (March 1991): 33–51.

Li, Jin-Shan. "Analyse critique des indices de disproportionalité électorale et de stabilité. Application aux cas de l'Allemagne et du Japon." *Revue Internationale de Politique Comparée* 2, no. 2 (September 1995): 369–388.

Lijphart, Arend. *Electoral Systems and Party Systems: A Study of Twenty-Seven Democracies, 1945–1990.* Oxford: Oxford University Press, 1994.

Monroe, Burt L. "Disproportionality and Malapportionment: Measuring Electoral Inequity." *Electoral Studies* 13, no. 2 (June 1994): 132–149.

Pennisi, Aline. "Disproportionality Indexes and Robustness of Proportional Allocation Methods." *Electoral Studies* 17, no. 1 (March 1998): 3–20.

Reynolds, Andrew, and Ben Reilly. *The International IDEA Handbook of Electoral System Design.* Stockholm: Institute for Democracy and Electoral Assistance, 1997.

Taagepera, Rein, and Matthew Soberg Shugart. *Seats and Votes: The Effects and Determinants of Electoral Systems.* New Haven, Conn.: Yale University Press, 1989.

PROXY VOTING

Proxy voting is the casting of a vote on behalf of another person, with that person's authority. It is commonly used in the commercial world as a mechanism for enabling stock- and shareholders to influence decisions at meetings of corporations, but at times it has also been used at legislative elections to provide for those who are unable to vote in person. In some situations it can therefore serve as an alternative to absentee voting.

All schemes of proxy voting must specify the criteria for determining whether a person is entitled to have a proxy vote cast on his or her behalf; the process for the appointment of the proxy; and the mechanism by which the appointed proxy is to cast the proxy vote.

Underlying any proxy voting system is the assumption that the person appointed to cast the proxy vote will do so in accordance with the wishes of the person who made the appointment. In most schemes of proxy voting at legislative elections, however, there is no transparent mechanism for guaranteeing the validity of this assumption, nor could such a mechanism be implemented without violating the secrecy of the ballot. Proxy voting, when reduced to its essentials, is therefore a process for allowing some people to cast multiple votes on the strength of the fact that others are unable to vote at all. This clearly gives rise to opportunities for abuse. In Australia the constitutional prohibition on plural voting has been taken to prevent the use of proxy voting.

Because of its susceptibility to abuse, proxy voting is generally regarded as a poor substitute for a properly administered system of absentee voting.

See also *Absentee Voting.*

MICHAEL MALEY, AUSTRALIAN ELECTORAL COMMISSION

BIBLIOGRAPHY

Blackburn, Robert. *The Electoral System in Britain.* London: Macmillan Press, 1995.

Administration and Cost of Elections Project website: *www.aceproject.org*

PSEPHOLOGY

See *Election Studies, Types of*

PUBLIC AID TO PARTIES AND CANDIDATES

Public aid to parties and to candidates in elections refers to the support provided from the public purse to assist in the work of political parties, in the selection and nomination of candidates running for public office, and in the partisan conduct of the election campaign itself. Public aid may be provided in three forms. First, and most important, it may involve direct financial subsidies to various party organs or to individual candidates. Second, it may involve indirect financial subsidies in the form of provisions for tax-free contributions to party or election funds, for free or low-cost access to public broadcasting, for free or low-cost mailings to voters, or for free travel for candidates or public representatives on publicly owned transport networks. Third, it may involve support in kind in the form of provisions for the secondment of state officials for party work or for the inclusion in the public bureaucracy of party appointees.

If political parties help democracy work, then it is in the interests of democracy that they survive and prosper. And it is this that justifies, or has been claimed to justify, the sometimes lavish public aid that is now bestowed on parties in many democracies. One of the first actions taken in many of the new postcommunist democracies in Europe, for example, was the funding of emerging political parties by the state. Without public subventions, proponents argued, the parties would find it difficult to get going; without these new parties, democracy might not be secured. There are also more practical reasons why parties and candidates need help with funding, and why this might best be provided by the state. Within contemporary politics, political work is increasingly capital intensive. Policy research, campaigning, and modern communications require a major capital investment, whereas relatively cost-free, labor-intensive electioneering activities, including canvassing and one-on-one political persuasion, are now often believed to be outmoded and ineffective. Parties and candidates therefore require substantial resources in order to compete, and since party memberships are almost universally in decline, the principal ways in which they can now get these resources are either through donations from the private sector or through subventions from the state. Given this choice, the preference is often given to state subventions, since these are seen as more neutral and evenhanded. The reliance of parties and candidates on private-sector donations, on the other hand, is often regarded more skeptically, since such donations may be directed only at certain types of party and hence may induce biases in the system, or may even encourage corruption and patronage.

In many contemporary Western democracies, and in almost all newly established democracies, a major source of party funding has therefore become the public purse. The provision of direct financial subsidies, which is the more important component of this public aid, operates in a variety of ways. In most countries, even in those where a system of public funding is still not well developed, state subventions are provided to support the work of parties in parliament. These are the equivalent of Britain's so-called Short Money, which is offered to the opposition parties in the British parliament. The amounts involved, however, usually far exceed the very limited funds available in the United Kingdom. Second, public funding is increasingly provided to party central offices in order to help staff and maintain organizational work between elections. This source of funding also facilitates research work on policy development, as well as on political campaigns that encourage participation in politics, particularly among young people and minorities. Subventions are also sometimes made available to specific party bodies, including research and educational institutions. In Germany, for example, the bulk of state money is directed toward research and education, with the result that all of the German parties now maintain richly endowed party foundations. In addition, subsidies are also sometimes made available for party work at the local or regional level. Finally, public money can be made available specifically for election campaigning. This tends to be more developed in the United States than in Europe, where the parties are more centralized and cohesive and where the funds that are transferred to the party central offices are assumed to filter through to help with the costs of electioneering.

Taken together, these various public subsidies represent a substantial and increasing transfer of public resources to the political parties. By the end of the 1980s, for example, the opposition Social Democratic Party in Germany was receiving an annual total of more than 260 million marks from the state—the equivalent of 12 marks for every vote that it received in the federal elections. In Norway, where per capita state funding is among the most lavish in western Europe, the national and local party organizations together commanded an annual total of some 125 million crowns (the equivalent of 50 crowns per vote), with yet additional subventions targeted specifically for the parties in parliament and the party educational institutions. The equivalent American figure for the 1988 presidential elections was a $46.1 million subvention to the two major-party candidates (or roughly 51 cents per vote received).

Although there is obviously a good case to be made for this sort of public funding of parties and candidates, particularly insofar as it offers a reasonably neutral and evenhanded method of distributing resources, there are also obviously good reasons to be wary of such practices. The decision to introduce a system of public funding in the first place, as well as the decision about how much money should be transferred to the parties, is usually taken by the legislature, which means that it is the parties themselves that act as both paymaster and beneficiary. This risks a system that functions more to the benefit of the parties than to the benefit of the public. Second, since public aid is usually related to prior electoral performance, with the amounts dispensed based on the parties' shares of the vote or their seats in parliament, the positions of established parties may simply be reinforced while those of emerging parties may be hindered. Third, the idea of public aid to parties runs counter to the more traditional notion of parties as voluntary bodies that rely exclusively on the resources that they can generate themselves from their voters, members, or supporters. Increased reliance on state subventions is likely to push the party center of gravity even more markedly toward its leadership in parliament and central office, and away from its grassroots membership and societal base. If parties no longer require members for the purposes of campaigning or for political work more generally (since these activities are increasingly taken over by professional consultants), and if they also no longer require fee-paying members as a source of funds for party work (since these funds are now provided by the state), then the likelihood increases that parties will move away from an emphasis on voluntary mass membership and become increasingly elite-driven organizations. In Germany an effort to counteract this danger prompted reforms of the system of public funding. These changes sought to link state subsidies specifically to the parties' efforts to build and maintain a membership base.

More generally, the increased reliance of parties on the state for financial support and other resources, coupled with their growing absorption within the regulatory frameworks that typically accompany the introduction of state subventions, has led to two more fundamental concerns. First, the links between parties and the wider society may become eroded. Parties will instead evolve into agents of the state, thus endangering both their legitimacy and the legitimacy of the political systems in which they are involved. Second, as parties become more dependent on a common pool of public resources, they risk losing their individual identities. A loss of party identity could render party competition less meaningful. Indeed, some observers have suggested that this process may encourage interparty collusion rather than competition, which in turn may lead to a cartelization of the party system. In order to counteract this tendency, observers argue that parties should become more dependent on their members and supporters and that they should renew their links with the wider society. How such renewal can coexist with a developed system of public aid for parties, however, remains a difficult question.

See also *Campaigning; Election Finance.*

PETER MAIR, UNIVERSITY OF LEIDEN

BIBLIOGRAPHY

Alexander, Herbert E., and Rei Shiratori, eds. *Comparative Political Finance Among the Democracies.* Boulder, Colo.: Westview Press, 1994.

Gunlicks, Arthur B., ed. *Campaign and Party Finance in North America and Western Europe.* Boulder, Colo.: Westview Press, 1993.

Hofnung, Menachem. "Public Financing, Party Membership and Internal Party Competition." *European Journal of Political Research* 29 (January 1996): 73–86.

Katz, Richard S., and Peter Mair. "Changing Models of Party Organization and Party Democracy: The Emergence of the Cartel Party." *Party Politics* 1 (January 1995): 5–28.

———, eds. *Party Organizations: A Data Handbook on Party Organizations in Western Democracies, 1960–90.* London: Sage Publications, 1992.

Scarrow, Susan E. *Parties and Their Members: Organizing for Victory in Britain and Germany.* Oxford: Oxford University Press, 1996.

PUBLIC OPINION POLLS: HOW THEY WORK

A public opinion poll measures the attitudes and behavior of a representative sample of a defined population. Even though predicting an election (or making any predictions) is one of the functions for which polls and survey research are least ideally suited, it is undoubtedly the function with which they are most identified in the public's mind.

There are five things that we can discover with the techniques of public opinion research (which include not only quantitative surveys, or the traditional poll, but also qualitative methods, including depth interviews and focus groups). We can measure behavior (what people do); knowledge (what people know—or think they know); and views (people's opinions, attitudes, and values). Polls are not ideal at predicting behavior because respondents often cannot predict it themselves. In elections, however, polls—though certainly imperfect—are much better predictors than any of the alternatives.

Election polls are a survey of political opinion. They may be commissioned either by news organizations or political actors such as candidates or parties. The function of news organizations is to inform, entertain, and educate. The role of modern newspapers, radio, and television is to let their audiences know what is happening in the world in which they live. Media organizations attempt to do so in an entertaining way and, as a result, improve audiences' understanding of the circumstances surrounding the events being reported. When an election is reported, however, a further element is present: in a democracy the consumers of this information are also the participants in the electoral process. Opinion polls, on the one hand, can be a help to the public's understanding of this process; they are one of the few systematic and objective parts of the information flow and thereby hold an important democratic role. Private polling, on the other hand, is market research conducted to aid campaigning by a candidate and his or her political party.

METHODOLOGY

Polls marry the "art of asking questions," as Stanley Payne put it, and the science of sampling—asking the right question of the right sample and adding up the figures correctly. A good question in an election poll enables the pollster to deduce how the respondent will vote. The best questions for this purpose will vary from time to time and from culture to culture. In the United States and Britain, polls usually simply ask how the respondent will vote as well as how likely he or she is to turn out at all. In Germany, by contrast, pollsters have developed extra questions to measure and correct for a "spiral of silence" effect (the process by which voters become successively more reluctant to admit supporting an apparently unpopular or unfashionable party or candidate).

A good sample is designed to maximize the probability that the sample is truly representative of the entire population being surveyed—which may be all adults, registered voters only, or likely voters only, depending on poll design and the laws and customs of the country. Interviewing may be either by telephone or face to face; surveys by mail are not adequate. A face-to-face interview may take place in the home or on the street. Again these details are dependent on national circumstances. The United States, with high telephone penetration and a large geographic area across a number of time zones, relies almost entirely on the telephone method, whereas in developing countries many voters do not have telephones (and those who have them are unrepresentative). Although face-to-face methods are less convenient, they offer advantages such as the practicality of longer interviews, the ability to present the respondent with visual aids (such as the symbols representing the parties in countries where illiteracy is high), and possibly tighter control of the nature of the sample. In Britain, for example, both methods are used, with little difference between them in terms of accuracy.

Whichever the interviewing mode, sampling may be by either of two methods—probability (random) sampling or quota sampling, and variations on these. Probability sampling involves giving each member of the sampling universe (adult, registered voter, or whatever) a mathematically equal probability of being selected for interview and then making repeated attempts at contact; this method is often considered the purer of the two. If done strictly, however, it is very time consuming, which can be a disadvantage in a fast-moving election. Moreover, a significant fraction of those whose names are selected refuse to participate or cannot be contacted; this inability to reach the entire sample may distort the sample and thus the result. Quota sampling attempts to replicate the results of a good random sample without its disadvantages. Ideally, a survey based on quota sampling identifies target numbers to reach respondents who share a known profile with the broader population—so many of each gender, so many in each age group, and so on. The characteristics used in designing the quota ideally should be closely related to voting behavior. Although quota sampling may appear crude, properly conducted it has a generally good track record in many countries. In Britain, for example, the empirical evidence suggests that quota sampling is more, not less, accurate than probability sampling.

Reputably conducted, scientifically designed opinion polls need to be distinguished from straw polls and from the phone-in, write-in, or e-mail-in "polls" that frequently infest elections. In a straw poll the interviewer selects respondents but without making a systematic attempt to achieve a representative sample; the sample may also be very small. In what is sometimes called a voodoo poll, members of an audience are invited to select themselves as respondents—for example, by phoning a particular number to register an opinion or preference. These sham polls have become popular as a marketing exercise, especially at election times. The limitations of self-selecting samples should be obvious. The unscientific polls are representative of nobody: they measure only the opinions of self-selecting members of the audience who saw the invitation to vote in the first place, and they are subject to multiple voting and manipulation by pressure groups.

The reported results of private polls for the parties or candidates are also subject to misuse. It is not unknown for these results to be leaked selectively to the press, in an attempt to put the best "spin" on the findings so that the party or candidate appears in the best light. In some countries, such as Britain, private polling for the parties is conducted almost exclusively by the professional market research organizations that produce the public polls, making it unlikely that the findings of private polls will systematically diverge from public poll findings. The polling companies could not afford to let their public polls be less accurate than their private polls, especially as polling makes up only a small fraction of the wider market research business of all the companies.

In the United States, where there are many more elections and fewer restrictions on election spending, the market for election polling is a great deal larger. Many of the pollsters work only for candidates, frequently exclusively for either Republicans or Democrats. In these circumstances, it might be conceivable that the private polls, by using different techniques, could diverge from the public polls, although it is unlikely that they would be more accurate. So-called push polling has become a feature of American elections. This type of telephone poll seems legitimate as the call begins, but questions are framed in a way that induces reactions favorable to a particular candidate or position, with the intention of not simply producing a distorted polling result but of influencing the respondent's future opinions. No reputable pollster would conduct push polling.

HISTORY

Public opinion polling began in 1935 as a journalistic exercise, when George Gallup and Claude Robinson introduced a syndicated newspaper column describing the findings of sample surveys of American public opinion. Almost immediately the new tool became associated with election prediction, as Gallup and his rivals Elmo Roper and Archibald Crossley successfully called the result of the 1936 presidential election. The established but unscientific straw poll conducted through the mail by the *Literary Digest* had predicted a landslide win for the Republican candidate, Alf Landon, over the Democratic candidate, Franklin D. Roosevelt.

Polling quickly crossed the Atlantic, reaching Great Britain in 1937 and France in 1938, again in both cases proving itself by impressively accurate predictions of the first elections where it was used. All other democracies have since followed suit, and the number of polling companies in each country has also burgeoned, ensuring that most elections are now measured by a variety of surveys and lessening the risk that sampling error might give a misleading impression. The polls continue to be conducted for the national news organizations, and their primary purpose is journalistic rather than academic.

The prediction record of the polls in both Britain and the United States has on the whole been good, though exceptions have been highly publicized. In the U.S. presidential election of 1948 and the British general election of 1970 the polls picked the wrong winner; in both cases the primary cause of the error seems to have been that the surveys were completed too early, enabling a late swing by voters to confound the polls' forecasts. In 1970 the one poll that included last-minute reinterviews of some of its respondents managed to pick up the trend and correctly predicted a narrow Conservative Party win.

On neither of these occasions were the polls grossly inaccurate: in Britain in 1970 the error of the polls taken collectively was 3.2 percent on the vote share of the leading parties (or 6.4 percent on the lead), but this error proved too large in a close election. In the British general election of 1992 the 4.2 collective error was larger; although subsequent investigation uncovered some methodological errors, a late swing in the vote was a major cause of the polls' inaccuracy. The polling companies disagreed over the exact solutions and altered their methodologies in different ways. At the next (1997) election all the pollsters had improved on their 1992 performance; as a group they averaged only a 1.5 percent error on their predictions of the major parties' share of the vote.

Over fifteen British general elections, polls have usually been within sampling tolerance, given their sample size, and not allowing for any design error or the fact that they are judged as a forecast of the future when they claim only to be a measure of the present. The average error on measuring the major-party share over the fifteen elections has been 1.9 percent, well within the plus or minus 3 percent that a two-sigma test of statistical significance would expect from perfect random samples.

The limitations of election polls need to be recognized. Sometimes in a close campaign, all the polls can tell a cautious commentator is that the race is too close to call. Still, the alternative to polls is pundits who predict by instinct rather than measurement or politicians who have a vested interest in concealing the truth.

Opinion polls provide a wealth of other detail that tends to be largely ignored. Measurement of the voting behavior of subgroups; the impact of particular issues, events, or personalities; how well informed the voters are—all these can be and are regularly measured in the public opinion polls. Furthermore, such information is enlightening even with a far less exacting standard of accuracy than is preferable for election prediction. Analyses can be made of demographic, geographic, attitudinal, and even value-based differences. Techniques include factor and cluster analysis, correspondence analysis, perceptual mapping, and many others. Such techniques are also used widely by academic analysts of electoral behavior, some of whom both commission their own polls and make use of the public polls. Between elections, regular polls of public opinion are conducted on numerous subjects, both political and nonpolitical. In the United States in particular, these are closely watched by politicians for their relevance to future elections and sometimes guide their behavior. During the impeachment of President Bill Clinton, the president used his continued high ratings in the polls as a lever to discourage his opponents from voting to unseat him—a vote that the polls suggested would be unpopular and therefore electorally damaging to them.

EFFECT ON VOTING BEHAVIOR

One question often raised is whether opinion polls influence voting behavior. In a number of countries, the publication of polls immediately before elections is forbidden. Yet the evidence in most countries on the influence of polls is unconvincing.

A week after the British election of 1997, five in six people said they recalled what opinion polls had been saying, and over half correctly recalled them as saying the election would be a Labour landslide. But only 2 percent of voters admitted that opinion polls had had a great deal of influence on their decision about what they would do on election day.

Undoubtedly, some voters base their voting decisions partly on how they perceive the race, and this perception is probably in most cases based directly or indirectly on opinion poll findings. Yet such voters would be likely to take competitive information into account whether or not it was derived from opinion poll data; in this case polls form an objective and reasonably reliable basis of information against which to judge other claims from the electoral participants or the media. Where the publication of polls is banned, a sort of black market in finding out public opinion immediately takes their place, with foreign media, banks, and the parties all commissioning private polls and then, sometimes, misleadingly leaking the results.

Voters' desire for information about the likely behavior of their fellow citizens may be quite rational: in many democracies the electoral system places the voter in a position where to maximize the value of his or her vote it is necessary to be informed about the likely voting behavior of others. In plurality-based electoral systems using single-member districts, such as the Anglo-American and French models, accurate polling data can supply vital information to facilitate tactical voting. Tactical voting will take place whether or not opinion polls are published; in their absence the media will continue to speculate about current standings, "experts" will continue to fill the information gap, and, inevitably, parties will further their cause by selectively leaking private polls and manipulating (or simply fabricating) canvass returns. In other words, the effect of the polls in this case is not to create a change in voting behavior but to ensure that voters have reasonably accurate information about other voters. A voter should be given every chance to understand what his or her vote will mean before casting it. A general election should not be a guessing game.

See also *Bandwagon Effects; Campaigning; Citizen Juries; Election Forecasting; Exit Polls; Public Opinion Polls: Legal Regulation; Voting Behavior, Influences on.*

ROBERT M. WORCESTER, MORI INTERNATIONAL;
LONDON SCHOOL OF ECONOMICS AND POLITICAL SCIENCE

BIBLIOGRAPHY

Noelle-Neumann, Elisabeth. *Spiral of Silence: Public Opinion—Social Skin.* Chicago: University of Chicago Press, 1984. Originally published as *Die Schweigespirale: öffentliche Meinung—unsere soziale Haut.* Munich: R. Piper, 1980.

Payne, Stanley. *The Art of Asking Questions.* Princeton: Princeton University Press, 1980.

Price, Vincent. *Public Opinion.* Newbury Park, Calif.: Sage, 1992.

Traugott, Michael W., and Paul J. Lavrakas. *The Voter's Guide to Election Polls.* Chatham, N.J.: Chatham House, 1996.

Worcester, Robert M. "Lessons from the Electorate: What the 1992 British General Election Taught British Pollsters about the Conduct of Opinion Polls." *International Social Science Journal* (December 1995): 617–634.

———. "Why Do We Do What We Do? A Review of What It Is We Think We Do, Reflections on Why We Do It, and Whether or Not It Does Any Good." *International Journal of Public Opinion Research* 9 (spring 1997): 2–16.

PUBLIC OPINION POLLS: LEGAL REGULATION

On May 5, 1998, Hungary's National Election Committee accused Gallup Hungary of violating the country's electoral law. Gallup had published the results of an opinion poll conducted in Hungary four days before the country's national elections on its World Wide Web homepage. Electoral law in Hungary prohibits the publication of opinion surveys eight days before an election. Six days later, on May 11, 1998, the Philippine government launched a last-minute appeal against a court ruling allowing exit polls in the presidential election being held that very day. The country's Supreme Court had overturned a ban on exit polls imposed by the authorities. These are recent examples of the legal problems that public opinion polls encounter in some countries of the world.

PREVALENCE AND FORMS OF RESTRICTIONS

Hungary and the Philippines are democracies. Undemocratic political systems have, of course, at all times prohibited the free conduct of opinion surveys and the publication of their results. The former German Democratic Republic is a case in point. In 1964 the Communist Party founded a survey research center that produced data exclusively for the use of

party leaders. When in 1972 the center published the results of a survey indicating that a majority (53 percent) of the East German population had a favorable opinion of Willy Brandt, then chancellor of the capitalist Federal Republic of Germany, it was not allowed to ask the respective survey questions again. In 1979 the center was closed down when its surveys showed for the first time an erosion in the support for the communist political system.

Legal regulations and constraints on public opinion polls are not restricted to undemocratic political systems. Many countries have implemented regulations, arguing that polls exert undue influence on the political process, particularly in times of elections. Since representative surveys first appeared on the political scene in the 1930s in the United States, such assumptions have nourished discussions about their legitimacy. For many, the precise indication of where a party or a political figure stands in the opinion of the electorate, or even which party or which candidate would likely win an election, was not a legitimate part of the political process. The opponents of free opinion polling argue first that poll results are usually wrong and therefore misleading (sometimes deliberately so), and second that, right or wrong, results about a party or candidate's standing in public opinion might influence the election outcome.

In 1996 a joint research group of the European Society for Opinion and Marketing Research (ESOMAR) and the World Association for Public Opinion Research (WAPOR) investigated the legal status of polls around the world. In thirty of the seventy-eight countries examined, it found some kind of restriction on the publication of poll results. In most of these cases, the publication of poll results twenty-four hours before an election was prohibited. In some instances, the prohibition extended for a week. The longest period of this kind occurred in South Africa, which observes a six-week moratorium. The list of countries that have placed restrictions on the publication of public opinion polls includes such traditional democracies as France (seven days) and Canada (three days). Minor restrictions relate to exit polls (interviews conducted on election day with representative samples of citizens who have already cast their votes). For example, Germany prohibits the publication of exit poll results until all polling stations have closed. Comparing the 1996 ESOMAR/WAPOR results with its findings in preceding years, the authors concluded that the number of countries that enforce publication moratoriums prior to elections had risen.

Another form of restriction relates to the topics addressed in a survey. In only a very few countries do restrictions on survey subject matter exist as official legal regulations. More often they are informal in nature and concern questions about which there is implicit agreement that they are better left unasked. The ESOMAR/WAPOR study found that in Japan and Thailand questions about royalty should be avoided. In Albania, China, Hong Kong, Croatia, Indonesia, Mexico, North Korea, Turkey, Venezuela, and some Middle Eastern countries questions on topics such as foreign and defense policies or political leaders and parties are not permitted. The results of this international study have to be judged in light of the fact that only a minority of all countries in the world were included or supplied information. The majority of those *not* included in the study were countries with less liberal political systems.

PROS AND CONS OF LEGAL RESTRICTIONS

Critics of prohibitions on conducting and/or publishing survey results in times of elections (or at any other time) claim that these regulations conflict with the rights of citizens. First, they contend, pollsters have a right to conduct free research and inform anyone who is interested about the results. Second, such restrictions violate the press's freedom to publish information that is both available and of interest to the public. Third, and most important, such regulations take away the right of every citizen to become informed about relevant information on the political process that other members of the political system may possess.

Besides affecting individual rights, the banning of polls also might conflict with two basic norms of the political system. First, poll results are usually the best possible expression of public opinion. For a democracy to make information about public opinion illegal is decidedly strange. Second, as most countries with restrictions prohibit the *publication* though not the conduct of opinion polls, there are always two classes of citizens: those who have access to poll results and those who do not. Examples of the former include politicians, who can use the results of such polls for strategic planning; business people, who might speculate on the effects on the stock market of a specific election outcome; or journalists, who may pretend that their ability to accurately predict election results derives from a special empathy with public sentiment. Those in the dark, ordinary citizens who are deprived of this information, become targets of manipulation by those in the know. Numerous examples exist of how a few who were privy to such information used it to gain a political or economic advantage. After France enacted its law prohibiting publication of poll results seven days prior to elections in the mid-1970s, French public opinion in favor of legalizing published poll results rose sharply, from 52 percent in 1974 to 76 percent in 1988.

Proponents of unrestricted polling counter with their own arguments. First, they claim, in the flood of interest-driven assertions about who will win a forthcoming election the sta-

tistical figures of pollsters are the only scientific and neutral source about the potential outcome. Indeed, media content analyses have shown that politicians and journalists are much more often the sources of misinformation than are poll figures. And though election forecasts sometimes are wrong—be it because of rapid changes in the voters' opinion, unavoidable statistical sampling error, flawed methodologies, or the political corruptness of a single pollster—the accuracy of leading survey institutes is impressive. For example, the mean deviance between the predictions of Germany's Allensbach Institute and official results has been less than 1 percentage point for all elections since the early 1950s. Second, to date no empirical studies have provided clear evidence that the publication of poll data or even election forecasts influence the electorate.

Supporters of unrestricted public opinion research claim that in a representative democracy the influence of survey data might even be desirable. They contend that the results of public opinion surveys would enable citizens to engage in tactical voting. Tactical voting involves casting a vote with the aim of achieving a certain election result—for instance, establishing a specific coalition—rather than simply voting for the party or candidate of one's choice. Finally, critics of legal restrictions to polls point to the fact that the earliest post-colonial elections in the United States were almost always carried out in full public view. In Virginia, for example, the voter entered the courtroom, stood before the sheriff, and announced his vote. In some cases, the candidates were even present to shake hands and thank him.

See also *Bandwagon Effects; Campaigning; Election Forecasting; Exit Polls; Open Voting; Public Opinion Polls: How They Work; Regulation of Television at Elections; Voting Behavior, Influences on.*

WOLFGANG DONSBACH, TECHNICAL UNIVERSITY OF DRESDEN

BIBLIOGRAPHY

Donsbach, Wolfgang. "Survey Research at the End of the Twentieth Century: Theses and Antitheses." *International Journal of Public Opinion Research* 9, no. 1 (1997): 17–28.

European Society for Opinion and Marketing Research/World Association for Public Opinion Research. *Guide to Opinion Polls.* Amsterdam: ESOMAR, 1998.

Foundation for Information. *The Freedom to Publish Opinion Polls: Report on a Worldwide Study.* Amsterdam: ESOMAR, 1997.

Meyer, Philip. *The New Precision Journalism.* Bloomington: Indiana University Press, 1991.

Schmitt-Beck, Rüdiger. "Mass Media, the Electorate, and the Bandwagon: A Study of Communication Effects on Vote Choice in Germany." *International Journal of Public Opinion Research* 8, no. 3 (1996): 266–291.

West, Darrell M. "Polling Effects in Election Campaigns." *Political Behavior* 13, no. 2 (1991): 151–163.

Worcester, Robert M. "Why Do We Do What We Do?" *International Journal of Public Opinion Research* 9, no. 1 (spring 1997): 2–16.

QUAKER DECISION MAKING WITHOUT VOTING

Quakers, also called the Religious Society of Friends, observe traditions first enunciated in England by George Fox (1624–1691). Fox criticized formal creeds and sacraments, believing there is "that of God" (also referred to as an "inner light") in each person. Quakers, having no clergy, gather in silence during their meetings for worship and wait for individual members to share "leadings" drawn from their inner light. Each individual's leadings are considered a contribution to the meeting for worship. Quakers number approximately 200,000 worldwide; they are concentrated in Great Britain, the United States, and Kenya.

DECISION-MAKING PROCESS

Quaker meetings for business follow the spirit of Quaker meetings for worship. Although a clerk, who is selected temporarily from among the members, directs the meetings for business, each individual's leadings are considered a contribution to the ongoing decision-making process. When the clerk believes unanimity has been achieved on a given issue, the clerk summarizes his or her sense of the meeting. If there is no objection, the sense of the meeting is incorporated into a written minute, and a decision has been made through consensus. But if any member in attendance feels his or her leading is not in accord with the sense of the meeting, that member may say so. The discussion is then renewed, and an effort is made to incorporate that individual's leading into a reconsidered, unanimous sense of the meeting. No votes are taken. Resolution of differences by majority rule is not an option.

On occasions when consensus is difficult to achieve, the clerk may call for a period of silence, when members can seek in a meditative manner a resolution incorporating everyone's leadings. After the period of silence, discussion continues until consensus is achieved or until it is agreed that consensus cannot be achieved, in which case the discussion is postponed to a later meeting.

A major difficulty in this form of decision making is the veto power each attending member possesses. Any dissenting member may block consensus. When such a situation arises, several alternatives are possible. Dissenting members may state that they disagree with, but do not wish to stand in the way of, a consensus decision. Or the dissenting members may ask that the minute record their opposition to the consensus decision but also their desire not to block consensus. Either of these statements enables the consensus decision to be made and "minuted" and the meeting to move on to other business, even though full unanimity has not been achieved. Or the dissenting members may state that they cannot unite with the proposed consensus. In such cases, the discussion is tabled, the absence of consensus is minuted, and the meeting moves on to other business.

The Quakers' hope, and often the actuality, is that the consensus decision finally reached is better than any individual suggestions made at the start of the meeting. The commitment to finding consensus often stimulates otherwise dormant creative energies.

A strength of the Quaker decision-making process is the absence of a disaffected minority. When a Quaker meeting for business reaches consensus regarding a decision, the community is usually united to implement that decision. This outcome can differ from that of some majority-rule decisions, where the decision may remain largely unimplemented because of resistance by the disaffected minority.

HISTORICAL PARALLELS

Historical parallels exist to the Quaker form of decision making. In the sixteenth century, the first Roman Catholic Jesuits practiced "communal discernment," whereby through prayer and discussion they reached virtually unanimous decisions. However, communal discernment ended with the establishment of a Jesuit hierarchy requiring obedience to one's superiors. In the latter half of the twentieth century, small groups of Roman Catholics, following the Second Vatican Council summoned by Pope John XXIII in 1962, began experimenting again with communal discernment.

Another parallel to Quaker decision-making is *satyagraha* ("truth-force"), a process Mohandas Gandhi developed first in South Africa, in his struggle against racism, and later in India, in his struggle to free it from British rule. The essence of Gandhi's *satyagraha* is identifying the truth in opposing sides and synthesizing a greater truth that can unite all sides.

Scholars studying political-party decision making in Switzerland have identified two types of "consociational" decision making that resemble Quaker processes: decision making by amicable agreement, and decision making by interpretation (in which a participant offers an interpretation of the sense of a discussion, and other participants tacitly accept that interpretation). Critics of consociational decision making argue that it blocks change by giving veto power to those wanting no change. Consociational decision making has also been praised for producing decisions that are likely to be implemented because of their widespread support.

Some forms of consensus decision making that use terminology similar to that of the Quakers have little in common with Quaker procedures. The U.S. Senate sometimes records decisions by "unanimous consent." However, the Senate often uses unanimous consent to handle matters that are trivial or noncontroversial. Similarly, requirements for unanimous consent in the United Nations lead some of the most serious international negotiations to be conducted off-stage and behind closed doors. U.N. unanimous-consent requirements often conceal sharp differences or even noncompliance by nations, while providing those same nations with face-saving procedures for appearing to be good international citizens.

Much of the business in corporate board rooms is carried out by unanimous consent. However, unanimous consent in board rooms often merely reflects an absence of dissatisfaction among board members with actions of the corporate directors. When board members are sufficiently dissatisfied with those actions, they are likely to express their dissatisfaction by firing the directors, rather than seeking to find consensus with them. Making a decision through compromise is sometimes thought of as paralleling Quaker decision making. But compromise (or splitting-the-difference) lacks the element of a creative solution forged from originally divergent points of view.

From the perspective of Quaker decision making, what is lacking in each of these other cases is the group's commitment to listen thoughtfully to, and incorporate the best from, all points of view (or each member's leadings) in order to create a unanimous decision without voting and without resorting to majority rule.

See also *Acclamation, Election by; Approval Voting; Choice, Elections as a Method of; Citizen Juries; Papal Elections.*

JOSEPH W. ELDER, UNIVERSITY OF WISCONSIN-MADISON

BIBLIOGRAPHY

Baltzell, Edward Digby. *Puritan Boston and Quaker Philadelphia: The Protestant Ethic and the Spirit of Class Authority and Leadership.* New York: Free Press, 1979.

Bartoo, Glenn. *Decision by Consensus: A Study of the Quaker Method.* Chicago: Progresiv, 1978.

Brinton, Howard Haines. *Reaching Decisions: The Quaker Method.* Wallingford, Penn.: Pendle Hill, n.d.

Juergensmeyer, Mark. *Fighting With Gandhi: A Step-by-Step Strategy for Resolving Everyday Conflicts.* San Francisco: Harper and Row, 1984.

Sheeran, Michael J. *Beyond Majority Rule: Voteless Decisions in the Religious Society of Friends.* Philadelphia: Philadelphia Yearly Meeting of the Religious Society of Friends, 1983.

Steiner, Jürg, and Robert H. Dorff. *A Theory of Political Decision Modes: Intraparty Decision Making in Switzerland.* Chapel Hill: University of North Carolina Press, 1980.

Trueblood, D. Elton. "The Quaker Method of Reaching Decisions." In *Beyond Dilemmas: Quakers Look at Life,* edited by Sceva B. Laughlin, 104–124. New York: Lippincott, 1937.

QUALIFICATIONS FOR THE RIGHT TO VOTE

See *Absentee Voting; Administration of Elections; Age of Voting; Compulsory Voting; Disqualification of Voters, Grounds for; Noncitizens and the Right to Vote; Overseas Voting; Plural Voters; Poll Tax; Proxy Voting; Registration of Voters: United States; Tendered Ballots; Women: Enfranchisement*

QUALIFIED MAJORITY VOTING

Most contemporary elections of individuals require either an absolute majority of the votes cast (the first whole number of votes more than 50 percent) or a relative majority or plurality of the votes cast (more votes than any other candidate). In theory, however, more could be required, for example an absolute majority (or some other specified percentage) of the total electorate, a majority of the votes cast greater than 50 percent, or a majority or plurality of the votes cast with the additional requirement that turnout exceed some floor. All of these more rigorous alternatives would have the potential disadvantage of leaving no one elected—a "problem" that occasionally arose in communist elections when so many voters crossed out the name of the single candidate that the candidate did not achieve the required 50 percent of votes cast. As a result, they generally are not used to elect individuals to public office. However, they are sometimes used in some kinds of votes in legislatures and in referendums, for which the bias in favor of a negative outcome that results from limiting the simple majority principle may be regarded as desirable. In the past they were used for elections within the Catholic Church and for the election of some public officials.

ORIGINS OF QUALIFIED MAJORITY VOTING

The roots of qualified majority voting, like those of many other modern electoral institutions, appear to lie in the practices of the medieval Catholic Church, which was the only Western institution of the period to hold elections or to be concerned with the participation of the ruled in the choice of their rulers. The purpose of a church election, however, was not to identify the choice of the voters, but through their prayerful votes to identify the choice of God. Given this purpose, church authorities believed the choice ought to be unanimous, and indeed the first clear case of a pope being chosen other than by general assent, that of Innocent II in 1130, led to a schism. Unanimity could not always be achieved, however, and to deal with this problem the church evolved the principle of *sanioritas,* which remained central to the theory of canonical elections for at least six hundred years. One of the clearest and most influential statements of this principle is found in the Rule of St. Benedict, which decreed that an abbot should be chosen unanimously by the monks on the basis of his merit, but failing unanimity, the new abbot should be the choice of that "part of the community who, however few, in view of their judgment are the most wise."

That the standard for canonical election was agreement by the *maior et sanior pars* (the larger and the wiser parts) presented two problems: if the larger and wiser parts do not agree, there is no natural way to resolve the conflict; and it is rarely obvious to one party that the other is the wiser. For nonpapal elections, these problems could be resolved by appeal to an ecclesiastical superior; for the papacy, however, there is no superior. The solution adopted by the Third Lateran Council in 1179 was to continue the principle of election by *maior et sanior pars,* but with the explicit assumption that a qualified two-thirds majority included the *sanior* part. The requirement of a qualified majority was also adopted in the secular realm; the Venetian Republic, for example, established in 1328 that the election of the doge (the chief magistrate) would require twenty-five votes from the council of forty-one.

Even if not used in the original choice of an official, a qualified majority may be required for that person to retain office. For example, judicial vacancies in Illinois are filled by competitive election, with a plurality required for election; incumbent judges, however, may seek retention through a simple "yes" or "no" vote, but they must attain a three-fifths majority.

NONELECTORAL USES

Although the use of a qualified majority is uncommon for election to office, it is quite common for a variety of votes in assemblies of various types. Among the most common is the requirement of a two-thirds majority for constitutional amendments in, for example, Costa Rica, Germany, India, and the United States; in Italy a constitutional amendment adopted by absolute majority can be challenged by referendum, but one adopted by two-thirds majority cannot be. Other possible majorities are exemplified by the requirement of a three-fifths majority for a constitutional amendment in the Czech Republic and the requirement of a three-fourths majority (or popular referendum) to change an "entrenched" part of the electoral law in New Zealand. In the U.S. Senate, sixty of one hundred votes are required to shut off debate. Until 1936 a Democratic presidential candidate required a two-thirds majority of the convention delegates to win the party nomination. In 1965 the British Conservative Party adopted a rule for the selection of its leader that allowed a first-ballot victory only to a candidate who had both an absolute majority of the votes cast and a lead of at least 15 percent over the runner-up.

Various qualifications of the simple majority principle also are common for referendums. Some types of issues may require more than 50 percent for approval; public borrowing in West Virginia, for example, must be approved by a three-fifths majority in a referendum. Another possibility is to require a minimum level of participation; Italian referendums are void unless turnout is at least 50 percent. Alternatively, the affirmative votes may have to represent a set percentage of the total electorate rather than a majority of the votes cast, as exemplified by the Scottish and Welsh devolution referendums in Britain in 1979. For the devolution referendums to pass, they had to be supported by an absolute majority of the votes cast *and* at least 40 percent of the entire electorate. In the Scottish referendum, devolution was approved by a majority of those voting, but the referendum failed because on turnout of only 64 percent, the 52 percent of those voting who favored devolution were only about one-third of the total electorate. A similar requirement is imposed in Massachusetts, where a referendum passes only if it is approved by a majority of those voting, and those approving are at least 30 percent of the total ballots cast in the last election. In federal systems some form of double majority may be required, as for Swiss constitutional amendments, which must be approved by an overall majority of those voting *and* by majorities in a majority of the cantons. Similarly, Australian national referendums require a national majority plus majorities in four of the six states.

See also *Papal Elections; Referendums: Europe; Referendums: Latin America; Referendums: United States.*

RICHARD S. KATZ, JOHNS HOPKINS UNIVERSITY

BIBLIOGRAPHY

Kobach, Kris W. *The Referendum: Direct Democracy in Switzerland*. Aldershot, England: Dartmouth, 1993.

Moulin, Leo. "Les origines religieuses des techniques electorales et deliberatives modernes." *Revue Internationale d'Histoire Politique et Constitutionnel* (April–June 1953): 106–148.

QUOTAS AND DIVISORS

Quotas and divisors are the building blocks of mathematical formulae to allocate seats by proportional representation in multimember constituencies. Quotas work by subtraction. A quota is established and that number is subtracted from each party's vote for every seat it is awarded. Divisors work by dividing a party's vote by a predetermined divisor each time a seat is allocated to it.

QUOTA SYSTEMS

The four major types of quota are Hare, Droop, Hagenbach-Bischoff, and Imperiali. The Hare quota is the simplest to calculate: the total number of valid votes is divided by the number of seats to be allocated. The system is named after Thomas Hare, the inventor of the single-transferable-vote system. To calculate the Hagenbach-Bischoff quota, the number of votes is divided by the number of seats plus one; for the Droop quota, the number of votes is divided by the number of seats plus one, and one is added to the resulting quotient; and for the Imperiali quota, used in Italy from 1948 to 1993, the number of votes is divided by the number of seats plus two. Thus, in a constituency with 60,000 votes and five seats, the respective quotas would be: Hare, 12,000; Hagenbach-Bischoff, 10,000; Droop, 10,001; Imperiali, 8,572. The Hare quota is the largest quota that allows even the possibility that all seats will be allocated by full quotas.

After the electoral quota for a constituency has been determined, the next step is to allocate the seats among the parties. In the largest remainder system, the seat distribution takes place in two stages. In the first stage the vote for each party is divided by the electoral quota. A seat is awarded to each party for each bloc of votes equal to a quota. If, as is usually the case, all the seats have not yet been allocated, there is a second allocation stage. In the second stage, any party that did not win a seat in the first stage will have all of its votes counted as a remainder, and any party that did win seats will have a remainder equal to its total votes minus a quota for each seat it was awarded in the first stage. The remaining unallocated seats are then allocated in strict sequence to the parties with the largest remainder. This system enables a small party to win a seat in a constituency even if its share of the vote is less than a quota, provided that its initial vote is greater than the remainders of parties that have already won a seat.

In the example in Table 1, 24,000 votes have been cast in a five-member constituency. The Hare quota is therefore 24,000/5 = 4,800. In the first stage, parties A, B, and C each secure a seat, but party D does not because its total vote is less than the quota. Two seats remain to be allocated at the second stage. One quota is subtracted from the votes cast for parties A, B, and C because they have each won a seat; party D's vote remains unchanged. Since party A has the largest remainder and party D the second-largest remainder, they are awarded the two remaining seats.

The quota is also used in allocating seats under the single-transferable-vote system. This system is widely used in elections to local government and regional assemblies (for instance, in Tasmania, Australia, and Cambridge, Massachusetts), but only rarely in nationwide elections, where it is currently employed in Ireland (since 1922) and for elections to the Australian senate (since 1949). In this system, the number of stages in the seat allocation depends on the number of parties awarded a number of votes equal to or greater than the quota in each of a series of counts.

DIVISOR SYSTEMS

The most common form of seat allocation using a divisor is the highest-average system. The most common type of highest-average system is the d'Hondt system. In round one, a seat is awarded to each party for each bloc of votes equal to a quota. In the second and subsequent rounds of seat allocation, each party's vote is divided by one plus the number of seats it has been allocated in the earlier rounds, and a seat is allocated to the party that has the highest average vote. Table 2 shows the seat allocation by the d'Hondt system in a five-seat constituency contested by four parties, with the same distribution of votes as in Table 1.

In the first round, parties A, B, and C each win one seat. In the second round, the divisor for parties A, B, and C is therefore two, whereas the divisor for party D remains at one. In the second round, party A has the highest average and there-

Table 1. Distribution of Seats by the Largest Remainder System

Party	First-round votes	Hare quota	Seats	Second-round remainder	Seats	Total seats
A	8,700	4,800	1	3,900	1	2
B	6,800	4,800	1	2,000	0	1
C	5,200	4,800	1	400	0	1
D	3,300	4,800	0	3,300	1	1
Total	24,000		3		2	5

Table 2. Distribution of Seats by the d'Hondt Highest Average System

Party	First Round			Second Round			Third Round			
	Votes	Hare quota	Seats won	Divisor	Average	Seats won	Divisor	Average	Seats won	Total seats won
A	8,700	4,800	1	2	4,350	1	3	2,900	0	2
B	6,800	4,800	1	2	3,400	0	2	3,400	1	2
C	5,200	4,800	1	2	2,600	0	2	2,600	0	1
D	3,300	4,800	0	1	3,300	0	1	3,300	0	0
Total	24,000		3			1			1	5

Table 3. Distribution of Seats by the Saint Laguë Highest Average System

Party	First Round			Second Round			Third Round			
	Votes	Hare quota	Seats won	Divisor	Average	Seats won	Divisor	Average	Seats won	Total seats won
A	8,700	4,800	1	3	2,900	0	3	2,900	1	2
B	6,800	4,800	1	3	2,267	0	3	2,267	0	1
C	5,200	4,800	1	3	1,733	0	3	1,733	0	1
D	3,300	4,800	0	1	3,350	1	3	1,117	0	1
Total	24,000		3			1			1	5

fore wins the seat; therefore, party A's divisor in round three is three. In round three, party B wins another seat. Party D wins no seats, since its average is still less than that of party B.

The procedure for allocating seats using the Saint Laguë method is identical to that for allocating seats using d'Hondt, but the divisors used are odd numbers; instead of being 1, 2, 3, 4, and so on, they are 1, 3, 5, 7, and so on (see Table 3). Because the increase in the size of the divisor is greater under the Saint Laguë system than under d'Hondt, it is more difficult for a party, once it has been successful, to win each additional seat. Saint Laguë is therefore more favorable to small parties than the d'Hondt system. In several countries, including Norway and Sweden, a modified version of the Saint Laguë system is used in which the initial divisor is 1.4 rather than one.

Division and subtraction can be combined in the distribution of seats to parties by allocating seats initially by quota and then by highest average rather than by remainder.

See also *Proportional Representation; Proportionality and Disproportionality.*

TOM MACKIE, UNIVERSITY OF STRATHCLYDE

BIBLIOGRAPHY

Carstairs, Andrew. *A Short History of Electoral Systems in Western Europe.* London: Allen and Unwin, 1980.

Cox, Gary. *Making Votes Count: Strategic Coordination in the World Electoral Systems.* Cambridge: Cambridge University Press, 1997.

Farrell, David. *Comparing Electoral Systems.* London and New York: Prentice-Hall, Harvester, Wheatsheaf, 1997.

Hand, Geoffrey, Jacques Georgel, and Christoph Sasse, eds. *European Electoral Systems Handbook.* London: Butterworths, 1979.

Lijphart, Arend. *Electoral Systems and Party Systems: A Study of Twenty-Seven Democracies.* Oxford: Oxford University Press, 1994.

REALIGNING ELECTIONS
IN THE UNITED STATES

In pluralist democracies, all elections are born more or less equal, but some are notably more equal than others. Narrative historians of U.S. history have stressed that elections such as those of 1860 and 1932 have been transforming moments that realigned political loyalties. Analogous moments exist in the history of electoral politics in other countries—for example, in Germany in 1930 and 1932 and in Britain in 1945 and 1979—but the vast bulk of research has been done by U.S. scholars identifying patterns in U.S. politics. Perhaps that is because realigning upheavals seem to have recurred with striking regularity during the past two centuries in the U.S. political system as they have not in other polities.

SYSTEMWIDE REALIGNMENT

Realignments at the mass level are immensely complex events, as is to be expected in a continent-sized country where electoral articulation has tended to focus, at least from the 1930s to the 1960s, on only two major partisan organizations. Parallel developments at the macrosystem level are also complex. And, at both levels, the significance of major regional and sectional antagonisms and aggregate preferences has often been profound. Moreover, realigning elections are only one dimension of system-modifying change.

Decisively abrupt, large-scale, and durable changes in aggregate voter preferences have been closely associated with the eclipse of time-specific regime orders and their replacement by orders with very different coalitional bases and policy agendas. Therefore one can credibly describe and analyze these successive regime orders and their policy choices (and often their constitutional choices) as systems. None is hermetically sealed from the others, yet the beginnings and ends of each have more in common than either has with what preceded or follows.

TYPES OF ELECTIONS COMPARED

The complement of a realigning election and the most frequent type of election is a "maintaining election," reflecting the underlying normal vote pattern. This pattern can be temporarily disrupted by a "deviating election," as in the United States in 1872, 1904, 1952, 1956, and 1972. In a deviating election, short-term forces, especially candidate popularity or unpopularity, play a major but temporary role. The counterpart of a deviating election is a "reinstating" (or counterdeviating) election, which restores something that looks like the status quo ante. In a "realigning election," however, the pattern of the normal vote is substantially altered, and a new pattern is created and maintained for decades.

The application of this typology to elections is not always easy. A durable realignment in the normal vote requires quite abnormal stimuli, major crises in the collective affairs of the nation that have an impact on many electors. No nationwide partisan realignment of voters has clearly occurred since the advent of scientific survey research, and the partisanship of electoral behavior was for a long time viewed by most researchers not as a historically contingent matter but as a given. For example, it was not until the 1990s that John Aldrich and Richard Niemi demonstrated conclusively that a critical realignment had occurred in the U.S. electorate between 1960 and 1972. It was not a classic partisan realignment but, instead, a shift that reconfigured parties as organizations and eroded traditional links between political entrepreneurs and ordinary citizens.

Three major conclusions follow from the identification of realigning elections. First, these events (or, better, compressed sequences of upheaval) are rare. At most they would take up somewhere between one-tenth and one-fifth of chronological time over a two-century span.

Second, realigning elections appear to come in cycles, with sequences of upheaval spaced a long generation apart from each other. This is a major reason why U.S. political historians have found the concept attractive, for it establishes boundaries between historically marked systems and thus identifies the periods central to historiography.

Third, event sequences have occurred that are critical but not strictly in terms of partisanship. For example, scholars of the early federal period in America are divided as to the partisan character of the period from the founding of the U.S. government to the democratizing revolution of the 1820s and 1830s. Many accept Ronald P. Formisano's summary formulation: "Federalists and Republicans: Parties, Yes—System, No." The major transformations of the Jacksonian era have been characterized by the historian Joel Silbey as "aligning realignment," building everything from partisan identification to characteristic partisan structures on a preceding vacuum.

CRITICAL ELECTIONS

In 1955 V. O. Key Jr. coined the term "critical elections" in political science and launched a large professional industry. But what may be regarded as a pioneer effort in this direction was offered to the public by the historian Arthur M. Schlesinger Sr. as early as 1939. His essay, "Tides of American Politics"—its title itself suggesting the existence of long-term rhythm—identified five elections that were major turning points in U.S. political history: 1800, 1828, 1860, 1896, and 1932. Schlesinger's identifications were entirely qualitative in character, but with refinements and qualifications the evidence for their pivotal character has grown with the years. Schlesinger's essay points to a cyclicality of rapid and semi-discontinuous change—the elections are 28, 32, 36, and 36 years apart—and is also the first modern effort to provide some systematic classification of elections.

Although Key called his article "A Theory of Critical Elections," it is essentially a first attempt to differentiate elections empirically on the basis of aggregate election results. In particular, he examined the differential forms of the 1896 and, in Massachusetts, the 1928 elections and the elections' durable consequences for the period from 1888 to 1952.

The abrupt realignments in the 1896 and 1928 elections differed. In 1896 there was a widespread surge in Republican support followed by stability through 1924, whereas in 1928 there was a differential "scissors" effect as pro-Democratic change was concentrated in specific urban environments with disproportionately large Catholic and working-class electorates.

Key used the quantitative analysis of election results to identify patterns of realignment—that is, moments of large-scale and durable changes in voting pattern. In so doing, he concentrated on system-level change instead of on the behavior of individuals because efforts to estimate individual behavior in the historic past are blocked by our inability to interview earlier generations. Key's approach required a sense of history and context unusual among political scientists. System-centered analysis, especially of realignment, is time-series analysis.

Key was well aware that, in a continent-sized country with effective choice usually limited to two rival parties, the determinants of voting behavior are diverse. The 1928 election was realigning only in environments like Massachusetts, where Catholics were numerous and substantial elements of ethnocultural conflict in society at large were already present. Different results occurred in industrial-urban environments such as Seattle, Los Angeles, or Flint, Michigan, where, in 1928, Catholics were less numerous and the surge was not to the Catholic Democrat, Al Smith, but to the Protestant Republican, Herbert Hoover.

Similarly, what looks like a surge at one level (the Northeast in 1896) becomes a case of dramatic polarization at another level (regionally in the same election). The differential scissors between rural and urban Massachusetts after 1928 corresponds to an across-the-board surge at other levels during the New Deal realignment sequence of 1932–1940.

PUNCTUATED EQUILIBRIUM

Some scholars have proposed to describe electoral systems in terms of a model of punctuated equilibrium first developed in the 1970s by the paleontologists Niles Eldridge and Stephen Jay Gould, who characterized bursts of semidiscontinuous change or transition from equilibrium I to equilibrium II. Frank Baumgartner and Bryan Jones use this approach in *Agendas and Instability in American Politics*. As William Riker and subsequent workers in the rational choice tradition have demonstrated, in politics equilibriums do not exist naturally. Any equilibrium-promoting processes in politics that we observe are artifacts of purposive human action. As such, they may be modified or even destroyed by the same or other human actors as contexts and motivations alter.

When equilibriums change, the change is likely to happen suddenly and with scant warning. A flip occurs as the universe of those concerned with politics abruptly expands in a crisis. Negative feedback is replaced by positive feedback, and there is a compressed burst of change—for a while feeding on itself—that conforms to a logistic- or S-curve time pattern. Thereafter a limit is reached and dampdown occurs as negative feedback and routine resume their sway. A historian of the English Puritan revolution of the seventeenth century, Michael Walzer, concisely summarized this stage: "The revolution dies when people get tired of going to meetings."

A focus on equilibrium entails explicit analysis of the various forces that sustain it over periods of time. An early and outstanding work pointing in this direction was by historian Charles G. Sellars, who wrote that a given state of affairs tends to survive more or less indefinitely unless or until a disruptive event collides with it. After all, the interests vested in maintenance of a situation and the stable predictability it yields are legion, and a large system shock is required to launch a positive-feedback flipover that may consign many or all of the forces of equilibrium to oblivion.

A clear example of a punctuated equilibrium was the rise of the Nazi vote (or contagion) among (largely) non-Catholic, non-Socialist components of the German electorate between October 1929 (the Baden state election) and July 1932 (the Reichstag election). It is also the most dramatic demonstration of Riker's nightmares about the fragility of political equilibriums, leading as it did to Hitler's Third Reich. At the same time, neither in Germany nor elsewhere outside the United States have detectable flipover events had a repetitive, cyclical character. This seems to be a central feature of realignments (or bursts of punctuated change) throughout America's history.

PROBLEMS OF METHODOLOGY

Key's pioneering study raised many questions that continue to attract attention and disputes. These include the following: What is a credible taxonomy of different kinds of elections? What methods are appropriate for identifying each kind of election? At what level is the analysis proceeding and to what extent can bridges be built from one level of election results to another? Within what contexts do certain kinds of elections break (or maintain) a repetitive pattern? And, more broadly, what sustains a long-term equilibrium—and when, how, and where is it substantially modified or destroyed?

The development of nationwide sample surveys of the electorate at the University of Michigan derives from the publication of *The American Voter* (1960), which classified voting at the individual level in ways that paralleled Key's aggregate analysis. The most important concept is the "normal vote"—that is, the vote each party can expect if individuals are not affected by short-term influences of issues, events, and personalities. The normal vote is anchored by individuals who have a long-term identification with a particular party.

Also, because of the social psychological frame of reference of survey research, differences in historical context raise questions about the appropriateness of projecting conclusions into earlier and different eras when the orientations of voters to politics may well have differed substantially from our contemporary outlooks. This particularly applies to the great and rare crisis-transition moments when the normal vote is substantially reshaped and other modes of mass participation erupt in conjunction with this process. Circumstantial aggregate evidence, such as much higher levels of voter turnout in the nineteenth century, points in this direction. At crisis-transition moments, it indeed seems as if abnormally large minorities of the electorate acquire an equally abnormal interest in politics and are strikingly proactive, leaving political entrepreneurs to catch up with them as best they can.

The relationship of voters to objects of political cognition is not a constant but is a historically contingent variable. Historic critical realignments have arisen out of crises that leaders of an existing regime order cannot master. Abnormally large minorities of voters suddenly not only cease doing what they have been habituated to doing; they also appear to behave proactively. At the individual level, decisively large minorities of voters quite abruptly stop what they have been doing (voting for a given party or not voting), begin doing something else, and keep doing it for quite a long time with only occasional deviations. The normal vote is transformed, and family- and locality-based political socialization more or less efficiently transmits reshaped preferences to a later generation or generations.

THE AMERICAN EXPERIENCE

Various lines of thought about the U.S. political experience combine to explain the pattern of realigning elections. As Louis Hartz and other students of dominant U.S. political culture have stressed, the U.S. culture has been dominated by consensus on many axes of potential conflict that elsewhere have resulted in actual conflict, including a general commitment to free enterprise, individual liberty, political egalitarianism, and religion (in general if not in particular). Although there has been political conflict in U.S. history, as the Civil War and Reconstruction experience in particular reminds us, political conflicts in the United States have been far less linked to protracted struggles among collectivities (whether national, religious, or social class) than in Europe. Moreover, at least from 1815 to 1940, no credible external military threat existed and, therefore, there was no incentive for centralized state building.

The historical experience of the American Revolution, decisively ratified in the 1800 election, demonstrated the popular rejection of a would-be Court Party and the embracement of Country Party ideology as a core value in our politics. Given this, it is not surprising that this consensus has also been profoundly antigovernment (or antistate). As described by James Bryce in 1888 and reiterated verbatim by political scientist Samuel P. Huntington in 1974, U.S. attitudes toward government in principle, if not always in operation, have included support for assertions such as "all government is based on and limited by law and the people," "when government activity is necessary, state and local government is to be preferred to federal," and "on the whole, the less government the better." If some of this seems reminiscent of Republican Party rhetoric of 1994—the Contract with America and Speaker of the House Newt Gingrich's opinions—it is no coincidence.

Established, major-party politicians, however, normally have no rational action incentives to accommodate an emergent public demand along a political axis of conflict different from the one they have routinized and from which they profit. Occasional bursts of significant third-party protest have swept like prairie fire through the system from time to time for two reasons: major change is always occurring in the world's most politically autonomous society and economy, producing not only winners but losers; and the losers, following the democratic and egalitarian cues in the culture, gravitate to government.

The U.S. Constitution may be regarded as a not-quite-perfect negative-feedback machine that places high barriers to the incremental adaptation of the government to demands for change. Most of the time, these demands either cumulate until some triggering event or events break this dam, or, because of other change, the initial demand evaporates. In comparative developmental terms, the Constitution is often viewed as archaic and the political order structurally very conservative. In the Constitution's practical operations, it reflects what Riker called "congealed taste" in a society for a system that is against big government.

And yet, as Chief Justice John Marshall observed in 1819, the Constitution is an instrument designed to be "adapted to the various crises of human affairs" and also to "endure for ages to come." It can adapt to crises in U.S. affairs only when the onset of crisis has produced exceptionally high pressures affecting both the mass electorate and those who wield power in separated institutions of government.

These factors provide a durable context for understanding that, out of long-term stasis and its contradictions, an explosive power is generated from time to time for equilibrium-destroying upheavals that lead to the creation of a new and very differently patterned political balance. Although realigning elections are not the sole vehicles for nonincremental change in U.S. politics, they are the most important mechanisms for permitting recalibration of the state's steering functions with the society it purports to govern.

See also *Election Forecasting; Swing; Volatility, Electoral.*

WALTER DEAN BURNHAM,
UNIVERSITY OF TEXAS AT AUSTIN

BIBLIOGRAPHY

Aldrich, John. *Why Parties?* Chicago: University of Chicago Press, 1995.

Baumgartner, Frank, and Bryan Jones. *Agendas and Instability in American Politics.* Chicago: University of Chicago Press, 1993.

Brady, David. *Critical Elections and Congressional Policy Making.* Stanford: Stanford University Press, 1988.

Burnham, Walter Dean. *Critical Elections and the Mainsprings of American Politics.* New York: Norton, 1970.

Campbell, Angus, Philip E. Converse, Warren E. Miller, and Donald E. Stokes. *The American Voter.* New York: Wiley, 1960.

Clubb, Jerome M., and Howard W. Allen, eds. *Electoral Change and Stability in American Political History.* New York: Free Press, 1971.

Clubb, Jerome M., William Flanigan, and Nancy H. Zingale. *Partisan Realignment.* Beverly Hills, Calif.: Sage, 1980.

Dodd, Lawrence C., and Calvin Jillson, eds. *The Dynamics of American Politics.* Boulder: Westview Press, 1994.

Gienapp, William E. *Origins of the Republican Party, 1852–1856.* New York: Oxford University Press, 1986.

Key, V. O., Jr. "A Theory of Critical Elections." *Journal of Politics* 17, no. 1 (1955): 3–18.

Kleppner, Paul. *Continuity and Change in Electoral Politics, 1893–1928.* Westport, Conn.: Greenwood, 1987.

Sellars, Charles G. "The Equilibrium Cycle in Two-Party Politics." *Public Opinion Quarterly* 29 (1965): 16–38.

Shafer, Byron E., ed. *The End of Realignment? Interpreting American Electoral Eras.* Madison: University of Wisconsin Press, 1991.

Sundquist, James D. *Dynamics of the Party System.* 2d ed. Washington, D.C.: Brookings Institution, 1983.

REAPPORTIONMENT AND REDISTRICTING

The apportionment (or allocation) of legislative seats over a given territory and the districting (or drawing) of the boundaries themselves are central to competitive elections. *Apportionment, reapportionment,* and *redistribution* are terms that refer to the allocation of districts, seats, or constituencies among the various units or regions of a political system. In the United States the 435 congressional districts are "reapportioned" among the fifty states every ten years, whereas in neighboring Canada the three hundred or so constituencies in the House of Commons are said to be "redistributed" among the ten provinces and two territories. In both countries the allocations, subject to guarantees of minimum numbers of districts to each federal unit, are based on a state or province's share of the country's total population as determined by the latest census.

"Redistricting," which is commonly described as "electoral boundary readjustments" in countries that base their parliamentary system on the Westminster model, is the act of determining the territorial boundaries or limits of the electoral districts, divisions, or electorates (as they are known in different countries) once they have been apportioned among the various units or regions. The diverse terms employed for allocating seats and drawing boundaries are often used interchangeably in the press, academic literature, and political discourse.

ABUSES OF THE PROCESS

Reapportionment and redistricting (which, in effect, are two stages of the same process) have long played an integral role in politics, so much so that politicians have historically used them to try to enhance their own partisan advantage. The time-honored practice of manipulating district boundaries for political benefit is referred to as "gerrymandering," after Gov. Elbridge Gerry of Massachusetts. In 1812 Gerry signed into law an electoral districting bill establishing odd-shaped districts whose design had no purpose other than to further one party's electoral interests at the expense of another's.

Malapportionment, which may be intentional, as with gerrymandering, or unintentional (more likely the former), is an often grossly unfair variation in population among districts. The greater the population inequality among electoral districts, the more the districts at the extremes of the population range are said to be "malapportioned."

Issues of apportionment, periodic boundary readjustments, and gerrymandering need never be raised in countries that do not employ a form of territorial representation. Israel, for example, uses a system of proportional representation to elect its 128-member Knesset from lists of party candidates on a countrywide basis. The entire country is treated as a single electoral district, rendering reapportionment and redistricting unnecessary. In countries using some other variant of proportional representation (such as Ireland and Malta), the election of members from multimember districts means that electoral boundaries must be delimited periodically. In countries employing single-member electoral districts (such as Canada, France, India, the United Kingdom, and the United States), the need to redefine the electoral boundaries periodically stems from shifts in population, although the interval between the boundary adjustments varies considerably from one country to another. The Canadian and U.S. constitutions require that district boundaries be redrawn following every decennial census; by contrast, India's last redistribution was in 1973, and its next will get under way no sooner than 2001. Since there are vastly more countries with at least some territorially defined districts than there are countries, like Israel, with none, the issues raised by apportionment and redistricting are of widespread importance.

WHO PARTICIPATES?

Two of the most basic questions in the process are who apportions the seats and who draws the boundaries within a country. The first part of the exercise (apportionment) is the easier of the two on which to reach agreement. Statutory laws typically determine the number of seats allocated to the various units in a country, for example, to England, Scotland, Wales, and Northern Ireland in the United Kingdom, or to the *länder* in Germany or the states in Australia. In some cases the total number of seats in the lower national house is fixed by law (since 1929 at 435 in the United States, for example). In other cases the size of a legislature or parliament changes from one reapportionment to another because of population

growth or movement (Canada and the United Kingdom) or the inclusion of additional population or territory (Germany following reunification in 1990).

The much thornier issue is that of redrawing constituency boundaries. The ways in which redistricting may be carried out range from entirely partisan, at one end of the spectrum, to nonpartisan and independent, at the other. As redistricting in the United States has shown, partisan involvement in the process guarantees considerable controversy among the principal political actors. Since the 1960s, each decennial redistricting has generated a large number of court cases. On the other hand, the work of independent commissions in countries that followed the pioneering lead of Australia tends to go largely unnoticed by the public and the press, which is not to say the politicians in those countries are unconcerned with the presumed electoral impact of boundary changes. Rather, the independent commissions' low profile reinforces the degree to which the process has been removed from the partisan political level and turned over to independent commissions whose decisions are final and incontestable.

The highly politicized process followed in the United States is also marked by its degree of decentralization of decision making. Once the 435 seats have been apportioned among the 50 states, the responsibility for drawing congressional district boundaries falls on the state legislatures. Therefore, partisan control of the legislative and executive (for veto purposes) branches at the state level is highly desirable when redistricting is under way. At the other extreme, Australia (since 1902) and Canada (since 1964) have opted in favor of independent commissions over partisan, government-dominated parliamentary committees. In both countries, commissions established within each state or province apply criteria and follow procedures established by federal statutes.

In spite of the obvious differences between the American and Australian/Canadian processes, the results of reapportionment and redistricting in the three countries show a degree of similarity that belies the extent to which the respective procedures are decentralized and are subject to the application of different political pressures or statutorily defined criteria. In the United States the redistricting process is a result of four decades of court involvement and the application of judicially sanctioned principles drawing on the doctrine of "one person, one vote." In both Canada and Australia, where there has been a demonstrable trend over the past few decades toward constructing an increasing number of districts with more equitable populations, the result stems from the rules included in the governing legislation and in the application of those rules by the independent commissions.

Public participation in the reapportionment/redistricting process also varies across nations. In Australia, for example, the governing statute requires that public input be sought at various points, including in advance of the commission's drafting its initial proposals. If at a later stage any individual or organization objects to the proposed boundaries, an inquiry must be held. Canada also encourages public participation by holding public hearings and welcoming written briefs on boundary proposals. In contrast to Australia, however, public participation in Canada comes at a single stage—after the commission has completed its initial set of maps. In the United Kingdom a public hearing is held only if local authorities or at least one hundred voters object to the boundary proposals. Politicians are permitted to participate in the hearings in the United Kingdom, with the result that objections may amount to little more than thinly veiled partisan self-interest.

On the question of public participation, as with most other questions relating to the drawing of electoral boundaries, the United States is different from other countries. The principal stage for voicing objections to proposed electoral districts is the court system. Since the early 1960s these have been numerous, having been launched by a wide variety of interest groups, individuals, and political parties. Their effect has been to turn the courts and court cases into major elements in the redistricting process.

COURT INVOLVEMENT

A 1962 U.S. Supreme Court decision started the "judicialization" of the electoral districting process. In that year the Court accepted in *Baker v. Carr* a fundamentally new doctrine in American law. For the first time, legislative apportionment was held to be a "justiciable question," and courts could subsequently accept the equal protection of the laws clause of the Fourteenth Amendment as grounds for overturning municipal, state, or congressional districts whose construction violated the principle that one person's vote should equal another's. Outdated or malapportioned districts (which tended to favor rural voters over urban) would no longer be permissible. "One person, one vote" became the new mantra of American legislative apportionment.

American courts have decided countless cases. These cases, together with the Voting Rights Act (initially passed by Congress in 1965 and amended in 1975 and 1982), have served to ensure that districts at all levels have been constructed as equitably as possible and that a racial minority whose population is sufficiently large and concentrated as to constitute a majority of a geographically defined area could turn to the courts to have district boundaries drawn to reflect that fact. "Majority-minority" districts were added to the list of judicially sanctioned apportionment principles. Their construction was reflected in the dramatic increase in the 1990s in the number of African American and Hispanic members of the House of Representatives. The drive to create majority-minority districts also led to the designing of some districts with unnatural and particularly odd configurations—one being likened by its critics to a bug splattered on a car windshield. Beginning with *Shaw v. Reno* in 1993, however, the U.S. Supreme Court began what would eventually become a case-by-case re-examination of the application of the doctrine of "racial gerrymandering," as the practice had become known. The Court held that the Fourteenth Amendment, in the absence of compelling interest, prohibited states from constructing districts in which race was the "predominant factor" motivating their design.

In no other country does the frequency of redistricting litigation even approximate that of the United States. In Canada, for example, courts have only begun to entertain (and at that, very rarely) cases alleging discriminatory treatment of voters under revised sets of electoral boundaries. The adoption of the Canadian Charter of Rights and Freedoms in 1982 opened up, under its "right to vote" clause, the possibility of individuals or groups challenging the results of an electoral boundary readjustment. The only significant case to have been decided to date by the Supreme Court of Canada (the *Carter* reference of 1991) implicitly accepted population limits of districts up to 25 percent above or below a province's average district population size. (This contrasts with much tighter variance limits in both the United States, by virtue of court decisions, and Australia, as a result of legislation). It also held that the principle of strict voter equality is not a constitutional requirement in Canada, but that "effective representation" and "relative parity of voting power" are. To determine these, factors such as geography, community history, community interests, and minority representation would need to be weighed carefully in the construction of the districts. The ruling has left proponents of "one person, one vote" less satisfied with the (admittedly limited) role of the Canadian courts than with the U.S. courts.

FREQUENCY OF REAPPORTIONMENT AND REDISTRICTING

The frequency with which reapportionment and redistricting are undertaken varies from one country to another. In some jurisdictions, as noted, they are carried out at ten-year intervals and are jump-started by the completion of the major census. New Zealand redraws its boundaries every five years. In Australia they are redrawn every seven years, or sooner if in one or more states population shifts warrant a readjustment. The United Kingdom has less rigid requirements, with electoral boundary reviews occurring not less than eight years and not more than twelve years apart. France, at the far end of the spectrum, has no specified time limit between redistributions.

There is also a wide variance among countries in the degree of partisan involvement in the process of redrawing electoral maps. At one extreme is the United States, in which virtually complete partisan control marks the entire process, including even some of the challenges to the courts. At the other end are countries like New Zealand and Australia, in which redistricting plans become effective immediately upon publication of the final report. The Canadian practice is similar, although it does allow members of Parliament, through consideration by a committee of the House of Commons, to voice objections to the proposed maps, which are then considered by the respective federal independent commission. The commissions have no obligation to accept the objections, and once the commissions' maps have been finalized, they are implemented. In the United Kingdom, by contrast, Parliament must accept the boundary recommendations before they are implemented, but their acceptance is generally viewed as a formality.

Countries that reapportion their seats more frequently than others demonstrate a stronger commitment to the principle of proportionality of seats among the various regions, states, or provinces, for they are attempting to track more closely the shifts in population that inevitably occur with time. The contrasting experience of Australia and India speaks directly to that point. In the former, the readjustments occur after a maximum interval of seven years, but they occur more often if population shifts warrant it; in India at least three decades will have elapsed since the last drawing of boundaries before the next is in place.

METHODS OF REAPPORTIONMENT

In addition to their frequency, reapportionments also vary from one country to another in the methods of determining the number of seats to which a region or federal unit is entitled. In the United States the so-called Huntingdon method is employed, which allows each state one district (in keeping with Article 1, section 2 of the Constitution) and divides the remaining 385 seats in succession, using the formula: state's population/$n(n$-1), where n is the number of seats. In Canada, by contrast, an electoral quotient is established by dividing the number of seats in the House of Commons in 1976 (282 less three seats assigned to the northern territories) into the national population (minus the population of the territories), then dividing the population of each province by that quotient to determine its number of seats. Canada augments this apportionment through various constitutional or legislated guarantees of additional seats in order to give some protection to smaller provinces and those with declining popula-

tions. The effect of these "add-on" constituencies in the reapportionment of the 1990s was to boost the Canadian Commons to a record 301 members.

The contrasting experience of these two neighboring countries in the apportionment among their federal units and design of their seats speaks to the variety of ways in which reapportionment and redistricting have evolved in different countries. The American approach to reapportionment of electoral districts among the fifty states underscores a commitment to balancing federalism and representation, with the emphasis on the latter once the constitutional minimum number of seats has been met. That is missing in Canada, where special treatment of small provinces and provinces with declining population has long been a feature of the reapportionment formula and has led to much greater population variance among districts than exists in the United States. Like other countries attempting to balance representational and territorial factors in their periodic reapportionment/redistricting exercise, Canada and the United States have each found an acceptable compromise that would be seen as out of place were it introduced in the other.

See also *Gerrymandering; Positive Discrimination in Redistricting in the United States; Rotten Boroughs; Safe Seat; Weighted Voting.*

JOHN COURTNEY, UNIVERSITY OF SASKATCHEWAN

BIBLIOGRAPHY

Administration and Cost of Elections (ACE) Project. "Boundary Delimitation," *http://www.aceproject.org*

Butler, David, and Bruce E. Cain. "Reapportionment: A Study in Comparative Government." *Electoral Studies* 4, no. 3 (December 1985): 197–213.

Courtney, John C. "Drawing Electoral Boundaries." In *Canadian Parties in Transition,* 2d ed., edited by A. Brian Tanguay and Alain G. Gagnon, 328–348. Scarborough: Nelson Canada, 1996.

———. "Electoral Boundary Redistributions: Contrasting Approaches to Parliamentary Representation." In *Comparative Political Studies: Australia and Canada,* edited by Malcolm Alexander and Brian Galligan, 45–58. Melbourne: Pitman, 1992.

———. "Parliament and Representation: The Unfinished Agenda of Electoral Redistributions." *Canadian Journal of Political Science* 21, no. 4 (December 1988): 675–690.

———. " 'Theories Masquerading as Principles': Canadian Electoral Boundary Commissions and the Australian Model." In *The Canadian House of Commons Essays in Honour of Norman Ward,* edited by John C. Courtney, 135–172. Calgary, Alberta: University of Calgary Press, 1985.

Courtney, John C., Peter MacKinnon, and David E. Smith, eds. *Drawing Boundaries.* Saskatoon, Saskatchewan: Fifth House Publishers, 1992.

Grofman, Bernard. *Voting Rights, Voting Wrongs.* New York: Priority Press, 1990.

Grofman, Bernard, Lisa Handley, and Richard G. Niemi. *Minority Representation and the Quest for Voting Equality.* New York: Cambridge University Press, 1992.

McLean, Iain, and David Butler, eds. *Fixing the Boundaries: Defining and Redefining Single-Member Electoral Districts.* Aldershot, England: Dartmouth Publishing, 1996.

O'Hare, William P., ed. *Redistricting in the 1990s: A Guide for Minority Groups.* Washington, D.C.: Population Reference Bureau, 1989.

Rallings, Colin, and Michael Thrasher. "The Parliamentary Boundary Commissions: Rules, Interpretations and Politics." *Parliamentary Affairs* 47, no. 3 (July 1994): 387–404.

Sullivan, Kathleen M. "Majority-Minority Districts: Do They Increase Minority Influence or Dilute It?" *Public Affairs Report* 36, no. 6 (1997): 1, 7–8.

RECALL ELECTIONS

The recall process in the United States permits voters to petition to place on the ballot the question of removing from office an elected official before the expiration of the official's term of office. The recall, like the initiative and the popular referendum, effectively empowers citizens to fire their elected officials. It also shares with its progressive cousins—the initiative and popular referendum—a faith in the voters to make these decisions and a desire to involve voters more in the governmental process. It is in many ways similar to a vote of no confidence in a parliament, except that in recall ordinary citizens force the issue and a majority of voters then decides the fate of the elected official.

HISTORY OF THE RECALL MOVEMENT

Proponents of the recall, like the early advocates of the initiative and the popular referendum, trace the roots of the recall to Athenian city-states and Switzerland. Again, as with the initiative and popular referendum, American progressive reformers of the first two decades of the twentieth century advocated the recall movement. But the recall also became part of the municipal reform movement that wanted to replace boss rule and party machine politics with nonpartisan local elections, changes in the structure of local governments, and—the ultimate check on abuse of power—the recall.

First adopted in 1903 when voters approved a new city charter for Los Angeles, the recall is now permitted at the state or the local levels in all but fourteen states. The first state to adopt the recall was Oregon in 1908, and within six years nine additional states had adopted recall provisions. As with the initiative, states that do not provide for the process at the state level permit local governments to use the process. Since their inception, recall elections have prompted intense debates over the roles of voters and elected officials.

WHO CAN BE RECALLED?

Recall provisions usually make all state, county, and local officials, excluding judges, subject to the recall. There are exceptions, however. Some states, like New Mexico, exclude state officials; others, like Minnesota, apply recall only to elected county officials. As many as eighteen states apply it only to local offices. Three states have unusual removal provisions that function without an election and are essentially impeachment provisions with varying modes of application.

Statewide recall elections have been relatively rare—only three recall petitions against governors have met the signature requirements: Gov. Lynn Frazier of North Dakota in 1921, Gov. Henry S. Johnston of Oklahoma in 1927, and Gov. Evan Mecham of Arizona in 1988. Governors Frazier and Johnston were recalled from office, but Governor Mecham was impeached before the recall election was held.

Removal of state legislators is equally rare; one scholar of the process tallies only nine state legislators in the twentieth century who were removed through recall. In one case, in Michigan in 1983, the recall of two senators meant the party control of the state senate switched from Democratic to Republican hands. Such outcomes are rare.

Local recall elections occur with somewhat greater frequency, especially in California, Oregon, and Michigan. Political scientist Thomas Cronin has estimated that at least three-fourths of the recall elections in the United States take place at the city council and school district levels. One of the most notable of these local recall elections happened in 1983 and was aimed at the San Francisco mayor, Dianne Feinstein. Mayor Feinstein had pushed for a strict handgun control measure and angered a small but vocal minority that reacted by forcing a recall election. The mayor effectively made the recall election a referendum on whether the use of the process was appropriate in her case. On election day, more than 80 percent of the voters who voted in the recall election voted to retain Mayor Feinstein.

Because of the infrequency of these elections, especially since the advent of survey research, we know comparatively little about how voters function in recall elections. Cronin found that turnout in recall elections is typically higher than turnout for the same level of contest in regular general elections.

Are federal officials, like members of the U.S. House of Representatives, subject to recall? The Wisconsin constitution provides voters with such a recall process, as do the constitutions of Michigan and New Jersey. Student of the recall process Joseph F. Zimmerman concludes that it will take an amendment to the U.S. Constitution before the recall applies to federal officers.

GOALS OF RECALL

The recall at its most basic can be seen as a means of removing a corrupt politician from office. But many thoughtful advocates of the recall device perceive elected officials as delegates in the Burkean sense and believe they should vote the views of their constituents; therefore, when representatives wander from their constituents' preferences, advocates of recall believe the representatives can and should be removed from office. But Edmund Burke also spoke of elected officials as trustees who should vote their conscience. Opponents of the recall believe it limits vision and leadership and discourages officials from leading public opinion instead of following it.

Recall can accomplish several goals. Proponents of adoption of the recall argue that it provides a safety valve for public sentiments and concerns and a means of resolving these concerns, it might check the power of special interests because officeholders will fear a recall if they behave inappropriately, it provides an alternative to impeachment, and it permits voters to hold elected officials immediately accountable for any action that offends a significant segment of the public.

Opponents of recall counter that recall of an official discourages leadership on vexing issues, the fear of a recall may discourage good people from seeking office in the first place, and recall elections effectively permit interest groups to harass officeholders by forcing divisive and disruptive elections.

HOW DOES IT WORK?

As with the initiative and the popular referendum, the recall is triggered when proponents meet a minimum-signature threshold, typically 25 percent of the vote for governor in the last gubernatorial election. The minimum-signature range for statewide recall is from 20 percent in California to 40 percent in Kansas. Should petitioners meet the signature threshold, the recalled official is often given a few days to resign, and, if the official does not resign, an election is often scheduled within 120 days.

Meeting the signature threshold does not always result in a recall election. For example, in 1988 Arizona citizens qualified a recall petition for Governor Mecham and a date was set for that election; but, before the election was held, the Arizona legislature impeached the governor.

Recall ballots provide voters with a succinct summary of the reasons for the recall of the public officer as well as the elected official's response and counterarguments. Some jurisdictions provide for a voter handbook in such elections; in San Francisco the handbook can include paid advertisements. Many jurisdictions provide for voters to decide only whether or not to remove the recalled official from office, but in some jurisdictions alternate officials are also on the ballot.

Polling data demonstrate that the public favors the idea of recall even though most Americans have never been asked to sign a recall petition and have never voted in a recall election. Such public support for a process so infrequently used suggests that it reflects broad public attitudes toward direct democracy.

See also *Democracy and Elections; Initiative: United States; Plebiscites; Referendums: Europe; Referendums: United States; Term of Office; Term Limits.*

DAVID B. MAGLEBY, BRIGHAM YOUNG UNIVERSITY

BIBLIOGRAPHY

Cox, Gail D. "The Trials of Gov. Evan Mecham." *National Law Journal* 10 (March 28, 1988): 1, 8–9.
Cronin, Thomas E. *Direct Democracy: The Politics of Initiative, Referendum, and Recall.* Cambridge: Harvard University Press, 1989.
Ford, Mark L. *When Voters Change Their Minds: Recall Elections.* Lexington, Ky.: Council of State Governments, 1984.
Price, Charles M. "Recall at the Local Level: Dimensions and Implications." *National Civic Review* 72 (April 1983): 199–206.
Zimmerman, Joseph F. *The Recall: Tribunal of the People.* Westport, Conn.: Praeger, 1997.

REDISTRICTING

See *Positive Discrimination in Redistricting in the United States; Reapportionment and Redistricting*

REFERENDUMS: EUROPE

A referendum is, in the words of David Butler and Austin Ranney, a vote on some public issue by a mass electorate. Virtually all modern European states are basically representative democracies, in which the people elect a parliament that elects a government, which then makes effective decisions on most issues. But in a significant number of countries there is provision for the people to decide certain issues directly.

Across Europe the practice varies considerably. In only one country, Switzerland, can the referendum be said to be a central and routine part of the political decision-making process. Switzerland has, on average, from six to ten referendums per year, and, indeed, over the years it has held more national referendums than the rest of the world put together. Other countries that make extensive use of the referendum include Italy, Ireland, France, and Denmark. In contrast, the referendum has played little or no part in the post-1945 governance of Germany, Britain, Belgium, or the Netherlands.

INITIATIVE

Referendums can come about in many ways and for many reasons. In just a few countries is there provision for the initiative, by which a designated number of voters, by signing a petition, can bring about a referendum on a particular issue. The initiative exists in both Switzerland and Italy, which is why these two countries top the list of popular votes. In Switzerland the rejective initiative (also known as the optional referendum) allows 50,000 voters to launch a challenge to any bill recently passed by parliament. Most bills are not challenged in this way, but about half of those that are challenged do not survive. The provision has effect not only when it leads to the defeat of a bill in a popular vote but also when those framing a bill take care to assuage potential sponsors of a rejective initiative during the process of formulating the bill, in order to preempt any challenge through the initiative. Swiss voters can also bring about an initiative in an effort to change the constitution or to challenge an international treaty that the government intends to sign.

In Italy, too, voters can bring about a popular vote, to attempt to strike down a constitutional amendment or a piece of legislation. In contrast to Switzerland, where only recently passed bills can be challenged, in Italy any item of legislation, no matter how old, can be made the subject of a popular vote. Moreover, the objective may be amendment rather than abrogation of the law. In addition to these established democracies, there is also provision for the initiative in some of the new postcommunist regimes in eastern Europe, notably Lithuania, Russia, Slovenia, and Slovakia.

In countries other than Italy, Switzerland, and the east European states noted above, use of the referendum can come about only through a decision of a representative organ, that is, a parliament (or some percentage of the members of parliament), government, president, or some combination of these. For example, in Denmark a third of the members of parliament may insist that a referendum be held on a bill. Even though this provision has been invoked only once, on a package of four bills on land reform in 1963, it may still be important by compelling the parliamentary majority to pay more consideration to the views of the minority. This kind of provision has been termed by the leading referendum scholar Pier Vincenzo Uleri "decision-controlling," indicating that its role is to enable one actor to challenge a decision made by another actor rather than to promote a measure of its own devising. Besides Denmark, a number of other countries (such as Austria, Greece, Iceland, Ireland, Spain, and Sweden) provide for such decision-controlling referendums, but in practice they have been rarely or never used.

FREQUENCY OF REFERENDUMS

The use of the referendum, as noted earlier, varies widely across Europe, and in a manner that defies easy explanation. It is not invariably the case that small countries use the referendum more than large ones, or vice versa, or that federal states use it more than unitary states, or vice versa. Different historical traditions, political cultures, and constitutional provisions all play their part in accounting for the variation.

The use of referendums in Europe is increasing, though this is due largely to an upsurge in a few countries rather than to a general pattern. Italy held very few referendums prior to the 1970s, but in 1970 the passage of a constitutional law opened the floodgates: Italy held thirty-nine referendums over the next twenty-five years, including twelve on the same day in 1995. In Ireland, too, use of the referendum has been increasing; there were only four referendums prior to the 1970s, but since 1970 there has been, on average, more than one every two years.

REFERENDUM ISSUES

Referendum issues embrace both the adoption of a new constitutional regime and the choice of policy outputs within that regime. The former is accepted more widely than the latter as a suitable issue for resolution by popular vote: some countries that have employed the referendum to affirm the establishment of a new regime have not routinely, if at all, employed it as a means of political decision-making. In these countries, referendums are most widespread at times of regime-building. For example, referendums on whether the state should be a monarchy or a republic were held in Belgium and Italy following World War II, and Icelandic independence from Denmark was endorsed overwhelmingly in 1944. Similarly, in France the first eight referendums held after 1945, up to and including the 1962 vote on the direct election of the president, can be seen as regime-establishing. Neither Belgium nor Iceland has held any further referendums, and in France there were only four more in the thirty-six years after the vote on direct election of the president.

In the 1970s, after the ending of military dictatorships, voters decided by referendum to establish a democratic republic in Greece and a democratic monarchy in Spain. Less dramatic examples of regime change occurred in Denmark in 1953 and Ireland in 1937, where new constitutions were adopted by direct vote of the people. In Norway in 1905 there was a 99.9 percent vote in favor of the country becoming independent of Sweden. The Norwegian vote demonstrates another role for the referendum; the outcome of the vote was never in doubt, and the value of the referendum lay not in resolving a contentious issue but in allowing the people to affirm a shared and fundamental value.

Another issue, akin to regime change, that has led to a recent increase in use of the referendum in certain countries is participation in the process of European integration within the European Union. Ten countries have held European Union–related referendums. In some member-countries it was necessary, according to the written constitution, to hold a referendum before joining; Denmark and Ireland in the 1970s, and Austria in the 1990s, held such popular votes. In others, the unwritten constitution is generally felt to require the consent of the people before such a step is taken, given its major implications for national sovereignty. Thus both Finland and Sweden held referendums in 1994 at which the people gave their consent to joining the Union. Similarly, on two occasions, in 1972 and 1994, when Norway applied to join and was accepted, the people voted narrowly against joining, although each time a clear majority of members of parliament were in favor of membership. Even in Britain, where the supremacy of parliament was traditionally unchallenged, a referendum on membership was held in 1975; on this occasion the referendum was not on the question of joining, this decision having been made in 1973 by parliament, but on the question of withdrawing. In addition to these votes, several countries of the European Union (Denmark, France, and Ireland) subsequently held referendums on aspects of the deepening of European integration. Thus far, every vote in every country, except for the two votes in Norway on membership and a 1992 referendum in Denmark, has been in favor of European integration.

Beyond such major constitutional questions, the referendum is used infrequently in most European countries to settle issues that could be regarded as the staple fare of day-to-day politics. In only five countries have such issues become the objects of referendum. In Switzerland the initiative provision means that a sufficiently large group of voters can put virtually any issue on the agenda, if it is framed as a constitutional amendment, so a highly disparate range of questions has been the object of popular votes; examples include abolishing the army, the sale of strong liquor, nuclear energy, various agricultural topics, and restricting motor traffic. In Italy, similarly, the agenda is set by groups of voters, who can challenge any aspect of an existing law, so Italians have been called on to vote not only on major moral issues, such as divorce and abortion, but also on technical or even trivial issues such as the trade unions that should be accorded negotiating rights in certain situations, or the amount of advertising permitted during the broadcasting of films on television.

The other three countries where a number of referendums have concerned what might be seen as routine policy matters are Denmark, Ireland, and France. In Denmark and Ireland, as in Switzerland, every change to the constitution requires the approval of the people, voting in a referendum. Consequently, both countries have held referendums on issues that, in most countries, would have been settled by parliament. In Denmark it took five referendums between 1953 and 1978 simply to reduce the voting age from twenty-five to eighteen years. In Ireland several votes have been held on minor or technical constitutional changes—such as altering the way the largely powerless upper house of parliament is elected or amending the rule regarding the confidentiality of government discussions—which have produced voter indifference and led to a low turnout. Having said this, in both countries more substantive matters have also been referendum issues.

In Denmark the most keenly contested referendums have concerned the European Union; turnout at each of the referendums on the subject has been high, on one occasion exceeding 90 percent, and partly as a result the Danes are better informed about the Union than are citizens in other member states. In Ireland, besides the European Union, major topics have included the electoral system (voters decided on two occasions to retain the single transferable vote rather than adopt a single-member-plurality system) and the same moral issues that have arisen in Italy. (Ireland held six referendums on divorce and abortion between 1983 and 1995.) In addition, in 1998 there was an overwhelming vote in favor of the agreement reached on Northern Ireland among the Irish and British governments and the political parties in Northern Ireland, an agreement that entailed the Republic of Ireland dropping its constitutional claim over Northern Ireland.

The French experience is slightly different. Whereas in Denmark and Ireland the referendum takes place under prescribed conditions, in France there has been a long tradition of rulers calling an ad hoc popular vote for opportunistic reasons. In the nineteenth century several referendums supposedly produced virtually unanimous support for authoritarian leaders. Twentieth-century referendums, by contrast, were genuine democratic exercises, but several were clearly designed to boost the position of the rulers rather than to resolve a political problem. For example, in 1972 and 1993 the presidents of the day, Georges Pompidou and François Mitterrand, respectively, called referendums on aspects of the European integration process. Neither referendum was necessary under the French constitution, and in each case the main motive was to exacerbate splits among the opposition parties, whose views on European integration differed greatly.

In other countries, referendums on nonconstitutional policy issues have been exceptional. Nuclear energy has surfaced as a referendum issue in both Austria and Sweden, and indeed Sweden has held popular votes on matters that have not been the subject of referendums anywhere else, such as whether to drive on the right or the left and the complicated technical issue of supplementary pension schemes. A number of countries have held referendums at a subnational level, including some, such as Germany, Spain, and the United Kingdom, that have no strong tradition of holding national referendums. In the United Kingdom these subnational referendums have had strong constitutional implications: the people of Scotland and Wales voted in favor of devolution measures in 1997, after earlier schemes failed to get enough support in 1979 referendums; and in 1998 the people of Northern Ireland accepted an agreement that entailed significant changes in the government of Northern Ireland and its relationship with the Republic of Ireland.

POLITICAL PARTIES
AND REFERENDUMS

The issues that are settled by referendums, not surprisingly, often do not correspond to the lines of conflict that structure the party system. Issues that do correspond, after all, are more likely to feature centrally in general election campaigns. In consequence, referendum issues often divide parties internally, so parties are not always the main actors in referendum campaigns. In a number of countries the main actors are instead ad hoc groups drawing on activists from several parties or from none, and parties sometimes keep out of the fray altogether, either so as not to expend scarce resources on an issue that is probably not of central importance to them or to avoid exacerbating internal divisions.

When parties are sufficiently unified on a referendum issue to get involved in the campaign, their cues to their supporters undoubtedly have an effect, yet they cannot be confident that all their usual supporters will follow their lead. If things were otherwise, that is, if all electors voted as their party leaders bade them, then there would be little point in referendums, which would be simply an expensive way of registering a decision that reflected the balance of party forces. When parties are internally divided on an issue and the party system cannot resolve it satisfactorily, the referendum may be a particularly appropriate method of reaching a decision.

Partly for this reason, the referendum is sometimes seen as a threat to existing parties and party systems. Referendums may be bruising and traumatic events for parties if they concern an issue that divides a party internally. Given that in most European countries the party system is still based on the left-right cleavage, many of the issues that arise in contemporary European politics, such as "postmaterialist" issues or questions of national sovereignty, do indeed divide parties. Yet this is not necessarily disruptive of parties or party systems. After all, such issues would cause problems for parties in any case, whether or not there was a referendum. Indeed, it has been argued that referendums on such issues actually help preserve the party system status quo, by acting as a "lightning rod," removing a difficult issue from the party political agenda and allowing it to be resolved in a different arena.

THE IMPACT OF REFERENDUMS

For many involved in politics, the most important question about referendums concerns their political impact. Do referendums favor conservative or progressive causes, are the outcomes more often welcomed by the political right or by the left? On these questions, as on many other aspects of the referendum, generalization is not easy. Elitist "fear of the mob" views would hold that the referendum might result in radical policies being imposed upon the body politic, but more often

it has been conservatives who have looked to the referendum as a means, sometimes a last means, of preventing a change proposed by representative institutions. In Britain, in the early years of the twentieth century, opponents of the proposal to grant home rule to Ireland argued in favor of a referendum, in the hope that what they believed was the "innate conservatism" of the people would be mobilized to defeat the proposal. In Norway the referendum has worked to preserve the status quo; in both 1972 and 1994 a majority of members of parliament favored joining the European Union, but the people voted against it. In Italy conservatives have attempted to employ the referendum to prevent or reverse change, but mostly without success. After parliament legalized divorce in the early 1970s, conservative Catholic groups succeeded in bringing about a referendum in 1974, at which they hoped the people would vote to annul the legislation, but instead the people voted to affirm the laws permitting divorce. Similarly, in 1981 Italians voted down a proposal that would have made abortion illegal. In Ireland the people voted against a proposal to legalize divorce in 1986, but they voted in favor of legalization in 1995.

The effects of the referendum on policy outcomes, then, vary from case to case. What can be said is that the referendum ensures that policy change, or even a decision not to change, has a legitimacy that it might not possess if made by parliament or the judiciary.

CONCLUSION

In the great majority of European countries, Italy and Switzerland being the main exceptions, representative institutions (parliament or government) control access to the referendum. This is a major constraint on the potential of the referendum to disturb the political agenda set by the established political forces. Used in this way, the referendum can complement representative democracy without threatening it. When the initiative is possible, matters are different; the political elite no longer controls the agenda, and the effect can be quite destabilizing, as was shown in Italy in the late 1980s and early 1990s. In most of the rest of Europe, the referendum is used only in prescribed circumstances and at the instigation of representative institutions. It is fair to conclude that the referendum has generally worked to enhance rather than to subvert the quality of democracy in Europe.

See also *Choice, Elections as a Method of; Initiative: Europe; Qualified Majority Voting; Recall Elections; Referendums: Latin America; Referendums: United States.*

MICHAEL GALLAGHER, TRINITY COLLEGE, UNIVERSITY OF DUBLIN

BIBLIOGRAPHY

Bogdanor, Vernon. *The People and the Party System: The Referendum and Electoral Reform in British Politics.* Cambridge: Cambridge University Press, 1981.

Budge, Ian. *The New Challenge of Direct Democracy.* Oxford: Polity Press, 1996.

Butler, David, and Austin Ranney, eds. *Referendums around the World: The Growing Use of Direct Democracy.* Basingstoke, England: Macmillan, 1994.

Gallagher, Michael, and Pier Vincenzo Uleri, eds. *The Referendum Experience in Europe.* Basingstoke, England: Macmillan, 1996.

Kobach, Kris W. *The Referendum: Direct Democracy in Switzerland.* Aldershot: Dartmouth, 1993.

Suksi, Markku. *Bringing in the People: A Comparison of Constitutional Forms and Practices of the Referendum.* Dordrecht: Martinus Nijhoff, 1993.

REFERENDUMS: LATIN AMERICA

With the exception of Uruguay, Latin American countries do not have a long tradition of direct democracy in the sense of institutional mechanisms for direct participation of citizens in substantial political decision making. Even in Uruguay, where such mechanisms have existed since 1918, the use of referendums until recently remained limited to the approval (or rejection) of constitutional amendments. However, since the late 1970s direct political decision making has gained importance at the level of formal institutions as well as in practice in a number of Latin American countries. By the end of 1999 fourteen Latin American countries (excluding the Caribbean islands) had constitutional provisions for the holding of referendums.

CURRENT INSTITUTIONAL FORMS

The institutional mechanisms regulating the conditions and procedures for holding referendums differ widely among the Latin American countries. The same is true for the frequency with which those mechanisms are used. For a systematic, comparative description of the respective provisions it is useful to distinguish various levels of analysis.

First, a distinction must be drawn between obligatory and optional (facultative) referendums. Referendums may be held on the basis of constitutional provisions that require certain questions be decided directly by the electorate. Typical examples are amendments to the constitution or a redesign of the territorial structure of the country. In Latin America referendums are obligatory in certain situations in Chile (for any constitutional amendments that are disputed between the executive and legislative branches), El Salvador (any project aiming at the reconstruction of the Central American Union), Guatemala (certain constitutional amendments), Panama (international treaties regarding the canal and certain amendments to the constitution), Peru (constitutional amendments not approved by a two-thirds majority in the national parliament), Uruguay (any constitutional amendment), and Venezuela (general reform of the constitution).

With regard to the optional referendums, it is useful to distinguish between those that are held upon initiative of state organs and those that are designed as a political recourse of the citizens themselves. In seven countries—Argentina, Brazil, Colombia, Ecuador, Guatemala, Nicaragua, and Paraguay—referendums may be held only upon initiative from "above." In Argentina, Brazil, Nicaragua, and Paraguay only the national parliament is entitled to call for a referendum with binding results, in the first two countries by simple majority vote of the members of parliament, in the last two by qualified majority vote. The public opinion poll *(consulta popular)* that the Argentinean president may call for does not produce legally binding results. In Guatemala and Colombia both the national parliament and the president may initiate a referendum. In both countries the prevailing interpretation of the constitution holds that the president has to reach an agreement with parliament on this question (in Colombia, with the Senate). On the other hand, in Colombia the Congress may call for a referendum only with regard to the question of whether a constitutional assembly should be elected. In no country of the region does the parliamentary minority or opposition have the right to call for a referendum as a means of challenging a decision of the legislative majority.

In Ecuador the referendum is clearly designed as a resource of the president to reach decisions on questions of "national importance"—a vague constitutional formula that also exists in Guatemala and Colombia and leaves ample space for interpretation—without any relevant intervention of the parliament. The national parliament has the right only to "request" *(rogar)* that the president submit to a referendum a law he has vetoed, but in the end it remains his decision to do so or not.

In Colombia, Peru, and Uruguay citizens themselves can set the agenda for direct decision making. Generally, a distinction can be made in these countries between the referendum as a means to abrogate a law already passed by the legislature and as a means of positive law making. In all three countries citizens can urge state organs to submit an existing law to a referendum. In Colombia and Peru the signatures of 10 percent of the electorate are required to initiate a referendum "from the bottom"; in Uruguay, upon request of 0.5 percent of the voters, the Electoral Court opens a three-month period in which citizens may sign as supporters of a demand to hold an "abrogative" referendum. The referendum has to be held if it is supported by 25 percent of the electorate.

Positive direct law making also is possible in these three countries. In Uruguay, again 25 percent of the registered voters may initiate a referendum on a law formulated by citizens without intervention of the parliament. For initiatives aiming at a constitutional amendment, 10 percent of registered voters suffice. In Colombia and Peru legal initiatives supported by 10 percent of the electorate enter the regular lawmaking procedure within parliament. If the law is rejected by the legislative majority, it has to be submitted to referendum upon request of 10 percent of the voters. In Peru, however, this is possible only if the law was approved by at least by two-fifths of the members of parliament.

With regard to the range of issues that may be subject to direct decision making, in Argentina, Brazil, and Nicaragua no explicit provisions exist in the constitution. In the other countries some restrictions apply. In Paraguay as well as in Colombia, Peru, and Uruguay certain legal subjects (for example, fiscal issues, international relations, defense) are excluded; and in Ecuador, Guatemala, and Colombia a vague positive delimitation is drawn by the above-mentioned formula that only questions of "national importance" can be decided by referendum.

RECENT POLITICAL PRACTICE

All in all, the existing mechanisms of direct democracy in Latin American countries—with the exception of Colombia, Peru, and Uruguay—are not strong elements of the respective political systems on the formal institutional level. Empirically, the relevance of these mechanisms for the functioning and development of the political systems has been limited in most cases, although in the last twenty years more referendums have been held in the region than in any earlier phase of political development. Between 1978 and the end of 1999 twenty-two national referendums (some of them with separate decisions on various issues) took place in nine Latin American countries. Six of the twenty-two referendums were "ad hoc"—held in a nonconstitutional political order or in the absence of any constitutional norms regulating the respective mechanism of decision making. Another seven referendums were obligatory ones related to constitutional reforms. The nine facultative referendums that were held on the basis of existing constitutional provisions took place in only three countries: four in Ecuador and one in Guatemala were related mainly to reforms of the institutional structure of the political system (all initiated by state organs); the other four, which were held in Uruguay, dealt with substantial policy questions and resulted from popular initiatives.

Thus, only in Uruguay and Ecuador have referendums become an important and recurrent feature of the political process in the last few years. Nevertheless, it should be kept in mind that a number of other countries in the region have the institutional potential to enhance direct participation of citizens in the political decision-making process. In any case, theoretical discussions of political scientists regarding the effects or the relative merits and perils of specific institutional forms of referendum may (and should) take into account the Latin American experience more than in the past.

See also *Choice, Elections as a Method of; Referendums: Europe; Referendums: United States.*

BERNHARD THIBAUT, UNIVERSITY OF HEIDELBERG

BIBLIOGRAPHY

Butler, David, and Austin Ranney, eds. *Referendums around the World. The Growing Use of Direct Democracy.* Basingstoke, England: Macmillan, 1994.

Nohlen, Dieter. *Encyclopedia electoral Latinoamericana y del Carribe.* San José: IIDH/CAPEL, 1993.

Pérez Pérez, Antonio. *Referéndum y democracia directa.* Montevideo: Asociación Americana de Juristas, 1987.

Suksi, Marku. *Bringing in the People. A Comparison of the Constitutional Forms and Practices of the Referendum.* Dordrecht: Martinus Nijhoff Publishers, 1993.

Thibaut, Bernhard. "Instituciones de democracia directa." In *Tratado del derecho electoral comparado de América Latina,* edited by Dieter Nohlen, Sonia Picado, and Daniel Zovatto, 65–88. México: Fondo de Cultura Económica, 1998.

REFERENDUMS: UNITED STATES

The United States is one of only five democracies that has never held a national referendum. The idea of amending the U.S. Constitution to provide for a national referendum has come up from time to time but the idea has not been a serious one.

One example of such a proposal was the Ludlow Amendment, a constitutional amendment proposed in the 1930s that would have required a national referendum before war could be declared, although it excluded such a requirement in cases of invasion or attack. Named for Louis L. Ludlow (D, Ind.), the amendment was defeated in Congress before it reached the electorate. More recent advocates of a national referendum process have been Sen. James Abourezk of South Dakota and former vice presidential candidate Jack Kemp. Although the idea of direct legislation at the national level enjoys strong support in occasional polls, it has never generated much interest in Congress, and no recent president has advocated the process.

PURPOSE OF REFERENDUMS

The term referendum has multiple meanings. It is often used as a generic noun to describe any vote on an issue. Most referendums in the United States are the result of a unit of state or local government putting a constitutional change or other question to the voters; this can be called a legislative referendum. A third kind of referendum occurs when citizens force a referendum to the ballot on a piece of legislation; this can be called a popular initiative. A fourth application of the referendum is the advisory referendum. Several local governments and some states have put before the voters advisory referendums on foreign policy and other national political issues. The nuclear freeze movement in the United States in the 1980s was in part an advisory referendum movement.

STATE REFERENDUMS

The popular referendum, like the initiative process, was largely adopted during the first two decades of the twentieth century; only three states have added the process since 1920. At the state level, every state except Delaware requires that changes to the state constitution be submitted to a referendum, and many local governments also provide for referendums on changes in government structure, the formation of new government units, and significant changes in tax policy. These constitutional or legislative referendums are effectively ratification votes on proposals taken to the ballot by the legislature or a constitution- or charter-revision commission. Voters approve such measures approximately two-thirds of the time, in contrast with the substantial rejection rate for citizen-initiated ballot propositions, which pass only about one-third of the time.

Half of the states permit citizens to refer to a vote of the people nonbudgetary legislation to which they object that has been enacted by the state legislature. This process is often linked to the initiative process. Only Kentucky, Maryland, and New Mexico provide for this form of popular referendum but do not provide for the initiative. The fact that the popular referendum is almost always paired with the initiative is the result of the two processes, along with the recall, being considered at the same time and usually being adopted together. Proponents of the initiative and the popular referendum contend that the popular referendum corrects for legislative sins of commission while the initiative permits voters to correct for legislative sins of omission.

The state most experienced with the popular referendum is North Dakota, owing in part to the low signature threshold for the process there. Ballot qualification for popular referendums is similar to qualification in the initiative and recall processes. Citizens sign petitions calling for a referendum, and if they meet the signature threshold and do so within the specified time, they have their measure on the ballot.

STATE AND LOCAL REGULATIONS

Signature thresholds for the popular referendum range from 2 percent in North Dakota to 15 percent in Wyoming. The median signature threshold for popular referendums is 5 percent. Approximately half of the states with a popular referendum require petitioners to meet a geographic distribution requirement, usually a minimum number of signatures in half or more of the counties of the state. State laws vary about the length of time petitioners have to gather signatures. Some states give petitioners as many as 120 days. Maryland, however, has a two-stage requirement, and the first stage needs to be met in thirty days. Most states do not suspend the referred legislation pending a vote of the people, but five states do suspend that legislation. In states that do not suspend the re-

ferred legislation, they reverse the legislation if the referendum is approved and the legislation effectively vetoed.

REFERENDUM AND INITIATIVE COMPARED

In states that provide both the initiative and the popular referendum, the initiative is much more frequently used because the rules that regulate ballot access for initiatives are more flexible. Popular referendums often have a shorter petition circulation period and sometimes have a higher petition signature threshold than statutory initiatives.

Initiatives and popular referendums can also achieve the same policy objectives. One example is the 1964 initiative in California that overturned the state's open housing act, the Rumford Act. The summary of this initiative stated: "prohibits state, subdivision or agency thereof from denying, limiting or abridging right of any person to decline to sell, lease, or rent residential real property to any person as he chooses." Proposition 14, the initiative that overturned the act, passed with 65 percent of the vote. Opponents of the open housing legislation placed an initiative reversing the Rumford Act instead of a popular referendum. The California initiative vote was later reversed by the California Supreme Court, a decision upheld in 1967 by the U.S. Supreme Court in *Reitman v. Mulkey*.

Because many popular referendums reverse or overturn legislation, they often are confusing to voters. Instead of voting in favor of the legislation previously enacted, voters are asked to overturn it. Hence it is not a referendum on fluoridation, school vouchers, or providing benefits to gay partners; instead, it is generally reversing or overturning actions on these or other issues.

The same tendencies found in initiative voting apply to referendum voting. Voters are not more inclined to vote on referendums than on the candidate races at the top of the ballot. Also, voters' opinions change substantially during the course of a referendum campaign.

See also *Choice, Elections as a Method of; Initiative: United States; Plebiscites and Plebiscitary Politics; Qualified Majority Voting; Recall; Referendums: Europe; Referendums: Latin America.*

DAVID B. MAGLEBY, BRIGHAM YOUNG UNIVERSITY

BIBLIOGRAPHY

Bowler, Shaun, Todd Donovan, and Caroline J. Tolbert, eds. *Citizens as Legislators: Direct Democracy in the United States.* Columbus: Ohio State University Press, 1998.

Bowler, Shaun, and Todd Donovan. *Demanding Choices: Opinion, Voting and Direct Democracy.* Ann Arbor: University of Michigan Press, 1998.

Cronin, Thomas E. *Direct Democracy: The Politics of Initiative, Referendum, and Recall.* Cambridge: Harvard University Press, 1989.

Hahn, Harlan, and Sheldon Kamieniecki. *Referendum Voting: Social Status and Policy Preferences.* New York: Greenwood Press, 1987.

Hamilton, Howard D., and Sylvan H. Cohen. *Policy Making by Plebiscite: School Referenda.* Lexington, Mass.: Lexington Books, 1974.

Lupia, Arthur. "Shortcuts Versus Encyclopedias: Information and Voting Behavior in California Insurance Reform Elections." *American Political Science Review* 88 (March 1994): 63–76.

Magleby, David B. *Direct Legislation: Voting on Ballot Propositions in the United States.* Baltimore: Johns Hopkins University Press, 1984.

Magleby, David B., and Kelly D. Patterson. "Consultants and Direct Democracy." *PS: Political Science and Politics* (June 1998): 160–169.

Wolfinger, Raymond E., and Fred Greenstein. "The Repeal of Fair Housing in California: An Analysis of Referendum Voting." *American Political Science Review* 62 (September 1968): 753–770.

REGIME CAPACITAIRE

See *Franchise Expansion; Plural Voters*

REGIME CENSITAIRE

See *Franchise Expansion; Plural Voters*

REGISTRATION OF VOTERS

See *Administration of Elections; Registration of Voters in the United States*

REGISTRATION OF VOTERS IN THE UNITED STATES

In the United States, prospective voters generally must identify themselves before an election by registering with a government agency. Registration typically must occur at least a month before an election, but this length of time varies by state. Many Americans must reregister frequently, since a new registration form is required every time a citizen moves. Reregistration at each new residence is a particular difficulty in the United States, since its citizens move more often than the citizens of most other democracies.

Institutionally derived voting qualifications, such as voter registration, are thought to reduce voter turnout, since the difficulty of registration adds to the effort and knowledge necessary to vote. Among modern democracies, the United States requires an unusually high degree of individual-citizen responsibility in voter registration, encumbering Americans with greater voting "costs." These costs are not financial, but involve activities such as gathering political information and registering to vote. Additionally, citizens have unequal skills and abilities to overcome registration costs, leading to differ-

ential turnout between social groups. In the United States, those at the bottom of the socioeconomic scale vote less, and complex registration provisions may be a factor. Thus, by permitting or limiting ballot access, registration laws influence total turnout and certain groups' turnout. This, in turn, affects the representativeness of democratic government.

CURRENT PROCEDURES

A variety of voter registration methods are currently employed in the United States, but all require voters to be responsible for their own registration. Whereas voter registration once typically required traveling to a specific government office during certain restricted hours and meeting with a particular elected official to sign a notarized application, today U.S. voter registration is generally easier. In the 1970s several U.S. states began permitting registration on election day (often at polling places), while other states experimented with "motor voter" registration—so termed because it combined the act of registration with motor vehicle bureau procedures. This variety of procedures arose because U.S. voter registration systems are largely the domain of individual states or counties.

In the 1990s the federal government standardized registration somewhat by mandating that most states provide certain minimum access to registration. Among other provisions, the National Voter Registration Act of 1993 requires all states to make voter registration available in motor vehicle bureaus, by mail, and at various government social service agencies, and it forbids states from removing citizens from the registration rolls simply for not voting. Even with this federal mandate, though, diversity remains in registration laws. North Dakota, for example, does not require voter registration, and a half-dozen states were exempted from the law because they permit registration on election day.

Even with greater uniformity and more voter registration opportunities, the United States is atypical in that the registration onus remains on the individual citizen. Most other democracies maintain voter registration lists for their citizens. This is often accomplished by issuing citizen identification cards and requiring citizens to notify the government of a move, or by periodic enumeration of residents, as was done in Canada until the mid-1990s.

HISTORICAL ORIGINS

Voter registration did not become commonplace in the United States until the end of the nineteenth century. The origins of U.S. voter registration are controversial and may have derived from one or both of the following motivations: to prevent lower-class voting, or to hinder electoral fraud. At the fore in promoting the former interpretation are political scientists and sociologists who argue that the decline in turnout after the 1896 election was due largely to institutional requirements designed to restrict poorer citizens from exercising the franchise. Key among these requirements was the implementation of voter registration. They contend that voter registration was implemented to restrict poorer citizens from exercising the franchise.

Alternatively, others suggest that limiting voter fraud was the motivation behind U.S. voter registration efforts. In a 1929 survey of voter registration systems, Joseph Harris noted that "registration laws have followed the exposure of widespread election frauds, such as voting of the graveyard, persons who had moved away or died, or persons not qualified to vote." The extent of such fraud in the high voter turnouts of nineteenth century elections is unknown. Some authors suggest that the turnout decline that occurred after the election of 1896 may have been partly caused by limiting voting to only those truly eligible. Whatever motivations lie behind it, voter registration spread through the United States and had been adopted in nearly every state by the end of the 1920s.

THE SOUTHERN STATES

There is little doubt, though, that southern whites used a variety of tactics to block the access of minority citizens to voting booths. Among the registration and poll restrictions used from the late nineteenth century until the 1960s to disenfranchise African Americans were exceptionally complex literacy tests and lengthy residence requirements.

The Voting Rights Act of 1965 included remedies and powerful sanctions to fight these registration restrictions and other impediments to voting, including the poll tax. In addition to prohibiting the use of these registration barriers, this act mandated efforts to overcome generations of registration and electoral discrimination against minorities. Most notably, federal government registrars went into the South, registering African Americans to vote.

These efforts increased minority voter registration in the South and markedly increased African American voter turnout in that region. Initially, there was an increase in white registration coincident to the African American registration gains. Over time, in many areas of the South the gap between African American registration and white registration has been closing. This is truly remarkable, since the African American voter registration level trailed white registration by almost 50 percentage points in the average southern state before the Voting Rights Act of 1965.

EASIER REGISTRATION INCREASES VOTING

Voter registration has also become easier outside the South since the 1970s. Relaxing registration rules is generally in-

tended to increase the proportion of the population registered, and therefore to increase turnout. A simple analysis suggests that policies easing voter registration restrictions should facilitate voting. Much current research focuses on these expected turnout effects.

The reduction of U.S. registration impediments has been accompanied by modest increases in turnout or reductions in the turnout decline plaguing the U.S. electorate in recent decades. Most estimates place the one-time turnout boost associated with removing almost all prevoting registration requirements (that is, allowing election-day registration) at about 5 to 9 percent. This means that, all things being equal, a state that allows citizens to register to vote on election day can expect about 5 to 9 percent higher turnout the first time in the next election. Making registration easier does not appear to have a cumulative effect across subsequent elections; that is, the increase occurs only once, and then that state's voters continue to vote consistently at this relatively higher rate in future elections.

Short of removing almost all preelection registration requirements, other modifications in registration restrictions have a lesser effect. Motor voter, mail-in registration, and other, more modest methods used to facilitate voter registration slightly increase turnout. As with election-day registration, after these reforms are implemented, turnout does not grow over time but experiences a one-time bump when the new registration program begins, and then turnout remains at this elevated level in subsequent elections.

While removing most preelection registration requirements increases turnout, the effect is not spread evenly across the citizenry. In the United States, unlike in most other democracies, voter turnout is linked to social class; put simply, Americans with higher educational and income levels are much more likely to vote. Some argue that the tougher U.S. voter registration laws may be a principal factor in the country's skewed turnout. If the registration barrier is lowered, those in the lower classes may vote more frequently. But the evidence does not support this conclusion. Where election-day registration was offered, all social classes' turnout increased, but the middle class experienced the biggest boost. This likely stems from the fact that the middle class already has access to the requisite political knowledge to facilitate voting, while the poor and less educated have diminished access to political information. Most of those in the upper class already vote, so there is little room for growth in turnout among the wealthy and well educated.

The political consequences of reducing registration barriers—outside the South—appear minimal. Survey research finds that nonvoters' policy preferences closely resemble those of voters. In the South, however, the effect of reducing registration barriers and introducing federal registrars (in some areas) has been dramatic. Not only has the southern electorate become less racially skewed, but African American representation in elected office is now commonplace.

Restrictive voter registration systems that place the registration responsibility on the individual reduce U.S. voter turnout. During the 1990s voter registration was standardized and made easier across much of the country. Easing voter registration provisions has increased turnout. Middle-class citizens are more likely to vote once registration is easier, with this group seeing the largest one-time turnout boost.

See also *Administration of Elections; Canvassing; Compulsory Voting; Democracy and Elections; Disqualification of Voters, Grounds for; Franchise Expansion; Open Voting; Poll Tax; Turnout; Voting Behavior, Influences on.*

CRAIG LEONARD BRIANS, VIRGINIA POLYTECHNIC INSTITUTE

BIBLIOGRAPHY

Brians, Craig Leonard. "Residential Mobility, Voter Registration, and Electoral Participation in Canada." *Political Research Quarterly* 50 (March 1997): 215–227.

Brians, Craig Leonard, and Bernard Grofman. "When Registration Barriers Fall, Who Votes? An Empirical Test of a Rational Choice Model." *Public Choice* (April 1999): 161–176.

Fenster, Mark J. "The Impact of Allowing Day of Registration Voting on Turnout in U.S. Elections from 1960–1992." *American Politics Quarterly* 22 (January 1994): 74–87.

Grofman, Bernard, Lisa Handley, and Richard G. Niemi. *Minority Representation and the Quest for Voting Equality.* New York: Cambridge University Press, 1992.

Harris, Joseph P. *Registration of Voters in the United States.* Washington, D.C.: Brookings Institution, 1929.

Knack, Stephen. "Does 'Motor Voter' Work?: Evidence from State-Level Data." *Journal of Politics* 57 (August 1995): 796–811.

Kousser, J. M. *The Shaping of Southern Politics: Suffrage Restriction and the Establishment of the One-Party South, 1880–1910.* New Haven, Conn.: Yale University Press, 1979.

Powell, G. Bingham, Jr. "American Voter Turnout in Comparative Perspective." *American Political Science Review* 80 (March 1986): 17–43.

Wolfinger, Raymond E., David P. Glass, and Peverill Squire. "Predictors of Electoral Turnout: An International Comparison." *Policy Studies Review* 9 (spring 1990): 551–574.

Wolfinger, Raymond E., and Steven J. Rosenstone. *Who Votes?* New Haven, Conn.: Yale University Press, 1980.

REGULATION OF TELEVISION AT ELECTIONS

Politicians strive for a frequent and extensive presence on television, especially during election campaigns. Among the different mass media that reach a wide audience, television is more and more regarded as the most important for campaign communication. Although television is not the most influential of media, political actors trust in its effectiveness to influence voters, both directly in their voting decision and indirectly through changes in their knowledge and attitudes about parties and candidates.

Political actors seek appearances on television's mediated and unmediated formats. Mediated programming (news or current affairs coverage) and partly mediated programming (talk shows or interviews) have the advantage of seemingly objective reporting; unmediated formats (political advertising), in contrast, are controlled by the campaigners and thus are seen by the media audience as political propaganda. Nevertheless, because electoral advertising is produced by the parties or the candidates themselves, it remains "undistorted" by journalistic selection processes.

In order to provide for equal opportunity of television access, diverse regulations affect what can and cannot be done on television during elections. Many countries rigorously limit or even forbid political advertising during the campaign. Regulations range from general rules on impartiality and equal opportunity for politicians or parties, to limits on election expenditures that affect advertising campaigns, to detailed restrictions on the time and the content of electoral broadcasts or even a total prohibition on political advertising.

Regulations can be differentiated according to whether they apply to political broadcasts that are under the editorial responsibility of the broadcasting station (mediated and partly mediated) or to political advertising (unmediated). Because governments often are not allowed to interfere with editorial freedom, provisions concerning political broadcasting are typically very general. Decisions about the coverage of political issues and events are left to the discretion of the broadcasters. Regulations usually set forth requirements for complete, impartial, and fair information.

REGULATION OF CAMPAIGN BROADCASTS

In the United States, section 315 of the Federal Communications Act guarantees equal opportunity for each political candidate. This applies to television programming controlled by the broadcasters as well as to political advertising. Exemptions from the equal opportunity requirement include bona fide news and events. In general, a broadcaster may not influence the election by preferential treatment of one candidate. The conditions framing presidential candidate debates are subject to negotiation in the bipartisan Commission on Presidential Debates. For example, in 1992 Ross Perot was permitted to participate as a third candidate in that year's presidential debates, but four years later, in 1996, a federal district court agreed with the commission's decision to exclude him from the debates because of his low chance of winning the election. In Germany, where the courts have played an important role in determining the guidelines for the parties' access to broadcasting time during election campaigns, it is left to the discretion of broadcasters to decide who appears in discussion programs. In recent years, smaller parties from time to time have successfully used court orders to prevent their exclusion from TV discussions.

In order to guarantee equal opportunities for candidates and parties, France prescribes the conditions for campaign broadcasts in detail. While paid political advertising on television and radio is prohibited in general, the French broadcasting authority, Conseil Supérieur de l'Audiovisuel, regulates the allocation of broadcast time for the political actors during the official campaign and sets the guidelines for the formats. (Free media, in contrast, is not regulated by law.) The French broadcasting production society also works to ensure that each candidate or party is provided with equal opportunities during the election campaign. Campaign broadcasts are permitted to contain "clips" (spot advertising). At the beginning of the 1990s, restrictions on the use of certain production techniques and the use of certain audiovisual material were relaxed; this helped foster the modernization of the television campaign.

The extent to which the publication of polls during the election campaign affects the vote remains controversial. The impact of such phenomena as the "bandwagon effect" and the "underdog effect" have been hotly debated. While the United States and Great Britain do not place restrictions on polling, many other countries do impose moratoriums on the publication of poll results prior to elections. Most of these take effect twenty-four hours before the election date; some begin as early as a week prior to the election. At the extreme, South Africa imposes a six-week moratorium. France passed a law in 1977 prohibiting the publication of and comments on opinion polls that directly or indirectly relate to an election during the week preceding a ballot. The same law also established a polling commission and required that certain technical data accompany each publication (for example, time of survey, number of respondents). Italy prohibits the publication of the results of preelection polls within a period of twenty-eight days before an election. A commission monitors the quality and the publication of survey findings.

The organization of a country's broadcasting system and the role of television advertising in particular influence the conditions for electoral advertising. In the United States, with its long tradition of commercial broadcasting in which advertising is the single source of financing, regulation of advertising, including political advertising, is kept to a minimum. In contrast, many west European governments guarded their monopolies on public broadcasting until the 1980s, when adver-

tising either began to supplement broadcast financing through fees and taxes (as in Germany) or was totally prohibited (as in Denmark and Sweden). These different philosophies about the role of advertising were repeated in the stance taken by legislative bodies and broadcasters toward political advertising. As long as public broadcasting prevailed in western Europe, electoral advertising was restricted in one way or another. This strict regulation of campaign advertising is often also regarded as a means by which to limit overall campaign spending.

Research into the regulation of electoral advertising in Western democracies reveals a variety of models concerned with the nature of the regulating body, the amount of advertising, ad content, and methods of allocation. Sponsorship of television spots by the candidates themselves is found only in the United States. In west European countries, the parties are responsible for electoral advertising. Political advertising in European countries is only allowed in preparation for an election, meaning that it is restricted to the official campaign period or even just to the "hot" phase (last weeks) of the election. Most countries also limit the number and length of campaign commercials; some even impose restrictions on content and visual styling.

In the United States, the market is regarded as the best provider of equal opportunity to all candidates. Open access and equivalent rates for advertising time are believed to level the playing field. In addition to the general regulations imposed by the Federal Communications Act, most U.S. states have laws concerning political advertising, the most common requirement being the disclosure of ad sponsorship. For decades, advertising time for candidates was available only through purchase, which meant in effect that the amount of time available depended on the financial potential of the respective candidates. But in 1996 the major U.S. networks for the first time gave free airtime to presidential candidates. However, the format for these segments of time was determined by the networks, resulting in a disappointing homogeneity.

The equal opportunity principle underlies the practice of giving free airtime to parties during election campaigns. However, this does not necessarily mean an equal amount of time for all parties. Some countries follow a system of graded allocation of airtime, with smaller parties getting less time and bigger parties getting more. Allocating free airtime gives all parties the opportunity to present their program and their candidates to the public and reduce dependence on electoral advertising. In Great Britain, for example, free airtime is allotted to the parties by the Committee on Political Broadcasting, which is made up of British Broadcasting Company (BBC) and Independent Television Commission representatives as well as of members of the parties in Parliament. Criteria such as the share of votes received in the previous general election determine the amount of time allotted. The main parties typically receive equal time relative to each other, and the smaller parties receive less time relative to the larger parties. The BBC applies the same ratio to achieve balance among the parties in news and current affairs programs during election campaigns. The length of British party electoral broadcasts lies between five and ten minutes. In Italy a parliamentary commission controls electoral advertising on public television. The same commission also allocates the amount of time for the parties' election broadcasts. In Germany, where broadcasting is in the hands of the sixteen federal *länder*, broadcasting laws oblige the public stations to provide airtime for all parties running for election. Since the 1960s free airtime for each individual spot has been fixed at 150 seconds. For the parliamentary election in 1998 the broadcast time allotted to party spots on public TV was shortened to 90 seconds. The number of spots for each party is rationed mainly according to the proportion of votes. Denmark, in contrast, allots equal time to all parties. The Canada Elections Act requires that public and private TV stations make airtime available for party broadcasts. Allocation of free time is based on a formula involving the number of seats contested, the number of seats won, and the proportion of votes received in the previous election. The same formula determines how much time each party can purchase for its advertising spots.

INTRODUCTION OF THE DUAL BROADCASTING SYSTEM IN EUROPE

The situation framing electoral advertising in western Europe changed somewhat with the introduction of commercial broadcasting in the 1980s. A dual broadcasting system emerged in which private broadcasters supplemented public broadcasters. Although the establishment of commercial stations brought an increase in media outlets, deregulation of political advertising and direct access for parties through unrestricted purchase of airtime did not immediately follow. Most European countries continue to set narrow limits on electoral advertising, underlining their suspicion of political actors' unfiltered self-portrayals.

In Finland, where political ads are broadcast exclusively on the commercial channel that was introduced only in 1993, parties are allowed unrestricted purchase of advertising time. With the exception of Great Britain, Italy is the European country with the longest tradition of dual broadcasting. It permitted parties to buy airtime until 1993, when a new law was enacted that bans TV spots from running during the hot phase of the campaign. Germany, too, made unrestricted purchase of airtime on commercial television possible. During the 1994 national campaign, only four of the twenty-four parties running for election bought airtime on commercial

television; twenty-two of the parties produced spots that were broadcast at no charge on public television.

Spots become shorter when airtime has to be purchased. In Germany the parties tend to use the full 90 seconds they are allocated for a single spot on public television; however, spots on German commercial television average just 30 seconds. A comparison of spots from the United States, Israel, and several west European countries indicates that unrestricted purchase of airtime leads to shorter spots, while party broadcasts in countries with controlled allocation of airtime are longer.

Even after deregulation of broadcasting and market entry of commercial stations in western Europe, much of the old philosophy toward political advertising persists. Unlike in the United States, legislative bodies in western Europe are reluctant to permit unrestricted purchase of airtime for electoral advertising. This reflects a restrictive attitude toward advertising in general, which is regulated even in commercial broadcasting. Moreover, in Europe the market is not seen as the best guarantor of equal opportunity for all political actors. Unrestricted purchase of airtime is regarded as inconsistent with the objective of giving an equal chance to all of the parties running in an election. Unlimited purchase is viewed as favoring the richer, more well established parties or those with the best connections to sponsors.

As party ties loosen and the number of swing voters increases, election campaigns will continue to regain importance. Electioneers will increasingly seek to influence the voters through effective campaign communication. Their increased use of unmediated formats such as television advertising may in the future push the pendulum back in the direction of renewed legislative regulation of television campaigning.

See also *Administration of Elections; Bandwagon Effect; Campaigning; Manifesto, Election; Public Opinion Polls: Legal Regulations; Voting Behavior, Influences on.*

CHRISTINA HOLTZ-BACHA, UNIVERSITY OF MAINZ

BIBLIOGRAPHY

Barendt, Eric M. *Broadcasting Law: A Comparative Study.* Oxford: Clarendon Press, 1995.

Fletcher, Fred J., ed. *Media, Elections and Democracy.* Toronto: Dundurn Press, 1991.

Hoffmann-Riem, Wolfgang. *Regulating Media: The Licensing and Supervision of Broadcasting in Six Countries.* New York: The Guilford Press, 1996.

Kaid, Lynda L., and Christina Holtz-Bacha, eds. *Political Advertising in Western Democracies: Parties and Candidates on Television.* Thousand Oaks, Calif.: Sage, 1995.

Swanson, David L., and Poalo Mancini, eds. *Politics, Media, and Modern Democracy: An International Study of Innovations in Electoral Campaigning and Their Consequences.* Westport, Conn.: Praeger, 1996.

RELEVANT PARTIES

The number of parties affects the nature and performance of party systems and, consequently, political systems. One problem that scholars encounter in this matter is how to assess the number of parties, that is, how parties are to be counted. How many "relevant" or "effective" parties are there? Too many parties points to a fragmented system; and a fragmented system is a dysfunctional one. Yet how many parties are too many?

Parties cannot all be counted equally; their relative weight in votes or seats should also be assessed. If all parties were counted at their face value, the United Kingdom could be said to have eight parties, whereas it is generally, and rightly, classified as a two-party system, inasmuch as single-party government alternates between the Conservative and Labour Parties. Likewise, in India one can count some sixteen parties, yet for a number of decades the absolute majority predominance of the Congress Party has brought about single-party governance. Maurice Duverger, the seminal author in the field of party studies, did not address the counting problem, and his work was weaker for this omission. Subsequently, Douglas Rae (1967) and Giovanni Sartori (1976) confronted the issue. Rae developed a measure called the "fractionalization index." Sartori established the notion of "relevant party." In 1989 Rein Taagepera and Matthew S. Shugart introduced the notion of "effective party" and a means of measuring their number.

Rae's fractionalization index (F) has long been the most used measure of party fragmentation. Rae does not actually count the parties. When the measure is applied to parliamentary seats (F_p), fractionalization is the probability that two members drawn at random from a parliament belong to different parties. The fractionalization varies from zero (maximal concentration: only one party) to one (maximal atomization: as many parties as there are seats). For example, a 50 percent split of parliamentary seats between two parties is indicated by 0.5. While Rae does not identify party systems as being two-party, three-party, five-party, ten-party, and so forth, his F index measures both the number and the relative sizes of the parties in any given polity.

The technical weakness of Rae's measure is that it overvalues the larger parties and its curve compresses far too quickly the smaller ones. Indeed, a party with 10 percent of the seats almost disappears in Rae's calculation, whereas the notion of relevant party may attribute relevance to very small parties, even those with 2 or 3 percent of the seats. Beyond the statistical defects of the F index, Sartori pointed out that the measure cannot distinguish among different kinds of party fragmentation (such as the difference between a segmented fragmentation, as in the Netherlands, and a polarized one, as in Weimar Germany); misses the "position value" of parties, for example, whether or not they are pivotal; is insensitive to overall systemic characteristics; and cannot account for the discrete nature of real-world party systems.

RELEVANCE

Sartori's notion of "relevant party" approaches the counting of parties differently. It is not a quantitative measure, but a qualitative assessment disciplined by two criteria. According to Sartori, a party is relevant if and when it has a coalitional potential for government or obtains blackmail potential. Conversely, parties that have neither coalitional nor blackmail leverage must be discounted as "irrelevant." Whether they enter into or exit from a party system makes no difference to the relevant actors.

The first criterion, "coalitional potential," means that a given party actually enters a coalition or would be a necessary partner in one of the possible governing majorities. More specifically, a party is considered irrelevant in any given legislature if it has neither entered nor supported (at the vote of confidence) at least one government. Likewise, a party is discounted if it votes for a government but its support is unnecessary and disowned by the government. The notion also applies to electoral alliances; if a party is asked to enter an electoral cartel, it acquires relevance. It is self-evident that this criterion applies only to multiparty parliamentary systems. This limitation is not severe, however, since parliamentary multipartism describes a large majority of democratic polities and the number of parties does not need to be discerned exactly in presidential systems (where party government gives way to presidential government).

The second criterion, "blackmail potential" is used in the Downsian understanding of the term: a blackmail situation exists whenever an "out party" becomes feared by the "in parties" to the point of affecting the direction—whether centripetal or centrifugal—of party competition.

The focus on relevant parties allows the characteristics of different kinds of party systems to be established in the terms in which political actors and voting publics actually perceive them. The notion delivers a sixfold classification of party systems: one-party, hegemonic party, predominant party, two-party, limited pluralism, and extreme pluralism. This classification sorts out the systemic characteristics missed by quantitative measures, for the counting of relevant parties is indicative, according to Sartori, of two structural configurations: the "mechanical predispositions" and "systemic propensities" of any given political system. This approach has been largely neglected by scholars because it requires a substantive understanding of the countries under investigation. Moreover, the limitation of Sartori's "relevant party" is that it does not adequately account for the size of parties, while it is clear that the number of parties relates to "how strong" any party is vis-à-vis the others.

EFFECTIVE PARTY

Taagepera and Shugart replaced the notion of *relevant party* with *effective party* since they needed a new label to distinguish their new technique. However, the problem of how to count parties remains regardless of whether the parties that matter are called relevant or effective.

Taagepera and Shugart (like Rae) sought a measure of the number of parties that took into account their relative sizes. They argued that the least arbitrary way to measure size is to leave aside arbitrary cutoff points and to let the vote shares determine their own weights. For example, a party with 40 percent of the votes receives a weight of .40; its weighted value is $.40 \times .40 = 0.16$. The sum of the weighted values of the party votes is an index designated as *HH*. This index varies, like the fractionalization index of Rae, from zero (extreme concentration) to 1 (extreme fractionalization). It also displays, by and large, the same merits and failings of the *F* index. Systemic properties are missed, and the empirical fit of the final Taagepera-Shugart rule (in their claim a single quantitative expression for Duverger's laws on the effects of electoral systems) is, by their own admission, unsatisfactory.

Thus there is a trade-off between the quantitative precision of the Rae and Taagepera-Shugart measures (the *F* and *HH* indexes), which provide numerical values for party system fragmentation but no systemic information, and the notion of relevant party, as defined by two criteria, which supplies systemic explanatory power. These different approaches to assessing party system fragmentation should not be considered mutually exclusive but, rather, as complementary.

See also *Downsian Model of Elections; Duverger's Law; Fractionalization Index.*

GIOVANNI SARTORI, COLUMBIA UNIVERSITY

BIBLIOGRAPHY

Rae, Douglas. *The Political Consequences of Electoral Laws.* New Haven, Conn.: Yale University Press, 1967.

Sartori, Giovanni. *Parties and Party Systems: A Framework for Analysis.* New York: Cambridge University Press, 1976.

Taagepera, Rein, and Matthew Soberg Shugart. *Seats and Votes: The Effects and Determinants of Electoral Systems.* New Haven, Conn.: Yale University Press, 1989.

RESIDENCE REQUIREMENT

See *Administration of Elections; Overseas Voting*

ROTTEN BOROUGHS

The term "rotten boroughs" was popular in England during a period of agitation for parliamentary reform that lasted intermittently from about 1760 until 1832. The phenomena it referred to were well known long before as "decayed boroughs." It originally referred to English boroughs with extremely small to nonexistent populations that nevertheless returned two members to the House of Commons. At the time of the reform bills of the 1830s, 36 of the 202 boroughs allegedly had fewer than 25 inhabitants, while 115 had fewer than 200. They were deemed "rotten" on the misleading assumption that in former centuries they had had much larger populations, a reasonable surmise given the fact that a majority of the parliamentary boroughs had been enfranchised in the thirteenth century. However, many boroughs with very small populations had not been large towns when originally enfranchised. For example, the little village of Gatton was enfranchised in 1450, probably to allow the Duke of Norfolk to nominate its two members. Indeed, beginning in the fifteenth century and increasingly in the sixteenth, many tiny boroughs were enfranchised or had their franchises restored at the instigation of large landowners able to determine their elections.

Rotten boroughs with very small populations were bound to have tiny electorates. The term was sometimes also used to designate all boroughs with such electorates, regardless of population size. Thus, Thomas Oldfield, the foremost late eighteenth-century authority on English boroughs, referred to Buckingham (population 2,605 in 1801) as a rotten borough since the franchise resided in the thirteen members of its governing corporation. There were 25 boroughs at the time, the largest having only seventy voters and the majority far fewer. Other borough franchises, whether freeman, burgage, or scot and lot (payment of local taxes), could also produce tiny electorates bearing no relationship to their populations. In Cornwall, notorious for its rotten boroughs, about two-fifths of its twenty-one parliamentary boroughs at the beginning of the nineteenth century possessed no more than twenty-five voters, while four-fifths had fewer than one hundred voters.

Boroughs with very small electorates were far less likely than larger ones to have contested elections; they were known as "close," or "pocket," boroughs where one or two wealthy patrons determined how the nominal electorates chose their MPs. Land that allowed someone to control an election appreciated considerably in value, with the result that several proposals for abolishing rotten boroughs included compensation for their "owners." Patrons used their boroughs to bring themselves or friends, relations, and political allies into the

Commons; to allow the government to fill the seats, often in return for favors; or to sell the seats to men willing to pay the price. In all but the last case, recipients usually were expected not to vote against the wishes of the patron, but the purchaser of a seat might vote as he wished. Ironically, by the end of the eighteenth century parliamentary reformers sometimes purchased seats in order to work toward the abolition of rotten boroughs.

Rotten boroughs were criticized continually from the reign of Elizabeth I (reigned 1558–1603) down to the Reform Act of 1832. In calling his first parliament in 1603, James I charged sheriffs not to direct a precept for election to "any auncient borrough town within their counties, beying soe utterly ruyned and decayed that there are not sufficient resyantes to make such choice." The charge was completely ignored. After the overthrow of the monarchy, the Instrument of Government of 1653, England's first and only written constitution, included an electoral reform resembling the Reform Act of 1832 in its disfranchisement of almost all of the small boroughs eliminated by the later statute. Following the death of Oliver Cromwell in 1659, the reform was reversed.

Opponents of rotten boroughs argued that the principle of "equal representation"—whether of persons or of property—was grossly violated by the existence of tiny constituency electorates controlled by wealthy patrons. Such places had as much representation as populous counties and boroughs at a time when several very large towns had no representation at all. Defenders of rotten boroughs put forward pragmatic arguments that they allowed certain interests in English society to be better represented, provided seats for government ministers, and, most emphasized, allowed talented young men to enter the House of Commons.

The authors of the reform bills of 1830–1832 were determined to eliminate most if not all of the rotten boroughs. The Reform Act disfranchised fifty-six small boroughs, and a further thirty had their members reduced from two to one. The introduction of a uniform £10 householder franchise in the boroughs increased the number of voters in about half of them and destroyed the corporation boroughs. After 1832, all but thirty-one of the English boroughs contained more than three hundred registered voters, with only five having fewer than two hundred. The small electorates existing after 1832 permitted forty-two pocket boroughs to survive the act.

See also *Gerrymandering; Reapportionment and Redistricting; Safe Seat.*

WILLIAM B. GWYN, TULANE UNIVERSITY

BIBLIOGRAPHY

Cannon, John. *Parliamentary Reform 1640–1832.* Cambridge: Cambridge University Press, 1973.

Gash, Norman. *Politics in the Age of Peel.* London: Longmans Green, 1953.

The History of Parliament. 6 vols. London: History of Parliament Trust, 1964–1968.

Porritt, Edward, and Annie G. Porritt. *The Unreformed House of Commons.* 2 vols. Cambridge: Cambridge University Press, 1903.

Seymour, Charles. *Electoral Reform in England and Wales.* New Haven, Conn.: Yale University Press, 1915.

RUNOFF

See *Second Ballot (or Runoff)*

S

SAFE SEAT

A safe seat is a seat in a parliament or a congress in which the vote for the winning party or candidate is so consistently high that the incumbent party or candidate is secure against normal fluctuations in electoral support from one election to another, fluctuations caused by swings in the popularity of the incumbent's party or by events. In a safe seat the incumbent can be confident of re-election as long as he or she does not lose the nomination of the party with the big majority. The term is most often used in single-member districts of a first-past-the-post electoral system. In a list proportional representation system, one may speak of a "safe position" on a party list, a position high enough to guarantee an individual's election because the party invariably wins a big enough share of the vote to return their top candidates.

The lead required to make a seat safe depends on the extent of electoral volatility from one election to the next. For example, if a series of elections shows that a party's net loss of support never exceeds 5 percent and the challenger's vote never rises by more than that, then a margin above 10 percent can be sufficient to make a seat safe. The extent of electoral volatility varies among countries and, more important, from one decade to the next within a country.

The margin required to make a seat safe rises if elections over a decade or more are taken into account. Although a lead of 12 percent is almost always safe from one election to the next, if the party holding the seat suffers big setbacks in two successive elections, the seat could be lost. Since U.S. Senate seats are contested every six years, a safe seat can guarantee a politician a place in the Senate for more than a decade. But since the U.S. House is contested every two years, a safe margin there can erode in much less than a decade.

In the American system, individual representatives seek to use incumbency to make their seat safe. An incumbent candidate does not need to convert opponents to keep a seat safe; the activities of an incumbent are sufficient if they prevent support from eroding. An incumbent can court voters by doing favors for individuals and by advancing the district's common, cross-party interests. An incumbent with seniority may hold a committee or leadership assignment that can bring special benefits to the district. Where a personal vote is of substantial importance, as in the United States, incumbency can be very important in safeguarding a seat. In Britain, where voting by party label is more important, incumbents are less able to protect their seat against a big national swing against their party, as occurred in 1997 from Conservative to Labour.

In a safe seat, intraparty politics are a greater threat to a member of a parliament or congress than interparty competition. In a proportional-representation system, a member of parliament who falls out of favor with the party organization can lose his or her seat by being placed lower on the list. In a system with primary elections, a sitting member can lose the party nomination to another party member. In the Irish single-transferable-vote system, members of parliament are always vulnerable to losing their seat to another member of the same party, since voters in a multimember district cast preferences among candidates of the same party.

Population change in a district can make a seat safer or less safe. For example, more African Americans moving into a constituency with a white member of Congress might make the member's seat less safe; or a marginal constituency held by a conservative might become "gentrified" by more middle-class people moving into it making it safer. The movement of population in and out of districts periodically leads to the redrawing of boundaries, which also can alter the composition of a previously safe or marginal seat. Redistricting of boundaries can take a large number of voters away from the majority party or can add voters who make the seat safer for the majority party. In an extreme example, in an inner city area with contracting population, the reduction of population might cause two safe seats to be merged into one, thus forcing two incumbents from the same party to fight each other for nomination to represent the dominant party in the single safe seat that results.

See also *Gerrymandering; Reapportionment and Redistricting; Unopposed Returns; Wasted Votes.*

RICHARD ROSE, UNIVERSITY OF STRATHCLYDE

BIBLIOGRAPHY

Cain, Bruce, John Ferejohn, and Morris Fiorina. *The Personal Vote: Constituency Service and Electoral Independence*. Cambridge, Mass.: Harvard University Press, 1987.

Jacobson, Gary C. *The Electoral Origins of Divided Government*. Boulder, Colo.: Westview Press, 1990.

Ornstein, Norman J., Thomas E. Mann, and Michael J. Malbin. *Vital Statistics on Congress, 1997–1998*. Washington, D.C.: Congressional Quarterly, 1997.

SECOND BALLOT (OR RUNOFF)

Second-ballot systems are systems in which, if a candidate or list does not surpass a specified vote threshold, a second vote (a runoff) is held at a later date, normally between the top two finishers from the first round. Second-ballot runoffs are employed throughout the world to elect presidents, subnational executives (for example, governors, mayors), national legislators, and subnational legislators.

Almost without exception, second-ballot systems are used in conjunction with single-member districts. However, there is no reason why the second-ballot method could not be used with multimember districts, as was the case in the 1973 Argentine Senate elections.

VOTE AND TURNOUT THRESHOLDS

A key component of any second-ballot system is the threshold that determines whether a runoff is necessary. The most common threshold is 50 percent + 1 of the valid votes cast in the first round of the election. If a candidate surpasses this threshold, then he or she is elected. If no candidate surpasses this threshold, then a runoff is held between the two candidates who received the most votes in the first round of the election. Countries that employ a 50 percent + 1 threshold for the election of their president include Brazil, Chile, France, Guatemala, Madagascar, Poland, and Portugal.

Other countries employ a 50 percent + 1 threshold but do not use valid votes cast as the denominator. In Peru (in 1985 and 1990), Lithuania, and Russia the denominator also includes null and blank votes, while in Romania and Slovakia the denominator is the number of registered voters.

In a few instances, second-ballot elections have been held using thresholds below 50 percent. For example, Costa Rica and Nicaragua elect their presidents with respective thresholds of 40 percent and 45 percent, while the U.S. state of Georgia elects its governor using a 45 percent threshold.

Argentina (for its presidential election) employs a more complex threshold. If the plurality winner in the first round garners more than 45 percent of the vote, or garners at least 40 percent of the vote and is more than 10 percent ahead of the runner-up, then he or she is elected. If neither of these conditions is met, a runoff is held between the top two candidates from the first round.

In addition to the candidate vote threshold, some of the formerly communist countries have included a turnout threshold in their presidential election law. In countries such as Bulgaria, Russia, and Ukraine, a second ballot is necessary if less than half of the registered voters turn out to vote in the presidential election (regardless of the percentage of votes won by the candidates). Similar rules apply in some of these countries' legislative elections, in which legislators are elected from single-member districts using the second-ballot method.

Whereas in most cases only two candidates can take part in the runoff, in a few instances more than two candidates can participate if certain conditions are met. The most well known of these exceptions is for the election of members of the French National Assembly during the Fifth Republic (1958–). Any candidate who wins a number of votes equal to 12.5 percent of the registered voters in the district may compete in the runoff (prior to 1978 the threshold was 10 percent, with the exception of 1962, when it was a mere 5 percent of the votes cast). In the second round of French legislative elections, the plurality vote winner is elected (this is also the case in nearly all other run-off systems, regardless of the number of candidates participating in the second-round runoff).

The most common form of runoff is another direct popular election. Under the majority congressional run-off method, however, the second election is held in the congress, which chooses between the top two (or three) candidates from the first round in the event that no candidate surpassed the requisite threshold (generally 50 percent of the valid votes). In the past this method was very popular in Latin America, and Bolivia continues to utilize it.

PRESIDENTIAL ELECTIONS

A substantial amount of theoretical and empirical work (for example Duverger's propositions) undergirds the hypothesis that use of the second-ballot method (especially where a vote threshold of 50 percent or greater is used, a situation that I will refer to henceforth as the majority run-off formula), all other things being equal, results in a greater number of relevant candidates than use of the plurality formula (the majority run-off formula's principal rival). This hypothesis is based primarily on two assumptions. First, since only one candidate can win a plurality election, whereas two can win the first round of a majority run-off election, strategic behavior by political elites and voters should result in a greater number of relevant candidates in the latter type of election. Second, the majority run-off formula provides candidates with an added incentive to run. In majority run-off elections, presidential candidates often campaign with the secondary (or even the primary) goal of obtaining a sufficiently large number of votes that, in the event they do not finish first or second, they can bargain for benefits, in exchange for their endorsement, from a position of strength with the two candidates who do reach the runoff (for example, Alexander Lebed's deal with Boris Yeltsin between the first and second rounds of the 1996 Russian presidential election, in which Yeltsin promised Lebed a high-profile post in exchange for Lebed's public support in the runoff).

Second-ballot systems (particularly those where the majority run-off formula is used) are more favorable than their single-ballot counterparts to candidates without strong traditional party ties (for example, presidential election victors Fernando Collor de Mello [1990–1992] in Brazil, Alberto Fujimori [1990–] in Peru and Jorge Serrano [1991–1993] in Guatemala were political outsiders). As a result of the majority run-off formula's permissive nature, first-round votes often tend to be dispersed among several candidates. This dispersion opens up a potential route to the presidency for political outsiders whose strategy is to finish second (but force a runoff) in the first round and then win against their more established competitor (who often is hampered by his or her identification with one specific party or coalition) in the runoff. Many people argue that the majority run-off formula (and to lesser extent second-ballot systems with lower thresholds) assures a strong popular mandate for the executive. The mirror image of this position is that the majority run-off formula avoids those highly negative situations in which a president is elected with a very low percentage of the popular vote, such as the 24 percent won by former Philippine president Fidel Ramos in 1992 or the 31 percent won by former Venezuelan president Rafael Caldera in 1993.

On average, second-ballot systems provide popular mandates that are modestly superior to those supplied by the single-ballot plurality formula. However, the mandate won in a runoff is not equivalent to a mandate won in the first and only round in a plurality-formula system. The electoral majority won by the executive in the runoff does not represent any unified coalition, party, or group or even a homogeneous electorate. Thus the "strength" of the electoral mandates in second-ballot systems is questionable.

SUBNATIONAL ELECTIONS

In addition to its use to elect presidents, the second ballot has been employed in a large number of countries to elect subnational officials such as governors and mayors (for example, in Brazil, Russia, the United States). In the United States the second-ballot method currently is employed to elect the mayor in major cities such as Detroit, Los Angeles, Miami, and New York in a nonpartisan primary, partisan primary, or general election. When the second-ballot method is employed for a nonpartisan primary, a runoff generally is held between the top two vote winners from the first round, irrespective of the percentage of the vote won by the candidates.

The second-ballot method also has a long history of use in many of the intraparty primaries in the states of the U.S. South. First adopted in 1902 by Mississippi, the second-ballot method has been used at one time by all of the states of the former Confederacy as well as a handful of other states (including Arizona and South Dakota).

Prior to the 1980s the southern states were dominated by the Democratic Party. The winner of the Democratic primary was virtually assured of winning the general election. The second ballot was adopted in large part to insure that no candidate would win the Democratic primary without strong intraparty support, and in particular to prevent a candidate from winning the Democratic primary, and hence the governorship, with a small percentage of the primary vote. Another explanation often given for the adoption of the second ballot in the South is that it reduced the capacity of African Americans to influence the outcome of the election, and in a similar manner reduced the ability of African Americans to be elected in the Democratic primary, particularly for statewide offices.

Louisiana has perhaps made the most widespread use of the second-ballot system in the U.S. South. Since 1975, for the election of the governor, U.S. senators and representatives, state legislators, and many other state government officials, Louisiana has employed an open-primary second-ballot system in which candidates from all political parties compete together in a first round, with a runoff held between the top two finishers from the first round if no candidate wins 50 percent + 1 of the valid vote.

Several Louisiana elections supply further evidence of the link between the second-ballot system and the success of political outsiders. For example, three candidates dominated Louisiana's 1992 gubernatorial election: Buddy Roemer (the Republican incumbent governor who had been elected as a Democrat four years earlier), Edwin Edwards (a Democratic former two-term governor who had been plagued by charges of racketeering and other unethical behavior during his previous term), and David Duke (a former grand wizard of the Ku Klux Klan who was running as a Republican, although he was disavowed by most of the Louisiana Republican Party). In the first round, Edwards won 34 percent of the vote, Duke 32 percent, and Roemer 27 percent (the remainder was divided among nine other candidates). Following a massive bipartisan campaign on his behalf, Edwards won the general election with 61 percent of the vote, although Duke's electoral success and presence in the runoff severely tarnished Louisiana's reputation.

NATIONAL LEGISLATIVE ELECTIONS

France as well as many other countries (a majority of which are former French colonies, such as Gabon, Haiti, and Mali) employ a second-ballot method for their legislative elections. In France the continuous use of this arrangement since 1962 (with the exception of the 1986 election) to elect the National Assembly has had a profound effect on the French party system. The use of the second-ballot method contributed to the formation of two broad electoral/political alliances: one on the right (consisting principally of Rally for the Republic and the Union of Democratic Forces), and one on the left (consisting principally of the Socialist Party and the Communist Party). At times other political forces have participated in these respective alliances.

Generally, the constituent members of these two respective alliances have coordinated their electoral activities. They either present a joint candidate at the district level or agree that, where they each present a candidate, the candidate with the fewest votes will not compete in the runoff (and will support the other party's candidate). This preelection cooperation is normally carried into the National Assembly, where the legislators from the electoral alliance function as a relatively cohesive bloc, either supporting an alliance-run government or functioning as a unified opposition to the government of the day.

See also *Alternative Vote; Condorcet Theorems; District Magnitude; Duverger's Law; Effect of Elections on Government; Fractionalization Index; Presidential Electoral Systems; Primary Elections; Tactical Voting.*

MARK P. JONES, MICHIGAN STATE UNIVERSITY

BIBLIOGRAPHY

Bullock, Charles S., III, and Loch K. Johnson. *Runoff Elections in the United States.* Chapel Hill: University of North Carolina Press, 1992.

Cox, Gary W. *Making Votes Count: Strategic Coordination in the World's Electoral Systems.* New York: Cambridge University Press, 1997.

Duverger, Maurice. *Political Parties: Their Organization and Activity in the Modern State.* London: Methuen, 1954.

Elgie, Robert. "Two-Ballot Majority Electoral Systems." *Representation* 34 (spring/summer 1997): 89–94.

Jones, Mark P. *Electoral Laws and the Survival of Presidential Democracies.* Notre Dame, Ind.: University of Notre Dame Press, 1995.

Schlesinger, Joseph A., and Mildred Schlesinger. "A Reaffirmation of a Multiparty System in France." *American Political Science Review* 84 (December 1990): 1077–1101.

Shugart, Matthew Soberg, and John M. Carey. *Presidents and Assemblies: Constitutional Design and Electoral Dynamics.* New York: Cambridge University Press, 1992.

Shugart, Matthew Soberg, and Rein Taagepera. "Plurality Versus Majority Election of Presidents: A Proposal for a 'Double Complement Rule.'" *Comparative Political Studies* 27 (October 1994): 323–348.

SECOND-CHAMBER ELECTIONS

Classical constitutionalism derived from Anglo-American experience tends to prescribe that parliaments be composed of two houses, each acting as a check on the other (as in the United States) or the second acting as a brake on the first (as in Britain). In view of the influence these two countries have exercised on constitution making in the world, what is surprising is not that bicameralism (or two-chamber parliaments) has been so common in constitutional polities, but rather that it is absent in so many countries today.

THE DECLINE OF BICAMERALISM

Prior to World War I, second chambers—or what was once more commonly referred to as "upper" chambers—were almost *de rigueur* in sovereign countries with working parliaments and in British autonomous dominions. Those that had none (Greece, Bulgaria, Montenegro, Luxembourg, Panama, Guatemala, Honduras, El Salvador, and Costa Rica) were small in size and population, and few were considered examples of advanced democratic development.

Dramatic changes have taken place since then, with the result that in a world that includes about 190 sovereign countries, bicameral parliaments can now be found in just 64 of them. The crucial factor determining which states will have bicameral parliaments appears to be whether a state is unitary or federal in structure. While only a quarter of unitary states have second chambers, practically all existing federations with working parliaments have second chambers. The only exceptions are St. Kitts and Nevis and Micronesia. Micronesia's "senate," as it is styled, includes members apportioned on the basis of population as well as members who serve longer terms and who represent one of the four states. To an American reader, this structure sounds very much like a house of representatives and a senate fused into a single body. Larger countries in terms of size or population are more likely to have bicameral legislatures than are smaller countries. And while second chambers are sometimes branded as undemocratic, given their roots in the estates-oriented institutions of medieval times, in fact most long-established democracies, such as the United States and Great Britain, have bicameral parliaments.

FUNCTIONS OF SECOND CHAMBERS

The fact that second chambers are most prevalent in large, federal countries highlights one of their chief functions—namely, the representation of regions within the national legislature. However, the notion of "regional" representation is somewhat ambiguous. Some equate a region with its state government or legislature. For them, only individuals acting as delegates of state authorities can truly represent a region. Some hold that representing a region simply means being elected to represent an electoral district that coincides with regional rather than with local boundaries. For others, regional representation is about inflating the weight of the smaller regions in the senate. Whichever of these views holds, in actual practice many second chambers fail as regional representatives because their members are bound by party discipline and put party ties before regional considerations.

Second chambers historically functioned as tools by which a typically wealthy membership could block any radical and threatening measures that had been adopted by the more populist first chamber. The British House of Lords served this purpose throughout the nineteenth century, and as a result of its obstruction to David Lloyd George's budget saw its powers severely curtailed under the Parliament Acts of 1911 and 1949. This opposition to change, exhibited by many bodies similarly constituted, drew strong public and doctrinal criticism against second chambers as tools of vested interests and led in many instances to their abolition. Certainly in today's democratic age, such interference is considered unacceptable.

Second chambers are often touted as houses of legislative review. They provide an opportunity for "sober second thought" on sometimes hastily adopted measures. This function is considered valuable in a democracy, especially in the absence of judicial review of legislation.

SELECTING SENATORS

Members of nineteenth-century upper chambers were typically appointed for life by the Crown. The second chambers of today are recruited in a more democratic way. Britain and Lesotho were unique in their use of hereditary and life peers. In 1999 the right of hereditary peers to sit and to vote in the British House of Lords was abolished. There are also twelve senates, most of them in former British colonies, with memberships that are entirely appointed. Indirect election by lower bodies occurs in sixteen countries, with France, Russia, and India being the largest of these, while seven countries combine indirect election with some form of appointment. Norway provides a unique example of the use of indirect election. Following each general election, the Norwegian Parliament elects one-fourth of its membership to serve in the second chamber. That the party composition of the latter mirrors in miniature that of the former significantly reduces the dangers of a collision between the two chambers.

AN OVERVIEW OF DIRECTLY ELECTED SECOND CHAMBERS

Direct election remains the most common method for selecting members of second chambers. In 1998 some twenty-seven countries used this method (see Table 1).

In most cases, the entire membership is elected by direct election. In seven countries, however, a minority of the membership is selected by a method other than direct election. For example, in addition to its 315 directly elected members, the Italian Senate includes up to five members appointed for life by each president of the republic, selected from among "citizens who have brought honor to the country through their exceptional merits in social, scientific, artistic and literary fields," as well as former presidents of the republic (also for life). Venezuela granted the same privilege to former presidents under its 1961 constitution, a privilege that might be withdrawn upon the adoption of a new constitution still in preparation at the time of writing. In the Chilean Senate, the presence of nine members appointed for eight-year terms reflects the efforts of former dictator Augusto Pinochet and his supporters, who wished to preserve their position within the newly democratized country. Lifetime membership in the Senate for Pinochet himself started upon his retirement as commander in chief of the armed forces in March 1998. The Spanish Senate includes forty-nine members indirectly elected by the assemblies of autonomous communities. The Belgian Senate includes twenty-one members elected by the assemblies of the three language communities plus ten members co-opted by the directly and indirectly elected senators. The children of the king are also entitled to sit in the Senate as a matter of right from the age of eighteen. In Croatia the president of the republic may appoint up to five members. Finally, the vice president of Uruguay is an ex-officio member of the Senate.

All U.S. state senates are directly elected, as are all legislative councils in Australian states. Only Nebraska and Queensland have unicameral state legislatures. All Canadian provinces, Swiss cantons, Austrian bundesländer, and (since the abolition of the Bavarian Senate in 1998) German länder have unicameral legislatures, too.

Whether or not second chambers should be directly elected by the people remains a topic of contention in many countries. In addition to the obvious point that direct election is the most democratic method, its proponents argue that no other method can endow the second chamber with enough clout to hold its own against the directly elected first chamber and thereby give it meaningful impact on the legislative process. Opponents of the idea argue that having two directly elected chambers is redundant—the party composi-

Table 1. Directly Elected Second Chambers, 1998

Country	Government structure	Size[a]	Term (years)	Renewal	Electoral formula		Districts	Other members
					Second chamber	First chamber		
Asia and Oceania								
Australia	Federal	76	6	S	PR	AV	Reg	—
Japan	Unitary	252	6	S	Mixed	Mixed	Nat+Reg	—
Kyrgyzstan	Unitary	35	5	S	Majority	Majority	SM	—
Palau	Unitary	14	4	W	FPTP	FPTP	Reg	—
Philippines	Unitary	24	6	S	FPTP	Mixed	Nat	—
Americas								
Argentina	Federal	72	6	S	FPTP-MR	PR	Reg	—
Bolivia	Unitary	27	5	W	FPTP-MR	Mixed	Reg	—
Brazil	Federal	81	8	S	FPTP	PR	Reg	—
Chile	Unitary	48	8	S	FPTP-MR	FPTP-MR	Reg	9 appointed; former president (lifetime member)
Colombia	Unitary	102	4	W	PR	PR	Nat	—
Dominican Republic	Unitary	30	4	W	FPTP	PR	Reg	—
Haiti	Unitary	27	6	S	Majority	Majority	Reg	—
Mexico	Federal	128	6	W	Mixed	Mixed	Nat+Reg	—
Paraguay	Unitary	45	5	W	PR	PR	Nat	—
United States	Federal	100	6	S	FPTP	FPTP	Reg	—
Uruguay	Unitary	31	5	W	PR	PR	Nat	vice president (member ex officio)
Venezuela	Federal	52	5	W	PR	Mixed	Reg	2 former presidents (lifetime members)
Europe								
Belgium	Federal	74	4	W	PR	PR	Comm	21 indirectly elected; 10 co-opted; 3 royal family
Croatia	Unitary	68	4	W	PR	Mixed	Reg	5 appointed
Czech Republic	Unitary	81	6	S	Majority	PR	SM	—
Italy	Unitary	326	5	W	Mixed	Mixed	Local+Reg	11 appointed for life
Poland	Unitary	100	4	W	FPTP	PR	Reg	—
Romania	Unitary	143	4	W	PR	PR	Reg	—
Spain	Unitary	257	4	W	LV	PR	Reg	49 indirectly elected
Switzerland	Federal	46	4	Var	Majority	PR	Reg	—
Africa								
Liberia	Unitary	26	9	W	PR	PR	Nat	—
Nigeria	Federal	91	4	W	FPTP	FPTP	Reg	—

Abbreviations: AV, alternative vote; S, staggered elections; W, whole chamber renewed at each election; SM, single-member constituencies; Var, varies from state to state; FPTP, first-past-the-post; FPTP-MR, first-past-the-post with minority representation; PR, proportional representation; Majority (two-ballot) system; LV, limited vote; Reg, regional or state; Nat, national; Comm, linguistic communities.

[a] Includes "other members."

tion of the second chamber will simply mirror that of the first. Alternatively, two directly elected chambers may lead to deadlock if the two bodies happen to be dominated by opposed majorities. The latter fear is frequently raised in parliamentary systems. The most dramatic case of deadlock was the refusal of the opposition-dominated Australian Senate to pass key money bills in 1975, a move that led the governor general to sack his Labor prime minister, appoint the Liberal leader as his successor, and call an early election to both houses that resulted in a crushing defeat for the Labor Party. That the ensuing furor was directed against the representative of the Crown rather than against the Senate illustrates how solidly entrenched the bicameral tradition is in Australia.

The case of the Canadian Senate exemplifies the obstacles in the way of direct election. Members of the Canadian Senate are executive-appointed. These appointees hold office until the age of seventy-five. Opponents complain that this system is weak and discredited. They argue that the second chamber could be invigorated through use of direct elections. However, this idea is strongly resisted by many key elements of the Canadian polity. Senatorships as political rewards are enjoyed both by the prime ministers who bestow them and by all actual or potential appointees. Many members of the House of Commons fear that elected senators could become strong competitors in the federal legislative arena. Some provincial premiers fear that their own role as regional champions would be undermined by an elected senate. Westerners and Maritimers advocate a senate in which all provinces have an equal number of seats, but the Francophones of Quebec object that such a division would reduce their weight from one-fourth of the membership to just one-tenth of the total. All of these factors combined in 1992 to ensure the rejection, at a referendum, of a constitutional reform package that included a directly elected senate.

CONSTITUENCIES FOR SECOND CHAMBERS

Governments have encountered much trouble solving the famous dilemma of second chambers posited by Emmanuel-Joseph Sieyès during the French Revolution: either they are recruited in a less democratic way than the elected chamber, in which case they are pernicious, or they are also elected by the people, in which case they are superfluous. In an effort to avoid this dilemma, some governments have established that the membership of their second chambers be directly elected, but within larger constituencies and with seats apportioned such that the voting power of the smaller regions is inflated. This approach has proven most effective in federations. In such a context, the one person, one vote, one value doctrine is arguably too simplistic. Smaller states are entitled to a

stronger voice within the national parliament, supporters contend; otherwise, they run the risk of being swamped on every issue by the larger states. As a result, seats in the second chambers of many federal countries are distributed equally among the various states: the example set by the United States has been followed by Australia, Switzerland (except that half-cantons have one seat whereas cantons have two), and all Latin American federations. The same rationale has been accepted in Spain, a decentralized unitary country, and even in a few unitary countries such as Bolivia, the Dominican Republic, and Haiti. Such a system often leads to staggering disparities in citizens' voting power: the ratio of the voting power of a resident of the largest state to that of a resident of the smallest state is 13:1 in Australia, 26:1 in Mexico, 46:1 in Spain, 66:1 in the United States, 145:1 in Brazil, and 181:1 in Argentina. However, in none of these countries has the existence of such a discrepancy become a significant public issue.

Another approach is to have the whole country form a single district for purposes of second-chamber elections. This is done in the Philippines, Colombia, Paraguay, Uruguay, and Kyrgyzstan. Portions of the Mexican and Japanese second chambers are also elected this way. A risk associated with this solution is that representation may be monopolized by members from a few larger regions. This might happen if lists of candidates are prepared by parties with no consideration for regional balance. Such a fear was expressed in Mexico in 1996, when one-quarter of its senators were made electable in a national constituency. In fact, the major parties have been careful to acknowledge Mexico's federal nature by placing one resident from every state on their lists of candidates.

Members of second chambers tend to be elected to represent constituencies that are identical to, or broader than, those that members of first chambers are elected to represent. The one exception is the Czech Senate, whose members are elected from single-member districts, while members of the first chamber are elected by proportional representation from wider districts. Being returned by a larger district presumably endows senators with more prestige and a wider view of issues, though this has generally (with the possible exception of the U.S. Senate) not translated into de facto superiority for the second chamber.

ELECTORAL SYSTEMS FOR SECOND CHAMBER ELECTIONS

Second chambers are almost universally smaller than first chambers. The size of directly elected second chambers varies from 14 members in Palau to 326 members in Italy. The average size is 87.2 members. Their small size, especially when coupled with the need for respecting regional boundaries, severely restricts the options available for selecting an electoral system, since district magnitude (the number of seats in a district) may be as low as two or three.

As a result, most second chambers are elected by plurality or majority formulas, even in countries where proportional representation is used for first-chamber elections. The so-called first-past-the-post system (a plurality electoral system) is the most common formula, mitigated in a few cases (Argentina, Bolivia, and Chile, for example) by a provision for some representation within each district for the party that comes in second. The same concern for providing minority representation in a plurality context has led to the selection of the limited vote for electing Spanish senators. Majority (or double-ballot) systems prevail in the Czech Republic and in Switzerland. Proportional representation functions in Australia, Belgium, Romania, Venezuela, and Uruguay. Mixed systems are found in Japan, Mexico, and Italy. In Italy three-quarters of the senators are elected by plurality in single-member districts, and the remainder are elected by regional proportional representation using a complex formula that corrects to some extent the distortions generated by the first-past-the-post system. In Mexico, following the most recent reform, three-quarters of the senators (three for each state) are elected within each state under the following mixed superposition system: the leading party in the state wins two seats, and the third seat goes to the runner-up party. The other senators are elected under a noncorrective proportional-representation system in a national constituency. The Japanese House of Councilors offers a similar mix of regional and national constituencies. The 47 districts return 152 members under the single-nontransferable-vote system, while 100 members are elected by a noncorrective proportional-representation system in the national constituency.

Directly elected second chambers raise the issue of electoral system congruence. At first glance, logic dictates that the systems used for both chambers be roughly the same so that voters not be confused by the coexistence of two criteria of legitimacy. However, many hold that the second chamber should be distinct from the first, or be used to counter any negative consequences the formula employed for first chamber elections is likely to generate.

The rationale for electoral system congruence has been accepted in fifteen countries. However, no less than twelve others have selected a different formula for the second chamber. Australians are alone in combining the alternative vote for the House of Representatives with the single transferable vote for the Senate (prior to 1948, the same formula was used for both houses). Seven proportional-representation countries, including Switzerland, Spain, and the Czech Republic, use a majoritarian formula for the second chamber. Of the seven countries with mixed systems for first-chamber elec-

tions, Venezuela and Croatia use proportional representation for the second chamber, whereas Bolivia prefers a majoritarian system.

TERMS OF OFFICE

It is commonly assumed, based on the U.S. case, that senators serve for substantially longer terms than members of the first chamber. This is so, however, not because the U.S. senatorial term is very long, but because the term served by representatives (two years) is exceptionally short. In practice, more than half of the world's directly elected senators serve four- or five-year terms, much like their colleagues in the lower chambers. Six-year terms exist in eight countries and exceed first-chamber terms by only one or two years, except in Australia, where representatives serve terms half that figure. Brazil and Chile grant their senators eight-year terms, while Liberian senators are now the only ones that serve nine-year terms, a distinction they shared until 1994 with their Argentinean counterparts.

STAGGERED ELECTIONS

In contrast with the almost universal practice of electing *all* members of the first chamber at the same time, constitution makers have been more willing to provide for staggered elections for second chambers. The U.S. practice of renewing one-third of the Senate every two years has been emulated, subject to variations in fractions and time periods, by ten countries, including Australia, Japan, Argentina, and Brazil. Switzerland obtains the same result by allowing each state to determine the length of the term of its elected delegates. The majority (sixteen) of elected second chambers, however, are renewed in toto. Whether elections are staggered or not depends on the term length of the second chamber. Staggered elections occur in just two of the sixteen second chambers with "standard" (four or five year) terms, but in nine of the eleven chambers with longer terms.

Direct election in most cases has not made second chambers equal in clout to first chambers. Most are clearly junior partners in the legislative arena, reacting to the initiatives taken by the first chamber rather than imposing their own. In parliamentary systems, governments are made and unmade in the first rather than in the second chamber. The relative weakness of second chambers is due in some cases to constitutional limitations of power or to the fact that the same political parties control both houses. The strength and prestige of the U.S. Senate is atypical and may be cited as an example of American exceptionalism. However, direct election provides second chambers with the legitimacy that universal suffrage now confers, allowing them a decisive impact in the legislative arena without challenging basic democratic principles.

See also *Designing Electoral Systems; Estate and Curia Constituencies; Federal Countries, Elections in; Majority Systems; Mixed Electoral Systems; Plurality Systems; Simultaneous Elections; Staggered Elections; Term of Office.*

LOUIS MASSICOTTE, UNIVERSITY OF MONTREAL

SECOND-ORDER ELECTIONS

The concept of second-order elections was first presented in 1980 by Karlheinz Reif and Hermann Schmitt and has since been elaborated by Reif and others. Reif and Schmitt undertook a study of the pattern of results in the first direct elections to the European Parliament. While those who promoted the reform of a directly elected European Parliament hoped that these elections would be fought on European issues, Reif and Schmitt suggested they would be better understood not as primarily European elections but as a type of *national* election. They argued that in the eyes of the parties and the public, the national political arena is the most important one in European nation-states. Hence, elections for national public office are the most salient and dominate all other elections. Reif and Schmitt defined elections for national office as first-order elections and elections for local and state offices as second-order national elections. By inserting the term "national" into their definition, Reif and Schmitt emphasized the fact that local and state office elections are essentially national elections, just less important ones. In most parliamentary systems, general elections for parliament are first-order elections and those for local government bodies are second-order elections. Elections to choose a nonexecutive head of state and European parliamentary elections are also second-order elections. The most important distinction between first-order and second-order elections is that in the latter less is at stake.

Second-order elections cannot be separated from first-order elections conducted in the same political system. Concerns that are appropriate to the first-order arena will affect the second-order arena, even though second-order elections are ostensibly about something quite different. Of particular importance is the political situation of the first-order arena at the moment when the second-order election is being held.

Descriptive accounts of second-order election campaigns make it clear that for both voters and parties, national issues and the politics of the first-order arena are of paramount importance. Opposition parties commonly invite voters to make the election a referendum on the government's performance to date, particularly when the government appears to be less popular than it was at its inauguration. Popular governments have also been known to ask the voters to reward them. Issues such as unemployment, inflation, and the functioning of the welfare state usually dominate national elections; these same issues feature prominently in the list of issues highlighted by the parties, the media, and the voters in European Parliament election campaigns. More narrowly European issues, even those as important as monetary union, get less attention.

Based on these arguments, Reif and Schmitt offered three broad propositions to characterize regular differences between aggregate behavior in European Parliament elections and previous (and subsequent) national elections:

1. Turnout will be lower in European Parliament elections than in national elections

2. National government parties will suffer losses in European Parliament elections

3. Larger parties will do worse and smaller parties will do better in European Parliament elections

Analyses of election results have generally validated these propositions. To begin with, over the first four sets of European Parliament elections (1979, 1984, 1989, and 1994) the average turnout was 63 percent, 19 percent lower than turnout in the previous national election. This means that almost one in four of those who vote in a national election do not vote in a European election. If we discount those countries where voting is compulsory, or where national and European Parliament elections take place on the same day, the drop in turnout is even more pronounced.

It is also true that governments perform poorly in European Parliament elections. If we compare the vote garnered by the government parties in the European Parliament elections with the vote they secured in the last national election, we find that over the first four sets of European Parliament elections support for governments falls, on average, by 6 percent. Finally, it is also evident that there is a net shift of votes from larger parties to smaller parties. In the fifth set of European Parliament elections, held in 1999, these patterns held, with turnout dropping to just 49 percent and the support for governments again dropping by 6 percent.

WHY VOTERS BEHAVE DIFFERENTLY

What individual motivations underlie these electoral changes? While Reif and Schmitt made no attempt to develop a complete model of individual electoral choice, they did highlight some aspects of European elections that help explain aggregate patterns in terms of individual change. There are several types of change to consider. First is the change from voting to not voting. As noted above, a crucial feature of second-order national elections is that less is at stake. To the extent that this view is shared by the main actors in the political process, notably the voters, the parties, and the mass media, this fact generally serves to reduce the expected benefits and increase the expected costs of voting for the individual elector. As such, we would expect to find that fewer people vote.

Second is the change in party choice. Here contextual factors must be taken into consideration. First of all, it is significant that European Parliament elections, unlike national elections, do not involve the selection of a governing body but only of a representative body. This distinction is important because in the European elections voters are freed from having to consider the secondary implications of their vote. Voters who opt for a given party in a national election because they believe that that party can best contribute to the formation of a government but who actually prefer another party (whether on grounds of ideology, group identity, or personality) can be said to have cast an "insincere" vote. To the extent that larger parties reap the benefits of insincere voting in national elections, it follows that they will be the more likely to lose support in European elections, where less is at stake. The benefits would instead accrue to small, relatively insignificant parties. Reif and Schmitt describe this process of change as one in which voters choose to vote with their hearts rather than with their heads.

A second contextual consideration involves the timing of the European election within each national election cycle. These circumstances might see a voter move from a sincere choice (in the previous national election) to an insincere choice. Voters may use second-order elections to send a message to parties, particularly government parties. There are different views about when such behavior might be most pronounced. Initially, Reif and Schmitt suggested that the extent of defection would be largely a function of a government popularity cycle that would reach its nadir just after midterm, and there is some evidence of this pattern in European Parliament election results. An alternative view (van der Eijk, Franklin, et al. 1996), given some support by survey data, is that the nature of defection will vary according to the perceived importance of the second-order election within the national context. When European Parliament and national elections overlap, little or no attention is paid to European Parliament elections, and voters may simply vote "with their heart"; however, when a European Parliament election takes place just before a national election, the results of the former are a significant indicator of the results of the latter. In this case, protest voting will be much more pronounced as voters can signal their discontent and know someone will be listening. Interestingly, variations in turnout can also be explained by election timing. The fall-off in turnout in European Par-

liament elections relative to national elections is less pronounced when a national election is set to follow soon after a European Parliament election.

THE CONSEQUENCES FOR NATIONAL AND EUROPEAN POLITICS

Because they are essentially national in character, European Parliament elections can have significant consequences for national politics. Indeed, as has already been indicated, voters often expect them to have such consequences.

A party's level of support in European elections is a good guide to its performance in later national elections. In fact, support in European elections is a better guide than is the level of support in the preceding national election, a point that underlines the national character of European elections. Organizations that take a stand in European elections may as a result face consequences, whether negative or positive, in the ensuing national election. New parties may gain visibility and credibility that will help them in the future. Many have argued that the growth of Green parties in particular owes much to their initial success in European elections. Governments can become destabilized by European elections. Although the government as a whole will usually lose support, the loss may affect some members of the government to a much greater extent than others and thus increase tensions within a coalition. Some governments are occasionally strengthened. For example, in 1989 the Spanish government called for an early election in order to capitalize on the support shown for it in the European elections. The elections can also promote policy changes in the national arena. For example, in Germany the government was influenced by challenges from the right-wing Republikaner Party when it changed policy toward Eastern Europe in 1989.

Because the elections are essentially about something other than Europe, they do not function in the manner normally expected of elections. They do little to increase awareness, create legitimacy, or stimulate debate about European integration. This is because European elections are fought along exactly the same partisan lines as national elections. The major exception to this is in Denmark, where a somewhat different party system functions in the European elections. In consequence, the election in Denmark has less of a second-order character; it in fact does help raise awareness and channel debate. Elsewhere, the very fact that the elections are dominated by parties that focus on the national political arena ensures that differences on European matters will be submerged beneath differences on national matters. A further, somewhat perverse consequence of the national character of European elections is that the European Parliament may contain a disproportionately large number of national "opposition" party representatives, resulting in a parliament with a partisan majority that differs from that of the European Council, which represents member governments.

GENERALIZING THE CONCEPT

While Reif and Schmitt put forth their second-order model as a way of explaining the pattern of results in European Parliament elections, Reif has noted that the model's intellectual origins lie in the analysis of German state elections and, to a lesser extent, U.S. midterm elections. Certainly, local and regional elections, elections for a weak president (as in Ireland), by-elections (in Britain), and to some degree even referendums show second-order effects. But they do not all display such effects to the same degree. In Britain, for example, classic second-order effects are more pronounced in European elections than in local elections. And the existence of second-order effects in European Parliament elections is much more pronounced in some countries than in others, notably those where the link between election results and government formation is clear cut and there is alternation in the control of government power (for example, in Britain, Ireland, and Germany but not in the Benelux countries). One implication of this is that the difference between first- and second-order elections is not a simple dichotomy; rather, both types lie on a continuum with a classic first-order election at one end and a classic second-order election at the other. The notion of how much is at stake seems to be an important criterion by which to define this continuum. Viewed in this way, we can see that what we now call a second-order election has some first-order properties, while what we call a first-order election has some second-order properties.

See also *Barometer Elections; Federal Countries, Elections in; Paradox of Voting; Suppléant; Turnout; Turnout, Minimum Requirement.*

Michael Marsh, Trinity College, University of Dublin

BIBLIOGRAPHY

Marsh, Michael. "Testing the Second-order Election Model After Four European Elections." *British Journal of Political Science* 28 (October 1998): 591–607.

Reif, Karlheinz. "European Elections as Member State Second-order Elections Revisited." *European Journal of Political Research* 31 (February 1997): 115–124.

Reif, Karlheinz, and Hermann Schmitt. "Nine Second-order National Elections: A Conceptual Framework for the Analysis of European Election Results." *European Journal of Political Research* 8 (March 1980): 3–44.

van der Eijk, Cees, Mark Franklin, and Michael Marsh. "What Voters Teach Us About Europe-wide Elections: What Europe-wide Elections Teach Us About Voters." *Electoral Studies* 15, no. 2 (May 1996): 149–166.

van der Eijk, Cees, and Mark Franklin et al. *Choosing Europe? The European Electorate in the Face of Unification.* Ann Arbor: University of Michigan Press, 1996.

SECRET BALLOT

Although secret voting had been used for elections in the Roman Republic and by citizen juries in classical Athens, not until the end of the eighteenth century did the secret ballot begin to replace oral voting in national elections.

The debate about the secret ballot was part of the nineteenth century debate about the expansion of suffrage. Radicals who demanded adult suffrage, such as the British Chartists, also called for the ballot to be secret to protect the newly enfranchised from pressure by their employers or aristocratic landowners. Some supporters of the secret ballot also claimed that its introduction would lessen the efficacy of bribery at election times. Opposition to the secret ballot was not limited to upper-class conservatives who saw it as a threat to their influence. Some liberals who supported a wider electorate, such as John Stuart Mill, regarded the vote as a trust that should be exercised openly.

The principle of the secret ballot was introduced in France during the Revolution (1789–1815), but its implementation there was incomplete until the early twentieth century. The innovation caught on earliest in the British colonies. In 1856 the British colony of Victoria (in southern Australia) introduced two key elements of a genuinely secret ballot: an official ballot provided by the electoral authority rather than a party or candidate, and a voting booth where the voter could mark the ballot unobserved. The official, government-provided ballot, known as the Australian ballot, became a model for reformers elsewhere in the English-speaking world. It was adopted by most of the other British colonies in Australia over the next decade, by New Zealand in 1870, by the United Kingdom in 1872, and by Canada two years later.

In the United States elections did not become fully secret until the end of the nineteenth century, because the parties each distributed their own ballot, known as a "party strip" or "unofficial ballot." Each party made its ballot identifiable by printing it on a different size of paper and in a different color than its rivals. It was therefore easy for party workers at the polling place to see which party's ballot the voter picked up. In 1888 Massachusetts introduced a state-prepared ballot that listed all of the parties and candidates, an innovation modeled on Australian practice. Within eight years, 90 percent of the states had followed suit.

In continental Europe the introduction of the secret ballot generally preceded or coincided with the introduction of adult male suffrage, as in Italy in 1861 and Belgium in 1877. But there were important exceptions to this pattern. Countries where peasant farmers already enjoyed the vote tended to delay introducing the secret ballot: Denmark until 1901, Iceland until 1906, and Finland until 1907, for example.

Countries with a politically powerful landowning class often resisted the secret ballot even longer. Prussia retained open voting until after World War I (1918). Open voting was restored in rural Hungary in 1922. In France, although the vote had been secret in principle for many years, secrecy was not generally observed until 1913, with the introduction of a polling booth and an envelope to conceal the ballot.

Although the secrecy of the ballot is now an almost universally accepted principle, its implementation in some countries has been limited by political or social factors. In communist countries the provision for a secret ballot remained largely formal. In the Soviet Union, in the absence of a choice of candidates, voters could either drop an unmarked ballot into a box under the scrutiny of election officials or use a screened voting booth to cross off the name of the sole official candidate. The use of the secret ballot could thus be interpreted as disloyalty to the regime.

In countries with a large number of illiterate voters, the protection of secrecy can be problematic. In the British colonies illiterate voters frequently needed the help of election officials to identify their chosen candidate on the ballot. Such voters would tell the election official in a low voice which candidate they wished to vote for, and the official would then mark the vote on a sheet. The integrity of these "whispering votes" depended on the honesty of the election official. The use of separate ballots for each party in the French colonies and their successor states compromised secrecy, too. Group voting or family voting, where male family heads cast ballots for their wives, children, or elderly relatives, has been observed in some former communist countries, such as Azerbaijan and Kazakhstan.

See also *Absentee Voting; Acclamation, Election by; Administration of Elections; Australian Ballot; Franchise Expansion Lot; Open Voting.*

TOM MACKIE, UNIVERSITY OF STRATHCLYDE

BIBLIOGRAPHY

Friedgut, Theodore. *Political Participation in the USSR.* Princeton, N.J.: Princeton University Press, 1979.

Furtak, Robert, ed. *Elections in Socialist States.* New York: Harvester; London: Wheatsheaf, 1990.

Garrigou, Alain. *Le Vote et la Vertu: Comment les français sont devenus électeurs.* Paris: Presses de la Fondation Nationale des Sciences Politiques, 1992.

Markoff, John. "From Center to Periphery and Back again: Reflections on the Geography of Democratic Innovation." In *Explaining Citizenship, Reconfiguring States,* edited by Michael Hanagan and Charles Tilly. Boulder, Colo.: Rowan and Littlefield, 1999.

Mill, John Stuart. *On Liberty and Representative Government.*

Millar, Fergus. *The Crowd in Rome in the Late Republic.* Ann Arbor: University of Michigan Press, 1999.

Rokkan, Stein. *Citizens, Elections and Parties: Approaches to the Comparative Study of the Processes of Development.* Oslo: Universitetsforlaget, 1970.

Smith, Trevor. *Elections in Developing Countries.* London: Macmillan, 1960.

Wiebe, R. *The Search for Order 1877–1920.* New York: Hill and Wang, 1967.

SIMULTANEOUS ELECTIONS

Elections are called simultaneous when various categories of officeholders are elected on the same day. At the national level, in addition to members of the first chamber, those categories may include senators and the president. At the local level, council members and, in some cases, the mayor are elected. In federal countries, residents of each state elect their legislators and governors, as do residents of regions in some unitary countries with decentralized regional governments. In the United States various executive, administrative, and judicial officials are elected as well.

The simultaneous character of elections is reinforced when a single ballot is used for the election of different officeholders and when a single vote on that ballot is counted as a vote for each of the candidates sponsored by a given party for each position. However, in this article, only the timing dimension will be examined.

There are many practical obstacles to holding simultaneous elections. The most obvious is that the term of office often differs from one category of officials to another. In France, for example, the president of the republic is elected for a seven-year term, compared with five years for members of the National Assembly and members of the European Parliament, nine years for senators, and six years for members of regional councils and departmental councils. A supplementary obstacle is that presidential and National Assembly elections may be held sooner than scheduled, for example, if the president dies or resigns or if the National Assembly is dissolved. As a result, the French normally vote for at least one category of officials almost every year; from 1978 to 1998 only four years were "election-free."

The United States, and presidential systems generally, find it easier to hold elections at the same time because all electoral terms are usually fixed. Typically, they range from two years (for the U.S. House of Representatives, the governors of Vermont and New Hampshire, and most state legislators), to four years (the president, most governors, and some state legislators) or six years (U.S. senators). Legislatures cannot be dissolved, and vacancies in executive offices are normally filled for the remainder of the term by other officeholders. It is technically possible to elect on a single day the president, all members of the U.S. House of Representatives, and one-third of U.S. senators and to schedule elections to state and local offices for the same day.

ADVANTAGES OF SIMULTANEOUS ELECTIONS

Many people advocate holding elections simultaneously as a cost-saving measure. Elections are expensive operations, which necessitate compiling electoral registers, purchasing election materials, and paying poll officials. Filling various offices on the same day may save much money, both for the government and for candidates, for the latter because they may pool their resources if they belong to the same party.

American political scientist Mark Jones recommends simultaneous elections in U.S.-type presidential systems because they minimize the likelihood of divided government, that is, the possibility that the presidency and Congress will be dominated by different political parties. The argument is plausible, even if recent American experience suggests that electing all representatives and the president on the same day does not preclude divided government: seven of the thirteen presidential elections held since World War II coincided with the election of a House of Representatives dominated by the other party. In countries with second chambers, the same rationale can be extended to legislative elections: electing senators and representatives on the same day presumably reduces the danger of colliding majorities in the two houses.

Electing numerous officials at the same time also can help increase turnout for less salient offices. In the United States and France turnout is higher for presidential than for legislative elections, and also higher for national than for local elections. Turnout for elections to the U.S. House of Representatives is invariably higher in presidential election years than at midterm elections. Proponents of simultaneous elections contend that if elections to less salient offices are held simultaneously with elections to the most salient ones, the latter will drag turnout higher than it would otherwise be. Sweden, where turnout for local elections is among the highest in the world, seems to bear that out; local elections there are held on the same day as national legislative elections.

DISADVANTAGES OF SIMULTANEOUS ELECTIONS

Simultaneous elections have drawbacks as well as advantages. They may necessitate administrative precautions if the franchise is slightly different (in age or residence) for each kind of simultaneously held election. If a distinct ballot is used for each election, voters must take care putting each ballot in the right box. Results may be slower to come because of the higher number of ballots to be counted. Voting machines help solve many of these problems. That such devices were invented in the United States, a country where many offices are filled concurrently, is probably not coincidental.

When elections are held simultaneously, the campaigns for less salient offices will likely be overshadowed in the media by the big races, and the latter will determine the outcome of the former (the "coat-tail" effect). This may be why, in mature federations (like Australia, Austria, Canada, Germany, and Switzerland), state elections rarely if ever coincide with federal elections. The same can be said for the Belgian and Italian regions and the Spanish autonomous communities and will be true for the Scottish Parliament and the Welsh Assembly. Among the forty-eight American states in which gubernatorial terms are of the same duration as the presidential term (four years), only nine elect their governor on the same day as they elect the president, whereas in the other thirty-nine, gubernatorial elections either coincide with midterm legislative elections (thirty-four states) or are held in odd-numbered years (five states).

The timing of Canadian provincial and Australian state elections also varies from one province or state to another. However, it is not uncommon for a few German and Austrian *länder* to schedule their legislative elections for the same date, presumably in order to increase the political significance of the results for the nation as a whole. In the United States, primary presidential elections are sometimes scheduled by the states with the same purpose in mind, as the southern "Super Tuesday" suggests.

In the emerging democracies of Africa, democratic transitions in the early 1990s, following the adoption of new constitutions, required immediate elections to various local and national offices. But national leaders often felt it more appropriate to hold elections sequentially, for example at about three-month intervals, starting with the least sensitive positions (like local councils), moving upward to national legislators and then to the president. Electorates and election officials who were unfamiliar with competitive elections were thus given a chance to hone their skills in anticipation of the more important contests.

See also *Designing Electoral Systems; Federal Countries, Elections in; Second-Chamber Elections; Staggered Elections; Term of Office; Ticket Splitting; Turnout; Turnout, Minimum Requirement.*

LOUIS MASSICOTTE AND ANDRÉ BLAIS, UNIVERSITY OF MONTREAL

BIBLIOGRAPHY

Jones, Mark P. *Electoral Laws and the Survival of Presidential Democracies.* Notre Dame, Ind.: University of Notre Dame Press, 1995.

SINGLE NONTRANSFERABLE VOTE IN MULTIMEMBER DISTRICTS

A system of voting currently used only in Taiwan but also used in Japan from 1947 through 1993, the single nontransferable vote (SNTV) in multimember districts (MMDs) is a simple extension of British-style single-member districts (SMDs). Under SMD, each voter casts a single vote and the candidate with the most votes wins the seat. British-style SMD is also called "first past the post" because only the top vote-getter is awarded a seat.

Under SNTV/MMD, each district elects more than one legislator, but voters still cast just one vote each. The number of seats in a district is M, the district magnitude, and the top M candidates are awarded seats. For example, if M=3, the first, second, and third candidates win seats, while the fourth, fifth, and lower candidates do not. In precisely the same way that British-style SMD can be called the first-past-the-post system, SNTV/MMD can be called the Mth-past-the-post system. In fact, we might well label the British system SNTV/SMD.

Given the structural similarities between SNTV/MMD and SNTV/SMD, we should expect to find similarities in how the two systems operate and what effects they produce. And, indeed, the most celebrated generalization about single-member districts, Duverger's Law, has been extended to SNTV/MMD. Duverger's Law states that SMD tends to produce a two-party system or, more accurately, competition between two serious candidates per district. Steven Reed proposed the "M+1 rule," which posits that the number of serious candidates under SNTV/MMD will, at equilibrium, be equal to the number of seats in the district plus one. He also demonstrated the empirical validity of this rule for Japanese elections. Gary Cox extended the M+1 rule and provided a mathematical proof based on rational choice assumptions. John Hsieh and Richard Niemi demonstrated the validity, with modifications, of the rule to Taiwanese elections. Finally, Reed and John Bolland extended the analogy between Duverger's Law and the M+1 rule by showing that, in the Japanese case, not only does the effective number of candidates tend toward M+1, but each candidate tends to be supported by a different campaign organization.

The analogy between Duverger's Law and the M+1 rule is so strong that one might argue that Duverger's Law is simply a special case of the more general M+1 rule. Whether or not this is true, the fruitfulness of comparing SNTV/SMD with SNTV/MMD has been amply demonstrated. However, the major difference between these two systems—single-member versus multimember districts—also produces significant effects. The importance of M, the number of seats per district, can best be illustrated by comparing SNTV/MMD with STV/MMD (single transferable vote in multimember districts), which is used in Ireland.

SNTV/MMD as it was used in Japan and STV/MMD as it is used in Ireland differ only in the transferability of the vote. Under STV/MMD, each voter lists his or her preferences among several candidates, and his or her vote can be transferred to other candidates if necessary. In both countries, district magnitude varies between three and five. To win a majority in multimember districts, a large party must run more than one candidate per district, forcing candidates from the same party to compete against one another. Such intraparty competition tends to be based more on the cultivation of the personal vote and on the provision of personal and constituency service than on policy differences. Candidates in both Japan and Ireland have developed geographical bases as a way of managing intraparty competition, concluding agreements "not to campaign in your area if you do not campaign in mine." It is also noteworthy that Ireland is second only to Japan in the number of national legislators who, in some sense, "inherited" their seats from previously elected relatives.

Finally, the fact that votes are nontransferable produces some effects quite different from those produced by either single-member districts or the transferable vote. Cox and Emerson Niou found that large parties are forced to run more than one candidate per district under both systems, but under SNTV/MMD they are also forced to make strategic decisions about how many candidates to run in a district. If a party runs too many candidates, it risks splitting its vote too many ways and losing winnable seats. For example, a party with 50 percent of the vote in a three-member district might run three candidates who finish third, fourth, and fifth, winning only one seat. However, if the party runs only two candidates, those candidates will finish first and second, winning two seats. The phenomenon of running too many candidates and thereby losing a seat is called *tomodaore* (falling together) in Japanese. Similarly, a party can lose a winnable seat if it does not divide its vote evenly among its candidates. For example, a party with 50 percent of the vote in a three-member district might win only one seat if one of its candidates won 40 percent of the vote, leaving only 10 percent of the vote for its other candidate. The transferable vote was designed to eliminate both of these problems, and in practice it largely succeeds in doing so.

See also *District Magnitude; Duverger's Law; Pooling Votes; Preference Voting; Single Transferable Vote.*

STEVEN R. REED, CHUO UNIVERSITY, JAPAN

BIBILIOGRAPHY

Cox, Gary W. "Strategic Voting Equilibria under the Single Non-Transferable Vote." *American Political Science Review* 88 (September 1994): 608–621.

Cox, Gary W., and Emerson Niou. "Seat Bonuses under the Single Nontransferable Vote System: Evidence from Japan and Taiwan." *Comparative Politics* 26 (January 1994): 221–236.

Hsieh, John Fuh-sheng, and Richard G. Niemi. "Can Duverger's Law Be Extended to SNTV? The Case of Taiwan's Legislative Yuan Elections." *Electoral Studies* 18 (March 1999): 101–116.

Ishibashi, Michihiro, and Steven R. Reed. "Hereditary Seats: Second Generation Dietmen and Democracy and Japan." *Asian Survey* 32 (April 1992): 366–379.

Reed, Steven R. "Structure and Behaviour: Extending Duverger's Law to the Japanese Case." *British Journal of Political Science* 20 (July 1990): 335–356.

Reed, Steven R., and John M. Bolland. "The Fragmentation Effect of SNTV in Japan." In *Elections and Campaigning in Japan, Korea and Taiwan,* edited by Bernard Grofman et al. Ann Arbor: University of Michigan Press, 1999.

SINGLE TRANSFERABLE VOTE

The idea of the single transferable vote dates from the middle of the nineteenth century when, independently of each other, Thomas Hare in Britain and Carl Andrae in Denmark devised it. The main attraction of this electoral system is the power it gives to voters to express preferences among individual candidates standing for election. It is also attractive to those studying elections, since the counting process reveals a lot of information about voting behavior. On the negative side, the conversion of votes into seats is less transparent under the single transferable vote than under most other electoral systems, and it is unpopular with some practicing politicians because of the very competitive nature of elections held under the single transferable vote.

DESCRIPTION

The essence of the single transferable vote is that the voters are presented with a ballot listing all candidates standing for election and can rank order these candidates in order of preference, by marking 1 for their most favored, 2 for their second favorite, and so on. There is no obligation on voters to take heed of party affiliation when ranking candidates; indeed, the single transferable vote works perfectly well in nonparty elections.

The counting process is relatively complicated and time-consuming, and some of the minor details vary between countries. Of necessity only a brief description can be given here. The process revolves around the Droop quota: the number of votes that ensures a candidate's election. This is calculated by the formula:

$$Q_{DROOP} \frac{\text{votes}}{(\text{seats} + 1)} = + 1, \text{ disregarding any fractional remainder}$$

Thus, for example, if 100,000 votes are cast in a four-seat constituency, the Droop quota equals one more than the integer part of 100,000/5; that is, it equals 20,001. This is the smallest number of votes possessing the property that only four candidates can obtain it.

Any candidate whose total of first-preference votes equals or exceeds this quota is declared elected. The surplus votes of such a candidate (that is, the number of first-preference votes he or she received over and above the quota) are redistributed; that is, they are transferred to the other candidates, in proportion to the number with a second preference marked for each of the other candidates. For example, if a candidate received 24,000 first preferences in a four-seat constituency with 100,000 votes, that candidate would have secured election and would have 3,999 surplus votes. To distribute the surplus votes, all 24,000 votes would be examined, and if a third of these carried a second preference for one particular candidate, then that candidate would receive a third of the surplus, or 1,333 votes.

If at some stage of the count no candidate has a surplus, the counting proceeds by eliminating the candidate with the lowest number of votes. His or her votes are distributed among the other candidates, in line with the next preference marked upon them. This process, of transferring the surplus votes of elected candidates and transferring all the votes of eliminated candidates, continues until all the seats are filled.

Although the details of the counting process can seem complex, the rationale is straightforward. Among other things it aims to minimize the number of wasted votes, so if a voter's choice of candidate is so popular as not to need that vote, or so unpopular that he or she has no chance of election, the vote is not wasted but can pass on to the voter's second choice.

The simplest case of the single transferable vote occurs when there is only one seat to be filled; the electoral system is then termed the *alternative vote*. The quota then is a simple majority of the votes, and the counting process consists of the successive eliminations of the lowest placed candidates until one of the remaining candidates has a majority of the votes. This process bears some resemblance to a run-off election with successive rounds of voting, each round excluding the candidate placed lowest in the previous round, except that under the single transferable vote there is no need for repeated voting, since all the information is conveyed by the voter on the initial ballot.

The single transferable vote in multimember constituencies is often termed PR-STV, that is, proportional representation by means of the single transferable vote, to distinguish it from the alternative vote. Although the mechanics of counting the votes are much the same under both the alternative vote and PR-STV (except that under the alternative vote the question of transferring the surplus votes of elected candidates does not arise), the aspect of multimember constituencies under PR-STV compared with single-member constituencies under the alternative vote makes a significant difference to the political consequences of these electoral systems.

USE OF THE SINGLE TRANSFERABLE VOTE

Since the Danish branch of the family died out, the single transferable vote has been employed almost exclusively in English-speaking countries, and it has the image of being the "Anglo-Saxon" version of proportional representation. Only two countries use it to elect their national parliament: the Republic of Ireland, which has used it for all elections since independence in 1922; and Malta, for all elections since 1921. In addition, it is employed to elect the state legislature in Tasmania. In Northern Ireland the single transferable vote was used in the 1920s before being replaced by single-member plurality, but it was readopted in the 1970s and has been used since for elections at virtually all levels. There is only one exception to the "Anglo-Saxon" pattern of use: partly due to the influence of the political scientist Rein Taagepera, the single transferable vote was used for Estonia's first postcommunist election in 1990 but was then replaced by a variant of list proportional representation.

POLITICAL CONSEQUENCES OF THE SINGLE TRANSFERABLE VOTE

PR-STV, as a particular version of proportional representation, can be expected to deliver proportional election outcomes, and it does so. Proportionality is conventionally measured by comparing the share of votes won by political parties with the share of seats they obtain in parliament. By this criterion, PR-STV delivers proportional outcomes in the countries where it is used—broadly speaking, outcomes that are as proportional as under other versions of proportional representation. For example, in Ireland Fianna Fáil, the largest party at every election for more than sixty years, has won on average 45 percent of the votes at postwar elections and 48 percent of the seats, while the third party, Labour, has won an average of 12 percent of the votes and 11 percent of the seats.

This criterion is imperfect because not all votes cast for a candidate of a particular party are necessarily votes for the party per se. Voters are free to award preferences on the basis of whatever factor is most important to them individually; for example, they might rank candidates according to their stance on some issue that cuts across party lines, or they might give their highest preferences to female candidates regardless of party. Thus a voter might give a first preference to a candidate of party A and a second preference to a candidate of party B. Treating this as a vote for party A, as conventional measures

of proportionality inevitably do, involves making simplifying assumptions that might not always be valid. In practice, voting across party lines is more common in Ireland than in either Malta or Tasmania, where voters are more likely to vote a straight party ticket.

The beneficiaries of disproportionality, that is, differences between vote shares and seat shares, are larger parties (which receive a higher share of seats than votes under virtually every kind of electoral system) and center parties. Center parties stand to benefit because they are a natural second choice; for example, in a three-party system, with one left-wing party, one right-wing party, and one center party, the likelihood is that most supporters of the left-wing party will prefer the center party to the right-wing party, and, likewise, right-wing supporters will rank center-party candidates ahead of left-wing candidates. Thus the center party may finish with a higher proportion of seats than of votes, but this is not a manifestation of disproportionality; it occurs because the single transferable vote takes into account the full preference ordering of the voters.

Party systems in different countries using PR-STV vary considerably, and it is clear that PR-STV does not deterministically lead to a specific configuration of parties. For many years Ireland was often cited as a partial exception to Duverger's Law, since it had only three significant parties, but in the 1980s and 1990s the number of parties with parliamentary representation increased. Malta, in contrast, has had a pure two-party system since its first postindependence election in 1966.

Under the single transferable vote, as under list systems with preference voting, candidates of a party are in competition with each other as well as with candidates of other parties. It may be that a party nominates, say, four candidates in a multimember district but receives enough votes for only two seats, so the personal support received by each of its four candidates determines which of them will get elected. In Ireland, Malta, and Tasmania this intraparty competition manifests itself mainly in assiduous attention to the grass roots and diligent performance of casework duties. This is not to say that PR-STV causes the casework loads about which some parliamentarians in these places complain. In each case the ratio of voters to members of parliament is relatively low (fewer than 4,000:1 in Malta), and a close relationship between members of parliament and voters would be likely whatever electoral system was employed.

Party cohesion might be expected to be jeopardized by the intraparty competition for votes generated by PR-STV, yet in practice it is not. The parliamentary parties in Ireland and Malta are exceptionally cohesive, with members very rarely deviating from the party line.

Incumbents are at risk of losing their seat not only to a candidate of another party but also to a fellow candidate of their own party. For this reason, some incumbents in countries using PR-STV would prefer an electoral system that reduced the risk of their being defeated. Nevertheless, turnover is relatively low under PR-STV: in both Ireland and Malta around 80 percent of incumbents who seek reelection are successful. In Malta most defeated members of parliament are ousted by a running mate from their own party, though in Ireland most defeats are sustained at the hands of a candidate from another party.

Proponents of PR-STV have argued that it promotes consensus by giving each candidate an incentive to seek support from voters of all political persuasions, since even a fifth or sixth preference vote may make a difference. Critics allege that for this very reason PR-STV may lead to blandness, with every candidate aiming to be all things to all voters. The evidence suggests that both claims are exaggerated. In Ireland elections are peaceful and consensual, with few differences between the parties, which might support both arguments. But in Malta, despite a lack of major policy differences between the parties, elections are often tense and are sometimes accompanied by violence. And in Northern Ireland, which has a deep division (with ethnic, national, and religious dimensions) between Protestants and Catholics and where PR-STV is used for the election of the provincial assembly and local councils, there are fundamental differences between the political parties. PR-STV in Northern Ireland has not led the parties to look for votes across the sectarian divide, and the great majority of votes are cast for parties that draw almost all of their support from one community alone.

Like other electoral systems based on candidate eliminations or runoffs, the single transferable vote does not guarantee monotonicity. That is, in theory it is possible that a candidate may miss out on election due to *increased* support, because the set of elected candidates may be determined by the order of elimination of lower-placed candidates. Some critics of the single transferable vote, especially those writing from an abstract social-choice perspective, see this as a powerful reason to object to it; for some, even the possibility that additional support could under any circumstances reduce a candidate's prospects of election is a fatal flaw in an electoral system. But defenders tend to take a more pragmatic view, arguing that the likelihood of this occurring in practice is so remote as to be not worth worrying about.

See also *Alternative Vote; Duverger's Law; Preference Voting; Proportional Representation; Proportionality and Disproportionality; Single Nontransferable Vote.*

MICHAEL GALLAGHER, TRINITY COLLEGE, UNIVERSITY OF DUBLIN

BIBLIOGRAPHY
Dummett, Michael. *Principles of Electoral Reform.* Oxford: Oxford University Press, 1997.

Farrell, David M. *Comparing Electoral Systems.* Hemel Hempstead, England: Prentice-Hall, 1997.
Gallagher, Michael. "The Political Consequences of the Electoral System in the Republic of Ireland." *Electoral Studies* 5, no. 3 (December 1986): 253–275.
Representation 34, no. 1 (winter 1996–1997); special issue on the single transferable vote.
Sinnott, Richard. "The Electoral System." In *Politics in the Republic of Ireland,* edited by John Coakley and Michael Gallagher. 3d ed. London: Routledge, 1999.

STAGGERED ELECTIONS

Elections are said to be staggered when the membership of a legislative body is renewed by fractions at elections held at different times. The standard type of staggered elections is exemplified by the U.S. Senate, whose members serve identical terms but are elected in different years. A much less prevalent type exists in Micronesia, where a minority of legislators serve a longer term than the others, since they are elected for wider constituencies. A similar arrangement was abolished in Ecuador in 1998.

Two countries—Argentina and Micronesia—and one American state have staggered elections for their first chamber. Under what appears to be the world's fourth-oldest national constitution still in force (1853), half of the membership of the Argentinean Chamber of Deputies is renewed every two years. In 1997 North Dakota amended its constitution so that by the year 2000 half of its representatives would be elected every two years.

Even in the past, staggered elections for the first chamber were rare. From 1795 to 1824 part of the French chamber (one-third until 1799, one-fifth thereafter) was renewed every year. The Low Countries had a much longer experience, beginning in 1815 in the Netherlands, followed by Belgium in 1831 and Luxembourg in 1841. All three chambers were renewable by halves, except when the chamber was dissolved, in which case all deputies were up for reelection. Staggered elections were abolished—in the same order as they were introduced—in the Netherlands (1887), in Belgium (1921), and in Luxembourg (1956).

Staggered elections are more widespread for second chambers, probably because they are seen as consonant with the role of second chambers as moderating bodies. In addition to the United States, ten countries (including Argentina, Australia, Brazil, and Japan) hold staggered elections for their directly elected second chambers, as do many countries with indirectly elected second chambers, like France and India. Yet a majority (sixteen) of directly elected senates in sovereign countries are renewed in their entirety. Among the forty-nine American state senates, twenty-six (including those in California, Florida, and Texas) are renewable by halves, whereas in the other twenty-three, all senators are elected on the same day. All but one of the five Australian states with legislative councils (the exception is Western Australia) also have staggered elections.

Redistricting raises problems when elections are staggered, because a reapportionment necessitates a statewide election. The State of Illinois provides that the entire Senate be re-elected following each decennial redistricting. However, legislative districts are thereafter divided into three groups. For the first group, the terms of legislators for the decade to come will be four, four, and two years. For the second group, the terms will be four, two, and four years. For the third group, they will be two, four, and four years. This staggering means that each biennial election held between two decennial reapportionments will cover either one-third or two-thirds of the seats.

The U.S. Senate, Lord Bryce poetically wrote in *The American Commonwealth,* "undergoes an unceasing process of gradual change and renewal, like a lake into which streams bring fresh water to replace that which the issuing river carries out" (pp. 112–113). Staggered elections allegedly foster greater stability in the composition of the legislature, thus reducing the likelihood of sharp breaks in policy. Such stability is claimed to be fitting if the second chamber has special responsibilities in the field of foreign policy. Staggered elections also help preserve the traditions and customs of a legislative body, as the new members, being in a minority, can be more easily assimilated. They also help make longer legislative terms (six to nine years) more palatable to the public by guaranteeing that changes in public opinion will be reflected to some extent in the composition of the second chamber.

The claim that staggered elections foster stability has been questioned, however. The downside of this feature is that it increases the *frequency* of elections, which is precisely why they were abolished in France: each annual renewal brought a new batch of different-minded members, and staggered elections soon came to be indicted as a cause of instability. In Luxembourg staggered elections led to the multiplication of preelection periods (one every three years) and to a periodical state of restlessness that undermined political stability. The coexistence, within a single body, of members representing yesterday's and yesteryear's will of the people is a possible source of confusion as to what the people really want; the most recently elected members may come to question the legitimacy of their colleagues elected a few years earlier, if the latter reflect a sharply different opinion.

Staggered elections have the advantage of providing the public with an additional opportunity to react to the initiatives of the government of the day. The value of such political tests increases when some turnover occurs within each region (as is the case for the Argentinean Chamber of Deputies and the Australian Senate), instead of being concentrated in only some regions (as was the case in Belgium and Luxembourg), at each renewal. The advantages of staggered elections have not been found decisive, judging by the decreasing number of countries that have them.

See also *Federal Countries, Elections in; Second-Chamber Elections; Simultaneous Elections; Term of Office.*

LOUIS MASSICOTTE AND ANDRÉ BLAIS, UNIVERSITY OF MONTREAL

BIBLIOGRAPHY

Bryce, James. *The American Commonwealth.* 2d ed. Vol. 1. New York: Commonwealth Publishing, 1908.

SUPPLÉANT

Death or resignation often produces vacancies in a parliamentary body. Rather than leave these seats unfilled, most systems employ one (or more) of three devices to replace departing members.

The most common device in single-member-district systems is a special election (by-election) to fill the vacancy. In list systems, the norm is that the next available candidate on the same list as the departing member succeeds to the position. Although those who become members of a parliament in these ways are sometimes called *substitutes* (in French, *suppléants;* in German, *ersatzkandidaten),* this term more properly is reserved for those elevated to office by the third device, which may be used in either single-member or list systems.

This third device is to elect individuals to the role of potential substitute at the same time as the original members are elected. In this case, a departing member is replaced by the corresponding substitute. This last possibility, however, may also allow for the filling of temporary vacancies, as when illness or travel make it impossible for a member to participate in the work of the parliament, or vacancies that result when a member of parliament assumes an office deemed incompatible with parliamentary membership. In many countries, membership in the national cabinet disqualifies a member from parliamentary service.

The designation of substitutes can take place through three basic means. In France, which employs single-member districts, and Benin, which uses a list system, each candidate for parliament is associated with a specific substitute who will take his or her place if required. This method is also used for the two single-member districts (Ceuta and Melilla) of the Spanish Congreso de los Diputados. In Belgium, which uses a list system, substitutes are elected from separate lists that are tied to the lists of regular candidates, but there is no tie between an individual candidate for a titular seat and an individual substitute; when a vacancy occurs, it is filled by the next available candidate from the list of substitutes. Finally, as in Bulgaria, Iceland, and Norway, a member who assumes a position in the cabinet is replaced by the next available candidate from the party's original list; however, this procedure is distinguished from the normal process of filling a vacancy with the next available candidate from the original list in that should the original member leave the cabinet, he or she can reclaim the seat in parliament, with the substitute returning to the top of the list of available unelected candidates.

The use of substitutes has three primary advantages over the other ways of filling vacancies. First, it provides for the immediate filling of vacant seats, without the delay required to organize a by-election; it also affords representation to the constituents of members who have long-term illnesses without requiring those members to give up their seats permanently. Second, in filling vacant seats it preserves the partisan decision of the last general election, unaffected by later swings in opinion and distortions resulting from the second-order nature of by-elections. Third, it provides a mechanism by which ministerial office can be made incompatible with membership in parliament while allowing former ministers to return to their original parliamentary seats and providing representation for their constituencies while they are in the cabinet.

See also *By-Elections; Candidates: Selection; Second-Order Elections.*

RICHARD S. KATZ, JOHNS HOPKINS UNIVERSITY

BIBLIOGRAPHY

Converse, Philip, and Roy Pierce. *Political Representation in France.* Cambridge: Harvard University Press, 1986. Chapter 17.
Sternberger, Dolf, and Bernhard Vogel, eds. *Die Wahl Der Parlamente und Anderer Staatsorgane.* Berlin: Walter De Gruyter, 1969.

SUPRANATIONAL ELECTIONS

See *Second-Order Elections*

SWING

Swing is a measure of the net change in votes for two parties between one election and the next. It is much more appropriate for two-party contests, such as those for the U.S. House of Representatives, than for multiparty contests in proportional-representation systems or for presidential elections in which the number of significant candidates shifts from two to three or vice versa, as has happened frequently in the United States since 1948.

Swing is normally measured as the change in a party's percentage of the vote. The simplest formula calculates the change in the vote that party A receives at two successive elections in a district; subtracts from this the change in the vote for party B; and then divides the total by two. If party A's vote goes up 2 percent and party B's goes down 2 percent, the swing is 2 percent (that is, $2 - -2 = 4/2 = 2$). The formula can be applied to results at the constituency level or to national vote totals. In a contest with only two parties, a rare circumstance in free competitive elections, the arithmetic value of one party's gain is equal to the other party's loss.

When more than two parties contest an election, the change in votes for parties A and B are unlikely to be exactly complementary. For example, if party C contests the second of two successive contests, then the two original parties can both have their vote go down. In the United States in 1992, the entry of Ross Perot into the presidential race was accompanied by the Republican presidential vote falling by 16.3 percent from 1988 and the Democratic vote falling by 2.7 percent. These results produced a net swing to the Democrats of 6.8 percent (that is, $-16.3 - -2.7 = 13.6/2 = 6.8$), because the fall in their vote was substantially less than that of the Republicans' vote.

The concept of swing was developed by David E. Butler in the Nuffield College election studies to analyze British elections from 1945 onward, when two-party competition was at its height. Since the Liberal Party failed to contest a majority of seats, constituency competition was confined to Conservative and Labour candidates, thus mirroring competition at the national level. Butler demonstrated that the net change in votes across constituencies was arithmetically very similar. Thus, the swing in the first few constituency results to be declared on election night could be used to project the national swing between the government and opposition parties and to forecast the winner before nine-tenths or more of the results had been declared. Butler's observation established the use of swing in British election-night broadcasting.

To control for the effect of third parties, swing can be calculated as the change in the vote share of parties A and B as a percentage of the combined vote for the two parties. In the 1992 U.S. presidential example, the Democrats and Republicans together won 80.0 percent of the total vote; the Democratic share was 53.6 percent of the two-party vote, compared with 46.0 percent in 1988, and the Republican share was 46.4 percent, compared with 54.0 percent in 1988. Thus, the swing in the two-party vote was 7.6 percent to the Democratic Party (that is, $-7.6 - +7.6 = 15.2/2 = 7.6$).

The election of the U.S. House of Representatives has not met the British conditions for using swing. In a significant number of districts, one of the two major parties declines to nominate a candidate. Furthermore, swing does not have the same meaning in all congressional districts. For example, because of the Democrats' longtime dominance in the South, Republican candidates were scarce in that region for many years, leading to differences in voting behavior between the South and non-South. The effect of incumbency on the vote for members of Congress is another reason for the absence of a relatively uniform swing in votes in all congressional districts.

In the great majority of established democracies, the concept of swing is not relevant, because of the multiplicity of parties competing for seats. In a substantial proportion of elections, the votes won by the various members of a government coalition can go in opposite directions, and this is even more likely to happen to the votes for multiple opposition parties. Furthermore, in proportional-representation systems, vote changes between parties are not so significant. The more proportional the system, the more important is the absolute share of the vote won by each party, independent of changes among a multiplicity of competitors.

Proponents of swing have always recognized that the gross movement of individual voters is far greater than the net change in votes between the two leading parties. Butler and Donald E. Stokes analyzed panels of voters who had been interviewed at two elections to demonstrate that most changes involve individuals leaving the electorate through death or entering by coming of age; voting at one election and not voting at another; or moving between a major party and a lesser party. Individuals who switch between the two biggest parties have always been a limited minority of all changers. By concentrating on net changes, swing takes into account the effects of all changes, but it does so by obscuring rather than identifying the different types of changes that together determine swing.

The underlying assumption of uniformity in voting across constituencies was challenged by Stokes in the 1960s, who noted that a swing of the same numerical value can represent very different proportionate changes if the initial two-party distribution of the vote differs. In a constituency in which the vote divides almost 50:50, a 2 percent swing represents a change in each party's vote of approximately 4 percent (that is, 2/50ths of its total). But a 2 percent swing in a constituency in which the vote is divided 80:20 represents a change of 2.5 percent (2/80) in the larger party's share of the vote and a change of 10 percent (2/20) in the smaller party's. Stokes suggested an ecological cause for the tendency of the dominant party in a constituency to experience a lesser decline in its proportionate share of the vote. Where a party is dominant, its supporters are less likely to defect.

The growing strength since 1974 of the British Liberal Party, and of nationalist parties in Scotland and Wales and Northern Ireland, has made swing an increasingly stylized abstraction in Britain rather than a fair representation of aggregate changes in the competitive strength of parties. Third parties have usually advanced by taking votes from both of the established parties, but they have done so unevenly. In hundreds of British constituencies, the "third" parties now finish first or second, making it more realistic there to speak of the swing between parties A and C, or B and C, or in Northern Ireland between parties D and E. The increasing geographical diversity of party competition has also made the relationship between seats and votes (the cube law) less predictable. To represent three-party competition, William Miller has developed a method of plotting movements within a triangular set of relationships that can be used to measure degrees of change as in points of a compass.

The limitations of swing as an analytical tool can be overcome, as Richard Rose has shown, by measuring the change in votes to reflect the ups and downs of parties. The starting point, as in swing, is to calculate the change in the share of the vote in two successive elections for party A; and then do the same for the change in the vote share of parties B, C, D, and so forth. The figure for each party is thus descriptively accurate. The sum of the ups and downs is zero, since gains and losses must cancel out. However, there is no necessity that the pattern of change be symmetrical. In a five-party system, one party could enjoy all of the gain or all of the loss; three parties could go down while two parties go up, or vice versa; or partners in the governing coalition could see their share of the vote move in opposite directions.

A measure of ups and downs is particularly apt in showing the impact of a third-party candidate, since that candidate's entry can cause both major parties' share of the vote to go down differentially at one election, and that candidate's subsequent withdrawal can differentially push up their vote. Unlike swing, a model of electoral change that allows for asymmetric changes in the electoral strength of competing parties is applicable to electoral competition across all established democracies. It also prompts consideration of the reason why differences should occur in the degree as well as the direction of changes in the votes of competing parties.

See also *Cube Law; Election Forecasting; Election Studies, Types of; Volatility, Electoral.*

RICHARD ROSE, UNIVERSITY OF STRATHCLYDE

BIBLIOGRAPHY

Butler, David E. "Appendix III." In *The British General Election of 1945,* by R.B. McCallum and Alison Readman, 277–292. London: Oxford University Press, 1947.

Butler, David E., and Donald E. Stokes. *Political Change in Britain.* 2d ed. London: Macmillan, 1974.

Butler, David E., and Stephen D. Van Beck. "Why Not Swing? Measuring Electoral Change." *PS: Political Science and Politics* 23 (1990): 173–184.

McLean, I. "The Problem of Proportionate Swing." *Political Studies* 21 (1973): 57–63.

Miller, William L. "Appendix: Analyzing Three-Way Voting." *The End of British Politics? Scots and English Political Behaviour in the Seventies,* 265–270. Oxford: Clarendon Press, 1981.

Rose, Richard. "The Ups and Downs of Elections, or Look Before You Swing." *PS: Political Science and Politics* 24 (March 1991): 29–33.

T

TACTICAL VOTING

When voters forgo voting for their most-preferred candidates or lists because they believe that casting votes for some other candidates or lists will likely secure a better outcome, they are said to vote tactically (or strategically). Tactical voters are those who use their votes as instruments to affect the outcome, rather than as vehicles to express their true preferences. Tactical voting can be divided into three broad categories: tactical voting in order to affect the allocation of seats; tactical voting in order to affect the formation of governments; and some forms of what is usually called protest voting.

The best example of tactical voting affecting the allocation of seats occurs in single-member districts. Imagine a race in which a right-wing candidate, R, faces a centrist C and a leftist L. One of R's supporters, upon seeing a poll that places C and L in a close fight for first, with R a distant third, may decide that voting for the second-most-preferred candidate, C, is more likely to produce a better outcome (electing C rather than L) than is voting for R (which would waste the vote, as far as affecting the outcome is concerned). In single-member districts, then, tactical voting tends to diminish the number of votes cast for candidates placed third or lower in the polls, effectively limiting competition to two candidates.

Tactical voting with an eye to affecting seat allocations can also arise in multimember districts. In the single-nontransferable-vote system formerly used in Japan, many districts had three seats. In these districts, candidates placing fifth or lower in the polls were sometimes seen as out of the running and hence were deserted by their supporters—which reduced the competition to a four-candidate fight for three seats. Under a wide range of electoral systems, including plurality rule and many forms of list proportional representation, the general rule is that tactical voting tends to reduce competition in an M-seat district to M+1 candidates or lists.

Tactical voting is important in part because it can affect the party system. For example, in single-member districts,

tactical voting helps promote bipartism in each district (*see* Duverger's Law) by transferring votes from hopeless to hopeful candidates. In other small-magnitude systems, tactical voting similarly tends to restrain the number of parties in the system. The number of parties in a system in turn has important consequences for the nature of governing coalitions (for example, single-party majority governments are common in two-party systems but rare in multiparty systems).

Tactical voting does not always reduce the number of viable competitors in elections. In electoral systems using multimember districts, there is often the possibility of transferring *excess* votes from strong candidates, in addition to the possibility of transferring *wasted* votes from weak candidates. This sort of tactical voting deconcentrates the vote, rather than concentrates it, and does not reduce the number of viable parties in the system.

The second broad category of tactical voting, in which voters seek to secure a better allocation of ministerial portfolios, has three subcategories. *Strategic sequencing*—or voting so as to affect which party gets the first opportunity to form a government—may have been important in Israeli elections prior to 1996, when the president selected one of the Knesset members, usually the leader of the largest party, to form a government. *Strategic balancing*—or voting so as to prevent any single party or coalition from securing control of all bodies in a system of separated powers—is argued to play a role in German and American elections. In the American case, the argument is that some voters vote for one party's presidential candidate but the other party's congressional candidate, intentionally seeking to deny either party control of both policy-making branches of government. In the German case, a similar argument has been made to explain the opposition's consistent success in midterm state elections, which determine control of the upper house at the federal level. *Strategic threshold insurance*—or voting so as to keep a prospective coalition partner's vote above a legally defined threshold to qualify for proportional-representation seats—has clearly been important in German elections and may become so in other countries that have parties hovering around the relevant threshold values.

The third broad category of tactical voting is protest voting—voting against one's most preferred party, even though it stands a good chance of winning, in order to chasten it and modify its behavior in the future. As an example, consider a voter who prefers that party A win the seat in a single-member district but is nonetheless unhappy with some aspects of A's performance. Such a voter may try to "send a message" by abstaining, casting an invalid vote, voting for a third party, or (if the voter is confident that A will nonetheless win) voting for A's main opponent. The point is not to defeat A but to reduce A's margin of victory and hopefully scare it into better behavior in the future. Protest voting fits the general definition of tactical voting given at the outset of the article if one considers the result of future elections to be the "better outcome" that the voter seeks.

See also *Bandwagon Effects; Coordination, Electoral; Cross-Filing; Duverger's Law; Election Forecasting; Second Ballot; Wasted Votes.*

GARY W. COX, UNIVERSITY OF CALIFORNIA, SAN DIEGO

BIBLIOGRAPHY

Blais, André, and Richard Nadeau. "Measuring Strategic Voting: A Two-Step Procedure." *Electoral Studies* 15 (February 1996): 39–52.
Cox, Gary W. *Making Votes Count: Strategic Coordination in the World's Electoral Systems.* Cambridge: Cambridge University Press, 1997.

TECHNICAL ASSISTANCE IN ELECTIONS

Election assistance in the narrowest of senses refers to assistance given by other governments, nongovernmental organizations, or intergovernmental bodies to national or local election officials, or both, in organizing and administering election-day activities in their jurisdiction. More broadly, assistance can include help with the establishment or modification of constitutional, legislative, or regulatory texts governing the conduct of and participation in elections; voter registration activities; voter education activities; delineation of electoral boundaries; procurement, distribution, and recovery of electoral equipment and materials; establishment and training of political parties; assistance to civil society organizations and the media in fulfilling their respective roles in the election process; and the proper handling of election-related disputes under the principles and provisions of the country's legal system.

Electoral observation is also sometimes considered a form of election assistance, especially when an effort is made to develop recommendations for legislators, election officials, civil society organizations, and others about how to improve the quality of future elections or when an explicit effort is made to convince voters that the presence of observers will reduce or eliminate the incidence of fraud.

OBJECTIVES OF ELECTION ASSISTANCE

Objectives of a technical election assistance program are the strengthening of the capacity of the institutions of democracy to play their assigned roles in the process; assuring that the election is conducted under internationally accepted principles for eligibility to vote, access, and transparency; and promoting the long-term credibility and sustainability of democratic institutions. International election assistance is often part of a larger package of activities intended to promote sustainable human development, the goal of which is to encourage long-term socioeconomic development and political pluralism. Related forms of assistance include activities that promote the rule of law, strengthen civil society, and foster good governance practices.

The rationale for election assistance is straightforward: democracy is seen as contributing to world peace, internal stability, and socioeconomic development; and elections are a necessary feature of any democracy. Election officials and others in countries emerging from sustained periods of non-democratic rule are often not sufficiently familiar with what goes into organizing and administering democratic elections to undertake these activities on their own. Emerging democracies also often lack the economic resources needed to equip and train election officials. If left to administer elections without such assistance, these countries could find that the elections were questioned to such an extent that the resulting government would be considered illegitimate, leading to widespread instability. Some also argue that, all else being equal, citizens are more likely to participate in elections if they believe their election administrators know how to administer free and fair elections and are doing so.

International technical assistance projects require local partners for implementation. In fact, the principal limiting factor in the delivery of election assistance is that, given the extreme political sensitivity of elections in general, technical assistance can be provided by invitation only. At the same time, because democratic elections have gained in importance as a conditioning factor for the provision of other types of development assistance, nations have become more interested in international electoral assistance.

The goal of such assistance projects usually is to transfer to the local partners skills and materials sufficient for them to fulfill their respective roles with declining levels of international assistance in both the impending election and future elections. Local partners for technical assistance activities are usually the competent election authorities (at both national and subnational levels), political parties, parliamentary oversight committees, nongovernmental organizations, the courts and police, the armed forces, and news organizations.

OVERVIEW SINCE 1976

Between 1976 and 1990 the United Nations Development Program (UNDP) financed a number of electoral assistance projects that were designed to strengthen the capacity of national election bodies. Through the time of the Namibian election in 1989, however, direct, large-scale United Nations (UN) involvement in election assistance was confined to electoral events in territories emerging from UN trusteeship. The Haitian and Nicaraguan elections in 1990 were the first that the United Nations verified in independent nations. Activity soon increased as requests from member states for electoral assistance grew from seven from 1989 through 1991 to thirty-two in 1992 alone. Much of the increase can be attributed to the end of the cold war, the collapse of the Soviet Union, and successful peace processes in Africa.

EXAMPLES OF
ASSISTANCE PROGRAM ACTIVITIES

Time is a critical factor because elections are complex undertakings. Assistance activities should be timed so that they can have the desired impact; assistance that is rushed in at the last moment often turns out to be wasted. If constitutional changes are necessary, they must be made far enough in advance to allow the laws that implement them to be drafted, debated, and passed; and these in turn must be in place far enough ahead of the election to allow for adequate training of those who must enforce the laws and for all possible contenders to take them into account when they decide whether or not—and how—to run for office.

Assessments and determination of needs. One of the most important steps in carrying out election assistance activities is determining the nature and extent of the needs. The legal framework is an important consideration. Does adequate constitutional, legislative, and regulatory language exist for the orderly holding of the elections? Do laws and regulations allow sufficient liberty of expression and assembly to ensure that the elections are free and fair?

Material needs are important as well. Are there sufficient ballot boxes, voting screens, ballot-box seals, communications equipment, and computer equipment? Is it possible to distribute equipment and materials? Staffing is also important. Is there sufficient staff to organize and administer the elections? If not, is there a plan for recruiting the needed staff? Training and education are necessary. Are training materials adequate

for everyone involved in delivering the elections? Is there an adequate plan for training those individuals? Do the materials encourage citizens to vote and instruct them in how to mark their ballots so that their vote is counted? Do the materials meet the differing needs of various constituencies in the country, such as minority language groups, the disabled, and first-time voters?

Adequate financing is necessary. Has the government allocated sufficient resources for the administration of the elections, or, if the government does not have sufficient resources, are there international donors prepared to assist so that all needs are reasonably met? Security and general administration are additional factors. Is a plan in place for ensuring the safety and integrity of election offices, election materials, election workers, polling places, and voters? Are there workable plans for the registration of candidates, the distribution and recovery of election equipment and materials, administrative communications, and the counting of votes and transmission of results?

Donor coordination. Because the number of organizations that provide election-related assistance has increased during the latter years of the twentieth century, coordination has taken on increased importance. Without coordination, countries preparing for elections might receive multiple offers of one type of assistance and none of others. With proper coordination of donor efforts, adequate assistance can be rendered in each area without duplication of effort. Donor coordination relies on the availability of a comprehensive assessment of the needs, as well as agreement between election officials and other government officials from the country preparing for elections on the one hand and representatives of donor countries on the other.

Legislation and regulation. In many cases, countries preparing for their first elections do not have adequate constitutional, legislative, or regulatory provisions to facilitate the orderly administration of elections. In these instances, assistance organizations are able to offer the advice and counsel of experienced lawyers, legislators, and election officials from other countries who work with local legislators and election officials to draft the necessary laws and regulations.

Equipment and supplies. The range and quantity of equipment and materials necessary for administering a national election is often far greater than imagined by the average politician and can place a significant financial burden on the national treasury. This is especially true of durable goods and equipment that are intended for use in a number of elections over an extended period. Various international election assistance organizations have undertaken to provide some or all of the equipment and supplies needed for a number of national elections.

The durable equipment (metal ballot boxes, radio equipment, and lamps, for example) donated for an election ideally would serve for future elections as well, leading over time to a decrease in the amount of material assistance necessary, although this has not always been the case owing to improper storage, rapid obsolescence, or theft. With sufficient lead time, it may also be possible to manufacture adequate supplies of certain items locally, although transitional elections are often held on very short notice.

Donated equipment and supplies should be appropriate for the recipient country. Cardboard ballot boxes might not be appropriate, for example, if the country is subject to frequent heavy rains and damp conditions. Ballots with high-tech security features such as color shifting and microprinting might not be necessary if the means for illicit duplicating of a simpler ballot do not exist in the country. The equipment and supplies provided by the international community should not be so sophisticated that participants in the electoral process expect that similar materials will be financed at future elections by an already-depleted national treasury.

Planning and logistics. This area often reflects the inexperience of election officials in emerging democracies. Assistance often begins with the development of a calendar of steps necessary for the election as well as a budget, followed by a staffing plan and the assignment of responsibilities to various individuals or groups within the election body. After staff is in place, assistance personnel can work with them to establish more detailed plans to cover the entire process and to refine the budget as needs change and any financial assistance arrives.

Security. Security plays two critical roles during an election process: it assures voters that it is safe for them to go to the polls, and it ensures that election supplies and equipment are safe from theft or alteration before, during, and after the election.

Training. In countries without a tradition of democratic elections, training of those involved in administering the elections—from national election commission members to midlevel operational staff to the pollworkers themselves—is often the most critical activity supported by international assistance organizations. Support can include financing existing projects, designing training materials, and training local trainers.

After adequate training materials have been developed by the election authorities—with or without outside assistance—projects usually proceed with the training of local trainers who are first taught the subject matter and modern instructional techniques. These local trainers then become an important resource for future elections. After that (or initially, if there is not training of trainers), an effort is usually made to familiarize everyone involved in the process—from national election commission members to pollworkers—with the constitution and electoral law. Training then becomes more specialized: midlevel managers receive training in their specialties, while pollworkers receive training in the procedures they are to carry out at the polling places. Those providing security for the elections may require special training as well. Increasing importance is also being given to training for the handling of special cases such as handicapped voters or attempts to commit election fraud.

Civic and voter education. In countries without a tradition of democratic elections, most voters are unfamiliar with the election process, both as a necessary element of a democratic society and as a series of concrete steps they must go through for their votes to be counted.

Civic education addresses the nature of democracy and what it means to live together in a democratic society, while voter education deals with the concrete steps that citizens must take to participate in an election and have their votes counted (for example, the requirement to register; the deadline, locations, and hours for registering; documents required for registering; the date of the election; the location and hours of operation of polling stations; and the manner in which the ballot must be marked).

Election offices as well as parties and nonpartisan civic groups can provide both civic education and voter education. The school system is often responsible for civic education, although in new democracies most adult electors will have left school before free elections have been introduced. Assistance to groups engaged in civic or voter education can range from financing projects that have already been designed to teaching election officials and others how to develop educational materials that will attract the attention of citizens and transmit to them the information they need to participate in the election process.

Educating citizens about the importance of and procedures for registering and voting has proved to have a positive effect on turnout and the success of elections.

Strengthening of parties and the press. Political parties and an independent press play critical roles in elections. Because many emerging democracies have had neither active political parties nor a strong media in their recent histories, assistance is often required. Political party assistance addresses ways to establish a party organization, recruit members and candidates, and run campaigns. Media assistance focuses on providing the resources necessary for the establishment of independent news organizations and on training journalists in research techniques and accurate reporting of news.

Evaluation. Both assistance organizations and election bodies benefit if they work together toward improving future elections. A number of assistance agencies have undertaken to work with election officials, legislators, party and civic leaders, unsuccessful candidates, the media, and other interested individuals and groups to identify problems with past elections and develop recommendations for ways to improve future elections. Interest is increasing among the donor community in the evaluation of the effectiveness of various types of election assistance.

Information resources and research. In countries with some ongoing experience of administering democratic elections, the need for assistance lies more in the area of learning about how other countries handle specific situations so that those experiences can inform efforts to improve future elections. This need has led to the establishment of election-related publications, resource centers, and research efforts to promote the collection, organization, analysis, and dissemination of election-related information and materials. Such resources can also be valuable to those responsible for setting up first-time elections in a country because they provide ready models of manuals, forms, ballots, and other materials used in election processes under similar circumstances elsewhere.

Election observation. The term "election observation" is popularly used to denote any presence of individuals from other countries to examine various aspects of the electoral process, but this represents several misconceptions. First, election observation can be, and increasingly is, carried out by domestic groups. Second, there are a number of variants that are not considered election observation by the United Nations and other assistance providers; these include election organization and administration, which was done in Cambodia in 1992–1993 when the United Nations was responsible for all phases of the election process; election supervision, which involves certifying both the electoral and the political elements of the process, often at each step of the process; and election verification, which focuses on specific, previously defined aspects of the electoral process. Supervisors and monitors are usually accorded powers to intervene in an electoral process, whereas observers are not.

Technical assistance in the area of election observation initially referred to assistance given to election bodies in preparing for the presence of international observers, but it increasingly refers to assistance in the development of an indigenous capacity—often through civic groups—to monitor elections. This generally includes training in how to recruit volunteers, how to develop training materials and training programs, and how to construct samples and produce reports.

INSTITUTIONAL PROVIDERS OF ASSISTANCE

International election assistance can be delivered either directly through the international organizations that provide most of the funding for such activities or indirectly through agreements negotiated with nongovernmental organizations to provide particular services in support of an election process.

On December 17, 1991, the UN General Assembly passed a resolution authorizing the secretary general to establish a trust fund for electoral assistance and designate an individual to coordinate the UN's electoral assistance activities. This resolution led to the establishment of the Electoral Assistance Unit (now the Electoral Assistance Division) on April 1, 1992. Since that time, the UN has provided some type of election assistance to more than seventy member nations. Other UN entities that have been involved in providing election assistance are the UNDP; UN Volunteers (UNV); the Office for Project Services (UNOPS); the Center for Human Rights (UNCHR); and other offices within the Department of Political Affairs (DPA), the Department of Economic and Social Affairs (DESA), and the Department of Peacekeeping Operations (DPKO).

The UN divides its activities into two categories: standard assistance activities and major electoral missions. The latter, which are usually much larger in scope and part of a comprehensive peacekeeping operation, require a mandate from the General Assembly or the Security Council.

Other international organizations engaged in providing technical election assistance are the Organization of American States (OAS), which has created the Unit for the Promotion of Democracy (UPD); the Organization for Security and Cooperation in Europe (OSCE) and its Office of Democratic Initiatives and Human Rights (ODIHR); the European Union (EU); the International Institute for Democracy and Electoral Assistance (IDEA); the Commonwealth Secretariat; the Southern African Development Community (SADEC); the Inter-Parliamentary Union; and the Inter-American Development Bank (IDB), which has created a Civil Society Unit to provide support for strengthening civil society in Latin America and the Caribbean.

The principal bilateral agencies and election bodies active in funding or providing technical election assistance are the U.S. Agency for International Development (USAID), the Canadian International Development Agency (CIDA), the United Kingdom's Department for International Development (DFID), the German aid agency GTZ, the Danish International Development Agency (DANIDA), the Swedish International Development Agency (SIDA), the Norwegian Aid Agency (NORAID), the Australian Agency for International Development (AUSAID), the Japanese International Cooperation Agency (JICA), assistance agencies of a number of other European nations, Elections Canada, and the Australian Electoral Commission.

The principal nongovernmental organizations that conduct technical assistance programs are the International Foundation for Election Systems (IFES), the Carter Center, the National Democratic Institute (NDI), the International Republican Institute (IRI), the African-American Institute (AAI), the Asia Foundation (TAF), the Konrad Adenauer Foundation, the Friedrich Ebert Foundation, the Friedrich Naumann Foundation, the European Media Institute, the Electoral Reform Society's Consultancy Services branch, the Study and Research Group on Democracy and Economic and Social Development (Groupe d'Etude et de Recherche sur la Démocratie et le Développement Economique et Social en Afrique, or GERDDES) located in Benin, the Electoral Institute of Southern Africa (EISA), and the South African groups IDASA and the Cooperative for Research and Education (CORE). The Soros Foundation, through its Open Society Institutes in a number of countries (mostly former Soviet republics), has also become an active provider of election-related assistance.

Quasi-governmental organizations such as the National Endowment for Democracy (United States) and the Westminster Foundation for Democracy (United Kingdom) have also provided certain types of assistance, notably civic education and civil-society building, particularly in early phases of transition.

Regional associations of election bodies have also emerged as active coordinators and even providers of technical election assistance. The oldest of these associations is that of Central America and the Caribbean, which was established by the Protocol of Tikal in 1985. In 1989 the Protocol of Quito established a parallel organization in South America. In 1991 these two organizations set up an umbrella organization called the Inter-American Union of Electoral Organizations (Unión Interamericana de Organismos Electorales, or UNIORE). The Center for Electoral Promotion and Assistance (Centro de Asesoría y Promoción Electoral, or CAPEL) serves as secretariat for these groups, which have played an active role in encouraging the exchange of experiences and expertise among election officials in the region through reciprocal observation missions, professional courses, and sharing of expertise.

The success of these groups in Latin America has led to the formation of similar groups in other regions: the Association of Central and Eastern European Election Officials (ACEEEO), which grew out of a 1991 meeting in Budapest and by 1999 included thirteen countries; the African Association of Electoral Authorities (AAEA), which was formally constituted in 1997, had fifteen members by 1999 and sent an observation mission to the historic elections in Nigeria in 1999; the Pacific Islands, Australia and New Zealand Electoral Administrators (PIANZEA) Network, established in October 1997 at the South Pacific Electoral Administrators Conference; the Asian Association of Electoral Authorities (AAEA), which was formally constituted in Manila in 1998 after an exploratory meeting in 1997 and sent an observation mission

to the elections in Cambodia; the Association of Caribbean Election Officials (ACEO), which was formally constituted in San Juan, Puerto Rico, in 1998 with IFES and the OAS as cosecretariats following an exploratory meeting in 1997 in Kingston, Jamaica.

A number of private enterprises have offered technical election assistance in recent years. Notable among them is Thomas De La Rue and Company, headquartered in the United Kingdom. De La Rue prints currency, postage stamps, and other government documents for many developing countries and has used its familiarity with many of these countries and their governments to offer turnkey elections to a number of countries. Under such an arrangement, De La Rue assumes responsibility for production and distribution of all election materials—from ballots and tally sheets to instruction materials and ballot boxes—and trains pollworkers in the conduct of the election.

Another private enterprise is CODE, headquartered in Canada. CODE had significant experience with shipping educational materials to developing countries and has been directly or indirectly involved in providing equipment and supplies for most of the key elections of the 1990s.

IMPACT OF ASSISTANCE

One of the most difficult aspects of electoral assistance has been the measurement of impact. Although it has usually been true that elections have been more successful in countries when assistance was rendered than in those when it has not, determining the precise impact of the assistance has remained difficult. In only some cases has it been possible, through rigorous postelection survey work, to ascertain what percentage of an electorate actually received election information through voter education projects. Because of declining levels of international assistance, it may soon be possible to determine if election officials are able to maintain reasonable standards on their own.

Fareed Zakaria, a critic of the development community's focus on elections, in 1997 lamented the rise of societies that are formally democratic on the basis of their periodic elections but that are not liberal in their recognition of basic freedoms. However, a USAID publication argued that election assistance "exerted subtle and not-so-subtle pressure for ensuring 'free and fair' elections, and in many cases persuaded major contestants to accept the voters' verdict."

STRATEGIES AND PROGRAMS FOR FUTURE ELECTION ASSISTANCE

The number of countries that have held founding elections grew significantly during the 1990s, and most of these countries received some level of election assistance from the international community. Many of these countries now have a small but committed cadre of experienced election officials who are committed to a career in this field and who have developed a knowledge base for their respective institutions. With the emergence of regional associations of election officials, this cadre has also begun to function as an international network of professionals able to assist one another on the basis of their own personal experience, decreasing the need for international assistance.

One of the major challenges remaining is to ensure that local election officials are able to benefit from a deepening level of experience and develop an institutional memory at the national level. Some of the traditional assistance providers are beginning to target their assistance at the local level, encouraging and enabling national election officials to share their accumulated knowledge with their local counterparts. This is especially true in the field of observation because funds that would otherwise have to be spent on international airline tickets and lodging for foreigners can be redirected to more productive uses if there is a strong domestic capacity—partisan and nonpartisan—to observe the elections. The funds can also be used for the training of domestic observers.

Closely related to the deepening of experience is the strengthening of institutions involved in the electoral process. There is increasing recognition that electoral bodies are best able to improve the quality of their work from one election to another when they are permanent and use the time between elections to plan and to train their personnel.

Future assistance activities might also become narrower in scope, focusing on specific deficiencies identified during previous elections, at the same time as they become longer in duration. Much early assistance was provided under such tight timetables that little learning took place—the international teams had to do much of the work themselves, often in the absence of a permanent election body. With permanent bodies in place and with elections becoming increasingly predictable in their timing, assistance can focus more on the transfer of knowledge.

Technology represents an area of great potential for election administrators around the world, and assistance may focus increasingly on this area. Maintenance of a permanent voter or civil registry is made much easier through the use of modern computer technology, with greater accuracy an additional benefit. Assistance providers can work with election and civil registry bodies to ensure that the solutions proposed by providers of goods and services are the best, most appropriate, and most cost effective for the given context.

Transparency and ethics are two other areas that are beginning to attract the attention and resources of the donor community. These are two areas that are vitally important for maintaining the confidence of the electorate in the professionalism of their election administrators.

CONCLUSION

International assistance has played an important role in ensuring that most elections held in emerging democracies during the 1990s have met basic standards of openness and fairness. The challenge for the future will be to find ways of ensuring that assistance continues to be provided where needed at levels that are affordable for the donor community and appropriate for recipient countries.

See also *Elections in Developing Countries; Electoralism; Founding Elections: Africa; Founding Elections: Latin America; Free and Fair Elections; Observation of Elections; Postconflict Elections; Premature Closure.*

J. Ray Kennedy and Jeffrey W. Fischer, International Foundation for Election Systems, Washington, D.C.

BIBLIOGRAPHY

"Debating Democracy Assistance." *Journal of Democracy* 10, no. 4 (October 1999).

Diamond, Larry. *Promoting Democracy in the 1990s: Actors and Instruments, Issues and Imperatives.* Washington, D.C.: Carnegie Commission on Preventing Deadly Conflict, 1995.

Elections and the Electoral Process: A Guide to Assistance. London: Foreign and Commonwealth Office, 1998.

From Bullets to Ballots: Electoral Assistance to Postconflict Societies. Washington, D.C.: U.S. Agency for International Development, 1997.

Kumar, Krishna. *Postconflict Elections, Democratization, and International Assistance.* Boulder, Colo.: Lynne Rienner, 1998.

Plattner, Marc F. "Liberalism and Democracy." *Foreign Affairs* 77, no. 2 (March–April 1998).

Shattuck, John, and J. Brian Atwood. "Defending Democracy." *Foreign Affairs* 77, no. 2 (March–April 1998).

Support by the United Nations System of the Efforts of Governments to Promote and Consolidate New or Restored Democracies. New York: United Nations General Assembly, 1995.

United Nations Guidelines on Special Arrangements for Electoral Assistance. New York: United Nations/UNDP, 1992.

Wentges, Taylor. *Multilateral Electoral Development: A Comparative Review of the Electoral Development Activities of the Organization of American States, Organization for Security and Cooperation in Europe, the Francophonie, the Commonwealth, and the United Nations.* Ottawa: Department of Foreign Affairs and International Trade, 1998.

Zakaria, Fareed. "The Rise of Illiberal Democracy." *Foreign Affairs* 76, no. 6 (November–December 1997).

TENDERED BALLOTS

Tendered ballots (or votes) are conditional votes used in some electoral systems when a prospective voter is not allowed to cast his or her vote, either because the electoral register shows that the prospective voter has already voted or because the voter cannot be found in the electoral register. The tendered ballot is kept under separate cover and is included in the final count only if later checks by the election administration confirm the voter's eligibility to vote and if the tendered ballots might be decisive for the outcome in the constituency in question.

Provisions for tendered ballots are needed—and found—primarily in countries where the quality of the electoral register is low or where the registration administration has been unable to cope with internal migration across administrative borders because of civil unrest, war, or some other complicating factor.

When it appears that a prospective voter has already voted, the explanation could be that somebody has fraudulently voted as if he or she were the person lawfully registered (impersonation). However, the appearance of having voted could also result from a simple error by a polling staff member who inadvertently marked the voter in question as having cast a ballot, when, in fact, somebody else should have been marked. Regardless of the cause—fraud or clerical error—a bona fide voter who is not allowed to cast his or her vote can be considered as having been disenfranchised by an improperly functioning electoral administration system because of insufficient control. Tendered ballots are thus a reasonable way of addressing legitimate complaints from aggrieved citizens. But they are also a commendable way of defusing difficult situations that might disrupt the voting process at the polling station, leading even to physical violence or destruction of voting material by aggrieved voters.

The same arguments in favor of tendered ballots apply when duly registered voters learn on election day that they are not allowed to vote because they cannot be located in the electoral register. A clear distinction must be made, however, between duly registered voters—who may even be carrying sufficient registration documentation—not appearing in the proper place in the electoral register and voters not duly registered but otherwise fulfilling the eligibility requirements. The latter are not entitled to a tendered ballot, even though they may be given such ballot to diffuse a complicated situation, the election official knowing that it would never be counted.

The inclusion of tendered ballots in the vote count is sometimes complicated, because the necessary administrative checks are time-consuming and might include various administrative offices. Moreover, tendered ballots are usually so few in number that, in majoritarian electoral systems (such as first-past-the-post), they rarely would change the outcome of an election from that based on a count of the ordinary votes. Some election laws are not very clear on how or when tendered ballots should be verified or counted, and probably more than once tendered ballots have not been given full attention after a majoritarian election. The situation is slightly different in proportional-representation systems because the probability of tendered ballots affecting the allocation of the last seat is higher. Regardless of electoral system, the handling of tendered ballots is often poorly documented.

Tendered ballots are used primarily as a pragmatic means of defusing potentially difficult situations at polling stations. More principled rationales for using tendered ballots are subordinate, as can sometimes be seen from the handling of tendered ballots after polling.

See also *Absentee Voting; Administration of Elections; Australian Ballot; Overseas Voting.*

JØRGEN ELKLIT, UNIVERSITY OF AARHUS

TERM LIMITS

Term limits are legal prohibitions on the reelection of public officials designed to limit the amount of time for which any individual may serve. Historically, limits have most widely been applied to presidents, although recently they have been extended to legislators in a few countries as well.

FORM AND STATUS
OF TERM LIMITS

Term limits on presidents were adopted throughout the newly independent Latin American countries in the nineteenth century as a protection against abuse of executive office to rig elections and maintain incumbents in power. By 1910 the demand for *¡No reeleccionismo!* served as the initial rallying cry of the revolution that removed Mexican president Porfirio Díaz after thirty-four years in office. In the United States, despite the lack of any constitutional limit, there was a widely acknowledged norm, dating to George Washington's refusal to stand for reelection in 1796, that no president should serve more than two terms. After Franklin Delano Roosevelt violated this norm by winning a third term in 1940 and a fourth in 1944, the U.S. Constitution was amended in 1951 to prohibit any person serving more than two terms.

Whereas arguments in favor of presidential term limits have tended to focus on preventing electoral fraud and intimidation of opponents, arguments against such limits have gained currency recently on the following grounds. First, technological advances in communications and computerized vote-counting, coupled with international observer organizations, make electoral abuse more difficult, facilitating clean elections and rendering the original rationale for term limits moot. Second, the prospect of facing judgment at the polls at the end of a presidential term encourages accountability by incumbents to the electorate. Third, presidential leadership is a rare commodity. If a chief executive maintains sufficient support among political party leaders and citizens after serving a term in office, it is counterproductive to prohibit such an effective politician from serving another term—and to do so legally might even encourage incumbents to maintain themselves in office extra-legally.

In the late twentieth century the Latin American nations appeared again to be leading the way in reforming presidential term limits—by scaling them back. During the 1990s, incumbent presidents in Peru, Argentina, and Brazil secured constitutional amendments to allow for their reelection to a second term. Opponents of Presidents Alberto Fujimori in Peru and Carlos Saúl Menem in Argentina would argue that these politicians relied on extra-legal methods to push through the relevant reforms, but both subsequently won reelection by substantial margins. Two consecutive terms are also allowed under the Russian constitution of 1993, which allowed Boris Yeltsin to win a second term in 1996.

Term limits for legislators are much less common than those for presidents. At the national level, they have been imposed on legislators in Mexico since 1936, in Costa Rica since 1949, in Ecuador from 1979 to 1996, and in the Philippines since 1986. In the first three countries, term limits prohibited any consecutive reelection, whereas in the Philippines lawmakers may serve up to three consecutive three-year terms. The rationale behind term limits for legislators has generally mirrored that for presidents—to prevent politicians from using the resources of incumbency to their electoral advantage. In Mexico, however, it is widely accepted that leaders of the embryonic Institutional Revolutionary Party (Partido Revolucionario Institucional; PRI) favored term limits in order to centralize power, cutting regional politicians off from their local support bases and making them dependent on the party leadership in Mexico City for career advancement.

LEGISLATIVE TERM LIMITS IN THE UNITED STATES

In the United States, legislative term limit reforms swept across the country in the early 1990s. During the late 1980s, the success rate for incumbent members of Congress seeking reelection soared above 95 percent, and that for state legislators rose steadily as well. These trends fueled widespread belief that staff and fund-raising advantages for incumbents were undermining the competitiveness of U.S. elections. Republicans attributed the perpetuation of a Democratic majority in the House of Representatives for nearly forty years to incumbency advantage. As a reaction, between 1990 and 1994 groups in twenty-three states that allow for direct democracy by means of citizens' initiatives placed term-limit measures on state ballots. The initiatives, limiting legislators to between six and twelve years of consecutive service, were overwhelmingly popular.

Most of these measures aimed at both state legislators and members of Congress. In 1995, however, the U.S. Supreme Court ruled that the Qualifications Clauses (Art. I, Section 2) of the Constitution are exhaustive, that the states may not impose additional qualifications for reelection (such as nonincumbency), and that legislative term limits at the national level would require amendment of the U.S. Constitution (U.S. Term Limits v. Thornton). Although the Republican Party in Congress has expressed support for such an amendment, its own members' enthusiasm cooled as they evaluated their positions as incumbents of the majority party. The prospect of a successful constitutional amendment appears remote. What remain, however, are term limits on state legislators in eighteen states as well as limits on a large number of municipal officials, which have for the most part passed judicial scrutiny and appear likely to endure.

Expectations about how term limits will affect legislative behavior have been diverse and, until recently, highly speculative. Because the United States had no experience with legislative term limits between the Articles of Confederation and the 1990s, and because the experiences of other countries do not necessarily generalize to the United States, hard evidence by which to evaluate term limits has been in short supply. Moreover, term limits violate a central assumption in most legislative theory—that legislative behavior and organization can best be explained with respect to reelection incentives. Prominent scholars of the U.S. Congress, including Morris Fiorina, credit legislators' efforts to secure reelection with encouraging pork-barrel spending, excessive government regulation, and bureaucratic inefficiency. Others, among them Alan Ehrenhalt and George Will, contend that legislative careerism encourages the recruitment and election of individuals philosophically predisposed toward larger, more activist government. If reelection accounts for who runs for and wins legislative office, how legislators behave, and how legislatures operate, then term limits might well be expected to alter the nature of legislative representation radically.

EFFECTS OF TERM LIMITS

There are three areas in which term limits might be expected to have a measurable impact on legislatures: composition, behavior, and institutions. The first has to do with the types of individuals who seek and win office; the second, with their priorities and activities in office; and the third, with the manner in which power is distributed, both within legislatures and between legislatures and other policy makers. Studies of the early effects of term limits on U.S. state legislatures suggest that they have had virtually no effect on composition, mixed effects on behavior, and marked effects on the institutional organization of legislatures.

With respect to composition, many term-limit supporters argued that the reform would not only encourage legislative turnover but would attract a new kind of person to run for and win office. One might have expected to see changes beginning as soon as term limits were on the books, to see new candidates stepping to the foreground in the new electoral environment. However, in the mid-1990s John Carey, Richard Niemi, and Lynda Powell found no measurable differences between first-term legislators in term-limit states and those in non-term limit states in terms of race, ethnicity, religion, educational or career backgrounds, income, or ideology. Term limits may have had some influence on the proportion of women elected, but the effect here is slight enough to be statistically uncertain.

With respect to behavior, advocates of term limits have also suggested that prohibiting reelection should encourage individuals who are less interested in their own careers and are more interested in service to the state or nation and in legislative accomplishment. The results here, based on surveys of thousands of state legislators and interviews with many more, are mixed. Term-limited legislators are as likely to regard politics as a career as their colleagues who face no restrictions on reelection. Neophyte legislators in term-limit states tend to be more active in proposing new legislation, although senior legislators are generally unimpressed with the thoughtfulness and expertise of the newcomers. Term-limited legislators also express slightly less concern with the specific demands of their geographical districts. One possible interpretation for this is that term limits encourage a sort of Burkean detachment from narrow district concerns, and correspondingly, perhaps, a greater attention to the good of the polity as a whole. Many legislators, however, emphasize the imperative under term limits to position themselves either for a run at statewide office after service in the legislature or for other postlegislative employment connected to their current political performance. Thus, term limits do not appear to be producing "citizen legislators" devoid of personal ambition. Their ultimate effect on behavior may depend on where politicians are able to build postlegislative careers. Information about these career trajectories will become available only as term limits kick in in more states.

With respect to institutional effects, expectations have been starkly polarized. Some scholars argue that term limits should increase the power of party leaders over novice legislators; others argue that it should decrease their authority because access to legislative resources will mean little to term-limited politicians. Similarly, some argue that limits will decrease the influence of lobbyists because legislators ineligible for reelection will be uninterested in the campaign contributions, whereas others contend that lame-duck legislators will curry favor with corporations and interest groups in exchange for postlegislative employment. Some suggest that by undermining legislative competence, term limits will increase the power of governors, whereas others hold that term limits will fortify the deliberative independence of legislatures vis-à-vis the ex-

ecutive. Surveys of and interviews with state legislators overwhelmingly support the idea that term limits shift influence toward the executive branch, civil servants, lobbyists, and legislative staffers and away from party leaders and committee chairs in the legislature. These changes are consistently attributed to asymmetries in information and expertise between legislators and other actors in the policy-making process as the level of experience in term-limited legislatures declines.

To sum up, term limits appear to be similar to many other electoral reforms in that their impact does not correspond perfectly to initial expectations. Presidential term limits abroad may have discouraged the development of personal fiefdoms by requiring turnover in the highest office, but they have been overturned in recent years in some prominent cases. Legislative term limits enjoyed a surge of intense popularity in the United States in the early 1990s, but the momentum behind the reform appears to have stalled, both in the courts and in Congress, and the most important early effects of term limits in the states may be to weaken the legislative branch relative to other policy-making actors.

See also *Recall Elections; Term of Office, Length of.*

JOHN M. CAREY, WASHINGTON UNIVERSITY, ST. LOUIS

BIBLIOGRAPHY

Carey, John M. *Term Limits and Legislative Representation.* New York: Cambridge University Press, 1996.

Carey, John M., Richard Niemi, and Lynda Powell. "The Effects of Term Limits on State Legislators." *Legislative Studies Quarterly* 23, no. 2 (May 1998): 271–300.

Ehrenhalt, Alan. *The United States of Ambition: Politicians, Power, and the Pursuit of Office.* New York: Times Books, 1991.

Fiorina, Morris. *Congress: Keystone of the Washington Establishment.* New Haven, Conn.: Yale University Press, 1989.

Linz, Juan J. "Presidential or Parliamentary Democracy: Does It Make a Difference?" In *The Failure of Presidential Democracy,* edited by Juan J. Linz and Arturo Valenzuela, 1–87. Baltimore, Md.: Johns Hopkins University Press, 1994.

U.S. Term Limits, Inc. v. Thornton (115 S. Ct. 1842).

Weldon, Jeffrey. "Political Sources of *Presidencialismo* in Mexico." In *Presidentialism and Democracy in Latin America,* edited by Scott Mainwaring and Matthew S. Shugart, 225–258. New York: Cambridge University Press, 1997.

Will, George F. *Restoration: Congress, Term Limits, and the Recovery of Deliberative Democracy.* New York: Free Press, 1992.

TERM OF OFFICE, LENGTH OF

A term is the period of time a person may fill an office. In politics, terms of office are measured in years.

Appointments by the executive may be made for life, until the occupant reaches a specific age, at pleasure, or for a specific term. In contrast, all elections are for a specific term. The only exceptions known to these authors were the colonial assemblies of the now Canadian provinces of Nova Scotia,

New Brunswick, and Prince Edward Island in the late eighteenth century, which were elected for an indefinite term. This feature reinforced the position of the governor vis-à-vis the assembly: a restive assembly could be dissolved soon after its election, whereas a compliant one could be maintained in office for a long time. One Nova Scotia legislature lasted fifteen years.

FIXED OR FLEXIBLE TERMS

Terms of office can be abridged through dissolution, impeachment, or recall. Dissolution of the legislature by the executive is a standard feature of parliamentary systems (Norway being an exception). It is routinely used in Westminster parliamentary systems and empowers the executive to select the date of the next election. Impeachment, which allows the legislature to remove a president or another civil officer from office on criminal grounds before the expiry of his or her term, is peculiar to presidential systems. Recall, a procedure that allows the electorate, by way of a petition, to call a referendum on whether the term of an official (executive, legislative, or judicial) should be terminated immediately, is in force only in a few American states and in the Canadian province of British Columbia. In general, presidential terms are fixed, as impeachment and recall are rare occurrences. In parliamentary systems, legislative terms are often abridged in practice.

LENGTH OF TERMS

One-year terms were not uncommon in the past in American states, and twelve-year terms have existed in Iceland. At present, the vast majority of countries with a working, directly elected parliament elect their first or single chamber for either four years (seventy-two countries) or five years (eighty-five), with 4.5 years being the average (see Table 1). Two-year terms (exemplified by the U.S. House of Representatives), three-year terms (found notably in Australia and New Zealand), and six-year terms are relatively rare. Terms for second chambers are normally longer than those for first chambers.

Directly elected presidents tend to serve slightly longer terms, 5.1 years on average, than parliamentarians in a first chamber. The most common terms are five years (fifty-one countries), four years (twenty), and six years (fourteen). The French *septennat* (seven years) has been emulated by few countries, most of them former French colonies. An amendment reducing the French presidential term to five years failed only narrowly in 1973.

Terms of office might be expected to vary little over time, if only because they are usually set out in constitutions and, as such, often require supermajorities or even referendums for alteration. Yet changes do occur. The duration of the U.K. Parliament was reduced from seven years to five in 1911, as part of a broader reform package intended to reduce the

Table 1. Length of Executive and Legislative Terms in Countries with a Working, Directly Elected Parliament, 1998

Term (years)	Number of directly elected presidents who serve the term	Number of first chambers whose members serve the term
2	0	2
3	0	9
4	20	72
5	51	85
6	14	3
7	8	0
Complex case	0	1*
Total	93	172
Average length	5.15 years	4.51 years

* In Micronesia most legislators are elected for two years, but a few are elected for four years.

power of the House of Lords. New Zealand went from five years to three in 1879. Extensions have been even more common than reductions. Three-year terms were increased to four years in Denmark (1915), Switzerland (1931), Norway (1938), and Finland (1954).

The general trend toward longer terms is exemplified by American states. In the 1830s, nine states elected the members of their first chambers for two-year terms, and the seventeen remaining states elected their members for one-year terms. One-year terms have disappeared everywhere, and in 1998, forty-four states had two-year terms, while six had four-year terms.

The same trend has affected gubernatorial terms. One-year terms, which existed in one-third of the states in the 1830s, are nowhere to be found today. The number of states with four-year terms has increased from six (out of twenty-six) in the 1830s, to twenty-four prior to World War I, to forty-eight today (New Hampshire and Vermont, with two-year terms, remain the sole exceptions). All Canadian provinces have similarly extended their legislative terms from four years to five. Over the last two decades, the term of Australian state legislative assemblies was extended from three to four years in New South Wales, Victoria, and Western Australia, and it was reduced from five to four in Tasmania. The thrust of reforms in the twentieth century has been to increase the terms that had been set below four years and to decrease those that exceeded five years.

A few countries have been inclined to alter legislative terms more frequently. Germany's Reichstag was elected for three years until 1888, then for five years until 1918. Since then (except for the Nazi and immediate postwar periods), four years has been the rule. Sweden's first chamber was elected for three years until 1919, for four years until 1970, then for three years again. A 1994 amendment brought the duration of the Riksdag back to four years. The pattern is much the same for France, where the term of the first chamber was set at five years in 1814, three years in 1848, six years in 1852, four years in 1875, and five years since 1946.

ISSUES FOR DEBATE

Selecting a specific term necessitates a trade-off between competing values. Proponents of longer terms argue that short terms will deter legislators from adopting necessary but unpopular measures. They also argue that short terms lead to a multiplication of elections over time, a feature that bothers the electorate and costs money. Short terms are advocated on the ground that elected officials should be kept accountable to the people. The fear that elected officials might try to perpetuate themselves in office is alleviated either by providing for short terms or by limiting the number of terms that may be served by the same individual. The latter restriction is common for elected presidents. For example, no one can be elected to the American presidency more than twice, whereas Mexican presidents cannot be reelected. In Mexico and Costa Rica, the prohibition against immediate reelection extends even to legislators.

Should elections be postponed in wartime or during internal disturbances? They were in many democratic countries during both world wars. An extreme case is the British Parliament elected in 1935, whose term was extended after the outbreak of World War II by annual acts up to 1945: meanwhile, by-elections became the only way for the people's voice to be heard. In France the term of the existing chamber was extended in 1939 by executive decree. The Canadian constitution includes a provision whereby Parliament or a provincial legislature may extend its term beyond five years in time of war, invasion, or insurrection, real or apprehended, provided the extension is not opposed by more than one-third of its membership.

Prior to the multiplication of opinion polls, it was plausible, in the absence of reliable indicators to the contrary, to assume that officeholders enjoyed the confidence of the people, even late in their term. We now know this is far from being always the case and that some governments can become highly unpopular yet still remain in a position to make fateful decisions for the future of the country. An extreme case is the government of Brian Mulroney in Canada, which in the early 1990s was supported at times by not more than 11 percent of respondents in opinion polls. Occurrences like these may stimulate public demand for recall procedures.

See also *By-Elections; Recall Elections; Second-Chamber Elections; Simultaneous Elections; Staggered Elections; Term Limits.*

LOUIS MASSICOTTE AND ANDRÉ BLAIS, UNIVERSITY OF MONTREAL

THRESHOLD OF EXCLUSION

The term *threshold of exclusion* refers to the legally established minimum share of the valid votes that parties must attain in order to participate in the distribution of parliamentary seats. Thresholds of exclusion are one of the most effective instruments for influencing political representation and for structuring the party system. They operate against party fragmentation, not only by excluding minor parties when transforming votes into seats but by influencing voters' thinking. In their electoral behavior, voters anticipate the possible consequences the threshold may have with regard to their political option. They may want to avoid wasting their vote by voting for only those parties with a better chance of overcoming the legal threshold.

There are different types of thresholds. The main criteria differentiating them are:

1. The level of application: the threshold may be applied at the constituency level (for example, Spain), the national level (as in Germany), or at both levels (as in Sweden).

2. The stage of application: the threshold may be applied at the first, second, or any subsequent round of seat allocation. Countries where this differentiation is relevant are, for example, Greece and Poland.

3. The percentage of the threshold: the most common thresholds are 3 percent, 4 percent, and 5 percent, but the worldwide range of thresholds is 1.5 to 12 percent.

4. The graduation of the threshold: variations are established with regard to parties and party-alliances; for example, 5 percent for parties, 8 percent for a two-party alliance, 10 percent for a three-party alliance.

Certainly, the effects of the threshold depend on these details. For example, a 5 percent threshold at the national level (as in Germany) may be very important, whereas a 3 percent threshold in multimember constituencies, where already the magnitude of these constituencies does not permit the representation of parties with a share of votes lower than 5 percent (as in Spain), may be nearly insignificant. A threshold at the national level, for instance, will affect all small parties, whereas a threshold at the constituency level will not affect small parties in their regional base or strongholds.

A distinction must be made between legal thresholds, called "artificial thresholds," and natural thresholds, which may result from districting. Or, to put it another way, the size of constituencies can be considered as a threshold, too. In general, the smaller the constituency (that is to say, the fewer seats there are to fill), the higher the natural threshold. Voters perceive the effect. This can be demonstrated empirically by looking at Spain, where the multimember constituencies are of different sizes. There, small parties get a lower percentage of the vote in small districts than they do in large ones.

Since the two types of threshold have the same effect on the exclusion of parties, it is logical, for analytical purposes, to combine them into a common variable—the effective threshold—when comparing electoral systems. However, it is important to remember that the two types may (and in fact do) exert different effects on the proportionality of the electoral results. Whereas natural thresholds tend to widen the proportionality gap between the share of votes and seats, favoring especially the biggest party, legal thresholds foster a more proportional distribution of seats among those parties that passed the threshold. Empirical evidence for this proposition can be found in Germany and Spain. Taking the proportionality index developed by Richard Rose as an indicator, Germany, with a 5 percent national threshold, exhibits a high degree of proportionality; Spain, with a natural threshold higher than the 3 percent artificial threshold at the constituency level, exhibits a low degree of proportionality.

Another kind of threshold is the requirement of winning a certain number of constituencies in order to take part in the proportional distribution of seats at the national level. The most prominent example is Germany, where parties that gain three constituency seats participate in the proportional distribution of seats regardless of whether they have passed the threshold of 5 percent of the national vote. Where it is applied, the seat-oriented threshold is designed as an alternative requirement, not an additional one, for receiving proportionally distributed seats, and thus it does not operate in the same direction as the threshold determined by a share of the popular vote. By contrast, it is likely to undermine the effect of the latter.

See also *Designing Electoral Systems; Proportional Representation; Proportionality and Disproportionality.*

DIETER NOHLEN, UNIVERSITY OF HEIDELBERG

BIBLIOGRAPHY

Lijphart, Arend. *Electoral Systems and Party Systems. A Study of Twenty-Seven Democracies, 1945–1990.* Oxford: Oxford University Press, 1994.

TICKET SPLITTING

If in marking a ballot a voter endorses the candidates of two different parties, it is called ticket splitting. The alternative is to vote a straight-party ticket, that is, to endorse all the candidates that a party nominates. Whether ticket splitting is possible depends on the number of offices at stake in an election and the ballot form. The greater the number of separately elected offices, the greater the voter's opportunity to cast preferences for different parties at the same election.

SYSTEMS THAT PREVENT TICKET SPLITTING

Ticket splitting is not possible when only one office is at stake, since a voter can then express only a single preference. This is the case in parliamentary elections in Britain, where each constituency returns but a single member to the House of Commons, and no other office is voted on at the same election. Thus, a voter can only express a preference for a single candidate as his or her member of Parliament. Until 1885 the majority of British members of Parliament were elected in constituencies that returned two or more members. In that case, each voter had as many votes as there were seats to be filled, and the voters could (and sometimes did) split their votes between candidates of two different parties. These constituencies were completely abolished before the 1950 British general election.

Ticket splitting is also impossible when the voting for two different offices is fused, that is, when a single vote is counted as the voter's endorsement of candidates for different offices, for example, both houses of a national assembly, or a legislative candidate and a presidential candidate. A fused vote is cast in Uruguay, and this ballot form has also been used in some other Latin American countries. In the United States the popular vote for presidential and vice presidential candidates is fused.

In a proportional-representation system in which the voters choose only among party lists, it is not possible to split votes between parties unless another office is being filled at the same time. An inability to split the ticket is the case in parliamentary elections in the Netherlands, and it was the case in Israel until the introduction of two votes—one for a party list for the Israeli parliament and another for an individual candidate for prime minister. In nonpartisan elections, by definition it is impossible to split a ticket, even if a multiplicity of offices are being contested, since none of the candidates has a party label.

SYSTEMS THAT PERMIT TICKET SPLITTING

More offices are filled by popular election in federal systems than in nonfederal systems because there is an additional tier of government. In the strict sense, ticket splitting occurs only if both regional and national offices are filled on the same day. But usually they are not. State or provincial governments can consciously hold elections apart from the national election in order to avoid the latter contest influencing the result of the former. Such considerations are particularly significant when, as in Canada, the structure of party competition is very different at the provincial and national levels.

The United States is exceptional in having a very long ballot listing candidates for many different offices; in giving voters the opportunity to endorse candidates for each office separately; in being a federal system with different structures of party competition at different levels of government; and in holding "big bang" elections once every four years in which a single ballot offers voters a chance to vote for officials at every level from the White House to the local court house.

Mixed systems that elect some representatives to parliament by proportional representation and others from single-member districts give each voter two ballots, one for each system, thus making ticket splitting possible. This system is used in the Federal Republic of Germany, in Italy since 1994, and in the 1999 election of the new Scottish Parliament and the Welsh Assembly. In the Scottish and Welsh balloting, a large majority of voters cast their two votes for the same party, but a noteworthy minority split their choices. A weak form of mixed system is found in countries in which a president is elected at a different time than the parliament, as is the case, for example, in Austria, Finland, France, and Ireland. The nonsimultaneous balloting creates the possibility of a voter favoring candidates of different parties for different posts in different years.

In Ireland seats are allocated by proportional representation, but its single-transferable-vote system assumes voters will rank candidates contesting a multimember constituency in the order of their preference. Irish voters usually give their initial preferences to the candidates of the same party, but the further down the list of candidates in a constituency with four or five parties nominating candidates, plus independents, the greater the likelihood of ticket splitting.

Although members of the Australian House of Representatives are elected from single-member districts, the country's alternative-vote system allows preferential voting, a form of ticket "spreading" if not splitting. In casting an alternative vote, the voter ranks candidates in order from the most preferred to the least, and the votes of the lowest ranking candidate or candidates are transferred until one candidate secures an absolute majority of all votes cast. In France most members of parliament are elected in constituency contests that involve two rounds of balloting, the first identifying the leading candidates, and the second a runoff in which fewer candidates run, thus forcing some voters to switch their support from one party to another if no second-round candidate represents their initial party preference.

See also *Alternative Vote; Federal Countries, Elections in; Fused Votes; Mixed Electoral Systems; Nonpartisan Elections; Offices Filled by Direct Election; Simultaneous Elections; Single Transferable Vote; Ticket Splitting in the United States.*

RICHARD ROSE, UNIVERSITY OF STRATHCLYDE

BIBLIOGRAPHY

Bawn, Kathleen. "Voter Response to Electoral Complexity: Ticket Splitting, Rational Voters and Representation in the Federal Republic of Germany." *British Journal of Political Science* 29 (July 1999), 487–505.

Jesse, E. "Split-voting in the Federal Republic of Germany." *Electoral Studies* 7, no. 2 (June 1988): 109–124.

Sinnott, Richard. *Irish Voters Decide.* Manchester: Manchester University Press, 1995.

TICKET SPLITTING IN THE UNITED STATES

Ticket splitting is the casting of votes for candidates of different parties during a single trip to the polls. In the United States this might involve voting for half Democrats and half Republicans or voting for nineteen Democrats and one Republican, for example. Ticket splitting is different from straight-ticket voting, which occurs when the voter marks the ballot for candidates of only one party.

Because voters in the United States are called on to decide many offices, they have many opportunities to split their tickets. In contrast, most other democracies call their citizens to the polls simply to vote for one member of parliament or for a party list. Some countries elect both a president and a parliament but, typically, at different times. Only a few countries ask their citizens to vote for more than one office at one time, and perhaps only Switzerland and the Philippines present voters with nearly as many opportunities to vote for candidates of different parties as does the United States. Hence, the ticket splitting that is practiced regularly during U.S. elections is unparalleled outside the United States.

HISTORY OF TICKET SPLITTING IN THE UNITED STATES

Until the twentieth century, ticket splitting was rare in the United States because voting procedures did not facilitate it. Throughout the nineteenth century, the political parties printed on colored paper a straight ticket that listed all of their candidates. Most voters took a ticket from one of the local party leaders and dropped it into the ballot box. In theory a voter could cross out the name of a particular candidate and write in the name of another party's candidate for that office, but in practice this was rare.

At the beginning of the twentieth century, a ballot procedure first used in Australia—thus known as the Australian ballot—was introduced to discourage the buying of votes. Under this system, the state printed each party's nominees for each office and provided voters with the opportunity to make their choices in secret. The change to a secret ballot made it much more difficult for party leaders to pay people for their votes; and, perhaps more important in the long run, voters could now pick and choose from the two tickets, voting for Republicans for some offices and for Democrats for others.

In 1970 political scientist Jerrold C. Rusk showed that the adoption of the Australian ballot in the United States was associated with the rise of ticket splitting. He also found that the format of state-printed ballots had an impact on the strength of the straight-ticket vote.

Massachusetts pioneered the office-bloc format on its ballots: each office was presented separately, and the candidates from each party were presented randomly. The office-bloc format thus forced voters to search the ballot for the members of one party in order to cast a straight ticket. In contrast, states such as Indiana arranged their ballots to be composites of the tickets that the parties had formerly distributed separately. In each column could be found each party's candidates for the various offices. This format continued to make it easy to cast a straight ticket. Today, however, even in Indiana—the founder of the party-column ballot—most counties vote with small punch cards that make it impossible to print all of the candidates of a single party in a single column.

No official statistics on ballot format are kept, but it is probable that, as computer punch cards have become the standard method for voting throughout the United States, relatively few U.S. voters now receive a party-column ballot. The last vestige of institutional support for straight-ticket voting is the single-punch option that allows voters to support the candidates of a particular party with one ballot punch. Currently, only sixteen of the fifty states offer their voters this option.

TICKET SPLITTING ON THE INCREASE IN THE UNITED STATES

Analysis of U.S. voting patterns in the twentieth century reveals a clear and steady increase in ticket splitting. Although sample survey evidence is limited to the relatively recent period for which data are available, examination of aggregate election results over time leads to a far more extended historical perspective on ticket splitting. If people cast straight party tickets, results for different offices will be similar. For example, if a Democratic candidate wins the presidential race in a given district or state, other Democratic candidates on the same ballot should also win—by roughly the same margin. If, however, many voters split their tickets, the result may be differing outcomes—victories for some candidates on the ticket and losses for others.

Walter Dean Burnham, a political scientist, showed in 1985 that in states outside the South the correlation between the vote for president and the vote for senator, representative, and governor has declined almost continuously throughout the

twentieth century. These correlations indicate that, at the turn of the century, observers could predict almost perfectly from a state's presidential vote how the state would vote for its congressional representatives and governor. By midcentury, voters in a state would often follow the same pattern in voting for president as they did for other offices but with a number of exceptions. By the 1980s, knowing a state's presidential vote was of almost no help in predicting its vote for other offices because the voting patterns were hardly correlated at all.

Although an examination of aggregate election returns provides clear evidence of increased ticket splitting over a long period of time, only analysis of individual-level survey data makes it feasible to gauge the scope of party-line voting. Data collected since 1952 by the National Election Study of the University of Michigan make it apparent that split-ticket voting has at least doubled in the second half of the twentieth century. In the elections of 1952 and 1956, only 14 percent of voters split their tickets when they voted for president and a member of the House of Representatives; in 1992 and 1996 the average was 30 percent. Even excluding Ross Perot voters—who are classified as ticket splitters because there were almost no congressional candidates running on the Perot ticket—analysis of returns shows 20 percent of U.S. voters in the 1990s supported different major party candidates for the two offices.

Some scholars have argued that this behavior is due simply to the nomination of presidential candidates whom many party identifiers could not support. Yet long-term increases in ticket splitting can also be found in measures that do not involve presidential voting. For example, in the 1950s the average incidence of voters splitting their ballots when they voted for House and Senate candidates was 9 percent; during the 1990s the average was 22 percent.

IS THERE A FUTURE FOR STRAIGHT-TICKET VOTING?

The future of parties might still be secure because in each case approximately three-quarters of all voters continue to vote for two candidates who are of the same party. Note that if people voted completely at random, however, half of all their choices would still appear to be party votes simply by chance. Thus, when one-quarter of the electorate splits a ticket between two offices, the halfway mark toward voting without regard to party has been reached. With many offices from which to choose and with most states not offering a straight-ticket option, it is becoming increasingly rare for voters to cast a perfectly straight ticket. In fact, in 1996 an astonishing 71 percent of voters said they usually split their tickets.

The results of this widespread ticket splitting have distinct political significance, which is clear in the unprecedented level of split party control of both federal and state governments in the late twentieth century. Most visible has been the division of partisan control of the presidency and Congress from 1969 through 2000. The same party has controlled the presidency and the House of Representatives only 19 percent of the time, compared with a historical average of 74 percent experienced from 1861 to 1968. The party of the president has recently had better success in the Senate thanks to the fact that the first six years of the Reagan presidency saw a Republican Senate. Nevertheless, from 1969 to 2000 the presidency and the Senate were controlled by the same party only 38 percent of the time compared with the historical average of 81 percent.

In the state capitals, divided party control also remains the norm. In 1997 only 38 percent of the states had one-party control of the governorship as well as both legislative houses, compared with 85 percent in 1947. Less recognized, however, is the regularity with which control of statewide executive offices is split between the major parties. Only eleven states had all of their executive offices filled by members of the same party in 1997. In the eighteen states that have a separately elected lieutenant governor, only ten were of the same party as the governor in 1997. Similarly, only twenty-two of the forty-three elected attorneys general were of the same party as their governors after the 1996 elections.

Divided party government, once an oddity, has become the normal state of affairs in U.S. government as the result of widespread ticket splitting. The American preference at the end of the twentieth century for voting for the person rather than for the party is good reason to expect that split-ticket voting might reach even higher levels in the future. A 1988 survey by political scientist Larry J. Sabato found 92 percent agreed with the statement: "I always vote for the person who I think is best, regardless of what party they belong to." Voters' attitudes about the potential for ticket splitting have consistently been greater than their practice of it, and recent trends can be interpreted as reflecting the tendency for voters' behaviors to come into line with their attitudes.

See also *Federal Countries, Elections in; Fused Votes; Ticket Splitting.*

MARTIN P. WATTENBERG, UNIVERSITY OF CALIFORNIA, IRVINE

BIBLIOGRAPHY

Beck, Paul Allen, et al. "Patterns and Sources of Ticket-Splitting in Subpresidential Voting." *American Political Science Review* 86 (December 1992): 916–928.

Burnham, Walter Dean. "The 1984 Elections and the Future of American Politics." In *Election 84: Landslide Without a Mandate?* edited by Ellis Sandoz and Cecil V. Crabb Jr. New York: Mentor, 1985.

Fiorina, Morris P. *Divided Government.* New York: Macmillan, 1992.

Rusk, Jerrold C. "The Effect of the Australian Ballot Reform on Split Ticket Voting: 1876–1908." *American Political Science Review* 64 (December 1970): 1028–1049.

Sabato, Larry J. *The Party's Just Begun: Shaping Political Parties for America's Future.* Glenview, Ill.: Scott, Foresman, 1988.

Wattenberg, Martin P. *The Decline of American Political Parties, 1952–1996.* Cambridge, Mass.: Harvard University Press, 1998.

TIE, METHOD OF RESOLVING

See *Administration of Elections*

TRIBAL AND ETHNIC VOTING

See *Colonial Elections; Elections in Developing Countries*

TURNOUT

Turnout is the proportion of eligible voters who make use of their right to vote in a particular election. Voting is the most basic form of political participation. Compared with other forms of political participation—both conventional, such as working in election campaigns or contacting government officials, and unconventional, like participating in demonstrations, boycotts, and rent and tax strikes—electoral participation differs in three important ways: it is the least intensive and least time-consuming form of political participation; many more people vote than participate in other political activities; and while there tends to be a class bias in electoral participation—citizens with greater wealth and more education turn out to vote in greater numbers than less privileged citizens—this bias is smaller in voter turnout than in any of the other forms of participation.

High turnout in democratic elections is usually considered important for two reasons. One is democratic legitimacy: can a government that has gained power in a low-turnout election really claim to be a representative government? For instance, President Bill Clinton won the 1996 presidential election with about 49 percent of the votes cast and with only about 49 percent of those eligible to vote actually doing so; he therefore received the support of fewer than 25 percent of all eligible voters. His mandate would have been considerably stronger had he won, even by a small margin, in a high-turnout election. The second reason why high turnout is important in democracies is that low turnout almost inevitably means that certain groups vote in greater numbers than other groups and hence gain disproportionate influence on the government and its policies.

Two arguments, now both discredited, used to be advanced in favor of low turnout. One was that low turnout simply reflected a high degree of citizen satisfaction. However, survey research has shown that it is the people who are dissatisfied—and who have good reasons to be dissatisfied because they belong to the underprivileged sectors of society—who make less use of their right to vote than satisfied citizens. The second argument, based especially on the experience of the last four elections (1930–1933) in the German Weimar Republic, in which increasing turnout coincided with the growth of the Nazi vote, was that high turnout could undermine democracy: in periods of crisis, sudden jumps in turnout may mean that many previously uninterested and uninvolved citizens have come to the polls to support extremist parties. This, however, is less an argument for low turnout than for turnout that is steadily at such high levels that there is simply no room for sudden jumps caused by crises and charismatic antidemocratic leaders. Besides, more recent comparative evidence shows that high voter turnout is actually associated with less citizen turmoil and violence than low turnout.

In principle, it is easy to calculate the turnout level in an election: it is the number of people who cast votes, divided by the number of citizens who are eligible to vote. In practice, however, there are problems with both the numerator and the denominator. With regard to the numerator—the number of people who vote—some countries, like the United States, include only voters who cast valid votes, whereas others, like most European democracies, include everyone who turns up at the polls, including those who cast blank and invalid ballots. Because blank and invalid ballots are a very small portion of the total number of ballots, this problem is a relatively minor one.

The denominator problems are much more serious, because the denominator that is commonly used is the number of registered voters. In the United States, registration is voluntary and often rather cumbersome, and it is the individual citizen's responsibility instead of the government's; as a result, fewer than 70 percent of all eligible voters are registered to vote. In Zambia the registration rate was only 51 percent in 1996. For most other democracies, which have automatic registration or make it the government's responsibility to register voters, the number of registered voters more nearly approximates the number of eligible voters, but sizable inaccuracies remain: voter registers may still not include all eligible voters, and they may include names of voters who have moved or died. Many scholars who study turnout levels in different countries therefore use the voting-age population as the denominator. Unless adult noncitizens are specifically subtracted from the voting-age populations, which is usually not the case, a degree of inaccuracy remains. Therefore, turnout rates

for countries with relatively large numbers of resident aliens, such as the United States, Switzerland, France, Germany, and Belgium, are likely to be understated by a few percentage points. Nevertheless, the voting-age population is the preferred denominator for turnout calculations. It tends to result in turnout figures that, on average, are 4 to 8 percentage points lower than turnout percentages based on registered voters.

VARIATIONS IN TURNOUT RATES

Turnout rates differ a great deal. Universal turnout—with literally everyone voting—does not occur in mass elections, but in the 1996 parliamentary election in Malta, the turnout (as a percent of voting-age population) was 98 percent. At the other extreme, only 5 percent of eligible voters turned out for a New York City school board election in the same year. Differences in turnout are especially large from country to country, but they are also substantial within countries: between elections held for different levels of government, between elections at the same level over time, and between different groups of voters.

The most reliable turnout data that are available for large numbers of countries are the rates of participation in the most important national-level elections: parliamentary elections in countries with parliamentary systems of government and presidential elections in democracies with strong presidents. These most important national elections are usually referred to as *first-order elections.* In the 1990s the turnout rates in first-order elections ranged from higher than 90 percent in Malta, Uruguay, and Italy to lower than 40 percent in Switzerland and Colombia. The difference between the highest and lowest percentages (averages of 97 percent in two elections in Malta and 32 percent in three elections in Colombia) was an astounding 65 percentage points.

Turnout rates in second-order elections—elections of national legislatures in presidential systems, subnational elections (like state, provincial, and local elections), and supranational elections like those of the European Parliament—which together form the vast majority of democratic elections, tend to be considerably below those in first-order elections. In the United States, turnout in the 1988, 1992, and 1996 presidential elections was 50, 55, and 49 percent, respectively, but it has been only about 35 percent in recent midterm congressional elections and only about 25 percent in local elections. Turnout in German and Spanish parliamentary elections and in French presidential elections in the 1980s and 1990s averaged between 75 and 80 percent, but in local elections and in German state elections it was only slightly above 60 percent. In the English-speaking democracies, which have roughly comparable national-level turnout levels, local turnout has been considerably below the Continental European levels: 53 percent in New Zealand, 40 percent in Great Britain, 35 percent in Australia, and 33 percent in Canada. In the 1994 European Parliament elections, the average turnout in the twelve member-countries was 58 percent, well below the average for the most salient elections in these countries, and in three countries—the Netherlands, Portugal, and the United Kingdom—only 36 percent of registered voters participated. Turnout in the first European Parliament election in newly admitted Sweden in 1995 was a mere 42 percent.

Turnout rates also vary over time. They tend to vary from one election to the next: ups and downs between 5 and 10 percentage points are not unusual. There are also two general trends: turnout tends to increase from the first democratic election to the subsequent two or three elections, but the overall trend in recent decades has been downward almost everywhere. In the United States the presidential elections of the 1890s had turnout rates as high as 75–80 percent, but they fell to 60–65 percent during the 1950s and 1960s, 50–55 percent in the 1980s, and 49 percent in 1996. In Switzerland, the European country with the poorest voter participation, turnout in the national legislative elections fell from 66 percent in 1947 to 36 percent in 1995. In other industrialized democracies the decline is also unmistakable, although not as dramatic: in western Europe average turnout went down by about 5 percentage points from the early 1960s to the late 1980s, and it declined even further in the 1990s, by more than 4 percentage points, in twenty-three Western democracies plus Japan. The pattern is similar for second-order elections. For instance, turnout levels in Germany have been declining, especially since the mid-1980s, at all four levels: local, state, national, and European Parliament elections. For all of the member-countries, average turnout in the elections to the European Parliament went down steadily, from 66 percent in the first elections held in 1979 to 64 percent, 63 percent, and 58 percent in the next three elections.

Finally, different groups of people within the same country often have different rates of voter turnout. One clear difference that is often noted is that people who pay more attention to politics, who frequently engage in political discussions, and who have stronger party identifications are more likely to vote than people who have little interest in politics, who do not discuss politics, and who do not or only weakly identify with political parties. This is not a surprising finding, and hence not a very interesting finding: all of these variables, including voter turnout, are part of the overall syndrome of political interest and participation.

Of greater interest are the links between demographic and socioeconomic variables, on the one hand, and turnout on the other: age, gender, involvement in social networks, education, income, and wealth. In most countries, age and turnout are strongly related in a curvilinear fashion: turnout increases with age, especially between whatever the voting age is (usually eighteen or twenty-one years) and thirty-five years, and declines after about age sixty-five. There also used to be a marked tendency for men to have higher turnout rates than women in many democracies. In the United States this pattern survives but only as a weak tendency; the pattern is reversed but also relatively weak in Japan; and in most other countries the difference has disappeared altogether. Membership in organizations and, generally, involvement in social networks tends to increase turnout.

By far the most important social characteristic (other than age) that affects differences in voter turnout is socioeconomic status: more-privileged citizens—those with higher incomes, greater wealth, and better education—vote in greater numbers than less advantaged citizens. This pattern of unequal and socioeconomically biased turnout is especially clear and strong in the United States. In American presidential elections from the 1950s through the 1980s, turnout among the college-educated was 26 percentage points higher than that among the population as a whole, whereas for people without a high-school diploma it was 16 percentage points lower—a difference of 42 percentage points between the two groups. In Switzerland, the other major Western democracy with low levels of turnout, the participation gap between the least and most highly educated citizens was about 25 percentage points in voting in national referendums in the 1980s, and it reached 37 percentage points in a 1991 referendum.

In countries with higher turnout, the link between socioeconomic status and turnout tends to be less strong, but it is strong enough to show up to some extent even in elections with very high turnout. In Australia, for instance, where as a result of compulsory voting laws about 95 percent of the registered voters usually vote in parliamentary elections, slightly higher turnout in particular elections has been found to entail the participation of slightly more working-class voters and hence a small but perceptible boost to the Labor Party. Another example is the last parliamentary election held under compulsory voting in the Netherlands in 1967: turnout was high among all educational groups but still a bit lower among the least-educated—93 percent—than among the most highly educated—97 percent.

A hypothetical example can illustrate why low turnout tends to spell unequal turnout. Assume that a country is divided into two groups of equal size, group A and group B. If turnout is 100 percent, the members of the two groups participate in exactly equal proportions. If turnout declines to 80 percent, it is possible that the actual voters are composed of all members of group A—accounting for 50 percentage points of the turnout—and only three-fifths of the members of group B—accounting for only 30 percentage points of the total turnout. With a turnout of 50 percent or lower, it is possible that the actual voters belong solely to group A and that nobody in group B votes. These are extreme possibilities, not probabilities, but they show that, when there is a basic tendency for groups to participate at different rates, the differences are minimal when overall turnout is high but can become, and tend to become, much larger as overall turnout goes down.

In addition to the clear connection between socioeconomic status and turnout, political scientists have found two further important links. The first is between socioeconomic status and party choice: lower-status people tend to support progressive parties, and higher-status people tend to vote for conservative parties. The second is between these types of parties and the policies that they pursue when they are in power: with regard to welfare, redistribution, full employment, social security, and overall government spending, parties pursue policies that are broadly in accordance with their party programs and with the interests and preferences of the socioeconomic groups that support them. Therefore, who votes, and who does not, has important consequences for who gets elected and for the content of public policies. A study of national elections in nineteen countries from 1950 to 1990 found that the left's share of the total vote decreased by almost one-third of a percentage point for every percentage point decrease in turnout. Since other, more intensive, forms of participation suffer from even greater socioeconomic biases than participation in elections, voting can serve as a democratic counterweight—but it can do so effectively only when turnout is high and hence substantially equal.

THEORETICAL EXPLANATIONS

Three main theories have been proposed to explain variations in turnout—as well as other forms of participation—based on individual resources, individual benefits, and mobilization. Resource theory is based on the fact that political participation has its costs: it requires knowledge, time, and money. People who have these resources can therefore be expected to participate more than people with fewer resources. This explanation can plausibly account for the socioeconomic differences in political participation mentioned above. However, it works less well for turnout than for other forms of participation, because voting requires relatively few resources. Even when there are cumbersome requirements to register well in advance of the election and in government offices that are not easy to locate—and in most democracies such obstacles do not exist—voting requires some skill, foresight, and persistence, but not a higher education or large amounts of time and money.

Resource theory performs even less well in explaining differences in turnout between countries, between national and less important elections, and over time. If variations in individual resources could account for differences in turnout, we would expect turnout to vary cross-nationally with levels of economic prosperity. Such a connection exists only at the low end of the prosperity scale: in the poorest countries with high rates of illiteracy, turnout indeed tends to be lower than in countries where almost everyone is literate. In the latter group, however, there are no clear differences between the wealthiest countries and those with less wealth. In fact, among Western democracies, two of the richest and most highly educated countries—the United States and Switzerland—have by far the lowest rates of voter turnout. Differences in individual resources obviously cannot explain why turnout is so much lower in second-order than in first-order elections nor why turnout goes up and down from election to election. Finally, according to resource theory, we would expect turnout to go up as countries become more prosperous; however, as indicated earlier, turnout levels have actually decreased in the industrialized democracies in spite of dramatic increases in levels of education and economic well-being since the 1950s.

The second theory takes into account not just the cost of voting but also, and with greater emphasis, the benefits that individuals derive, or think they can derive, by affecting the outcome of elections. This individual-benefits theory is especially strong in explaining variations in turnout over time: turnout tends to be higher when there is more at stake—when an election is a close contest or when there are large differences between the main parties and candidates. It also plausibly explains the lower turnout in second-order elections, in which less is at stake than in national parliamentary or presidential elections. And it explains why some of the institutional differences between countries, like their electoral systems and whether their elections are held separately or concurrently—to be discussed below—have such a strong impact on their turnout rates.

A weakness of individual-benefits theory is that, in a mass election, the chance that an individual will decide the outcome of an election is infinitesimally small. Because voting requires the investment of some time and effort, it does not make rational sense for an individual to pay this cost, regardless of how much is at stake. What needs to be added therefore is that individuals tend to have an inflated sense of the potential influence of their vote—just as people tend to vastly overestimate their chances of winning lotteries. A second weakness is that, while the theory can explain why turnout is lower in second-order than in first-order elections, it does not explain why it is so much lower in most countries; after all, the cost of voting at the different levels is the same and quite low. Especially in federal systems such as the United States and Germany, state elections are obviously of great importance—which is not reflected in voter turnout levels. Similarly, in presidential systems of government in which the executive and the legislature are coequal branches of government, congressional elections should rank close to presidential ones in importance—but turnout in midterm congressional elections in the United States is dramatically lower.

Mobilization theory is also a costs-versus-benefits theory but one in which parties, interest groups, and the media are the crucial actors. Its proponents argue that citizens turn out to vote largely as a result of deliberate efforts to persuade them to vote. Generally speaking, the differences in turnout that can be explained by individual-benefits theory can also be explained by mobilization theory: when more is at stake in an election, individuals can be expected to be more highly motivated to vote, but political parties and other groups can also be expected to try to make stronger efforts to mobilize them to vote. However, the wide gap in turnout between more and less important elections is more plausibly accounted for in terms of mobilization, because mobilization carries very substantial costs, like the price of advertising—in contrast with the almost negligible cost of an individual's voting. One specific difference in turnout that is explained well by mobilization theory is the higher turnout of people who are embedded in denser social networks. It makes good sense for parties and other groups to target their mobilization efforts at these persons because they can reach more of them at lower costs and because they are likely to respond not just by voting themselves but also by persuading their friends and acquaintances to vote as well.

INSTITUTIONAL DIFFERENCES

Of all of the differences in turnout—between countries, between levels and importance of elections, over time, and between groups within countries—the largest differences are those between countries. As shown earlier, the difference between the highest-turnout and lowest-turnout country in the 1990s was 65 percentage points, whereas the largest within-country difference was the 42 percentage points between the most and least educated Americans—a very large gap, but smaller than the 65 point between-country difference. The second outstanding feature of cross-national differences in turnout is that they can be shown to be heavily influenced by formal institutional features of the electoral and overall governmental systems: registration rules, whether or not elections are by proportional representation, whether or not different elections are held concurrently, the frequency of elections, the availability of mail ballots, weekend or workday voting, and the presence or absence of compulsory voting.

The relationships between these institutional characteristics and voter turnout rates in different countries are among the oldest and most solidly established propositions in political science. The findings reported as early as the 1930s in the two classic studies of voter turnout—*Why Europe Votes,* by American political scientist Harold F. Gosnell, and *Political Behavior,* by Swedish political scientist Herbert Tingsten—have by and large been validated by more recent, methodologically more sophisticated, research.

In the United States burdensome registration requirements have long been recognized as a major institutional deterrent to voting. Especially if the deadline for registration is far in advance of the election and if only limited hours are available to eligible voters who wish to register, registration requires considerable knowledge, time, and energy—a significantly higher cost than the cost of voting itself. Many studies have been conducted to determine the extent to which American registration requirements have depressed turnout. Comparisons between nationwide turnout and turnout in the few states with either no registration requirement or same-day and same-place registration—that is, the possibility of registering at the polls on election day—show differences of about 15 percentage points. On the basis of cross-national evidence, the adoption of a European-style system in which registration is automatic or the government's responsibility could boost turnout by up to 14 percentage points. Other estimates have been somewhat lower, but we can safely assume that a system of automatic registration would increase turnout by at least 10 and possibly by as much as 15 percentage points.

Another important institutional mechanism that affects turnout is the electoral system. Proportional representation tends to stimulate voter participation by eliminating the problem of wasted votes—votes cast for losing candidates or for candidates that win with big majorities—from which systems using single-member districts suffer. This makes it more attractive for individuals to cast their votes for parties and for parties to mobilize voters, even in areas of the country in which the parties are weak—in line with the individual-benefits and mobilization theories of turnout. It is also often suggested that the multiparty systems fostered by proportional representation stimulate turnout by offering more choices to the voters. However, empirical analyses have shown that multipartism slightly depresses turnout, probably because less is at stake and the election result is less likely to be decisive than in two-party competition in which the winning party becomes the government. On balance, however, the effect of proportional representation is still positive, and recent multivariate comparative studies have estimated that the turnout boost from proportional representation, all other factors being equal, is somewhere between 5 and 10 percentage points, depending on the degree of proportionality of the system.

These estimates of the benefits of proportional representation are all based on the most salient first-order elections. In contrast, the level of participation in second-order elections using proportional representation is much less impressive. The European Parliament elections provide a striking example: turnouts have been low even though eleven of the twelve member-countries choose their representatives by proportional representation. In the 1995 elections, by proportional representation, of the provincial legislatures in the Netherlands, turnout was only 50 percent. A recent American example is the 1996 New York City school board election, mentioned earlier—one of the rare cases of proportional representation in the United States—in which turnout was a mere 5 percent.

A high frequency of elections has a strongly negative influence on turnout. In the United States, on average, voters are asked to come to the polls between two and three times each year—much more often than in all except one other democracy. The one country with even more frequent dates on which elections and referenda are conducted, about six or seven times per year, is Switzerland. The United States and Switzerland are also the two Western democracies with by far the lowest levels of turnout. The most plausible explanation is that frequent elections entail a substantial increase in the cost of voting. If frequent elections depress turnout in first-order elections, it is logical to expect that they hurt turnout in second-order elections even more. This may be the explanation for the wide gap in the United States between presidential elections, on the one hand, and the less important—but, in a system of separation and division of powers still very important—midterm congressional elections as well as state executive and legislative elections on the other.

The American case of both separation and division of power as well as bicameralism is also unusual because even in the most important election—the election of the president—there is much less at stake than, at the other extreme, in the election of a unicameral parliament in a parliamentary and unitary system of government. This leads to the prediction that turnout in the most important national elections will be lower in presidential systems, if there is an elected upper house of parliament, and if the country is a federation—and if the presidential, lower house, upper house, and state elections are not held at the same time. This hypothesis has been confirmed in comparative research.

According to the same logic, we would expect the smaller and less-populous democracies to have very high turnout in their national elections, especially if they have parliamentary systems of government, because their national elections are the only elections that really count. This expectation is also correct: all other factors being equal, turnout in countries with populations of about 100,000 is substantially higher than in countries with larger populations.

Low voter turnout in Swiss national elections—the lowest in the Western world—is often cited as a special case of the phenomenon of low turnout when the stakes in elections are low: Switzerland is a federation, and most members of its upper house are directly elected, but the executive is not popularly elected. This last factor, it is argued, is counterbalanced by the fact that national legislative elections are minimally decisive because the four largest parties have formed the same broad coalition government for almost the entire period since 1943. If this explanation is correct, we would expect higher turnout in the two exceptional elections of 1955 and 1959, when the incumbent government was a three-party coalition and the Socialists were in the opposition. However, turnout (as a percent of voting-age population) did not increase from the 63 percent in 1951; instead, it declined to 61 percent in 1955 and to 58 percent in 1959. Switzerland's crowded election schedule appears to be the better explanation of its extremely poor turnout rates.

The individual-benefits and mobilization theories also lead us to expect that concurrent (simultaneous) elections will increase turnout, since the benefit of voting and of mobilizing people increases while the cost remains almost the same. In particular, second-order elections should have better turnout when combined with the most important national elections. The available evidence shows this hypothesis to be correct. Portugal and Ireland held their European Parliament elections at the same time as their national parliamentary elections in 1987 and 1989, respectively, and they yielded turnouts more than 20 percent higher than the preceding or next separate European Parliament election in these countries. The 1979 local elections in England and Wales happened to be conducted simultaneously with House of Commons elections, and, as a result, local election turnout virtually matched the participation in the parliamentary election. Combining a first-order election with one or more second-order elections may even help turnout in the former to some extent: in the United States the inclusion of a gubernatorial race can increase turnout in presidential elections by about 6 percentage points.

In contrast, the daunting accumulation of very many elections and referendum questions on one long ballot—a phenomenon unique to the United States, with its extremely large number of elective offices, primary elections, and, in many states, numerous referendums—is generally regarded as a deterrent to turnout, although the benefits of voting would appear to increase with increasing ballot length. Moreover, when a large number of choices have to be expressed on one ballot, many voters vote for the most important offices and referendum questions but fail to vote for less important offices and questions—a phenomenon known as roll-off.

Minor measures to facilitate voting, such as the possibility of absentee voting (by mail ballot or proxy) and the scheduling of elections on weekends instead of weekdays, can also be a small but distinct stimulus to turnout. A multivariate analysis of turnout in 29 countries found that, other factors being equal, weekend voting increases turnout by 5 to 6 percentage points and that mail ballots are worth another 4 percent in first-order elections. In the second-order European Parliament elections, weekend voting adds about 9 percentage points to turnout.

The strongest of all the institutional factors is compulsory, or mandatory, voting. Compulsory "voting" is a misnomer because even when voters are obligated to deposit a ballot in the ballot box, as they are in Australia, the secrecy of the ballot allows them to place a spoiled or blank ballot in the box. In other countries, like the Netherlands until 1970, mandatory "voting" merely entails the requirement to appear at the polling station on election day, without any further duty to mark a ballot or even to accept a ballot. In most comparative analyses of election turnout in the industrialized democracies between 1960 and 1990, compulsory voting has been found to raise turnout, other factors being equal, by 10 to 16 percentage points. A similar study of Latin American elections in the 1980s and early 1990s found that mandatory voting boosted turnout by 11 percent in presidential elections and 16 percent in congressional elections.

A systematic study of within-country differences—variations over time in Australia and the Netherlands, and variations among different areas in the same country in Austria—has produced further persuasive evidence. In all three countries, compulsory voting effectively and consistently raised turnout. Moreover, the exact increase in turnout depended on the baseline of participation without compulsory voting. Mean turnout in all three countries under mandatory voting was higher than 90 percent, but the increment due to mandatory voting in Austria was only about 3 percentage points, because turnout even under conditions of voluntary voting was well above 90 percent. In the Netherlands the abolition of compulsory voting in 1970 caused a larger drop, of about 10 percentage points, to the average voluntary-voting baseline of around 84 percent. And in Australia the mean turnout difference was even larger—more than 28 percent—because the average turnout under voluntary voting before 1925 was only about 62 percent.

Brazil and Venezuela are additional examples of low baselines and hence high turnout boosts due to compulsory vot-

ing. Average official turnout in Venezuela from 1958 to 1988 was 90 percent, but, after the abolition of mandatory voting in 1993, turnout fell to 60 percent. A public opinion poll in Brazil in 1990 found that, under hypothetical conditions of voluntary voting, turnout would undergo a similar drop of about 30 percentage points, from the 85 percent turnout in that year's election to 55 percent. Clearly, the impact of mandatory voting laws is especially pronounced in elections that would otherwise have very low turnouts.

This conclusion has special significance for all second-order elections, because these less important elections tend to be the ones with the lowest turnouts. In a multivariate analysis of the 1989 European Parliament elections, compulsory voting was found to raise turnout by 26 percentage points. In all four of the European Parliament elections from 1979 to 1994, the mean turnout was 84 percent in the countries with compulsory voting but only 46 percent in those with voluntary voting—a difference of 38 percentage points. In Belgium and Italy voting is compulsory in both national and local elections, and, as a result, turnout is high at both levels. Belgian local elections from 1976 to 1994 had an average turnout of 94 percent of the registered voters—the same percentage as the average turnout in the nonsimultaneous parliamentary elections during this period. In Italy from 1968 to 1994, mean turnout in local elections was 84 percent, compared with 86 percent in nonsimultaneous national parliamentary elections—a difference of only 2 percentage points. In Dutch provincial and municipal elections from 1946 until the abandonment of mandatory voting in 1970, turnout was almost always above 90 percent of registered voters, often close to 95 percent, and usually only a bit lower than that in parliamentary elections. In 1970 it dropped to 68 percent in provincial and 67 percent in municipal elections. After a brief improvement in turnout levels later in the 1970s, they declined even further. The 1994 and 1995 figures were 65 percent in municipal, 50 percent in provincial, and 36 percent in European elections.

It is somewhat surprising that making voting compulsory is so effective, because the penalties for failing to vote are typically minor, usually involving a fine roughly equal to that for a parking violation. Moreover, enforcement tends to be very lax. Because of the large number of people involved, compulsory voting cannot be strictly enforced; parking rules tend to be enforced much more strictly! For instance, with about 10 million registered voters in Australia, even a typical turnout of 95 percent means that half a million people did not vote, and it is obviously not practical to impose such a large number of fines. Australia is actually among the strictest enforcers of mandatory voting, but even there only about 4 percent of nonvoters end up having to pay the small fines. In Belgium fewer than one-fourth of 1 percent are fined. The strong effect of the obligation to vote is easily explained by the theory of individual costs and benefits: because the cost of voting is very low (except when there are burdensome registration requirements), the inducement of compulsory voting, small as it is, can still neutralize a large part of this cost.

LESSONS FOR PUBLIC POLICY

As indicated earlier, high turnout in democratic elections is usually considered a democratic virtue. How can turnout be maximized? The empirical evidence concerning cross-national differences summarized in this article contains several practical lessons. However, not all of the conditions that improve turnout can realistically be adopted or may carry too high a price.

Three categories of difficulty can be distinguished. First, the finding that a very small population size is conducive to high turnout is obviously not helpful at all for more-populous countries. Second, several turnout enhancers are not impossible but very difficult to adopt because they entail drastic changes in other important institutions of government: democracies that have majoritarian electoral systems, or presidential systems of government, or bicameral legislatures with two popularly elected houses, or a federal division of power, or many elective offices and referendums will probably not want to get rid of these institutions merely for the sake of improving their turnout rates. Third, several measures to increase turnout can be adopted much more easily in the sense that they do not require radical changes in other institutions: automatic voter registration, absentee ballots, weekend voting, concurrent voting for local elections, and compulsory voting.

Some of the institutional problems in the second category can be partly solved by conducting presidential, national legislative, and state executive and legislative elections concurrently as much as possible. The principal limitation here is that the different terms of office may not be equal and, even if equal, may not coincide. For instance, in the United States full concurrence would require the standardization of terms of office—say, a four-year term—for president, for members of the House of Representatives and the Senate (alternatively, an eight-year term for senators), and for all state governors and state legislators, as well as a single election day every four years. These would clearly still involve radical institutional changes. In countries with parliamentary systems, legislative terms of office are usually not fixed terms but maximum terms that can be shortened when parliaments are dissolved prematurely. For this reason, it is only rarely possible to hold elections to the European Parliament at the same time as national parliamentary elections. Moreover, when the number of elective offices and referendums is extremely large, as in the United States, concurrent elections do improve participation in the less important elections, but there is also a sizable roll-off by voters who do not fill out their entire ballots.

The least intrusive measures, belonging to the third category described above—that is, measures that do not necessitate simultaneous changes in other rules and institutions—still offer very effective possibilities for boosting turnout. Three lessons are of special importance. First, high turnout in the most important national elections can be assured by combining four of these measures: automatic registration, absentee ballots, weekend voting, and compulsory voting. For instance, the comparative evidence suggests that turnout in American presidential elections might be raised by some 30 percentage points, to about 80 percent, by adding the three missing features to the ready availability of mail ballots that already exists. The second lesson is that the less important (second-order) elections, and local elections in particular, can have high turnouts, too, if they are conducted on the same days as the most important national elections and if the latter have high voter turnouts. Finally, compulsory voting can be used as one of several turnout boosters, but it is an exceptionally strong mechanism that can yield high turnout by itself, in both national and local elections.

See also *Absentee Voting; Boycott of Elections; Competitiveness of Elections; Compulsory Voting; Cube Law; Day of Election; Downsian Model of Elections; Paradox of Voting; Primary Elections; Proportional Representation; Registration of Voters in the United States; Second-Order Elections; Simultaneous Elections; Turnout, Minimum Requirement; Wasted Votes.*

Arend Lijphart, University of California, San Diego

BIBLIOGRAPHY

Blais, Andre, and Agnieszka Dobrzynska. "Turnout in Electoral Democracies." *European Journal of Political Research* 33 (March 1998): 239–261.

Crewe, Ivor. "Electoral Participation." In *Democracy at the Polls: A Comparative Study of Competitive National Elections,* edited by David Butler, Howard R. Penniman, and Austin Ranney, 216–263. Washington, D.C.: American Enterprise Institute, 1981.

Franklin, Mark N. "Electoral Participation." In *Comparing Democracies: Elections and Voting in Global Perspective,* edited by Laurence LeDuc, Richard G. Niemi, and Pippa Norris, 216–235. Thousand Oaks, Calif.: Sage, 1996.

Gosnell, Harold F. *Why Europe Votes.* Chicago: University of Chicago Press, 1930.

International IDEA. *Voter Turnout from 1945 to 1997: A Global Report on Political Participation.* 2d ed. Stockholm: International Institute for Democracy and Electoral Assistance, 1997.

Jackman, Robert W., and Ross A. Miller. "Voter Turnout in the Industrial Democracies During the 1980s." *Comparative Political Studies* 27 (January 1995): 467–492.

Lijphart, Arend. "Unequal Participation: Democracy's Unresolved Dilemma." *American Political Science Review* 91 (March 1997): 1–14.

Pacek, Alexander, and Benjamin Radcliff. "Turnout and the Vote for Left-of-Centre Parties: A Cross-National Analysis." *British Journal of Political Science* 25 (January 1995): 137–143.

Piven, Frances Fox, and Richard A. Cloward. *Why Americans Don't Vote.* New York: Pantheon Books, 1988.

Powell, G. Bingham, Jr. "American Voter Turnout in Comparative Perspective." *American Political Science Review* 80 (March 1986): 17–43.

Rosenstone, Steven J., and John Mark Hansen. *Mobilization, Participation, and Democracy in America.* New York: Macmillan, 1993.

Teixeira, Ruy A. *The Disappearing American Voter.* Washington, D.C.: Brookings Institution, 1992.

Tingsten, Herbert. *Political Behavior: Studies in Election Statistics.* London: P.S. King and Son, 1937.

Verba, Sidney, Norman H. Nie, and Jae-On Kim. *Participation and Political Equality: A Seven-Nation Comparison.* Cambridge: Cambridge University Press, 1978.

Wolfinger, Raymond E., and Steven J. Rosenstone. *Who Votes?* New Haven, Conn.: Yale University Press, 1980.

TURNOUT, MINIMUM REQUIREMENT

A minimum level of turnout can be required for an election to be valid. The rule may apply to legislative elections, presidential elections, or both. Most of the time, the minimum level required is 50 percent, as is the case in many former Soviet republics, such as Belarus and Georgia. Minimum turnout rules are rare outside of the former Soviet republics.

The threshold need not be 50 percent. It is 25 percent, for instance, in Russian legislative elections. In Hungarian legislative elections the threshold is 50 percent on the first ballot. If that threshold is not met, another vote takes place, in which the required turnout is 25 percent. There is also a minimum required turnout of 25 percent in the first round of French legislative and departmental elections.

It is possible to make the electoral formula dependent on the level of turnout. On the first ballot of a Lithuanian presidential election, a candidate needs more than half of the votes cast to be elected, provided the turnout is at least 50 percent. If turnout is less than 50 percent of registered voters, a winning candidate must get the votes of at least one-third of the electorate (which means 67 percent of the vote if turnout is 49.9 percent, or 83 percent of the vote if turnout is 40 percent).

The rationale for imposing a minimum level of turnout is simple: when the majority of electors abstain, no candidate can pretend to have the strong support of constituents. The logic behind the use of a minimum turnout is similar to that behind adoption of the majority formula (and indeed turnout thresholds are more frequent in elections held under the majority rule). If it can be claimed that the support of a majority of voters should be required for a candidate to be elected, it can also be argued that a majority of electors should turn out to vote for an election to produce a legitimate winner.

The objection to a minimum turnout is largely pragmatic. What should be done when the threshold is not reached? How often does the vote have to be repeated before a winner is proclaimed? Who is to fill the office meanwhile? Pragmatic considerations have led most political elites in the world to conclude that the imposition of a turnout threshold is counterproductive. Although a low turnout may endanger the legitimacy of an election, it is not clear that forcing another vote solves the problem.

The potential problems associated with the minimum turnout requirement are illustrated by the Ukrainian parliamentary elections of 1994 and 1995. At the time, Ukraine had a run-off electoral system: to be elected in the first round, a candidate had to obtain more than 50 percent of the votes cast, and turnout in the given electoral district had to exceed 50 percent of the potential electorate; otherwise, a second round would be held between the two leading candidates under the same conditions. In both rounds, voters had the option of voting against all of the candidates on the ballot. There were, therefore, two conditions for being elected: obtaining a majority of votes cast and having a turnout over 50 percent.

After the first two rounds, held in March and April 1994, 112 seats remained unfilled. The main reason for the low number of valid elections, however, was not turnout, which averaged 75 percent in the first round and 67 in the second.

Additional rounds of elections were held in July–August 1994, November–December 1994, and December 1995. In this fourth series of elections (there were two rounds each time), there were 45 seats to be filled, but turnout failed to reach the 50 percent mark in 31 constituencies.

Unsurprisingly, the seemingly endless series of elections led Ukraine to change its electoral system (which is now mixed) and to abolish its minimum turnout requirement.

See also *Boycott of Elections; Compulsory Voting; Second-Order Elections; Simultaneous Elections; Turnout.*

ANDRÉ BLAIS AND LOUIS MASSICOTTE, UNIVERSITY OF MONTREAL

BIBLIOGRAPHY

Birch, Sarah. "The Ukrainian Parliamentary and Presidential Elections of 1994." *Electoral Studies* 14 (1995): 93–99.

———. "The Ukrainian Repeat Elections of 1995." *Electoral Studies* 15 (1996): 281–282.

UNFREE ELECTIONS

Today, elections take place in nearly every part of the world. But even in this age of more or less successful democratic transitions, many of these contests leave voters without a real choice. The contrast between those countries where "the people" truly choose, as in the Anglo-American liberal tradition, and those where the state, in its effort to acquire a forged legitimacy, compels voters to choose what it wants them to choose remains very real. Moreover, the careful student of electoral institutions in countries that now boast democratic competitive elections will find evidence of the extent to which these countries in the past did not meet the very standards that they now prescribe for others. Yet, with sporadic exceptions, political scientists have concentrated on supposedly free and competitive elections while ignoring those in which one candidate, one list of candidates, or one party gains 99 percent of the vote.

Holding free and competitive elections is viewed by politicians and social scientists as well as by the public at large as the most crucial element of legitimacy for any pluralist democracy. Indeed, political scientists conceive themselves as being concerned primarily with democratic multiparty systems characterized by competitive elections. For this reason the diverse and refined technologies of manipulation of legitimacy and consent that have been developed in noncompetitive political contexts, such as one-party elections or other types of state-controlled or clientelist elections, remain unexamined. (The word "clientelist" describes informal reciprocal power relations between individuals or groups in unequal positions, based on the exchange of benefits between "patrons," such as big landowners, and "clients," such as poor peasants, in the form of protection, access to state- or party-provided benefits, material rewards, jobs, prestige, and so forth.)

Scholars who study elections that offer no real choice focus on the significance of such elections to the rulers of the countries concerned rather than on their significance to individual voters. Rulers who do not rely on the ballot box to maintain their hold on power use elections to mobilize public opinion and acquire the appearance of legitimacy in a world where election by the masses has replaced election by God in conferring authority.

DEFINING NONCOMPETITIVE ELECTIONS

It might be argued that all electoral processes are inevitably undemocratic. Such procedures allow the cleverest and most powerful elites to make the "sovereign" people yield power to them in an acceptable way. From this point of view, the distinction between truly democratic elections—that is, those that are free and competitive—and their unfree, noncompetitive variants is of little importance. Both rely on some kind of misrepresentation of the people's will. According to this interpretation, the only way to avoid misrepresentation is through direct democracy or through use of a lottery selection of powerholders, as was done in ancient Greece.

Elitist thinkers have long expressed skepticism about the free and competitive nature of elections. For Gaetano Mosca, "The representative is not elected by the voters but, as a rule, has himself elected by them" (quoted in Thomas Bottomore, *Elites and Society*. London: C. A. Watts, 1966, 5). According to Joseph Schumpeter, "The choice of the electorate does not flow from its initiative but is being shaped, and the shaping of it is an essential part of the democratic process" (Schumpeter, *Capitalism, Socialism and Democracy*. New York: Harper and Brothers, 1947, 282). For Anthony Downs, "Parties in democratic politics are analogous to entrepreneurs in a profit-seeking economy. So as to attain their private ends, they formulate whatever policies they believe will gain the most votes just as entrepreneurs produce whatever products they believe will gain the most profit for the same reason" (Downs, *An Economic Theory of Democracy*. New York: Harper and Brothers, 1967, 295).

These criticisms hold that totally democratic procedures are distant ideals, unattainable in view of the weight of institutional, economic, ideological, social, and human factors. At best, elections are *relatively* free and competitive. In fact, it is these two points, the freedom of voters and competition between candidates, that constitute the most generally accepted criteria for distinguishing between "free" and "controlled" elections. A third consideration, the effects of elections on government policies, must be added to complete this distinction. Classical elections commonly have a direct effect on government, while nonclassical ones do not, or at least not directly. (Table 1 offers a summary of electoral situations and their characteristics relative to these three considerations.)

Voter freedom as a criterion for identifying free elections. In practical terms, the difference between free and controlled elections is indicated by the opportunity a voter enjoys to (1) have his or her franchise recognized through correct registration (an opportunity that was not always available in the United States, for example); (2) use the electoral franchise without being segregated into categories that divide the electorate and

revoke the universality of popular sovereignty (as occurred for many years in South Africa, in particular); (3) cast his or her ballot free from external hindrances (such as those that existed, for example, in revolutionary France or, more recently, in the Soviet Union); (4) decide how to vote, even to destroy his or her ballot if desired, without submitting to external pressure, whether official or clientelist; and (5) expect his or her vote to be counted and reported accurately, even if it goes against the wishes of those who govern (Mexico and Egypt, for example, resisted this norm for quite a long time, and Indonesia still does). Controlled elections are those that do not fulfil one or more of these requirements. In effect, the freedom of elections is judged here by the voters' degree of freedom.

This definition omits the indirect social pressures exerted upon voters, especially by a dominant culture or ideology or

Table 1. Electoral Situations

Election type	Control of competition	Examples	Freedom of vote	Political consequences
Competitive elections	Prohibition of candidatures exceptional; influence of a dominant culture	Western-type democracies	Universal suffrage, no coercion, and fair counting of results	Alternation of government and shifts of policies possible
Semicompetitive (exclusionary) elections	Class exclusion	England, early nineteenth century	Suffrage limited to property owners	Alternation of government and shifts of policies possible
	Racial exclusion	Apartheid, South Africa	Suffrage limited to whites	For white power structure only
	Exclusionary multiparty elections	Turkey, 1950–1960; Algeria since 1997; Mexico until 1994	Universal suffrage; little coercion	Effective alternation of government in Turkey but not in Algeria
	Coexistence of state-controlled movement and weak parties	Indonesia; Mexico until the 1980s	Strong coercion; results unverifiable	Without direct consequences; no alternation of government
Controlled one-party or no-party elections	National Fronts with dominant official party and common list	Poland and East Germany under communist rule	Results determined beforehand	Ritualistic elections without political consequences
	Declining one-party systems with candidates representing various "streams"	Egypt and Spain in the 1970s	Universal suffrage, limited coercion	Used as a political barometer by government
	One-party with competition among several candidates	Soviet Union in the 1980s or post-totalitarian	Little coercion	Ritualistic, without political consequences other than arbitration among internal factions
	One-party monopolistic	Stalinist Soviet Union	Compelled voting	Designed to show "unanimous consent" for governing actors

by caste associations and communitarian environments. In fact, cultural or societal domination can distort the freedom a voter enjoys, as no one living in a human organization can remain totally independent of the in-group pressures common to any social system.

Multiparty competition as a criterion for identifying free elections. The second criterion for identifying free elections is met by the presence of several candidates or lists of candidates for an office; an election where only a single candidate or list of candidates is presented to the electorate is definitely not competitive. Yet, even in multiparty democracies, two limits to competition generally remain. One is the financial limitation that handicaps certain parties more than others. The other is a legal and normative limitation, such as that expressed in West Germany when the government there outlawed the Communist Party, or as expressed elsewhere in the outlawing of parties directly inspired by a racist doctrine (for example, the efforts to outlaw the Front National in France).

An intermediate category, semicompetitive elections, must be considered here as it covers an enormous variety of limitations. Electoral competition can be suppressed in clientelist states such as those that existed for a long time in Mediterranean Europe, Latin America, Turkey, and parts of Southeast Asia or even at one time in western Europe.

Faked electoral competition also occurs. Faked elections are most visible in authoritarian and totalitarian regimes where use of single-party, no-party, or single-list systems is common. These systems offer voters an official slate and no other, precluding any possibility of competition and legal opposition or dissension. What remains a mystery is not so much the vote itself but the miraculous computation of triumphal electoral results determined beforehand by the state (a phenomenon that still occurs in China, Cuba, North Korea, and Vietnam).

A less drastic brake on competition involves the imposition of limits on the number of parties that are tolerated. Such limits were imposed in postwar Turkey, Brazil (after 1964), and Iran (before 1975). They still exist today in Egypt, Indonesia, Iran (since 1979), Singapore, and among the Islamist parties of Algeria. Regimes that limit competition in this way often erect procedural barriers to check the growth of the few small, legal parties or electoral groupings that operate in their countries. These parties are tolerated only to reinforce the disputable democratic legitimacy of the dominant government party. Portugal before 1974, Mexico until 1994, and, before the Soviet bloc's demise, some eastern European communist countries all made this common practice.

Finally, some governments limit competition by allowing voters to choose from among the two or three candidates that appear on an approved official list (this was done in Francisco Franco's Spain as well as in many African countries and in the so-called popular democracies of eastern Europe at the end of the communist era).

Electoral outcomes as a criterion for identifying free elections. The effect of electoral outcomes on government provides the third criterion by which to distinguish free from controlled elections. In truly democratic regimes, control of office is normally determined by the outcome of the election. Officeholders are appointed based on the wishes of the majority of the electorate as a matter of routine, and government policies are modified in kind. In undemocratic regimes, electoral results do not alter the power structure. Powerholders claim to stand above parties and above voters. Elections function as no more than a political barometer, the readings of which do not create any obligation for the government.

Free democratic elections combine voter freedom, multiparty competition, and outcomes that affect what happens in government in a fairly positive and coherent manner. Conversely, undemocratic, controlled elections manipulate these three elements in so many ways that they induce a sort of taxonomic confusion. While some semicompetitive or noncompetitive elections may effect political consequences, elections that are not free at all will have no impact for the voters, even though several candidates for office may have been offered up in a pretense of competition.

This empirical scale distinguishes two forms of electoral manipulation: semicompetitive "exclusionary" elections and coerced "unanimity" elections. In the case of exclusionary elections, the government aims to prevent the manifestation of mass expectations, restricting the right to vote or the number of parties or candidates allowed to compete. Within these limits, however, those allowed to vote may make a choice. This kind of semicompetitive election was practiced by a number of military or civilian strong governments between 1950 and 1980 in Brazil, Indonesia, Mexico, Morocco, Paraguay, Taiwan, and Turkey. Egypt, Indonesia, Iran, Morocco, Senegal, and Tunisia still practice, or only recently abandoned, this type of election. Controlled pluralist elections remain the electoral method of choice for conservative authoritarian regimes that disguise themselves as semidemocracies.

The revolutionary, totalitarian, and post-totalitarian regimes of the ex-communist bloc and of the former developing world have demonstrated a predilection for the unanimity secured by one-party or single-list elections. Multiparty elections, even forged ones, are rare in these countries, especially in Africa. However, purely single-candidate or single-list elections have gradually become less frequent, except in presidential elections. In addition, the nonpluralist though formally competitive elections typical of declining dictatorships frequently give the voters some influence, particularly in some East African authoritarian states where they might be interpreted as something like "consent" elections.

These considerations ignore many electoral modalities that complicate noncompetitive ballots. In particular, they ignore the individual voter's private perception of such elections as well as voters' collective evaluation. A more comprehensive analysis would extend itself to historical and socioeconomic dimensions. For example, as they evolve toward some possibilities of limited choice or gradually acquire at least some opportunities for abstention, state-controlled elections have not always demonstrated the same repressive meaning. Francisco Franco's Spain, the Kuomintang's Taiwan, and the communist countries of Hungary and Poland during their communist eras all demonstrated different degrees of repression.

PURPOSES
OF NONCOMPETITIVE ELECTIONS

State-controlled elections provide a global insight into the negative aspects of electoral processes at large. They also offer a means of penetrating the unseen political management of governance in authoritarian regimes. But the electoral histories of many democracies also demonstrate that these countries have seen liberal phases alternate with disguised or overt authoritarian phases over the course of their political development. The United States, for example, did not effectively enforce the right of blacks in the South to vote until after the civil rights demonstrations of the 1960s.

The consideration of noncompetitive elections also provides greater knowledge of the worldwide electoral process as it pertains to political development in nonindustrialized countries, particularly those of the former developing world, by bringing to light the mechanisms through which socially undifferentiated and tradition-bound peoples are—or are not—transformed into self-conscious electorates. In the nineteenth century, and even more recently in the American South, this maturity was usually reached in the electoral purgatory of those who were excluded from voting under the poll tax and literacy test systems. Has this changed today? Do noncompetitive elections really generate political deprivation among the would-be citizens of dictatorships of all types, or do they, on the contrary, accelerate the course of democratic apprenticeship?

To answer this question, we must first consider the legal framework and institutional environment of elections. We must study the extension of suffrage; the object, frequency, and form of elections; the organization of campaigns; the shaping of constituencies; the counting of votes cast; and the "processing" of results (that is, the importance that the government publicly attributes to election results). We must then observe actual campaign behavior: the machinery, whether hidden or openly fraudulent and coercive, affecting the number of people actually allowed to vote; the content of propaganda; the ties existing between the candidates and those in power or in some officious political network; and the effective freedom of the vote. In some circumstances, the relative fairness of semicompetitive elections justifies consideration of their formal and public aspects; the extreme distortion of many others, however, forbids any serious evaluation.

The description of the formal and actual features of noncompetitive elections does not exhaust their complex meaning, since electoral practice is always embedded in a political tradition or historical path and a specific socioeconomic and cultural environment. Noncompetitive elections do not have the same significance in a complex industrialized society as they do in a predominantly peasant society, where the population is fairly homogeneous and largely illiterate. They also have a different meaning according to the specific electoral history of each country. For instance, the population of the Democratic Republic of the Congo (formerly Zaire) had no experience of free elections during the colonial period (when it was known as the Belgian Congo), whereas the inhabitants of British and French colonial territories did acquire some experience of free elections before independence. Similarly, some of these countries have been influenced at a given moment by the Western electoral model and experienced at least short periods of relatively democratic politics after independence that others did not.

Noncompetitive elections provide a rare opportunity to document and analyze the public manifestations of the governments that organize them. In those states with emergent economies—typically countries of the former developing world, whether authoritarian or post-totalitarian, populist or reactionary—political conflict and its resolution remain largely hidden. The political battles of these countries are concealed behind an opaque screen that shields a very small ruling elite from public scrutiny. It is this secrecy that makes noncompetitive elections, for those who care to consider them, an exceptional source of information about a political reality that at other times remains hidden from view.

Observation of the candidate-selection machinery offers a wide and useful base for understanding, for example, the rivalries, compromises, and co-optation and intimidation that frequently constitute the real purpose of noncompetitive elections. Indeed, the composition of the lists of candidates offered to the voters reflects an infinite number of ideological or programmatic nuances representing covert political streams or groups within nominally single-party regimes. In the same way, the content of electoral campaigns and electoral literature may be very informative to the astute observer. In all of its stages, nonclassical elections represent at least one occasion when autocratic governments cannot avoid the public formalization of an official program and espousal of ideological position. They also offer a rare opportunity to assess the ability of such regimes to mobilize mass support.

In some parts of the world, elections were never held at all. (Fidel Castro once declared, "Revolution has no time for elections.") In countries under communist rule, however, mobilizational elections were generally held. In the Soviet Union in 1984, for example, turnout for one such election was 99.99 percent, with 99.94 percent of the vote going to the official slate. These elections served to demonstrate to the populace that its rulers cared about them, in spite of the fact that many of the Russian and east European voters who were duly registered never physically appeared at the polls. Today, few political leaders can do without some type of election. For present-day authoritarian and post-totalitarian regimes, noncompetitive elections function as an escape valve to relieve the internal or external pressures that build in the wake of opposition and dissent. Noncompetitive elections force a ruler to be explicit in establishing his or her stance. At the same time, they identify the type of relations, coercive or participative, that the governing circle has with the population.

The function of one-party elections for fully totalitarian regimes differs from their function for post-totalitarian or authoritarian regimes. Totalitarian regimes make a show of high electoral turnout precisely because of the mobilizational character of totalitarianism combined with their desire to display the ideological adhesion of the population. In contrast, authoritarian and post-totalitarian regimes like Franco's in Spain, the post-1964 military government in Brazil, or Wojciech Jaruzelski's dictatorship in Poland do not place any emphasis on apparent electoral unanimity. They undertake more of a *laissez faire* attitude that corresponds to their relative indifference or skepticism toward ideological persuasion.

Analysis of the voters' attitudes is also possible in a few cases. At the local and sometimes even the national level, the results of some noncompetitive elections are not significantly falsified, either because the government considers it unnecessary or because it expressly wishes not to do so. In these situations, the proportion of votes attributed to each candidate generally does not matter, except in detailed studies of results by constituency, where it may be interesting to contrast the characteristics of successful and unsuccessful official or semi-official candidates. More promising is the study of abstentions, provided they have not been falsified. When the government gives no other opportunity to express an opposing view, withholding one's vote may become a challenge to the government. This is especially true when abstention occurs on a large scale and is clearly concentrated in certain regions of a country or in specific sectors of the population. In these

circumstances, abstentions are politically significant, permitting an interpretation in terms of differential regional, social, religious, or ethnic conformity toward the established authorities. While study of abstention in the Soviet Union resulted in little new information, it proved more valuable when applied to Spain during the time of Franco, where a clear correspondence existed between the vote for the left before the 1936–1939 civil war and abstention under the succeeding dictatorship.

Competitive elections are expected to provide a peaceful succession of officeholders and to legitimize leaders and governments and the policies they undertake. But what are the practical aims of state-controlled elections? A totalitarian, authoritarian, or post-totalitarian government that calls for an election that it is not strongly obliged to hold expects such an event to have a specific, and naturally self-gratifying, outcome. While the compulsory and multipurpose character of competitive elections does not require a precise strategic calculation, such calculations in state-controlled elections involve four specific functions: communication, education, legitimation, and distributional adjustment.

Communication. The communication function of these elections is well-documented and incontrovertible. Electoral processes normally provide an immediate and authoritative occasion for the transmission of orders, explanations, and cues from the government to the population. They also offer the opportunity to recruit intermediaries to act on behalf of those in power.

In authoritarian regimes, where public controversy is anathema, election time sometimes looks like a period of exceptional politicization, albeit directed solely to the advantage of those who govern. Authoritarian leaders cannot escape the obligation of "indulging in" politics from time to time, but they do it in as direct, massive, and unilateral a manner as possible. Moreover, the governments of new states, where illiteracy, linguistic fragmentation, and lack of preestablished channels are hindrances to easy communication with the people, can use electoral campaigns as an efficient though occasional means to reach the masses. This is particularly the case when the ruling party or administration is unable to ensure continuing nationwide political activity by its own elites (as occurred in the sub-Saharan military dictatorships of Africa).

Education. The educational concern of state-controlled elections reflects the paradox that, whereas the very exercise of the vote instills in citizens an awareness that they ought to have the ability to influence their rulers, it at the same time hides real inequalities of power through nominal equality at the ballot box. The result of this process is both educational and anesthetic. In situations where governments believe that general conformity strengthens stability, elections tend to invalidate the opposition while reinforcing the institutionalization of the authoritarian or post-totalitarian regime.

Alternatively, where a ruler believes that limited pluralism without real freedom holds advantages for social and political stability, state-controlled or falsely competitive elections provide an opportunity to introduce various types of bipartisan or multipartisan combinations that exclude radical opposition parties or give such parties no real political chance. The ruler's hope is that the population will get used to having no real choice other than that imposed by the political planning of the government, or even that it will forget the less-restricted choices of the past and learn moderate electoral behavior, making control unnecessary. This strategy has been common in Africa, Latin America, and the Middle East. The Turkish Republican Party inaugurated it in the 1950s, while the Revolutionary Institutional Party in Mexico, the Brazilian military government, and the Senegalese Socialist Party followed it in the 1960s, 1970s, and 1980s. And while contrary to their attitudes toward the Islamist movements, the strategies of the Algerian, Iranian, and Tunisian regimes appear to be the same today.

Legitimation. No less controversial, the legitimation function of state-controlled elections can take two forms: national legitimation or international legitimation. Elections are a symbol of good conduct to the outside world. For example, in Rwanda the U.S. administration of Bill Clinton demanded elections at any price, even though in practical terms they could not be very convincing according to the usual norms of democratic correctness.

At the same time, internal electoral legitimation is a resource of great importance in states where national unity remains fragile, if not altogether fictitious. In these countries, elections generally constitute the most efficient method for promoting popular, nationwide mobilization that transcends local, ethnic, religious, or socioeconomic cleavages. By simultaneous application of traditional political processes (for example, palaver norms favoring unanimity, feudal patronage) and modern techniques (for example, ideological references, single or dominant parties with or without deferent and tolerated opposition, the practice of voting), elections appear semi-festive and even cathartic. In Africa, south of the Sahara especially, they are a sort of national festival. As a result, they lend themselves to interpretations that suit the rural populations, town-dwellers, prosperous Westernized elites, and radical have-nots alike.

Distributional adjustments. Noncompetitive elections reflect and influence the internal distribution of power among the groups that control the state or single-party apparatus. In regimes where there is no real compulsory term for consulting the population, a call for elections is often motivated by the need for public sanction of the power elite, by the wish to capture the support of new elements in the political mix, or, in some circumstances, by a desire to weaken the hold of traditional influences such as religion (as in Algeria).

Sometimes, the purpose of state-controlled elections is to "consult" the people in order to ratify or enforce an already-negotiated compromise. These elections may also help reestablish a firm hand on anarchistic or unenthusiastic sectors of society by compelling their members to adopt greater political conformity, at least at the surface, or by attracting nonradical opponents with the promise of reform. Under all circumstances, noncompetitive elections generally help rejuvenate political elites and simultaneously weaken dissenting groups or individuals by conveniently isolating them.

Elections are multifunctional, and to some extent noncompetitive elections combine elements of each of the various functions discussed here. Nevertheless, one or two of these purposes are clearly more specific, even crucial, to the totalitarian or authoritarian regime. The last function in particular—influencing the distribution of power inside the governing apparatus—becomes more and more important as decaying authoritarian or post-totalitarian autocracies approach their collapse and consequently try to refashion their image. The final days of the Soviet Union under Mikhail Gorbachev or of Poland under Jaruzelski illustrate this point. These leaders were thinking ahead in an effort to secure their own futures within the successor regimes.

State-controlled elections reflect more or less original blends of clientelism and corruption together with a huge variety of social and historical contexts, multiple distortions or reinterpretations of imported American and European prototypes, new forms of popular civic involvement, and strategic maneuvering to ensure a reputable exit from the political arena. Yet most research dealing with these types of elections remains, with very few exceptions, purely descriptive. Interest in the monopolistic elections that still take place in China, Cuba, North Korea, and Vietnam has been eclipsed by a focus on the semicompetitive elections now taking place in countries like Algeria, Iran, Romania, Syria, and Ukraine. The so-called third wave of democratization that began after the fall of the Berlin Wall in 1989 and the replacement in the 1990s of one-party systems and "saber-rattler" dictatorships by pseudo-multiparty systems in Africa south of the Sahara is generating another problem. The competitive character and fairness of the elections organized in these new post-totalitarian or post-authoritarian democracies have been too rapidly taken for granted, and the remnants of a past that many still carry with them must be more seriously examined.

There is no doubt that free, competitive elections alone are not sufficient to establish a sound democracy. The birth and consolidation of a young democratic regime require as well the support of a civil society, the restoration of state authority, and the implementation of the rule of law, among other things. Yet, at the same time, there can be no democracy without elections that allow citizens to dismiss, peacefully, those who govern them.

See also *Boycott of Elections; Democracy and Elections; Effect of Elections on Government; Electoralism; Free and Fair Elections; Functions of Elections; Observation of Elections; Postconflict Elections; Premature Closure; Technical Assistance in Elections.*

GUY HERMET, INSTITUT D'ÉTUDES POLITIQUES, PARIS

BIBLIOGRAPHY

Barkan, Joel D., and John J. Okumu. " 'Semi-Competitive' Elections, Clientelism, and Political Recruitment in a No-Party State: The Kenyan Experience." In *Elections without Choice,* edited by Guy Hermet, Richard Rose, and Alain Rouquié, 88–107. London: Macmillan, 1978.

Diamond, Larry. "Is the Third Wave Over?" *Journal of Democracy* 7, no. 3 (autumn 1996): 20–37.

Elklit, Jorgen, and Palle Svensson. "What Makes Elections Free and Fair?" *Journal of Democracy* 8, no. 3 (autumn 1997): 32–46.

Hermet, Guy. "Electoral Trends in Spain: An Appraisal of the Polls Conducted under the Franco Regime." *Iberian Studies* 2 (1974): 5–10.

———. "State-Controlled Elections: A Framework." In *Elections Without Choice,* edited by Guy Hermet, Richard Rose, and Alain Rouquié, 1–18. London: Macmillan, 1978.

Hermet, Guy, and Lilly Marcou, eds. *Des partis comme les autres? Les anciens communistes en Europe de l'Est.* Brussels: Éditions Complexe, 1998.

Hermet, Guy, Richard Rose, and Alain Rouquié, eds. *Elections Without Choice.* London: Macmillan, 1978.

Linz, Juan J. "Political Identities and Electoral Sequences: Spain, the Soviet Union, and Yugoslavia." *Daedalus* 121, no. 2 (1992): 123–140.

———. "Totalitarian and Authoritarian Regimes." In *Handbook of Political Science,* Vol. 3, edited by Fred I. Greenstein and Nelson W. Polsby, 175–411. Reading, Mass.: Addison-Wesley, 1975.

Rose, Richard. "Is Choice Enough? Elections and Political Authority." In *Elections Without Choice,* edited by Guy Hermet, Richard Rose, and Alain Rouquié, 196–212. London: Macmillan, 1978.

Rose, Richard, William Mishler, and Christian Haerpfer. *Democracy and Its Alternatives: Understanding Post-Communist Societies.* Oxford: Polity Press; and Baltimore: Johns Hopkins University Press, 1998.

Shlapentokh, Vladimir. *Public and Private Life of the Soviet People.* New York: Oxford University Press, 1989.

White, Stephen, Richard Rose, and Ian McAllister. *How Russia Votes.* Chatham, N.J.: Chatham House, 1997.

UNOPPOSED RETURNS

An election offers an opportunity for choice, but voters will have a choice only if two or more candidates or parties put themselves forward in competition for their vote. In many nonpolitical contexts, it is common for an individual to be elected unanimously if there is a consensus in favor of the incumbent, if no one else wants the job, or if it is considered desirable that the electorate show its commitment to the winner of a multicandidate race (as in papal elections, for example).

In a proportional election system, voters are almost always offered a choice between parties; the fact that at least two parties are likely to win seats in a multimember district encourages competition. By contrast, in a single-member, first-past-the-post system many seats are "safe." A party that has a good chance of winning the most seats nationally may find it difficult to field a standard-bearer in a district where another party is dominant, and the more hopeless the party's cause in that district, the greater the possibility that the dominant party's standard-bearer will face only token opposition. In the U.S. House of Representatives elections of 1998, in thirty-one districts the majority-party candidate faced opposition from only a fringe candidate, usually a Libertarian securing a derisory vote.

In nineteenth-century Britain many members of Parliament were returned unopposed because most constituencies were safe; campaigning was costly due to the voters' expectation that candidates would offer payment, favors, or hospitality in exchange for votes; and the rewards were few, since members of Parliament did not receive a salary. In the first election held on a reformed (although not universal) franchise in 1832, a quarter of the members were elected unopposed. The proportion rose to more than half by 1841 and as high as 58 percent in 1859 before falling, as the expansion of the franchise encouraged the organization of nationwide parties that contested every seat to boost their total national vote. The enactment of anticorruption legislation made it easier for candidates to afford to wage a campaign. The British general election of 1885 was the first in which more than 90 percent of the seats were contested. The 1931 election was the last in which more than 10 percent were unopposed. Since 1945 very few seats have been unopposed.

Where ethnic or racial considerations make seats extremely safe, the likelihood of unopposed candidacies increases. When the Northern Ireland Parliament was elected in single-member districts (until 1969), securing the nomination of the Nationalist Party was tantamount to election in a Catholic constituency, and securing the Unionist nomination was tantamount to election in a Protestant constituency. Until the Northern Ireland civil rights campaign erupted in 1968, between two-fifths and one-half the seats were uncontested.

In the American South when African Americans were effectively disfranchised, the critical choice occurred in the Democratic Party primary. Winning the Democratic nomination was tantamount to election, and often the Democratic nominee had no Republican challenger. Winning a primary election for a congressional seat remains tantamount to election in both Republican and Democratic strongholds today.

Candidates have run unopposed at the congressional level in the majority of states at one time or another in the past quarter-century.

When a candidate is unopposed, no vote need be held in the constituency, resulting in the preferences of voters there not being included in the national total of votes. Since uncontested seats would produce a very lopsided distribution of the vote among parties, this can alter the distribution of the total national vote. For example, in the December 1910 United Kingdom election, the Liberal Party won 43.9 percent of the total vote, but an average of 49.5 percent in constituencies it contested.

Regional or nationalist parties concentrate their appeal on a restricted number of constituencies. In the 1997 United Kingdom parliamentary election, the Scottish National Party contested all seventy-two seats in Scotland and won 22.1 percent of the vote there. But because the Scottish Nationalists did not contest any seats in England, Wales, or Northern Ireland, they had only 2.0 percent of the total United Kingdom vote.

See also *Acclamation, Election by; Competitiveness of Elections; Downsian Model of Elections; Papal Elections; Safe Seat; Unfree Elections; Wasted Votes.*

RICHARD ROSE, UNIVERSITY OF STRATHCLYDE

BIBLIOGRAPHY

Craig, F.W.S. *British Electoral Facts, 1832–1987.* Chichester, England: Parliamentary Research Services, 1989.

Elliott, Sydney. *Northern Ireland Parliamentary Election Results, 1921–1972.* Chichester, England: Political Reference Publications, 1973.

Key, V.O., Jr. *Southern Politics in State and Nation.* New York: Knopf, 1949.

VOLATILITY, ELECTORAL

Electoral volatility commonly refers to an index for measuring change in aggregate voting patterns between two or more elections. This index first achieved prominence in the wake of a now classic article on the dynamics of European party systems by the Danish political scientist Mogens N. Pedersen (1979). Earlier versions of such an index had been proposed by Adam Przeworski (1975) and William Ascher and Sidney Tarrow (1975). Pedersen's version was simplicity itself. It stated that total (or aggregate) electoral volatility (TV) is the net change within the electoral party system resulting from individual vote transfers. TV can be measured as the cumulated (aggregate) electoral gains of all winning parties in a given election or, alternatively, as the cumulated (aggregate) electoral losses of all losing parties in a given election. In practice, since the rounding of the figures can lead to anomalies, TV is usually calculated by summing the absolute values of cumulated gains and cumulated losses and dividing by two, according to the following formula:

$$\sum_{i=1}^{n} |\frac{P_{it} - P_{i(t+1)}}{2}|$$

where n is the number of parties in the system and P_{it} and $P_{i(t+1)}$ are the percentage of electoral support for party i at time t and time $(t+1)$, respectively.

By definition, this index runs from a minimum value of 0 (which indicates that there is no change in the aggregate distribution of support for the parties) to a maximum value of 100 (which indicates that all of the existing parties have lost all of their support and are being replaced by wholly new parties). Table 1 summarizes the election outcomes in Sweden in 1991 and 1994. The cumulated gains of the Left Party, the Social Democrats, the Conservatives, and the Greens are 11.3 percent. The cumulated losses of the Center Party, the People's Party, the Christian Democrats, and New Democracy are 11.2 percent (the difference is due to rounding). Support for "Others" remains unchanged. The index of TV, therefore, is 11.25.

Two features of this mode of measuring electoral change must be emphasized. First, the change that is measured is usually, although not necessarily, that which occurs from one election to the next. In other words, TV is typically applied to the measurement of short-term electoral change. This means that should a party or parties lose or gain small amounts of electoral support steadily over a long period of time, say from 30 percent to just 5 percent over the space of ten or more elections or from 5 percent to 30 percent over the same amount of time, this change will barely register in the conventional indices of volatility. As such, these measures of volatility are best suited to the identification of short-term propensities to electoral instability.

Second, change at the aggregate level may well conceal the real amount of individual-level change. For example, if the total number of voters who switch from party A to party C is countered by the number of voters who switch from party C to party A, then the aggregate index will not give an accurate estimate of the real levels of instability. For this reason analysts of electoral change often prefer to use survey data, despite problems in the accuracy of reported vote-switching, or other estimation techniques. On the other hand, the aggregate index does have the major advantage of being applicable to elections for which no survey estimates are available, an important consideration in long-term historical analyses. Moreover, although it may well underestimate the real levels of individual-level change, there is no logical reason to assume that underestimation is likely to be inconsistent over time, and in this sense, whatever its limits, variation in the aggregate index may usefully be employed as a valid *indicator* of variation in individual-level change.

Later analyses of electoral volatility have somewhat refined the original and introduced new variations. Ivor Crewe and David Denver (1985), for example, distinguished between net aggregate volatility, as measured by Pedersen, and gross volatility, which employs survey data to measure change at the individual level. Stefano Bartolini and Peter Mair (1990) distinguished three separate aggregate measures: total volatility (TV), as measured by Pedersen for the party system as a whole; bloc volatility (BV), which is derived by combining

Table 1. Volatility Calculation: Elections in Sweden, 1991 and 1994

Party	Percentage of votes		Percentage change
	1991	1994	
Left Party	4.5	6.2	+1.7
Social Democrats	37.7	45.2	+7.5
Center Party	8.5	7.7	-0.8
People's Party/Liberals	9.1	7.2	−1.9
Conservatives	21.9	22.4	+0.5
Christian Democrats	7.1	4.1	−3.0
New Democracy	6.7	1.2	−5.5
Green Party	3.4	5.0	+1.6
Others	1.0	1.0	—

Note: Total aggregate volatility = 11.25

the different parties into two or more blocs and measuring the net gains/losses of each of these blocs; and within-bloc volatility (WBV), which is the aggregate volatility that remains when BV is subtracted from TV. Although Bartolini and Mair restricted their subsequent analysis of BV to those blocs of parties that could be distinguished in terms of class cleavage, this mode of cross-party aggregation of BV can also be applied to other combinations of parties, including religious versus secular parties, incumbent versus nonincumbent parties, traditional versus new parties, and so on.

Although the index of total volatility does offer a very useful and intuitively meaningful summary measure of patterns of electoral stability or instability, there are three reasons why it may be misleading or misinterpreted. First, it is a very crude measure. All electoral changes are treated as equivalent, and a net aggregate shift in votes between two allied parties in a coalition government is given the same weight as a similar shift between two hostile parties. While the level of electoral instability is the same in both of these cases, the implications for the party system may be quite different. Second, the index figures that are cited by analysts may sometimes exaggerate the real levels of instability in that they sometimes fail to take into account vote shifts that result purely from splits in parties from one election to the next. In 1987 in Italy, for example, the Communist Party (PCI) won 26.6 percent of the vote. By the time of the following election in 1992, the PCI had split into two "new" parties, the Democratic Party of the Left (PDS), which polled 16.1 percent of the vote, and the Communist Refoundation (RC), which polled 5.6 percent of the vote. One measure of volatility in the 1992 election might interpret the PCI, which ceased to exist, as having lost 26.6 percent of the vote, with two new parties (PDS and RC) emerging to win 21.7 percent of the vote. Once other party gains and losses were taken into account, this would inevitably yield a very high level of volatility. An alternative measure of volatility, however, would compare the total

vote of the PDS and RC in 1992 to that of their joint predecessor, the PCI, in 1987, and would then add just 4.9 percent (26.6 percent minus 21.7 percent) to the overall volatility index to reveal a more muted level of change. Third, the index measures change in terms of the distribution of votes among the parties, and analysts usually fail to build into their measures those changes that result from movements in and out of the electorate, whether because of differential turnout levels, age qualifications, or death.

See also *Election Studies, Types of; Realigning Elections in the United States; Swing.*

PETER MAIR, UNIVERSITY OF LEIDEN

BIBLIOGRAPHY

Ascher, William, and Sidney Tarrow. "The Stability of Communist Electorates: Evidence from a Longitudinal Analysis of French and Italian Aggregate Data." *American Journal of Political Science* 10 (August 1975): 475–499.

Bartolini, Stefano, and Peter Mair. *Identity, Competition and Electoral Availability: The Stabilisation of European Electorates, 1885–1985.* Cambridge: Cambridge University Press, 1990.

Crewe, Ivor, and David Denver, eds. *Electoral Change in Western Democracies: Patterns and Sources of Electoral Volatility.* London: Croom Helm, 1985.

Katz, Richard S., Hans Rattinger, and Mogens N. Pedersen. "The Dynamics of European Party Systems." *European Journal of Political Research* 31 (February 1997): 83–97.

Pedersen, Mogens N. "The Dynamics of European Party Systems: Changing Patterns of Electoral Volatility." *European Journal of Political Research* 7 (March 1979): 1–26.

Przeworski, Adam. "Institutionalization of Voting Patterns, or Is Mobilization a Source of Decay?" *American Political Science Review* 69 (March 1975): 49–67.

VOTING BEHAVIOR, INFLUENCES ON

The public's regular choice of political leaders through elections is one of the bases of representative democracy, and the rationality of the public's choices is a measure of the meaningfulness of the democratic process.

Discussions about voting choice begin with a basic paradox: political decisions are complex, so how do voters select the "right" candidates or parties to represent their preferences? For instance, how does the average voter in a California primary know whom to vote for among several competitors for the governorship, whom to select for congressional and senatorial positions (as well as the state legislature), whether a school bond is economically justified, whom to elect to the local water board, whether a new parcel tax is needed, or whether English should be required in classroom instruction? Even more complicated is the question of how voters, collectively, can make the right choice, not just for themselves but also for their community or nation. Much of the literature on voting behavior has attempted to explain not only the factors that people use in making their voting choices but also how these choices provide a rational basis for public policy in a democracy.

THE EVOLUTION OF VOTING BEHAVIOR RESEARCH

Political pundits have always speculated about what motivates voters and have interpreted election outcomes based on their political observations. But voting-behavior research made a tremendous leap forward with the development of scientific public opinion polls in the late 1940s and early 1950s. For the first time, researchers could assess what a representative group of voters thought about the candidates, issues, and political parties of the day. Early voting-behavior research emphasized the social basis of voting choice. Individuals voted for a party that represented their class, religion, or other social group. In addition, most voters entered each election with standing preferences based on the parties' historical representation of specific social-group interests; thus campaigns mobilized partisans more than convinced people which party to support. Proponents of the sociological model argued that people acted politically as they were socially. In other words, sociological variables defined the common group interests that shaped party coalitions and popular images of which party was most attuned to the needs of various types of people.

Social-group voting simplifies decision making by giving voters sociological cues to guide their voting choices. Instead of trying to be informed on all the issues of the campaign, voters focus on the party (or parties) that historically have supported the social groups to which they belong. A voter who identifies with a specific social group can decide among competing parties based on cues such as the endorsements of labor unions, business associations, religious groups, and the like—as well as on the group appeals of the parties themselves. These cues provide a shortcut to rational vote choice. For instance, an autoworker in Detroit who voted for the party that disproportionately supports labor (the Democrats) was making a vote choice that in most instances reasonably represented his or her political interests. The stable group base of each party in the 1940s and 1950s also meant that many voters held partisan predispositions that endured across elections, further simplifying the decision process.

In Europe the sociological model linked the development of party systems to the historical evolution of social cleavages. In comparison with social forces in the United States, those in Europe seemed to exert an even stronger influence on the voting choice of Europeans, further underpinning the value of the sociological model. Social class appeared to be a standard influence on voting choice, with the middle class disproportionately supporting conservative parties and the working class supporting parties of the left. In nations with mixed religious denominations or strong anticlericalism, religion often

proved to be an even stronger influence than class on voting choice. Region, ethnicity, and rural/urban differences were other potentially important influences on party preferences. In summarizing these findings, Seymour Martin Lipset and Stein Rokkan (*Voting Systems and Party Alignments,* 1967, p. 50) voiced their now-famous conclusion that "the party systems of the 1960s reflect, with but few significant exceptions, the cleavage structure of the 1920s."

Our understanding of voting behavior made a major scientific advance with the publication by Angus Campbell et al. of *The American Voter* in 1960. This study introduced a social-psychological model of the vote. Campbell and his colleagues posited that voting choice was determined by individual attitudes and political beliefs, rather than by social factors. The model held that voters' opinions on the issues and evaluations of the candidates were the most direct influences on voting behavior and that they reflected the convergence of long-term political orientations and the short-term effects of the issues and personalities of the campaign.

The American Voter introduced many of the concepts that still guide electoral research today. The study described the elements of a political-belief system that voters use to conceptualize the political process. Other findings defined the specific elements of the issue opinions and candidate evaluations that determined vote choice and showed how they varied over time. These psychological variables were described as having an immediate impact on voting behavior, since they were more directly related to voting decisions than the social characteristics of the sociological model.

But these scholars also raised questions about the sophistication of contemporary electorates, and they asked whether voters possessed the abilities to make informed choices on the wide variety of issues potentially discussed at election time. Thus, researchers still needed to explain how voters simplify their electoral calculus and make reasonable voting choices.

The simplifying structure in the psychological model was the special role of long-term affective attachments to a preferred political party, or "party identification." Party identifications were supposedly formed early in life, often inherited from one's parents and then generally reinforced by habitual support for one's preferred party. These party identifications filter individuals' views of the political world, providing them with a means not only for making voting decisions (support one's own party) but also for interpreting and evaluating political phenomena. If the parties consistently represented distinct policy preferences, then habitual support of one's preferred party was both a simple and rational way to make voting decisions. Furthermore, partisanship was the ultimate cue for making political judgments, because virtually all issues and candidates could be linked to party supporters or opponents. Partisanship also influenced turnout and other forms of political participation. Partisans cared more about election outcomes, paid closer attention to the campaign, and were more likely to participate in the campaign and to turn out to vote.

The psychological approach of *The American Voter* was exported to other democracies through a series of collaborative cross-national research projects. Although these studies often illustrated the peculiarities of American electoral politics, and thus the difficulty of exporting American concepts, researchers often observed a functional equivalence between Europe and America in the central elements of the psychological model. The influence of this approach was so pervasive that party identification—and the model it represents—became the central theoretical concept in electoral research. In summary, the psychological model explained how individuals efficiently made their voting decisions and how they used psychological reference points in managing the complexity of political learning and political decision making.

The American Voter model remains the dominant paradigm in voting research, and most analysts of electoral politics would at least implicitly turn to the concepts and frameworks of this model in explaining voting behavior. In the last two decades, however, scholars have made several attempts to modify the psychological model. Some researchers argue that voters are not the habitual partisan voters implied in the psychological model. As the volatility in vote outcomes increased in American elections of the 1960s and 1970s, it became apparent that many individuals were shifting their votes from one party to another. Scholars reconceptualized party attachment as the cumulation of past experiences—not just a habitual attachment to a party learned early in life. Other scholars suggested that changes in the nature and context of democratic politics in advanced industrial societies were affecting the way that voting choices were made. In short, voting analysts came to believe that citizens are more rational and issue-oriented than implied in the sociological or psychological models, and that voting decisions are more dependent on the voters' evaluations of the issues and candidates of each campaign.

A CHANGING POLITICAL CONTEXT

Ironically, just as electoral researchers were describing how most Western party systems were frozen around the social cleavages of the 1920s or structured around enduring partisan attachments, dramatic changes began to affect these same systems.

One source of change was a transformation of the social bases of contemporary democracies. For example, virtually all industrial democracies have shared in increasing affluence for two generations. The rising incomes of the working class narrowed differences in living conditions between class strata and attenuated the importance of class-based political conflict. The growth of the service sector and government employment further reshaped the structure of labor forces, creating new postindustrial societies. These changes were paralleled by other shifts in the social structure. For instance, modern societies require a more educated labor force, and access to education expanded dramatically. Changing employment patterns also stimulate increased geographic mobility and urbanization. The traditional closed community life—be it in a rural village or working-class neighborhood—was gradually supplanted by more open, fluid, and cosmopolitan life styles for many citizens.

One consequence of these trends was a dramatic increase in the political skills and resources possessed by contemporary electorates—as best represented by increases in educational levels. For instance, almost half of the 1948 American electorate had only a primary education or less, and only a tenth had some college education. By 1996 these percentages had changed dramatically. American voters with some college education outnumbered those with only primary education by an eight-to-one ratio, and the college-educated made up almost two-thirds of the electorate.

The context for electoral decision making also changed. The expansion of the mass media created an information explosion. Where once a concerned citizen might have difficulty getting access to current political information, contemporary voters live in a hypersaturated media environment. It is easy to forget that our contemporary world of instant news and twenty-four-hour cable news services differs markedly from the information environment of even one generation ago. This change in the information environment lowers the effort voters must make to stay informed about politics and increases their potential exposure to a wider array of information. The development of the mass media also transformed how politics are conducted, placing more emphasis on candidates, their video style, and media-centered campaigning.

The political interests and values of contemporary electorates also shifted. Traditional economic concerns remain important, but their social base was blurred by rising affluence and a more complex labor-force structure. New issues have emerged onto the political agenda: concerns about environmental protection, minority rights, the role of women, and various lifestyle issues. Often these issues cut across the political and social cleavages that historically structured party competition; for example, social groups that were traditionally conservative on economic issues might be divided on these new cultural and lifestyle issues. At the least, the addition of new sources of party competition make stable and habitual patterns of party preferences less useful in making voting choices.

EROSION OF
TRADITIONAL INFLUENCES

The social trends transforming advanced industrial democracies have changed the structure of electoral choice and thus the influences on the voting behavior of contemporary electorates. For instance, one of the pillars of the sociological model was the importance of class voting. One of the most consistent patterns in voting behavior across nations in the post–World War II decades was that the working class leaned toward left-wing parties and the middle class toward conservative parties. This pillar has cracked and crumbled over the past generation; class voting is decreasing in virtually every established democratic party system. The simplest and most frequently used measure of class voting is the "Alford index," which computes the simple difference between middle-class and working-class support for left-wing parties. For example, in the 1957 West German election the two class strata differed by nearly 40 percentage points in their support for the Social Democratic Party; in recent German elections this difference has averaged about 10 percent. Similar declines are observed for other northern European democracies where class voting was initially strong. Even the class-based rhetoric that has emerged in recent campaigns—such as debates about the negative effects of economic globalization, the marginalization of labor, and the spread of "McJobs"—has not revived class voting differences in the United States or other Western democracies.

Because class voting has been one of the most broadly analyzed aspects of modern electoral research, evidence of its decline has generated substantial academic discussion. One line of research argues that crude measures of social class do not capture the present complexity of social structure and thus miss the continued relevance of class cues to voting. A variety of alternative class measures have been suggested. Yet the empirical reality remains: even these complex class frameworks have only a modest value in explaining how citizens vote. Class-based cues have become a less important influence on voting behavior in nearly all advanced industrial democracies.

Religion was the second main pillar of the sociological model. Early empirical voting research found that religious affiliations were often strongly linked to voting choice. The religious cleavage, however, has followed the same pattern of decline as the social class cleavage. In most Western democracies religious involvement has declined over the past forty years. In the Catholic nations of Europe, for instance, the number of people who attend church frequently has decreased by nearly half since the 1950s. Predominately Protestant countries, such as the United States and the nations of northern Europe, began with lower levels of church involvement but nevertheless have followed a similar downward trend. By definition, secularization means that fewer voters are integrated into religious networks and exposed to the religious cues that can guide the vote. The link between religious leaders and political parties has also weakened in most Western democracies. A generation ago, it was routine for Dutch priests or German pastors to remind their congregation of what God expected of them at election time. Now, direct church involvement in partisan politics is more often viewed as an intrusion. Despite the recent revival of fundamental religious movements in some Western democracies, the empirical evidence points to a declining influence of religion on voting behavior.

A similar erosion of influence can be observed for most other sociological characteristics. For instance, urban and rural voters display only modest differences in voting patterns, and these differences have generally narrowed as modernization has decreased the gap between urban and rural lifestyles. Despite repeated proclamations of an emerging gender gap, differences between the genders in voting behavior are small.

Perhaps the clearest exception to the rule of declining social cleavages is the case of race in the United States, in which one can identify pockets of solid partisan support—such as African Americans for the Democratic Party. At the same time, voting patterns of other ethnic groups in the United States (such as Latinos and Asian Americans) are not heavily biased toward one party, and racial minorities are smaller and less politically distinct in most European democracies. Region has shown some persisting importance for voting, but mostly when it overlaps with linguistic or ethnic conflict within nations, such as the language differences in Belgium and Canada or the identity politics of Spain's and Britain's regions. In most nations, however, region exerts only a minor influence on voting preferences.

When all the evidence is assembled, one of the most widely repeated findings of modern electoral research is the declining influence of sociological factors on voting behavior. The rate and timing of their decline varies across nations. In party systems like the United States and Japan, where social group-based voting was initially weak, the decline has occurred slowly. In other electoral systems, such as Germany, the Netherlands, and Italy, where sharp social divisions once structured the vote, the decline has been steady and dramatic.

Two sets of factors explain the decline in the sociological model of voting behavior. First, the ties between individuals and their respective social groups have weakened. Social cues may still be a potent influence on voting behavior for people who are integrated into traditional class or religious networks, but today fewer people are integrated into stable social structures, such as the working class milieu and religious networks that originally furnished the basis of the class and religious cleavages. Second, the connection between a political party and its social group constituency has blurred in many party systems. For instance, the constituency of the U.S. Democratic Party is now split along class, racial, and value lines. It is a monumental task to unite such diverse constituencies at election time, and even more difficult to sustain agreement during the governing process. A similar fragmentation of constituencies has affected social-democratic and conservative parties in Europe.

Furthermore, the broadening of political discourse, to include a wider range of political issues, and the increasing exposure to other information sources erode the value of fixed social characteristics as a guide to electoral choice. Even when economic conflicts are salient—for example, on issues such as tax reform, trade policy, or deficit reduction—social class is a poor guide to determining a voter's positions on these issues. Class cues carry even less value in determining positions on environmental quality, affirmative action, or gay rights. For the majority of the electorate, therefore, social position and the attendant political cues no longer provide a very useful shortcut to political decision making. It is not that voters do not have a social location (of course they do), or that voters cannot identify the parties in terms of traditional class positions (they can), but that these cues are of decreasing relevance to contemporary voters.

The psychological model maintains that partisanship is continually relevant, because most elections are partisan contests. And yet, party ties also have weakened in most advanced industrial democracies—producing a pattern of *partisan dealignment*. For instance, approximately 75 percent of the American electorate identified themselves as partisans prior to 1964; by 1972 the percentage of partisans had dropped to 64 percent, and it has remained in that range since. Electoral research finds evidence of weakening partisan ties in Europe that is remarkably similar to the partisan dealignment in the United States. Over 40 percent of the British public were strong partisans during the late 1960s; this percentage was cut in half in less than a decade. Comparative evidence uncovers similar patterns for most contemporary electorates.

Partisan dealignment means, by definition, that partisanship is becoming less important as an influence on vote choice. Furthermore, the new apartisans have distinct social characteristics and differ from the traditional partisan independents, who were uninformed and uninvolved in politics. The new independents are apartisan, rather than uninvolved. They are active participants in politics, although often outside party-related activities such as campaigns and elections. These new independents are also less consistent in their voting patterns because voting behavior is not dependent on long-standing party predispositions. Because apartisans are concentrated among the young, the better educated, and citizens

with postmaterial values, the continuing socioeconomic development of advanced industrial societies may reinforce the dealignment trend that has emerged over the past decade. The weakening of party ties also manifests itself in electoral results. For instance, the erosion of partisanship is visible in the declining stability of voting patterns. In addition, many of these voters express doubts about parties as institutions of representative democracy. Finally, voter turnout has decreased in most Western democracies, at least partially as the result of weakened partisanship.

What is stunning about these findings on the weakening of partisanship, as with the weakening of the sociological model, is the relative simultaneity of these trends across nations. There are several explanations for the spreading pattern of partisan dealignment. One involves the declining role of parties as political institutions. Many of the parties' traditional input functions have been taken over by other institutions. Special-interest groups and single-issue lobbies press their policy interests without relying on partisan channels. Similarly, the mass media are assuming many of the information and input functions that political parties once controlled. These and other developments lessen the importance of parties in the political process and therefore weaken the significance of parties as political reference points. In addition, the decline of partisanship reflects the growing sophistication of contemporary electorates and the growing ability of voters to make electoral decisions independent of traditional political cues such as social-group ties or hereditary partisanship.

CONTEMPORARY ELECTORAL CHOICE

Rather than thinking of an electorate's voting behavior in terms of a single model—such as a sociological or a psychological model—voting behavior is now fragmented into different subsectors or influenced by multiple factors. Thus different subgroups of the electorate may base their decisions on different criteria. For instance, although sociological influences on voting have generally decreased in importance, these cues remain potent for the small subsector of the population that is strongly integrated into traditional social networks. A Midwest farmer who attends the local church each Sunday may remain strongly committed to the Republican Party, just as a French industrial worker living in Paris may continue to support the Communist Party. For individuals embedded in such social milieus, social cues remain a powerful, and highly relevant, cue for voting behavior.

Other individuals are guided by their emotional attachments to a preferred party. Although the number of partisans has generally decreased, for those who retain such ties they provide a strong cue on which party to support. Such political loyalties also remain a potent influence on other aspects of political behavior, such as the evaluation of political actors and the tendency to participate in elections.

Today, however, fewer voters approach the election with such sociological or psychological predispositions. Many individuals base their decisions on the issues and candidates of the campaign and the influences of friends, colleagues, and other political cue-givers, which produces an individualization of voting choice. These voters are more likely to make their own political decisions without relying on group or party cues. This shift in the source of voting cues leads to an eclectic and egocentric pattern of political decision making, as voters base their electoral decisions on policy preferences, performance judgments, or candidate images.

There is still considerable debate on whether most voters fulfill the requirements of rational issue voting. Skeptics question whether voters are sufficiently informed about most issues to base their decisions on an appropriate evaluation of party stances on the issues, or whether apparent issue-based voting is merely the projection of other political orientations. Nevertheless, if social cues and partisanship are less central in electoral decision making, then voters must be turning to other factors—such as issues and candidates—to make their political decisions. Electoral research indicates that the decline in social group–based voting over time has been matched by an equivalent rise of issue voting.

One form of issue voting involves what are known as "position" issues. These are issues that divide the public into proponents and opponents, such as issues of nationalizing industry, increasing (or decreasing) spending on a policy area, or allowing abortion. An issue must meet several criteria to influence voting decisions. The issue must be salient in a campaign and to the voters, the parties must take contrasting stances on the issue, and voters must correctly perceive the parties' positions and vote for the one closest to their own policy position. Scholars have engaged in considerable debate on whether these requirements are fulfilled for most issues, and early electorate research tended to discount the likelihood of issue voting meeting these criteria.

Another form of issue voting involves "valence" issues. Valence issues are generally favored by the populace, and thus voters' evaluations focus on the performance of the government (or the opposition) in achieving these desired goals. For example, which party can best provide for a healthy economy, lessen crime, or ensure the nation enjoys peace? Such performance evaluations are important criteria that many voters use in making their political choices.

Election researchers have focused considerable attention on economic performance as a criterion for voting choice. Substantial evidence documents the importance of macroeconomics on micropolitics, both in the United States and Europe. Prosperous times often insulate a government from challenge at election time, and when times turn bad, the government's vulnerability increases.

Although the influence of such economic evaluations is noncontroversial, the evidence on its scope and nature remains a point of debate. One question concerns whether voters base their political evaluations on their own personal economic situation (egocentric voting) or on the performance of the broader national economy (sociotropic voting). Most of the evidence seems to suggest that voters follow the sociotropic model, which implies that policy outcomes, rather than narrow self-interest, are the driving force behind performance voting. Researchers also disagree on whether voters base their judgments on past economic performance or on prospective expectations for the economy's future performance. In either case, judgments about party and candidate performance along specific policy dimensions are shaping electoral choices, not long-term sociological or partisan predispositions.

Either form of issue voting—position or valence—raises the basic question of how voters gain the information to evaluate issues and the policy choices facing the government. One way that individuals deal with the information costs of issue voting is to take shortcuts: voters focus their attention on a few issues. The "issue public" for a given policy is normally a small subgroup of voters who are concerned about the policy and follow events more closely than the normal voter. Individuals in the subset of the public concerned with health care spending, for example, are more likely to be informed on the issues and make their electoral decisions based on which party represents their positions. Such issue publics, which exist for other policy areas as well, comprise the core of voters concerned with the policy and willing to incorporate this into their electoral choice. Issue publics also illustrate the patterns of fragmentation and individualization that characterize contemporary voting patterns.

In addition to focusing on a few topics, voters cope with the information costs of issue voting by using information shortcuts in deciding their position on issues and the appropriate electoral choice. Voters may follow the cues of friends, social groups, or the media to develop issue preferences. Such short-cuts, or *heuristics,* are especially apparent on referendum voting, where normal party cues may be lacking. But even in normal electoral politics, voters can turn to a variety of political cues to decide how to vote on specific issues.

Whereas electoral analysts have always thought of issues as desirable influences on the vote, they traditionally have viewed candidate evaluations less positively. Many analysts view voting on the basis of personality characteristics to be irrational. The cynical view of candidates is that they are attractively packaged commodities devised by image makers who manipulate the public's perceptions by emphasizing traits with special appeal to the voters. People's judgments about alternative candidates are, in this view, based on superficial criteria such as the candidate's style or looks.

Recently, some researchers have suggested a very different approach to candidate assessments. This approach holds that candidate evaluations are not necessarily superficial, emotional, or purely short-term. Voters may focus on the personal qualities of a candidate to gain important information about characteristics relevant to assessing how the individual will perform in office. This approach presumes that individuals organize their thoughts about other people into broad preexisting categories. These category "prototypes" are then used in making judgments when only limited factual information is available. Traits such as integrity, reliability, and competence are hardly irrational, for if a candidate is too incompetent to carry out policy promises, or too dishonest for those promises to be trusted, it makes perfect sense for a voter to reject a politician regardless of his or her party.

Candidate images often play an important role in American elections, because the electoral system and weak parties enable the candidates themselves to be the focus of the voters' electoral choices. In most parliamentary systems, the candidates' images are often subsumed within a political party's general appeal. In many nations the ballot lists a choice of parties, not individual candidates. Nevertheless, there is growing evidence that candidate images are increasing in importance in many parliamentary systems.

VOTING IN NEW DEMOCRACIES

Voting choice in the emerging democracies of eastern Europe is apparently similar to that we have just described in the mature Western democracies. These new party systems are unlikely to be based on stable group-based cleavages, especially since the democratic transition occurred quite rapidly. In the first rounds of elections following the collapse of communism in eastern Europe, the political images of many parties were ill-defined, a large number of parties competed in each election, and the party choices varied greatly between elections. Politics were too fluid for stable social coalitions to form as a basis of party support. Public opinion surveys also found that these electorates were less likely to hold long-term party attachments that might guide their behavior. If partisanship develops as citizens repeatedly support a preferred party, and these partisan ties are transmitted from generation to generation, then partisanship may develop over time.

The apparent similarity between the volatility of east European partisanship and the partisan dealignment in Western democracies is only superficial, however. Advanced industrial democracies are experiencing an evolution in the patterns of electoral choice that flow from the breakdown of long-standing alignments and party attachments, the development of a more sophisticated electorate, and efforts to move beyond the restrictions of representative democracy. The new electoral forces in Western democracies also are developing within a political and social setting in which traditional group-based and partisan cues still exert a significant, albeit diminishing, influence.

The new democratic party systems of eastern Europe face the task of developing the basic structure of electoral choice—the political frameworks that historically defined electoral choices in the West. A framework of social-group and partisan cleavages may provide a valuable starting point for this research, and the party-identification model may provide a basis for studying how new political identities form. At the present time, however, a stable framework for political competition has not yet developed.

There continues to be considerable electoral volatility in these new democracies. The volatility in electoral outcomes in nations such as Poland and Hungary mimics a pattern that occurred when Spain and Portugal undertook their democratic transitions in the 1970s. And yet, in the world of global television, greater knowledge about electoral politics (at the elite and public levels), and fundamentally different electorates, eastern Europe is unlikely to create party systems along the pattern of western Europe in the 1920s. The changing political context and the substantial economic and social problems facing these nations are likely to perpetuate a pattern of volatility for the near future.

THE CHANGING NATURE OF VOTING CHOICE

Electoral research has demonstrated how the influences on voting behavior have changed over time. Voter choices in most Western democracies traditionally were highly structured and relatively stable over time. Social institutions such as the unions and churches were major political actors, influencing both political elites and their membership. Because individuals were often ill-prepared to deal with the complexities of politics, they relied on the political cues of external reference groups in reaching political decisions. However, the decline of social group–based voting is one of the common developments affecting virtually all advanced industrial democracies.

One possible benefactor from the erosion of social-group cues could have been the political parties. Electoral politics are, after all, the primary mechanism of citizen mobilization in most democracies. And yet, people have also lessened their psychological ties to the political parties. Thus partisanship is also eroding as an influence on voting. This erosion has produced a decrease in party-line voting and an increase in partisan volatility, split-ticket voting, and other phenomena that indicate the public is no longer voting according to a party line.

These trends lead to the individualization of electoral choice. Electorates have shifted toward a more individualized and inwardly oriented style of political choice. Instead of following the pronouncements of party elites and social groups, more citizens now attempt to make their own political decisions. An eclectic and egocentric pattern of political decision making is developing. Rather than basing their electoral decisions on socially structured and relatively homogeneous personal networks, contemporary publics are more likely to base their decisions on policy preferences, performance judgments, or candidate images.

Voters' increasing reliance on the mass media contributes to these trends and reinforces them. The contemporary media provide voters with a greater variety of information sources and, potentially, a more critical perspective of established political actors such as parties, labor unions, and industries. Access to a diverse media environment enables people to become active selectors of information rather than passive consumers of political cues provided by others. In addition, the ability to see candidates and parliamentary leaders up close and "in person" on television has caused voters to pay more attention to the personal attributes of politicians, such as competence and integrity.

The individualization of politics also displays itself in the increasing heterogeneity of the public's interests, as seen in diverse issue publics; environmentalism, women's rights, and life-style choices have joined the already full agenda of advanced industrial democracies. In addition, schema theory argues that citizens are becoming fragmented into a variety of distinct issue publics. Individual citizens focus on the specific issues of immediate or personal importance.

These developments have the potential either to improve or to weaken the "quality" of the democratic process and the representation of the public's political interests. The nature of contemporary political beliefs means that public opinion is simultaneously becoming more fluid and less predictable. Uncertainty forces parties and candidates to become more sensitive to public opinion, or at least to the opinions of those who vote. Motivated issue voters are more likely than the average voter to at least have their voices heard, even if they are not accepted. Furthermore, the ability of politicians to communicate directly with voters can strengthen the link between politicians and the people. To some extent, the individualization of electoral choice revives the images of the informed independent voter that are found in classic democratic theory.

At the same time, there is a potential dark side to these new forces in electoral politics. The rise of single-issue poli-

tics handicaps a society's attempts to deal with political issues that transcend specific interests. A focus on issue publics also leaves the electorally inactive disenfranchised. Too great an interest in a single issue, or too much emphasis on recent performance, can produce a narrow rational motivation that is harmful to democracy. In addition, direct unmediated contact between politicians and citizens opens the potential for demagoguery and political extremism. Both extreme right-wing and left-wing political movements probably benefit from this new political environment, at least in the short term.

Early opinion analysts called for a mix of stability and change in mass politics as an essential feature of democracy. Today, the balance of this mix has changed significantly—there is far more change than stability, and the nature of electoral politics has been permanently altered.

See also *Bandwagon Effects; Citizen Juries; Downsian Model of Elections; Election Studies, Types of; Political Business Cycle; Public Opinion Polls: How They Work; Public Opinion Polls: Legal Regulation; Regulation of Television; Tactical Voting; Wasted Votes.*

RUSSELL J. DALTON, UNIVERSITY OF CALIFORNIA, IRVINE

BIBLIOGRAPHY

Butler, David, and Donald Stokes. *Political Change in Britain: The Evolution of Electoral Choice.* 2d ed. New York: St. Martin's, 1974.

Campbell, Angus, Philip Converse, Warren Miller, and Donald Stokes. *The American Voter.* New York: Wiley, 1960.

Dalton, Russell. *Citizen Politics: Public Opinion and Parties in Advanced Industrial Democracies.* 2d ed. Chatham: Chatham Publishers, 1996.

Evans, Geoffrey, and Pippa Norris, eds. *Critical Elections: British Parties and Voters in Long-term Perspective.* Thousand Oaks, Calif.: Sage, 1999.

Franklin, Mark, Tom Mackie, and Henry Valen, eds. *Electoral Change.* New York: Cambridge University Press, 1992.

Inglehart, Ronald. *Culture Shift in Advanced Industrial Society.* Princeton, N.J.: Princeton University Press, 1990.

LeDuc, Larry, Richard Niemi, and Pippa Norris, eds. *Comparing Democracies: Elections and Voting in Global Perspective.* Thousand Oaks, Calif.: Sage, 1996.

Lipset, Seymour Martin, and Stein Rokkan, eds. *Party Systems and Voter Alignments.* New York: Free Press, 1967.

Kiewiet, D. Roderick. *Macroeconomics and Micropolitics.* Chicago: University of Chicago Press, 1983.

Miller, Warren E., and Merrill Shanks. *The New American Voter.* Cambridge: Harvard University Press, 1996.

Nie, Norman, Sidney Verba, and John Petrocik. *The Changing American Voter,* enlarged edition. Cambridge: Harvard University Press, 1979.

Niemi, Richard G., and Herbert Weisberg, eds. *Controversies in Voting Behavior.* 3d ed. Washington, D.C.: CQ Press, 1992.

Popkin, Samuel. *The Reasoning Voter.* Chicago: University of Chicago Press, 1991.

Wattenberg, Martin. *The Decline of American Political Parties 1952–1966.* Cambridge: Harvard University Press, 1998.

VOTING MACHINES

See *Administration of Elections*

WASTED VOTES

Votes can be described as wasted when they do not influence the election outcome, either because they are cast for a candidate with no chance of winning in a single-member, first-past-the-post system, or because they have no chance of influencing the distribution of seats among parties in a proportional-representation system.

The idea of a wasted vote is complicated by uncertainty over which candidate will win. In first-past-the-post elections in which a close outcome is anticipated, a voter cannot be sure in advance of voting whether a vote will be wasted. Uncertainty is even greater in a proportional-representation system, where votes that might be wasted in district or regional counts are often pooled to assign seats at the national level. In a proportional-representation system, relatively few votes are wasted—only those cast for a party that fails to win the small percentage of votes needed to qualify for the distribution of seats in a district or nationwide.

The idea of a wasted vote is clearest in a first-past-the-post electoral system, since votes cast for all but the first place candidate are wasted. In a presidential election, votes cast for the losing candidate or candidates can be described as wasted, since a person who votes for a Republican when a Democrat is elected does not have his or her preferred representative heading the government. In safe seats that the same party consistently wins by a large margin, a person who votes against the incumbent party can reasonably expect this vote to be wasted. However, even if a vote does not support a winner, it does express an opinion and as such is not entirely wasted. A person who favors a Republican in a Democratic year or is a Conservative in a Labour constituency may regard it as desirable to give public evidence of this view. Insofar as the size of victory is important, a vote cast for a local loser is not completely wasted, as it either adds to the size of the party's national support or reduces the size of the lead of the national winner.

In a single-member district where there is a choice between three or more candidates, a voter whose preferred can-

didate is likely to finish third or lower can avoid wasting a vote by voting tactically for a second-choice candidate with a better chance of winning. When the fear of wasting a vote leads people to change their vote, the actual underlying division of opinion in the electorate will be distorted. In a proportional-representation system, one can vote for a party that does not come in first place locally while simultaneously voting for the winning party nationally.

Indirectly, a voter's readiness to support party or candidate X can influence party or candidate Y, causing Y to alter policies that appeal to those who might otherwise vote for X. Candidate Y may even have won as a consequence of moving closer to the position of X and thereby capturing some of X's votes. In such circumstances, a vote for X to support particular policies influences the victorious opponent to move close to positions that X favors. If it does, this vote will have had some effect. In the extreme case, when both candidates favor the same policies and differentiate themselves only in terms of symbolic party labels or personality, those sharing the views dominant in the electorate cannot waste their votes, for whichever candidate wins, both winner and loser have adopted their position.

The logic of indirect influence is equally applicable to the policies pursued by the government of the day. Those who vote for the losing candidates or parties are usually not ignored by the election winner; they are likely to be viewed as potential supporters in the next election, especially if the victor's margin is slight. The government of the day may regard it as essential to gain the support of former opponents in order to replace defectors from the coalition that initially elected it.

From the point of view of a candidate, a seat that he or she has little or no chance of winning is a hopeless seat. Why should a politician fight for a hopeless seat? In the British system, where candidacy is not restricted to the district in which a politician lives, fighting for a hopeless seat is often a way of gaining campaign experience, supporting the party cause, and subsequently being nominated for and winning a safe seat. Less ambitious candidates may serve as standard-bearers from a sense of loyalty or because they already have a position in local politics. In some cases, candidates do not know they are virtually certain of defeat and accept nomination for a hopeless seat in the belief that it could be won and that their effort would therefore not be wasted.

See also *Coordination, Electoral; Downsian Model of Elections; Effect of Elections on Government; Paradox of Voting; Safe Seat; Tactical Voting; Voting Behavior, Influences on.*

RICHARD ROSE, UNIVERSITY OF STRATHCLYDE

BIBLIOGRAPHY

Cox, Gary W. *Making Votes Count: Strategic Coordination in the World's Electoral Systems.* New York: Cambridge University Press, 1997.

Downs, Anthony. *An Economic Theory of Democracy.* New York: Harper, 1957.

Lakeman, Enid. *How Democracies Vote: A Study of Majority and Proportional Electoral Systems.* 3d ed. London: Faber and Faber, 1970.

WEIGHTED VOTING

Weighted voting refers to election systems in which voters are able to cast votes of varying values. One obvious example is a company meeting where shareholders cast votes weighted to reflect the number of stock shares they own. Votes cast by delegates at political party conventions provide another example of weighted voting. In this instance, the individuals who are casting the weighted votes have been elected to represent a state or district. A third example can be found in the United States in the structure of the electoral college, which is responsible for the election of the U.S. president. There, the number of electoral votes assigned to each of the fifty states reflects the size of each state's representation in Congress.

Weighted voting provides a solution to the problem of how to represent political subdivisions of varying population sizes in a body that makes decisions that are binding on the whole community. For many years, New York State's Nassau County used weighted voting for its six-member County Board of Supervisors. Members of the board were able to cast either one, two, or four votes at the board meetings, depending on the size of the towns or cities they represented. During the same period, New York City's Board of Estimate also used a weighted voting strategy: the mayor and two other city-wide elected officials cast two votes each, while the presidents of the five boroughs were able to cast one vote each.

Problems with weighted voting systems have been apparent for quite some time. In 1842 the U.S. House of Representatives debated a bill prohibiting the use of statewide, at-large elections for the selection of its members. Such a system resulted in state delegations composed of members of only one political party. Those delegations combined to form a single bloc of votes. One critic of the plan predicted that if all

states followed this system, the six states with the largest blocs of votes would together constitute a majority able to determine the passage or defeat of all proposed legislation, effectively leaving all other states powerless.

As this early example demonstrates, a problem with most weighted voting systems is that the proportion of *votes* allotted to a unit is not the same as the proportion of *power* that the unit is able to wield in the legislature. It was this feature of weighted voting that New York courts found unacceptable in the 1960s. The courts ordered Nassau and other counties to adopt for their Board of Supervisors a system of weighted voting that was proposed by mathematician John Banzhaf. Banzhaf argued that weighted voting systems could be made fair if a unit's share of power—not its share of votes—is made proportionate to the unit's share of the population. Banzhaf defined power as the number of times, given all possible combinations of yea–nay votes among board members, that a unit's member would be able to cast the decisive vote resulting in either the passage or the defeat of a bill. As of 2000, some twenty counties in New York State continue to use this system, relying on a computer program to calculate the number of votes to be allotted to each unit to produce proportionate power shares. In 1989, however, the U.S. Supreme Court refused to allow New York City's Board of Estimate to adopt Banzhaf's system, arguing that the assumption on which it is based—that board members are autonomous, independent actors as likely to vote one way as to vote the other way—is totally unrealistic.

A second problem with weighted voting systems became evident in the wake of the Supreme Court's 1964 *Reynolds v. Sims* decision requiring that state legislative districts be made substantially equal in population. One way of meeting that requirement, some believed, would be for states to continue using counties or other units of local government as units of representation in the state legislature, but now having the elected representatives cast votes weighted to reflect the size of their unit's population. Critics of this plan successfully argued that legislators do much more than cast votes: they make speeches, serve on committees, and provide service to constituents. Legislators from units of varying size cannot be expected to serve constituents equally well in these several roles.

Internationally, the best known example of weighted voting is seen in the Council of Ministers of the European Union, where each of the four largest nations are given ten votes each, while the other members of the council are given anywhere from two to eight votes each.

See also *Plural Voters; Reapportionment and Redistricting.*

HOWARD SCARROW,
STATE UNIVERSITY OF NEW YORK, STONY BROOK

BIBLIOGRAPHY

Banzhaf, John. "Weighted Voting Doesn't Work." *Rutgers Law Review* 19 (winter 1965): 317–343.

Board of Estimate v. Morris, 489 U.S. 688 (1989).

Felsenthal, Dan, and M. Machover. *The Measurement of Voting Power.* Northampton, Mass.: Edward Elgar Press, 1998.

Reynolds v. Sims, 317 U.S. 533 (1964).

Scarrow, Howard. *Parties, Elections, and Representation in the State of New York.* New York: New York University Press, 1983.

WINNING AN ELECTION

Winning an election can refer to three different but linked achievements: winning the most votes; winning the most seats in a parliament or congress; or winning control of government. There is no empirical or logical necessity that at a given election the same party be declared the "winner" on all three criteria. The relation between winning votes and winning seats depends on the rules of the electoral system in use and the distribution of votes. The relation between votes and seats and gaining control of government depends on the number of offices contested; for example, there can be only one winner of a presidential ballot, whereas a multiplicity of parties usually win seats in a parliamentary election. In countries where there is a separate contest for the legislature and the presidency and they share concurrent powers, such as the United States, it is possible for different parties to win control of different parts of the same government.

WINNING A CONSTITUENCY

Every election invariably results in one candidate or party winning the most votes; a tie outcome in a constituency is very unlikely when thousands of votes are cast, and even less likely in the total national vote. In a first-past-the-post system the candidate with the most votes is the winner, except where turnout must exceed a set figure, usually half the registered electorate, in order to make the election result valid or where a supermajority is required in order to secure a consensus, as in papal elections. However, the leading candidate will be certain to receive an absolute majority only if there are just two candidates on the ballot.

In the first-past-the-post electoral systems used to elect members of the U.S. Congress or the British Parliament, the leading candidate does not need an absolute majority to become the winner. When three or more candidates compete, it is possible that the leading candidate will have less than half the vote. The more evenly matched the competitors are, the greater the possibility that the leader in a three-candidate race will have less than 40 percent of the vote. In a five-candidate contest in the Scottish constituency of Inverness in the 1992 British general election, the Liberal candidate won with 26.0 percent of the constituency vote.

In the election of the Australian House of Representatives the alternative vote system is used to ensure that the winning candidate secures more than half the vote. To make this happen, each voter is asked to list candidates in order of preference. If the leading candidate has less than half the first-preference vote, then the second preferences of candidates at the bottom of the count are distributed to higher-ranking candidates until one gets an absolute majority.

In a first-past-the-post system the normal way of ensuring that the winner has more than half the vote is to hold a second ballot if no candidate secures half the vote in the first ballot. In this "run-off" round, only the leading candidate and the runner up are entered as contestants. This is the case in the election of a French president. Since half a dozen or more candidates may compete in the first round, the outcome of the second round can reverse the order of candidates. For example, in the first round of the 1995 French presidential ballot the Socialist candidate, Lionel Jospin, led with 23 percent of the vote, and Jacques Chirac, a Gaullist, came in second with 21 percent. But in the second round runoff, Chirac won, taking 53 percent of the vote when competing solely against Jospin. A similar system operates in the election of governors in some American states. France also has a two-round system for electing members to the National Assembly from single-member districts. To be eligible to contest the second round, a candidate must win at least 12.5 percent of the vote in the first round. If more than two candidates choose to contest in the second round, a simple plurality is sufficient to be the winner.

WINNING SEATS IN THE LEGISLATURE

At the national level, the party that has won an absolute majority of seats or the party that has won the most seats in parliament, even if not a majority, may be described as the leading party. Since the number of seats in a legislature is relatively small, it is possible in a parliament with an even number of seats for there to be a tie, that is, for the governing coalition to have half the seats and the opposition to have half the seats. To avoid this, the Swedish Riksdag changed its composition from 350 to 349 seats before the 1976 election.

The outcome of a proportional-representation election invariably produces a leading party, but that party usually falls well short of winning half the seats because seats in Parliament as well as votes are shared among half a dozen or more parties. The likelihood of winning one or more seats encourages a large number of parties to contest elections, since a party with a few percent of the votes can win a few seats in parliament. In the Netherlands, for example, so many parties have some popular appeal that the "winning" (that is, leading) party can have less than one-quarter of the popular vote, and in Belgium the winning party can have as little as one-sixth of the popular vote.

The electoral system's method of translating votes into seats also affects the identification of a winner. A proportional-representation system normally produces a leading party with a plurality of seats; but that leading party is usually not the winner in the sense of having more than half the seats. Moreover, a leading party that sees the size of its plurality reduced as a consequence of losing seats to its competitors may not be considered the winner, even if it remains the largest party in parliament.

The first-past-the-post system usually manufactures a majority in the House of Commons for a party with less than half the vote, making it easier to fix responsibility for government than is the case with a coalition government. No British party has won half the popular vote since the 1935 election.

The first-past-the-post system can even manufacture a majority of seats for a party that was not first in votes. In the 1951 British general election, the Conservative Party won fewer votes than the Labour Party but won a majority of seats in Parliament, and in February 1974 the Labour Party won more seats than the Conservatives even though the latter won a larger share of the popular vote. Such reversals can occur if one party "wastes" votes by piling up big majorities in some constituencies while losing by a narrow margin in others.

WINNING CONTROL OF GOVERNMENT

If control of government is in the hands of a prime minister accountable to parliament and there is no president with strong executive powers, then a party that wins an absolute majority of seats wins control of government. However, the use of proportional representation in many parliamentary systems normally results in no party winning a majority of the seats.

When no party wins half of the seats, the party with the most seats is usually, but not always, asked to nominate its choice for prime minister. In such circumstances a coalition government requires the support of a majority of the members of parliament to remain in office. If the largest party has seen its share of the vote fall, then it may be excluded from the new coalition government. For example, in 1991 the Swedish Social Democratic Party, then in government, saw its seats in parliament fall from 156 to 138, and the leader of the second-ranking party, with 80 seats, formed a four-party coalition government without the Social Democrats. When several parties form a coalition government, the vote for one coalition partner often goes up while that for another goes down.

A presidential election produces a single winner, whatever the method of election. But in the United States, members of both houses of Congress are elected on the same day as the president. This makes it possible for one party to win the White House and the other party to win a majority in one or both houses of Congress, thus producing an election in which both parties can claim to be winners and control of government is divided. In France the situation is more complex because the powers of the French president in relation to the French National Assembly are greater than the American president's in relation to Congress. Furthermore, the French president is elected for a seven-year term of office, whereas the maximum term of the National Assembly is five years. The presidential election is therefore regarded as the "biggest" election to win. The same is true in the Russian constitution drafted by President Boris Yeltsin. However, if a parliament elected more recently than a president has a majority that is opposed to the president, then its fresh electoral mandate and legislative powers may force the president to reach a "power-sharing" arrangement.

The media reporting of public opinion polls introduces a double distortion in the identification of an election winner. The candidate or party coming first in a public opinion poll has not won anything (except a headline), since no election has taken place. Furthermore, the reporting of popular preferences takes no account of the conversion of votes into seats according to the rules of the national election system. Polls also influence expectations, so that a candidate or party that draws significantly more votes than expected can be described as having done "well."

See also *Accountability, Elections as one form of; Alternative Vote; Bonus Seats; Choice, Elections as a Method of; Cube Law; Double Simultaneous Vote; Duverger's Law; Effect of Elections on Government; Fractionalization Index; Government Formation and Election Outcomes; Manufactured Majorities; Papal Elections; Proportionality and Disproportionality; Public Opinion Polls: How They Work; Second Ballot (or Runoff); Wasted Votes.*

RICHARD ROSE, UNIVERSITY OF STRATHCLYDE

BIBLIOGRAPHY

Cole, Alistair, and Peter Campbell. *French Electoral Systems and Elections since 1789.* 3d ed. Aldershot: Gower, 1989.
Cox, Gary W., and Samuel Kernell, eds. *Divided Government.* Boulder, Colo.: Westview Press, 1991.

Mackie, Thomas T., and Richard Rose. *The International Almanac of Electoral History.* 3d ed. Washington, D.C.: CQ Press, 1991.

Rose, Richard. *What Is Europe?* New York: Addison Wesley Longmann, 1996.

Rose, Richard, and Thomas T. Mackie. "Incumbency in Government: Asset or Liability?" In *Western European Party Systems,* edited by Hans Daalder and Peter Mair, 115–137. London and Beverly Hills: Sage Publications, 1983.

Taagepera, Rein, and Matthew Soberg Shugart. *Seats and Votes: The Effects and Determinants of Electoral Systems.* New Haven, Conn.: Yale University Press, 1989.

WOMEN: ENFRANCHISEMENT

The enfranchisement of women is the process whereby they are granted the right of citizenship, including the right to vote (suffrage), to contest for political office, and to participate equally in governmental decision making.

Citizenship refers to the rights and duties of inhabitants—however defined—of countries or municipalities and certain regions. Pericles, the Athenian statesman, omitted slaves and women from his definition of the ideal democratic citizen. The U.S. Declaration of Independence and the French Revolution's Declaration of the Rights of Man and Citizen also excluded women. It was not until the twentieth century that the definition of citizen was expanded to include women. In 1948 the United Nations Universal Declaration of Human Rights stated that everyone has a right to take part in the governing of her or his country, that the right of equal citizenship in political life should be held by women as well as by men. This includes not only the right of women to elect others and to stand for election, but to have an equal opportunity to be elected to the nation's governmental bodies and to participate fully in decision making.

The United Nations Platform of Action, adopted by 188 countries in Beijing at the Fourth World Conference on Women in 1995, stated the significance of women's equality in decision making: "Women's equal participation in decision making is not only a demand for simple justice and democracy but can also be seen as a necessary condition for women's interests to be taken into account."

CHRONICLING WOMEN'S ENFRANCHISEMENT

Beginning in 1906 and extending through 1920, the first legal enfranchisement of women occurred in just a few countries, comprising only 10 percent of the world's nations. By 1994, 95 percent of the world's nations had enfranchised women. In the accompanying box are listed those countries where women had an unrestricted right to vote (for example, no property or older age requirements) as well as the right to be candidates for public office. (Missing from the available sources are accounts of women's enfranchisement in some African, Asian, and Pacific matriarchal societies and in the frontiers of colonial powers and elsewhere in the non-Western world. This explains why mostly Western nations are listed as the first to gain early enfranchisement. However, the worldwide movement for enfranchisement developed a short time later.)

For women of the nineteenth and twentieth centuries, enfranchisement was a matter of equal justice: if men could vote and stand for election, then women should have the same rights. Although men's vote was not extended initially to all classes and races, universal male enfranchisement generally preceded women's by some fifty years. In some countries it took much longer. Men won universal suffrage in France in 1848, but it was not until 1944 that French women achieved national voting and standing rights.

By the end of the twentieth century there were only a few countries where only men were granted the right to vote, as in Kuwait. In a few others both men and women were denied the right to vote and to stand for election. The latter includes Saudi Arabia, Qatar, Oman, and the United Arab Emirates. Although the right to stand for election—to be a candidate and be elected—follows in theory from the right to vote, early on several countries granted women the right to vote without giving them the right to stand for office. In these countries, women's suffrage was restricted to the right to vote for male candidates only. For example, New Zealand granted women's suffrage very early, in 1893, but did not allow women to stand for office until over a generation later, in 1919.

Conversely, some countries gave women the right to stand for office before they gave women the right to cast a vote. Norway, the Netherlands, and Guyana, for example, allowed women to run for office and be elected by an all-male electorate. This denied a woman candidate her vote, as well as votes of a possible women's constituency.

THE CONTEXT OF WOMEN'S ENFRANCHISEMENT

In each country and within regions, the movement for women's political rights generally grew in three phases. Phase I, the development phase, took place amid the fervor of reform social movements, including men's franchise, the rights of labor, socialism, alcohol temperance, and national independence. During this phase women organized and mobilized for their political and social rights, including the right to private property. Phase II, the achievement phase, is when women's legal enfranchisement was most often won, toward the end of wars, coups, or revolutions and upon the gaining of national independence. Phase III is implementation, which will be considered in the last section.

WOMEN'S UNRESTRICTED RIGHT TO VOTE AND STAND FOR ELECTION, BY YEAR

Year	Countries	Year	Countries
1906	Finland	1955	Cambodia, Ethiopia, Honduras, Nicaragua, Peru
1913	Norway	1956	Benin, Comoros, Egypt, Gabon, Mali, Mauritius, Somalia
1915	Denmark, Iceland		
1918	Austria, Estonia, Germany, Kyrgyzstan, Latvia, Poland, Russian Federation	1957	Malaysia
		1958	Burkina Faso, Chad, Guinea, Hungary, Lao People's Democratic Republic
1919	Belarus, Luxembourg, New Zealand, the Netherlands, Ukraine	1959	Madagascar, Tunisia, United Republic of Tanzania
1920	Albania, Czech Republic, Slovakia, United States	1960	Canada, Cyprus, Gambia, Tonga
1921	Armenia, Azerbaijan, Georgia, Lithuania, Sweden	1961	Burundi, El Salvador, Malawi, Mauritania, Paraguay, Rwanda, Sierra Leone
1924	Mongolia, Saint Lucia, Tajikistan	1962	Algeria, Australia, Monaco, Uganda, Zambia
1927	Turkmenistan	1963	Congo, Equatorial Guinea, Fiji, Iran, Kenya, Morocco
1928	Ireland, United Kingdom		
1931	Spain, Sri Lanka	1964	Bahamas, Libyan Arab Jamahiriya, Papua New Guinea, Sudan
1932	Maldives, Thailand, Uruguay		
1934	Brazil, Cuba	1965	Afghanistan, Botswana, Lesotho
1937	Philippines	1967	Ecuador, Kiribati, People's Democratic Republic of Yemen, Tuvalu
1938	Uzbekistan		
1942	Dominican Republic	1968	Nauru, Swaziland
1944	Bulgaria, France, Jamaica	1970	Yemen Arab Republic, Zaire
1945	Croatia, Indonesia, Italy, Senegal, Slovenia, Togo	1971	Switzerland
1946	Cameroon, Democratic People's Republic of Korea, Guatemala, Liberia, Myanmar, Panama, Romania, Trinidad and Tobago, Venezuela, Vietnam, Yugoslavia	1972	Bangladesh
		1973	Andora, San Marino
		1974	Jordan
		1975	Angola, Cape Verde, Mozambique, São Tomé and Príncipe
1947	Argentina, Japan, Malta, Pakistan, Singapore	1976	Portugal
1948	Belgium, Israel, Niger, Republic of Korea, Seychelles, Suriname	1977	Guinea Bissau
		1978	Zimbabwe
1949	Bosnia and Herzegovina, Chile, China, Costa Rica	1979	Micronesia (Fed. States), Palau
		1980	Iraq, Vanuatu
1950	Barbados, Haiti, India	1984	Liechtenstein
1951	Antigua and Barbuda, Dominica, Grenada, Nepal, Saint Kitts and Nevis, Saint Vincent and the Grenadines	1986	Central African Republic
		1989	Namibia
		1990	Samoa
1952	Bolivia, Côte d'Ivoire, Greece, Lebanon	1994	Kazakhstan, South Africa
1953	Bhutan, Guyana, Mexico, Syrian Arab Republic		
1954	Belize, Colombia, Ghana		

Note: Oman, Qatar, Saudi Arabia, and the United Arab Emirates lacked enfranchisement for women and men as of 1994.
Source: Democracy Still in the Making. Geneva: Inter-Parliamentary Union, 1997, 28.

In the developmental phase in the United States, many women leaders of the suffrage movement had been active in the movement to abolish slavery and in the alcohol temperance movement while also advancing women's rights. Women's suffrage in the United States was achieved shortly after World War I. Women in the Nordic countries of Finland, Iceland, and Norway gained the right to vote and contest for office during the struggle for national independence. Nearby Russia proclaimed women's voting and standing rights as its socialist revolution developed. Enfranchisement followed in neighboring Estonia, Latvia, and Poland and in Germany, Austria, and the Netherlands. Thus, the northern and eastern

European region achieved enfranchisement at the end of World War I as independence and revolutionary movements neared completion.

The enfranchisement trend continued throughout the first half of the twentieth century in a few European countries (Belgium, France, Ireland, and the United Kingdom). Beginning in the 1930s the movement succeeded in some Asian (Thailand and Sri Lanka), South American (Brazil, Cuba, and Uruguay), and African (Senegal, Togo) countries. In these countries, the context of success was phase II conditions—following coups, revolutions, and independence movements.

During the second half of the twentieth century, from 1950 to 1994, demands for national independence accelerated in the developing countries. As decolonization gained force, more than one hundred countries achieved independence or loosened their ties with their former colonial rulers. Most gave enfranchisement simultaneously to women and men. Some countries within regions seemed to move together: Antigua, Barbados, and Saint Kitts and Nevis in the Caribbean achieved suffrage in the 1950s. The African nations of Congo, Kenya, Uganda, and Zambia did so in the 1960s. For most, independence meant suffrage and standing rights for all.

AFTER LEGAL ENFRANCHISEMENT, WAS EQUAL CITIZENSHIP ACTUALLY ACHIEVED?

Although the twentieth century was the time of equal voting rights, it was only minimally a time of equal citizen rights for women. The UN goal of equality in governmental decision making generally was not achieved in the twentieth century. In 1997, nearly a hundred years after enfranchisement was first

obtained, the average percentage of women national legislators in the world was only 12 percent, while men lawmakers were 88 percent. In developing nations women comprised only 9 percent of legislators. The average in long-standing democracies was 20 percent.

The above averages conceal the fact that in a few countries at the end of the twentieth century there was a definite trend toward the implementation of legal enfranchisement. In about 6 percent of democratic nations, women have garnered 25 to 40 percent of the national legislative seats. Their political representation has been growing in the older democracies and in the newer ones as well. These developments portend more women cabinet members, for the proportion of women in the cabinet generally follows their presence in the national legislature. Although women prime ministers and presidents at the close of the twentieth century were only about 5 percent of the world's elected leaders, their numbers are on an upswing.

Table 1 lists the leading countries in implementing women's enfranchisement. On the cusp of the twenty-first century, these countries had at least 25 percent women legislators. Note that long-standing women's enfranchisement is not a prerequisite for advancing women's political rights. In Table 1 Argentina's and South Africa's leadership demonstrate that developing democracies that were later in achieving the vote may rather quickly move toward equal citizenship for their women.

What distinguishes these leading eleven states? First, most have an electoral arrangement that usually favors women—namely the party-list proportional representation system. The number of representatives in each district usually averages seven to twelve, which gives ample room for women to be

Table 1. Leading Countries in Women's Citizenship: Countries with a Minimum of 25 Percent Women Parliamentarians, 1997

Country	Year of enfranchisement	Percent women MPs	Electoral system	Quota for women's nominations
Sweden	1921	40.4	party-list PR	yes
Norway	1913	39.4	party-list PR	yes
Finland	1906	33.5	party-list PR	yes
Denmark	1915	33.0	party-list PR	yes
Netherlands	1919	31.3	party-list PR	yes
New Zealand	1919	29.2	mixed PR and majority/plurality	yes
Austria	1918	26.8	party-list PR	yes
Germany	1918	26.2	mixed PR and majority/plurality	yes
Iceland	1915	25.4	party-list PR	yes
Argentina	1947	25.0	party-list PR	yes
South Africa	1994	25.0	party-list PR	yes

Source: Democracy Still in the Making. Geneva: Inter-Parliamentary Union, 1997, 64–77, 90–97.

added to a political party's list of candidates. Two of the countries listed in Table 1 have a mixed proportional representation/majoritarian electoral system. Second, they have taken deliberate steps to nominate 30 to 50 percent women on their party lists, with left and Green parties having the largest quotas. There are quota laws, as in Argentina, or simply affirmative party rules, as in the Nordic countries.

Looking back at women's legal enfranchisement at the start of the twentieth century, only 10 percent of the world's nations enfranchised women, but by the end of the century that figure was at 95 percent. Yet in spite of widespread voting rights, the twenty-first century begins with only a small number of countries leading the way toward women's equal participation in political decision making. If present trends continue, other countries will follow, and the twenty-first will be the century of equal citizenship for women.

See also *Candidates: Selection; Franchise Expansion; Gender Quotas; Proportional Representation; Women: Representation and Electoral Systems.*

WILMA RULE, UNIVERSITY OF NEVADA, RENO

BIBILIOGRAPHY

Flexner, Eleanor. *A Century of Struggle: The Women's Rights Movement in the United States.* New York: Atheneum, 1970.

Haavio-Mannila, Elina, et al. *Unfinished Democracy: Women in Nordic Politics.* New York: Pergamon, 1985.

Meleisea, Penelope Schoeffel. "Women and Political Leadership in the Pacific Islands." In *Suffrage and Beyond: International Feminist Perspectives,* edited by Caroline Daley and Melanie Nolan, 107–123. New York: New York University Press, 1994.

Pateman, Carole. "Three Questions about Womanhood Suffrage." In *Suffrage and Beyond: International Feminist Perspectives,* edited by Caroline Daley and Melanie Nolan, 331–348. New York: New York University Press, 1994.

Ramirez, Francisco O., Yasemin Soysal, and Suzanne Shanahan. "The Changing Logic of Political Citizenship: Cross-National Acquisition of Women's Suffrage Rights, 1890 to 1990." *American Sociological Review* 62 no. 5 (October 1997): 735–745.

Rule, Wilma. "Political Rights, Electoral Systems, and the Legislative Representation of Women in 73 Democracies: A Preliminary Analysis." In *Global Policy,* edited by Stuart Nagel. New York: Marcel Dekker, forthcoming.

Southard, Barbara. "Colonial Politics and Women's Rights: Woman Suffrage Campaigns in Bengal, British India in the 1920's." *Modern Asian Studies* 27 (May 1993): 397–439.

United Nations. "The Beijing Declaration and the Platform for Action." New York: United Nations Department of Public Information, 1995.

WOMEN: REPRESENTATION AND ELECTORAL SYSTEMS

Debates about electoral reform have revolved around the practical impact of changes to the status quo. Underlying these arguments are contested visions about the fundamental principles of representative democracy and the central normative criteria that an electoral system should meet. In addition is the question of whether the virtues of strong and accountable government are more or less important than social representation, including the inclusion of women and ethnic minorities.

It is well known that women continue to be strongly under-represented in elected office despite trends in the family and the work force that have transformed almost every aspect of women's and men's lives during the post–World War II era and the growth of the women's movement that has altered the political culture. In the spring of 1999 there were just under 5,000 women in parliaments worldwide, representing 13.3 percent of the membership of lower houses and 10.6 percent of upper houses.

The situation varies markedly by region; women do best in the Nordic region (topped by Sweden) where they make up, on average, 38.3 percent of the members in the lower houses. Compare this with a representation of only 3.6 percent in the Arab states (such as Djibouti, Kuwait, and the United Arab Emirates) that have few or no female representatives in parliaments. The proportion of women members elsewhere falls between these extremes: the Americas (15.4 percent), Europe (15.0 percent), Asia (14.3 percent), sub-Saharan Africa (11.6 percent), and the Pacific (11.5 percent). The rank order of countries reveals that the level of socioeconomic development is not a necessary condition for women's success. In South Africa, Mozambique, and Costa Rica, for example, female representation is far higher than in the United States, Italy, and Japan.

The key issue is how electoral systems affect the structure of opportunities for women's representation. Since the seminal works of Maurice Duverger (1954) and Douglas Rae (1971), a flourishing literature has classified the main types of electoral systems and sought to analyze their consequences. The two most important factors that affect women's representation are the basic electoral formula that determines how votes are counted to allocate seats and the use of legal strategies of affirmative action.

THE ELECTORAL FORMULA

Electoral formulas are commonly categorized into four main types. Proportional representation systems include open and closed party lists in regional or national constituencies and make use of largest remainders or highest averages formulas. Semiproportional systems include the single transferable vote, cumulative vote, and limited vote. Majoritarian electoral systems include plurality, second ballot, and the alternative vote. Mixed systems are those like the additional member system; they combine majoritarian and proportional elements.

Studies have established that party-list proportional representation facilitates the entry of women into elected office in established democracies. In Western democracies the difference in women's representation between proportional representation and majoritarian systems was quite modest until the 1970s, but the gap expanded in the 1980s. District magnitude is commonly seen as particularly important; more women are usually elected from large, multimember constituencies. Three reasons are often given for this phenomenon.

First, in multimember districts, parties attempting to maximize their appeal have an electoral incentive to produce a balanced ticket and to include in lists of candidates for each district all social groups, such as northerners and southerners, farmers and shopkeepers, and women and men. Second, balancing the slate in proportional representation systems also avoids internal conflict between party factions—trade unions or women's branches, for example—struggling to influence the selection process. Last, proportional representation facilitates the use of measures of affirmative action and gender parity to encourage the selection of more women candidates.

Some of these qualities are also present in semiproportional systems, such as the single transferable vote used in Ireland, but these systems usually have a smaller number of candidates (4–5) in each district. In contrast, in majoritarian systems, candidates are selected for single-member districts. Where the selection process is in the hands of the local constituency party, there is no incentive for local members to pick a ticket that is balanced at the district or national level. In these systems, party members often select a member who they believe will maximize their chances of winning in that constituency, irrespective of the broader consequences for

parliament. In mixed systems, such as in elections to the German Bundestag, it is likely that far more women are elected through party lists instead of through single-member districts.

One important question is whether the relation between electoral systems and female representation continues to hold in the late 1990s in a wider range of newer and established democracies. We can compare the representation of women based on the proportion of women elected to all lower houses in May 1999. The comparison is restricted to fifty-three democratic or semidemocratic states, defined as those countries with a combined Freedom House Gastil index of 4 or less, thereby excluding parliaments in authoritarian systems or under military rule that cannot exercise more than a symbolic role.

The comparison confirms that in the 1990s women continue to be better represented under proportional representation list systems. As a simple rule, women proved twice as likely to be elected under proportional representation than under majoritarian electoral systems. Women were 10.8 percent of the members of parliament in majoritarian systems, 15.1 percent in mixed or semiproportional systems, and 19.8 percent of members in proportional representation systems.

The pattern was far from linear *(see Figure 1)* because of intervening systemic factors such as the structure of opportunities to enter legislative office. In particular, the process of recruitment within parties, including the informal and formal rules and the party organization, strongly influences the opportunities for women in elected office. More women were

Figure 1. Percentage of Women MPs in the Lower House, by Electoral System, 1999

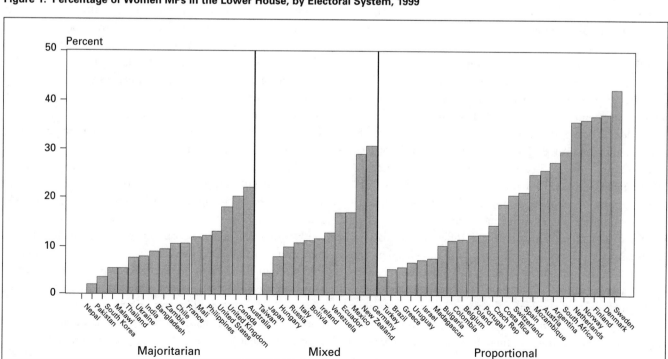

elected in some majoritarian systems like Australia's and Canada's than in some highly proportional party-list systems like Israel's and Belgium's.

By itself the electoral system is neither a necessary nor a sufficient condition to guarantee women's representation. Nevertheless, the electoral system functions as a facilitating mechanism that expedites implementation of measures within parties—affirmative action, for example—for female candidates.

The role of the electoral system is independent of levels of socioeconomic and political development. A regression model has been run that predicts the proportion of women in parliament in the fifty-three democracies where the electoral system was coded from majoritarian (0), to mixed (0.5), to proportional (1). The model controlled for levels of socioeconomic development (measured by per capita gross domestic product), providing an indication of the growth of the service sector and women's employment in the paid work force as well as the level of political development based on the Freedom House Gastil democratization index. The results confirmed that the type of electoral system continued to prove significant (standardized beta regression coefficients of .29 with sig. .016) even after controlling for socioeconomic development (beta .28 with sig .09) and level of democratization (beta .24 not sig).

STATUTORY REGULATIONS OF AFFIRMATIVE ACTION

Statutory quotas—when women must make up at least a minimal proportion of the legislature or of parliamentary candidates—are also part of some electoral systems. In a handful of states by law women must make up a certain proportion of the list ballot—such as 50 percent in Italy and 30 percent in Argentina. France has actively debated the use of gender parity in elected office through constitutional reform. In India, 33 percent of seats on local municipal elections are reserved for women; this practice has also been proposed for India's lower house, the Lok Sahba. Reserved seats are also designated in Bangladesh (30 of 330 seats), Eritrea (10 of 105), and Tanzania (15 of 255). Affirmative action strategies like these can also serve political minorities based on regional, linguistic, ethnic, or religious cleavages, although the effects depend upon the sizes and spatial concentrations of such groups. Reserved seats are used in countries as different as Jordan (for Christians and Circassians), Pakistan (for non-Muslim minorities), New Zealand (for Maori), and Slovenia (for Hungarians and Italians).

As an alternative, affirmative action or positive discrimination strategies have commonly been introduced through party rules to promote the training, funding, or selection of women candidates. Gender quotas adopted in party rules have been used all over the world, including in South Africa by the African National Congress, in Mexico by the Democratic Revolutionary Party, and throughout Scandinavia. The British Labour Party, for example, used all-women shortlists for nomination in half its target marginal seats in the period preceding the 1997 general election. Although this policy was subsequently dropped under legal challenge, it still proved highly effective, contributing toward the doubling between 1992 and 1997 of the number of women in the Westminster parliament.

A worldwide review of practices in the early 1990s by the Inter-Parliamentary Union found that twenty-two parties made use of gender quotas for legislative elections, while fifty-one parties used them for elections to internal party posts. These measures were commonly introduced in western Europe during the 1980s by parties of the left (Social Democratic, Labour, Communist, Socialist, and Greens). In contrast, in the first free elections in central and eastern Europe, parties there moved in the opposite direction and abandoned gender quotas largely in reaction to the old Communist regimes.

CONCLUSIONS: A TWIN-TRACK STRATEGY

We can conclude that debates about electoral reform have often produced conflict about means (What would be the effects on party fortunes of alternative systems?) but even more fundamentally about ends (What is the primary objective of the electoral system?). Those concerned with increasing women's representation have advocated two strategies: the adoption of proportional representation with large multimember constituencies and the use of affirmative action rules in candidate selection and in legislative bodies.

The electoral system influences the incentives facing party selectorates when they decide whether to choose male or female candidates. In large multimember districts, parties have greater incentives to create a balanced ticket in the attempt to maximize their electoral appeal. This incentive is absent in single-member districts at the local level, where the choice of candidate is often decided.

Affirmative action strategies can be adopted in any electoral system, but they may be easiest to implement when they are applied to balancing the social composition of party lists. Examples are zippering—designating every other position on the list for male or female candidates—or balancing the list by region, occupation, or religion.

Although insufficient by themselves, proportional representation electoral systems in combination with affirmative action strategies adopted by law or by party selection procedures can serve to increase social representation and produce parliaments that look more like the people they serve.

See also *Candidates: Selection; Franchise Expansion; Gender Quotas; Proportional Representation; Women: Enfranchisement.*

PIPPA NORRIS, HARVARD UNIVERSITY

BIBLIOGRAPHY

Dahlerup, Drude. "Using Quotas to Increase Women's Political Representation." In *Women in Parliament: Beyond Numbers,* edited by Azza Karam. Stockholm: IDEA, 1998.

Duverger, Maurice. *Political Parties.* New York: Wiley, 1954.

Inter-Parliamentary Union. *Electoral Systems: A Worldwide Comparative Study.* Geneva: IPU, 1993.

———. *Women in National Parliaments.* 1999. www.ipu.org/wmn-e/world.htm.

———. *Women in Parliament, 1945–95.* Geneva: IPU, 1995.

Lijphart, Arend. *Electoral Systems and Party Systems.* Oxford: Oxford University Press, 1994.

———. and Grofman, Bernard. *Choosing an Electoral System.* New York: Praeger, 1984.

Lovenduski, Joni, and Pippa Norris. *Gender and Party Politics.* London: Sage, 1993.

Matland, Richard E. "Enhancing Women's Political Participation: Legislative Recruitment and Electoral Systems." In *Women in Parliament: Beyond Numbers,* edited by Azza Karam. Stockholm: IDEA, 1998.

———. "Women in European Legislative Elites." *West European Politics* 8 (October 1985): 90–101.

Rae, Douglas. *The Political Consequences of Electoral Laws.* New Haven: Yale University Press, 1971.

Reynolds, Andrew, and Ben Reilly, eds. *The International IDEA Handbook on Electoral System Design.* Stockholm: IDEA, 1997.

Rule, Wilma, and Joseph F. Zimmerman. *United States Electoral Systems: Their Impact on Women and Minorities.* New York: Praeger, 1992.

Taagepera, Rein, and M. S. Shugart. *Seats and Votes.* New Haven: Yale University Press, 1989.

APPENDIX

ELECTORAL SYSTEMS IN INDEPENDENT COUNTRIES

TABLE 1
Basic Features of Parliamentary Elections

TABLE 2
Basic Features of Presidential Elections

DIETER NOHLEN

FLORIAN GROTZ

MICHAEL KRENNERICH

BERNHARD THIBAUT

TABLE I

BASIC FEATURES OF PARLIAMENTARY ELECTIONS

The following table includes data on parliamentary elections in 144 independent countries with a constitutional form of government and a population of more than 500,000. Also included are a number of countries that, while not meeting these criteria, are important for the comparative study of electoral systems, for example, Malta.

Many of the countries included cannot be considered democratic, nor their elections free and fair. For that reason, this table incorporates the Freedom House rating for political and civil liberties.

In two-chamber systems, the method of election described is that for the lower house, for example, the U.S. House of Representatives or the House of Commons in the United Kingdom.

The cross references within parentheses in this introduction to the table refer to articles in the main body of the encyclopedia.

EXPLANATIONS OF COLUMN HEADINGS AND CELLS

Country (year). Name of the country and the year for which election data are reported. Generally, these elections took place under the procedural and technical norms indicated in the other columns of the given row. Any exceptions to that rule are indicated.

FH rating. Freedom House's 1997/1998 classification, based on a detailed assessment of civil rights and political liberties. The categories are free, partly free, and not free. The rating is indicative of the political significance of elections in the respective country. For full details, see *Freedom in the World: The Annual Survey of Political Rights and Civil Liberties, 1997–1998.* New York: Freedom House.

Voting age. The minimum age at which a person is eligible to vote. *(See also "Age of Voting.")*

Compulsory voting. Indicates whether individuals who are eligible to vote are obligated (yes) or not obligated (no) by law to cast a ballot. *(See also "Compulsory Voting.")*

Classification of electoral system. Categorization of the electoral system based on its technical elements, such as decision formula(s), constituency size(s), and mode(s) of seat allocation. Since in the real world the technical elements can be combined in many different ways, the categories expand the classic distinction in the abstract between "majority system" and "proportional representation" to correspond with the wide variety of systems that can be found around the world. *(See also "Majority Systems"; "Proportional Representation.")*

The categories highlight important technical features of the electoral system and assess the system's effect on the proportionality of seat shares to vote shares. The following range from the most majoritarian to the most proportional in well-institutionalized party systems:

- *Plurality system.* The candidate (in a single-member constituency) or list (in a multimember constituency) with the largest number of votes, whether more or less than half, is elected. Plurality systems are differentiated one from another by district magnitude and form of candidacy. *(See also "Plurality Systems.")*

- *Single nontransferable vote.* The candidate with the most votes wins. The voter has fewer votes to cast than there are seats to be filled in a two-member or multimember constituency. The fewer votes that each voter has to cast, and the larger the constituency, the more the system tends toward proportionality. *(See also "Single Nontransferable Vote.")*

- *Absolute majority system.* Election requires more than one-half the vote. Absolute majority systems are differentiated one from another by district magnitude. If no candidate achieves the required majority, a second-round runoff may be held or the winning candidate may be determined by an alternative vote. *(See also "Alternative Vote.")*

- *Binomial system.* Two members are elected from each district. *(See also "Binomial Electoral System.")*

- *Segmented system.* One portion of the parliamentary seats is allocated by a majority formula and the other by a proportional formula and each method is applied separately;

for example, plurality in single-member constituencies and proportional representation in one national district. In segmented systems the disproportional effects of the majoritarian part of the electoral system are not compensated by the proportional-representation element. The overall proportionality of a segmented system depends mainly on the ratio between the majoritarian and proportional-representation elements. For example, in Russia the ratio is one to one, whereas in Guinea only 33.3 percent of the seats are allocated by plurality.

- *Compensatory system.* Majority and/or proportional-representation system with certain technical elements (for example, a special contingent of seats) to compensate parties that are disadvantaged by the disproportional effects of the initial seat-allocation system. In contrast to segmented systems, in compensatory systems votes that were unsuccessful in the initial seat-allocation procedure are taken into account in the allocation of compensatory seats. *(See also "Additional Member System.")*

- *Proportional representation in multimember constituencies.* These systems are differentiated one from another by district magnitude. The categories applied are: small MMCs (two-to-five seats to be allocated), medium MMCs (six-to-nine seats), and large MMCs (ten or more seats). Generally, the larger the MMC, the more proportional the system. A special subcategory of this type of system has a number of seats to compensate for slight deviations in proportionality (as in Denmark, Norway, and Sweden, for example). In contrast to compensatory systems, this type of electoral system lacks any majoritorian part.

- *Proportional representation in multimember constituencies with an additional national list.* Some electoral systems based on proportional representation in small or medium multimember constituencies provide for an additional national list in order to enhance overall proportionality, for example, Angola and Poland. In contrast to segmented systems, in this type of electoral system both parts of the system work under a proportional-representation formula, and in contrast to compensatory systems (and like segmented systems), there is no technical procedure assuring that unsuccessful votes are compensated.

- *Single transferable vote.* Seats are allocated in multimember constituencies, and voters rank candidates in order of preference; in most cases rank ordering is optional. Seats are allocated at various stages of counting, and votes are redistributed according to preferences. Ireland is the classic example.

- *Mixed-member proportional system.* A special subcategory of proportional representation. This subcategory stands out because of its specific combination of decision formulas: the overall distribution of seats among parties is determined according to proportional representation; however, a certain number of candidates are elected directly in single-member constituencies according to the plurality formula. From the seats any party has achieved according to the proportional-representation procedure, the party's successful single-member-constituency candidates are subtracted; that is to say, application of the plurality formula normally does not influence the proportionality of the system as a whole. This configuration is known as the German model. *(See also "Additional Member System.")*

- *Pure proportional representation (PR).* Achieves proportionality between vote share and seat share for all parties as nearly as possible; the disproportional effects of natural or legal thresholds are minimized. The Netherlands is an example.

Number of seats. This figure is the total number of regularly elected members of the lower house of the parliament as stipulated by the electoral law or the constitution. In some countries, however, the number of elected seats may vary from election to election due to special legal provisions (for example, surplus mandates, as in Germany, or special minority seats that are filled only under certain conditions, as in Colombia).

There may also exist nominated members of parliament (as in Kenya and Tanzania). In these cases, a note indicates the size of the current parliament and explains the respective methods. Where the elected seats are awarded by two different methods, the total number of seats is given first, and the numbers allocated by the different methods are indicated in the following lines.

Constituencies. The three columns are:

- *Number of constituencies.* In plurality or majority systems with single-member constituencies, the number of constituencies is identical to the number of elected seats; in proportional-representation systems, the number of constituencies is always less than the number of seats.

- *Seats per constituency.* This column provides the number of seats awarded per constituency (district magnitude).

    Magnitude can be uniform, as in nationwide single-member constituencies (for example, the U.S. House of Representatives) or in proportional-representation systems where the whole country is a single multimember constituency (for example, Israel). Where magnitude is uniform, only one number is given.

Magnitude also can vary, due to different methods of allocating seats (for example, Germany), or it can vary within a proportional-representation system due to the dispersion of population across administrative areas. When constituencies vary in size, the range from the smallest to the largest constituency is given.

- *Mean number of seats in a constituency.* The mean is indicated if constituencies are of unequal size. For combined electoral systems, the figures refer separately to the different seat categories.

Form of candidacy. A ballot may offer the voter a choice among individual candidates (who usually but not necessarily have to be nominated by parties) or a choice among lists containing the names of a multiplicity of candidates nominated by a party or an electoral alliance of parties. Such lists may be closed (the voter endorses the entire list without any possibility of changing the order in which seats are allocated to the candidates or adding other individuals of his or her choice); nonblocked (the voter may express a preference for certain candidates by casting a certain number of preferential votes); or open (the voter may completely rearrange the list by casting preferential votes and by supplementing the list with candidates from other lists in a practice known as *panachage).*

Ballot form. A voter can cast a single vote for an individual candidate; a single vote for a (party) list of candidates; a series of preference votes for candidates who run individually or are nominated on a party list; or separate votes (generally two) in combined electoral systems. The term *multiple vote* indicates that voters may cast as many votes as there are seats to be filled in the constituency.

Levels of seat allocation. Parliamentary seats may be allocated to candidates at the constituency level, as is the case in uniform systems such as plurality in the single-member constituencies of the U.S. House of Representatives. They may be allocated at two or more constituency levels, where elections are held in different but combined constituencies (for example, a single-member constituency combined with a regional or national multimember constituency in segmented or compensatory systems). Or seats may be allocated on a higher (regional or national) level, as in proportional-representation systems that have remainder or additional seats. Where the higher level is used only for the allocation of remainder seats in proportional-representation systems, this is indicated in parentheses.

Mode of seat allocation. Seats may be allocated under various procedural norms and especially by different decision formulas.

In systems of majority representation the decision rule may be plurality or absolute majority. In the latter case provisions have to be established for a subsequent procedure if no candidate (or party list) achieves an absolute majority in the first round. This subsequent procedure (for example, a runoff between the two strongest candidates of the first round) is indicated in parentheses.

In proportional-representation systems (or the proportional-representation part of combined systems) there may exist a legal threshold of votes that parties must achieve in order to be entitled to proportional-representation seats. Then, seats may be allocated by different modes, which are defined in the articles "Proportional Representation" and "Quotas."

Turnout. The figures indicate the percentage of the population eligible to vote who voted at the parliamentary election referenced in column 1.

Strongest party. The percentage of the national vote won by the strongest party at the parliamentary elections referenced in column 1. In segmented and compensatory systems, the figure refers only to the proportional representation part of the electoral system.

Rose proportionality index. The degree to which the allocation of seats matches the distribution of the national vote at the parliamentary elections referenced in column 1. To calculate this index, the sum of the differences of each party's share of votes and its share of seats is divided by two and the result is subtracted from one hundred.

ABBREVIATIONS

EC	Electoral coalition
MMC	Multimember constituency
n.a.	not available
PR	Proportional representation
SMC	Single-member constituency
TMC	Two-member constituency

The authors are grateful to André Blais and Richard Rose for their helpful comments on an early draft, and to Jørgen Elklit and Bernard Grofman for providing detailed information on several countries.

Country (year)	FH rating	Voting age	Compulsory voting	Classification of electoral system	No. of seats	No.	Seats	Mean seats	Form of candidacy	Ballot form	Levels of seat allocation	Mode of seat allocation	Turnout (%)	Strongest party	Rose index
Albania (1997)	partly free	18	no	compensatory system	*155:*					*two votes:*			72.6	53.4	82.3
					115	115	1		individual	personal vote	SMC	SMC: absolute majority (runoff among two strongest candidates)			
					40	1	40		closed lists	list vote	national MMC[1]	MMC: threshold of 2% of national vote; Hare-Niemeyer applied separately for the two strongest and the rest of the parties			
Algeria (1997)	not free	18	no	PR in small, medium, and large MMCs	380	48	4-24	7.9	closed lists	single vote	MMC	threshold of 5% of national vote; Hare quota; largest remainder	65.6	33.6	85.8
Angola (1992)	not free	18	no	PR in medium MMCs with additional national list	*220:*								91.3	53.7	94.1
					90	18	5		closed lists	single vote	regional MMC	d'Hondt			
					130	1	130				national MMC	Hare quota; largest remainder			
Argentina (1997)	free	18	yes	PR in small, medium, and large MMCs	257	24	2-25	10.7	closed lists	single vote	MMC	d'Hondt; threshold of 3% of constituency vote	81	36.4	91.9[2]
Armenia (1995)	partly free	18	no	segmented system	*190:*					*two votes:*			55.6	42.7[3]	66.9
					150	150	1		individual	personal vote	SMC	25% of constituency vote if more than 2 candidates run, 50% if 1 or 2 candidates run			
					40	1	40		closed lists	list vote	national MMC	threshold of 5% of national vote; Hare-Niemeyer			
Australia (1998)	free	18	yes	alternative vote in SMCs	148	148	1		individual	ranking of all candidates	SMC	absolute majority[4]	95.2	40.0	81.0
Austria (1995)	free	19	no	PR in medium and large MMCs	183	9	6-102	20.3	nonblocked lists	one preferential vote	MMC regional level (for remaining seats)	threshold of 4% of national vote; Hare quota; remaining seats are allocated in two regions with d'Hondt	86	38.3	99.3
Azerbaijan (1995)	not free	21	no	segmented system	*125:*					*two votes:*			86.1	n.a.	n.a.
					100	100	1		individual	personal vote	SMC	absolute majority (runoff among two strongest candidates)			
					25	1	25		closed lists	list vote	national MMC	threshold of 8% of national vote; Hare quota; largest remainder			
Bangladesh (1996)	partly free	18	no	plurality system in SMCs	300[5]	300	1		individual	single vote	SMC	plurality	75.6	37.5	83.7

1. The 40 compensatory (officially, supplementary) seats in Albania are allocated separately: 10 seats for the two strongest parties, and 30 seats for other parties with at least 2 percent of the national vote. Since the two strongest parties usually get more than 25 percent of the votes, the minor parties are favored by the allocation of the national seats. Insofar as they are favored, the electoral system contains a compensatory element.
2. The proportionality index for Argentina is calculated on the basis of the results of the 127 seats renewed in 1997.
3. The figure for strongest party in Armenia refers to the list vote for the party coalition Republican Bloc.
4. In Australia, if none of the candidates obtains an absolute majority of the first-preference votes, the candidate with the least number of votes is eliminated and his/her votes are redistributed among the remaining candidates on the basis of the voters' second preferences. This procedure is repeated until one candidate obtains an absolute majority.
5. In addition to the 300 elected seats, 30 special seats for women are chosen by the directly elected representatives.

Country (year)	FH rating	Voting age	Compulsory voting	Classification of electoral system	No. of seats	Constituencies No.	Constituencies Seats	Constituencies Mean seats	Form of candidacy	Ballot form	Levels of seat allocation	Mode of seat allocation	Turnout (%)	Strongest party	Rose index
Belarus (1995)	not free	18	no	absolute majority system in SMCs	260	260[6]	1		individual	single vote	SMC	absolute majority (runoff among two strongest candidates)	64.7	n.a.	n.a.
Belgium (1995)	free	18	yes	PR in small, medium, and large MMCs	150	20	2-33	7.5	nonblocked lists	single vote, preference possible	MMC provincial level (for remaining seats)	Hare quota; remaining seats are allocated at provincial level with d'Hondt[7]	91.2	13.2	92.7
Benin (1995)	free	18	no	PR in small and medium MMCs	84	18	3-6	5.3	closed lists	single vote	MMC	Hare quota; greatest average	75.8	14.6	72.1
Bolivia (1997)	free	18	yes	mixed-member proportional system	130: 68	68	1		individual	two votes: personal vote	SMC	party share of seats is determined at MMC level with d'Hondt (threshold of 3% of national vote). SMC: plurality (each party's SMC seats are subtracted from its contingent of total seats)	70	22.3	91.8
					62	9	5-31	6.9	closed lists	list vote	MMC				
Bosnia (1998)	partly free	18	no	PR in two large MMCs	42	2[8]	14, 28	24.0	closed lists	single vote	MMC	Saint Laguë	70.0	33.8	87.6
Botswana (1994)	free	18	no	plurality system in SMCs	40	40	1		individual	single vote	SMC	plurality	76.6	54.7	87.2
Brazil (1998)	partly free	16	yes	PR in medium and large MMCs	513	27	8-70	19.0	nonblocked lists	one preferential vote	MMC	Hare quota; greatest average	78.5	76.0[9]	82.0
Bulgaria (1997)	free	18	no	PR in one MMC	240	1	240		closed regional lists	single vote	national MMC	party share of seats is determined by d'Hondt at the national level; threshold of 4% of national vote; each party's seats are allocated to regional lists	58.3	52.3	92.5
Burkina Faso (1997)	partly free	18	no	majority system in SMCs and PR in small, medium, and large MMCs	111	45	1-11	2.5	SMC: individual. MMC: closed lists	single vote	SMC/MMC	SMC: plurality MMC: Hare quota; greatest average	44.1	68.6	77.6
Cambodia (1998)	not free	18	no	PR in MMCs (with 8 SMCs)	120: 112	15	3-18	7.5	closed lists	single vote	MMC	Hare quota; greatest average	90.8	41.4	85.4
					8	8	1		individual		SMC				

6. In 1995 only 199 seats were allocated in Belarus because the minimum participation rate (50 percent of the registered voters in the respective constituency) was not met in the other constituencies.

7. In Belgium, seats unallocated at the constituency level are distributed among "party cartels" formed by each party's lists within the respective province. Only parties that have attained at least two-thirds of the Hare quota in one of the constituencies in a province are allowed to participate in the allocation of the remaining seats in that province.

8. The two constituencies in Bosnia are the two territorial entities of the state: Serbian Republic, 14 seats; Federation of Bosnia and Herzegovina, 28 seats. Within each constituency, pure PR is applied.

9. The percentage for the strongest party in Brazil refers to an alliance of different parties collaborating within the subnational constituencies.

Country (year)	FH rating	Voting age	Compulsory voting	Classification of electoral system	No. of seats	Constituencies No.	Constituencies Seats	Constituencies Mean seats	Form of candidacy	Ballot form	Levels of seat allocation	Mode of seat allocation	Turnout (%)	Strongest party	Rose index
Cameroon (1997)	not free	20	no	majority system in SMCs and MMCs	180	n.a.	1-7	n.a.	SMC: individual. MMC: closed lists	single vote	SMC/MMC	SMC: plurality. MMC: absolute majority or PR with bonus for strongest party[10]	75.6	48	86.6
Canada (1997)	free	18	no	plurality system in SMCs	301	301	1		individual	single vote	SMC	plurality	68.7	38.4	82.4
Central African Republic (1998)	partly free	18	yes	absolute majority system in SMCs	109	109	1		individual	single vote	SMC	absolute majority (second round among candidates with more than 10%; plurality)	55.2	n.a.	n.a.
Chad (1997)	not free	18	no	absolute majority system in SMCs and MMCs	125	59	1-	2.1	SMC: individual. MMC: closed lists	single vote	SMC/MMC	SMC: absolute majority (runoff among two strongest candidates). MMC: absolute majority or PR with d'Hondt[11]	45.6	40	72.8
Chile (1997)	free	18	yes	binomial system	120	60	2	2.0	nonblocked lists	one preferential vote	TMC	plurality list gets the 1st seat; it gets the 2nd only if it doubles the vote share of the second-best list (identical to d'Hondt)	68.6	23	85.8
Colombia (1998)	partly free	18	no	PR in MMCs	160[12]	33	n.a.	4.8	nonblocked lists[13]	single vote for candidate	MMC	Hare quota; largest remainder	44.4	54.0	87.8
Costa Rica (1998)	free	18	yes	PR in medium and large MMCs	57	7	4-21	8.1	closed lists	single vote	MMC	Hare quota; largest remainder[14]	70	41.3	84.9
Côte d'Ivoire (1995)	not free	21	no	plurality system in SMCs and MMCs	175	157	1-4	1.1	SMC: individual. MMC: closed lists	single vote	SMC/MMC	plurality	56.2	64.9	79.8
Croatia (1995)	partly free	18	no	segmented system	108[15]					two votes:					
					28	28	1		individual	personal vote	SMC	plurality	68.8	45.2	86
					80	1	80		closed lists	list vote	national MMC	threshold of 5%/8% (2 EC), 11% (3+ EC) of national vote; d'Hondt			

10. In an MMC in Cameroon, if a list wins an absolute majority of votes, it gets all the seats; otherwise, the strongest party gets 50 percent + 1 of the seats, and the rest of the seats in the MMC are distributed according to the Hare quota and largest remainder among the other party lists that exceed a 5 percent threshold.

11. In an MMC in Chad, if a list wins an absolute majority of votes, it gets all the seats; otherwise, the seats are distributed according to d'Hondt.

12. The number of elected seats in Colombia is a minimum of 160. In addition, a maximum of 5 seats may be allocated in special minority districts. In 1998 one such seat was allocated.

13. Strictly speaking, there are no party lists in Colombia, but a plurality of lists that adhere to parties.

14. In Costa Rica, remaining seats are distributed among only those parties that achieved at least half of the Hare quota.

15. Parliamentary seats total 127. In addition to the 108 "general" seats, 12 PR-seats are filled by party-list vote of Croatians living abroad and seven PR-seats are filled by party-list vote of ethnic groups from the national constituency.

Country (year)	FH rating	Voting age	Compulsory voting	Classification of electoral system	No. of seats	Constituencies			Form of candidacy	Ballot form	Levels of seat allocation	Mode of seat allocation	Turnout (%)	Strongest party	Rose index
						No.	Seats	Mean seats							
Cuba (1998)	not free	16	no	absolute majority system in SMCs	601	601	1	1	individual	one vote	SMC	absolute majority (no repeat election)	98.4	n.a.	n.a.
Cyprus (1996)	free	18	yes	PR mainly in small, medium, and large MMCs	80[16]	6	1-21	13.3	nonblocked lists	up to 4 preferential votes	SMC/MMC	Hare quota; thresholds for remaining seats[17]	92.2	34.5	95.6[18]
Czech Republic (1998)	free	18	no	PR in large MMCs	200	8	14-41[19]	25.0	nonblocked lists	up to 4 preferential votes[20]	MMC national level (for remaining seats)	threshold of 5%/7% (2 EC), 9% (3 EC), 11% (4+ EC) of national vote; Droop quota. Remaining seats: Droop quota at national level; largest remainder	74	32.3	88.5
Denmark (1998)	free	18	no	PR in small, medium, and large MMCs with compensatory seats	135	17	2-16	7.9	nonblocked MMC lists	single vote (preference possible)	MMC	modified St. Laguë	85.9	35.9	99.1
					40[21]	1	40				national MMC	threshold of 2% of national vote; Hare quota; largest remainder; seats gained at the MMC level are subtracted from the number of seats to which a party is entitled according to a proportional, national allocation of all 175 seats. The difference is the party's share of the 40 compensatory seats[22]			
Djibouti (1997)	not free	18	no	plurality system in MMCs	65	5	4-37	13.0	closed lists	single vote	MMC	plurality (winning list gains all seats)	56.9	78.6	78.6
Dominican Republic (1996)	partly free	18	yes	PR in MMCs	120	30	2-31	4.0	closed lists	single vote	MMC	d'Hondt	78.6	42.7	93.2

16. Of the 80 seats, 56 are elected by the Greek-Cypriot community and 24 by the Turkish-Cypriot community.

17. In Cyprus, remaining seats are distributed among parties or electoral coalitions that have gained at least one seat in any constituency pursuant to the first distribution or, for single parties, at least 1.8 percent of all valid votes cast throughout the island. (For coalitions of two or more parties, the applicable figures are 10 percent and 20 percent, respectively). Single party lists that participate in the second distribution must receive 3.6 percent of the total number of votes cast in order to be entitled to a second seat.

18. The proportionality index is calculated only for the Greek community.

19. Constituency sizes in the Czech Republic are determined ex post facto by the following formula: "Number of valid votes in the respective constituency" divided by "Total number of valid votes at the national level" multiplied by "Total number of seats to be filled." Therefore the number of seats to be distributed at the constituency level depends not only on the electoral body but also on the differences in participation rates among constituencies. In 1998 three seats were allocated in constituencies other than they would have had the constituency sizes depended only on the size of the electoral body.

20. Preferential votes are taken into account only if 10 percent or more of the voters for the respective list have made use of the option of preferential voting. Within any list, only those candidates who have received at least 10 percent of the list votes as preferential votes move to the top of the list.

21. In addition to these 175 seats, Greenland elects two members and the Faroe islands two members.

22. In Denmark, possible alternatives to the 2 percent threshold are: one or more MMC seats or as many votes as on average were cast per MMC seat in at least two of the three regions of Denmark, that is, mathematically a Hare formula is applied. The parties' shares of the 40 compensatory seats, which are calculated at the national level, are first distributed to the three regions (by Saint Laguë) and then to the respective MMC (by the "Danish divisor method").

Country (year)	FH rating	Voting age	Compulsory voting	Classification of electoral system	No. of seats	Constituencies			Form of candidacy	Ballot form	Levels of seat allocation	Mode of seat allocation	Turnout (%)	Strongest party	Rose index
						No.	Seats	Mean seats							
Ecuador (1996)	partly free	18	yes	plurality system in small, medium, and large MMCs with additional national list	121:\n101	21	2-18	5.0	open lists	multiple vote for provincial deputies	provincial MMC	plurality of votes for the candidates	73.1	27.3	88.2
					20	1	20		closed lists	single list vote for national deputies	national MMC	d'Hondt			
Egypt (1995)	not free	18	yes[23]	absolute majority system in TMCs	444[24]	222	2	2	individual	two votes	TMC	absolute majority (2nd round among four best-placed candidates)	47.9	n.a.	n.a.
El Salvador (1997)	partly free	18	yes	PR in MMCs with additional national list	84:\n64	14	3-16	4.6	closed lists	single vote	MMC	Hare quota; largest remainder	61.3	35.4	95.6
					20	1	20				national MMC	Hare quota; largest remainder			
Estonia (1995)	free	18	no	PR in medium and large MMCs	101	12	7-12	8.4	nonblocked MMC lists; closed national lists	single vote for MMC-list candidate	MMC national level (for remaining seats)	Hare quota at MMC level (applied first to candidates; then to MMC lists). Remaining seats: modified d'Hondt at national level with 5% threshold	69.6	32.2	87.2
Ethiopia (1995)	partly free	18	no	plurality system in SMCs	547	547	1		individual	single vote	SMC	plurality	93.6	82.9	96
Fiji (1994)	partly free	21	no	plurality system in SMCs and small MMCs	70[25]	52	1-3	1.3	individual	single vote	SMC/MMC	plurality	74.8	n.a.	n.a.
Finland (1995)	free	18	yes	PR in medium and large MMCs	200	14	7-30[26]	14.3	nonblocked lists	one preferential vote	MMC	d'Hondt	68	28.3	92
France (1997)	free	18	no	absolute majority system in SMCs	577[27]	577	1		individual	single vote	SMC	absolute majority. 2nd round: plurality[28]	67.9	23.5	74.5
Gabon (1996)	partly free	18	no	absolute majority system in SMCs	120	120	1		individual	single vote	SMC	absolute majority (runoff among two strongest candidates)	n.a.	n.a.	n.a.
Gambia (1997)	not free	18	no	plurality system in SMCs	45[29]	45	1		individual	single vote	SMC	plurality	69.3	52.1	73.8

23. Voting is compulsory only for men in Egypt.

24. In Egypt, in addition to the elected seats, 10 members of parliament are nominated by the president.

25. Of the 70 elected seats, 37 are reserved for Fijians, 27 for Indians, 1 for Rotumans, and 5 for members of other races.

26. There is one SMC in Finland (Åland).

27. This figure, 577, includes 15 for overseas departments and 7 for overseas territories and *collectivités territoriales*.

28. In France, if no candidate receives an absolute majority in the first round, a second round is held among candidates who received votes from at least 12.5 percent of registered voters. If only one candidate fulfills this condition, the runner-up of the first round may also run in the second round.

29. In addition to the 45 elected members, four members are nominated.

Country (year)	FH rating	Voting age	Compulsory voting	Classification of electoral system	No. of seats	Constituencies No.	Constituencies Seats	Constituencies Mean seats	Form of candidacy	Ballot form	Levels of seat allocation	Mode of seat allocation	Turnout (%)	Strongest party	Rose index
Georgia (1995)	partly free	18	no	segmented system[30]	235:				*two votes:*	*two votes:*			68.3	23.7	59.2
					85	85	1		individual	personal vote	SMC	absolute majority (2nd round among candidates with more than 33%; plurality)			
					150	10	5–24	13.6	closed lists	list vote	MMC; national level (for remaining seats)	threshold of 5% of national vote; Hare-quota; remaining seats allocated at national level by d'Hondt			
Germany (1998)	free	18	no	mixed-member proportional system	656:[31]				*two votes:*	*two votes:*			82.2	40.9	94.0
					328	328	1		individual	personal vote	SMC	party share of 656 seats is determined at the national level according to list vote, with a threshold of 5% of national vote. Each party's seats are allocated to regional lists. Formula for each procedure: Hare-Niemeyer. SMC seats: plurality (each party's SMC mandates are subtracted from its seat contingent)[32]			
					328	1	328		closed regional lists	list vote	national level				
Ghana (1996)	partly free	18	no	plurality system in SMCs	200	200	1		individual	single vote	constituency	plurality	65	53	86.2
Greece (1996)	free	18	yes	PR in MMCs with additional national list	300:								76.3	41.5	87.6
					288	56	1–36	5.1	nonblocked MMC lists	1–5 preferential votes depending on constituency size	SMC/MMC; regional and national level (for remaining seats)	SMC: plurality. MMC: Droop quota; remaining seats are allocated in 13 regional districts with Hare quota; seats still remaining are allocated to the strongest party at national level.			
					12	1	12		closed national lists		national MMC	national MMC threshold of 3%; Hare quota; largest remainder			
Guatemala (1995)	partly free	18	yes	PR in small and medium MMCs with additional national list	80:				*two votes:*	*two votes:*			46.7	41.7	68.2
					64	23	n.a.	2.8	closed lists	regional list vote	SMC/MMC	d'Hondt			
					16	1	16		closed lists	national list vote[33]	national MMC	d'Hondt			
Guinea (1995)	not free	18	yes	segmented system	114:				*two votes:*	*two votes:*			61.9	53.5	91
					38	38	1		individual	personal vote	SMC	plurality			
					76	1	76		closed lists	list vote	national MMC	Hare quota; largest remainder			
Guinea Bissau (1994)	partly free	18	no	plurality in SMCs, PR in small and medium MMCs	102	29	1–6	3.5	closed lists (individual in SMC)	single vote	SMC/MMC	d'Hondt (plurality in SMC)	88.9	46.4	82.7

30. Twelve members of parliament are elected in Abkhazia by a plurality system in SMCs.

31. In addition to the elected seats, surplus seats may emerge: parties gaining more SMC-seats than they are entitled to under the PR formula applied in the respective region (*land*) keep all seats without any compensation for the other parties. In 1998 there were 13 surplus seats.

32. The 5 percent threshold is not applied to parties that have gained at least 3 SMC seats.

33. The national vote in Guatemala is at the same time a vote for a presidential candidate.

Country (year)	FH rating	Voting age	Compulsory voting	Classification of electoral system	No. of seats	Constituencies No.	Constituencies Seats	Constituencies Mean seats	Form of candidacy	Ballot form	Levels of seat allocation	Mode of seat allocation	Turnout (%)	Strongest party	Rose index
Guyana (1997)	partly free	18	no	pure PR	53	1	53		closed lists	single vote	national MMC	Hare quota; largest remainder	97.8	55.3	98.7
Haiti (1995)	partly free	18	no	absolute majority system in SMCs	83	83	1		individual	single vote	SMC	absolute majority (runoff among two strongest candidates)	31.1	n.a.	n.a.
Honduras (1997)	partly free	18	yes	PR in MMCs	128	18	n.a.	7.1	closed lists	single vote	MMC	Hare quota; largest remainder	65	49.7	96.5
Hungary (1998)	free	18	no	compensatory system	386:				*two votes:*				56.3	32.9	83.5
					176	176	1		individual	personal vote	SMC	absolute majority (runoff among candidates with 15%+ of valid votes)			
					152	20	4-28	7.6	closed MMC lists	list vote in MMC	regional MMC	threshold of 5%/10% (2 EC), 15% (3+ EC) of national vote; Droop quota; largest remainder			
					58	1	58		closed national lists		national MMC[34]	threshold is identical to regional MMC; d'Hondt[35]			
Iceland (1995)	free	18	no	PR in medium and large MMCs with additional national list	63:					single vote			87.3	37.1	97.3
					50	8	5-19	6.3	Closed MMC lists		MMC	Hare quota; largest remainder (MMC threshold is two-thirds of Hare quota)			
					13	1	13		closed national lists		national MMC	d'Hondt			
India (1998)	partly free	18	no	plurality system in SMCs	543	543	1		individual	single vote	SMC	plurality	62.0	25.9	87.4
Indonesia (1997)	not free	17	no	PR in small, medium, and large MMCs	425[36]	27	4-68	15.7	closed lists	single vote	MMC	Hare quota; largest remainder	88.9	74.3	97.7
Iran (1996)	not free	15	no	majority system in SMCs and MMCs	270	196	n.a.	1.4	individual	multiple vote	SMC/MMC	qualified majority is one-third of the votes in SMC / votes of one-third of the voters in MMC (runoff among leading candidates: twice the number of seats to be filled)	77.2	n.a.	n.a.
Iraq (1996)	not free	18	no	plurality system in small and medium MMCs	250	52	3-6	4.8	closed MMC list	preferential votes[37]	MMC	plurality	93.5	n.a.	n.a.
Ireland (1997)	free	18	no	single transferable vote	166	41	3-5	4.0	nonblocked lists	single vote[38]	MMC	Droop quota	65.9	39.3	89.3

34. In Hungary, on the national level, nonsuccessful votes of the two other levels are counted. By this procedure, a compensatory element is introduced in the electoral system.

35. In the SMC run-off election, the three best-placed candidates of the first round may run. To qualify for seats at the PR-MMC level, lists must have received at least two-thirds of the electoral quota; otherwise, the remaining seats are added to the compensatory seats and are allocated at the national level (1998: 24 seats). The minimum participation rate is 50 percent of registered voters, both at the SMC (first round) and MMC level. If this minimum rate is not achieved, the elections are repeated once (in SMC without any further rounds).

36. In addition to the 425 elected members, 75 members of parliament are appointed.

37. Voters may express their preferences by crossing out candidates within the (single) MMC list.

38. Voters in Ireland may express their preferences by ranking the candidates within one list.

Country (year)	FH rating	Voting age	Compulsory voting	Classification of electoral system	No. of seats	Constituencies No.	Constituencies Seats	Constituencies Mean seats	Form of candidacy	Ballot form	Levels of seat allocation	Mode of seat allocation	Turnout (%)	Strongest party	Rose index
Israel (1996)	free	18	no	pure PR	120	1	120		closed lists	single vote	national MMC	threshold of 1.5% of national vote; d'Hondt	79.3	26.8	96
Italy (1996)	free	18	no	compensatory system	630: 475	475	1		individual	two votes: personal vote	SMC	plurality	82.9	21.1	89.8
					155	1	155		nonblocked regional lists	list vote	national MMC[39]	threshold of 4% of national vote; Hare quota. Remaining seats: n.a.; each party's seats are allocated to regional lists in the 26 provinces			
Jamaica (1997)	free	18	no	plurality system in SMCs	60	60	1		individual	single vote	SMC	plurality	65.4	55	70.3
Japan (1996)	free	20	no	segmented system	500: 300	300	1		individual	two votes: personal vote	SMC	plurality	59	32.8	81.6
					200	11	7-33	18.2	closed lists	list vote	MMC	d'Hondt			
Jordan (1997)	partly free	19	no	single non-transferable vote	80[40]	20	2-9	4.0	individual	single vote	MMC	plurality	47.5	n.a.	n.a.
Kazakhstan (1995)	not free	18	no	absolute majority system in SMCs	67	67	1		individual	single vote	SMC	absolute majority (runoff among two strongest candidates)	80.7	n.a.	n.a.
Kenya (1997)	not free	18	no	plurality system in SMCs	210[41]	210	1		individual	single vote	SMC	plurality	47.2	n.a.	n.a.
Korea (North) (1998)	not free	17	yes	absolute majority system in SMCs	687	687	1		individual	single vote	SMC	absolute majority[42]	99.9	n.a.	n.a.
Korea (South) (1996)	free	20	no	segmented system	299: 253	253	1		individual	single vote	SMC	plurality	62.9	34.5	86.4
					46	1	46		closed lists		national MMC	threshold of 5% of national vote or 5 SMC seats; Hare quota; largest remainder[43]			
Kuwait (1996)	partly free	21	no	plurality system in TMCs	50	25	2		individual (no party candidates)	two votes	TMC	plurality	83.4	n.a.	n.a.
Kyrgyzstan (1995)	partly free	18	no	absolute majority in SMCs[44]	70	70	1		individual	single vote	SMC	absolute majority (2nd round with plurality)	76.3	n.a.	n.a.

39. In Italy, MMC seats are allocated at the national level by the following procedure. For parties that gained SMC seats, the successful SMC votes (at least 25 percent of the total votes cast in the respective SMC) are subtracted from their list votes. This procedure introduces a compensatory element into the electoral system, because only after this subtraction is the Hare quota calculated for distributing the MMC seats.

40. Of the 80 seats in Jordan, 18 are allocated to confessional/ethnic minorities (9 for Christians, 3 each for the Circassian and Chechen, and 6 for Bedouins).

41. In addition to the 210 elected seats, 12 seats filled by nomination are distributed proportionally among the parties represented in parliament according to their share of elected seats.

42. A minimum participation rate of 50 percent of the registered voters in the constituency exists in North Korea.

43. In South Korea, parties with more than 3 percent but less than 5 percent of the national votes and less than 5 SMC seats get one national seat. Parties with more than 5 percent of the national votes and less than 5 SMC seats get 5 SMC seats.

44. Data refer to the Assembly of Peoples Representatives; the other chamber of the Kyrgyzstan parliament, the Legislative Assembly, has 35 members who also are elected in SMCs by absolute majority vote.

Country (year)	FH rating	Voting age	Compulsory voting	Classification of electoral system	No. of seats	Constituencies No.	Constituencies Seats	Constituencies Mean seats	Form of candidacy	Ballot form	Levels of seat allocation	Mode of seat allocation	Turnout (%)	Strongest party	Rose index
Laos (1997)	not free	18	no	plurality system in MMCs	99	18	3-14	5.5	closed lists	single vote	MMC	plurality (winning list gains all seats)	99.4	n.a.	n.a.
Latvia (1998)	free	18	no	PR in large MMCs	100	5	14-27	20.0	nonblocked lists	one preferential vote	MMC	threshold of 5% of national vote; St. Laguë	71.9	21.2	88.1
Lebanon (1996)	not free	21	no	plurality system in MMCs within fixed confessional PR[45]	128	5	n.a.	25.6	nonblocked lists	multiple vote	MMC	plurality within confessional groups	44.1	n.a.	n.a.
Lesotho (1998)	partly free	18	no	plurality system in SMCs	80	80	1		individual	single vote	SMC	plurality	71.8	60.7	62.0
Liberia (1997)	not free	18	no	pure PR	64	1	64		closed lists	single vote	national MMC	threshold of 1.56% of national vote; Hare quota; largest remainder	82.8	75.3	96.8
Lithuania (1996)	free	18	yes	segmented system	141: 71	71	1	1	individual	two votes: personal vote	SMC[46]	absolute majority (runoff among two strongest candidates)	52.9	29.8	75.5
					70	1	70		nonblocked lists	list vote (preferences possible)	national MMC	threshold of 5% / 7% (EC) of national vote; Hare quota; largest remainder			
Luxembourg (1994)	free	18	yes	PR in medium and large MMCs	60	4	7-23	15.0	open lists	multiple vote	MMC	Droop quota; highest average	88.3	30.3	91.6
Macedonia (1998)	partly free	18	no	segmented system	120: 85	1	85		individual	two votes: personal vote	constituency[47]	absolute majority (runoff among the two strongest candidates)	72.9	28.1	86.5
					35	35	1		closed lists	list vote	national MMC	threshold of 5% of national vote; d'Hondt			
Madagascar (1998)	partly free	18	yes	plurality system in SMCs and PR in TMCs	150	121	1-2	1.2	SMC: individual. TMC: closed lists	single vote	SMC/TMC	SMC: plurality. TMC: Hare quota; largest remainder	60.1	n.a.	n.a.
Malawi (1994)	free	18	no	plurality system in SMCs	177	177	1		individual	single vote	SMC	plurality	79.6	46.4	97
Malaysia (1995)	partly free	21	no	plurality system in SMCs	192	192	1		individual	single vote	SMC	plurality	71.8	n.a.	n.a.
Mali (1997)	free	18	no	absolute majority system in MMCs	147	55	n.a.	2.7	closed lists	single vote	MMC	absolute majority (runoff among two strongest candidates/lists)	21.6	75.3	88.2

45. In Lebanon, each confessional group has a fixed number of representatives: Maronites, 34; Sunnis, 27; Shiites, 27; Greek Orthodox, 14; Druses, 8; Greek Catholics, 8; Armenian Orthodox, 5; Alawites, 2; Protestants, 1; Armenian Catholics, 1; other minorities, 1. This "confessional PR" also determines the basic structure of the electoral system, since the electoral law defines how many representatives of each confession are to be elected in each constituency. Voters have as many votes as there are seats to be allocated in the respective constituency, but their choice is limited by the preestablished confessional structure of the candidature, that is, they must cast one vote for each confessional seat in the constituency.

46. In Lithuania, the minimum participation rate is 40 percent in the SMCs and 25 percent nationwide (for national-list seats).

47. The minimum participation rate is 33 percent in the Macedonian SMCs.

Country (year)	FH rating	Voting age	Compulsory voting	Classification of electoral system	No. of seats	Constituencies No.	Constituencies Seats	Constituencies Mean seats	Form of candidacy	Ballot form	Levels of seat allocation	Mode of seat allocation	Turnout (%)	Strongest party	Rose index
Malta (1996)	free	18	no	single transferable vote	65+[48]	13	5		nonblocked party lists	single vote[49]	MMC	Droop quota	97.2	50.7	98.5
Mauritania (1996)	not free	18	no	absolute majority system in SMCs, PR in TMCs	79	53	1-2	1.5	SMC: individual. TMC: closed lists	single vote	SMC/TMC	SMC: absolute majority (runoff among two strongest candidates). TMC: threshold of 10% of national vote; unspecified quota	52.1	67.6	79
Mauritius (1995)	free	18	no	plurality system in MMCs	70: 62 8[50]	21	2-3	3.0	individual	multiple vote	MMC community/party level	plurality "best losers"	79.7	64.7	68.5
Mexico (1997)	partly free	18	yes	segmented system	500: 300 200	300 1	1 200		party candidates closed lists	two votes: personal vote list vote	SMC national MMC	plurality threshold of 2% of national vote; Hare quota; largest remainder	58	40	90.7
Moldova (1998)	partly free	18	no	PR in one MMC	101	1	101		closed lists	single vote	national MMC	threshold of 4% of national vote; d'Hondt	72.3	30.1	76.3
Mongolia (1996)	free	18	no	plurality system in SMCs	76	76	1		individual	single vote	SMC	plurality	88.4	47[51]	86.7
Morocco (1997)	partly free	20	yes	plurality system in SMCs	325	325	1		individual	single vote	SMC	plurality	58.3	13.9	84.2
Mozambique (1994)	partly free	18	no	PR in large MMCs	250	11	11-54	22.7	closed lists	single vote	MMC	threshold of 5% of national vote; d'Hondt	87.9	44.3	85.7
Namibia (1994)	free	18	no	pure PR	72	1	72		closed lists	single vote	national MMC	Hare quota; largest remainder	76	73.9	98.7
Nepal (1994)	partly free	18	no	plurality system in SMCs	205	205	1		individual	single vote	SMC	plurality	61.9	34.5	82
Netherlands (1998)	free	18	no	pure PR	150	1	150		closed regional party lists	single vote	national MMC	threshold of 0.67% of national vote; d'Hondt	73	29	96.9

48. In Malta, to ensure that a party with more than 50 percent of the national vote gets an absolute majority of the seats, additional (bonus) seats are allocated to the leading party until it has 50 percent plus one of the parliamentary seats (currently 4 bonus seats).

49. Voters may express their preferences by ranking the candidates within one list.

50. A maximum of 8 parliamentary seats are allocated in Mauritius to under-represented communities (the first 4 on a purely community basis to the most under-represented communities, irrespective of party affiliation; the second 4 on a party and community basis).

51. The figure for strongest party in Mongolia refers to votes for an alliance of two parties.

Country (year)	FH rating	Voting age	Compulsory voting	Classification of electoral system	No. of seats	Constituencies No.	Constituencies Seats	Constituencies Mean seats	Form of candidacy	Ballot form	Levels of seat allocation	Mode of seat allocation	Turnout (%)	Strongest party	Rose index
New Zealand (1996)	free	18	no	mixed-member proportional system	120: 65[52]	65	1		individual	two votes: personal vote	SMC	party share of 120 seats is determined at national level according to list vote with St. Laguë (threshold of 5% of national vote). SMC: plurality (each party's SMC seats are subtracted from its list seats)	88.3	33.8	92.4
					55	1	55		closed party lists	list vote	national MMC				
Nicaragua (1996)	partly free	16	no	PR in MMCs with additional national list	90+:[53] 70	17	1-19	4.2	closed lists	two votes: MMC list vote	MMC	Hare quota; remaining seats are allocated at national level with the following quota: national sum of residual votes divided by the sum of remaining seats	77.1	46	95.8
					20	1	20		closed lists	national list vote	national MMC	Hare quota; remaining national list seats are allocated under a quota calculated as the mean of 4 regional electoral quotas			
Niger (1996)	not free	18	no	PR in small, medium, and large MMCs (with 8 SMCs)	83: 75	8	4-14	9.4	closed lists		MMC	Hare quota; largest remainder	39.2	56.7	86.7
					8	8	1		individual	single vote	SMC	plurality			
Norway (1997)	free	18	no	PR in small, medium, and large MMCs with compensatory seats	165: 157	19	4-15	8.3	closed lists	single vote	MMC	modified St. Laguë (no legal threshold)	78	35.1	94.3
					8	1	8				national MMC	national seats are allocated to those lists with the highest quotients remaining after the allocation of MMC seats; threshold of 4% of national vote			
Pakistan (1997)	partly free	21	no	plurality system in SMCs	207	207	1		individual	single vote	SMC	plurality	37	n.a.	n.a.
Palestinian Authority (1996)	n.a.	17	no	plurality system in SMCs and MMCs	88: 85	16	2-12	6.5	open lists	multiple vote	MMC	plurality	75.4	57.5	n.a.
					3	3	1		individual	single vote	SMC				
Panama (1994)	free	18	yes	plurality in SMCs and PR in small and medium MMCs	71	40	1-6	3.2	SMC: individual. MMC: non-blocked lists	multiple vote (optional in MMC)[54]	SMC/MMC	SMC: plurality. MMC in 3 steps: Hare quota, half Hare quota, and highest number of personal votes	73.7	22.9	n.a.

52. The 65 elected SMC seats include 5 Maori districts designed to ensure representation of the indigenous population.
53. In addition to the 90 elected seats, all unsuccessful presidential candidates whose number of votes meets or exceeds the quota used for the remaining national list seats in the legislative elections are entitled to a parliamentary seat. In 1996 three candidates met this criteria, so that the national parliament currently has 93 members.
54. MMC candidates in Panama may run on different party lists.

Country (year)	FH rating	Voting age	Compulsory voting	Classification of electoral system	No. of seats	Constituencies No.	Constituencies Seats	Constituencies Mean seats	Form of candidacy	Ballot form	Levels of seat allocation	Mode of seat allocation	Turnout (%)	Strongest party	Rose index
Papua New Guinea (1997)	partly free	18	no	plurality system in SMCs	109[55]	109	1		individual	two votes[56]	SMC	plurality	66.0	6.5	n.a.
Paraguay (1998)	partly free	18	yes	PR in small, medium, and large MMCs	80	18	1–14	4.4	closed lists	single vote	SMC/MMC	d'Hondt	80.5	53.8	96.5
Peru (1995)	partly free	18	yes	pure PR	120	1	120		nonblocked lists	two preferential votes (optional)	national MMC	d'Hondt ("cifra repartidora")	63.4	52.1	94
Philippines (1998)	free	18	yes	segmented system	260:[57] 208	208	1		individual	two votes: personal vote	SMC	plurality	70.7	42.4	87.8
					52	1	52		closed lists	list vote	national MMC	threshold of 2% of national vote; maximum of 3 seats per party[58]			
Poland (1997)	free	18	no	PR in medium and large MMCs with additional national list	460: 391	52	7–17	8.8	nonblocked lists	preferential vote	MMC	threshold of 5%/8% (EC) of national vote for MMC lists; d'Hondt	47.9	33.8	81.5
					69	1	69		closed lists		national MMC	threshold of 7% of national vote; d'Hondt			
Portugal (1995)	free	18	no	PR in small, medium, and large MMCs	230	22[59]	2–50	10.5	closed lists	single vote	MMC	d'Hondt	67.2	43.9	90.9
Romania (1996)	free	18	no	PR in small, medium, and large MMCs	343	42	4–29	8.2	closed lists	single vote	MMC national level (for remaining seats)	threshold of 3%/8% (EC) of national vote; Hare quota; d'Hondt	76	30.2	81.6
Russia (1995)	partly free	18	no	segmented system	450: 225	225	1		individual	two votes: personal vote	SMC	plurality	64.7	22.3	74.8
					225	1	225		closed lists	list vote	national MMC	threshold of 5% of national vote; Hare quota; largest remainder			
Senegal (1998)	partly free	18	no	PR in small MMCs with additional national list	140: 70	30	1–5	2.3	closed lists	single vote	SMC/MMC	SMC: plurality. MMC: Hare quota; largest remainder	38.8	50.2	83.6
					70	1	70				national MMC	national seats: Hare quota; largest remainder			

55. Of the 109 seats, 89 are distributed at the local and 20 at the federal level. Since all seats are allocated by plurality in SMCs, the electoral system cannot be classified as segmented, but as (two-tier) plurality.

56. Each voter casts two votes: one for a provincial and one for a local candidate.

57. In addition to the elected seats, 17 members of the Philippine parliament are appointed by the president of the republic.

58. One national seat is allocated for every 2% of votes obtained. In 1998 only 9 of the national seats were allocated in the Philippines because of the combined effect of legal threshold and maximum number of national seats per party.

59. Among the 22 MMC are 2 TMCs for Portuguese living abroad (one for European and one for non-European countries).

Country (year)	FH rating	Voting age	Compulsory voting	Classification of electoral system	No. of seats	Constituencies No.	Constituencies Seats	Constituencies Mean seats	Form of candidacy	Ballot form	Levels of seat allocation	Mode of seat allocation	Turnout (%)	Strongest party	Rose index
Sierra Leone (1996)	partly free	18	no	PR in one MMC	68	1	68		closed lists	single vote	national MMC	threshold of 5% of national vote; Hare quota; largest remainder	50.1	35.9	88.4
Singapore (1997)	partly free	21	yes	plurality system in SMCs and in small and medium MMCs[60]	83	24	1-6	3.5	SMC: individual. MMC: closed lists	single vote	SMC/MMC	plurality	95.9	64.9	67.5
Slovakia (1998)	partly free	18	no	PR in one MMC	150	1	150		nonblocked lists	up to 4 preferential votes	national MMC	threshold of 5% of national vote (for ECs applied to each party separately); Droop quota; largest remainder	84.2	27.1	94.0
Slovenia (1996)	free	18	no	PR in large MMCs (with 2 minority SMCs)	90: 88	8	11		nonblocked lists	single vote with optional preference	MMC national level (for remaining seats)	Hare quota. Remaining seats, d'Hondt at national level (threshold of 3 MMC seats)	73.7	27	88.7
					2	2	1		individual		SMC	plurality			
South Africa (1994)	free	18	no	pure PR	400: 200	9	4-43		closed provincial and/or national lists	single vote	MMC	party share of 400 seats is determined at national level; each party's seats are allocated to provincial and national MMC lists; electoral formula for both procedures is STV-Droop quota; largest remainder	86.7	62.6	98.8
					200	1	200				national level				
Spain (1996)	free	18	no	PR in MMCs (with 2 SMCs)	350: 348	50	2-34	7.0	closed lists	single vote	MMC	threshold of 3% of constituency vote; d'Hondt	77.5	38.7	91.2
					2	2	1		individual		SMC	plurality			
Sri Lanka (1994)	partly free	18	no	PR in MMCs with additional national list	225: 196	22	4-20	8.9	nonblocked lists	one list vote with preferences for 3 candidates	regional MMC	threshold of 5% of constituency vote; 1 bonus seat for strongest party; Hare quota; largest remainder	76.2	48.9	94.7
					29	1	29		closed lists		national MMC	Hare quota; largest remainder			
Sudan (1996)	not free	18	no	no-party absolute majority system in SMCs	275[61]	275	1		individual (no party candidates)	single vote	SMC	absolute majority (runoff among two strongest candidates)	55	no party	n.a.

60. In each Singaporean MMC–the so-called group representation constituencies–one of the elected representatives must come from the Malayan, Indian, or any other minority community. The membership of the House can be expanded by up to 3 "nonconstituency members" and up to 6 "nominated members."

61. In addition to the 275 elected members, 125 members of parliament are indirectly elected.

Country (year)	FH rating	Voting age	Compulsory voting	Classification of electoral system	No. of seats	Constituencies No.	Constituencies Seats	Constituencies Mean seats	Form of candidacy	Ballot form	Levels of seat allocation	Mode of seat allocation	Turnout (%)	Strongest party	Rose index
Swaziland (1998)	not free	18	no	no-party plurality system in SMCs	55	55	1		individual (no party candidates)	single vote	SMC	plurality	n.a.	no party	n.a.
Sweden (1998)	free	18	no	PR in small, medium, and large MMCs with compensatory seats	349: 310	29	2-34	10.7	nonblocked lists	single vote with optional preference	MMC	threshold of 4% of national vote or 12% of vote in one subnational MMC; modified St. Laguë	81.4	36.4	97.4
					39	1	39				national MMC	threshold of 4% of national vote; modified St. Laguë[62]			
Switzerland (1995)	free	18	no	PR in MMCs (with 5 SMCs)	200: 195	21	2-34[63]	3.3	open lists	multiple vote	MMC	Droop quota. Remaining seats: divisor method	42.2	21.8	91.6
					5	5	1		individual	single vote	SMC	plurality			
Syria (1998)	not free	18	no	plurality system in MMCs	250	15	n.a.	16.7	nonblocked lists	preferential vote	MMC	plurality	82.2	n.a.	n.a.
Taiwan (1995)	free	20	no	single nontransferable vote with additional national list	164:[64] 128	n.a.	n.a.		individual	single vote	MMC	MMC: plurality	67.7	46.1	94.2
					36	1	36		closed lists		national	national seats: threshold of 5% of national vote or 12% of votes in one subnational MMC; Hare-Niemeyer			
Tajikistan (1995)	not free	18	no	absolute majority system in SMCs	181	181	1		individual	single vote	SMC	absolute majority (runoff among two strongest candidates)	84	n.a.	n.a.
Tanzania (1995)	partly free	18	no	plurality system in SMCs	232[65]	232	1		individual	single vote	SMC	plurality	76.5	59.2	74.2
Thailand (1996)	partly free	18	no	plurality system in SMCs and small MMCs	393	155	1-3	2.5	individual	multiple vote	SMC/MMC	plurality	62.4	n.a.	n.a.
Togo (1994)	not free	18	no	absolute majority system in SMCs	81	81	1		individual	single vote	SMC	absolute majority (runoff among two strongest candidates)	65.1	n.a.	n.a.
Trinidad & Tobago (1995)	free	18	no	plurality system in SMCs	36	36	1		individual	single vote	SMC	plurality	63.3	48.8	97.8

62. In Sweden, a preliminary allocation of all seats—both "fixed" (constituency) and "additional" (national)—is made by modified Saint Laguë. Parties that receive more more seats in this preliminary allocation than they have in reality are allotted additional seats from the national pool of 39 additional seats.

63. Constituencies correspond to the federal states (cantons); their size varies according to the population of each canton. For the allocation of remaining seats, each party's votes are divided by the number of seats it has already been allocated plus one. The party with the highest quotient obtains the first of the remaining seats. This procedure is repeated until all remaining seats are allocated.

64. The data refer to the Li fa Yuan (Legislative Yuan) as the most important parliamentary chamber. Of the elected seats, six represent overseas Taiwanese.

65. In Tanzania, in addition to the elected seats, there are seats for the attorney general and five members of the House of Representatives of Zanzibar as well as thirty-seven special seats for women. The latter are distributed among the parliamentary parties in proportion to their share of seats.

Country (year)	FH rating	Voting age	Compulsory voting	Classification of electoral system	No. of seats	Constituencies No.	Constituencies Seats	Constituencies Mean seats	Form of candidacy	Ballot form	Levels of seat allocation	Mode of seat allocation	Turnout (%)	Strongest party	Rose index
Tunisia (1994)	not free	20	no	plurality system in small and medium MMCs with compensatory seats	163: 144 / 19	25 / 1	2-10 / 19	5.8	closed lists / closed lists	single vote	MMC / national MMC	plurality (winning list gets all seats) / Hare quota; highest average[66]	99.7	97.7	90.4
Turkey (1995)	partly free	18	yes	PR in small, medium, and large MMCs	550	79	2-21	7.0	closed lists	single vote	constituency	threshold of 10% of national vote; d'Hondt	85.2	21.4	83
Turkmenistan (1994)	not free	18	no	absolute majority system in SMCs	50	50	1		individual	single vote	SMC	absolute majority (runoff among two strongest candidates)	99.8	100	-
Uganda (1996)	partly free	18	no	no-party plurality system in SMCs	214[67]	214	1		individual (no party candidates)	single vote	SMC	plurality	60.7	no party	n.a.
Ukraine (1998)	partly free	18	no	segmented system	450: 225 / 225	225 / 1	1 / 225		individual / closed lists	two votes: personal vote / list vote	SMC / national MMC	plurality / threshold of 4% of national vote; Hare quota; largest remainder	70	24.7	90.8
United Kingdom (1997)	free	18	no	plurality system in SMCs	659	659	1		individual	single vote	SMC	plurality	71.6	43.2	78.5
United States (1996)	free	18	no	plurality system in SMCs	435	435	1		individual	single vote	SMC	plurality	66	52.8	n.a.
Uruguay (1994)	free	18	yes	pure PR	99	19	2-45	5.2	nonblocked lists[68]	single vote	MMC national level	party share of 99 seats is determined at national level with d'Hondt; regional MMC seats are first allocated by Hare quota (at the MMC level) and then may be reallocated between regional MMC in order to match the national distribution resulting from the d'Hondt method	91.4	32.3	99.5
Uzbekistan (1995)	not free	18	no	absolute majority system in SMCs	250	250	1		individual	single vote	SMC	absolute majority (runoff between two strongest candidates)	88.3	n.a.	n.a.

66. In allocating the national list seats in Tunisia, the votes of all unsuccessful lists at the MMC level are included in the calculation of the electoral quota, which introduces a compensatory element in the electoral system.

67. In addition to the 214 elected seats, 62 members of parliament are nominated.

68. Strictly speaking, electors in Uruguay vote for blocked lists. However, since within each party (lema) various lists (sublemas and listas) may compete (votes for all competing intraparty lists are summed), the system resembles one with nonblocked party lists.

Country (year)	FH rating	Voting age	Compulsory voting	Classification of electoral system	No. of seats	Constituencies No.	Constituencies Seats	Constituencies Mean seats	Form of candidacy	Ballot form	Levels of seat allocation	Mode of seat allocation	Turnout (%)	Strongest party	Rose index
Venezuela (1998)	free	18	yes	mixed-member proportional system	207.[69]					two votes:			60.2	21.7	83.7
					88	72[70]	1-7	1.2	individual	personal vote	SMC/MMC	party share of 189 seats is determined at regional MMC level according to d'Hondt. The 88 "personalized" seats (elected by plurality) are subtracted from each party's regional seat contingent			
					101	24	3-24	12.7[71]	closed regional lists	list vote	regional MMC				
					18	1	18				national level	Hare quota; maximum of 5 seats per party[72]			
Vietnam (1997)	not free	18	no	absolute majority system in small MMCs	450	158	2-3	2.8	one open list	multiple vote	constituency	absolute majority (plurality among all candidates)	99.6	n.a.	n.a.
Yemen (1997)	not free	18	no	plurality system in SMCs	301	301	1		individual	single vote	SMC	plurality	60.7	43.1	81.0
Yugoslavia (1996)	not free	18	no	plurality system in SMCs and PR in small MMCs	138[73]	43	1-5	3.2	closed lists	single vote	MMC	threshold of 5% of constituency vote; d'Hondt	53.3	42.2[74]	88.1[75]
Zambia (1996)	partly free	18	no	plurality system in SMCs	150	150	1		individual	single vote	SMC	plurality	58.7	61	73.7
Zimbabwe (1995)	partly free	18	no	plurality system in SMCs	120[76]	120	1		individual	single vote	SMC	plurality	56.7	81.4	83.1

69. In Venezuela there are 189 "fixed" parliamentary seats plus a variable number of compensatory seats (18 in the 1998 elections).

70. These 72 "personalized" plurality constituencies include 66 SMCs, 1 two-member constituency, 3 MMCs each returning 3 members, 1 MMC returning 4, and 1 MMC returning 7.

71. The mean size of subnational constituencies is calculated on the basis of the 189 "fixed" seats.

72. The variable contingent of seats (numbering 18 in 1998) is allocated to the parties in proportion to their national share of the votes for the 189 "fixed" seats. From this result, the seats already obtained are subtracted. The difference is the party's share of the additional compensatory seats assigned to those constituencies in which the party concerned is the most underrepresented on the basis of the number of votes won.

73. The two members of the Yugoslav federation constitute separate electoral areas: 108 seats are allocated in 29 Serbian MMCs, and 30 seats in 14 Montenegrin MMCs.

74. The figure for strongest party refers to the Serbian electoral area only.

75. The figure for proportionality index refers to the Serbian electoral area only.

76. In addition to the 120 elected seats, 30 members of parliament are nominated.

TABLE 2

BASIC FEATURES OF PRESIDENTIAL ELECTIONS

The following table includes data on presidential elections in eighty-eight independent countries with a constitutional form of government, a population of more than 500,000, and a head of state who is directly elected. The United States, whose president is indirectly chosen by an electoral college, is also included.

Many of the countries included cannot be considered democratic, nor their presidential elections free and fair. For that reason, the Freedom House rating for political and civil liberties is provided in Appendix Table 1. Footnotes in Table 2 indicate those countries where the constitution requires that presidential elections be held with a single candidate or where elections have been uncontested in practice.

EXPLANATIONS OF COLUMN HEADINGS AND CELLS

Country. Name of the country for which election data are reported.

Year. The year for which election data are reported.

Concurrent with parliamentary elections. Indicates whether presidential elections are held simultaneously with parliamentary elections. "Yes" may signify that the president and the parliament are elected on the same day. Where this is not the case and midterm elections are held, a footnote so indicates.

Presidential term of office. The regular, constitutional term of an elected president, in years.

Maximum consecutive terms. The maximum number of consecutive terms that a president may serve.

Electoral formula. The majority required for a presidential candidate to be elected in the first round or, where the single transferable vote is used, in the first round of vote counting.

Further procedure. Procedure to be followed if the required majority indicated in the "Electoral formula" column is not achieved. "Runoff" means that a second round takes place among the two strongest candidates of the first round.

Vote share of strongest candidate. National vote share of the candidate who received the most valid votes in the first round.

Country	Year	Concurrent with parliamentary elections	Presidential term of office (years)	Maximum consecutive terms	Electoral formula	Further procedure	Vote share of strongest candidate (first round)
Algeria	1995	no	5	2	absolute majority	runoff	61.0
Angola	1992	no	5	2	absolute majority	runoff	49.6
Argentina	1995	yes	4	2	45% or 40% and ten-point advantage	runoff	49.9
Armenia	1998	no	5	2	absolute majority	runoff	38.8
Austria	1998	no	6	2	absolute majority	runoff	63.5
Azerbaijan	1998	no	5	3	two-thirds majority	runoff	76.1
Belarus	1994	no	5	2	absolute majority	runoff	44.8
Benin	1996	no	5	2	absolute majority	runoff	35.7
Bolivia	1997	yes	5	no reelection	absolute majority	runoff	22.3
Bosnia-Herzegovina[1]	1998	yes	4	2	plurality	—	31.0
Brazil	1998	yes	4	2	absolute majority	runoff	87.5
Bulgaria	1996	no	5	2	absolute majority	runoff	44.1
Burkina Faso	1998	no	7	unlimited	absolute majority	runoff	87.5
Cameroon	1997	no	7	2	plurality	—	92.6
Central African Republic	1993	no	6	2	absolute majority	runoff	37.3
Chad	1996	no	5	no reelection	absolute majority	runoff	43.8
Chile	1994	no	6	no reelection	absolute majority	runoff	58.0
Colombia	1998	no	4	no reelection	absolute majority	runoff	34.6
Costa Rica	1998	yes	4	no reelection	plurality of 40%	runoff	45.5
Côte d'Ivoire	1995	no	5	unlimited	absolute majority	2nd round, plurality	96.0
Croatia	1997	no	5	2	absolute majority	runoff	61.4
Cyprus	1998	no	5	unlimited	absolute majority	runoff	40.8
Djibouti	1993	no	6	2	absolute majority	runoff	60.7
Dominican Republic	1996	no	4	no reelection	absolute majority	runoff	38.9
Ecuador	1998	yes	4	no reelection	absolute majority[2]	runoff	35.4
Egypt	1999	no	6	unlimited	absolute majority[2]	—	93.8
El Salvador	1994	no	5	no reelection	absolute majority	runoff	49.1
Finland	1994	no	6	2	absolute majority	runoff	25.9

1. The presidency of Bosnia-Herzegovina consists of three members who represent the main ethnic groups: one Bosniac and one Croat, each directly and separately elected from the territory of the Federation of Bosnia and Herzegovina, and one Serb directly elected from the territory of the Republic of Srpska.

2. In Egypt the one candidate nominated by the national parliament, the People's Assembly, is elected by popular referendum.

Country	Year	Concurrent with parliamentary elections	Presidential term of office (years)	Maximum consecutive terms	Electoral formula	Further procedure	Vote share of strongest candidate (first round)
France	1995	no	7	unlimited	absolute majority	runoff	23.3
Gabon	1998	no	7	2	absolute majority	runoff	66.6
Gambia	1996	no	5	2	absolute majority	runoff	55.8
Georgia	1995	no	5	2	absolute majority	runoff	74.3
Ghana	1996	yes	4	2	absolute majority	runoff	57.4
Guatemala	1995–1996	yes	4	no reelection	absolute majority	runoff	36.5
Guinea	1998	no	5	2	absolute majority	runoff	54.1
Guinea-Bissau	1994	no	5	2	absolute majority	runoff	46.2
Haiti	1995	no	5	no reelection[3]	absolute majority	runoff	87.9
Honduras	1997	yes	4	no reelection	plurality	—	52.8
Iceland	1996	no	4	unlimited	plurality	—	40.9
Iran	1997	no	4	2	absolute majority	runoff	69.6
Ireland	1997	no	7	2	absolute majority	single transferable vote	45.2
Kazakhstan	1991	no	5[4]	unlimited	absolute majority	runoff	100.0
Kenya	1997	yes	5	2	plurality (plus 25% in 5 of 8 regions)	runoff	40.1
Korea (South)	1997	no	5	no reelection	plurality	—	40.3
Kyrgyzstan	1995	no	5	2	absolute majority	runoff	71.6
Liberia	1997	yes	6	2	absolute majority	runoff	75.3
Lithuania	1997	no	5	2	absolute majority	runoff	45.3
Macedonia	1994	no	5	2	absolute majority	runoff	52.4
Madagascar	1996	no	5	2	absolute majority	runoff	36.6
Malawi	1994	yes	5	2	plurality	—	47.2
Mali	1997	no	5	2	absolute majority	runoff	87.4
Mauritania	1997	no	6	unlimited	absolute majority	runoff	91.0
Mexico	1994	yes[5]	6	no reelection	plurality	—	50.2
Moldova	1996	no	4	2	absolute majority	runoff	43.2
Mongolia	1997	no	4	2	absolute majority	runoff	60.8
Mozambique	1994	yes	5	2	absolute majority	runoff	53.3
Namibia	1994	yes	5	2	absolute majority	repeated rounds	76.3

3. In Haiti the president may serve one additional term only after an interval of five years.
4. The term of the Kazakh president elected in 1991 was prolonged until the year 2000 by a referendum held in 1995.
5. The House of Representatives of Mexico holds midterm elections, but presidential elections are always held together with parliamentary elections.

Country	Year	Concurrent with parliamentary elections	Presidential term of office (years)	Maximum consecutive terms	Electoral formula	Further procedure	Vote share of strongest candidate (first round)
Nicaragua	1996	yes	5	no reelection	45% + 1	runoff	51.0
Niger	1996	no	5	2	absolute majority	runoff	52.2
Palestinian Authority	1996	yes	transitional period[6]	unlimited	plurality	–	88.2
Panama	1994	yes	5	no reelection	plurality	–	33.3
Paraguay	1998	yes	5	no reelection	plurality	–	55.4
Peru	1995	yes	5	2	absolute majority	runoff	64.4
Philippines	1998	no	6	no reelection	plurality	–	46.4
Poland	1995	no	5	2	absolute majority	runoff	35.1
Portugal	1996	no	5	2	absolute majority	runoff	53.8
Romania	1996	yes	4	2	absolute majority	runoff	32.3
Russia	1996	no	4	2	absolute majority	runoff	35.3
Senegal	1993	no	7	2	absolute majority and quorum[7]	runoff	58.4
Sierra Leone	1996	yes	5	2	qualified absolute majority (55%)	runoff	35.8
Singapore	1993	no	6	unlimited	plurality	–	58.7
Slovenia	1997	no	5	2	plurality	–	55.5
Sri Lanka	1994	no	6	2	absolute majority	single transferable vote[8]	62.3
Sudan	1996	no	5	2	absolute majority	runoff	75.7
Syria	1991	no	7	unlimited	absolute majority[9]	runoff	100.0
Taiwan	1996	yes	6	2	plurality	–	54.0
Tajikistan	1994	no	5	2	absolute majority	runoff	60.0
Tanzania	1995	yes	5	3	absolute majority	runoff	61.8
Togo	1998	no	5	2	absolute majority	runoff	52.1
Tunisia	1994	yes	5	3	plurality	–	100.0[10]
Turkmenistan	1992	no	5[11]	unlimited	absolute majority	runoff	100.0[12]
Uganda	1996	no	5	2	absolute majority	runoff	74.2

6. According to the draft of the Basic Law for the Palestinian National Authority, the term of the president shall be the duration of the transitional period.

7. In Senegal the winning candidate must obtain not only an absolute majority of valid votes cast but also the votes of at least 25 percent of registered voters.

8. The single-transferable-vote system is used in Sri Lanka. Voters rank the candidates in the one round of balloting. If no candidate gets an absolute majority of first preferences, the lower-order preferences of losing candidates are redistributed until one candidate has a majority of preferences.

9. In Syria, one candidate stands for election.

10. The Tunisian election of 1994 was uncontested.

11. The term of the president of Turkmenistan elected in 1992 was prolonged until 2002 by a referendum in 1994.

12. The Turkmen election of 1992 was uncontested.

Country	Year	Concurrent with parliamentary elections	Presidential term of office (years)	Maximum consecutive terms	Electoral formula	Further procedure	Vote share of strongest candidate (first round)
Ukraine	1994	no	5	2	absolute majority	runoff	37.7
United States[13]	1996	yes	4	2	absolute majority within electoral college	election by House of Representatives (one vote per state)	49.2
Uruguay[14]	1995	yes	5	no reelection	absolute majority	runoff	32.3
Uzbekistan	1991	no	5	2	absolute majority	runoff	86.0
Venezuela	1998	yes	5	no consecutive reelection	plurality	—	56.5
Zambia	1996	yes	5	2	plurality	—	68.9
Zimbabwe	1996	no	6	unlimited	absolute majority	runoff	92.7

13. Strictly speaking, the U.S. president is elected indirectly. The members of the electoral college are elected on the state level, and the candidate with the plurality of the vote in a given state normally receives all of that state's electoral votes. The president is elected at the same time as the entire U.S. House of Representatives and one-third of the U.S. Senate.

14. The Uruguayan president elected in 1995 was elected under the plurality decision rule. A constitutional reform of 1997 introduced the absolute majority formula.

INDEX